The Grahams & The Donalds

Edited by Rab Anderson
and Tom Prentice

Scottish Mountaineering Club
Hillwalkers' Guides

With contributions from Rab Anderson, Dave Broadhead, Ken Crocket, Derek Fabian, Andrew Fraser, Alec Keith, Graham Little, Grahame Nicoll, Andy Nisbet, Meryl Marshall, Colin Moody, Fran Pothecary, Tom Prentice, Matt Shaw and Noel Williams

Published by the Scottish Mountaineering Press

Copyright © Scottish Mountaineering Club
Photographs © Copyright as credited

All rights reserved. No part of this publication may be reproduced, stored in or introduced into a retrieval system, or transmitted, in any form or by any means (electronic, mechanical, photocopying, recording or otherwise), without the prior written permission of the publisher.

Second Edition 2022

ISBN 978-1-907233-45-6
A catalogue record of this book is available from the British Library

SMC ® and Munro's Tables ® are registered trade marks
Some maps are derived from Ordnance Survey OpenData™ © Crown copyright and database right 2021

Front Cover: Beinn an Eòin, Stac Pollaidh and Suilven   *Dougie Cunningham (www.leadinglines.net)*
This Page: Sgòrr na Cìche (Pap of Glencoe)   *Cubby Images*

Produced and designed by Tom Prentice
Maps: Bernard Newman, Tom Prentice and Rab Anderson

Printed & bound in Europe by Latitude Press Ltd
Distributed by Cordee Ltd (t) 01455 611185 (w) www.cordee.co.uk

Stac Pollaidh from Sgùrr an Fhìdhleir (Rab Anderson)

	Introduction	6
	Notes	8
SECTION 0a	Galloway & The Lowthers	12
SECTION 0b	The Borders	40
SECTION 0c	The Midland Valley	76
SECTION 1a	Loch Fyne to Loch Lomond	84
SECTION 1b	Loch Lomond to Loch Tay	108
SECTION 2 & 3	Loch Tay to Loch Linnhe	130
SECTION 4	Loch Linnhe to Loch Ericht	148
SECTION 5, 6 &7	Loch Ericht to Glen Esk	158
SECTION 8	Deeside to Speyside	172
SECTION 9	Speyside to the Great Glen	186
SECTION 10a	Loch Linnhe to Glenfinnan	198
SECTION 10b	Glenfinnan to Glen Shiel	214
SECTION 11	Glen Shiel to Loch Mullardoch	236
SECTION 12	Loch Mullardoch to Glen Carron	248
SECTION 13	Glen Carron to Loch Maree	260
SECTION 14	Loch Maree to Loch Broom	270
SECTION 15	Loch Broom to the Cromarty Firth	282
SECTION 16	Loch Broom to the Pentland Firth	294
SECTION 17	The Islands: Arran, Jura, Mull, Rum, Skye, South Uist & Harris	316
	Table of Grahams	354
	Table of Donalds	360
	Grahams by Height	364
	Donalds by Height	366
	Index of Grahams	368
	Index of Donalds	370
	SMC & SMT Publications List	372

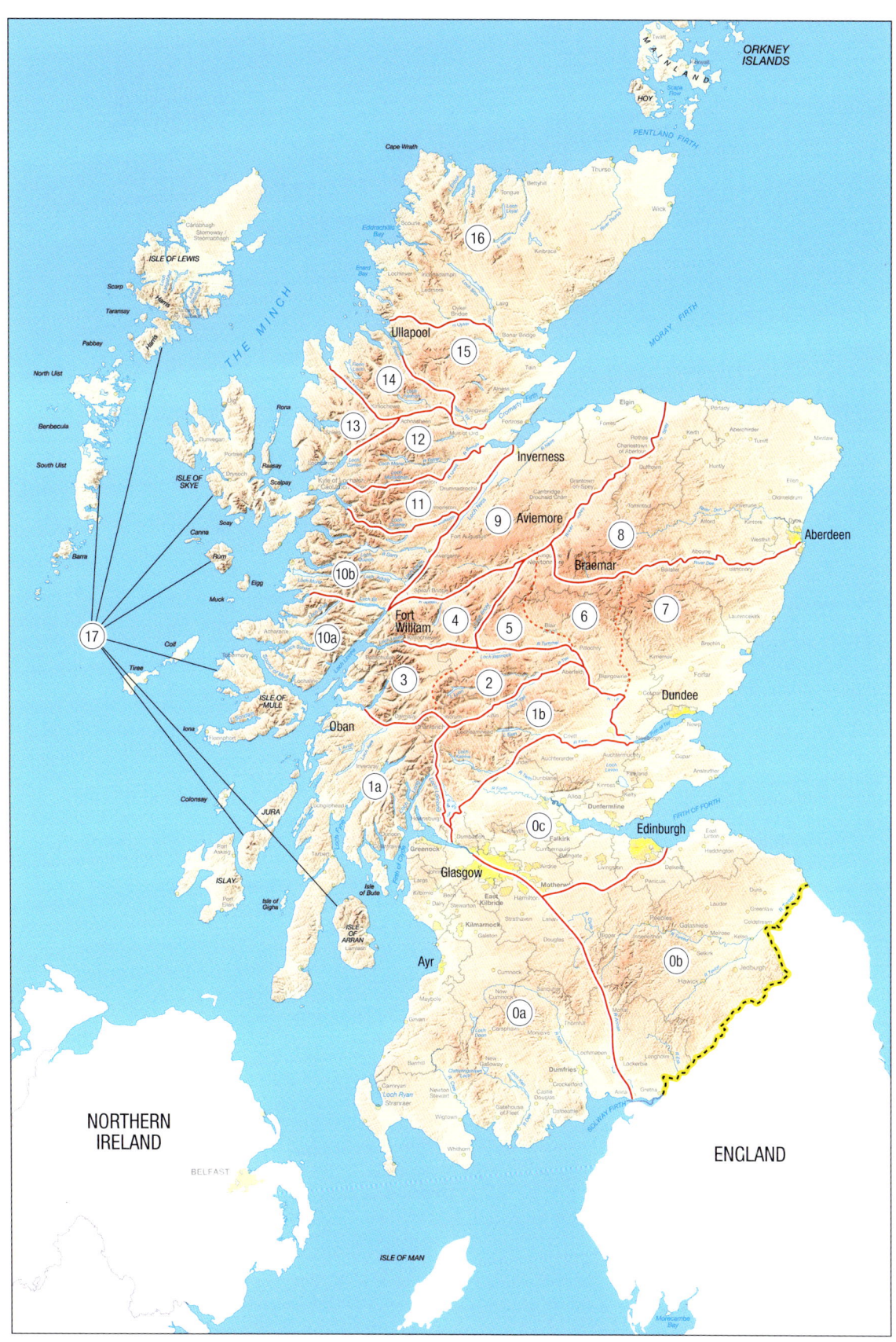

Introduction

Culter Fell and Chapelgill Hill from the flanks of Gathersnow Hill (Rab Anderson)

This guidebook to *The Grahams & The Donalds* follows in the footsteps of the Scottish Mountaineering Club's guides to *The Munros* and *The Corbetts*.

Most people, and not just hillwalkers, have heard of The Munros, the collective name given to the 282 mountains in Scotland above 3000ft which came into being following the 1891 publication by SMC member Sir Hugh Munro of his *Tables Giving All the Scottish Mountains Exceeding 3000ft in Height*. No one could have anticipated the influence Munro's Tables would have on generations of hillwalkers and that more than a century after their publication, they would still be the inspiration for many people's hill climbing activities.

In 1935 another hill listing came into being when Percy Donald published his *Tables Giving All Hills in the Scottish Lowlands 2000ft in Height and Above*. Donald was also a SMC member and, as with Munro, the hills on his list became known as The Donalds.

It wasn't until 1952 that the next listing was established with the posthumous publication of John Rooke Corbett's *List of Scottish Mountains 2500ft and Under 3000ft in Height*. Corbett was also an SMC member and, as with the other two, these hills became known as The Corbetts. Where his list differed from the others was that it included a height separation criterion based on a set number of map contour rings. This was interpreted to mean that the hills on his list had to involve a reascent of 500ft (152.4m) on all sides, thereby illustrating a hill's prominence, or what has become known as its drop.

Despite these early lists it was some time before a definitive listing of Scottish hills in the 2000ft to 2500ft range was finalised. Perhaps this should have occurred with William McKnight Docharty's listing of hills. Docharty, another SMC member, published a list of some 900 British and Irish Mountain Tops in 1954, followed by two supplements in 1962. These publications included all but four of what we now know as The Grahams, although his means of separating them was not the same as that used for the current listing.

But, unlike Munro, Donald and Corbett, who all published their lists in the Scottish Mountaineering Club Journal, Docharty published his lists privately. Perhaps if he had published them in the *SMC Journal*, then these hills would now be known as Dochartys? Over the following years, others produced lists which included the 2000ft hills, but none of them became accepted.

In 1992, Alan Dawson produced his book *The Relative Hills of Britain*. This lists all of the hills in Britain, regardless of height, so long as they have an all-round relative height of at least 150m compared to the surrounding land. In other words they had to be at least 150m high and have a 150m drop, or prominence. Numbering over 1500, these hills were named The Marilyns and in Scotland included all the hills in the 2000ft to 2500ft range, known at the time as Lesser Corbetts, abbreviated to LCs and known as 'Elsies'.

All of The Corbetts are listed as Marilyns, since the generally accepted height separation criterion for the Corbetts is 500ft (152.40m). However, not all of The Munros are Marilyns because Munro's selection was subjective, rather than based on a specific height separation criterion. Over the years, the fact that Munro set no absolute method of determining what is, and what is not, a Munro has been a cause of consternation to many.

Also in 1992, Fiona Torbet (née Graham) published her own list of Scottish hills in the 2000ft to 2500ft height range in the Scottish-based hillwalking magazine

The Great Outdoors. Dawson and Torbet subsequently met and agreed on a definitive drop-based listing for hills in this category with Torbet's maiden name of Graham being given to them; The Torbets no doubt too easily confused with The Corbetts!

In 1995, TACit Press published a booklet of Tables which included The Grahams, and in 1997 a new and updated edition of the SMC book *Munro's Tables* was published which included, along with Tables of Munros, Corbetts and Donalds, the list of Grahams as compiled by Alan Dawson. 1997 also saw publication of the first Grahams guidebook: *The Grahams A Guide to Scotland's 2,000ft Peaks* by Andrew Dempster.

The Grahams had become firmly established and accepted by the hillwalking community.

The Donalds

In compiling his Table of Lowland Hills, Percy Donald visited every elevation over 2000ft in what he considered the Scottish Lowlands, over a five-month period starting in December 1932. It was an impressive achievement, especially since he mainly used public transport, walked all bar one hill on his own and the choice of attire for all his walks was the kilt.

The format of Donald's Tables was similar to that of Munro's Tables where summits were originally classified as Hills and Tops, but are now known as Munros and Munro Tops. Likewise, the summits in Donald's Tables are now known as Donalds and Donald Tops and there are 141 hilltops made up of 89 Donalds and 52 Donald Tops. The inclusive nature of the Table means that it contains all of the Lowland Corbetts (7) and all of the Lowland Grahams (23). Donald's Tables, together with an explanation can be found on page 360.

The formula Donald chose to distinguish between those points which he classified as Hills and those which he considered to be Tops has, like Munro's Tables, been the subject of some discussion ever since!

Unlike the Munros though, where the majority only climb the principal Hills and perhaps less than 20% climb the Munro Tops as well, most of those bagging The Donalds actually climb all 141 Hills and Tops on the list. Much of the challenge of The Donalds is in the logistics required to incorporate the outlying Tops into the day's walk. As a result most of the Donald rounds are fairly substantial undertakings.

Confusing matters slightly is what are known as the New Donalds. Donald's formula and his categorisation into Hills and Tops was not neat enough for some, so a rigid drop-based criterion was applied to create this new list of hills in the Scottish Lowlands over 2000ft.

Regardless of this, as with The Munros, the challenge is in completing Percy Donald's original and historic listing, so the New Donalds are seen as something of an aberration. In any case, climb all 141 Donalds and Donald Tops and you climb all the New Donalds.

The Donald rounds described in this guidebook are by their nature generally quite long, but they are attainable to a fairly fit and competent walker. They can easily be broken down into smaller walks if required and they can also be extended into larger outings for those seeking to complete the list more rapidly. These Lowland hills might not have the same form and rocky nature as those of the Highlands, but they do have a charm all of their own and will undoubtedly provide the walker with an entertaining and thoroughly enjoyable experience.

The Grahams

The Grahams are defined as Scottish hills over 2000ft (609.60m) and under 2500ft (762m) in height, with a distinct all-round height separation of at least 150m.

Fiona Torbet's original list only included hills in the Highlands and involved a drop-based criterion of about 150m, together with a distance-based criterion of a listed hill being the highest all-round point for about two miles. Alan Dawson's list included all of Scotland and was based purely on a 150m drop.

Following Fiona Torbet's death in 1993, Alan Dawson has continued to maintain the official list of The Grahams, details of which can be found through his *The Relative Hills of Britain* (RHB) website and the *Database of British and Irish Hills* (DoBIH) website.

In order to align with the SMC's traditional Section numbers, as used in its hillwalking guidebooks to *The Munros* and *The Corbetts*, the way in which the Table of 219 Grahams that starts on p354 has been presented differs from the official listing of Grahams. Additionally, for ease of use, the entries in the Table have been laid out to run in the same order as the hills appear in the route text. A number of hill heights also differ from the official listing so as to align with the most widely-used maps in the field produced by the OS. In recent times, more accurate heights have been obtained by independent surveyors and recorded in the DoBIH – these heights are also noted in the Table.

Rather than just describing the ascent of a particular Graham, this guidebook aims to provide the walker with details of the best available route for a day's hillwalking. In many cases the Graham is combined with another nearby hill to produce a logical round and a number of Graham and Corbett combinations are described.

Since the 23 Lowland Grahams are also Donalds they have been incorporated into the Donald rounds. For the walker solely interested in The Grahams, brief Graham-only details have been given where relevant.

As more walkers compleat The Munros and The Corbetts, attention is being focused on The Grahams. However, it is still fairly unusual to encounter anyone, apart from on the most popular of Grahams. This lack of traffic also means that there are few distinct paths to follow, so despite their stature many Grahams provide quite arduous outings. The smaller nature of these hills means that their summits provide interesting perspectives of their larger neighbours and some of the dullest looking Grahams provide some of the finest viewpoints. Whilst there are Grahams that number amongst the most well known of Scottish peaks, there are a great many obscure ones that will be a revelation.

Oireabhal and Bìdigidh above Loch Chliostair, Harris (Noel Williams)

ROUTE DESCRIPTIONS
Hill Heights and Summit Locations

Height and summit location information has been taken from the Ordnance Survey as the national mapping authority and producers of the most widely-used maps for hillwalkers. The SMC recognises that independent surveys are being performed which contribute to our understanding of the hills, and while not all of this information is submitted to the OS, it is held in the Database of British and Irish Hills (DoBIH). Heights from the DoBIH that differ from, or are more accurate than, the OS are included in the Table of Grahams starting on p354; see note on the DoBIH at the end of this Table. A few summit locations differ and the relevant information on these is noted at the end of the Table and in the walk description.

Grahams are referenced G1 (Beinn Talaidh) to G219 (Creag Dhubh Mhòr), depending upon height. A full list of Grahams in order of height is given at the back of the book, together with a Table listing all the Grahams laid out in order of SMC Sections, which matches the chapters in this book. This differs from the offical listing.

Donalds are similarly referenced, D1 (The Merrick) to D89 (Innerdownie). Donald Tops have not been referenced in order of height and are simply identified – DT. A full list of Donalds and Donald Tops in order of height is given at the back of the book, together with Donald's Tables listing all the Donalds and Donald Tops.

Mapping

Route maps illustrate route descriptions and serve as aids to planning and have been drawn from out of copyright mapping supplemented by on-the-ground observation. The detail on these maps is not complete and they should not take the place of a proper map.

The recommended maps for hillwalking are the Ordnance Survey 1:50k Landranger Series, and in the heading for each walk the letter L, followed by a number, denotes the relevant OS map. The OS also produce an Explorer Series of maps at a larger scale of 1:25k. The heights of features are generally taken from either the OS 1:50k maps series or the 1:25k series.

Harvey Maps' 1:25k Superwalker and 1:40k British Mountain Maps series are on waterproof and tearproof paper and cover a number of popular mountain areas. Harvey also publish a number of summit map enlargements.

UK mapping uses metric measurements, so distances and heights in the text are in kilometres (km) and metres (m). Distances when approaching by car are sometimes in miles to aid measurement via a car mileometer.

Six figure grid references identify certain locations and are preceded by two OS grid letters to provide a unique reference to within 100m.

The maps in this book use the following symbols to indicate the status of a summit:

♦ **Graham** (219); 2000ft (609.6m) to below 2500ft (762m); minimum 150m drop

◇ **Graham Top**; 2000ft (609.6m) to below 2500ft (762m); minimum 30m drop

■ **Donald** (89); Lowlands, over 2000ft (609.6m). Note: 23 Donalds are also Grahams and 7 Donalds are also Corbetts. Others are Graham Tops and Corbett Tops. In all of these instances the 'other appropriate symbol' has been placed within the Donald symbol.

☐ **Donald Tops** (52); Lowlands, less-distinct summit heights over 2000ft (609.6m). Some Donald Tops are also Graham Tops. In these instances the Graham Top symbol has been placed within the Donald Top symbol.

▲ **Munro** (282); 3000ft (914.4m) and higher

△ **Munro Top** (226); 3,000ft (914.4m) and higher, less distinct summit heights

● **Corbett** (222); 2500ft (762m) to below 3000ft (914.4m); minimum 500ft (152.4m) drop

○ **Corbett Top**; 2500ft (762m) to below 3000ft (914.4m); minimum 30m drop

⊗ Other summit

Distances, Height Gain & Time
Distances and heights have generally been rounded up to the nearest 250m (0.25km) and 10m respectively. Ascent times are calculated on the basis of 4.5km per hour for distance walked, plus 10m per minute (1 hour per 600m) for climbing uphill. Times have generally been rounded up to the nearest 5 minutes.

Timings are a close metric approximation to Naismith's rule. No allowance has been made for stops but an allowance has made for difficult ground and for steep or difficult descents during the walk. This has been based on Langmuir's method of adding 10 minutes per 300m of difficult descent, a timing which has been applied a little more liberally and is particularly relevant to long descents at the end of the day.

Where descriptions relate to the traverse of two or more hills, the distance, height gain and time at selected summits are cumulative from the start. The overall distance, height gain and time has been highlighted in blue.

Parking, Roads, Tracks & Paths
Three levels of parking have been identified on the maps. 🅿 indicates an official, or publicly maintained car park, or a parking area such as a lay-by. 🅿 indicates that there is adequate off-road parking. 🅿 indicates that parking is limited or restricted, such as in small pull-offs or verge parking.

Throughout the text, road means a tarmac surface, usually public. Where a surfaced road is private, as in some estate roads, this is mentioned. Track means any unsurfaced way such as used by forestry or estate vehicles; usually private. Atv track means any less distinct route on the hill used by all-terrain-vehicles such as quad bikes. Tracks can usually be biked, whereas it is unlikely that atv tracks can be. Path means a clear pedestrian route on the ground, often a stalkers' or hillwalkers' path.

Routes
Continuous red lines on the maps indicate the principal routes and red dashed lines some alternatives or extensions. Yellow lines and yellow dashed lines generally indicate secondary routes together with their extensions and variations. These correspond with the overall route distance, height and times in the descriptions.

The objective of this book is to describe routes to the Grahams and the Donalds. However, the nature of these hills means that it is often possible to extend routes to take in nearby hills and routes have been described with this in mind. Without stating it every time, it will often be possible to shorten a walk after the principal objective has been climbed, either by returning via the route of ascent, or by some other route. Where extensions are logical these have normally been described or mentioned with full distances and times given.

Routes have generally been described to take in the principal objective first then perhaps a neighbouring higher hill. However, these are only suggestions. On the day, a reverse approach to the one described might better suit the conditions or the party.

MOUNTAIN SAFETY & WEATHER
Participation Statement
Mountaineering Scotland recognises that hillwalking, climbing and mountaineering are activities with a danger of personal injury or death. Participants in these activities should be aware of and accept these risks and be responsible for their own actions and involvement.

Navigation, Equipment & Planning
Good navigation skills, equipment, clothing and forward planning can all help reduce the chance of an accident. While mobile phones and GPS can help in communications and in locating your position, the former do not work over all of Scotland and both rely on batteries and electronics which can fail or be easily damaged. Consequently, they can never be a substitute for navigation skills with map and compass, first aid or general mountain skills. The potential hazards of winter conditions, rivers in spate, or challenging navigation from changes in weather should always be remembered.

Weather Forecasting
Although weather forecasting has improved over the years, it is not a precise science. The smaller nature of the hills covered in this guidebook means that they are generally less affected by low cloud and bad weather than the higher hills. The downside to this though is that many of the hills in this book have less defined routes and less defined features than their higher counterparts, so navigation in poor weather can prove challenging. There are many forecasts available but a few are worth mentioning. The Mountain Weather Information Service (MWIS) has forecasts covering Scotland in five areas. The Meteorological Office (Met Office) also has Mountain Weather forecasts covering the main mountain areas of Scotland in four areas, within which one can obtain forecasts for specific hills. Links to MWIS and the Met Office are also available through the Mountaineering Scotland website. In addition, BBC TV and Radio forecasts, which at times include a walkers' forecast, also have regularly updated web based forecasts. These are all available for mobile phones, together with other mobile phone app forecasts.

Notes

Avalanches
Avalanches occur with great regularity in the Scottish hills. The lower nature of the Grahams and Donalds means that for much of the time they can be less susceptible to avalanche risk than the higher hills. However, avalanches can happen wherever there is snow lying on ground of sufficient angle, so these lower hills are not avalanche risk free. Winter walkers should familiarise themselves with the principles of snow structure and avalanche prediction.

While the ability to make your own assessment of risk is vital, snow and avalanche predictions for the major mountain areas are produced by the Sportscotland Avalanche Information Service (SAIS) and are readily available throughout the winter. As well as on the SAIS website, which can also be linked to from the Mountaineering Scotland website, these reports can be found at police stations, sports shops, tourist information centres and on display boards in mountain areas. The About Avalanches section on the SAIS website makes useful reading. *A Chance in a Million?* is the classic work on avalanches and is recommended reading for anyone venturing onto the Scottish hills in winter.

Mountain Rescue
In the event of an accident, contact the police, either by phone (999) or in person. It is often better to stay with the casualty but in a party of two, one may have to leave to summon help. If the casualty has to be left, leave them in a warm, comfortable, sheltered, and well-marked place. Further information is available on the Mountain Rescue Scotland website.

Midges, Clegs, Deer Ked & Ticks
Biting insects such as midges, clegs and deer ked can make things unpleasant at times. Ticks, however, can carry Lyme disease and incidents appear to be increasing, so it is worth reading up on them. Mountaineering Scotland, the BMC and Lyme Disease Action UK all have relevant information.

OTHER USEFUL INFORMATION
Access
The Land Reform (Scotland) Act 2003 gives everyone statutory access rights to most land and inland water including mountains, moorland, woods and forests, grassland, paths and tracks, and rivers and lochs. People only have these rights if they exercise them responsibly by respecting people's privacy, safety and livelihoods, and Scotland's environment. Equally, land managers have to manage their land and water responsibly in relation to access rights. The Outdoor Access Scotland website and the Scottish Outdoor Access Code provide detailed guidance on these responsibilities.

Stalking, Shooting & Lambing
Deer management takes place during many months of the year but the sensitive period is the stag stalking season, from 1st July to 20th October. Few estates actually start at the beginning of the season and most stalking takes place from August onwards. Hinds continue to be culled until 15th February. Requests may be made to either avoid areas where stalking is taking place, or to keep to standard routes and ridgelines. Stalking does not normally take place on Sundays, although requests to avoid disturbing deer on the hills may still be made. There is no stalking on National Trust for Scotland land.

Heading for the Scottish Hills provides information and contact phone numbers to help hillwalkers and climbers find out where red deer stalking is taking place over the stag stalking season. This can be found online by entering Heading for the Scottish Hills into a search engine. A link is also available from Mountaineering Scotland's website.

The grouse shooting season is from 12th August until 10th December. If you are heading onto the hills with a dog it is important to avoid disturbance to sheep, especially during the lambing season between March and May.

Footpath Erosion, Cairns & Memorials
It is the responsibility of all walkers to minimise their erosive effect on the mountain landscape. The proliferation of navigation cairns detracts from the feeling of wildness and may be confusing rather than helpful as regards to route-finding. The indiscriminate building of cairns and memorials on the hills should be discouraged.

Bikes, Cars & Transport
A number of routes in this book advocate the use of mountain bikes for approaches along estate and forestry tracks. Bikes can cause erosion when used on footpaths and open hillsides and should only be used on prepared surfaces such as vehicular or forest tracks and some stalkers' paths. Access rights do not extend to vehicles being driven up private roads without permission.

Most walkers will arrive by car. For those using public transport, up-to-date timetables are best found via the internet.

Bothies
The Mountain Bothies Association maintains about 80 bothies on various estates throughout Scotland. None of these are owned by the MBA, but belong to estates which generously allow their use. A number of bothies are closed during the Stalking Season. Visit the MBA's website for further information.

Mountaineering Scotland
This is the representative body for climbers and hillwalkers in Scotland. One of its primary concerns is the continued free access to the hills. Information about bird restrictions, stalking and access issues can be obtained from them. Any hill user encountering problems regarding access should contact Mountaineering Scotland.

Scottish Mountaineering Club
The SMC produces guidebooks for Hillwalkers, Scramblers and Climbers. All profits from these guidebooks go to the Scottish Mountaineering Trust (SMT) and provide much of the SMT's revenue – see opposite.

Marsco and the Allt Dearg Mòr, Skye (Tom Prentice)

Scottish Mountaineering Trust

Profit from the sale of this guidebook helps to fund the Scottish Mountaineering Trust (SMT). The SMT is a Scottish charity that provides grants to projects, people and organisations promoting recreation, education and safety in the hills and mountains, especially those of Scotland.

The Scottish Mountaineering Trust supports:
- Footpath construction and maintenance
- Land purchases that ensure public access
- Publication of guides to, and information about, the hills and mountains of Scotland
- Mountaineering education and training, especially aimed at young people
- Mountain rescue teams and organisations, for equipment and facilities
- Renovation of club huts available to the wider mountaineering community
- Expeditions with educational or scientific objectives aligned with those of the Trust

In over 30 years the SMT has provided over £1.6m to people and organisations working in these areas.

The SMT is funded by donations from those who share its values, and from the publication of Scottish Mountaineering Club and Scottish Mountaineering Press books.
If you would like to find out more about how the SMT can help you, or your organisation, or to support the SMT with a donation, please go to *www.thesmt.org.uk*.

Mullwharchar with Dungeon Hill right, from the Devil's Bowling Green on Craignaw (Rab Anderson)

SECTION 0a
Galloway & The Lowthers

Section 0a – Galloway & The Lowthers

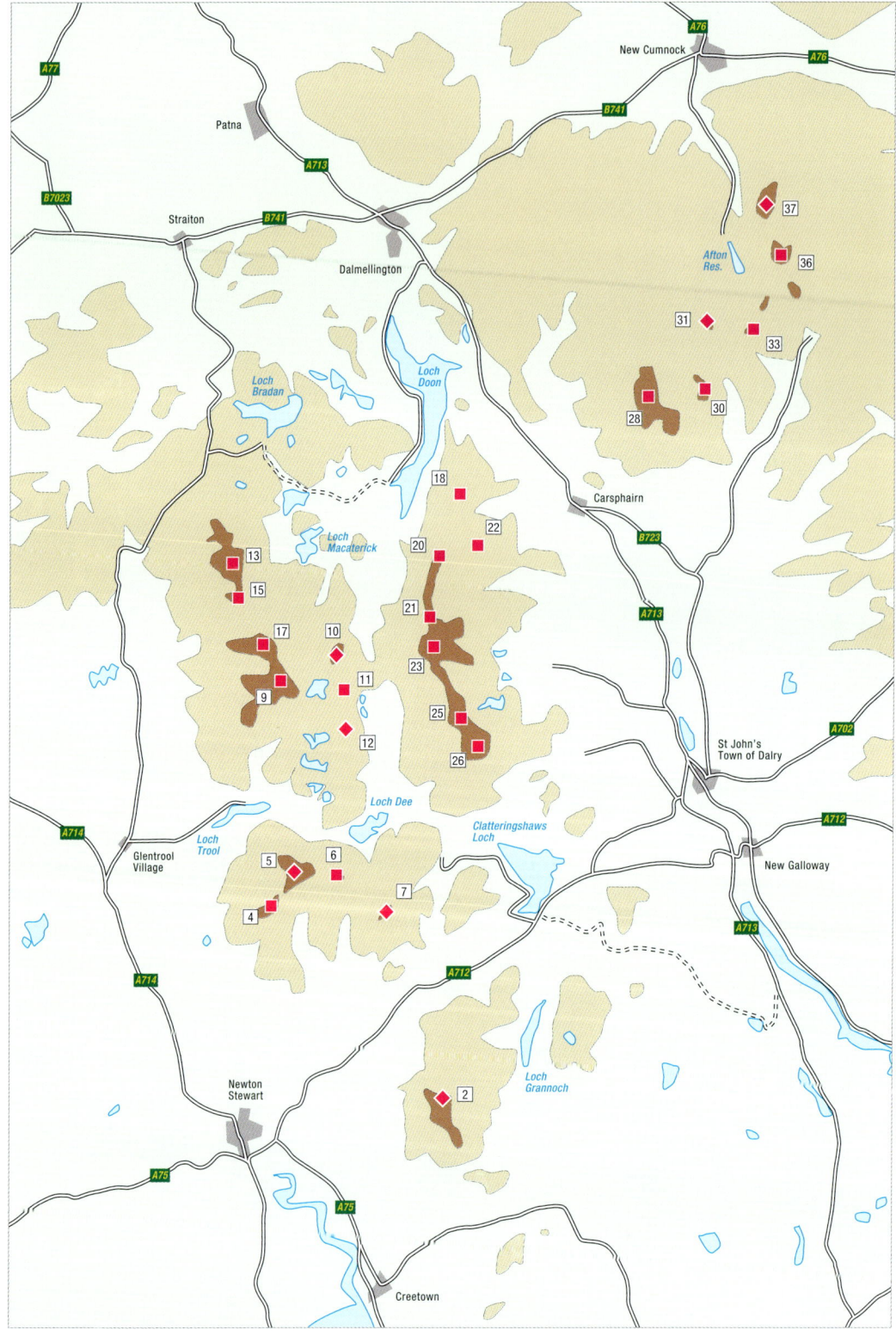

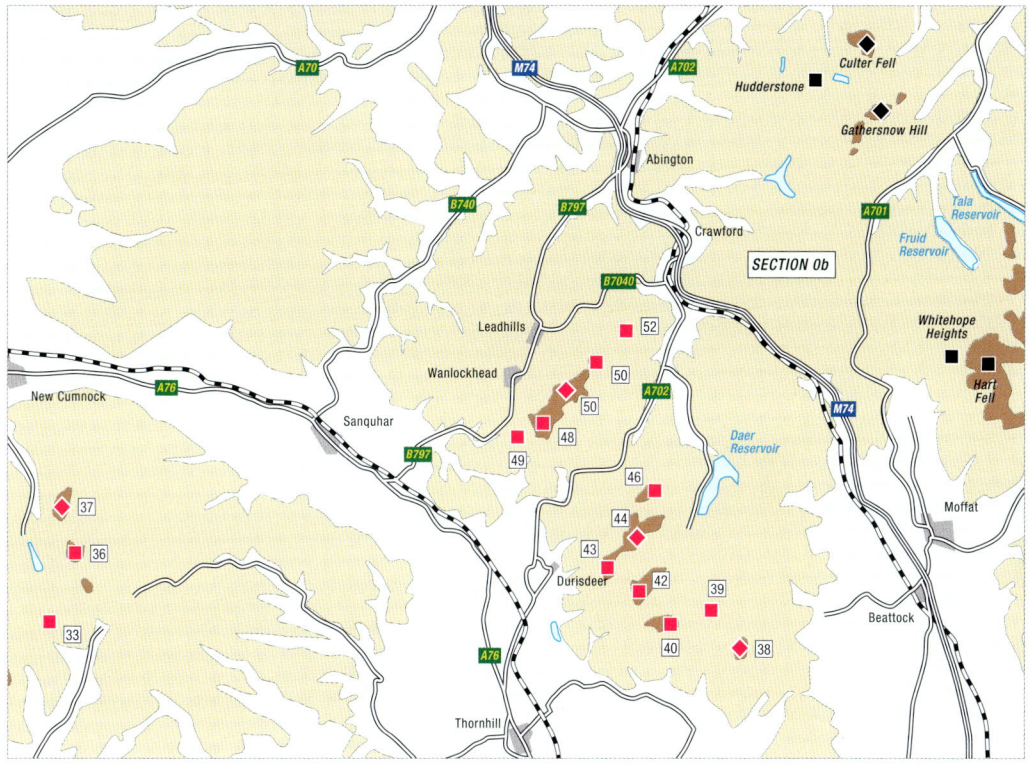

SECTION 0a

[1] Knee of Cairnsmore, [2] ◆ Cairnsmore of Fleet,
   [3] Meikle Mulltaggart   16
[4] Larg Hill, [5] ◆ Lamachan Hill, [6] Curleywee, [7] ◆ Millfore   18
[8] Benyellary, [9] The Merrick, [10] ◆ Mullwharchar,
   [11] Dungeon Hill, [12] ◆ Craignaw   21
[13] Shalloch on Minnoch, [14] Caerloch Dhu, [15] Tarfessock,
   [16] Tarfessock South Top, [17] Kirriereoch Hill   24
[18] Corran of Portmark, [19] Bow, [20] Meaul,
   [21] Carlin's Cairn, [22] Cairnsgarroch   26
[23] Corserine, [24] Millfire, [25] Milldown, [26] Meikle Millyea   28
[27] Beninner, [28] Cairnsmore of Carsphairn, [32] Dugland,
   [31] ◆ Windy Standard, [29] Keoch Rig, [30] Moorbrock Hill   30
[31] ◆ Windy Standard, [33] Alhang, [34] Alwhat, [35]
   Meikledodd Hill, [36] Blacklorg Hill, [37] ◆ Blackcraig Hill   32
[38] ◆ Queensberry, [39] Earncraig Hill, [40] Gana Hill   34
[41] Glenleith Fell, [42] Wedder Law, [43] Scaw'd Law,
   [44] ◆ Ballencleuch Law, [45] Rodger Law, [46] Comb Law   36
[47] Cold Moss, [48] Lowther Hill, [49] East Mount Lowther,
   [50] ◆ Green Lowther, [51] Dun Law, [52] Lousie Wood Law   38

Section 0a – Galloway & The Lowthers

Cairnsmore of Fleet

Cairnsmore of Fleet from the west (Tom Prentice)

Knee of Cairnsmore; 657m; DT; L83; NX509656; in Border Scots knee is usually from nose or promintory
Cairnsmore of Fleet; 711m; (G78); (D28); L83; NX501670; moor of cairns, above the Fleet. There are two prehistoric cairns on the plateau
Meikle Mulltaggart; 612m; DT; L83; NX512678; possibly big hill of the priest

A massive whalebacked granite intrusion, this southernmost Graham dominates the western reaches of the Solway Firth. In addition to Cairnsmore of Fleet itself, which is also a Donald, it includes the Donald Tops of Knee of Cairnsmore and Meikle Mulltaggart. On a clear day the views south from these hills extends to the Lake District, the Isle of Man and the Mountains of Mourne in Ireland.

A circular and relatively dry route taking in all three tops starts at the Big Water of Fleet Viaduct (NX557642). This is reached from Gatehouse of Fleet via the B796 north beside the Water of Fleet from where a minor road leads to the Nature Reserve Information Centre then along a track for 1km, to a parking area just after the viaduct. The viaduct is an imposing 20-arch structure which once carried the former Dumfries to Stranraer line and featured in the Hitchcock film of John Buchan's book *The Thirty Nine Steps*.

Take the track on the west side of the river and follow it north into the forest, past a turn-off right to Meikle Cullendoch, then west to exit the forest. Continue across trackless ground to climb the east ridge of the

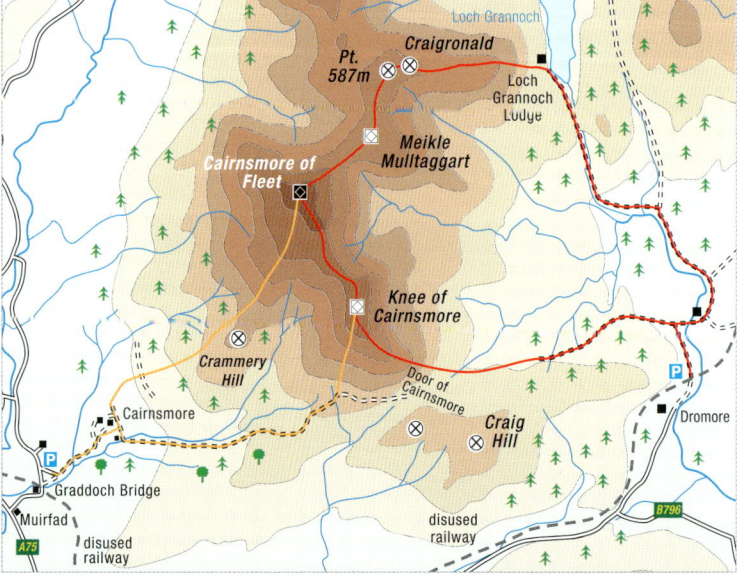

Knee of Cairnsmore. The OS 1:25k and 1:50k maps show the top at a cairn at NX509654, but the 1:10k map shows a point 200m to the north to be 1m higher. A faint path leads along the ridge, across the Nick of Clashneach, then up to the summit shelter and trig point on Cairnsmore of Fleet (**8km; 650m; 2h 50min**).

Immediately before the summit is a granite memorial to the crews of eight aircraft which crashed on the hill between 1940 and 1979, the earliest a Luftwaffe Heinkel bomber and the latest a USAF Phantom jet. The cairns on both Cairnsmore and the Knee are of Bronze Age vintage. The desolate corrie to the east hosts the remote Spout of the Clints Waterfall and is a National Nature Reserve; an example of open moorland ecosystem, common before blanket afforestation. On the north side of the hill lies Billy Marshall's Cave, used for smuggling by the legendary gypsy king who died in 1792, aged 120!

Drop north-east to Nick of the Saddle and climb Meikle Mulltaggart, picking up an atv track. The top is unmarked and the track bypasses the summit to the west of it (**9.5 km; 700m; 3h 15min**).

The return is made via Loch Grannoch Lodge at the end of Loch

South to Knee of Cairnsmore (Rab Anderson)

Grannoch. Trackless, rough going leads northwards over an unnamed 587m top, then east down the ridge of Craigronald. Cliffs immediately above the lodge can be avoided either north or south of it. From the lodge, follow the forest track south, taking a right turn after 2.5km, then another right after 2km at the house of Meikle Cullendoch, followed by a left shortly thereafter to reach the start (19km; 720m; 5h 35min).

Cairnsmore of Fleet can be climbed by itself via the path from Cairnsmore Farm near Newton Stewart, reached from the signposted parking area at NX464632 (**6km; 690m; 2h 30min**); (12km; 690m; 4h).

Meikle Mulltaggart and Knee of Cairnsmore can easily be added, climbing the former first then gaining the latter by back-tracking to pass beneath the summit of Cairnsmore of Fleet. Descend south-south-west off the Knee to gain a rough track at its higpoint at NX506642 and follow this back to the farm then the start (17km; 900m; 5h 35min).

Descending to Meikle Mulltaggart from Cairnsmore of Fleet (Keith Fergus)

Larg Hill, Lamachan Hill, Curleywee, Millfore

Curleywee, left, and Lamachan Hill over Loch Dee (Andrew Fraser)

Larg Hill; 676m; (D49); L77; NX424757; shank hill. Gaelic 'lorg', shank, thigh, leg (in shape)
Lamachan Hill; 717m; (G70); (D26); L77; NX435769; hill above Lamachan (farm). Mapped as Lommachan Hill (1654). Perhaps from Gaelic 'lomach', bare place
Curleywee; 674m; (D51); L77; NX454769; hill of the eagle? The burn in the northern corrie was mapped as Korreilleury Burn in 1654: maybe Gaelic 'coire', corrie, or 'corr', pointed hill, with 'na-h'iolaire', of the eagle
Millfore; 657m; (G167); (D62); L77; NX477754; cold hill from Gaelic 'meall fuar'. Mapped Mullfear (1654)

Lying between the A712 to the south and Loch Trool and Loch Dee to the north, these hills offer fine high-level ridge walking. They can be done in one long outing as described, although the inclusion of Millfore adds considerably to the day. Millfore can be climbed separately, and if so, is better approached from Craigencallie or the Black Loch, as described at the end. Start at the Bruce's Stone car park at the east end of Loch Trool. The stone commemorates Robert the Bruce's victory in 1307 at the Steps of Trool, the battle which opened the war of independence.

From the car park, follow the track down then eastward past the Falls of Buchan and Glenhead and across the vehicle bridge to the south side of the Glenhead Burn. Continue south-east on the forest track (National Cycle Route 7), rising through the trees for 1km until it crosses the Shiel Burn at NX435790. Leave the track here and follow the line of the burn then its right fork up to Nick of the Lochans, between Mulldonach and Lamachan Hill.

If omitting Larg Hill it is best to take the ridge to the left or east of the Shiel Burn which leads to Bennanbrack. A wall then leads right to the summit of Lamachan Hill.

To take in Larg Hill from Nick of the Lochans, climb the steep slope to the south onto Cambrick Hill until it starts to level out then traverse south along the western side of Lamachan Hill to gain the Nick of the Brushy col. A wall can then be followed south-west

Curleywee, left, and Millfore from Lamachan Hill (Tom Prentice)

Larg Hill, Lamachan Hill, Curleywee, Milfore

Section 0a – Galloway & The Lowthers

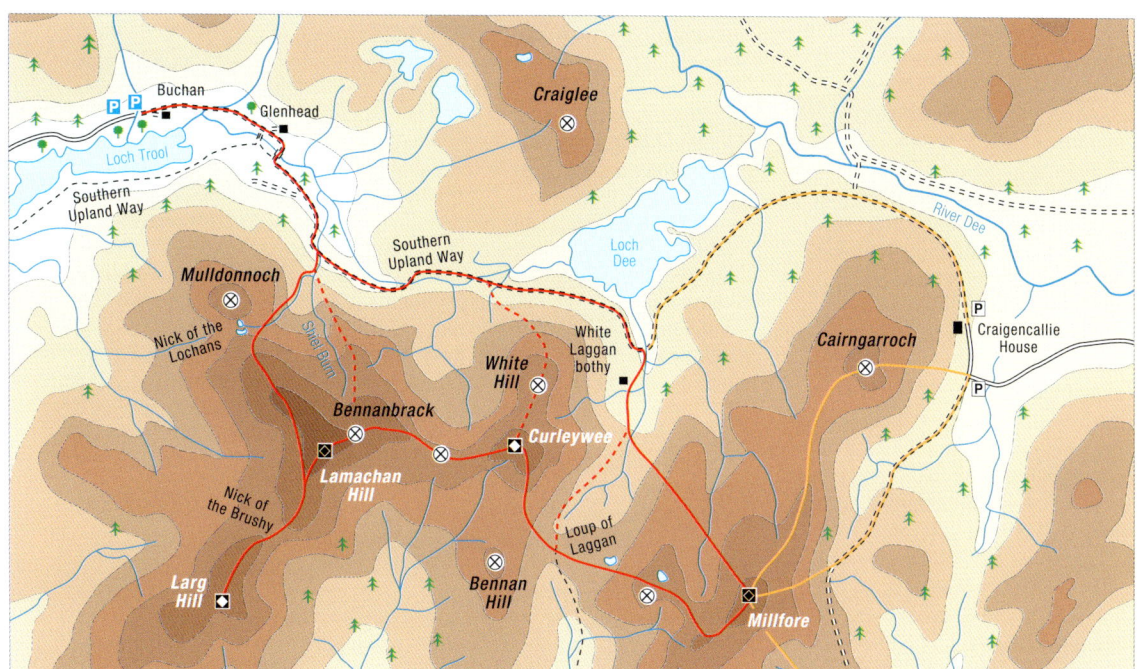

along the ridge to Larg Hill (**7km; 620m; 2h 35min**). Larg Hill was the site of an airship crash in 1917.

Return to Nick of the Brushy and follow the wall onto the summit plateau of Lamachan Hill. The main ridge now switchbacks for 2.5km of fine ridge walking, first east-north-east to Bennanbrack then south-east past Nick of Corners Gale and Nick of Curleywee to the shapely Curleywee (**11km; 920m; 4h 5min**). Known as the 'Matterhorn of the South' this peak is finely situated above Loch Dee.

If omitting Millfore, descend north over White Hill then drop through rough terrain, either direct or via an atv track, to pick up the route of the Southern Upland Way west of Loch Dee, which leads back to the start (**17.5km; 1010m; 5h 45min**).

Continuing to Millfore, take the ridge south for 800m to a wall, which is followed south-east to the Loup of Laggan; the col between the Pulnee and White Laggan Burns. From here, ▶

Millfore from the south (Jim Teesdale)

it is 2km of complex but interesting ground east to Millfore with its trig point (**14.5km; 1200m; 5h 25min**).

The ascent passes the Black Loch then the White Lochan of Drigmorn. White Lochan was used for curling in the 19th century, the stone structure on its northern shore having been built by soldiers stationed at Newton Stewart during the 1853–56 Crimean War.

From Millfore, the quickest descent is north-west for 2km, crossing the upper reaches of the Black Laggan Burn, over a small subsidiary ridge, then continuing downhill to the path on the west side of the White Laggan Burn. This leads past White Laggan bothy to join the forest track, which is followed west for 2.5km to the col between Loch Dee and Loch Trool.

Now on the Southern Upland Way, continue along this on the track through the forest on the south side of the Glenhead Burn. Cross the bridge over the burn at Glenhead and continue along the track back to the start (**24.5km; 1300m; 8h**).

Millfore can be climbed by itself by starting at the right-angled corner (NX503774) about 600m south of Craigencallie at the end of the minor road, which leaves the A712 and runs round the west side of Clatteringshaws Loch. Follow the burn up the edge of the forestry, go over Cairngarroch then past the Nick of Rushes (fence with stile at NX485769) and the bizarrely named Buckdas of Cairnbaber to reach Millfore (**4km; 560m; 1h 50min**).

Either return the same way or descend east-north-east for 1km to gain a forest track which leads back to the start (**7.5km; 560m; 2h 50min**).

Another route from the south starts at the Black Loch car park (NX499730) and follows a forestry track to a saddle then climbs the south-east ridge (**5km; 500m; 2h**); (**10km; 500m; 3h 25min**).

Another option is to bike to the south side of Loch Dee, quicker and easier from Craigencallie, then make a circuit of these hills, or both Grahams, via White Laggan bothy with Curleywee being climbed only the once then bypassed on its south side on the traverse between the Grahams.

Galloway Hills
The main group of Galloway Hills effectively comprises 19 Donalds and 7 Donald Tops, of which 5 are Grahams and 3 are Corbetts, including the highest hill in the South of Scotland, The Merrick. It is a fairly complex group of hills which is covered here in six walks, although there are many other ways of climbing the various hill groups, either in shorter, or more extended outings.

Those interested in climbing just the Grahams can tackle these as two pairs and a single. Cairnsmore of Fleet is easily split from its two attendant Donald Tops and quickly climbed via the path from Cairnsmore to the south-west, as mentioned in the route description on p17. Lamachan Hill and Millfore can be tackled from any of the starts described in the route description on p18, omitting Larg Hill, however Curleywee lies between them and although this can be avoided it is perhaps better to take it in. Similarly, Craignaw and Mullwharcher can be split from the Donald round opposite, which includes The Merrick, however the reality of the terrain and the fact that a good path leads to, or from, the summit of The Merrick means that there is in fact little to be gained in doing so.

The main northern group of hills is formed by three distinct south to north running parallel chains which lend themselves to long ridge walks along the crests, although getting back to the start points can prove a logistical problem due to forests and burns, unless transport can be arranged at either end, or overnight stays are made in bothies or by camping.

The seven hilltops on the western chain from Caerloch Dubh to Benyellary, of which five are known as The Awful Hand (Benyellary being the thumb and The Merrick the forefinger), can be climbed in a linear traverse from parking south of the Stinchar Bridge car park (see p25) in the north to the Glen Trool car park in the south (18km; 940m; 6h 15min). A circuit of these seven tops is also possible from the Kirriereoch car park (see p24) via the principal route described for Shalloch on Minnoch by continuing from Kirriereoch Hill over The Merrick to Benyellary. Either descend Kirn Brae (steep) or the north-west ridge to gain a forest track at NX386855 which leads back to the car park (27.5km; 1300m; 8h 45min). A descent can be made off The Merrick down the west ridge to gain a track at NX388868. These hills, in whole or in part, can also be climbed from Forest Drive via the forest track down the west side of Loch Riecawr, which opens up the possibility of extending the round to include Craignaw, Dungeon Hill and Mullwharchar with Tunskeen bothy (NX425906) perhaps being of use.

The eastern chain of nine hilltops from Corran of Portmark to Meikle Millyea is known as the Rhinns of Kells and although covered here in two walks, the ridge can be climbed in one linear outing. This can be done from Green Well of Scotland (see p26), as for the route taking in Meaul and Carlin's Cairn then continuing south to Meikle Millyea. There are three possible descents from here. The first is as for the route described for the Corserine to Meikle Millyea round on p28 to gain the Forrest Lodge car park (23km; 1130m; 7h 30min). The second gains the Southern Upland Way then the car park at NX558826 (22.5km; 1130m; 7h 25min). A third option is to continue over Little Millyea and Darrou to go down a rough firebreak directly to the Southern Upland Way and the River Dee crossing at NX496794 from where the road end can be reached at Craigencallie (24.5km; 1200m; 8h). This traverse relies on a secondary means of transport being available. It is possible to climb all these hills as a round from the Forrest Lodge car park. This is done by starting with Meikle Millyea then climbing the ridge northwards to Corran of Portmark then returning over Bow to climb Cairnsgarroch. A descent can be made from here south past Craigchessie then down a firebreak to gain a forestry track which is crossed to descend a felled area where the Polmaddy Burn can be crossed and followed east to a stile to reach another firebreak leading to a forest track which runs south then south-east back to the start (30km; 1340m; 10h). Further clear felling of the forest may open up the routes to the various tracks and provide other routes across the Polmaddy Burn.

The Merrick, Mullwharchar, Dungeon Hill, Craignaw

Looking across Loch Enoch to The Merrick, left, and Kirriereoch Hill (Andrew Fraser)

Benyellary; 719m; (DT); L77; NX414839; possibly hill of the eagle

The Merrick; 843m; (D1); L77; NX427855; branched or spreading mountain. Bin Maerack (1654), i.e. Gaelic 'beinn meurach'. Beinn was lost, replaced by "The" from 1755

Mullwharchar; 692m; (G115); (D39); L77; NX454866; hill of the lapwing. Gaelic 'meall na h-adharcan' or the hunting horn 'adhairce'. Mapped Mayllhorkun hill (1654), Millwharchar (1797)

Dungeon Hill; 620m; (D83); L77; NX460850; hill above the Dungeon lochs, there being another of the name 6km east. Perhaps from the rocky fastness appearance of the hill

Craignaw; 645m; (G179); (D68); L77; NX459833; Craggy hill of the rock. Gaelic 'creag na h' aill'. The hill's surface is a mass of rocks, including the Devil's Bowling Green. Mapped Kraigna (1654), Kraignall (1755). Possibly 'creag an atha', cliff of the ford, from the crossing of the Silver Flowe below

This superb route combines The Merrick, the highest hill in Southern Scotland, with the Dungeon of Buchan range as this area's most rugged and arguably finest hills. The first half to The Merrick is on good paths and easy walking, the Dungeon section is pathless and rough going. This reflects the different geology, metamorphic on The Merrick and granite on the Dungeon, the junction being clearly visible on the descent from The Merrick to Loch Enoch. It is possible to split the traverse into two equally fine walks, as described at the end, but the nature of the terrain means there is little to be gained in terms of time or effort by doing so.

Start at the Bruce's Stone car park at the end of the road in Glen Trool, where a path is signposted to The Merrick. Follow the path for 2km, first above the tumbling Buchan Burn, then to the basic bothy at Culsharg. From there, the path climbs up the left side of the Whiteland Burn to reach a forest track. Turn right across the burn to gain the continuation path and follow this up through a gate, then steeply on through forestry to emerge into the open. The path continues ahead, gradually swinging round to climb more steeply onto Benyellary. Thereafter, follow a wall across the ridge of the Neive of the Spit, then follow the path north-east across the slope (the Broads of The Merrick) to reach the trig point, which sits above the steep northern face (6.5km; 770m; 2h 45min).

The views are extensive, with the distant peaks of England's Lake District, the Mourne Mountains of Ireland, Arran and the Highlands all visible.

From here on is largely pathless. Descend to Loch Enoch by heading east-south-east at first to gain Redstone Rig then head for the north-west corner of Loch Enoch. The butterfly-shaped Loch Enoch is notable for a number of reasons. It is the highest and at 39.3m, the deepest loch in Southern Scotland. In his book *The Merrick and the Neighbouring Hills*, J.McBain describes how in 1918 he drilled holes in the partly frozen loch to check the depth by plumbline. The island on the loch has ▶

The Merrick, Mullwharchar, Dungeon Hill, Craignaw

Loch Enoch and the rounded cone of Mullwharchar from the south (Tom Prentice)

its own loch-in-loch, and the fine silver sand was once a prized commodity for sharpening scythes. The remains of a 1940 Whitley bomber lie on the southern shore.

To the north-east rises the cone of Mullwharchar, the remotest hill in Southern Scotland and the first of the Dungeon of Buchan range. The ascent involves weaving up through grass and rock (**9.5km; 970m; 4h**).

Mullwharchar became the unexpected focus of environmental protest in the early 1970s when a proposed nuclear waste repository on the hill was defeated at public inquiry.

From Mullwharchar, descend rough ground south to the Pulskaig Burn outfall from Loch Enoch, then head south-east onto the north ridge of Dungeon Hill, known as the Brishie. The summit (**11.5km; 1090m; 4h 50min**) gives a fine view south down the valley of the Cooran Lane, surely a prime candidate for 'rewilding' with the removal of forestry and tracks to reinstate a previous wilderness. The concentric rings of the floating bog of the Silver Flowe are prominent. This is a National Nature Reserve and home to the fine azure hawker dragonfly.

Descend west to the foot of the rise up to Craignairny then cut down the side of this to the Nick of the Dungeon col. Climb the increasingly rocky north-west ridge of Craignaw to the Devil's Bowling Green, an area of flat granite littered with boulders. Beyond, a steep rocky slope leads past a northern top to the summit (**14km; 1240m; 5h 45min**).

There are excellent views of The Merrick and Loch Enoch, as well as east to the Rhinns of Kells. Some 200m to the south-west, below a steep cliff, there is a memorial to the crew of an American F1-11 jet fighter, which crashed here in 1979.

Descend south for 600m then head down rough ground to cross the Mid Burn between Loch Neldricken and Loch Valley to gain a path. The path gives difficult and boggy going, past Loch Valley then down and

Dungeon Hill from the flanks of Craignaw (Rab Anderson)

The Merrick, Mullwharchar, Dungeon Hill, Craignaw

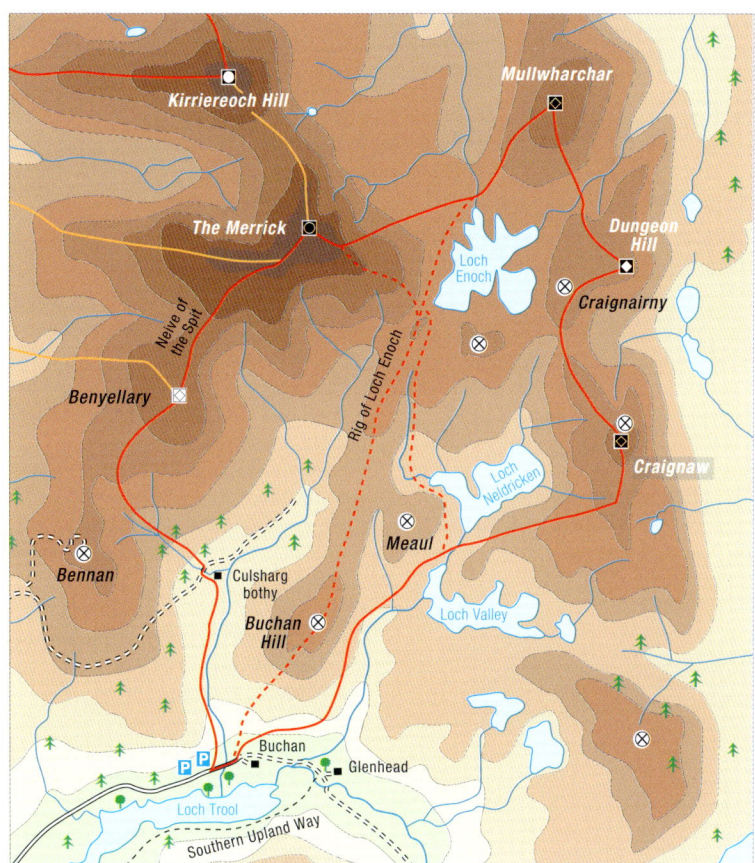

around the side of Buchan Hill above the Garland Burn. Gain the track at the farm at Buchan and follow this past the Falls of Buchan back up to the car park (**20km; 1260m; 7h 45min**).

The Merrick and the two Grahams of the Dungeon range can be done as separate walks. For both routes it will be necessary to gain or descend from the south-west end of Loch Enoch, either by the good but boggy path past Loch Valley and Loch Neldricken, or by Buchan Hill. Points of interest on the former are the rock face of the Old Man of The Merrick at NR437846 and the Murder Hole of Loch Neldricken. This latter is a grim eye of water immortalised in S.R.Crockett's book *The Raiders*.

The route via Buchan Hill starts on the east side of the Buchan Burn, immediately after the bridge on the road to Buchan farm. This is a drier, more scenic but perhaps rougher walk than by the lochs and leads over Buchan Hill to the Rig of Loch Enoch. From the south-west corner of Loch Enoch The Merrick is easily climbed by Redstone Rig, while Mullwharchar can be accessed via the rough west side of Loch Enoch.

South to Craignaw from Craignairny (Tom Prentice)

Shalloch on Minnoch, Tarfessock, Kirriereoch Hill

> **Shalloch on Minnoch**; 775m; (D13); L77; NX407905; hunting place on the middle hill? Gaelic 'sealg', hunt and 'meadhonach', middle. Mapped Shellach of Meannock (1654), Shalloch Cairn (1775)
>
> **Caerloch Dhu**; 659m; (DT); NX400920
>
> **Tarfessock**; 697m; (D35); L77; NX409891; bearded, shaggy hill. Gaelic 'tòrr feusagach'. Mapped Torfessock (1797)
>
> **Tarfessock South Top**; 620m; (DT); L77; NX413886
>
> **Kirriereoch Hill**; 786m; (D11); L77; NX421869; hill of the greyish quarter (or corrie). Gaelic 'ceathramh' (or 'coire') 'riabhach'. The hill seems to be named from Kirriereoch farm: 'ceathramh' is a land measure

These hills form the northernmost fingers of The Awful Hand, the ridge of hills of which The Merrick (the forefinger) is highest. A 4km forest track approach is more than compensated for by an interesting and characterful route. Access is via the unclassified road between Straiton and Glentrool Village, which bounds the hills on their west side.

About 4.5 miles (7.5km) north of Glentrool Village, and 2.5 miles (4km) south of the Barr road junction at Rowantree Bridge, turn onto a track signed Kirriereoch and park at a Forestry Commission picnic site by the Water of Minnoch (NX358867). The once popular route from the Rowantree Bridge car park via the farm at Shalloch on Minnoch is overgrown with forestry and no longer recommended.

From the parking area, continue along the track and turn sharp left followed by a sharp right just short of Kirriereoch farm. After 300m, a track comes in from the right. The return route from The Merrick and Benyellary (see the Galloway Hills information panel on p20) takes this track. Continue straight ahead and on for another 1.8km to cross a bridge over the Pillow Burn. About 250m beyond the bridge, keep right where the track forks and follow it to its end (NX389881). Providing The Merrick and Benyellary are not being included in the round, a mountain bike would assist this section since the track has only moderate inclines.

Just before the track ends, turn left onto a path beside old wooden fence posts and ascend the clearing between the plantations. It is worth noting that the return route ascends the continuation of the clearing and fence posts immediately below the track.

Head up the hill to gain gloriously easy walking on the west ridge of Tarfessock. Rather than follow the ridge, take a rising traverse northeast to gain the Nick of Carlach, the col between Tarfessock and Shalloch on Minnoch. After a further 800m the summit plateau of Shalloch on Minnoch is gained. The 775m summit is clearly marked on the 1:25k map and lies near the corrie edge, about 300m south-east of the 768m trig point (7.5km; 560m; 2h 40min).

The Donald Top of Caerloch Dhu is unhelpfully situated to the north and requires an out and back trip to attain its summit. This is the westernmost hill on Donald's List and is gained by descending the broad ridge north of the trig point (9km; 590m; 3h 5min). Whilst it only involves an ascent of 30m or so, it requires a more substantial 140m climb back to the

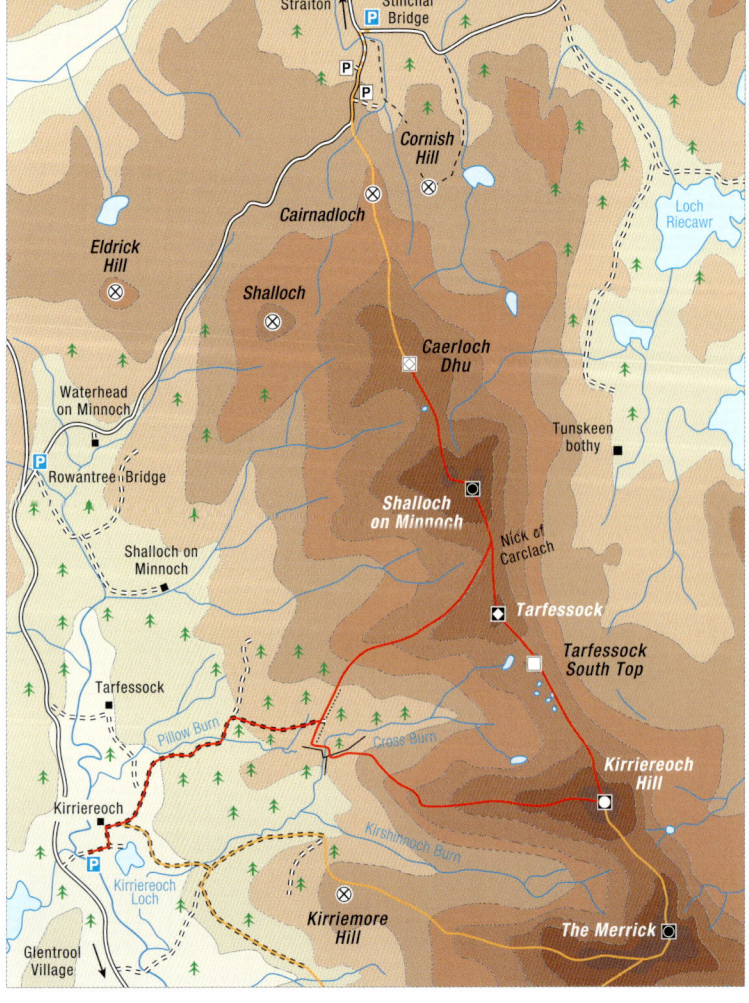

Shalloch on Minnoch, Tarfessock, Kirriereoch Hill

Kirriereoch Hill, left, Tarfessock and Shalloch on Minnoch from the south-east (Tom Prentice)

trig point on Shalloch on Minnoch.

From Shalloch on Minnoch, return south to the Nick of Carclach then continue onto Tarfessock. Rough and rocky ground studded with lochans leads over Tarfessock South Top to a fence at the col below Kirriereoch's screes. Avoid these on the left by a steep ascent on grass to arrive at a wall straddling the hill. The highest point is a boulder on rounded ground about 180m south-east of the wall (**15km; 1020m; 5h 15min**).

To descend, return to the wall and follow intermittent paths down the west ridge. Where the wall turns sharply south, pass through it and follow a rough path beside metal fence posts to reach a fence surrounding forestry in the glen. Follow the fence west towards the Cross Burn to an old stile on the right. Go over the fence here and follow the path north to meet the burn. Ford the burn and continue between a fence on your left and forestry on your right, to where the plantation ends. This is the clearing below the track, identified on the ascent. The start of the clearing is extremely marshy, but the track is soon gained and followed back to the start (**22.5km; 1030m; 7h 15min**).

It is possible to extend this walk to The Merrick and perhaps Benyellary; see the Galloway Hills information panel on p20 for details.

These hills can also be traversed via an out and back route from the north, using an atv track which starts from a passing place at NX394947, just south of where the single track road between Glentrool and Straiton exits, or enters the forestry. About 250m and 350m to the north of this passing place, track entrances provide space to park; the Stinchar Bridge car park lies a further 750m or so to the north. The atv track leads for 4km over Cairnadloch and Caerloch Dhu to Shalloch on Minnoch.

Tarfessock then Kirriereoch Hill are included as above (**10km; 740m; 3h 40min**) with a return along the tops (**20km; 1040m; 6h 50min**).

A variation could also be made over Cornish Hill (NX404941) using the waymarked trail to or from the Stinchar Bridge car park. A linear traverse to Glen Trool can also be made and is briefly described in the Galloway Hills information panel on p20.

Descending to Caerloch Dhu from Shalloch on Minnoch (Tom Prentice)

Corran of Portmark, Meaul, Carlin's Cairn, Cairnsgarroch

Carlin's Cairn, Meaul, centre, and Bow from the flanks of Corran of Portmark (Andrew Fraser)

Corran of Portmark; 623m; (D80); L77; NX509936; pointed hill, above Portmark (on Loch Doon), from Gaelic 'corr', pointed. Alternatively Gaelic 'corran', sickle, from shape of late snow wreath seen from Carsphairn. Mapped Corran (1797)

Bow; 613m; (DT); L77; NX508928

Meaul; 695m; (D37); L77; NX500909; hill. Gaelic 'meall', lumpy hill. At one point it would have had an adjective – e.g. 'meall buidhe', yellow hill, which perhaps explains the adjacent hill Bow 'buidhe'

Carlin's Cairn; 807m; (D8); L77; NX496883; the old woman's cairn. Scots 'carline'; in honour of a miller's wife who sheltered Robert the Bruce

Cairnsgarroch; 659m; (D60); L77; NX515913; pointed from Gaelic 'càrn sgòrach', or possibly cold and windy hill 'càrn sgàireach'. Mapped Kingswell Hill (1654), Cairnsgorroch (1797)

Lying on the eastern edge of the Galloway Forest Park, the Rhinns of Kells ridge runs for 18km, not falling below 620m for 10km. This route takes in the hills of the northern part of the ridge and offers open walking with superb views north to Cairnsmore of Carsphairn and west to The Merrick. Once on the tops the hills are generally grassier than the southern section of the ridge, but the descent north from Cairnsgarroch is rocky, rough and wet, and gives slow going. The Galloway Hills information panel (see p20) includes details of the full Rhinns of Kells traverse.

Parking is available on a section of old road on the south-west side of the A713 opposite the entrance to the cottage at Bridge-end and Green Well of Scotland. This is one mile (1.6km) north of Carsphairn village and on the south side of the bridge over the Water of Deugh. Walk across this bridge then turn left down the access road to Holm of Daltallochan and follow the track beyond for 2km to Garryhorn. In the 18th century, Garryhorn was the local headquarters of Grierson of Lag, whose dragoons hunted and killed numerous Covenanters. Believed to be in league with the devil, at his funeral a black corbie perched on the hearse all the way to the grave.

Continue for 1.8km to the abandoned Woodhead Lead Mines. In its heyday between 1839 and 1873, this had a population of 300 with its own school. All that remains are numerous ruined buildings and 11 shafts, the deepest of which is reputed to be 95m. Follow the track to the tree-surrounded highest ruins, the track fades as you get close, then take a clearer track on the right which leads north past a fenced-off ventilation shaft to a gate in a wall before a conifer plantation. Go through the gate and turn left onto an atv track which ascends the flanks of Knockower and on to Corran of Portmark (named Coran on OS maps). Leave the atv and ascend to the summit cairn, one of the finest viewpoints in Galloway (6km; 430m; 2h).

Cross the fence and follow another atv track on its west side over the Donald Top of Bow towards Meaul. At NX500917, near the atv track on the

Corran of Portmark, Meaul, Carlin's Cairn, Cairnsgarroch

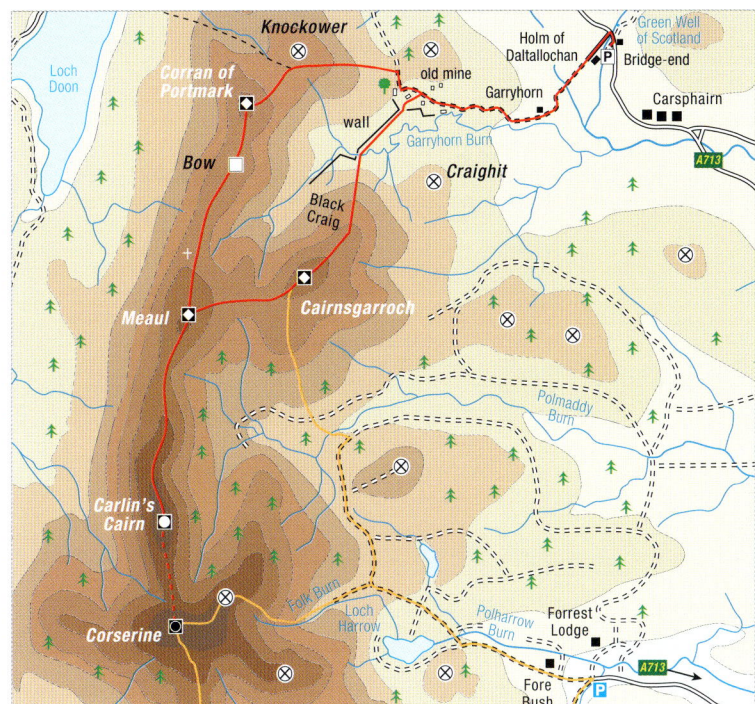

northern flank of Meaul overlooking Loch Doon, a single upright stone and plaque mark the spot where Covenanter John Dempster is said to have been shot in 1685, following a long chase by Lag's dragoons. A trig point marks the summit of Meaul (**9.5km; 610m; 3h**).

Descend to a col which once formed part of a drove road between the Ken and Girvan valleys by way of Loch Doon. An easy climb now leads to Carlin's Cairn (**12.5km; 790m; 4h**).

Legend attributes the building of the large cairn here to a miller's wife, who in return for aid offered to a fugitive Robert the Bruce was granted land in Polmaddy to the east.

From Carlin's Cairn it is possible to continue south to the Donald and Corbett of Corserine by way of the col known as the Riders' Gap then return to Carlin's Cairn; an additional 2.5km, 210m, 1h on the day.

Retrace the route north to Meaul then pick up a wall and follow this down eastwards then up onto Cairnsgarroch (**17km; 970m; 5h 20min**).

Descend Cairnsgarroch, initially north-east down a broad, rough and mostly pathless ridge, then in a more northerly direction to Black Craig. From there, descend the rough and tiring slopes east of the crags to a point where the Garryhorn Burn is crossed by a wall at NX524930.

Here, the girders of a ruined footbridge can be used to cross the burn. About 350m downstream, a log carries the fence from the col between Cairnsgarroch and Craighit over the burn, and this can also be used to cross over. Follow the wall towards the mine ruins to join the outward track and follow this back to the start.

Great care should be taken in the vicinity of the mines as deep vegetation may obscure open shafts from view (**23.5km; 980m; 7h**).

Carlin's Cairn, left, Meaul, Corran of Portmark and Cairnsgarroch, right, from Corserine (Rab Anderson)

Corserine and Millfire from Milldown on the ridge of the Rhinns of Kells (Rab Anderson)

> **Corserine**; 814m; (D6); L77; NX497870; crossing point of the Rhinns (of Kells, the parish). Gaelic 'crois na rinne'. Corserine lies athwart this north-south range (Gaelic 'rinn', point as in its eastern spur Craigrine; and its western spur Craigtarson, from Gaelic 'tarsuinn', transverse). Mapped Krosrang (1654)
> **Millfire**; 716m; (DT); L77; NX508847; probably Gaelic Meall Feoir, hill of hay, grass, pasture
> **Milldown**; 738m; (D18); L77; NX511839; brown hill. Gaelic 'meall donn'. Mapped Milldoon (1797)
> **Meikle Millyea**; 749m; (D14); L77; NX516825; big (grey) hill. Scots 'meikle' and Gaelic 'meall', plus possibly 'liath', so perhaps 'grey hill'. Mapped Mekle Mulle hill (1654). Locally pronounced Millyae

Corserine, the second highest hill in Galloway, and its attendant hills form the southern part of the Rhinns of Kells ridge, and can be climbed in a fine circuit of Loch Dungeon. The summits alternate between rough grass and rocky outcrops, characteristic of the granite underlying much of the area. The ridge gives tremendous views west over the Silver Flowe to craggy Dungeon Hill and Craignaw, backed by The Merrick.

Start at a car park at the end of the Forrest Lodge road, accessed off the A713 some 2 miles (3.5km) north of St John's Town of Dalry, or just beyond where the road crosses the Polharrow Burn if approaching from the north. The Galloway Hills information panel on p20 contains details of a long return circuit of all the hills on the Rhinns of Kells ridge from this car park, together with a complete linear traverse from Green Well of Scotland to the north, starting as for the previous walk.

Head north towards Forrest Lodge then go left (west) up the forest track, named Birger Natvig Road to pass the house at Fore Bush. After 2km take a right turn at a junction, Robert Watson Road, and cross the Polharrow Burn. Continue straight ahead at another three junctions until after a further 1.5km the track swings right at NX525874. Take to a track on the left and after 200m or so, follow a path off left into the forest on the south side of the Folk Burn, which is crossed (not immediately obvious) after a few hundred metres.

Once it emerges from the forest the path continues west onto Craigrine, the north-east ridge of Corserine, which is climbed to the summit plateau. The summit trig point can be difficult to locate in mist but by keeping the edge of the northern corrie just in sight to the right, it should be spotted on the left (**6.5km; 680m; 2h 35min**).

Carlin's Cairn lies just to the north and is an easy optional diversion with a return to Corserine, add (2.5km; 200m; 1h). From Corserine, descend the ridge south-south-east for 1.7km to the col below Millfire.

In the valley to the west of this can be seen the former shepherd's house at Backhill of Bush, which was last inhabited in the 1940s and is now a bothy. Prior to forestation, this was a truly remote spot, reached from Forrest Lodge by way of this col. All supplies, even funeral corteges had to come this way, transported on sleds pulled by ponies. The seriousness of this route in winter is highlighted by a cairn 1km to the east, which commemorates shepherd boy Ralph Forlow who died here in the blizzard of 27th January 1954.

Corserine, Milldown, Meikle Millyea

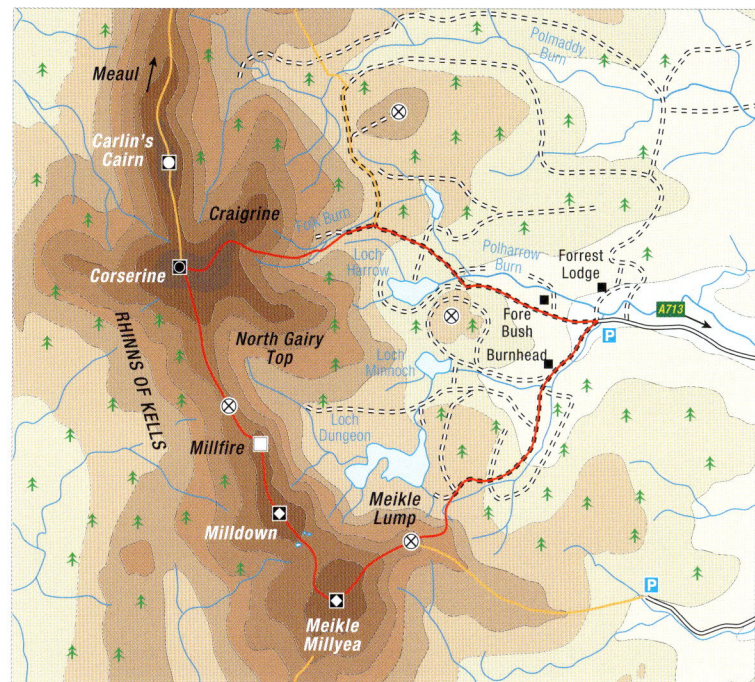

The northern top has a trig point and is the 746m highpoint shown on current OS maps. However, an OS confirmed survey shows the 749m summit to actually be located at NX51618255, some 400m further along the wall to the south-west (**11.5km; 920m; 4h 10min**).

Pass easily over the craggy Donald Top of Millfire and make the short ascent onto Milldown beside a drystane dyke. Thereafter, drop to the Lochans of Auchniebut and follow the dyke up Meikle Millyea.

From the trig point, descend the north-east ridge of Meikle Lump. A dyke that joins the one followed on the ascent runs down the ridge, swinging east then north-east towards the forestry and a track beyond. It is best to follow the wall almost to the edge of the forest where the track can be gained by going left over a burn to a stile (NX534838). Turn right at the junction and descend past a wooden watch tower. Alternatively, follow the boggy forest edge right for 500m where a break leads to the track.

Descend the track, named Prof. Hans Heiberg Road, for 3.5km, keeping straight ahead at all junctions, past Burnhead Farm to reach the car park (**17km; 920m; 5h 40min**).

Millfire from the Rhinns of Kells ridge to the north-west (Rab Anderson)

Cairnsmore of Carsphairn, Moorbrock Hill

Section 0a – Galloway & The Lowthers

Cairnsmore of Carsphairn, Beninner, Moorbrock Hill and Windy Standard from the south-east (Andrew Fraser)

> **Beninner**; 710m; (DT); L77; NX605971
>
> **Cairnsmore of Carsphairn**; 797m; (D10); L77; NX594979; moor of cairns, above Carsphairn (carse of alders). Mapped Kairnsmoort (1654), Cairnsmuir upon Deuch (1755), Cairns Moor (1797)
>
> **Dugland**; 612m; (DT); L77; NS602009
>
> **Windy Standard**; 698m; (G108); (D33); L77; NS620014; windy hill with cairn. Scots 'standard', hill cairn
>
> **Keoch Rig**; 611m; (DT); L77; NX617999
>
> **Moorbrock Hill**; 650m; (D65); L77; NX620983; mapped Kornsleu Hill (1654), Cornsclia (1797), Cornsolue (1826). Probably Gaelic 'cor an sliabh', point on the moor

Together with its neighbouring hills, Cairnsmore of Carsphairn forms part of a distinctive group towards the southern end of the range that to the north includes Blackcraig Hill and Windy Standard, both of which are Grahams and covered on the next pages. Being a Corbett, Cairnsmore of Carsphairn is the highest point in the range, as well as the highest of the three Cairnsmores, as celebrated in the old Galloway doggerel, 'There's Cairnsmore of Fleet and Cairnsmore of Dee, but Cairnsmore of Carsphairn is the highest of the three'.

Together with the adjoining Beninner, the round of this southern group includes Keoch Rig and Moorbrock Hill on the opposite side of the valley. Also taken in is Dugland, the new outlying Donald Top of Windy Standard, which is easier to include with this round than with the Afton Reservoir round, although it does make this route a bit tougher.

The start is from the valley of the Water of Ken, reached by the dead-end single track road which branches north from the B729 Carsphairn to Moniave road at Stroanfreggan Bridge. Drive up this road to Craigengillan where a forestry track starts next to a cottage at NX637948.

There is limited parking on the verge next to the wall around the cottage, which at the time of writing was acceptable to the owner; there is also room to squeeze off the road in a passing place just before this. A gated estate track to Moorbrock 500m further north has a No Parking sign at the entrance.

Follow the track north next to the Polifferie Burn and when the track swings left into the forest, continue ahead over an old bridge by an overgrown route to join the estate track at the entrance to Moorbrock. At the byre in front of the estate house, one possible route is to go west beside a wall then up the break in the forestry on the north side of the Poldores Burn, which is crossed to gain the open hillside.

However, this gives somewhat tortuous going through deep tussocks and perhaps a better route, which is only fractionally longer, is to keep to the track, taking the left branch uphill just beyond the estate house. This track traverses around Green Hill and from its lowest point the second firebreak can be descended to cross the burn and gain the hillside.

Whichever route is chosen, either climb directly up the steep slope left

Cairnsmore of Carsphairn, Moorbrock Hill

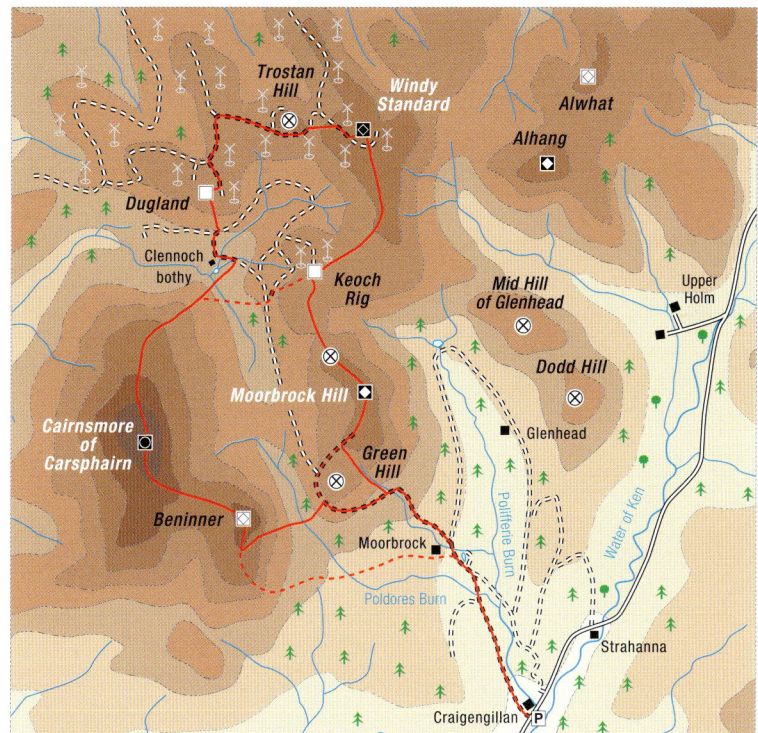

of Beninner Gairy then go up left by an obvious break through the minor rock outcrops in the upper section, or traverse across to the left of the steep ground then ascend to the top of Beninner (**5km; 540m; 2h 5min**).

Descend north-west to the Nick of the Lochans then continue up to the trig point and large cairn on the granite boulder-studded summit of Cairnsmore of Carsphairn. The view is extensive down the Ken and Dee valleys, with the Rhinns of Kells to the south-west particularly prominent (**6.5km; 700m; 2h 40min**).

Descend north onto Currie Rig then drop north-east off this towards Clennoch bothy, in the floor of the glen at the junction of the Bow, Clennoch and Hog Hill Burns. Near the bottom, swing right across a track then go through a gate in the fence at NX603998 and cross the Bow Burn. Ascend rough ground, either directly to the bothy, or up right to a track which leads to it. From the bothy, follow the track north to join another track then leave it to ascend steeply northwards to reach a wind turbine, then cross rough ground to the cairn marking the turbine-surrounded summit of Dugland (**10km; 920m; 4h**).

Drop east back to the track in the valley then follow it around the head of the Clennoch Burn and up the spur of Hog Hill through the windfarm onto Keoch Rig (**12.5km; 1060m; 4h 50min**).

It only takes an additional 20min to include Windy Standard from Dugland, following the windfarm track across Trostan Hill then short-cutting the loop by an atv track. From the summit, pass through a gap in the fence and descend beside another fence past the Deil's Putting Stone boulder, curving round to Keoch Rig.

Leaving the windfarm track on Keoch Rig, a rough atv track can be followed south-west then south to a col from where the ascent is made onto the long summit ridge of Moorbrock Hill (**14.5km; 1190m; 5h 30min**).

From the southern end of the summit ridge, descend a track for a short way towards the saddle, then short-cut directly downhill to the south-east by the Poltie Burn to rejoin the track. Descend to a junction, turn right across the burn and return past Moorbrock (**19km; 1190m; 6h 40min**).

Moorbrock Hill, right, from the estate track to Moorbrock (Rab Anderson)

Windy Standard, Alhang, Blacklorg Hill, Blackcraig Hill

Blackcraig Hill and Glen Afton from Cannock Hill (Tom Prentice)

> ***Windy Standard***; *698m; (G108); (D33); L77; NS620014; windy hill with cairn. Scots 'standard', hill cairn: there are nine Standard hills in Galloway and Ayrshire*
>
> ***Alhang***; *642m; (D71); L77; NS642010; from Gaelic 'allt', mountain stream (original meaning – steep slope): the river Afton rises on its north slope. Aldhing (1654), Alhinge (1797). Second element possibly Gaelic 'cumhaing', narrow*
>
> ***Alwhat***; *628m; (DT); L77; NS646020*
>
> ***Meikledodd Hill***; *643m; (DT); L77; NS660027; Scots for big lump*
>
> ***Blacklorg Hill***; *681m; (D45); L77; NS653042; black shank-shaped hill. Gaelic 'lorg', shank, thigh, leg (in shape)*
>
> ***Blackcraig Hill***; *700m; (G104); (D30); L71, 77; NS647064; black cliff hill. Mapped Black Craig (1755)*

Upper Glen Afton is surrounded by rolling hills including two Grahams, which give a fairly straightforward although quite long high-level route round the Afton Reservoir.

Lower Glen Afton, celebrated in song by Burns, is still an unexpected gem. Unfortunately, the same cannot be said of the visual intrusion created by the windfarms that extend along the west side of Upper Glen Afton onto Windy Standard and beyond.

From New Cumnock, take the B741 south-west for a few hundred metres then turn left into Afton Road (signposted Burns Cairn, which is passed) and ascend Glen Afton to the end of the public road. There is a parking area (NS627055) across a concrete bridge on the left, just beyond the Afton Water Treatment Works.

Follow the track south through a gate for 200m towards the dam then take a waymarked path on the right. This climbs past a rocky knoll known as Castle William, which has connections to William Wallace, to gain a higher track at some sheep pens.

Follow this track past a branch off left above the Afton Reservoir dam, and curve uphill past the first of the wind turbines on Black Hill. Go left at a fork to pass under the pylon line which marches eastwards across the head of the reservoir, cutting across the latter part of the route. Continue south past more turbines, keeping right when the track forks, and climb onto Wedder Hill. Descend the other side past the final two turbines to reach the end of the track.

Now on soft ground, gain the fence on the right and follow it across the slight rise of Millaneoch Hill then down to a col to step over another fence. Continue uphill beside a fence wired for power and go through a double metal gate to the other side. Finally, climb onto Windy Standard and cross a track to gain its turbine-surrounded trig point at the north-west end (**6km; 390m; 2h**).

Dugland (612m), an outlying Donald Top, lies to the west and can be picked up via the windfarm access tracks, short-cutting the initial loop by an atv track. However, this involves a there and back of 4.25km, 170m, 1h 15min, which when added to this round is a considerable extension. For this reason Dugland is included in the Cairnsmore of Carsphairn round.

From the top of Windy Standard, return north-east through the gate to the col and then descend south-east beside the fence to the marshy col below Alhang. Continue beside the fence up and over Alhang, then north-east over the Donald Top of Alwhat to a fence junction below Meikledodd Hill. The ill-defined summit of this Donald Top is gained by a short

Windy Standard, Alhang, Blacklorg Hill, Blackcraig Hill

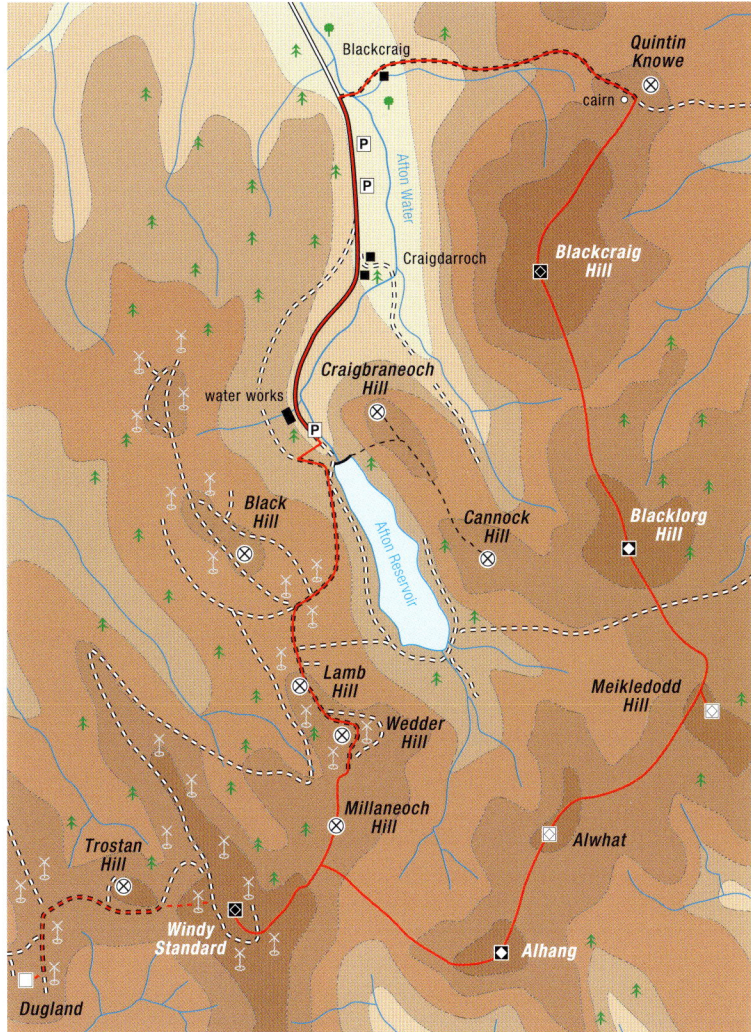

diversion south-east beside the fence (**11.75km; 710m; 3h 50min**).

Return to the junction and descend northwards to the col. Cross the track and pass beneath the power lines to make the steady ascent to the cairned top of Blacklorg Hill. Go over a stile and continue northwards, with occasional waymark posts, to the peat hag-covered col below Blackcraig Hill, best crossed via atv tracks on its west side, well away from the fence. Ascend to the trig point, which lies a short distance west of the fence. The highest point appears to lie 50m to the south-east of the trig point (**16km; 980m; 5h 15min**).

To descend, rejoin the fence and follow a path on the north ridge to Quintin Knowe. Go north-west, then west following a path down the north side of the Langlee Burn, which turns into a track leading past Blackcraig farm to the road. Turn left and follow the road up the glen for 2.75km back to the start (**23km; 1090m; 7h 15min**).

Blackcraig Hill can be climbed on its own from one of the many long laybys on the Glen Afton road, south of Blackcraig Farm, by reversing the descent described above (**4.5km; 440m; 1h 45min**). Return the same way (**9km; 440m; 2h 50min**).

If Windy Standard is to be climbed on its own, then this is best done from Glen Afton via the ascent route described opposite, with a return the same way (**12km; 450m; 3h 25min**).

Approaching the summit of Windy Standard (Tom Prentice)

34 Queensberry, Earncraig Hill, Gana Hill

Section 0a – Galloway & The Lowthers

Queensberry from Gana Hill (Rab Anderson)

Queensberry; 697m; (G110); (D34); L78; NX989997; the second element is probably from Old English 'beorg', rounded hill. Recorded as Queensberry (1633), Queinsberg (1648). First element obscure, though it may refer to a queen

Earncraig Hill; 611m; (D88); L78; NS973013; eagle crag, from 'erne' Scots for eagle and crag. Mapped Sergan Law (1773) or Sergeant Law (1817), from Scots word for a sheriff's officer

Gana Hill; 668m; (D54); L78; NS954010; hill above Gana Burn on its north slope. Another Gana Burn 5km north-west (see also Ballencleuch Law), might suggest a form of Scots 'kennel', channel (for a burn)

These three hills, one Graham and two Donalds, form the southernmost part of the high ridge of the Southern Lowther Hills. Although they can be tacked onto a large round from Daer Reservoir (see following route), they are more conveniently climbed in a good round from the farm at Mitchellslacks to the south-west. This is reached by a loop of the unclassified road to the east of Thornhill on the A702. There is limited parking on the verge at NX964961 beside a Scottish Rights of Way signpost, a little north of the access track to Mitchellslacks. Locations around Mitchellslacks were used in the 1978 adaptation of John Buchan's spy story, *The Thirty Nine Steps*, starring Robert Powell.

Cut down the bank onto the access track to Mitchellslacks and follow this over the Capel Water then swing left past the farm to head northwards through the fields. When the track forks after the last gate leading out onto the open hillside, the right-hand track is followed uphill, past a track off right, then across to the foot of the distinctive small hill The Law. Take the track on the right which contours The Law then cuts back downhill to a series of sheep pens in the valley floor. Loop around to the north of the pens on a rough track then cross the burn to the side of them and follow atv tracks south-east then east heading for the prominent cairn on High Church, which lies above an interesting rocky defile with a pond at its entrance. The ridge leads north-eastwards onto Craih Hill then down and across a gap where a short but steep climb gains the trig point on top of Wee Queensberry. Head north-east along the top on an atv track then drop down across a boggy area and continue on up the long slope of Peace Knowe to the top of Queensberry (**6km; 570m; 2h 20min**).

Descend north to pick up a fence and follow this as it swings north-west onto Penbreck. Earncraig Hill sits directly opposite but there is a deep and narrow glen in-between, which has to be circumnavigated north then west beside the fence. Cross the col at Capel Yetts then head south-west up Berry Rig to meet a wall at the summit of Earncraig Hill (**9.5km; 730m; 3h 25min**).

The route continues westwards beside the wall, dropping quite steeply to the col at Daer Hass where the wall turns away north. Now climb west up the slope across rough

Queensberry, Earncraig Hill, Gana Hill 35

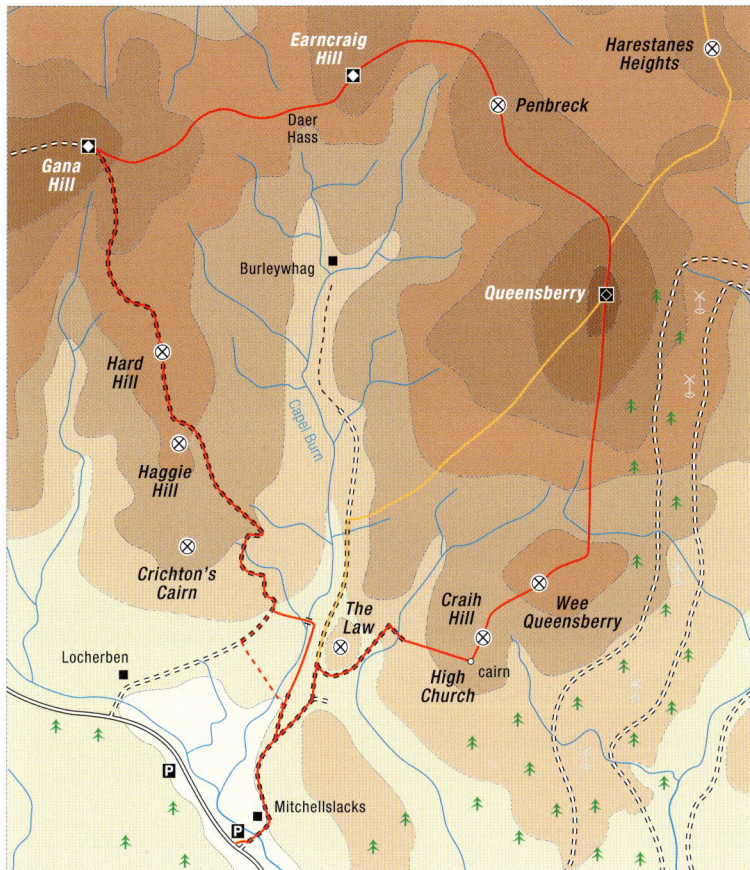

ground and pick up a fence which runs south-west then swings round to head north-west up the shoulder of Gana Shank. Join a track then go through a gate in another fence and stay on the track as it cuts the corner away from the fence to rejoin it again where it passes over the summit of Gana Hill (**12km; 910m; 4h 20min**).

Return along the track and follow it south down the spur of Gana Shank. At the foot of this the track swings round from one side of the ridge to the other, through a col, to pass over Hard Hill where it then descends along the upper slopes of the valley of the Capel Burn. Shortly after a right-hand hairpin bend the track crosses a burn then drops a little to where it makes another right-hand turn at NX968978.

At this point it is possible to cut down the steep slope on the left to re-cross the lower part of the burn just crossed to find a bridge at NX970978, which enables the Capel Burn to be crossed below The Law. Follow paths south beside the burn to a track which rises to meet the outward track at the gate in the wall just north of Mitchellslacks.

Another option is to continue on the track on the west side for a short way and where this swings towards Locherben leave it and follow an atv track south to flatter ground. After dropping down the bank, the Capel Burn can be crossed to gain the track on the other side then the gate in the wall. Continue through the fields past Mitchellslacks back to the start (**18.5km; 950m; 6h**).

Queensberry itself can be climbed more directly, but less interestingly, by keeping left where the track forks at the foot of The Law and continuing up the glen above the Capel Burn. After crossing a side burn an atv track, signposted to Queensberry, can be followed up right to the summit of the hill (**5.5km; 490m; 2h**), (**11km; 500m; 3h 30min**).

Another option for climbing Queensberry on its own is from the north-east above Beattock on the M74. The route starts from the end of the road which climbs past Beattock Hill; there is room to park before the bridge over the Kinnel Water at Kinnelhead (NT033016). Following Scottish Rights of Way signposts, initially take the track towards Kinnelhead then take another track back south-west to Lochanhead. Cross the burn just east of the cottage, then cross boggy ground and follow the edge of the forestry plantation uphill past the Pot of Ae (the head of the Water of Ae) to the summit of Queensberry (**5.5km; 450m; 2h**).

Rather than return the same way (**11km; 450m; 3h 20min**) the route can be varied by taking a slightly longer descent over Harestanes Heights and Craighoar Hill to the north-east.

North to Burleywhag bothy and Earncraig Hill (Tom Prentice)

South-east to Ballencleuch Law, left, and Scaw'd Law, right, from Well Hill (Andrew Fraser)

> **Glenleith Fell**; *612m; (DT); L78; NS922023; grey glen fell*
>
> **Wedder Law**; *672m; (D52); L78; NS938025; lamb hill. Scots 'wedder', castrated male sheep, usually a yearling lamb*
>
> **Scaw'd Law**; *663m; (D58); L78; NS922035; speckled, scabby or patchy hill. Scots 'scald', 'scawd', scabby, patchy. A common southern hill name*
>
> **Ballencleuch Law**; *689m; (G118); (D42); L78; NS935049; hill above Ballen Cleuch, the stream gorge (Scots 'cleuch') east of the summit. Mapped Ganaw hill (1755), the Gana Burn draining to the west*
>
> **Rodger Law**; *688m; (DT); L71, 78; NS945058*
>
> **Comb Law**; *645m; (D67); L71, 78; NS943073; arched ridge hill. Mapped Netherburn Hill (1755), from the burn on the west side, then as Comb Law in 1817: nearby is Coom Rig. Pont maps a Coom Head (1590s), which may be either*

The Southern Lowther hills comprise an area of elevated grouse moor, the summit ridge of which stretches some 14km from Ballencleuch Law in the north to Queensberry in the south, only once falling below 500m in altitude. Ballencleuch Law, also a Graham, is the highest hill in the northernmost part of this ridge which also includes three Donalds and two Donald Tops. Queensberry and the southern part are described on the previous pages.

The principal route described accesses these hills from the attractive village of Durisdeer. Parking is available in the village next to the church, although is likely to be in short supply on a Sunday morning. While now a sleepy hamlet, Durisdeer is strategically positioned at the southern end of the Well Path, a Roman road which for centuries was the principal route through these hills. There has been a church on this site since at least the 13th century and the present one contains a remarkable marble-carved mausoleum to the Dukes of Queensberry, underneath which lies a vault containing lead coffins of the Douglas family.

From Durisdeer, walk south back down the main road for 200m and turn left immediately before the cemetery onto a track leading to Glenaggart. Follow the track for 800m to a junction just after the burn at Glenimp then take the track on the left. This track traverses the hillside then climbs steadily to gain the ridgeline on the shoulder of Scaw'd Law, 500m south of its summit.

The Donald Top of Glenleith Fell lies to the south and is easily reached, either across deep heather, or by descending the track a short way, passing through a gate, then taking another track that cuts across the slope to pass just beneath the top, which is gained by a short climb west (**4.5km; 470m; 1h 45min**).

Return to the main track and follow this south-south-east downhill past a shed then quite steeply uphill to the top of Wedder Law, the summit being located at a fence just north of the track (**7km; 620m; 2h 30min**).

By this stage, signs of the intensive use of these hills for grouse shooting will be evident. While perhaps less

Wedder Law, Scaw'd Law, Ballencleuch Law, Comb Law

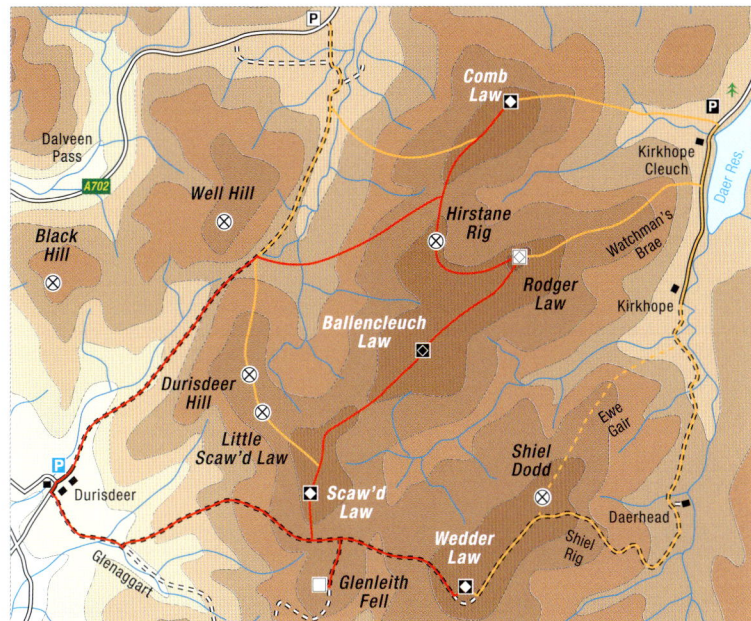

visually intrusive than say, windfarms, this particular track is a good argument as to why planning control of such tracks is necessary.

From Wedder Law, the simplest option is to return via the track, back through the gate in the fence just below the shoulder of Scaw'd Law, then branch off right on a grassy atv track where the main track swings left. On reaching a wall, go through a gate and climb onto double-topped Scaw'd Law. The DOBIH suggest that the north top at NS922037 may be higher (**9.5km; 760m; 3h 20min**).

Follow the wall, or the atv track just out from it, and where the wall veers off after 400m continue easily north-east beside, or just out from, the fence onto Ballencleuch Law then continue to Rodger Law with its trig point (**13km; 890m; 4h 20min**).

To the north east, the visual impact of the massive Clyde Valley Windfarm can be fully seen, whilst to the north-west the Northern Lowther Hills are more pleasing on the eye. To the south-east, Queensberry stands out over Earncraig Hill.

This now leaves the awkward outlier of Comb Law, and although this lies to the north, one has to first backtrack south-west for about 300m to pick up the fence again then follow this down the spur north-west. The fence swings round down Hirstane Rig then continues north-east to a junction of fences on top of Comb Law (**16.5km; 950m; 5h 10min**).

To descend, return to the col with Hirstane Rig then drop west-south-west down the hillside to gain the Well Path. This is followed south-west for 4km back to Durisdeer, past an elevated Roman fortlet reckoned to be one of the best preserved in Britain (**23km; 950m; 6h 50min**).

Those seeking to quickly bag the Graham of Ballencleuch Law can do so from Daer Reservoir. Park just before Kirkhope Cleuch at a track entrance at NS967073. Climb over Rodger Law via Watchman's Brae (**4km ;390m; 1h 30min**). Return the same way (**8km; 430m; 2h 30min**).

This round of Donalds can also be made from the same parking spot by following the south side of the wall around a forestry plantation to gain Comb Law then reverse the main route to Wedder Law. From there, continue north-east on the track to Shiel Dod then either follow the track back, south-east and east down Shiel Rig (easier and drier but a little longer), or cut more directly down the north-east ridge of Ewe Gair and rejoin the track in the floor of the valley. The track leads back to the reservoir (**21km; 720m; 6h 20min**).

A useful round can also be made from NS925085 on the A702 above the Dalveen Pass where there is parking opposite the start of a track between two telecoms masts. Follow the track south to the far end of a felled plantation, turn left across a burn then take the left-hand track across a bridge over another burn where the track loops round to a sheepfold and some buildings.

Now climb rough ground onto Comb Law and reverse the principal route over Rodger Law, Ballencleuch Law and Scaw'd Law to pick up Glenleith Fell and Wedder Law. Return to Scaw'd Law then descend over Little Scaw'd Law and Durisdeer Hill to gain the track on the line of the Roman Road and follow this back (**21.5km; 890m; 6h 30min**).

Comb Law, back left, and Ballencleuch Law from Scaw'd Law (Rab Anderson)

Lowther Hill, East Mount Lowther, Green Lowther, Dun Law, Lousie Wood Law

Looking across Wanlockhead to Green Lowther, left, and Lowther Hill (Andrew Fraser)

Cold Moss; 628m; (DT); L71, 78; NS898094

Lowther Hill; 725m; (D23); L71, 78; NS890107; an obscure name, unless it is a decomposed form of Gaelic 'meall odhar', dun-coloured hill: there are two hills called Me(a)lowther in south Scotland. Mapped Loders Hill (1654)

East Mount Lowther; 631m; (D76); L71, 78; NS878100; 1944 summit indicator states previously named Auchenlone Hill; possibly after a farm, now lost, called Auchenton or Auchenlon. Southern ridge still mapped as Auchenton Shank, 'shank' being the Scottish equivalent of Gaelic 'lurg', leg. Roy's map shows two farms with auchen-names further down the Mennock Water. Present name first recorded by the OS c.1850. Most westerly of the Lowther range and 'mount' very unusual in the Border hills

Green Lowther; 732m; (G43); (D21); L71, 78; NS900120; green for its vegetation to distinguish it from Dun Law and White Law just along the range. To south-west is Green Trough

Dun Law; 677m; (D48); L71, 78; NS916136; dull brown hill. Its neighbours include White Law, Black Law and Green Lowther

Lousie Wood Law; 619m; (D84); L71, 78; NS931152; hill above Lousie Wood Burn (and the burn from a wood, now lost) on its west. Pont's map (1590s) seemed to name it Wadderlaw (hill of wedders, lambs)

Lowther Hill's huge air traffic control 'golf ball' radome makes it a conspicuous landmark, although the highest point on this long upland ridge is actually Green Lowther, the sole Graham in the massif. An access road joins the two peaks and while these intrusions make neither hill particularly attractive, the full traverse of the ridge is still a satisfying and enjoyable outing.

The start is at a height of just over 300m, to the north of the top of the spectacular Dalveen Pass. Ample parking is available on a section of old road at NS931100, 500m to the north of Overfingland, where the Southern Upland Way (SUW) leaves the A702. Walk south up the road past Overfingland and Troloss Cottage then take the signposted SUW to the west. This waymarked route climbs uphill to the south of a small forestry plantation, passing through a gate then crossing a stile, before climbing over Laght Hill then Comb Head and the Donald Top of Cold Moss to ascend Lowther Hill (**5.5km; 570m; 2h 10min**). A fenced compound surrounds the radar station and there is no access to the highest point.

East Mount Lowther is an outlier to the south-west, climbed by an out and back route. Follow the SUW left over a stile before the compound is reached then skirt south of the summit to a stile over a fence by a small hut. Cross over to gain the

Lowther Hill, East Mount Lowther, Green Lowther, Dun Law, Lousie Wood Law

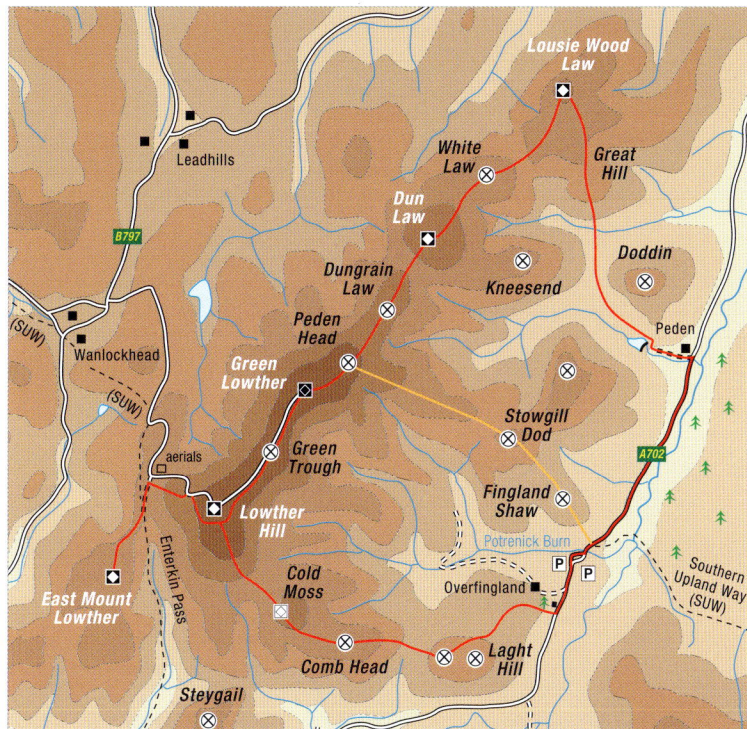

access road and follow this for a very short distance then cut back left to the fence and descend to gain a track opposite another aerial compound. Descend the track south-west to the head of the Enterkin Pass, then ascend beside the fence to the summit of East Mount Lowther (**7.5km; 650m; 2h 45min**). There are fine views down the Nith Valley to the Lake District and westwards to Arran.

It is now necessary to reverse the route back to Lowther Hill which gives good views to Wanlockhead, at 425m the highest village in Scotland. Lead has been mined here since Roman times and gold was discovered during the reign of James IV.

Either follow the road up and around the north side of Lowther Hill and on towards Green Lowther, or retrace the outward route south round the compound to gain an atv track on the east side of the fence beside the road. Follow this over Green Trough to Green Lowther (**11km; 880m; 3h 55min**). The trig point stands below a collection of rusting masts, surrounded by wind-blasted fencing and concrete bunkers.

Fortunately the rest of the route over Peden Head and Dungrain Law to gain the two Donalds, Dun Law then Lousie Wood Law, gives pleasant, unobstructed high-level walking following a fenceline. There are fine views to the village of Leadhills and north-east up the Clyde valley to Tinto and Culter Fell with Hart Fell to the east. This 5km ridge only has two main drops, either side of Dun Law. They are the Big and Little Windgate Hass, the origin of whose names possibly reflects the presence of Lake District miners in the area. The fence crosses the unmarked summit of Dun Law while the top of Lousie Wood Law is marked by a trig point 100m north-north-west of where the fences join (**16km; 1150m; 5h 35min**).

The descent is south by way of Great Hill then following faint tracks across rough ground between Kneesend and Doddin to reach paths on the north side of the Peden Burn. The A702 is met at Peden from where it is a 3km walk back along the road to the start (**22.5km; 1180m; 7h 10min**).

Although the quickest way of climbing Green Lowther is to use the access road from Wanlockhead, a more enjoyable route starts from the parking north of Overfingland. Follow the road north over the Potrenick Burn then ascend Fingland Shaw where an atv track leads to Stowgill Dod. From here a fence is followed to Peden Head then Green Lowther (**4.5km; 450m; 1h 45min**). Return the same way (**9km; 480m; 2h 50min**).

Approaching the summit of Lowther Hill (Tom Prentice)

Clockmore, left, distant Broad Law and Cramalt Craig from Cappercleuch (Rab Anderson)

SECTION 0b The Borders

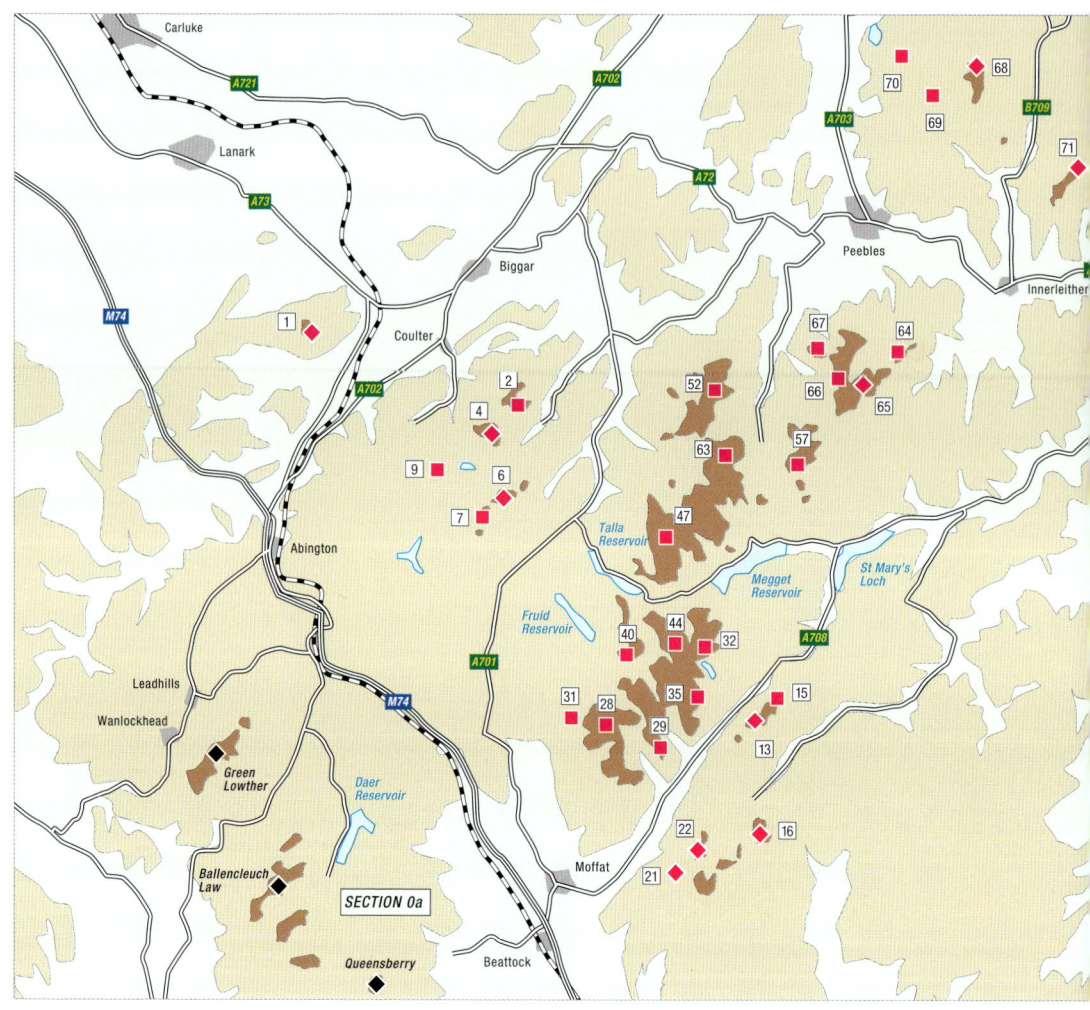

SECTION 0b

[1]♦ *Tinto*	44
[2] *Chapelgill Hill*, [3] *Cardon Hill*, [4]♦ *Culter Fell*	46
[5] *Coomb Hill*, [6]♦ *Gathersnow Hill*, [7] *Hillshaw Head*, [8] *Coomb Dod*	48
[9] *Hudderstone*	50
[10] *Bodesbeck Law*, [11] *Mid Rig*, [12] *Bell Craig*, [13]♦ *Andrewhinney Hill*, [14] *Trowgrain Middle*, [15] *Herman Law*	50
[16]♦ *Ettrick Pen*, [17] *Hopetoun Craig*, [18] *Wind Fell*, [19] *Loch Fell*, [20] *West Knowe*, [21]♦ *Croft Head*, [22]♦ *Capel Fell*, [23] *Smidhope Hill*, [24] *White Shank*	52
[25] *Nether Coomb Craig*, [26] *Swatte Fell*, [27] *Falcon Craig*, [28] *Hart Fell*, [29] *Under Saddle Yoke*, [30] *Saddle Yoke*	54
[31] *Whitehope Heights*, [28] *Hart Fell*	56
[32] *Lochcraig Head*, [33] *Nickies Knowe*, [34] *Firthhope Rig*, [35] *White Coomb*, [36] *Carrifran Gans*	58

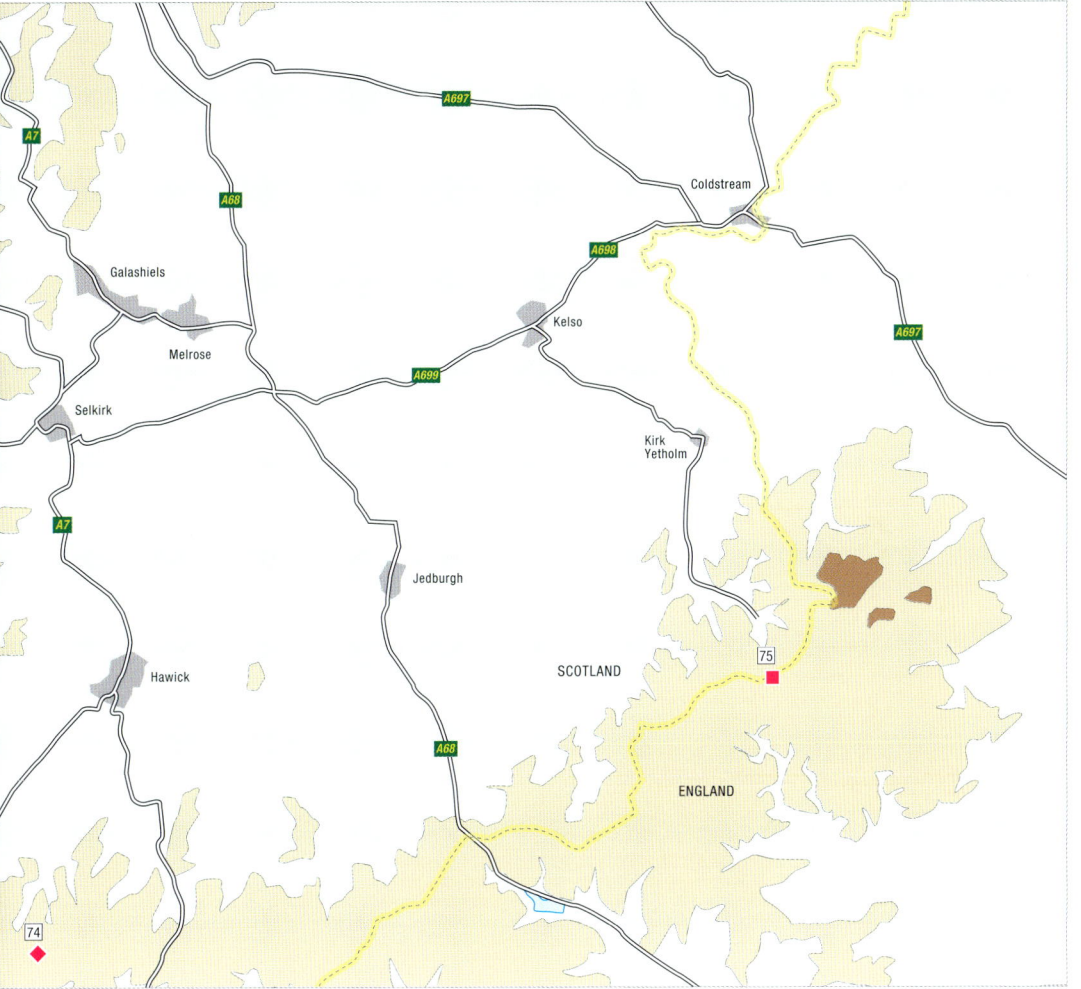

Section 0b – The Borders

[37] *Garelet Hill*, [38] *Lairds Cleuch Rig*, [39] *Erie Hill*,
  [40] *Garelet Dod*, [41] *Din Law*, [42] *Cape Law*,
  [34] *Firthhope Rig*, [35], *White Coomb*, [36] *Carrifran Gans*,
  [43] *Great Hill*, [44] *Molls Cleuch Dod*, [45] *Carlavin Hill*   60
[46] *Talla Cleuch Head*, [47] *Broad Law*, [48] *Hunt Law*,
  [49] *Cramalt Craig*, [50] *Clockmore*   62
[51] *The Scrape*, [52] *Pykestone Hill*, [53] *Middle Hill*,
  [54] *Taberon Law*, [55] *Drumelzier Law*   64
[56] *Black Cleuch Hill*, [57] *Black Law*, [58] *Conscleuch Head*,
  [59] *Deer Law*, [60] *Greenside Law*, [61] *Notman Law*,
  [62] *Fifescar Knowe*, [63] *Dollar Law*   66
[64] *Birkscairn Hill*, [65] ◆ *Dun Rig*, [66] *Glenrath Heights*,
  [67] *Stob Law*   68
[68] ◆ *Blackhope Scar*, [69] *Bowbeat Hill*, [70] *Dundreich*   70
[71] ◆ *Windlestraw Law*, [72] *Bareback Knowe*,
  [73] *Whitehope Law*   72
[74] ◆ *Cauldcleuch Head*   74
[75] *Windy Gyle*, [76] *Cairn Hill West Top*   74

Tinto

Tinto across the River Clyde from Lamington Hill to the south-east (Rab Anderson)

Tinto; 711m; (G79); (D29); L72; NS953343; Fiery hill. Gaelic 'teinnteach', suggesting a beacon hill where fires were lit in times of danger. Mapped Tintok Hill (1590s), reflecting old local name Tintock

Tinto stands proud and dominates the local landscape with its pointed profile and red-coloured screes. It occupies a solitary position north of the main Southern Uplands, rising above the flatlands between the Clyde and Douglas valleys. A large prehistoric cairn known as The Dimple adorns the summit, dwarfing the trig point, which stands to one side. Tinto's prominence and accessibility makes it a popular hill and its summit provides fine panoramic views which include the Lake District peaks, Arran and Lochnagar.

The hill is roughly shaped like a cross with ridges running to the four points of the compass and the simple up and down ascent of any ridge is just a short walk. However, if the hill is traversed a longer, more interesting walk can be constructed utilising quiet country roads to its north and south.

The northern approach is by far the most popular with a major path all the way. Start from the minor road that runs north of Tinto. There is a car park near Fallburn at NS964374, close to the junction with the A73, where there is a convenient tea room.

The path passes an iron-age fort with concentric ramparts to climb Totherin Hill then continues up the ridge and slope beyond to the summit (**3.4km; 480m; 1h 35min**). Descend the same way with fine views over the Midland Valley (**6.8km; 480m; 2h 30min**).

An ascent from the south is perhaps the most pleasant, and relatively unfrequented. Start at Wiston Lodge YMCA hostel (NS958322). There is limited parking on the roadside but, if courteous, visitors should be able to drive into the grounds and park near the hostel.

Walk due north by an avenue of trees, past a house and a water supply building. Pass through a gate and follow the edge of the field north, aiming directly for the peak. Large zigzags gain the top of Pap Craig where the path becomes less distinct in a mix of heather and red scree. Alternatively, a fenceline on the right leads direct to the summit (**2.9km; 440m; 1h 25min**). Descend the same way (**5.8km; 440m; 2h 15min**).

The west ridge has a secluded feel and starts at Howgate Mouth, a col that can easily be gained either from the south, from NS925331 on the B7055 road, or from the north by parking at NS919349 at the end of the public road just south of the houses at Howgate. A pleasant grassy walk over Lochlyoch Hill leads to the

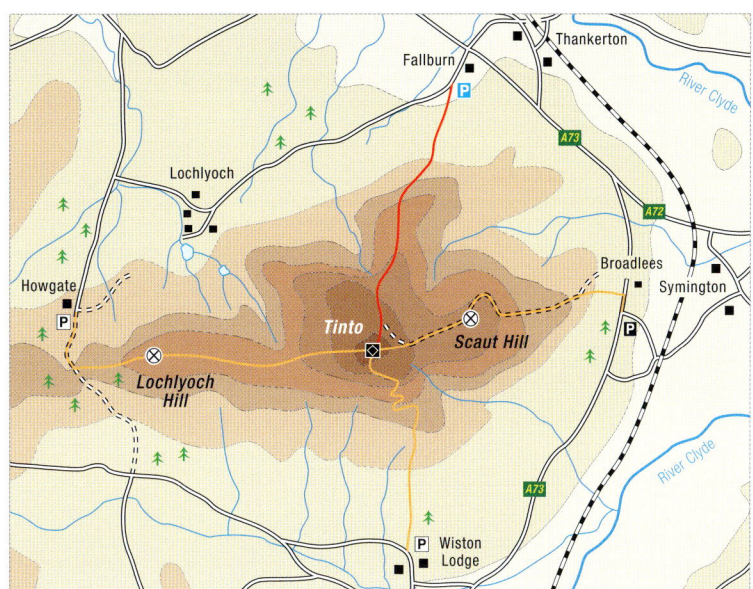

summit (**3.5km; 440m; 1h 30min**). Descend the same way (**7km; 490m; 2h 30min**). This west ridge also makes a pleasant descent if climbing the hill from the north or south.

The east ridge is probably the least climbed, partly because parking is difficult. The path starts from near Broadlees (NS984352), but the safest parking is probably on the minor road to Symington, 450m to the south. Walk through a field onto the ridge crest. A bulldozed track comes in from the north before zigzagging its way up to Scaut Hill. Either descend slightly from the crest to pick up this track, or turn to the south-west and ascend the ridge crest (**4km; 500m; 1h 45min**). Descend the same way (**8km; 530m; 2h 50min**).

Ascending Tinto's west ridge; Culter Fell in the distance (Rab Anderson)

Chapelgill Hill, Culter Fell

Culter Fell from Congrie Hill (Rab Anderson)

Chapelgill Hill; 696m; (D36); L72; NT066303; hill above Chapel Gill, a stream and farm (now lost names) on the east. 'Gill' is a Middle English word for stream in a ravine, and it and 'chapel' suggest an incomer from north England
Cardon Hill; 675m; (DT); L72; NT065314
Culter Fell; 748m; (G14); (D15); L72; NT052290; hill above Culter. Originally recorded as Fiends Fell early 17th century. Name changed late 17th century to that of the parish – Culter

This trio forms the northern group of the Culter Hills and is prominent when viewed from the north, with the highest hill in the area, the wedge-shaped Culter Fell (pronounced Cooter), forming a backdrop to Cardon Hill's rounded summit.

A pleasant and fairly short circuit of the three hills can be made from Glenkirk near the head of the Holms Water valley, south of Broughton. There is parking on grass at the end of the public road just before the house (NT079294). Follow the track on the right before the house to a barn and skirt it on its left side to gain the south-east ridge of Chapelgill Hill. The ascent is a sustained pull but easy underfoot. Higher up a fence is joined coming up from the east. A small cairn marks one of several possible summits on the flat, grassy top (**2km; 430m; 1h 10min**).

Cardon Hill is a short diversion to the north over the minor top of Birnies Bowrock (unnamed on the OS 1:50k map) from where easy ground leads to the summit; the views to the north are beautiful. In poor visibility the fence at the top of Chapelgill Hill runs to a T-junction from where a right (north-east) turn along the fence leads to Cardon Hill. Culter Fell is gained by retracing your steps southwards following the watershed, and the fence which runs all the way, over

Chapelgill Hill, right, from Culter Fell (Tom Prentice)

Chapelgill Hill, Culter Fell 47

tussocky, boggy ground around the head of Hope Burn and over Kings Bank Head. Continue up the north ridge to the summit where there is a trig point; on a clear day the views are excellent (6km; 650m; 2h 25min).

The shortest route back to Glenkirk is to return down the north ridge before dropping eastwards to gain a grassy track which runs down the ridge between the Glenharvie and Hope Burns then over Congrie Hill (10km; 660m; 3h 30min).

A descent can also be made to the south via Leishfoot Hill to gain Holms Waterhead, or extended to Holm Nick, the col at the head of the glen.

An alternative route of ascent for Culter Fell, together with Cardon Hill and Chapelgill Head if required, can be made from the Culter Water valley to the west. There is parking beyond Culter Allers Farm at NT031312 and beside the Culter River at NT031311, before the public road ends. Walk south along the road for about 700m before turning east and following the track beside Kings Beck. A small footpath continues pleasantly up the burn, beyond where the main track ends, and the beck can be followed in its entirety to emerge beneath the north ridge of Culter Fell which is climbed beside the fence to the summit (4km; 500m; 1h 45min).

The quickest descent is down the north-west ridge, Fell Shin. However, a better walk can be had by descending south to Holm Nick and then taking the track down to Coulter Reservoir. This track can also be gained from Culter Fell by a south-west descent over Knock Hill. A pleasant 4km walk leads back down the glen from the reservoir (13km; 530m; 4h).

The quickest ascent of both Grahams in this group on their own is made by approaching Culter Fell from Glenkirk, via the grassy track over Congrie Hill (4km; 480m; 1h 45min), followed by the onward link to Gathersnow Hill beside the fence up Glenwhappen Rig (8km; 720m; 3h).

The best descent is over Coomb Hill then down its north ridge to Holms Waterhead (13km; 760m; 4h 20min).

The ascent of both Grahams from the Culter Water side is longer (16km; 750m; 5h).

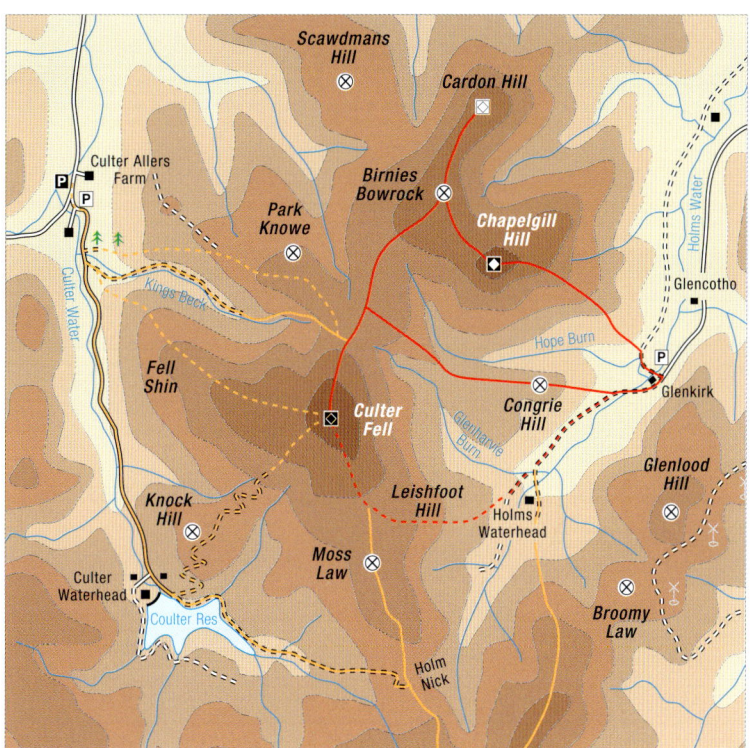

Culter Hills
This fine range of rolling hills lies on the watershed between the major valleys of the River Clyde and the River Tweed, the former draining into the Atlantic on one side of the country and the latter draining into the North Sea on the other side. Lying almost equidistant from Glasgow and Edinburgh, and being encircled by the main roads of the M74, the A701 and the A702, the hills are readily accessible.

The range as a whole falls into three distinct groups: Culter Fell and its two northern outliers, Gathersnow Hill and its three outliers in the south, and the western outpost of Hudderstone. Intruded into by a number of major valleys, which provide the access routes, it is a complicated group of hills with numerous ways of attaining the various summits. The principal routes described here are for tackling each of the three groups separately.

However, it is possible to link the hills, especially the Culter Fell and Gathersnow groups, which can be done as a fine round from Glenkirk (see opposite). They can also all be climbed in one long outing, as briefly described below.

The extended outing of five Donalds and three Donald Tops (which includes the two Grahams, Culter Fell and Gathersnow Hill) starts and finishes from the parking just beyond Culter Allers Farm in Culter Glen. Start by ascending towards Culter Fell up Kings Beck, or the path up its northern rim. Branch out north to visit the outliers, Chapelgill Hill and Cardon Hill, then double back south over Culter Fell. Another diversion is needed to visit Coomb Hill before the rest of this group is traversed; Gathersnow Hill, Hillshaw Head then the outlier Coomb Dod. Whilst not the most aesthetic onwards route, now simply follow the Clyde Wind Farm access track northwards across the west side of Hillshaw Head. Continue north-westwards, down and along the crest via the right-hand track, to reach the last turbine in this section where the track ends just beneath the top of Dod Hill. Now gain the fence and follow it onto Hudderstone. The descent from the top of Hudderstone via Cowgill Rig, as described for the route on p50, is very pleasant (29km; 1350m; 9h 30min).

Gathersnow Hill, Hillshaw Head

Gathersnow Hill viewed from the north-west across Coulter Reservoir (Tom Prentice)

Coomb Hill; 640m; (DT); L72; NT069263
Gathersnow Hill; 688m; (G120); (D43); L72; NT058257; the hill holds snow until late. Mapped Gathersnow (1755). There is a Snowgill Hill 3km west
Hillshaw Head; 652m; (D63); L72; NT048246; top above the hill wood. Hillshaw Burn on east: Scots 'shaw', small (natural) wood. Mapped Hillshaw Browhead (1775) and Culter Stane Hill (1817)
Coomb Dod; 635m; (DT); L72; NT046238

The Gathersnow Hill group of hills can be climbed from the Kingledoors valley to the south-east. The primary route described is that from the farm at Kingledoors at the foot of the glen. A small loop of old road at the east entrance to the farm affords good parking (NT109281). Walk up the tree-lined driveway, then turn left and walk through to the far end of the farmyard. From here there is a choice of routes to Coomb Hill.

The principal route heads up the glen by following the track across the burn to gain the access track to the 11 turbine Glenkerie Wind Farm. This leads on up the glen to ascend Kingle Rig onto Broomy Law. Continue beyond this on the track up the glen to reach the white farmhouse of Hopehead. From there, ascend a grassy track west then north towards the small col behind Point 429m (Glengary Knowe) and make a direct ascent of Coomb Hill on easy ground. The summit is delightfully grassy.

Easy walking then leads south-west along the grassy ridge following the fence to the top of Gathersnow Hill, marked by only a few stones (**7km; 500m; 2h 20min**).

The high tableland of the Manor Hills dominates the view to the east, whilst the view west and south-west is met by the 206 turbines of the Clyde Wind Farm, one of the UK's biggest onshore wind farms. The turbines extend onto Hillshaw Head, Coomb Dod and Glenwhappen Dod at the head of the valley, impinging on the next section of the walk.

Continue easily alongside the boundary fence separating Scottish Borders from South Lanarkshire to Hillshaw Head, marked by a small pile of stones east of the fence, then down and up to reach Coomb Dod with its trig point (**9.5km; 590m; 3h 5min**). The easiest return from here is to drop eastwards into the Kingledoors valley and walk along the track back to the start (**18.5km; 590m; 5h**).

An alternative from Kingledores Farm is to traverse the full length of the ridge on the north side of the glen, gained via a path up Cocklie Rig Head. To reach this path, follow the track to just beyond the farm where it crosses the burn, then break off right and climb north past a stand of Scots pines. The path gradually ascends above the Benshaw Burn, passing by two lonely rowan trees, after which it becomes indistinct. It is probably now easier to head onto the spur on the left to gain the wind turbine access road and follow this up left then right to the top of Cocklie Rig Head and step over the fence. Once on the

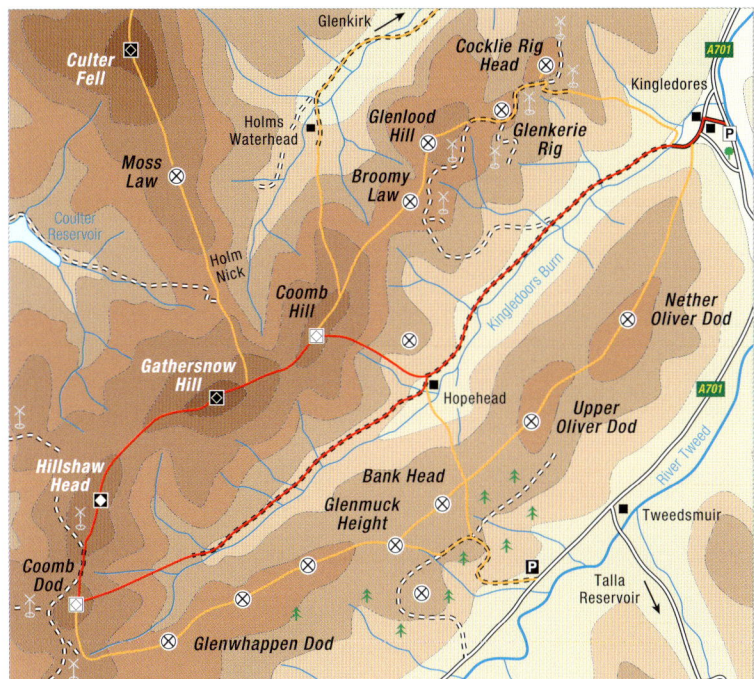

ridge, keep to the crest following the fence all the way over Glenlood Hill and Broomy Law onto Coomb Hill, then Gathersnow Hill (**8km; 670m; 3h**). Follow the previous route to Coomb Dod (**10.5km; 760m; 3h 45min**).

There are now two options.

(i) Descend into the Kingledoors valley to the track, as described opposite (**19.5km; 760m; 5h 40min**).

(ii) Continue along the chain of hills that form the south side of the glen to complete the fine Kingledoors Horseshoe. It should be noted that despite the lesser height of the hills on this side, the terrain proves more difficult and time consuming (**19.5km; 1000m; 6h 15min**).

Plans to extend the Glenkerie Wind Farm by erecting turbines on the Holms Water side of the ridge on Glenlood Hill, Broomy Law and Coomb Hill have been rejected, but may be resurrected. These were to be accessed using the existing track up Broomy Law.

The round of these hills can also be started from near Tweedsmuir on the A701. However, although shorter, this involves crossing the Oliver Dod ridge first. The path marked on the OS 1:50k map running north-west from the village has all but disappeared, not least because of some forestry planting. Instead, take a forestry track from NT091240 some 700m south of the junction of the Talla Reservoir road with the A701. There is some space for parking at the start of the forest track.

The track curves gently up the hillside. Just past the highpoint, close to the ridge crest, a junction is reached to the south-east of Bank Head. From here, leave the track and cross due north over rough ground for a short way, passing a small pond, to pick up the line of the burn dropping north into the Kingledoors valley. The burn follows a narrow defile before opening up into flat fields, which are crossed to the farmhouse of Hopehead; a bridge by the house crosses the Kingledoors Burn. From here, follow the route already described over Coomb Dod to Gathersnow Hill (**6km; 560m; 2h 20min**) and onwards to Coomb Dod (**8.5km; 630m; 3h 5min**).

The direct return to Tweedsmuir is made by continuing around the horseshoe over Glenwhappen Dod, but the going is distinctly tussocky and slow. Join a forest track just south-east of Glenmuck Height and turn left (north-east). This track gains the junction passed on the ascent, from where a right turn leads back down to the start (**15km; 700m; 4h 45min**).

The quickest way of ascending both Grahams (Culter Fell and Gathersnow Hill) is from Glenkirk. Climb Culter Fell via the grassy track over Congrie Hill, as described for the prinicpal route on p46 (**4km; 480m; 1h 45min**).

From there, the onward link to Gathersnow Hill is made via Moss Law and Holm Nick, following the fence up Glenwhappen Rig (**8km; 720m; 3h**).

The best descent is over Coomb Hill then down its north ridge to Holms Waterhead (**13km; 760m; 4h 20min**).

This route can be extended to include the Culter Fell and Gathersnow outliers, although this does involve some backtracking.

Gathersnow Hill from Coomb Hill (Rab Anderson)

Hudderstone

Hudderstone; *626m; (D78); L72; NT022271; stone in the heather, probably. Hill mapped Hatherstone (1817 and 1840) and Heatherstane Law (OS, 1860): 'hather' and 'hadder' are Scots renditions of heather*

Hudderstone is a remote outlier to the west and north-west of the main Culter Hills group, and being awkward to contrive into a reasonable Donald round with them, is generally climbed on its own.

Although an ascent can be made using the surfaced road up the Culter Water valley, then crossing the Coulter Reservoir dam wall to ascend Snowgill Hill, both the route and the parking are better from the road up the Cow Gill valley.

On the road in from Coulter, fork right just past the entrance to Culter Allers Farm and pass Birthwood Farm to park on the verge about 1km further on, just before a bridge over the burn (NT020306). Walk over the bridge, then in front of a cattle grid follow a track on the left uphill and round into a walled field. Leave the track and climb uphill on a grassy atv track which leads up the edge of the field to pass through a gate and gain the crest. The atv track passes just beneath the top of Ward Law and is followed over Woodycleuch Dod then uphill beside a fence to the top of Hudderstone (**4.5km; 470m; 1h 50min**).

What the summit lacks in drama is more than made up for on a clear day

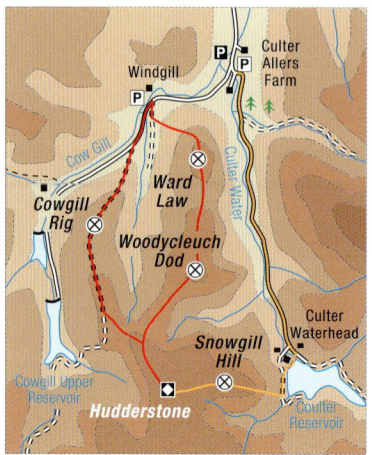

by its superb view: Culter Fell to the east with the high tablelands of the Manor Hills beyond, Broad Law over the shoulder of Gathersnow Hill then Hart Fell to the south-east, the distant Lake District fells to the south, Arran to the west and Tinto close by to the north-west.

Several obvious options exist for extending this outing but the simplest route is to return back down the north-west ridge beside the fence to pick up the obvious track which leads over Cowgill Rig to regain the road close to the start (**8.5km; 490m; 3h**).

Bodesbeck Law; 665m; (D57); L79; NT169104; hill above Bodesbeck (farm). Mapped Bodgeback Law in 1775; 'beck' is northern English for a stream

Mid Rig; 616m; (DT); L79; NT180122

Bell Craig; 623m; (D79); L79; NT186128; bald cliff. Scots beld (sometimes bell), 'bald': Bald Craig is the cliff just west of the summit

Andrewhinney Hill; 677m; (G136); (D47); L79; NT197138; obscure. Scots 'hinney' honey (as endearment). Known by farmers on west side as Andrew Whinny Hill which might suggest whin-covered

Trowgrain Middle; 628m; (DT); L79; NT206150

Herman Law; 614m; (D87); L79; NT213157; mapped Herskey Law (1755) perhaps Scots 'harsky' rough? Later Hermans Law (1773). OS Name Book states may be 'a contraction of Herd Man'. Farmers on west called it Hirmont Law, according to OSNB, which may be Britonnic 'hyr monith', long hill

Hudderstone and Coulter Reservoir from Gathersnow Hill (Rab Anderson)

Bodesbeck Law, Bell Craig, Andrewhinney Hill, Herman Law

The broad summit of Andrewhinney Hill seen from the flanks of Bell Craig to the south-west (Rab Anderson)

A chain of eight high-level grassy hilltops runs along the ridge between the valleys of the Moffat and Ettrick Waters opposite White Coomb and the Grey Mare's Tail waterfall. This ridge contains four Donalds and two Donald Tops, of which Andrewhinney Hill, a Graham, is the principal summit. Although the full traverse of the ridge, together with the return along the road, is fairly long it is a straightforward outing, especially since the start is at an altitude of 378m.

Drive up the Ettrick valley to the end of the public road and park considerately at the edge of the turning area, as much off the road as is possible. Head north-west on the right-hand track through the gate and follow this as it climbs, uphill through the forest above the Longhope Burn. The track zigzags out of the trees into the open onto a grassy shoulder where it becomes a grassy hill track which is followed westwards to swing round onto the top of Bodesbeck Law (**3km; 290m; 1h 10min**). On the other side, across the deep trench of Moffat Dale lie Under Saddle Yoke and the Hart Fell hills around Black Hope.

Ahead, a wall and fence run along the grassy crest to the aptly named Nowtrig Head (Pt.608m on the OS 1:50k map) where the wall turns away right. Continue beside the fence over Mid Rig (also unnamed on the OS 1:50k map) to Bell Craig. The hills on the opposite side of Moffat Dale are now Carrifran Gans and White Coomb. The highpoint of the day, Andrewhinney Hill, is easily gained after a short descent and a 100m ascent (**8km; 510m; 2h 40min**).

Loch Skeen and its surrounding hills, with the Grey Mare's Tail below, captivate the view on the other side, although one has to descend a little to the west to see the waterfall.

A choice of ridges gives an escape route from here back to the Ettrick valley. However, the minor bump of another Mid Rig then Trowgrain Middle (note that the summit lies some 80m north and 115m west of the tall cairn by the fence) offer little resistance on the easy walk out to the final summit of the day; Herman Law (**10.5km; 580m; 3h 20min**).

Head south from here and descend the narrow ridge between the waters of the Black Grain and Back Burn to reach the road at the white cottage of Brockhoperig. From here, 6km of road leads pleasantly alongside the Ettrick Water, gently uphill, following the route of the Southern Upland Way to provide an end to an enjoyable and satisfying day (**20km; 700m; 5h 40min**).

A swift ascent of Andrewhinney Hill itself can be made from Birkhill at the top of the A708 above Moffat Dale; parking just to the north-east of the farm. Take the signposted route at the farm, straight up the steep hillside beside the fence onto Herman Law then follow the fence over Trowgrain Middle and Mid Rig to Andrewhinney Hill. Return the same way, or descend from the col before Trowgrain Middle to pick up a rough track that drops back down to Birkhill (**8km; 440m; 2h 40min**).

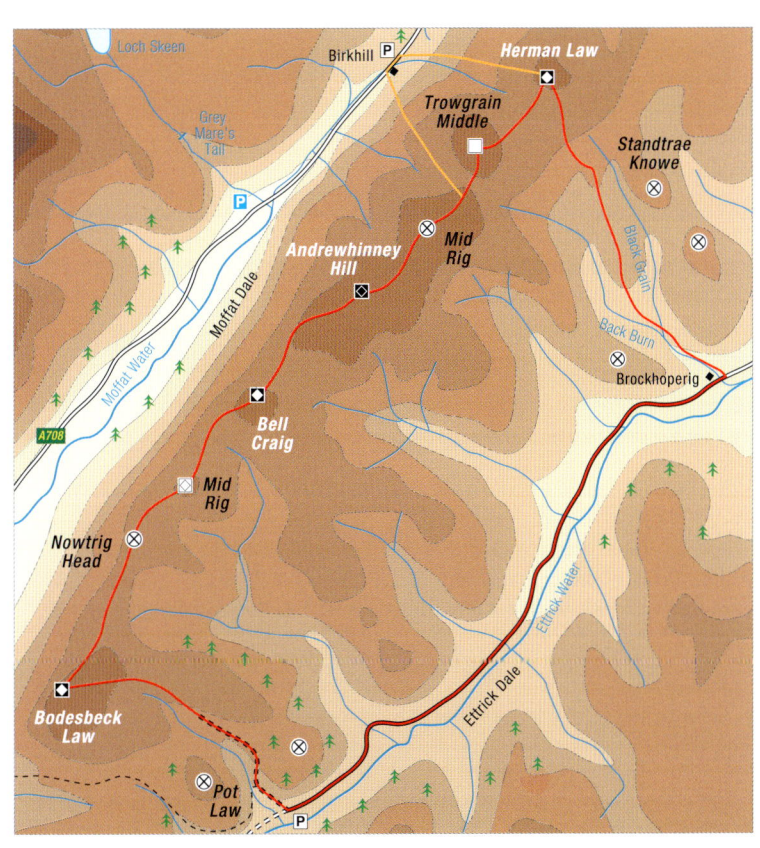

Ettrick Pen, Wind Fell, Loch Fell, Croft Head, Capel Fell

Section 0b – The Borders

Capel Fell, left, Ettrick Pen in the distance and Wind Fell from Croft Head (Rab Anderson)

Ettrick Pen; 692m; (G114); (D38); L79; NT199076; head point of Ettrick (dale). Mapped Penn of Ettrick (1654): also known 16th-18th centuries as Penn of Esdaile Moore, because it also stands at head of Eskdale, to the south

Hopetoun Craig; 632m; (DT); L79; NT187067

Wind Fell; 665m; (D56); L79; NT178061; windy hill. The pass beside it on the west was Windy Hass (1804), later Windy Nick (1860)

Loch Fell; 688m; (D44); L79; NT170047; no loch present here, so the name is obscure

West Knowe; 672m; (DT); L79; NT163052

Croft Head; 637m; (G186); (D72); L79; NT153056; hill above Crofthead (farm). Scots 'croft', smallholding

Capel Fell; 678m; (G132); (D46); L79; NT163069; horse hill? Scots 'cappell, capul', horse. Horses roamed wild on hills

Smidhope Hill; 644m; (DT); L79; NT168076

White Shank; 622m; (DT); L79; NT169083

These nine hills are clustered around and close to the afforested headwaters of the Ettrick Water. They can be conveniently combined into a very fine extension of the classic Border round known as The Ettrick Horseshoe. The walk described is one of only a few where three Grahams can be climbed in one logical outing.

Drive up the Ettrick valley to the end of the public road and park considerately at the edge of the turning area, as much off the road as is possible.

Take the left-hand track and follow this, the route of the Southern Upland Way, south-west past Potburn and cross the bridge over the Ettrick Water to reach the bothy at Over Phawhope. Break off left just beyond the bothy, cross the Entertrona Burn and head uphill on another track through a break in the forest.

When the track ends, continue on a rough path on the left, branching left at a cairn, to climb up through young trees onto the rounded spur. Turn right at the top and continue alongside the fence to reach the large cairn on top of Ettrick Pen (**3.5km; 320m; 1h 20min**).

It is a splendid viewpoint. To the south one can see from The Cheviot on one side of the country to the Solway Firth on the other.

The regional boundary continues around much of the high-level part of this walk and is marked on the ground by a fence, then a wall, which act as navigational aids. A long south-westerly section alongside the fence leads over Hopetoun Craig then onto Wind Fell.

Descend to where the fence splits and drop down beside the left-hand fence to Windfell Nick. From there, follow the fence southwards up the long spur to reach a junction of fences and the trig point on top of Loch Fell (**8.5km; 570m; 2h 50min**).

Take the right-hand fence to gain West Knowe where the next objective, Croft Head, can be seen on the opposite side of the valley with the sizeable drop and ascent in-between fully revealed. Descend steeply beside the fence towards the edge of the forest for a short way then break away from this to cut steeply down and across the slope to gain a sheep fank on the valley floor. Pause for breath, cross the Southern Upland Way, then climb the path which ascends the fine and narrow east

Ettrick Pen, Wind Fell, Loch Fell, Croft Head, Capel Fell

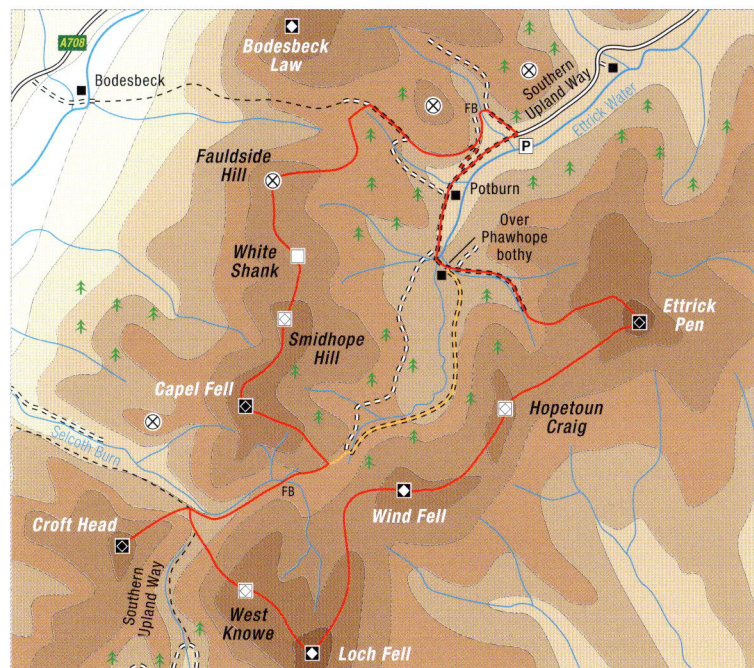

ridge via some zigzags to gain the Cat Shoulder leading to the top of Croft Head (**11km; 790m; 3h 50min**).

Savour the splendid view then return to the valley floor. Now follow the Southern Upland Way up the right side of the narrow valley opposite the Craigmichen Scar. Beds of sedimentary rock have been exposed here and shaped by the forces of nature into an impressive unstable high-angled hillside and a gorge through which the Selcoth Burn flows. The burn is crossed higher up by a bridge to gain Ettrick Head, the col where the path descends into the Ettrick valley. Climb north-west beside a fence onto the third Graham, Capel Fell (**14km; 1020m; 5h**).

Although there is still some distance to cover, the going becomes easier and the views ahead to Hart Fell, Carrifran Gans and White Coomb can be fully appreciated. Descend north-east beside the fence to the col to meet a wall, which now indicates the boundary, and follow this over Smidhope Hill then onto White Shank. Swing round beside the wall over the bump of Fauldside Hill then drop down to meet a track at the col in front of Bodesbeck Hill.

Now heading back to the valley floor on the track, descend through a break in the forest to reach a sheep fank where the main track dog-legs off right to Potburn. Continue straight ahead on a grassy track which leads to felled forest and contour the hillside. On joining a new felling track, either descend this to the track below and return to the start, or continue round the hillside to cross a burn by a footbridge at NT185094 then descend another track back to the road (**20km; 1100m; 6h 30min**).

A slightly shorter Graham-only route starts as for the described route onto Ettrick Pen (**3.5km; 320m; 1h 20min**) and continues to Wind Fell. Drop down to Ettrick Head then follow the Southern Upland Way and ascend Croft Head (**9.5km; 680m; 3h 15min**). Return to Ettrick Head then ascend Capel Fell (**12.5km; 910m; 4h 25min**) and return to Ettrick Head. Follow the Southern Upland Way back to the start (**17.5km; 910m; 5h 30min**).

Capel Fell from Loch Fell (Rab Anderson)

Swatte Fell, Hart Fell, Under Saddle Yoke

Nether Coomb Craig; 724m; (DT); L78; NT129109

Swatte Fell; 728m; (D22); L78; NT118113; obscure. The OS Name Book suggests Anglo-Saxon 'swaete', sweated. More likely is Old English 'swað', which developed to 'swathe', sward of grass

Falcon Craig; 724m; (DT); L78; NT122127

Hart Fell; 808m; (D7); L78; NT113135; hill of the stag. Hills named after stags are found in the Lakes (Harter Fell), the Hebrides (Hartaval) and elsewhere in Nithsdale

Under Saddle Yoke; 745m; (D16); L78; NT142126; saddle shaped like a yoke. Mapped Coripheran Yoke (1775), the Yoke (1790s), Saddleback (1820), this hill together with Saddle Yoke, form a classic narrow saddle

Saddle Yoke; 735m; (DT); L78; NT144123

Forming a natural circuit around the Blackhope Burn and the Black Hope valley, these hills can be conveniently climbed in one superb outing known as the Black Hope Round. This is one of the classic Border hillwalks. There are no Grahams on this round, but the highest point is Hart Fell, a Corbett.

The circuit starts from Blackshope cottage or Capplegill in Moffat Dale, 5.5 miles (8.8km) to the north-east of Moffat. Blackshope is the white cottage on the north side of the A708, just east of the farm at Capplegill and the bridge over the Blackhope Burn.

Limited parking is possible at the east side of this cottage, only on the east side of the entrance to the gated track into the Black Hope valley. Take care not to block access to the track, or the garage. There is also space to park on the grass in front of the white building opposite the entrance to Capplegill some 350m along the road to the west.

From either parking spot, walk along the road to a gate into a field, on the west side of a small building and on the right bank of the Hang Burn. Walk up the right side of this burn towards the obvious cleft of Hang Gill on the hillside. Pass through a gate and follow a sheep track steeply up the side of Hang Gill. Just above the waterfall, go through a gate at first one fence (electrified) then right through a gate in another fence. Head up rightwards to pick up a path which leads up the broad ridge running up the side of Black Craig to gain the top of Nether Coomb Craig (**2.5km; 580m; 1h 35min**).

The slope on the right plunges steeply into Black Hope and there are fine views across to Under Saddle Yoke and Saddle Yoke.

The better route continues close to the edge, and follows an atv track across the dip then up onto the flat top of Swatte Fell. Head across left to an old wall and go through a gate to find the highest point, which lies some 250m or to the south-west along the wall. The OS 1:50k map gives a height of 728m at this point, whilst the 1:25k map gives a height of 729m some further 300m to the north-east along the wall where there is a small cairn. The DoBIH confirm the former as being the highest point, but with a height of 730m.

Go back through the gate and follow the wall and fence over Falcon Craig; a cairn on the other side of the fence marks the top. At the narrow neck to the north, the Hass o' the Red Roads, the wall turns and drops

Hart Fell, left, and Under Saddle Yoke, right, from Croft Head (Rab Anderson)

Swatte Fell, Hart Fell, Under Saddle Yoke

Above the Hass o' the Red Roads on Hart Fell, with Under Saddle Yoke, left, and Saddle Yoke (Rab Anderson)

south-west down a fine valley, down which the Auchencat Burn flows into the River Annan. Continue uphill beside the fence then along the broad summit to reach the trig point on Hart Fell (**6.5km; 760m; 2h 40min**).

Those in a hurry to tick the Donalds might decide to pick up the outlier, Whitehope Heights, to the north-west. However, this involves a big drop-off and reascent, adding around 2h to the day. It is also off the natural round and is better collected via a separate walk from the other side. Albeit this climbs Hart Fell again, it takes in the Devil's Beef Tub and provides another enjoyable outing. The Whitehope Heights and Hart Fell route is described on p56.

Continuing with the circuit, swing around the head of the Black Hope valley following the fence north-eastwards then eastwards above Saddle Craigs and descend over Hartfell Rig. Break away from the fence just before the col with Cape Law then cut across the head of Whirly Gill and contour the slope southwards to another col. Ascend the broad ridge to the top of Under Saddle Yoke (**10.5km; 910m; 3h 50min**).

Descend steeply to a narrow col then back up the narrow ridge on the other side onto Saddle Yoke. Pause for breath, savour the view to the Ettrick Hills in front, Carrifran Gans and White Coomb to the side and the Eildons in the far distance, then plunge down the splendid long south ridge into Moffat Dale. Just before the foot of the ridge, head right to reach the track at a gate and follow this back (**14km; 970m; 5h**).

See following page for map

Moffat Hills

The Moffat Hills contain no Grahams, but there are 10 Donalds and 11 Donald Tops, which as their highest points include the Corbetts White Coomb and Hart Fell. Collecting these hills in a satisfactory logical fashion and in accordance with Donald's original list proves a little more awkward than it seems at first sight, due to a number of outlying Donald Tops. One of the attractions in compleating Donald's list is in deciding how to tackle these outliers. All of the Moffat Hills on Donald's List could essentially be climbed in two big rounds with some significant out and back detours to pick up the outliers, which the fit and those in a hurry to compleat might elect to do. However, this would miss out on some particularly fine walks, and for this reason The Moffat Hills are described here in four logical rounds and although these walks include two out and back detours they are not particularly significant. These rounds do overlap in places and some hills appear twice, however there is no great hardship in climbing hills such as White Coomb and Hart Fell from two different directions, so the majority should hopefully enjoy the experience. It is also possible to tackle the hills described here in smaller, or indeed different rounds to suit weather conditions and levels of fitness.

Whitehope Heights across the head of Annandale (Rab Anderson)

Whitehope Heights; 637m; (D73); L78; NT095138; height above Whitehope (Burn). Scots 'hope', small upland valley. Whitehope Top (1775)

Hart Fell; 808m; (D7); L78; NT113135; hill of the stag. Hills named after stags are found in the Lakes (Harter Fell), the Hebrides (Hartaval) and elsewhere in Nithsdale

Whitehope Heights is a Donald that can truly be classed as an outlier, being separated from Hart Fell, its nearest Donald neighbour, by a walking distance of 2.6km, a drop of 281m and an ascent of 110m. It can be climbed as a somewhat lengthy and arduous detour off the Black Hope Round, the preceding route, and a time is given in that walk for its inclusion. However, it is off the natural round and it could be argued that it detracts from that classic horseshoe walk.

For this reason Whitehope Heights is perhaps best left for an ascent on its own, and the walk to its summit from the west, together with an ascent of Hart Fell and a return by the Devil's Beef Tub, makes a fine round. The Beef Tub is a natural steep-sided corrie bowl at the head of Annandale where Border reivers hid stolen cattle.

At the top of the Devil's Beef Tub on the A701 some 5 miles (8km) north of Moffat, park considerately around the entrance to a gated track (NT055128) at a height of 395m. There is further parking downhill a little. The initial part of the route to just beyond Chalk Rig Edge is followed by the Annandale Way long-distance footpath.

Cross the fences to the side of the gate by stiles and climb to the trig point on top of Annanhead Hill (478m) then continue over to Great Hill (466m) with the slopes below falling steeply into the Beef Tub. Continue along the grassy crest of the ridge beside the fence, over Chalk Rig Edge (500m), then drop slightly and climb towards the top of Whitehope Heights. Cross the stile in the deer fence to gain the cairn (**5km; 420m; 1h 50min**), then return back over the fence.

Tick done, the simple option is to return. However, much the better walk is to continue on to Hart Fell whose vast bulk dominates the view ahead. Drop gently north-east through an odd corridor created by a sheep fence on the left and the deer fence on the right, then more steeply east to a narrow col. Draw breath and make a long, steep ascent beside the fence to reach the flat summit of Hart Fell where there are fine panoramic views (**7.5km; 710m; 2h 55min**).

Follow the fence south for 200m and where this swings away south-east, head south-west on an atv track down a long, grassy shoulder over Arthur's Seat. Go through a gate in the deer fence and continue down the narrow spur of Well Rig, through the gap between the burns, to pass above Hartfell Spa, a chalybeate spring felt to have health-giving iron salt properties. At the bottom, go right

Whitehope Heights, Hart Fell

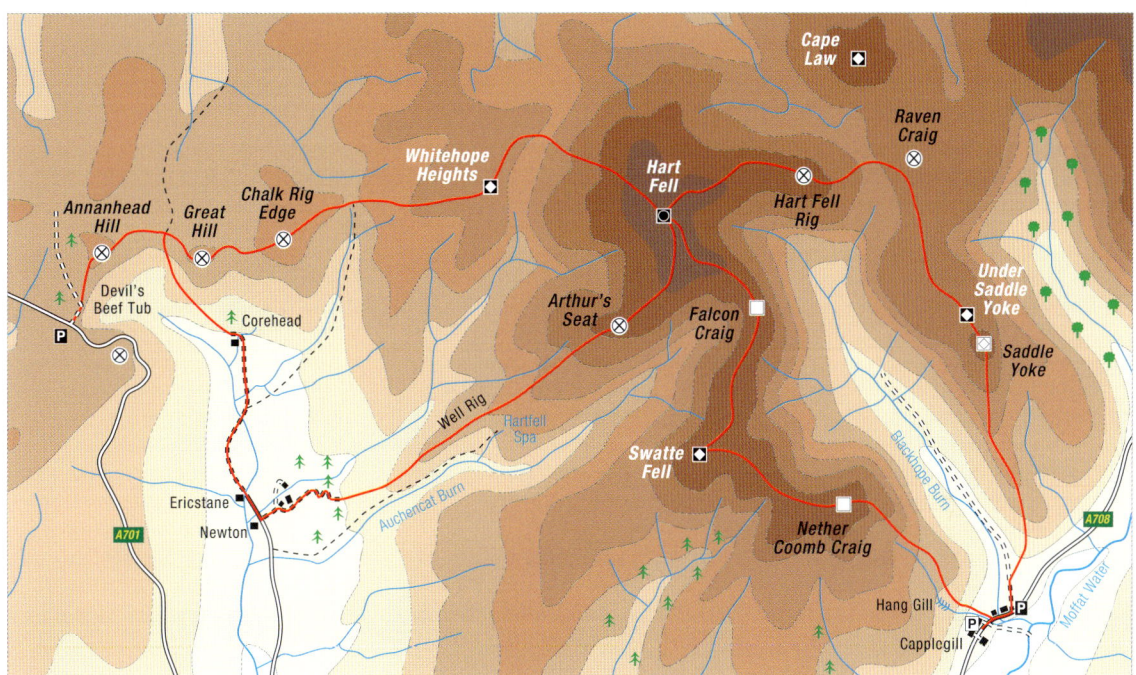

and through gates to gain a track leading to the minor road up the floor of the glen at Newton.

Turn right and follow the road around the east side of the buildings at Ericstane, then on to the buildings at Corehead, which are rounded in an anti-clockwise direction. A number of gates are passed through to gain an indistinct path which rises up the side of the Devil's Beef Tub to the heights above. This is certainly one of the highlights of the round and the final airy traverse to reach the col proves somewhat of a surprise, and not just for weary knees weakened by the ascent! All that remains is a short reascent of Annanhead Hill, beyond which lies the road (**17.5km; 1020m; 5h 55min**).

Great Hill, left, Whitehope Heights and Hart Fell from the Devil's Beef Tub (Tom Prentice)

Lochcraig Head, White Coomb

***Lochcraig Head**; 801m; (D9); L79; NT167176; hill above the cliff of the loch*
***Nickies Knowe**; 761m; (DT); L79; NT163191*
***Firthhope Rig**; 800m; (DT); L79; NT153153*
***White Coomb**; 821m; (D4); L79; NT163150; white arched ridge. A cornice often forms in winter over Coomb Craig, facing east. Mapped White Coom Edge (1775)*
***Carrifran Gans**; 757m; (DT); L79; NT159138*

This is an excellent and scenic Donalds circuit of Loch Skeen, taking in the Corbett White Coomb as its highest summit.

Park in the National Trust's pay and display car park at the foot of the Grey Mare's Tail waterfall, off the A708 in Moffat Dale. Follow a good path up the steep slope on the east side of the waterfall. Height is gained rapidly and the path soon traverses the hillside to easier ground beside the Tail Burn, which leads pleasantly to picturesque Loch Skeen. Lochcraig Head rises resplendent above the far end of the loch.

Walk along the east side of the loch for about 200m then break off right across heather to pick up a fence which is followed across a couple of boggy sections towards Lochcraig Head. Any other line is likely to prove more difficult. The fence and an old wall running beside it lead up the right side of the steep slope before swinging round and traversing across the flat summit area a short distance south of the actual top itself, which is easily gained alongside another fence (**4.5km; 570m; 2h**).

It is worth walking to the edge for the splendid view over Loch Skeen to the Graham Andrewhinney Hill on the ridge running above Moffat Dale.

The Donald Top of Nickies Knowe is an outlier to the north, easily picked up by following the fence to where it splits on Talla East Side then following the left-hand fence with a drop to a wide saddle and a short climb to the top (**6km; 600m; 2h 25min**).

Return to the saddle then pick up a sheeptrack which rises slightly then contours the hillside to reach the wall and remnants of the fence just above Talla Nick; the deep col between the hills. In poor visibility it might be better to keep to the fencelines.

From the col, ascend onto the top of Firthybrig Head to meet another old wall and a fence that run along the flat ridge. Follow a rough atv track south-west alongside the wall and fence, up an imperceptible rise onto Donald's Cleuch Head.

The Donald Top of Great Hill could be included by a detour to the north-west; an added 2km, 30m, 25min.

Another slight rise gains a junction of fences on the Donald Top of Firthhope Rig (800m). Make a right-angled turn to the left here and

White Coomb from Andrewhinney Hill to the south-east (Rab Anderson)

Lochcraig Head, White Coomb 59

Lochcraig Head and Loch Skeen from Andrewhinney Hill (Rab Anderson)

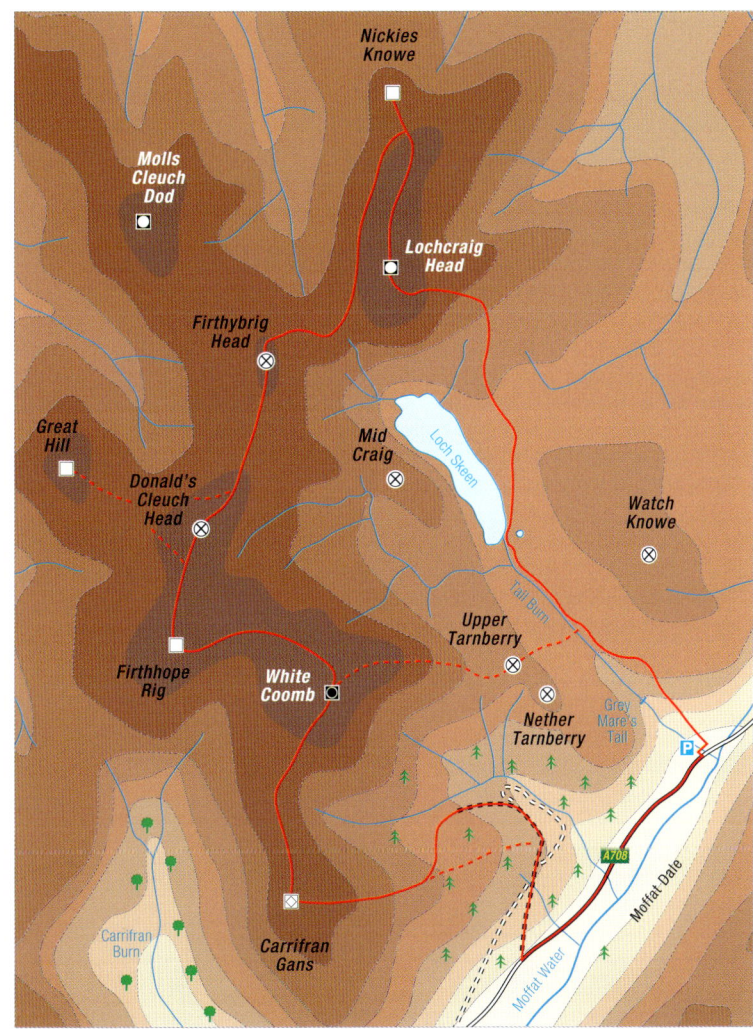

continue south-east on the atv track, still following the old wall and the fence. Where the fence makes a right-angled turn to the south-west, and the wall carries straight on, cut diagonally across to the rounded summit of White Coomb (**11.5km; 790m; 4h**).

The Donald Top of Carrifran Gans is an outlier less than 1.5km to the south and is easily included by descending south-west to a broad col with a tiny lochan then making a short ascent to the summit (**13km; 830m; 4h 25min**).

There are two descent options.

(i) Follow an atv track down the broad east ridge towards the forest. At a cairn, either drop northwards with the atv track to reach the head of a track through the forest, or continue down the crest to descend a break in the trees and gain the forest track lower down. Descend the track past a branch off left, then after crossing a burn take the left fork to gain the road and follow this for 2.5km back to the start (**18.5km; 870m; 5h 45min**).

(ii) Return to White Coomb and take the normal descent from there by heading north-east to the old wall, then follow this down the east ridge over the bump of Upper Tarnberry to reach the Tail Burn well above the waterfall. The crossing may entail getting wet feet. Descend the path to the car park (**17.5km; 940m; 5h 45min**).

Garelet Hill; 681; (DT); L72; NT124201

Lairds Cleuch Rig; 684m; (DT); L78; NT125195

Erie Hill; 690m; (D41); L78; NT124187; mapped Earickle (1775). Possibly from Gaelic 'elrick', a narrow pass used to trap deer

Garelet Dod; 698m; (D32); L78; NT126172; lump of the grassy stripes? Scots 'gair, gare', green grassy stripe on hillside where water has suppressed heather: east of the top is Speir Gairs

Din Law; 667m; (DT); L78; NT124156

Cape Law; 722m; (D24); L78; NT131150; coping-stone hill? Scots 'cape' can mean such a stone. The south end of the summit plateau was mapped Three Lairds Cairn (1775), indicating estates junction

Firthhope Rig; 800m; (DT); L79; NT153153

White Coomb; 821m; (D4); L79; NT163150; white arched ridge. A cornice often forms in winter over Coomb Craig, facing east. Mapped White Coom Edge (1775)

Carrifran Gans; 757m; (DT); L79; NT159138

Great Hill; 774m; (DT); L78; NT145163

Molls Cleuch Dod; 785m; (D12); L79; NT151179; lump above Molls Cleuch. Scots 'cleuch', ravine, possibly with a personal name. Mapped Maulscleuchshank (1775)

Carlavin Hill; 736m; (DT); L78; NT142188

Taking in all of the hills on Donald's List which lie around the Games Hope valley, this is one of the bigger Donald rounds. It provides a superb day out as well as a true test of stamina. There are no Grahams, but if desired (and most will no doubt do so) the Corbett of White Coomb can easily be included, perhaps with Carrifran Gans. These two hills are also on the round of Loch Skeen, described on the preceding pages.

Start at the south-east end of Talla Reservoir, beyond the farm at Talla Linnfoots. There is ample verge parking just before the bend where the road starts to climb out of the valley (NT134202).

Walk down the road for 100m or so and cross the footbridge over the Games Hope Burn. Ahead is a steep grassy slope, which provides an unrelenting but brutally satisfying climb, leading directly to the trig point on Garelet Hill. Stay to the right of the Witch Linn burn, stepping over a fallen fence partway up, and make best use of sheep tracks on firm ground up the slight ridge. If the fallen fence is ever fixed, there is a gate some 200m away on the other side of the burn (**1km; 380m; 50min**).

Step over the boundary fence which runs along the crest and walk south beside this onto the slightly higher Lairds Cleuch Rig then descend to the shallow col in front of the next hill. Break away from the fence here and make the short ascent to the top of Erie Hill before descending off the back to rejoin the fence. A gradual climb beside the fence leads up the spur of Common Law then around onto Garelet Dod, the top of which lies just out from the fence and wall (**4.75km; 620m; 2h**).

Drop off the back, cutting down and across steeply to rejoin the fence and follow this over Ellers Cleuch Rig to the rocky head of Ellers Cleuch, level with the head of the small Gameshope Loch. Head up the other side and climb to the rocky knoll that is the top of Din Law; the top is about 100m out from the wall. Rejoin the wall and follow this down then up to Cape Law (**7.5km; 830m; 3h 5min**).

Follow the wall along a level section out to Pt.709m. The slopes here are those skirted on the Black Hope Round on the way to Under Saddle Yoke from Hart Fell. Continue following the wall and fence towards Under Saddle Yoke, dropping to a small dip. The wall can be seen going over a slight rise ahead, then across the head of Rotten Bottom and up to Firthhope Rig. Just before the rise it is possible to cut the corner and

Erie Hill, left, and Lairds Cleuch Rig with Broad Law to the right (Rab Anderson)

Erie Hill, Garelet Dod, Cape Law, White Coomb, Molls Cleuch Dod

rejoin the wall at the foot of Firthhope Rig, saving some time and distance.

Two options exist from here.

(i) Cross flat ground, still following the wall and fence, then make the steep climb up and across to a junction of fences on top of Firthhope Rig. From here, White Coomb is an easy short detour, gained by dropping down slightly then following the fence and what is left of the wall gently uphill. Where these diverge, cut across to the top of White Coomb (**11.75km; 1070m; 4h 30min**).

(ii) This includes Carrifran Gans by cutting eastwards across the slope to swing round and make a rising traverse above the burn to gain the col, between White Coomb and Carrifan Gans. A fence leads to the summit. Return to the col then climb beside the fence to White Coomb. This detour only adds 1.25km, 20m, 20min over option (i).

From the summit of White Coomb, follow the wall and the fence to Firthhope Rig and stay with these onto Donald's Cleuch Head, an imperceptible rise. Leave the fence and head north-west along an old fence-

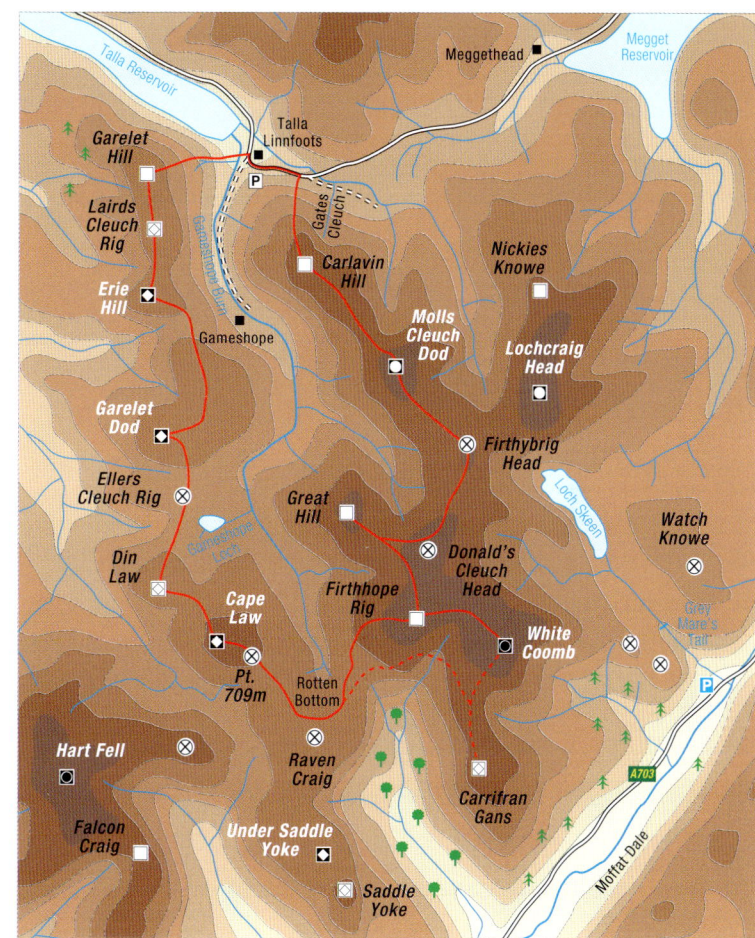

line onto Great Hill, then return to the fence and continue to Firthybrig Head. There is a junction of walls and fences here with the right-hand wall dropping to Talla Nick beneath Lochcraig Head.

The fit and the determined could detour from here to take in Lochcraig Head and Nickies Knowe. However, this is likely to involve a return time of about 1h 45min.

Now on the home run, drop down then gradually up beside the left-hand wall and fence to the top of Molls Cleuch Dod. There are two cairns, one next to the wall and another 100m to the north-east (**17.5km; 1210m; 6h 5min**).

Continue beside the wall and fence, down then easily up to the final summit of Carlavin Hill.

For the descent, follow the wall downhill a short distance then head north away from this as it drops into a shallow basin at the head of a burn that descends to the valley floor.

If the wall is followed it crosses the burn and traverses the hillside to an area of rock where it stops and a line of old fence posts drops down alarmingly steep slopes directly to the valley floor. This should be avoided. If one chooses to descend this way it would perhaps be better to follow the south side of the burn down into the valley, although this is still very steep.

Better and safer is to either descend north down the burn of Gates Cleuch to reach the road, or head away from the wall just after the summit and follow the northern shoulder of the hill down to the road, which is followed downhill to the start (**21km; 1230m; 7h 15min**).

If the outlying White Coomb, Carrrifan Gans and Great Hill are not taken in, having been included on the previous walk, then a saving of 4km, 100m, 1h can be achieved on the above distance and time.

Broad Law and Cramalt Craig, right, from Molls Cleuch Dod to the south (Rab Anderson)

Talla Cleuch Head; 691m; (D40); L72; NT133218; hill above Talla Cleuch, the cleuch (ravine) dropping to Talla Reservoir. Talla is probably Gaelic 'an t-alla', the crags, or 'talla' rocks, on account of the striking cliffs above the reservoir and Talla Water

Broad Law; 840m; (D2); L72; NT146235; broad (flat-topped) hill. Mapped Braidl Hill (1654) from Scots 'braid', and Hairstane Broad Law (1755), after the farm (now) Hearthstane at its foot

Hunt Law; 639m; (DT); L72; NT150264

Cramalt Craig; 831m; (D3); L72; NT168247; cliff above the Cramalt (Burn). The burn name is probably Gaelic 'crom 'llt', crooked torrent. Mapped Black Dody (1775), 'the black lump'

Clockmore; 641m; (DT); L72; NT183228

Another Donald round with no Grahams, this walk has the Corbett Broad Law, the second highest hill in the Southern Uplands, as its highest point. As with many Donald rounds there are two outlying Donald Tops which make the outing a little more difficult, though not unduly so.

Start from the highpoint of the road (450m) that crosses between Talla and Megget Reservoirs. There is space for a few well-parked cars at the cattle grid beside the Megget Stone boundary marker. Given that a return is made along the road, various other places to park can be found to the east.

Ascend an atv track up the hillside to the right of the fence above the cattle grid, onto Fans Law. Cross flat ground and swing round beside the fence continuing uphill a short distance before crossing the fence and cutting north-west up and across the slope to reach another fence coming down off Cairn Law. Follow an atv track just out from the fence to avoid boggy ground on the broad col and climb to the top of Talla Cleuch Head; the highest point lies on the east side of the fence about 100m beyond where it makes a right-angled turn (**2.5km; 250m; 1h**).

There are fine views across to the hills around the Games Hope Burn.

Return downhill then follow the fence uphill to join the fence left earlier on Cairn Law and make a gradual 2km ascent alongside this to gain the trig point on top of Broad Law (**6km; 460m; 2h 10min**).

Swing around north-east beside the fence, passing the crown-like aircraft beacon that adorns the summit, then pass one aerial to join a track and go through a gate to reach two larger aerials.

Descend east beside the fence, with the great bulk of Cramalt Craig lying ahead. The Donald Top of Hunt Law lies to the north and although well off to the side it is easier to take in than it looks. Rather than traverse directly to this from the col, it is

Talla Cleuch Head, Broad Law, Cramalt Craig 63

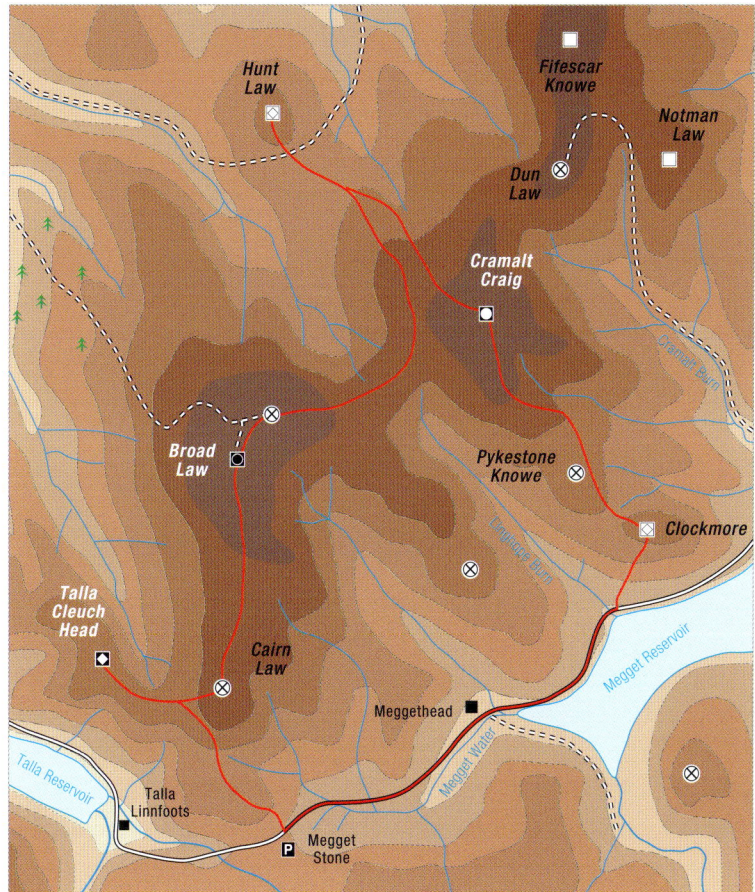

Manor Hills
Named after the Manor Valley which cuts into their midst, the Manor Hills occupy the area of hill country south of Peebles. They are separated from the Moffat Hills by the Megget and Talla Reservoirs and lie between the River Tweed on the west and the Yarrow Water on the east. There are 13 Donalds and 9 Donald Tops out of which Dun Rig is the solitary Graham and Broad Law, a Corbett, the highest point. All these hills can conveniently be climbed in four reasonable outings.

perhaps better to climb partway up the hillside next to the fence before stepping over and descending towards it. Pick up a rough atv track which descends from the summit of Cramalt Craig and follow this over the boggy col. Cross the bulldozed track which links the valleys on either side then continue up an atv track to the top of Hunt Hill. To the west across the Tweed Valley are the Culter Hills, then north the Drumelzier Hills with Fifescar Knowe and Dollar Law to the east.

Return across the boggy col and follow the rough atv track all the way up the spur to gain the summit of Cramalt Craig (**13km; 810m; 4h 20min**).

This hill is only 9m lower than Broad Law and until 1984 was classed as a Corbett, however the required drop is just short at c146m.

Head southwards from the summit across flat ground following an atv track which descends the shoulder then swings to the south-east before dropping to cross rough ground just to the east of the shepherds' cairn on Pykestone Knowe. Cross a shallow col and make the short ascent to the top of Clockmore.

Megget Reservoir lies below and after dropping southwards for a bit, the road bridge across the Linghope Burn comes into view. Descend steeply south-south-west down Appletree Brae towards the bridge and at the bottom pass beneath the power lines to go through first one, then another gate to reach the road.

Cross the bridge and follow the road past Meggethead at the end of the reservoir, then gradually uphill beside the Megget Water back to the start. The walk back along the road takes about 45min (**20.5km; 970m; 6h 30min**).

Talla Cleuch Head and Talla Reservoir from Garelet Hill (Rab Anderson)

Pykestone Hill, left, to Drumelzier Law, right (Rab Anderson)

The Scrape; 719m; (DT); L72; NT176324
Pykestone Hill; 737m; (D19); L72; NT173312; hill with pointed stones. The summit is scattered with many pointed boulders. Mapped Pikestone Craig (1755) and Pykitstane Hill (1775)
Middle Hill; 716m; (D27); L72; NT159294; middle hill, between the highpoints Pykestone Hill and Dollar Law: also, viewed from Tweed Valley, midway between Glenstivon Dod and Taberon Law
Taberon Law; 636m; (DT); L72; NT146288
Drumelzier Law; 668m; (D53); L72; NT149312; hill above Drumelzier. Mapped Great Law (1755 and 1775)

This round of Donalds and Donald Tops starts from Drumelzier, alleged to be the burial place of the wizard Merlin of Arthurian legend fame; the spot at NT134345 being marked by a plaque.

Leave the south side of the B712 between Peebles and Broughton at the west end of Drumelzier and go up the lane with a red post box at its start for 150m to reach a small parking area on the left.

Rather than start along the track past the large cattle shed, cross the Drumelzier Burn by a footbridge and go left around the side of Old Mill house to pass through a gate, then follow a grassy path southwards into the valley for 400m. Go through another a gate then cross the burn by a footbridge to join the track and continue along this.

After crossing a bridge and climbing through a break in a small forestry plantation, take the right-hand track which rises up the side of the spur of Dens Knowe. A little higher, take the left-hand track and continue to just below the summit of Pykestone Hill. Break off left here and contour to the fence then cross Broad Moss and make the short climb to the junction of fences on the broad, rounded summit of The Scrape.

Return across Broad Moss and climb to the trig point on top of Pykestone Hill (**7km; 580m; 2h 30min**).

Descend south onto the line of the old drove road, the 'Thief's Road', which is followed for a short way, over the bump of Grey Weather Law, before leaving it to continue beside the fence onto Long Grain Knowe. The old drove road heads south up onto Dollar Law.

At the junction of fences on Long Grain Knowe, a right-angled turn to the right leads across boggy ground beside the fence to a left turn to gain the top of Middle Hill, whose summit is covered in a lovely mossy carpet.

Pykestone Hill, Middle Hill, Drumelzier Law   65

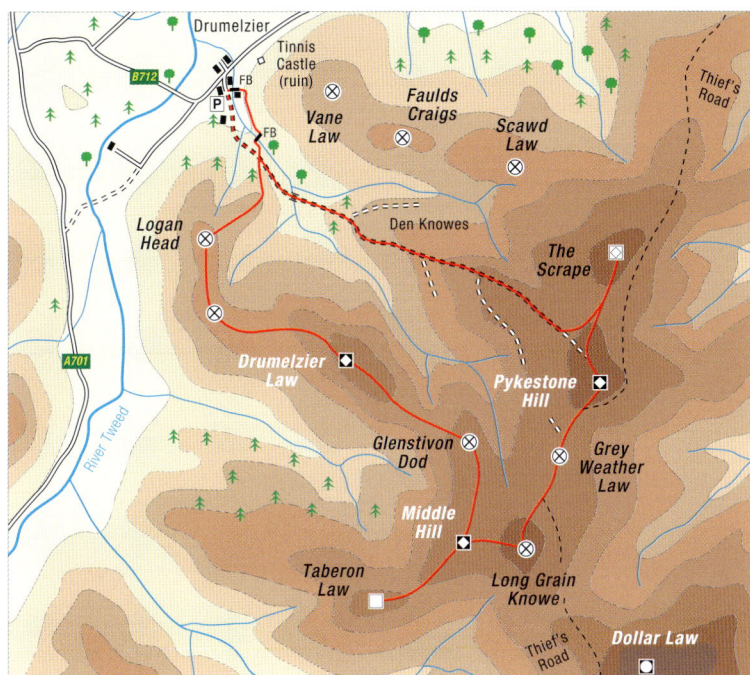

The actual top lies 50m to the south of the fence (**10km; 670m; 3h 20min**).

Now for the 55min there and back deviation to pick up the outlying Donald Top of Taberon Law, which lies 1.5km away to the south-west above afforested slopes. Keep to the atv track to avoid the boggy ground at the col to gain the top, which also lies south of the fence. On the other side of the Stanhope valley to the south is Hunt Law, the outlier on the Broad Law Round (see preceding route), whilst across the Tweed, Gathersnow Hill and Culter Fell stand out. Return to the top of Middle Hill then step over the fence and head north on the fenceless ridge to the tall shepherds' cairn on Glenstivon Dod. Continue north for a few hundred metres then drop north-west to a col and climb onto shapely Drumelzier Law whose summit lies at the north-west end of a level crest (**15.5km; 910m; 5h**).

Descend to the north-west and follow an atv track which swings west then north along the ridgeline onto Logan Head. On this section there are fine views up the Tweed valley and across to Broughton Heights. The track swings around again here and is followed north-east down Finglen Rig to a gate in the corner of a field.

Go through the gate and take either of two grassy tracks, the upper gives better views, to regain the track in the floor of the glen. Either follow the track back, or cross the foot-bridge and return past Old Mill house (**20km; 1160m; 6h 15min**).

Drumelzier Law from Middle Hill (Rab Anderson)

Black Law, Greenside Law, Dollar Law

Section 0b – The Borders

Black Cleuch Hill, left, and Black Law (Rab Anderson)

> **Black Cleuch Hill**; 675m; (DT); L73; NT222290
> **Black Law**; 698m; (D31); L73; NT222279; *black hill. From its heather cover. Mapped Blake Law (1775), from Scots 'blake', black*
> **Conscleuch Head**; 624m; (DT); L73; NT220262
> **Deer Law**; 629m; (DT); L73; NT222255
> **Greenside Law**; 643m; (D70); L72; NT197256; *hill with the green side. A contrast with its eastern nose, Black Rig*
> **Notman Law**; 734m; (DT); L72; NT185260
> **Fifescar Knowe**; 811m; (DT); L72; NT175270
> **Dollar Law**; 817m; (D5); L72; NT178278; *high meadow? Mapped Duillard hill (1654) and Duller Law (1755) might suggest Brittonic or Gaelic 'dol ard', meadow on the height. It has a broad flat grassy top*

Grouped around the head of the lovely Manor Valley, these Donalds and Donald Tops provide another sizeable outing. Begin not far from the end of the road up the Manor Valley where there is parking on the right next to the bridge over the Newholm Hope Burn (NT198307), just beyond a white cottage.

Walk south along the road across the bridge, go over a cattle grid then go left across the field and cross the Manor Water by a wooden bridge (there is another bridge a little further up by a Scottish Water facility). Climb steeply up the hillside, initially following sheeptracks, to gain the top of Langhaugh Hill (533m) and 100m beyond this pick up an atv track. Either follow this along the south side of the hill where it does swing round to the top, or break up onto the shoulder at some wooden shooting butts to reach a fenceline and follow this to a fence on the otherwise featureless top of Blackhouse Heights (named as this on the OS 1:50k map, but Black Cleuch Hill on the OS 1:25k map). Swing round then drop south to a col and climb onto Black Law (**4.5km; 450m; 1h 45min**); the summit is on the first rise.

Continue south-west to the second slight rise, which is 2m lower, and go through a gate to follow the fence which leads off at right-angles. This leads downhill to a col then easily over Conscleuch Head onto Deer Law where the fence swings away eastwards. A finger of rock cairn marks the top, 100m to the south-west.

Greenside Law is the next objective and lies to the west, on the other side of Glengaber Burn valley. Either head downhill cutting north-west across the slope on very tussocky terrain, aiming to the right of the summit of Greenside Law, or return to the col with Conscleuch Head then descend west down the slope. Cross the Glengaber Burn at around NT211260 and climb up the other side through deep heather on Black Rig, passing a wooden shed, to gain the through track between the Manor Valley and Megget Reservoir. From a cairn at the highpoint of the track, leave it and climb to the top of Greenside Law which lies on the other side of a fence (**10km; 700m; 3h 30min**).

Black Law, Greenside Law, Dollar Law 67

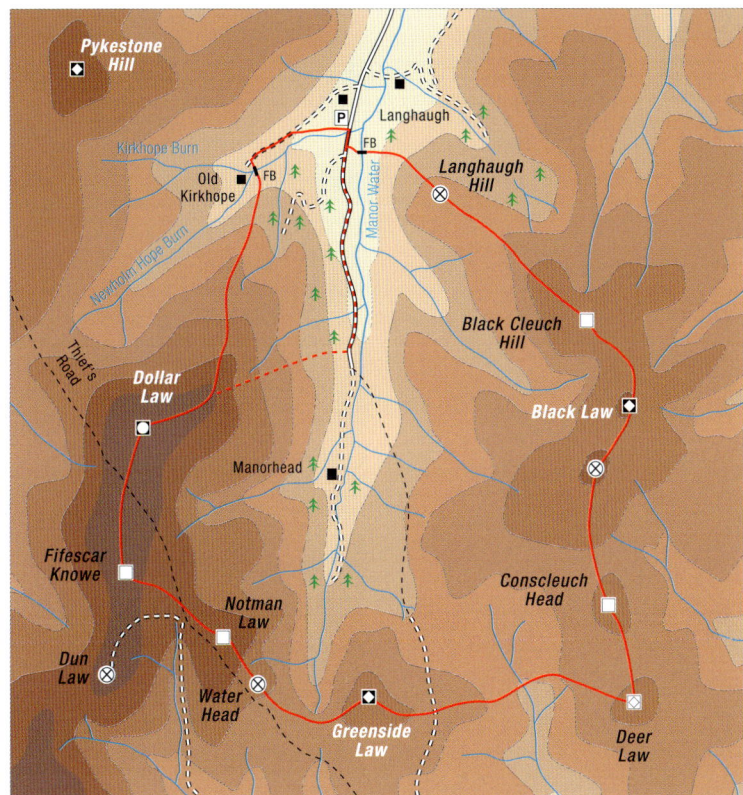

Head then up onto Notman Law.

Drop off the back and either follow the fence, or the grassy track. Where the fence swings left and the track passes through it by a gate, follow the fence uphill away from the track. Join another fence and an old wall then follow these north onto Fifescar Knowe. After a short descent, cross the track which heads across to Pykestone Hill and continue easily to the cairn and trig point on the summit of Dollar Law (**14.5km; 1010m; 5h**).

There are two descent options.

(i) Follow the fence and wall northeast all the way downhill to the southern end of the forest to reach the road which is walked back to the start.

(ii) Follow the wall and fence gradually downhill for 600m before crossing over and heading off at right-angles beside another fence that runs down the north spur, along the top edge of the forestry plantation. At the bottom, cross the bridge and go round the side of the sheep pens at the Old Kirkhope steading then follow a track back towards the road, passing a cross and font stone in a field on the left. Where the forestry ends, just before the white cottage, go through a gate and follow the burn back to the start (**19km; 1010m; 6h 20min**).

Descend south-west on an atv track alongside the fence and swing around the steep-sided corrie which forms the head of the valley where there are fine views down the Manor Valley. There is a rough track on the other side of the fence, marked as a path on the map, but this passes beneath the top of Notman Law. The direct route beside the fence is the better option, steep initially, over the bump of Water Head or Shielhope

Greenside Law at the head of the Manor Valley, far left, and Dollar Law, from the north (Rab Anderson)

Birkscairn Hill, Dun Rig, Glenrath Heights, Stob Law

Birkscairn Hill; 661m; (D59); L73; NT274331; cairn above Birks (farm). Mapped Birks Cairn (1775) by Armstrong who described 'a remarkable large and regular built pile of stones'. Scots 'birk', birch

Dun Rig; 744m; (G21); (D17); L73; NT253315; dull-brown ridge. Mapped 1775 as Coom or Blackcleugh Head

Glenrath Heights; 732m; (D20); L73; NT241322; heights above Glenrath (glen, farm). Gaelic 'gleann ràth', glen with a old fort: the farm lies beside a prehistoric fort called Macbeth's Castle

Stob Law; 676m; (D50); L73; NT230332; mapped Sandy Know Head (1775). Scots 'stobis' a stake, tree trunk or boundary post: there is no boundary here and the flat top is cairn-less

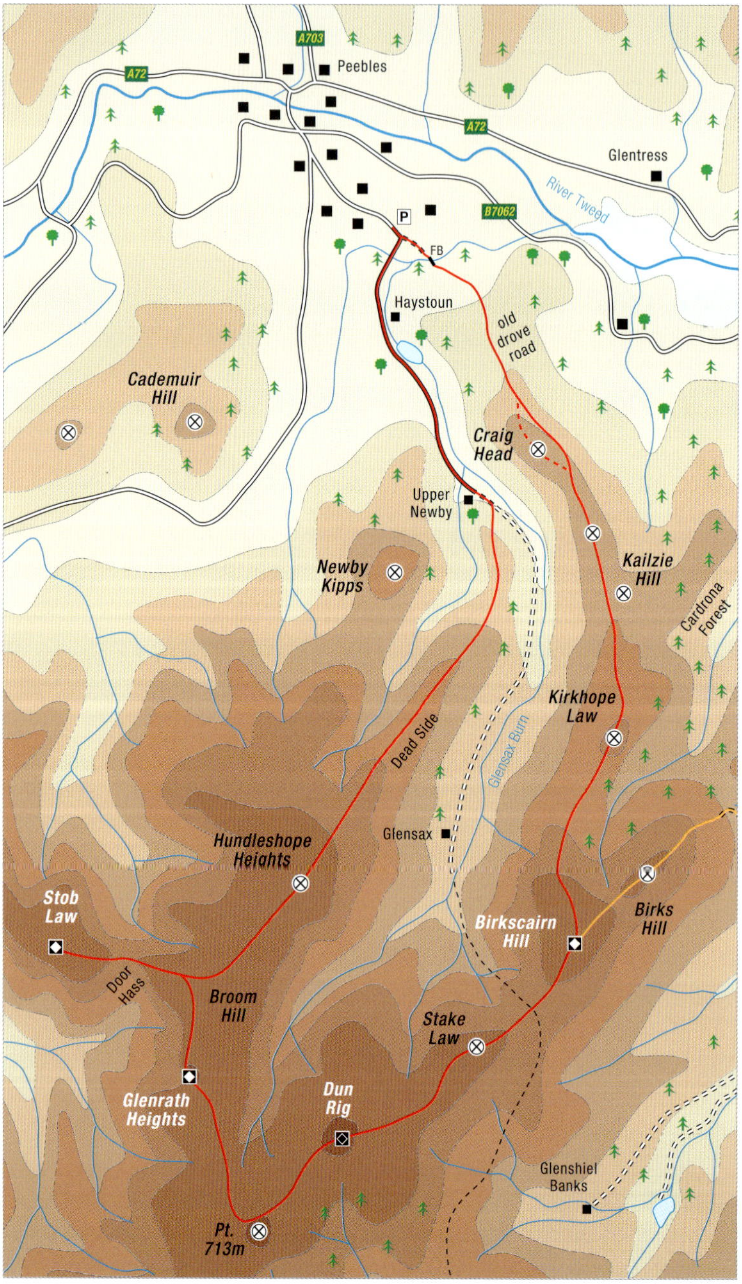

As well as being a Donald, Dun Rig is the only Graham in the Manor Hills. It sits in a commanding position at the head of the Glensax Burn, and when climbed as part of a round with its neighbouring Donalds, it gives a long but fine circuit. Park on the south-eastern edge of Peebles, at the end of Glen Road (NT260393), gained from Springhill Road.

Walk past the road off right to Haystoun, which is the return route, and take the Tweed Trails signposted track straight ahead. Cross the Glensax Burn via the bridge and follow the route up the hillside past fields then uphill through the trees where the track (an old drove road) runs between two drystane dykes for a way. When the walls open out, either skirt Craig Head on the drove road or go over it on a path. Continue uphill to meet the top edge of the Cardrona Forest then, with fine views opening up all around, climb over Kirkhope Law (537m) and leave the forest behind to climb Birkscairn Hill.

Drop south-west to where the drove road starts the descent towards the

Hundelshope Heights, left, Glenrath Heights and Stob Law from the Manor Valley to the north (Rab Anderson)

Yarrow Water and St Mary's Loch then head up over Stake Law on increasingly boggy ground through peat hags to reach the trig point on the flat top of Dun Rig. The highpoint is 50m further south-west, as shown on OS maps (**10km; 700m; 3h 20min**).

Descend south-westwards then break away from the fence on a boggy path that contours below Pt.713m and swing round to rejoin the fence where it drops north to a col. Climb onto Glenrath Heights (named as Middle Hill on OS maps) and continue beside the fence, descending slightly then passing through a gate to follow the left-hand fence onto the spur of Broom Hill. Drop north-westwards to a col, Door Hass, then easily climb the outlying Stob Law (**14.5km; 860m; 4h 40min**).

Return to Broom Hill then cut the corner to rejoin the other fence and follow this north-east onto Hundleshope Heights (685m) where there is a trig point. Break away from the fence here and follow an atv track down the long north-east spur of Dead Side to join the track along the floor of the glen. The track becomes surfaced and leads along the Glensax Burn, past the farm of Upper Newby then a pond and the large house at Haystoun, back to the start (**24km; 1000m; 7h 15min**).

A shorter Graham-only route is possible starting at NT305336 beside the Quair Water to the east, using the road to Glen House, the hill track onto Birks Hill to gain Birkscairn Hill, and on to Dun Rig (**7km; 620m; 2h 35min**), (**14km; 680m; 4h 20min**).

From the same start it is also possible to bike to Glenshiel Banks and climb the hill via its south ridge.

Dun Rig, left, and Hundleshope Heights from near Craig Head (Rab Anderson)

Blackhope Scar, Bowbeat Hill, Dundreich

Blackhope Scar from Bowbeat Hill (Rab Anderson)

Blackhope Scar; 651m; (G172); (D64); L73; NT315483; common grazing land of Blackhope (farm). Scots 'hope' upland valley

Bowbeat Hill; 626m; (D77); L73; NT292469; hill for summer grazing for cows. Scots 'bow', cattle and 'beat', hill-grazing

Dundreich; 623m; (D81); L73; NT274490; hill-fort with a good outlook, perhaps, from Britonnic 'din drich' or, less likely, Gaelic 'dùn dreach', hill-fort on the (hill) face. There are ancient earthworks on top

The Moorfoot Hills lie to the north of the Manor Hills above Peebles, and present a steep north-west facing scarp slope towards Edinburgh. The highest points on this slope, though not the highest point in The Moorfoots, which is Windlestraw Law, are formed by the Graham Blackhope Scar and its neighbouring Donalds, which sit around the headwaters of the River South Esk. It is a distinctive skyline and the round of all three hills gives a scenic and varied outing.

Start from the car park at NT292528 at the southern end of Gladhouse Reservoir, reached by a short section of public road.

Walk south-east along the road into the farmyard at Moorfoot, then swing round to the right and follow the track towards the valley formed by the River South Esk. Pass Gladhouse Cottage and cross the South Esk, then leave the track to follow a grassy track up left to the remains of Hirendean Castle. Continue on the grassy track, which traverses left off the crest, and go through a gate at the corner of the fence above the burn. Regain the crest and follow the grassy track steeply up the narrow spur onto Hirendean Hill. Although a direct line can be taken from here, it is best to remain on the track which swings right, dropping slightly, before ascending past a line of shooting butts onto The Kipps (541m).

Drop off the back and head

Hirendean Castle ruins above the South Esk (Rab Anderson)

Blackhope Scar, Bowbeat Hill, Dundreich

eastwards to pick up the fence which runs up the shoulder of Blackhope Scar. The going is generally better on the left of the fence and there is a small path through the heather. However, the going can be slow and some back and forth crossings of the fence may be required to avoid boggy bits. The fence leads to the summit where there is a trig point at a junction of fences (**6km; 410m; 2h**).

The view over Edinburgh and the Forth Valley is fabulous and extends to Beinn a' Ghlo and the Cairngorms, readily seen, especially when capped with snow.

Follow the fence which swings round south-west and descend Long Edge to reach Kings Road Nick in front of Emly Bank and the Bowbeat Windfarm. Climb south-west to easily take in Bowbeat Hill; purists may wish to flounder along on the north side of the fence whereas the sensible will use the turbine access roads. Swing around the head of the Bowbeat Burn onto Bowbeat Rig, moving easily or floundering depending on which side of the fence one sits!

Leave the windfarm behind and climb north-west following the bleak high ground. Swing south-west near the fence between Dundreich and Jeffries Corse to cross a fence ascending from below, then gain the cairn and trig point on the summit of Dundreich (**12.5km; 690m; 4h**).

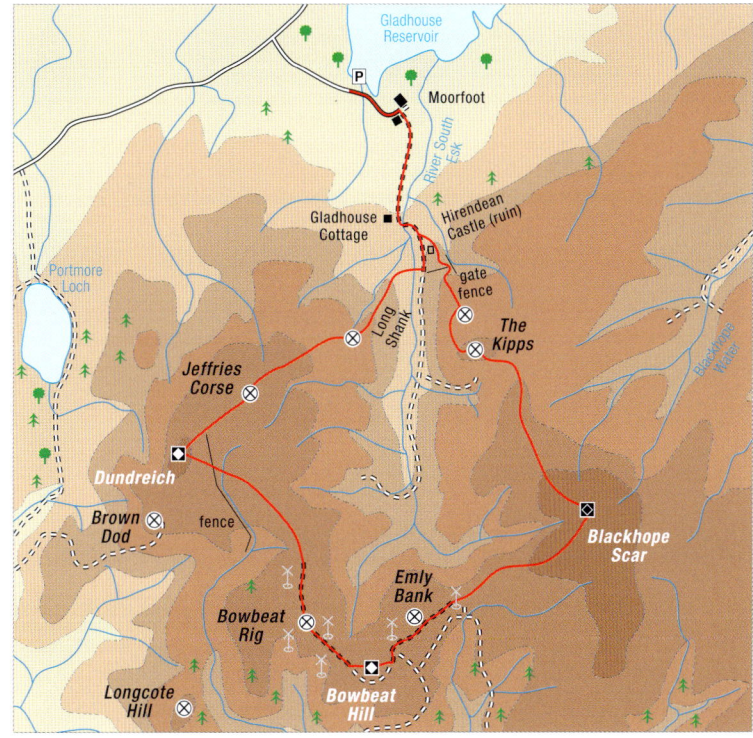

Although this part of the route is clear on the ground, the featureless terrain means it might not be so obvious in snow and mist. In these conditions it is possible to descend west from the high ground to gain a fence beside a burn. This leads to the summit slope, and is the fence crossed in the above description.

Continue north-east to Jeffries Corse, then break away from the fence to pick up an atv track which leads downhill to the north-east to swing east between burns and climb onto a small grassy knoll. Descend the fine ridge of Long Shank which leads to a crossing of the River South Esk and the track running beneath Hirendean Castle, back to the start (**18km; 710m; 5h 30min**).

Jeffries Corse and Dundreich from the track to Gladhouse Cottage (Rab Anderson)

Windlestraw Law, Whitehope Law

Windlestraw Law; 659m; (G161); (D61); L73; NT371430; hill covered in windlestrae (grass). Scots 'windelstrae', long spindly grass such as crested dogstail or tufted hair-grass
Bareback Knowe; 657m; (DT); L73; NT362420
Whitehope Law; 623m; (D82); L73; NT330445; hill above Whitehope (farm). Scots 'hope', upland valley

Although it is the highest point in the Moorfoot Hills, the Graham Windlestraw Law is an elusive summit which remains hidden from view from the roads which surround it. The hill only reveals itself to those travelling the B709 which runs through the middle of The Moorfoots along the secluded glen between Heriot and Innerleithen. It is from the north side of the Glentress Water in this glen that the route to its summit begins. Despite the drop back to the floor of the glen, it is easy to include an ascent of the Donald of Whitehope Law on the opposite side.

Start from the B709 at NT342436 some 400m south of Blackhopebyre and the obvious grassy track that leads onto the hill just south of these buildings. There is ample off-road parking beside the fence on the west side of the road, a little down from a wooden pole bridge over the Glentress Water, which is the return route, if doing Whitehope Law.

Walk northwards up the road and about 100m or so before Blackhopebyre, go through a gate onto the grassy track on the east side of the road. Follow the track up Glentress Rig, initially on a long traverse to the right, then east up the spur keeping to the more obvious tracks leading up Wallet Knowe. Higher, the track becomes less distinct and swings right, passing along a line of shooting butts to run alongside a fence. Where this fence reaches the fence on top, cross over then go left for 100m to the trig point (**4km; 380m; 1h 30min**).

Descend easily south-west alongside the fence then make the short climb onto the summit of Bareback Knowe, a Donald Top. Continue following the fence along the crest to reach another fence coming in from the left. Go past this fence for a short way and then cross over the fence and head westwards to pick up a fence then an atv track which leads down the north-west shoulder. There is a notable contrast between the heathery ground on the right side of the fence and the grassy ground on the left.

Just before the col with Dod Hill, take the less obvious left-hand atv track down the side of the fence and go through a gate to follow an atv track down the left side of the fence. Ignore a gate into the field on the right and continue to another fence then follow

Windlestraw Law, Whitehope Law

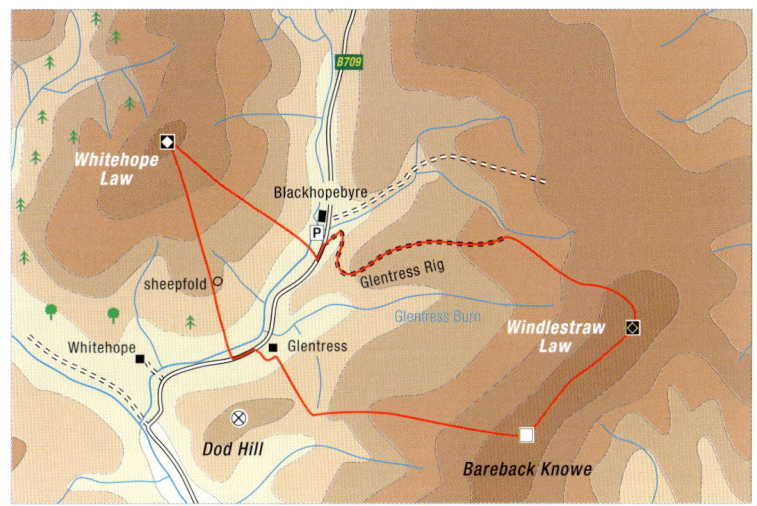

Above: Windlestraw Law from Whitehope Law (Rab Anderson)

this left a short way to its end, then cut straight down to the road a short distance south of Glentress cottage; about 1km from the start.

Looking across to Whitehope Law from this descent, a large circular sheepfold will have been seen to the right of a small forestry plantation; an objective on the ascent. Also spotted will be a bridge over the burn at NT337430 with some obvious sheep tracks leading from it. Walk southwest along the road for 200m beside a wall and fence then go through a gate into the field to cross the bridge and follow the sheeptracks that zigzag uphill to the sheepfold. Above this the going becomes more tedious through generally trackless heather and eventually leads up the shoulder to a fence then the summit of Whitehope Law (**10.5km; 780m; 3h 45min**).

On the way down, initially tussocky and awkward, simply head for the track up Glentress Rig on the opposite side of the valley and descend directly to the pole bridge across the burn. The burn can normally be easily crossed here to reach the parking area (**12km; 780m; 4h 15min**).

Whitehope Law from Bareback Knowe (Rab Anderson)

Cauldcleuch Head

Cauldcleuch Head (Rab Anderson)

Cauldcleuch Head; 619m; (G207); (D86); L79; NT456006; hill above the Cauld Cleuch. Scots 'cauld cleuch', cold gully, ravine, which runs north from the top

Windy Gyle; 619m; (D85); L80; NT855152; mapped Windygate Hill (1770). The OS had Windygate until 1907 (3rd edition); thereafter Windy Gyle, perhaps from 'ghyll', gully. There is a gate at the summit where the border is crossed

Cairn Hill West Top; 743m; (DT); L80; NT895193

Sitting in splendid isolation, Cauldcleuch Head forms the highpoint in the relatively unfrequented Border hills between Hawick and the Muckle Toon of Langholm. This Graham is a great whaleback of a hill, the ascent of which provides a fine and scenic round. The start is reached along a minor road through the lovely glen that runs eastwards off the A7 and down which the Carewoodrig Burn flows. There is parking at the entrance to a forest track at the highpoint of this road at NY439978, between Carewoodrig and Billhope.

Walk west along the road for 100m, then go through a gate and climb the hillside just out from the edge of the forest, initially following an atv track, then a fence to gain the trig point on Tudhope Hill (599m) (**2km; 310m; 1h**).

With the bulk of the climbing behind, and a clear view of the great rounded slopes of Cauldcleuch Head in front, follow the fence over to Millstone Edge, then swing around onto Langtae Hill at the head of the Billhope Valley. After a short descent, climb up and around peat hags, still beside the fence, to reach the flat top of Cauldcleuch Head (**6km; 470m; 2h 10min**).

Although the ground underfoot gives rough going at times, especially when wet, the fine views more than compensate for any hardship. In all directions, as far as the eye can see the landscape is a soothing blend of rounded green hills, glens and forest.

Descend south onto Muckle Land Knowe then break away from the fence and cross rough ground, passing over the minor bumps of Pennygant Hill, to reach the narrow top of Stob Fell. Just beyond the summit, drop off west and descend the prominent ridge of South Mid Hill to gain a track beside the Billhope Burn at a cottage. A short walk south along this track leads to the road at Billhope, which is followed uphill back to the start (**11km; 560m; 3h 30min**).

Windy Gyle is a solitary Donald in The Cheviot Hills and sits on the border with England. It can be combined with a walk along the border via the Pennine Way to Cairn Hill West Top. This hill appears in Donald's List as a Donald Top and the highest point on the border. However, Cairn Hill West Top is not really a summit, merely a south-west top of The Cheviot, the highest summit in The Cheviot Hills. Due perhaps to some odd quirk, the border with England does not run along the highpoint of The Cheviot as might be expected and the summit of The Cheviot lies wholly within England. However, its western flanks spill onto the Scottish side of the border, so it makes sense to combine it with an ascent of Windy Gyle.

Start from Cocklawfoot at the end of the road up the Bowmont Water valley, gained from the B6401 about 1km south of Town Yetholm. There is ample off-road parking in the vicinity of the road end where an onward track goes to Cocklawfoot via a bridge and ford over the river; the return route.

Take the track on the right to where it forks in front of the farm at Kelsocleuch. Follow the right fork uphill beside a wall for 400m then turn left along a path, still beside the wall, to run along the bottom of a plantation. The path swings round up a break between the trees and leads onto the grassy ridge of Kelsocleuch Rig. Expansive views of the whole circuit now open up, with the imposing bulk of The Cheviot at the end.

The route heads up around the edge of a grassy corrie bowl onto Windy Rig then climbs south-east to the large cairn (Russell's Cairn) and trig point at the summit of Windy Gyle (**4.5km; 390m; 1h 40min**).

Windy Gyle 75

Descend north-east along the ridge passing another large cairn. The long, broad and featureless frontier ridge stretches into the distance across ground which can be incredibly boggy and tiresome when wet. Any temptation to stay on the Scottish side of the fence is soon dispelled, especially when the Pennine Way path on the other side becomes a slabbed walkway. This may be a somewhat strange intrusion on the landscape, however it does prevent erosion and certainly makes the going easier. The pavement soon crosses the ancient cross border route of Clennel Street coming up Cock Law to the north and for those satisfied with their Donald tick, a return could be made to Cocklawfoot down this.

Continuing, swing north past the trig point on King's Seat to reach Score Head then climb north-east to Cairn Hill West Top, a mere bump but the highest point on the entire border. The Pennine Way makes a hairpin turn to the north-west here, however a short extension leads east up to Cairn Hill itself then north-east up to the elevated trig point on the great, rounded peaty dome of The Cheviot, at 815m the highest hill hereabouts (**13km; 600m; 4h**).

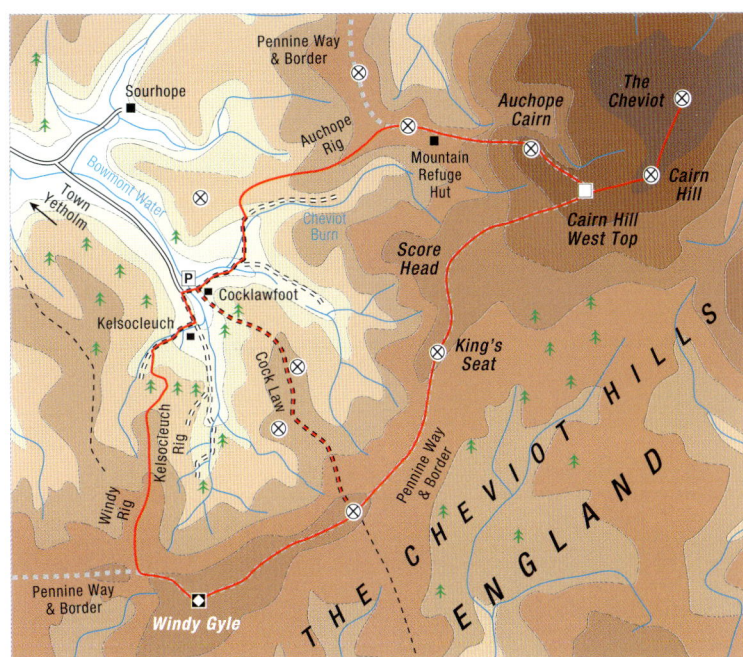

Return to Cairn Hill West Top and follow the Pennine Way to the cairns on Auchope Cairn then descend steeply beside the fence to the Mountain Refuge Hut. The valley on the right opens up to reveal the fine and craggy defile that is the Hen Hole. Continue along the Pennine Way for 500m or so, go through a gate to leave England, then follow a fence down the long ridge of Auchope Rig, south-west to a small flat col at the junction of four fences. Drop to the Cheviot Burn in the floor of the valley via the grassy track and follow this through the farm at Cocklawfoot back to the start (**19km; 620m; 5h 40min**).

Looking south to Cocklawfoot farm, Kelsocleuch Rig, right, and Windy Gyle, centre (Rab Anderson)

The Ochil escarpment rising above the River Forth at Stirling (Rab Anderson)

SECTION Oc
The Midland Valley

Section 0c – The Midland Valley

SECTION 0c

[1] **King's Seat Hill**, [2] **Andrew Gannel Hill**, [3] **The Law**,
  [4] ◆ **Ben Cleuch**, [5] **Ben Ever**   79
[6] **Blairdenon Hill**   81
[7] **Innerdownie**, [8] **Whitewisp Hill**, [9] **Tarmangie Hill**   82
[10] **Meall Clachach**, [11] ◆ **Uamh Bheag**, [12] **Beinn Odhar**,
  [13] **Beinn nan Eun**   83

Ben Cleuch, left, and Andrew Gannel Hill from King's Seat Hill (Ken Crocket)

King's Seat Hill; 648m; (D66); L58; NS933999; also known as Innercairn (1769)
Andrew Gannel Hill; 670m; (DT); L58; NN918006
The Law; 638m; (DT); L58; NS910996
Ben Cleuch; 721m; (G61); (D25); L58; NN902006; stony mountain. Gaelic 'beinn clach'. Mapped Benclach (1783)
Ben Ever; 622m; (DT); L58; NN893001

The Ochil Hills occupy a prominent position in the centre of the Midland Valley with the rounded dome of Ben Cleuch forming their highest point. The first of two routes described is a longer walk which as well as climbing Ben Cleuch takes in the other four of its attendant hills that appear on the list of Donalds. The second route is a more direct there and back ascent of Ben Cleuch via The Law. Both routes conveniently start from Tillicoultry, at the entrance to Mill Glen which is signposted from the west end of the town. There is parking at the top of Upper Mill Street, or nearby, just below the stepped entrance to the Glen.

Where the road swings left over the burn, turn right up a track signposted to Blackford and after 50m, turn left up the hill to follow a stepped path, which then zigzags up the open hillside. This provides a view down into the disused quarry on the opposite side above Mill Glen and leads to a fork. The left fork leads to the burn at the foot of The Law. Instead, take the higher fork on the right which contours the hillside above the lower path. After rounding the spur, climb uphill on the path and shortly after crossing a burn, take the right-hand fork to continue up the spur; the lower path heads for the col between the hills.

Partway up, a cairn (shown on OS maps) is passed, and further on the path swings round onto the top of King's Seat Hill with its open views to the Lomond Hills and across the Forth to the Pentland Hills. The highest point lies at the north-west end of the high ground, not at the large cairn to the south-east (**4km; 600m; 2h**).

Head north-west and take the path that drops to the col then make the short ascent to Andrew Gannel Hill. The summit is beside the fence, but a little nose just off to the side provides an excellent position overlooking the route. This is en route to Ben Cleuch and easily taken in, however, The Law requires a relatively short diversion, although it does entail some descent and reascent. Follow the fence towards Ben Cleuch with a short drop then climb to where it joins another fence. Cross over and descend south ▶

beside the fence to gain the top of The Law. From here, Andrew Gannel Hill and King's Seat Hill are prominent, with Tarmangie Hill peeping over between the two. Return north to the junction of fences then swing left and climb to the rock-strewn top of Ben Cleuch (**8.5km; 870m; 3h 30min**).

A stone wall round the trig point provides shelter. The view to the west and north-west is particularly fine. Arran is visible on a good day and moving round north, the Arrochar Alps, Ben Lomond, the Crianlarich Hills, the Ben Lawers group and the Cairngorms are all well seen.

Descend north-west on a path and swing round south-west to pick up the fence which leads to a col, an intersection of fences, which is crossed, then a grassy track leading to the top of Ben Ever. Continue along the south ridge on the grassy track to reach a fork then take the right fork which leads past sheep pens into Silver Glen and a farm track. Turn left, go over a gate, and continue down the track, now zigzagging, until a sign marked Public Footpath after the second zag left indicates a gate into Wood Hill Wood. Follow this path across the burn and on for about 1.5km, passing the Ochil Hills Woodland Park car park, which is an alternative starting point for the walk, to exit the wood above the golf course. Turn right at a tarmac road and go through shrubs on the left-hand side to gain Scotland Street which leads back to Upper Mill Street (**15km; 920m; 5h 10min**).

The direct route to Ben Cleuch normally passes through Mill Glen, however at the time of writing damage caused by rockfall has caused the Council to close this popular path. Funding has been found to rectify this but work has not yet begun. Instead, turn right at the top of Mill Street and follow the previous route for a short way to the fork in the path after the zigzags, then take the left fork. This contours above the glen then makes a short and steep scramble down to a wooden footbridge which crosses the Gannel Burn just before its confluence with the Daiglen Burn.

Now follow the well-trodden path up the slender ridge ahead, steeply at first then easing somewhat to gain the summit of The Law. Continue north beside the boundary fence over easy ground to eventually meet another fence then swing north-west to Ben Cleuch (**4km; 700m; 2h**).

Return via the route of ascent (**8km; 720m; 3h 20min**).

The Ochil Hills

The name Ochil comes from the ancient Cambric 'uchel', meaning high. When viewed from the south this is understandable, for The Ochils suddenly rear up to the north of the flat estuary of the River Forth.

Due to the proximity of these hills to the major centres of population, a large number of routes breach this steep introductory slope to gain access to the gently rounded and grassy high ground linking the various hill tops. The highest point in the Ochils is Ben Cleuch (721m), the only Graham of the range.

Lying south of the Highland Boundary Fault Line, The Ochils are classified as being in the Lowlands and are therefore included in Donald's Tables, there being five Donalds and four Donald Tops.

All these hills are covered here in three principal walks, although anyone interested in exploring this fine range of hills could break these down into smaller or different outings. The full 'Round of Nine' can be done in one outing starting at Menstrie and ending at Glendevon (**25.5km; 1200m; 8h 30min**).

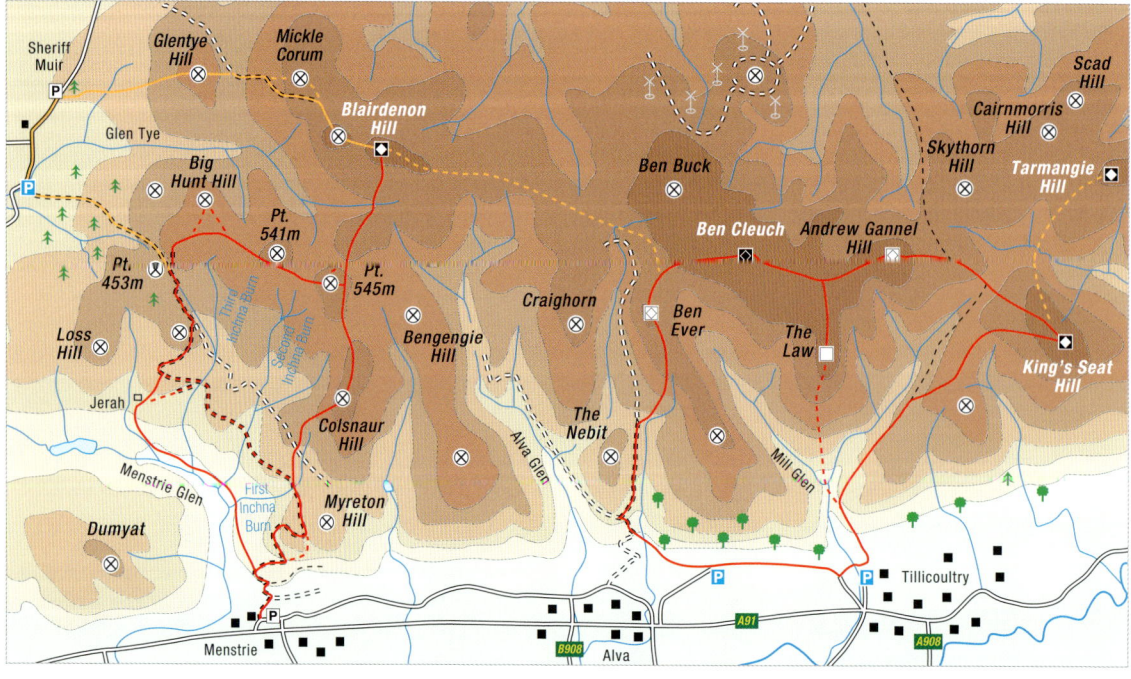

Blairdenon Hill 81

Blairdenon Hill from Sheriffmuir (Tom Prentice)

Blairdenon Hill; 631m; (D74); L58; NN865018; Gaelic 'blàr' means plain or flat ground; 'denon' is obscure

Blairdenon Hill lies at the western end of the Ochil Hills and is set back from the steep frontal scarp slope containing the other main highpoints. As a result it is more difficult to link into a circuit with these hills and is therefore generally climbed on its own, although there are a few ways of attaining its summit.

One route from the south starts at Menstrie and takes in Colsnaur Hill; an unusually quiet hill and a good viewpoint. Turn north off the A91 at the Hollytree Inn, go up Park Road and turn right into Ochil Road to park.

Walk up the track between the houses and follow this through a gate then on up the steep scarp slope in a series of zigzags. Above the initial zigzags the track meets then runs above a deer fence around the Jerah Woodland where 1.3 million trees have been planted north to Glen Tye.

After about 2.5km, pass through a gate into the planted area then cross the First Inchna Burn. Some 30m further on, leave the track and follow a path up the hillside between the trees. Pass through another gate, cross a track and continue on the path up the spur between more trees, finally swinging round to gain the summit of Colsnaur Hill (553m).

Head north along the ridge, leaving the planted area by a stile, then follow an atv track beside a drystane dyke. Where the atv track goes left (the return), continue across Menstrie Moss on a rough path beside the wall, then a fence. Drop down to cross the Old Wharry Burn then ascend to the flat top of Blairdenon Hill. The summit is marked by a small cairn on the far side of a junction of fences (**7km; 690m; 2h 45min**).

Return across the Old Wharry Burn then shortly after regaining the wall, leave the path alongside it for a path that joins the continuation of the atv track used earlier on Pt.545m. Follow this west then north-west across a boggy col to pass just beneath the top of Pt.541m and down to another col below Big Hunt Hill. The atv track turns south-west here then descends to a gate into the Jerah Woodland and a short track that drops to the main forest track at a col. Turn south down this track, passing a fork off left after 300m.

The easiest option is to follow the track all the way back, rejoining the approach route at the First Inchna Burn (**17km; 815m; 5h 30min**).

About 400m after passing through a gate beyond the fork, the track can be left for a path that leads to the ruined farmstead of Jerah. A path to the south-east leads down through the trees to Menstrie Glen and across all three Inchna Burns to rejoin the approach track; about 1km shorter.

An alternative route from the west, which is a circuit of Glen Tye, starts from verge-parking (NN832026) at a stand of trees 750m north of the former Sheriffmuir Inn; now a house of the same name. This is on the minor road between Dunblane and Greenloaning, which crosses Sheriff Muir at the west end of The Ochils.

Go through an open gate then the trees, following an atv track towards the hill, and drop down through a gate to cross a small burn. Millions of trees have been planted on this side of The Ochils and the route continues uphill on the atv track between the planting here onto the top of Glentye Hill (481m). Drop off the back then go through another gate and continue on the atv track, which climbs up and across the hillside onto the broad crest. The top of Mickle Corum (594m) is a good viewpoint and can easily be included by a short there and back alongside the fence.

Rather than follow the atv track, which involves crossing back and forwards over the fence at the summit, go through the open gate in the fence and follow the path on the other side. This leads over Greenforet Hill, past a memorial in the dip to a Tiger Moth which crashed in 1959, then on up to the top of Blairdenon Hill (**4km; 380m; 1h 30min**).

Cross the fences that meet on the summit by two stiles then follow a rough path downhill beside the southwards running fence. At the bottom, cross the Old Wharry Burn then continue uphill beside the fence and cross Menstrie Moss; boggy in places. Shortly after the fence meets a drystane dyke, leave the path beside the wall for a rough path which joins an atv track on Pt.545m. Follow this atv track west then north-west across a boggy col to pass just beneath the top of Pt.541m then down to another col below Big Hunt Hill; easily included by a short diversion. The atv track now turns south-west and drops to a gate leading to a track, then the main forest track at a col. Turn right along this track and follow it downhill to join the road at a small parking area then follow the road uphill past the former Sheriffmuir Inn to the start (**11.5km; 530m; 3h 40min**).

Section 0c – The Midland Valley

Innerdownie, Whitewisp Hill, Tarmangie Hill

Innerdownie summit and Whitewisp Hill, left, from the south (Tom Prentice)

Innerdownie; 610m; (D89); L58; NN966031; obscure. There is another Innerdouny Hill 8km to the north-east
Whitewisp Hill; 643m; (DT); L58; NN955013
Tarmangie Hill; 645m; (D69); L58; NN942014; hillock abounding in fawns. Gaelic 'tòrr mangaich'. Mapped Tarmangie Carn (1779)

These grassy hills offer an enjoyable high-level round with fine views east to Loch Leven and the Lomond Hills and south to the Forth. From the Glen Sherup Forestry Commission car park in Glen Devon, ascend the signposted path to gain a forest track beyond Whitens and follow it to where the Reservoir Trail (the return route) is signposted off right to Glensherup Reservoir dam. Just beyond this, turn left at a track junction and contour the hillside east down Glen Devon through felled and forested sections.

Near the end of the track, at NN975041, a Scotways marker indicates a narrow firebreak on the right, which is followed south-east through the conifers to a gate on the northern flanks of Innerdownie. Follow the wall to the cairned summit of Innerdownie where there are views south to rounded Whitewisp Hill, more pointed Tarmangie, and distant Ben Cleuch (**5km; 390m; 1h 45min**).

Continue beside the wall over the ill-defined bump of Bentie Knowe to a col, from where a steady ascent beside a fence gains a stile and the broad summit of Whitewisp Hill.

Return to the wall and fence then follow them to the summit of Tarmangie Hill, gained by a gate in the fence or a stile further on (**8.5km; 510m; 2h 45min**).

Descend, keeping right of the fence, to a gate in the deer fence below Cairnmorris Hill, from where an atv track begins. The atv track can be followed all the way to the base of Ben Shee, but it is worth making a short diversion en route to gain the top of Scad Hill with its large summit boulder.

As Ben Shee is approached, more and more seedlings line the route. Since buying the high ground from Cairnmorris to Ben Shee, Woodland Trust Scotland have removed the sheep, controlled deer numbers and planted millions of birch, oak, rowan and other native trees and shrubs. The atv track skirts Ben Shee to the west, but a sign indicates a path to the summit, which is easily gained (**12.5km; 610m; 3h 55min**).

Descend to regain what is now a gravel track and follow this over the ridge and down into Glen Sherup. Remain on the track to where the trees on the right end and continue to a gate in a fence. Cross the stile and descend to the right, beside the fence, to reach the road. Turn right then follow the road back up past Glen Sherup House to Glensherup Reservoir. Cross the dam over the reservoir, ascend to the track then turn left and continue back to the car park (**16km; 620m; 4h 40min**).

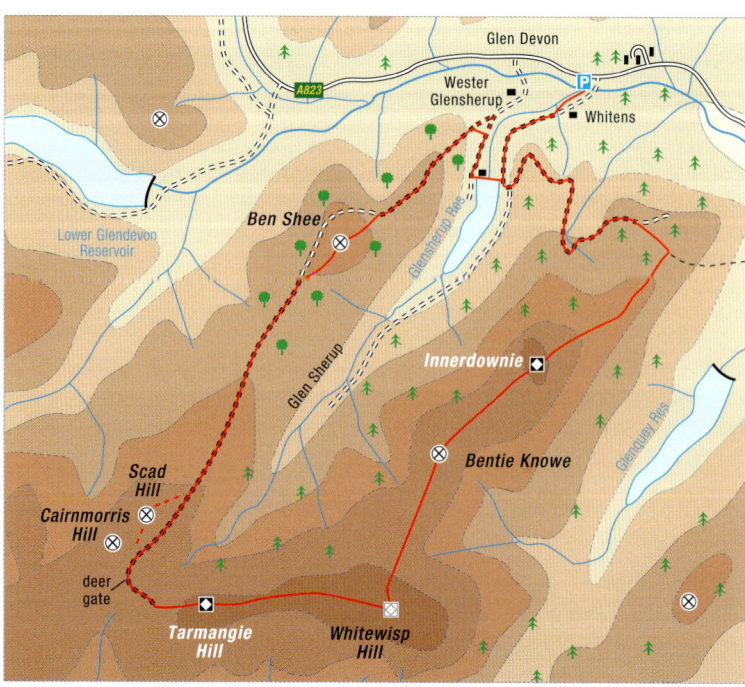

Uamh Bheag

Uamh Bheag, background, with Am Beannan in the foreground (Rab Anderson)

Meall Clachach; *621m; (DT); L57; NN688125*
Uamh Bheag; *666m; (G152); (D55); L57; NN691118; little cave*
Beinn Odhar; *626m; (DT); L57; NN714127*
Beinn nan Eun; *631m; (D75); L57; NN723131; mountain of the birds*

Positioned just south of the Highland Boundary Fault, these hills lie in the Scottish Lowlands and as such, fall within the geographical boundary of The Donalds. However, they were not included in Percy Donald's original list. Uamh Mhòr on the southern flanks of Uamh Bheag sports an impressive rock cleft at NN 687111, described by Walter Scott as 'a great den, or cavern... said, by tradition, to have been the abode of a giant. In latter times, it was the refuge of robbers and banditti...'. It is well worth a visit if time allows.

Unfortunately, these mountains are rather less interesting than their history. The finest hill on the round is shapely Am Beannan, an unclassified peak of 574m, which displays steep conglomerate common with other points along the Highland Boundary Fault such as the Menteith Hills, Conic Hill and Inchcailloch island.

Uamh Bheag is pleasant enough, but peat hags, bog and rough grass dominate the tops of Meall Clachach, Beinn Odhar and Beinn nan Eun, while the southern flanks of the latter two support wind turbines visible from most of the Forth valley.

Park at the car park below Glen Artney church and walk down the glen to the bridge over the Water of Ruchill. Go through the gate before the bridge to follow sheep and cattle paths along the south side of the river towards the Allt Ollach, with Am Beannan obvious ahead.

Ascend either side of the fence before the Allt Ollach to a bridge. Cross over and make a steep ascent of Am Beannan to arrive unexpectedly on its rounded top (**4km; 420m; 1h 35min**).

A broad hag-strewn ridge leads to Meall Clachach and a fence, which is followed through more hags to the summit of Uamh Bheag, marked by a cairn at the intersection of three fences (**6km; 570m; 2h 15min**).

If only climbing the Graham, return the same way (**12km; 610m; 3h 50min**).

The southerly fence leads to Uamh Mhòr and the cleft on its southern slopes. Continue alongside the easterly fence, making a short descent and ascent, to gain the trig point on the lower Pt.662m. The actual highpoint of the East Top (663m) lies about 150m to the north.

From the trig point, make a rough descent by a fence and boundary cairns to a col, followed by a heathery ascent past wind turbines to gain the featureless summit of Beinn Odhar (**9.5km; 720m; 3h 20min**).

Descend eastwards to a shallow col then ascend peat trenches to the summit of Beinn nan Eun, marked by a fence post in a pile of stones on a flat, peat hag summit riven with pools (**10.5km; 770m; 3h 35min**).

Head off down the north ridge past grouse butts to sheep pens and cross the Allt na Caillich to a track. Follow the track left to white gates, then turn left down the road to the car park (**14.5km; 770m; 4h 45min**).

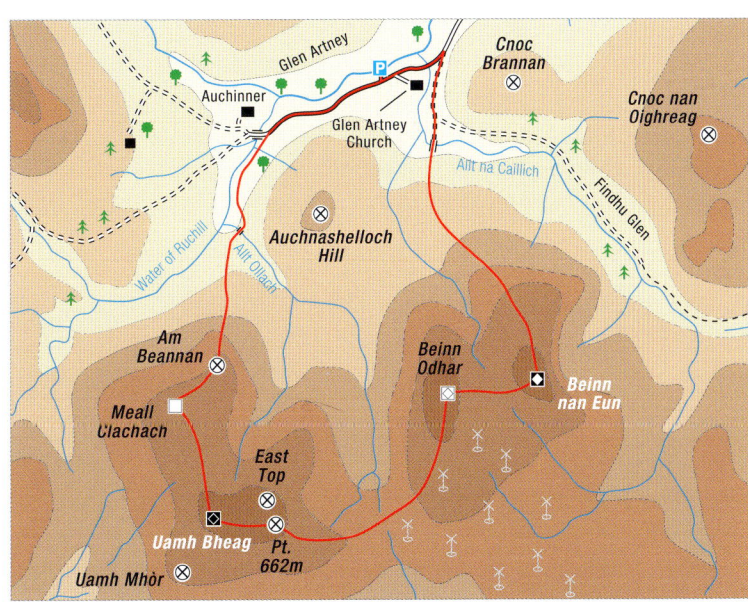

Beinn Chaorach from Beinn a' Mhanaich (Rab Anderson)

SECTION 1a
Loch Fyne to Loch Lomond

Section 1a – Loch Fyne to Loch Lomond

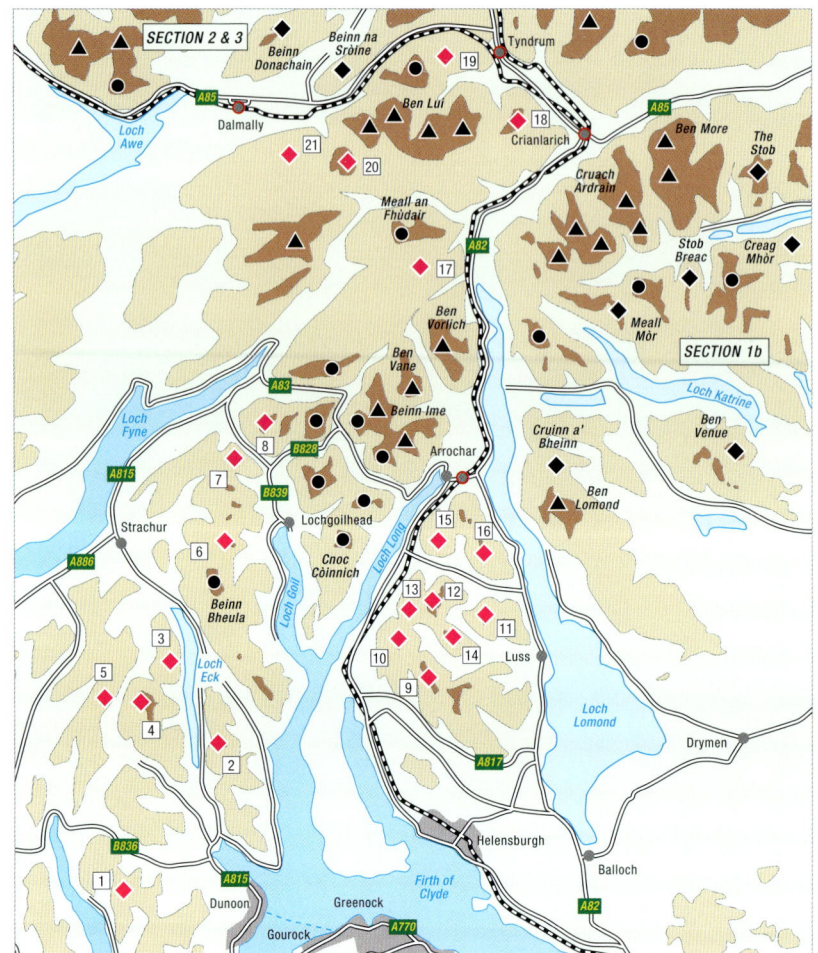

SECTION 1a

[1] *Cruach nan Capull*	87
[2] *Beinn Ruadh*	88
[3] *Beinn Bheag*, [4] *Beinn Mhòr*	89
[5] *Creag Tharsuinn*	91
[6] *Beinn Lochain*	92
[7] *Cruach nam Mult*	94
[8] *Stob an Eas*	95
[9] *Beinn Chaorach*, [10] *Beinn a' Mhanaich*	96
[11] *Mid Hill*, [12] *Doune Hill*, [13] *Cruach an t-Sìthein*, [14] *Beinn Eich*	98
[15] *Tullich Hill*, [16] *Beinn Bhreac*	101
[17] *Beinn Damhain*	103
[18] *Fiarach*	104
[19] *Meall Odhar*	105
[20] *Meall nan Gabhar*, [21] *Beinn Bhalgairean*	106

Cruach nan Capull

Cruach nan Capull from the Glen Lean approach past Corrachaive (Tom Prentice)

Cruach nan Capull; 612m; (G216); L63; NS095795; *heap of the horses*

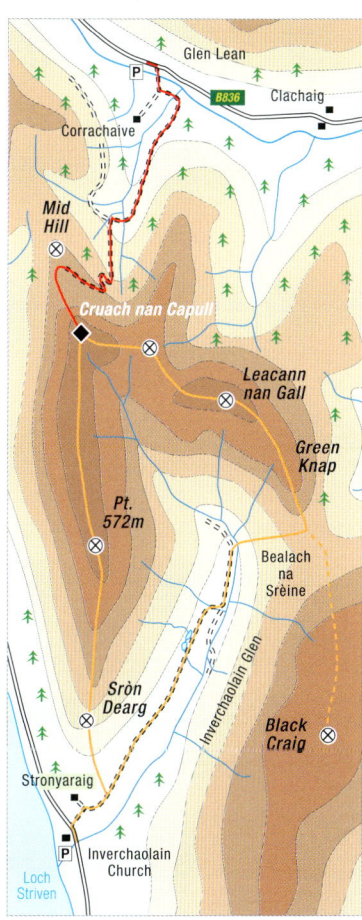

Surrounded on three sides by Loch Striven and the Firth of Clyde, Cruach nan Capull lies at a similar latitude to Glasgow and Edinburgh, making it the most southerly Graham in the Highlands. The mountain can be climbed from Glen Lean to the north or from Inverchaolain on Loch Striven to the south. For the general approach see the Cowal Hills panel on p89.

The northerly route starts from a large layby on the B836 about 400m west of the access track to Corrachaive. There is also limited parking at the start of the track. Follow the track, going left at a Y-junction to reach a gate. Cross the burn and continue through conifer plantations towards Cruach nan Capull, to a point where the track turns west and crosses the Corrachaive Burn. Just before the next and smaller Midhill Burn, turn left into the conifers (NS098808) onto an overgrown grassy track (shown on the OS 1:25k map).

Zigzag up the hillside on this track then make long, straight contours first south, then north to gain the shoulder of Mid Hill, from where the summit of Cruach nan Capull is easily gained (**4km; 510m; 1h 45min**).

Descend by the same route (**8km; 520m; 2h 45min**).

The southern route starts from a small parking area in front of Inverchaolain church, gained via the A815 south from Dunoon and a minor road north along Loch Striven. Go north up the road to the first track on the right and follow it past Stronyaraig to open hillside, from where the impressive Sròn Dearg is gained and climbed to a fence leading to a trig point on the rounded, grassy summit of Pt.572m. A long, grassy ridge then leads to the summit of Cruach nan Capull (**5km; 610m; 2h 10min**).

Descend steeply east, still following the fence, and go over a slight rise turning south-east to Leacann nan Gall. Continue south-east over Green Knap to the Bealach na Srèine on the old coffin route from Inverchaolain to Glen Kin and Glen Lean.

Black Craig (522m), a rounded Sub 2000ft Marilyn, lies to the south and can be included with a return to the bealach. However, most will wish to simply descend steeply west into Inverchaolain Glen, crossing the burn to pick up the track in the glen floor. Keep right where the track divides to gain a higher track and follow this back past Stronyaraig to the start (**12km; 690m; 4h**).

An approach is also possible from the east using forest tracks above Dunoon to gain Bishop's Seat and the Bealach na Srèine, as well as via the coffin route up forested Glen Kin.

Beinn Ruadh

Beinn Ruadh; 664m; (G155); L56; NS155883; red mountain

Beinn Ruadh's lower flanks are steep and forested, limiting access points and making circular routes awkward. The easiest approach is from the south, from the Forestry Commission Scotland Inverchapel car park (NS145865) on the east side of the A815, a few hundred metres north of the Stratheck holiday chalets at the south end of Loch Eck.

Cross the footbridge over the Inverchapel Burn, then turn right onto a waymarked path and ascend beside the burn. Keep left at a junction and zigzag up to join a higher path and follow it left towards a viewpoint over Loch Eck. Before reaching the viewpoint, gain the hillside at a wooden kissing gate and follow assorted animal tracks to a fence. Cross over and make a steep right traverse below the craggy south-west face to gain the south ridge.

The cairn on Pt.623m is soon reached, from where an intermittent old fenceline leads over the knobbly ridge, with fine views over Loch Eck to gain the summit trig point (**3km; 650m; 1h 45min**). Descend by the same route (**6km; 635m; 2h 45min**).

The mountain can also be climbed from the north, starting from the minor road which crosses the north end of the hill from Loch Eck to Ardentinny. Park on the north side by a gate at NS150924 where the Loch Eck cycle route crosses over. On the south side of the road the obvious cycle path leads to a track. Go left and descend to a fork, then right onto another track which is followed to its end, from where a path leads off left.

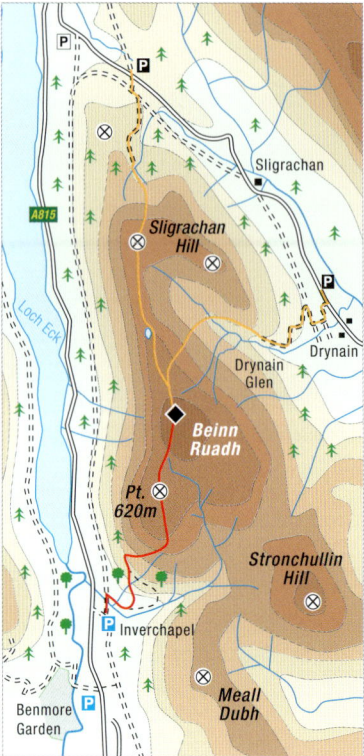

Cross over the burn and keep ascending on a path which leads up and round to a wide, grassy firebreak beside the burn. Follow this for a short distance to another burn and firebreak coming in from the left and go up these to open hillside beyond.

Go over a fence to gain the top of Sligrachan Hill, marked with a prominent tall cairn. An old fenceline leads up Beinn Ruadh's craggy north ridge to the summit trig point (**5km; 620m; 2h 20min**). Descend the same way (**10km; 720m; 3h 50min**).

An approach is also possible from the east via a Forestry Commission track (NS174896) near Drynain at the north end of Ardentinny. Ascend the track, keeping right where it divides to reach a higher track. Follow that right to a junction, then turn hard left and ascend to a turning area. A rough track goes sharp right to exit the forestry, from where an intermittent track leads to sheep pens in Drynain Glen. Head north-west to clear the trees at a fence and stile before the Drynain Burn, then turn due west and ascend to the north ridge and the summit (**4km; 650m; 2h**). Descend the same way (**8km; 650m; 3h 10min**).

Approaching the summit of Beinn Ruadh above Loch Eck. The Corbett Beinn Bheula is in the distance (Tom Prentice)

Beinn Mhòr, Beinn Bheag

Beinn Mhòr, left, and Beinn Bheag, right, in shade, from Beinn Ruadh (Tom Prentice)

Beinn Bheag; 618m; (G208); L56; NS125932; little mountain
Beinn Mhòr; 741m; (G28); L56; NS107908; big mountain

Loch Eck's western shore is dominated by a 10km wall of steep, rocky hillside and impressive corries. The northern end is capped by the rocky tops of Beinn Bheag and the unnamed Pt.568m with its trig point. The southern end is the vast sprawling bulk of Beinn Mhòr. As with most mountains in the area, steep hillsides and conifer plantations limit access points.

The well-established route from Glenmassan to the south suits an ascent of Beinn Mhòr by itself, but continuing to Beinn Bheag necessitates a rather tedious 370m reascent over Beinn Mhòr, and for this reason it is hard to recommend. The other popular route via Bernice on Loch Eck is more accommodating.

From the car park at Benmore Botanic Garden on the A815, cross the bridge over the River Eachaig, turn right and follow the track north round the garden to a right turn onto the track up the west side of Loch Eck. Pass Bernice after 7km, continue uphill to a junction then turn left and take the track up Bernice Glen, leaving it at its highpoint where it swings left (**8km; 160m; 2h**).

Ascend first on the right, then cross to the left side of the burn and climb to a faint path at the edge of the felled forest. Cross a fence and follow it down right to regain the burn and ascend to the Bealach Bernice. The col is marshy, so it is worth trying to cross the two fences on the right before arriving. Ascend north and east to skirt Pt.534m and Meall Breac, then continue to the west of Pt.601m to Beinn Bheag's summit cairn (**10km; 620m; 3h 15min**).

Return to the bealach, cross back ▶

Cowal Hills
Despite their proximity to Greenock and Glasgow, the Firth of Clyde complicates access to these hills, the most southerly of the Highland Grahams.

Although Cruach nan Capull, Beinn Ruadh and Beinn Mhòr are all clearly visible across the Firth, potential suitors from the central belt face a long drive north, west and then south via lochs Lomond, Fyne and Eck The alternative for anyone with easy access to the M8 or the rail network, is the 20 minute ferry crossing from Gourock or Greenock to Dunoon.

The total journey by ferry can take almost as long as driving, but makes a much more satisfying approach to the mountains, especially in summer when tourist traffic on Loch Lomond can significantly slow the journey.

Cars can be taken on the ferry, but it is also possible to leave the car at Greenock and use bicycles to access all five Cowal hills, although the Loch Striven approach to Cruach nan Capull and the Glenbranter approaches to Creag Tharsuinn, Beinn Mhòr and Beinn Beag involve longer distances.
Western Ferries: <www.western-ferries.co.uk>, Gourock to Dunoon (vehicle). A second vehicle service is expected to start in 2014-15.
Argyll Ferries: <argyllferries.co.uk>, Greenock to Dunoon (passenger only).

Beinn Mhòr, Beinn Bheag

over the fences and ascend the steady and rather monotonous northern slopes of Beinn Mhòr to gain the rocky upper corrie and the small summit plateau crowned with a trig point (**13.5km; 1050m; 5h**).

Return to the bealach then Bernice and the track back to Benmore (**24km; 1060m; 7h 30min**).

It is possible to bike to the track highpoint above Bernice saving about 1h 50min on the day.

If the Benmore to Bernice approach has been made on foot, this allows a very fine return route to be had. From the summit of Beinn Mhòr, follow the fenceline south-east then south to Capull Cloiche (577m), then cross the plateau south-east towards Creachan Mòr (571m). About halfway across, a diversion can be made to the north-east to take in the prominent Graham Top of Clach Bheinn (add 55min). From Creachan Mòr, an increasingly narrow and rocky ridge with stunning views south to Holy Loch and the Firth of Clyde leads over Creachan Beag and down to 482m A' Chruach.

From the summit, follow old fence posts straight down to a gate and stile. Turn right to gain a track which is followed steadily downhill to the fence surrounding Benmore Garden and a junction with the outward Loch Eck track. A right turn leads back to the car park (**22km; 1190m; 7h 20min**).

The full 10km ridge above Loch Eck offers a fantastic north-south expedition from Glenbranter to Benmore, taking in Beinn Bheag and Beinn Mhòr en route. The pre-placement of a mountain bike at Benmore significantly assists the return along the track on Loch Eck's western shore.

Start from Glenbranter Forestry Commission car park (NS111975) off the A815 at the head of Loch Eck; reached by following the access road round in front of the forestry office and toilets.

Walk south to a junction. Turn left over the river to Glenshellich, then left again (white waymarks) to pass below the farm on a gravel track. Continue round Loch Eck to a point just after a track junction on the right, where there is a wide break in the trees, with a burn and rocky watercourse (NS127960). Ascend this, cross an upper track and continue up the burn's left side to a bouldery corrie and the col between Cruach Bhuidhe and Pt.568m. Ascend to the trig point on Pt.568m, then down the rocky south face to a marshy col from where the summit of Beinn Bheag is easily gained (**6.5km; 740m; 2h 45min**).

From here, the route to Bheinn Mhòr and south over A' Chruach to Benmore is as described above (**18.5km; 1410m; 6h 50min**).

From Benmore return the 15km along the west side of Loch Eck to Glenbranter (**33.5km; 1450m; 9h 10min**).

Use of a bike, preplaced at Benmore Garden car park, can reduce this by around 1h 50min.

Use of a bike on the main track up the west side of Glen Shellish enables Beinn Bheag and Beinn Mhòr to be climbed via the Bealach Bernice, and Creag Tharsuinn (p91) via the Bealach na Croidhich.

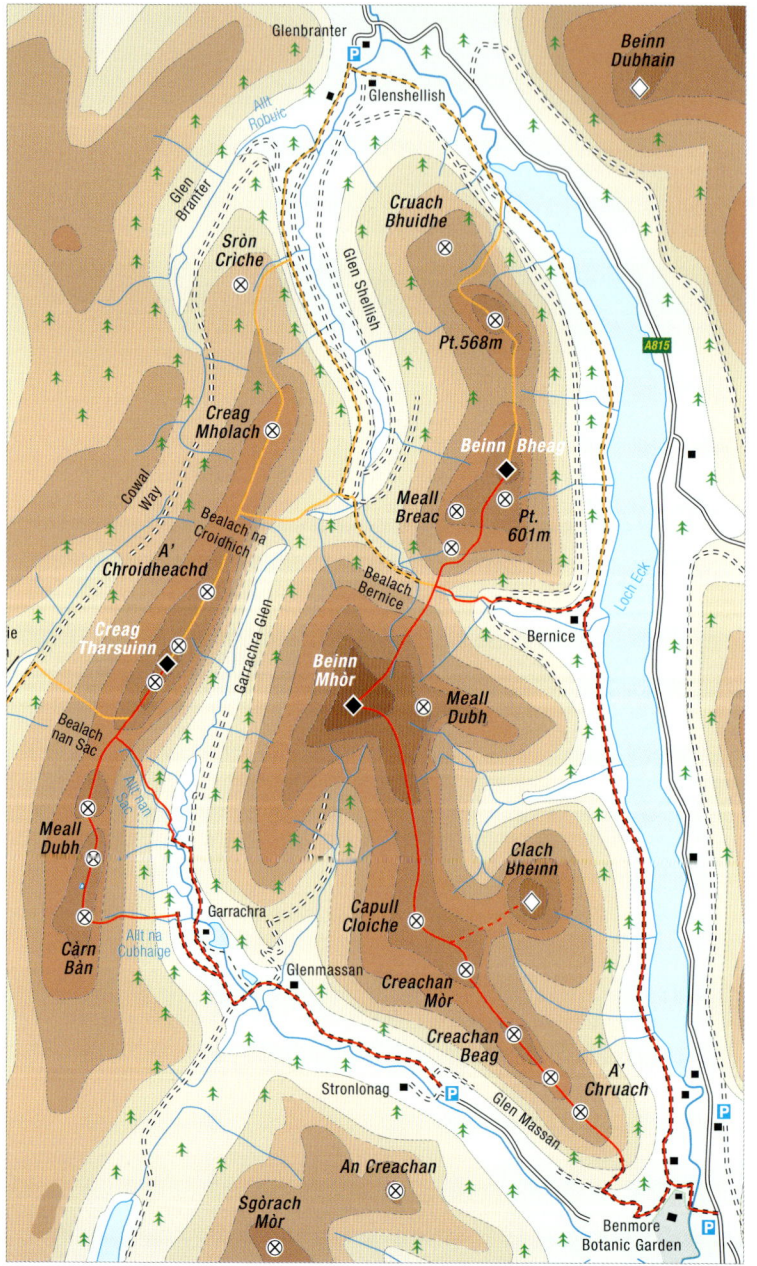

Looking north over the Bealach nan Sac to Creag Tharsuinn (Tom Prentice)

Creag Tharsuinn; 643m; (G182); L56; NS088913; transverse hill

New forest tracks (not shown on maps) and felling have improved access in the upper Garrachra Glen, making the approach from Glen Massan the route of choice for Creag Tharsuinn. The ascent and descent involve firebreaks, where good route-finding pays dividends.

The signposted road up Glen Massan is followed to its end at a small car park. Continue on the track past Glenmassan to a small loch and cross the bridge over the river to a track junction. Turn right and continue to a fork; the return route comes in from the left here. Follow the right track past the house and loch at Garrachra to a felled area where a new track goes left to the river.

The route follows the grassy gully of the Allt Nan Sac opposite and is worth noting from here, as trees restrict visibility in the lower section. Ford the river, a bridge may be constructed in the future, go right to the Allt nan Sac and follow it north. Care is needed as the trees close-up ahead and the firebreak pushes you left onto an off-route tributary rising to crags. Ascend ahead, easily through the trees on a short forested ridge (dividing the tributary and the Allt Nan Sac) to reach the wide and grassy upper gully.

Ascend steep grass on either side of the burn to a fence and continue north-east to the Bealach nan Sac, from where the south-west ridge leads over assorted rocky knolls to the top. While the summit is usually marked by a few stones, the highest knoll is hard to determine if they are missing (**7km; 580m; 2h 30min**).

Return to the bealach and continue south-west to the cairn on Meall Dubh, then over Pt.578m to skirt a lochan and gain the trig point on Càrn Bàn (**10km; 690m; 3h 20min**).

Descend east from the summit to the well-defined Allt na Cubhaige and follow its right (south) bank to the forest edge. Continue in the same line to cross over the burn and easily follow animal paths through the forest to a track. Turn right to the junction near Garrachra and follow the outward route back to the start (15km; 690m; 4h 40min). Biking to the fork before Garrachra saves 50min on the day. New forestry tracks and continued felling may alter the ascent and descent in the future.

An approach can also be made from the north, starting from the Glenbranter Forestry Commission car park (NS111975) off the A815 at the head of Loch Eck; reached by following the access road round in front of the forestry office and toilets. Walk past the turning to Glenshellish Farm and houses. The road turns to a track, crosses the Allt Robuic and forks. Take the right-hand fork uphill, keeping left where it bends sharply right, to enter Glen Shellish. After about 800m, an obvious wide firebreak containing the Alltan nan Dearc is reached on the right (NS103956). Ascend to the left of the burn, rough at the start, then easier through broadleaf woodland to the wide ridge south of Sròn Crìche. Heather, tussocky grass and boggy sections lead to Creag Mholach, from where a grassier ridge leads over A' Chroidheachd and assorted knolls to the summit (**7.5km; 650m; 2h 45min**). See earlier for summit details.

Descend by the same route (15km; 700m; 4h 35min).

The western approach from Garvie Farm on the A886 utilises the Cowal Way. Parking is very restricted at the start, otherwise it would be the easiest, if possibly the least interesting, route. Follow the track through the farm and east beside the Garvie Burn then north-east through forestry to a clearing at Tom a' Chromain (NS074915). A gate leads to open hillside and the Bealach nan Sac, to join the Glen Massan route described earlier (**7km; 610m; 2h 35min**).

Descend by the same route (14km; 610m; 4h 15min).

Beinn Lochain

Beinn Lochain, right, and its East Top from the flanks of Stob na Boine Druim-fhinn (Tom Prentice)

Beinn Lochain; *703m; (G96); L56; NN160006; mountain above the lochan*

Three Grahams and four Corbetts surround the village of Lochgoilhead at the northern end of the Cowal peninsula. Beinn Lochain is the most southerly of the three and along with its East Top and the neighbouring Graham Tops of Beinn Tharsuinn, Stob na Boine Druim-fhinn and Mullach Coire a' Chuir to the north, and the Corbett Beinn Bheula to its south, it forms part of an impressively mountainous escarpment on the west side of the head of Loch Goil, overlooking the village.

Beinn Lochain is best climbed in a round with Stob na Boine Druim-fhinn and Beinn Tharsuinn, although the route can be extended to include Beinn Bheula. It is also possible to start with the northern Graham Cruach nam Mult, and Mullach Coire a' Chuir, for a full traverse of the western escarpment. That route is described in the panel opposite.

Park just off the road in a dirt layby on the west side of Loch Goil (NN189006), where a lochside track goes left to a boat yard and the main road starts to ascend. The layby is almost opposite the south end of the Drymsynie chalets. It should be noted that there are a number of new forestry tracks on this route, not yet shown on OS maps.

Climbing Stob na Boine Druim-fhinn first, follow the main road south, about 180m uphill, and turn right towards the Drimsynie Estate Office (named Corrow on OS maps). Go through the farmyard to a gate and a track which heads left then back right and climbs to a track junction directly below what was once a firebreak in the felled hillside above. Go up the 'firebreak' on a clear animal path passing through gates and over a forestry track then through more gates beyond to gain the open hillside below a small bluff.

Skirt the bluff on either side to gain the broad ridge above and ascend this to its top where an obvious, deep cleft splits the cliffs. Ascend the grassy cleft beside a burn to gain the undulating upper ridge which leads to a final steep ascent past a short rock gendarme to the finely defined summit and trig point on Stob na Boine Druim-fhinn (**4km; 660m; 2h**).

Retrace your steps to the undulating upper ridge and descend

Superfortress undercarriage and Stob na Boine Druim-fhinn (Tom Prentice)

south-south-east to the col below Beinn Tharsuinn.

About 710m due west of here, on the edge of the forest in the glen below, lies the wreckage of a B-29 US Army Air Force Superfortress which clipped the top of Beinn Tharsuinn on 17th January 1949 and crashed with the loss of all 20 crew. The site is at NS161022 and can easily be visited as a diversion on the way to Beinn Tharsuinn.

To visit the site, descend due west above the south side of the burn. The extensive wreckage lies at the forest edge, headed by a stone memorial to the crew. From the site, steady slopes of tussocky grass lead south-east to the summit of Beinn Tharsuinn. This diversion adds 20min to the route, plus any time spent at the site.

The direct route ascends Beinn Tharsuinn's northern slopes from the col to gain a rocky ridge with fine views down to the village and over Loch Goil, to reach the 619m summit on top of an isolated knoll (**5.5km; 780m; 2h 35min**).

Continue down south to the col, cross a fence and make a steady ascent south then west to the cairned summit of Beinn Lochain and fine views south over Curra Lochain to the big eastern corries of Beinn Bheula (**7km; 970m; 3h 20min**).

Immediately east of the summit is a small knoll. From the col between it and the summit, descend surprisingly steep, grassy slopes towards the east end of Curra Lochain to meet a path (the Cowal Way) and follow it over a stile to stepping stones at the east end of the loch. If the water level makes these difficult, there is also a handrail crossing about 100m downstream. Cross over onto a rough path on the south side of the burn.

It is possible to include Beinn Bheula from here, although this is not described. Continue the descent via a path to the Sruth Bàn waterfall then zigzag down grassy terraces marked by occasional white posts. Beyond these, continue ahead through the firebreak to gain a forestry track. Turn right and descend, ignoring tracks off right, to the houses at Lettermay and the main road, which is followed back to the start (**12.5km; 970m; 4h 45min**).

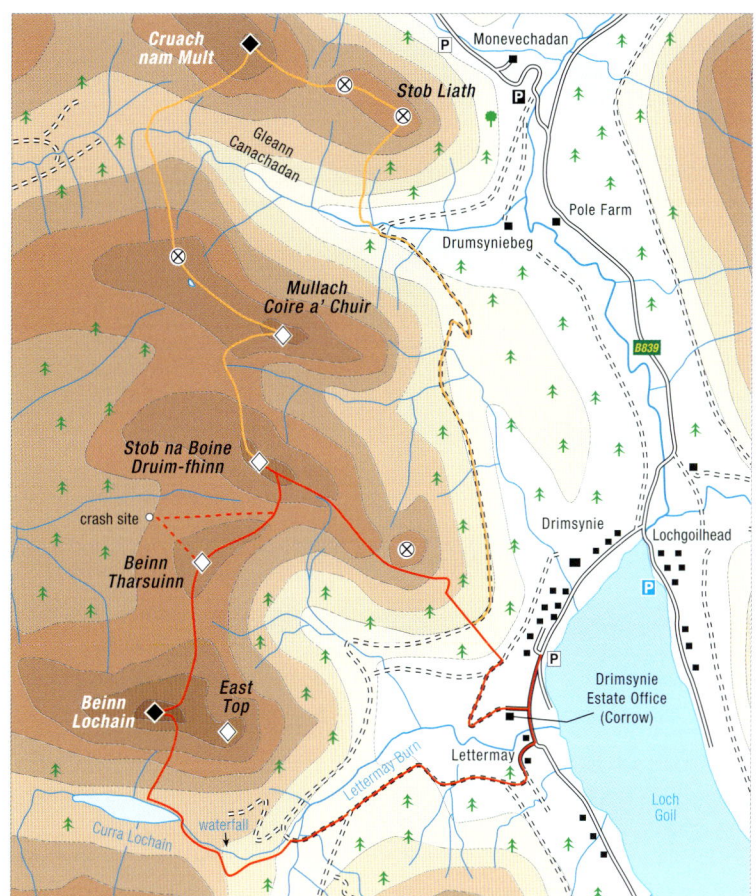

Lochgoilhead Western Escarpment Traverse
The two Grahams on the western escarpment above Lochgoilhead can be linked to make a fine round with spectacular views. Some 7km of the route is on forestry tracks, although most of this is downhill.

Start at the dirt layby on the west side of Loch Goil (NN189006) and continue as for Stob na Boine Druim-fhinn, described opposite. Pass through Drimsynie Estate Office (Corrow) and ascend the 'firebreak' to the forestry track. Turn right and follow the track north for 4km, mostly downhill but with a few short ascents. After a hairpin bend, the track descends into Gleann Canachadan, turns sharply right and crosses the glen's burn. Leave the track at the bend before the burn and follow a path into the forest to a log bridge. Cross the burn and continue to a wooden gate and the open glen.

Ascend left of the forestry to the top of Stob Liath then traverse west over prominent grassy knolls to the eastern flanks of Cruach nam Mult and climb them via a wide, grassy gully on the left (**8km; 850m; 3h 10min**).

Descend south-west towards the forest edge in the col at the head of Gleann Canachadan, then ascend the northern flanks of Mullach Coire a' Chuir to a grassy ridge, which leads south-east above the craggy north face to the summit (**11km; 1090m; 4h 20min**).

A south-westerly descent soon gains the next col, followed by a steeper ascent south-east to Stob na Boine Druim-fhinn (**12.5km; 1260m; 5h**).

From there, the route over Beinn Tharsuinn to Beinn Lochain is as described opposite (**15.5km; 1570m; 6h 20min**).

Descend to Curra Lochain then past the Struth Bàn waterfall to meet the track to Lettermay as described opposite (**21km; 1570m; 7h 45min**).

Cruach nam Mult

Approaching Cruach nam Mult from the east along the ridge from Stob Liath (Tom Prentice)

Cruach nam Mult; 611m; (G218); L56; NN168056; heap of the wethers (sheep)

When climbed from near the highpoint on the road through Hell's Glen, the quickest and most popular approach, 'heap of the sheep' seems an appropriate name for Cruach nam Mult. These rather dull western flanks are in complete contrast to the impressively steep and rocky north face which forms the south side of this deep-set glen, and the eastern end which terminates in the rocky stub of Stob Liath.

However, the advantage of this western approach, is that Cruach nam Mult and the Graham Stob an Eas on the north side of the glen can be climbed on the same day from the same parking spot.

Park at NN168074 just north of the highpoint on the B839, where tracks head east and west into the forest. In case of forest operations there is also space at a track entrance 350m to the north.

Go along the western track for almost 1.5km, to a point 100m beyond the end of a fence and a burn that runs down beside it. Follow a felling track up then right across the hillside. Where this heads more steeply uphill near the top, go right along another felling track on a rising traverse to exit the upper corner of the felled area at NN159059.

Ascend south-east up the grassy spur and swing eastwards up the easy-angled western flanks past some wooden posts to gain the summit. A recent survey confirms the highest point as being the north-west knoll. The knoll 90m to the south-east is half a metre lower, although this is the better viewpoint (**3.25km; 390m; 1h 25min**).

Return the same way (**6.5km; 410m; 2h 20min**).

A more interesting but longer circuit climbs the hill from the south-east. From the same parking spot, descend the road through the quiet and scenic Hell's Glen, passing alternative parking next to a communications mast at NN179061 and beside the Moses Well at NN185056. Cut the bend below Monevechadan by diverting through the trees to the bridge over the River Goil and a Forestry Commission track signposted Drimsynie.

Follow this track south then west up Gleann Canachadan to where it bends sharp left. Turn right at the bend and follow a path into the forest to a log bridge. Cross the burn and continue to a wooden gate and the open glen. Ascend left of the forestry to the top of Stob Liath (503m), which offers excellent views south over Loch Goil. Some prominent grassy knolls are now traversed west alongside a fence to the rocky eastern flanks of Cruach nam Mult, which are climbed via a wide grassy gully on the left (**8km; 650m; 2h 50min**).

Descend to the parking at the high-point in Hell's Glen by reversing the standard ascent route described first, taking care to find the top of the felling track at NN159059 (**11.5km; 650m; 3h 40min**).

Cruach nam Mult can also be combined with Beinn Lochain for a traverse of the western escarpment as described in the panel on p93.

Stob an Eas 95

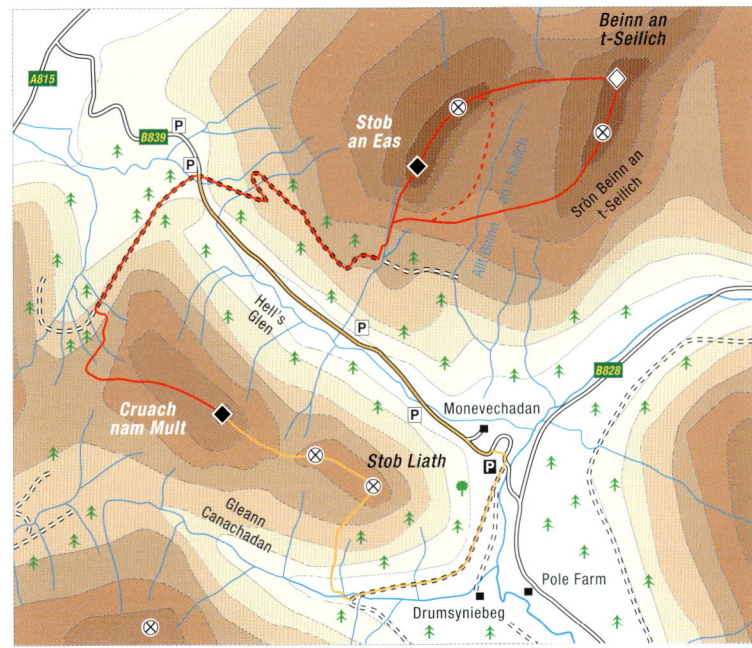

Stob an Eas; *732m; (G46); L56; NN185073; stub of the waterfall*

views (3km; 510m; 1h 30min).

Although a return can be made the same way (6km; 510m; 2h 20min), it is more enjoyable and perhaps less daunting to include the Graham Top of Beinn an t-Seilich (719m) in the circuit. To do so, follow the knobbly ridge north-east towards Glen Kinglas then descend east towards the col before Beinn an t-Seilich. A quick return can be made here by turning south here and traversing below Stob an Eas's rocky east face back to the approach route (8km; 510m; 2h 55min).

Continuing the round, cross the col and climb Beinn an t-Seilich's western slopes to the summit cairn (5km; 650m; 2h 15min).

The pleasant ridge of Sròn Beinn an t-Seilich now leads south above the long and rocky east face, until a descent is made south-west into the corrie. Cross the Allt Beinn an t-Seilich and traverse west back to the approach route and a return by the line of ascent (10km; 670m; 3h 30min).

The northernmost of the Lochgoilhead Grahams, Stob an Eas presents an unexpectedly impressive profile from many directions. One fine view is from its companion Graham Cruach nam Mult on the south side of Hell's Glen, from where it appears as a steep rocky pyramid. The two hills are often combined in a single day from the same parking spot on the B839 through the glen.

Park at NN168074 just north of the highpoint on the B839, where tracks head east and west into the forest. In case of forest operations there is also space at a track entrance 350m to the north. Ascend the eastern track round two bends, to where the main track ends and a rougher track continues, contouring east round the lower hillside of Stob an Eas then ascending more steeply to reach a burn in a recessed gully and a clearing in the conifers (NN182067).

Leave the track and ascend the left-hand side of the burn until it is possible to cross over. Now follow the right-hand side to gain and climb the increasingly steep southern nose of Stob an Eas, weaving in-between small cliffs of mica-schist to reach the summit trig point and spectacular

The impressive rocky pyramid of Stob an Eas (Tom Prentice)

Beinn Chaorach, Beinn a' Mhanaich

Section 1a – Loch Fyne to Loch Lomond

Beinn a' Mhanaich, left, and Cruach an t-Sìthein from the flanks of Beinn Chaorach (Tom Prentice)

Beinn Chaorach; 713m; (G73); L56; NS287923; *mountain of the sheep*
Beinn a' Mhanaich; 709m; (G85); L56; NS269946; *mountain of the monk*

Glen Fruin offers the easiest access to Beinn Chaorach and Beinn a' Mhanaich, the most southerly of the group of eight Grahams that make up the Luss Hills; see the information panel on p99.

The glen is best accessed by following the A82 past Balloch to the roundabout at Arden. Turn onto the A818 to Helensburgh, follow it to the next roundabout and take the second left signposted Glen Fruin. Follow this minor road north-west through the glen to park on the verge of a large layby at NS274900, about 250m north of Auchengaich and below a gated road; the old access road to Auchengaich Reservoir.

A second and newer road, the A817, contours the glen above its floor. This road was built for military

Beinn Chaorach from the Beinn Tharsuinn col (Tom Prentice)

Beinn Chaorach, Beinn a' Mhanaich

vehicles serving naval bases on Loch Long and the Gare Loch, and no parking, overtaking or stopping is allowed. However, it is possible to park at the start of the Auchengaich Reservoir access road where it is cut by the A817. This is best accessed from the west, as access from the east involves turning across the traffic on a blind summit.

From the layby north of Auchengaich, go through a gate and ascend a section of the old reservoir access road to the A817. Cross over with care as visibility is poor and continue up the continuation access road to a gate across it with a side gate and signpost for a footpath to Glen Luss.

Go through the gate and ascend the hillside on the right, marshy to start, following a line through the bracken, then diagonally north-east towards the col between Auchengaich Hill and Beinn Tharsuinn. Paths and an atv track lead to the top of Beinn Tharsuinn, marked with a small cairn. Follow the fence to a marshy col, avoided to the left, and ascend to the summit of Beinn Chaorach, marked with a cairn on the left-hand side of the fence and a trig point on the right (**3.5km; 610m; 1h 50min**).

Descend the broad ridge in a north-westerly direction over the knoll of Pt.667m, then more steeply left of the fence towards Beinn a' Mhanaich, to the bealach between Glen Fruin and Glen Luss and a stile. Do not cross over, but continue beside the fence, which turns north-east, to arrive at the foot of a shallow rocky gully on the south-east face of Beinn a' Mhanaich. Climb the right flank of this to the col south of the summit, from where it is easily gained (**7km; 980m; 3h 30min**).

Return to the col, cross a gate in the fence and descend south along the fine, well-positioned ridge, to pass over Maol an Fheidh (591m). Continue down The Strone, marred slightly by old shooting range signs, then descend steeply south-east towards Auchengaich Reservoir. Cross over the dam to gain the access road and follow it back to the start (**13km; 990m; 5h**).

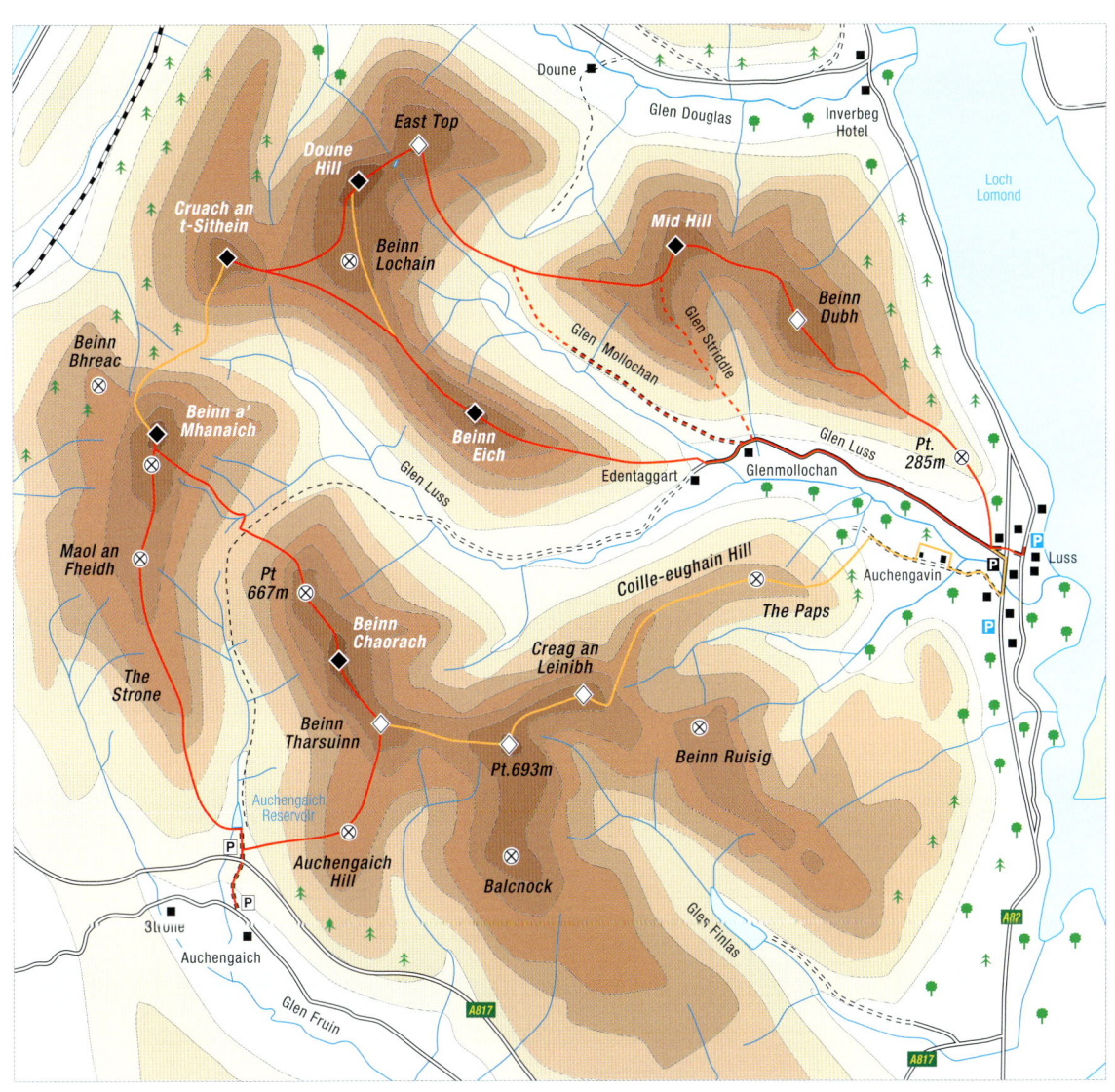

North from Beinn Eich to Cruach an t-Sìthein, left, Beinn Lochain, Doune Hill, centre, and its East Top (Tom Prentice)

Mid Hill; 657m; (G166); L56; NS321962; mid hill
Doune Hill; 734m; (G38); L56; NS290971; hill above Doune farm. Doune from Gaelic 'dùn', hillfort
Cruach an t-Sìthein; 684m; (G122); L56; NS275965; heap of the fairy knoll
Beinn Eich; 703m; (G95); L56; NS302946; mountain of horses

Mid Hill, Doune Hill and Beinn Eich form three sides of Glen Mollachan off upper Glen Luss and offer a horseshoe round of high quality, with a diversion west en route to pick-up Cruach an t-Sìthein.

The easiest parking for these central Luss Hills is the Argyll and Dute Council pay and display car park in the centre of Luss; £1 per hour in 2022. Limited parking is also possible on the minor road up Glen Luss, a short distance on from the turning off the A82. There is no parking as such at the end of Glen Luss and while it might be possible to squeeze a car off the road in passing places or in the turning area at the end of the public road, this may well prove more trouble than it is worth.

Exit the car park, turn left and follow the road to the first turning on the right. Go up this past Luss

Mid Hill and Ben Lomond from Beinn Eich (Tom Prentice)

Mid Hill, Doune Hill, Cruach an t-Sìthein, Beinn Eich

Beinn Chaorach left with Beinn Eich right from Mid Hill (Tom Prentice)

Primary School, from where a tarmac path ascends to the wooden bridge over the A82. Cross over and past a house, then straight ahead onto a gravel path. Go through a gate and turn right, then follow the fence to a stile and cross over.

Ascend to a metal gate with a stile and continue up the track above with increasingly good views over Loch Lomond and its islands. After a small section of woodland and a mobile phone mast, the track becomes more of a path and leads through bracken to the top of Pt.285m. Beyond this the path becomes marshy, but improves again as a fence is joined and followed via a stile to the top of 642m Beinn Dubh.

A broad expanse of open ridge now separates Beinn Dubh from Mid Hill, confusingly also named Beinn Dubh in Fiona Graham's original list. Continue north-west on the path until it deteriorates in an area of peat hags, then emerge from the other side to gain a cairn (NS322964), marked as the summit on OS 1:50k maps. About 145m to the south-west is a second cairn, with some quartz among the stones, which the OS 1:25k map correctly identifies as the summit (**5.5km; 690m; 2h 20min**).

Descend the broad summit area south-west for about 330m, then turn ▶

Luss Hills

Collectively known as the Luss Hills, the high ground between Loch Long and Loch Lomond contains eight Grahams; the highest concentration in such a small area, anywhere in the country. They are well proportioned hills, separated, by significant drops and deep glens, with outstanding views from the Southern Highlands to Arran and the Paps of Jura.

Glen Douglas splits the two northern hills from the main massif, which is partially sub-divided into a central and southern section by Glen Luss, the glen running west from the village of Luss on the shore of Loch Lomond.

*The hills lend themselves to a number of different approaches and are described in three main walks. However, it is also possible to link the six central and southern Grahams into a single high-level, high-stamina circuit of exceptional quality. From the parking in Luss, ascend Mid Hill as described on this page (**5.5km; 690m; 2h 20min**) and continue to the summit of Doune Hill (**10km; 1270m; 4h 30min**). Continue south and skirt rounded Beinn Lochain to the east, to gain and climb Beinn Eich's fine west ridge to the summit (**13km; 1430m; 5h 30min**). Reverse the ridge and contour north-west below Beinn Lochain, before descending to the col below Cruach an t-Sìthein, from where a short climb gains the summit (**16.5km; 1600m; 6h 35min**).*

*A steep descent is made south-west then south to the forested col below Beinn a' Mhanaich. Follow the forestry fence round the west side of Beinn a' Mhanaich and once clear of the frontal crags, veer south-east up the hillside to meet another fence rising from below, which passes over the col south of the top. Leave the fence east to gain the summit (**19km; 1980m; 8h 15min**)*

*Descend straight down the east face, keeping left of a fence and wooded gully to the burn in the col below Beinn Chaorach. Cross over and head south-east to the north ridge of Beinn Chaorach and follow it beside a fence to the summit trig point (**22.5km; 2350m; 9h 55min**). From here descend south-east beside a fence to the top of Beinn Tharsuinn. Continue east beside the fence to Pt.693m, then north-east to the top of Creag an Leinibh (**26km; 2550m; 11h**).*

*Route-finding at the start and finish of the next section requires a little concentration. Continue south-east beside the fence for about 165m, then turn sharp north and descend the steep north-east slope to the broad ridge of Coille-eughain Hill and continue to The Paps. From here descend well to the left of a larch plantation and the main mass of bracken. Head straight down to pass right of a small clump of birch trees in a burn above the main treeline to reach a track at NS344931. Follow this rightwards through rough pasture towards Auchengavin Farm. Before a barn, a diversion from the track takes you north to a stile and across pasture towards the farmhouse and round a hedge back to the track, which leads to the A82. Walk north to the Glen Luss road and turn left then right to gain the wooden bridge over the A82 back to Luss (**32km; 2570m; 12h 40min**).*

Mid Hill, Doune Hill, Cruach an t-Sìthein, Beinn Eich

west to gain the west ridge (slightly hidden from above), which leads past crags, boulders and three old birch trees to the flat, bog myrtle-covered col below Doune Hill.

A relentless 470m ascent now follows, keeping right of the tree-filled burn, initially on a grassy animal path to gain a shallow upper corrie and the summit of the domed East Peak (701m), a Graham Top.

Descend west to a small lochan at the col between the tops (Bealach an Dùin), then ascend to the trig point on Doune Hill. A small cairn some 45m to the south-south-west of the trig point marks the highest point (**10km; 1270m; 4h 30min**).

Gentler gound now leads south-west and south towards rounded Beinn Lochain. Skirt the top of this to the west and descend to the col below Cruach an t-Sìthein, from where a short ascent gains the summit (**12km; 1440m; 5h 15min**).

Return to the col, ascend a little way then contour east below Beinn Lochain to gain the south ridge connecting it with Beinn Eich. A short ascent up a fine grassy crest gains the shapely summit of Cruach an t-Sìthein (**15.5km; 1630m; 6h 25min**).

Descend the south-east ridge, heading for the Edentaggart farm in Glen Luss below, to reach a wall where it is joined by a gate in a fence. Cross the wall by a stile then continue down left to cross a stile over another wall. Skirt the farm to its north heading for a corner on the access track and cross a stile to gain this. Follow the track then road down Glen Luss (**22km; 1680m; 8h 15min**).

Biking to Glenmollochan farm to ascend Mid Hill by the path up its south-east ridge, thereby missing out the ascent over Beinn Dubh, reduces the overall time by about 50min. The road is steep at the start but makes for a speedy descent.

These hills are also easily divided into shorter routes. Mid Hill can be approached over Beinn Dubh followed by the path down the south-east ridge to Glenmollochan and the road back to Luss (**11km; 720m; 3h 50min**). Doune Hill, Cruach an t-Sìthein and Beinn Eich can be climbed as a circuit via Glen Mollachan (**21km; 1240m; 7h 15min**). Use of a bike would ease this walk by about 50min as well.

See previous pages for map

Cruach an t-Sìthein from the col between Beinn Lochain and Beinn Eich to the south (Tom Prentice)

Tullich Hill and Invergroin from the approach up Glen Douglas (Tom Prentice)

Tullich Hill; *632m; (G194); L56; NN293006; hill above Tullich farm. From Gaelic 'tulach', hillock*
Beinn Bhreac; *681m; (G126); L56; NN321000; speckled mountain*

Glen Douglas runs between Loch Lomond and Loch Long, separating the northern Luss Hills from the rest of the group, and the road through the glen provides easy access for this pleasant circuit from Invergroin. Tullich Hill gives fine views north across Loch Long to The Cobbler and the high peaks of Arrochar, while Ben Reoch (661m) and Beinn Bhreac drop steeply to Loch Lomond on their eastern sides and present open vistas up and down the loch and across to Ben Lomond.

While the central and southern Luss Hills are predominantly rounded and grassy, with sheep frequently found on the summits, these northern hills display craggier mica-schist terrain, similar to that which characterises much of the landscape of the Southern Highlands.

The route starts from a parking area at NS310987, about halfway through Glen Douglas, directly below the conifer plantation before the farm and houses at Invergroin.

Walk up the road to Invergroin past the houses and cross the bridge over the burn. About 100m beyond the bridge, go through a gate on the right, signposted Tullich Hill and follow an atv track up the hillside. Go left to cross a stile (the track goes right to a gate) then continue to an upper fence and go through a gate on the right. ▶

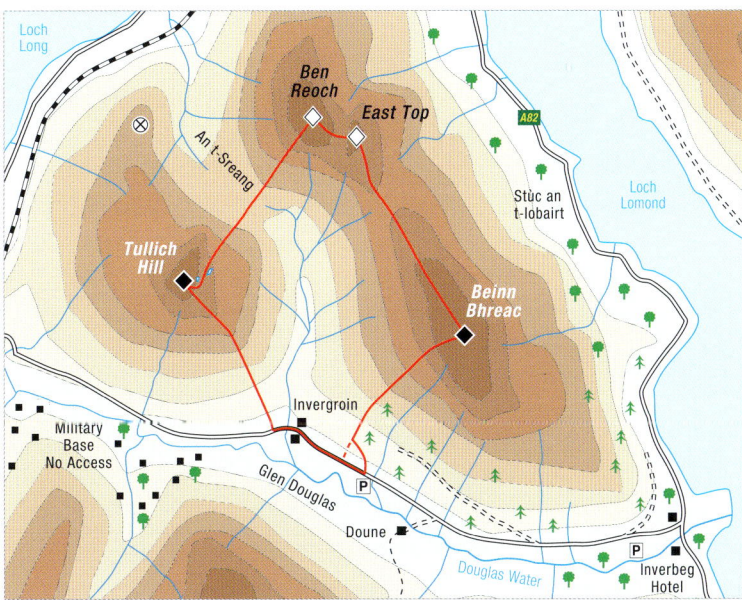

As height is gained the warren of military bunkers below Doune Hill on the south side of Glen Douglas come into view, and the silence is often broken by tannoy announcements.

The broad south-eastern ridge of Tullich Hill becomes better defined and leads to the summit area, which has a number of highpoints separated by a small lochan. The actual summit is the westernmost of these points, marked by a cairn of quartz and mica-schist rocks (**3km; 530m; 1h 30min**).

A line of steep crags guard the southern side of the north-east ridge leading to the An t-Sreang col below Ben Reoch. To avoid these crags, descend east from the summit to gain lochans below and east of the ridge and continue north-east to the col below. From here, a steep ascent in the vicinity of a line of old fence-posts leads to the cairned summit of Ben Reoch (**5km; 830m; 2h 40min**).

Drop down south then east over the rocky East Top and down to the col below Beinn Bhreac. A steady ascent up the broad rock-strewn ridge leads to the summit, marked by a prominent trig point on a small crag (**8km; 1020m; 3h 40min**).

Beinn Bhreac and Loch Lomond from Ben Reoch (Tom Prentice)

Immediately below the summit, the east face of Beinn Bhreac is riven by crevasses from extensive rock-slides, common among many mica-schist mountains in the area. On the shore of Loch Lomond at the very base of the face is Stùc an t-Iobairt, where Robert I (The Bruce) is said to have rested in 1306 after defeat at Dalrigh south of Tyndrum.

Head west then south-west from the summit to gain the western top corner of a conifer plantation. Follow the edge down, then the wall directly below it, and go through a gate to regain the road at Invergroin and follow this back to the parking area (**10.5km; 1020m; 4h 30min**).

Tullich Hill, left, above Arrochar on Loch Long (Tom Prentice)

Beinn Damhain

Beinn Damhain from Meall an Fhùdair (Tom Prentice)

Beinn Damhain; 684m; (G123); L50, 56; NN282173; *mountain of stags*

Lying well back from the main road through Glen Falloch, it is hard to get more than a fleeting glimpse of Beinn Damhain. Even the approach doesn't give much away and the hill's fine proportions and surprisingly rocky summit are only fully appreciated when viewed from the north across the Làirig Arnan.

The hill is easily accessed from lower Glen Falloch and provides an enjoyable up and down route, which can be extended into a circuit by including the Corbett Meall an Fhùdair and Troisgeach to the north.

Park at the base of a track on the north side of the A82, opposite Glen Falloch farm, at the foot of Glen Falloch (NN319197). Parking is limited, so maximise space for others and do not block access. Go over the locked gate and ascend over the railway to another gate. A steady ascent in a southerly direction leads to zigzags which can be clipped by ascending beside the burn to regain the track below electricity pylons. Turn left at the junction and skirt below Troisgeach until the track descends left to cross the Allt Arnan at a bridge over a rocky gorge below a hydro dam.

Remain on the track to where it ends, then follow sheep paths up the left bank of the main burn draining from Lochan Beinn Damhain on the mountain's eastern shoulder. At the top, where the ground levels out, stepping stones can be used to cross the burn. If they cannot be found, then the burn can be crossed at the head of the lochan, although this may necessitate wet feet if in spate.

Gain the heathery and rocky eastern ridge and follow it over successive humps to the surprisingly rocky and boulder-strewn summit cone, topped by a medium-sized cairn (**6km; 670m; 2h 25min**). Beinn Damhain's solitary position and well-defined summit means it holds its own among the surrounding hills and offers some fine views. Return the same way (**12km; 680m; 3h 55min**).

To continue to Meall an Fhùdair, descend north from the summit to the marshy watershed, to pass immediately left of the larger of some lochans. Ascend north-west up the slopes on the other side to the 764m summit (**8.5km; 1050m; 3h 50min**).

Now traverse the summit ridge east and north east towards Meall nan Caora, then south-east across a peaty plateau to 733m Troisgeach (**10.5km; 1130m; 4h 25min**). Descend eastwards down the broad ridge to reach the track near the pylons and follow it back to the start (**14.5km; 1130m; 5h 40min**).

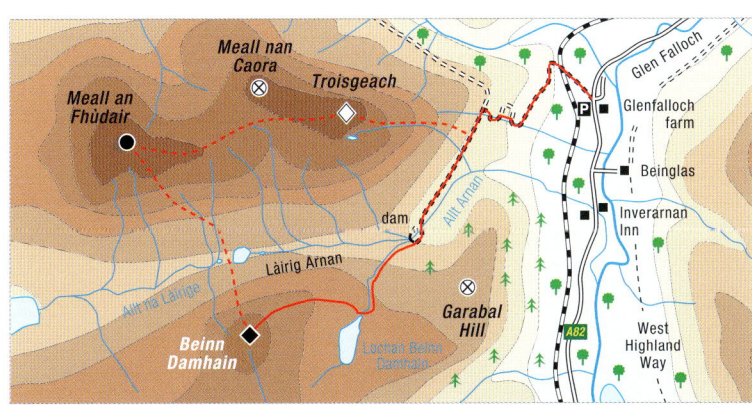

Fiarach

Cruach Ardrain from the dolerite dyke forming Fiarach's summit (Rab Anderson)

Fiarach; 652m; (G171); L50; NN344261; *slanting hill*

Fiarach lies at the southern end of the Ben Lui horseshoe of three Munros and one Corbett, which enclose the River Cononish south-west of Tyndrum. It offers particularly fine views east to the Crianlarich Munros at the head of Glen Falloch.

Its companion Graham Meall Odhar (see opposite) lies at the northern end of the horseshoe and it is possible to climb both hills in a day from Dalrigh, especially if a bicycle is used. Fiarach is a broad, elongated hill topped with a distinctive castle-like summit, set well back from the frontal face which overlooks the A82 at Dalrigh. The summit is unusual, being the highest point on a dolerite dyke which erosion has left standing proud of the surrounding moorland, like a high wall in the middle of nowhere.

An ascent of Fiarach is easily made from the large car park at Dalrigh (NN344291), using the track up Gleann Auchreoch. From the bottom of the car park, gain the old road and follow it south-east. Cross the bridge over the River Fillan, turn right onto a track and after 1km pass over the railway. Follow the track up Gleann Auchreoch, passing some fine stands of Scots pines to reach a gate at the edge of the conifer plantation.

Turn left and follow a fence uphill to gain a broad ridge. Continue

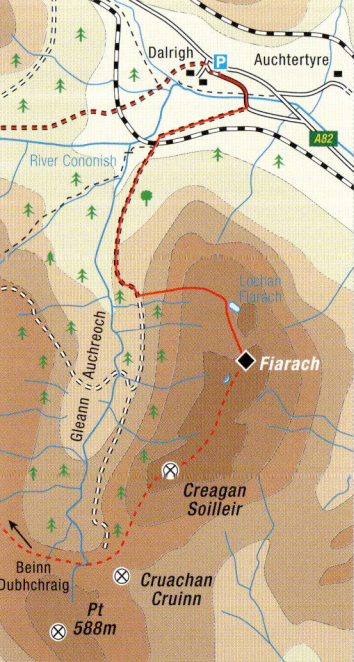

beside the fence and past Lochan Fiarach directly to the summit (**5km; 470m; 1h 55min**). Before descending, it is worth following the broad ridge south-west for a short way for a view of Fiarach's surprising dolerite 'wall'.

Return by the same route (**10km; 470m; 3h 10min**).

Anyone wanting to link Fiarach and Meall Odhar into a single hillwalking circuit without having to return first to Dalrigh, can climb the intervening Munro Beinn Dubhchraig (978m). This mountain's south ridge is easily gained from the southern end of Fiarach and leads directly to the summit; an ascent of about 480m.

A descent is then made north-west to the lochan on the shoulder, then north along the ridge to the fenceline marked on the OS 1:25k. Follow this north-west, then break off north to the footbridge over the River Cononish, just south of Cononish (NN304283); about 8.5km from Fiarach. Gain the access track in the glen then ascend and descend Meall Odhar as described opposite, returning to Dalrigh by the West Highland Way (approximately 25km total).

Meall Odhar

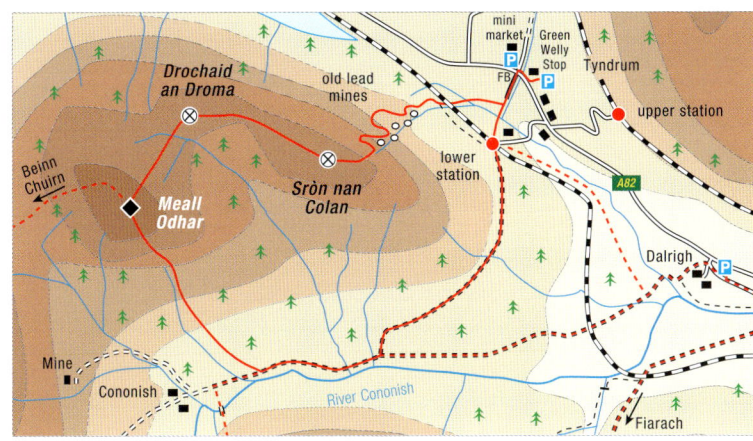

Meall Odhar; 656m; (G169); L50; NN298298; dun-coloured hill

Meall Odhar lies at the northern end of the horseshoe which has Fiarach (see opposite) at its southern end. As an up and down ascent from near Cononish, Meall Odhar doesn't offer the hillwalker much to chew on, but combined into a circuit with the minor hills to its east and a visit to the old lead mines above Tyndrum, it offers a very pleasant outing.

From one of the car parks in Tyndrum, follow the A82 north and go over the footbridge. Cross the A82 opposite the mini-market then descend the road and the West Highland Way past a row of cottages to a wide path leading to Tyndrum Lower Station. Go right over the level crossing and take the track on the left through the forest to reach the track from Dalrigh in Cononish glen.

Continue towards Cononish farm for about 1km to the second large area of rough pasture in the forestry covering the north side of the glen below Meall Odhar. Go through a gate and ascend to the obvious firebreak in the conifers. Cross over the fence and follow the firebreak to the open heathery hillside and ascend to the summit cairn (**5.5km; 460m; 2h 10min**).

Pass north over the summit, then head north-east to the rocky knoll of Drochaid an Droma. From here, continue round to Sròn nan Colan (590m) and descend east over knolls to a fence surrounding the old lead mine workings. Some of the workings are unfenced and all are unstable so keep your distance. From here, zigzag west on a good path through the mine debris littering the hillside to a scree cone and conifers. The scree becomes grassy then bare again, after which an ill-defined grassy path leads right and down through the trees to a cattle creep carrying the burn under the railway. If the level of the burn makes access difficult, the path and grassy track on the south side of the railway lead south-east to the lower station. Pass under the railway and follow the prepared path to the WHW and turn left back to Tyndrum (**10km; 540m; 3h 25min**).

Anyone climbing Meall Odhar and Fiarach in the same day (on foot or using a bike) should access the Cononish road direct from the car park at Dalrigh (NN344291) on the A82. Although the distance is the same as from Tyndrum, the circuit as described above from Dalrigh involves an extra 2km along the West Highland Way from Tyndrum Lower Station back to the car park.

Meall Odhar can be linked with the Corbett Beinn Chuirn via the col between the two. Follow the old boundary fence posts through a break in the forestry, go over a deer fence, and climb 410m up Beinn Chuirn's east face to the summit.

Meall Odhar from Gleann Auchreoch to the east (Tom Prentice)

Meall nan Gabhar, Beinn Bhalgairean

Meall nan Gabhar; 744m; (G20); L50; NN235240; hill of the goats
Beinn Bhalgairean; 636m; (G187); L50; NN202241; mountain of the fox

Meall nan Gabhar from Beinn Bhalgairean (Tom Prentice)

Were it not for Meall nan Gabhar's impressively steep north face, these two mountains would be lost among the giants of the Ben Lui massif, which tower above the A85 on the south side of Glen Lochy. Set back from the road and in full, unrestricted view, Meall nan Gabhar questions the mountain knowledge of passing hillwalkers and delivers a clear 'climb me' challenge. Something the retiring and less well-defined summit of Beinn Bhalgairean cannot do.

Both hills can be climbed together from the access track to Succoth Lodge, signposted Succoth, which is located off the A85 at NN193275, about 350m west of the turning to Glen Orchy and just east of the access track to the houses at Corryghoil. Park in a layby at the start of the track. It may also be possible to park further up the track at the bridge over the Eas a' Ghaill, saving about 1.8km on the day.

It should be noted that there has been extensive felling below both mountains with the construction of tracks for logging lorries. Further felling is certain and may significantly alter the landscape and both restrict and improve access in the future.

Follow the track to a four-way junction at a bridge over the Eas a' Ghaill river. Two routes are possible from here; one up the north-east side of the Eas a' Ghaill, which is the main route described, and the other up the south-west side (described at the end) which is more suitable for those using bikes, or happy with a total of 10km forest track walking.

The main route follows the old drovers' road from Dalmally to Inverarnan on Loch Lomond, via Succoth Lodge and while it can be wet in places and obstructed by fallen trees (all easily passable) it gives softer and more enjoyable walking. Turn left over the bridge, signposted Succoth, then keep right alongside the river, passing Railway Cottages and under the railway to a T-junction at Succoth. Turn right between two houses to a gated grassier track down on the right.

Follow this track as it ascends beside the river, firstly through beautiful broadleaf woodland then conifers, felled in places, to emerge at a clearing below electricity pylons. Ascend intermittant atv tracks below the pylon line for 400m to an upper forestry track. Cross over and continue on another grassy atv track up the clearing to a deer fence and gate at the forest edge. From here, continue up the corrie past the Ben Lui National Nature Reserve sign and two pylons, to below the east face of Meall nan Gabhar, which looks

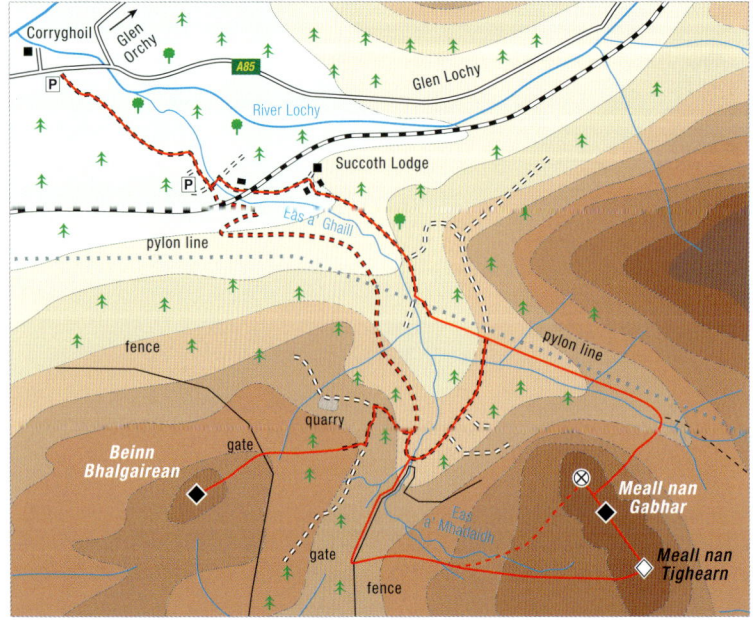

steeper and bigger than it is.

Cross south over the burn and ascend the face left of the craggier central section. This offers a surprisingly straightforward and grassy ascent to the col between Meall nan Gabhar's two summits. Although the OS 1:25k and 1:50k maps show the northern top as the 743m highpoint, the 1:10k map and a survey confirm the south-eastern top is 1m higher. Turn right and first ascend the north-east top for the view, then return to the col and climb to the south-east top (**7km; 700m; 2h 45min**).

Continue south-east to the top of Meall nan Tighearn (739m), then descend in a westerly direction close to the Eas a' Mhadaidh, heading for a gate at NN216239 in the deer fence enclosing the forestry surrounding Beinn Bhalgairean. The fence is not high and easily climbed if necessary.

Go through the gate and follow the fence north-east beside conifers then felling to reach the main forestry track where it loops around the Allt Coire Làir. Turn left and continue to a junction. This is where the alternative forest track route, which can be biked, up the south-west side of the Eas a' Ghaill arrives from below.

Turn left and ascend this track for 380m to NN217249, then turn left along another track. After 250m, turn right up a narrower track, then follow the continuation atv track across rough ground to a gate in the deer fence at NN209245. The gentle eastern flanks now lead to an old cairn on the most westerly of two hillocks (**13km; 1045m; 4h 50min**).

Ben Cruachan dominates the view to the north-west, with the Grahams of Beinn Donachain and Beinn na Sròine to the north and north-east.

Retrace the route to the junction on the main track. To return via Succoth, turn right and follow the track down to the pylon clearing and the outward route (**21km; 1045m; 7h**).

Alternatively, turn left and descend the forest track on the west side of the Eas a' Ghaill to the bridge and parking, in the same overall time and distance.

For the alternative route up the south-west side of the Eas a' Ghaill, which involves a greater distance on forest tracks, don't cross the bridge over the Eas a' Ghaill, but continue straight ahead and ascend to the track junction below Beinn Bhalgairean.

Ascend Beinn Bhalgairean (**7km; 590m; 2h 30min**) as already described, then Meall nan Gabhar (**12km; 985m; 4h 25min**) via the fence and the west face, before returning over Meall nan Tighearn.

Return to the track and retrace the ascent route to the start in the same overall time as the Succoth route (**21km; 1045m; 7h**).

For mountain bikers, the forest track on the south-west side of the Eas a' Ghaill offers a relentless uphill route, although the gradients are never excessive and the surface is generally good. The return is exhilaratingly fast, downhill almost the whole way to the parking and can save at least an hour on the day.

Beinn Bhalgairean from Meall nan Gabhar – Cruachan massif with Beinn a' Chochuill and Beinn Eunaich right. Distant Ben More and the Mull Grahams (Rab Anderson)

Creag na h-Eararuidh and Beinn Dearg from Glen Artney (Rab Anderson)

SECTION 1b
Loch Lomond to Loch Tay

Section 1b – Loch Lomond to Loch Tay

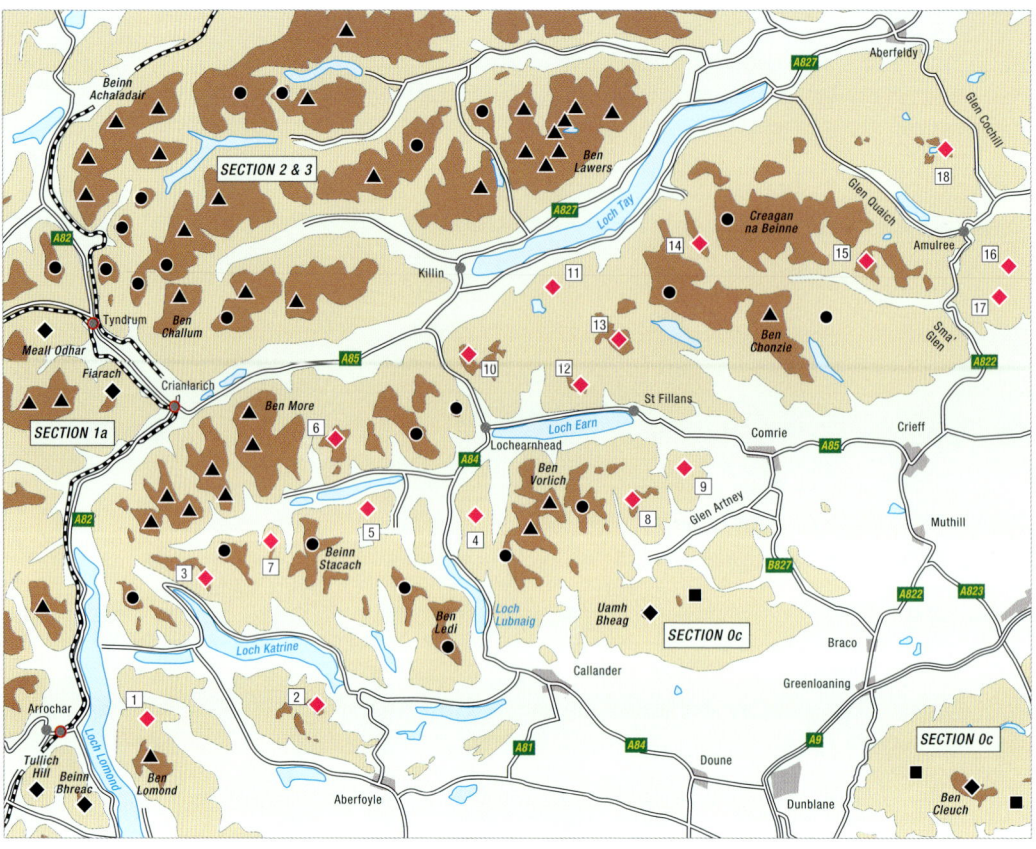

SECTION 1b

[1] *Cruinn a' Bheinn*	111
[2] *Ben Venue*	112
[3] *Meall Mòr*	114
[4] *Sgiath a' Chàise*	115
[5] *Creag Mhòr*	116
[6] *The Stob*	118
[7] *Stob Breac*	119
[8] *Creag na h-Eararuidh*	120
[9] *Mòr Bheinn*	121
[10] *Meall Buidhe*	122
[11] *Creag Gharbh*	123
[12] *Creag Each*, [13] *Creag Ruadh*	124
SHEE OF ARDTALNAIG [14] *Ciste Buidhe a' Claidheimh*	126
[15] *Beinn na Gainimh*	127
[16] *Meall nan Caorach*, [17] *Meall Reamhar*	128
[18] *Meall Dearg*	129

Cruinn a' Bheinn and Ben Lomond (Andrew Fraser)

Cruinn a' Bheinn; 632m; (G192); L56; NN365051; *roundness of the mountain*

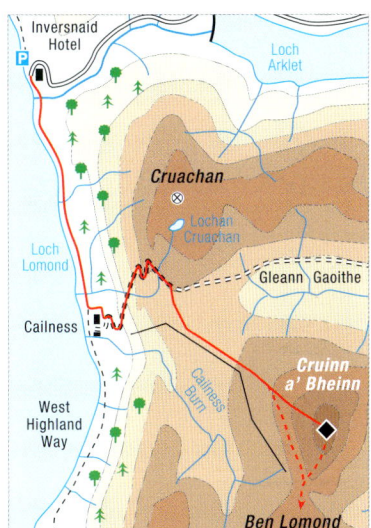

A number of fine Grahams flank the shores of Loch Lomond, their deep glens and craggy sides scoured by repeated periods of glaciation into classic mountain profiles. Unfortunately the glaciers gave Cruinn a' Bheinn fewer favours, grinding it into a bit of a rounded lump, compared with lofty and majestic Ben Lomond next door.

While the views from the summit are good, the hill's lowly height and set back position from the lochshore, means they aren't as grand as those from the Grahams perched on Loch Lomond's western shore.

However, what Cruinn a' Bheinn lacks in character it more than makes up for in the beauty of its approach. The route along the West Highland Way south from Inversnaid passes through glorious oak woodland, while the track above Cailness offers truly spectacular views across Loch Lomond to the surrounding mountains.

Park at the Inversnaid Hotel, follow the West Highland Way (WHW) signs south round the front of the hotel and cross the bridge over the Inversnaid falls. The WHW is now followed without deviation through the lochside woodland and out into open grassland to arrive at the red and white painted cottage of Cailness.

Before reaching the cottage, cut up the bank beside a bushy drainage channel to reach the fence above then go along this and pass through a gap where it meets the fence around the cottage. This gains a track which leads steeply up the hillside in a series of zigzags. Almost at its highest point, before it breaks over into broad Gleann Gaoithe, and with Cruinn a' Bheinn now visible to the south-east, leave the track to follow a fence down on the right across the moorland. When the fence swings away, continue uphill by the line of an old fence to a final short, steep slope leading to the relatively flat summit area. A small cairn at the south-western end of the high ground marks the top (**7.5km; 630m; 2h 40min**). Return by the same route (**15km; 640m; 4h 30min**).

An ascent of Ben Lomond's unfrequented north ridge is easily made from here by descending south-west to the Bealach Cruinn a' Bheinn, then climbing the ridge to join the well worn 'Ptarmigan' path beyond Pt.768m. The path leads up the rocky north-west ridge to the summit. Return to the bealach and follow the fence back; an added 6km, 520m, 2h 40min to the day.

Ben Venue

Ben Venue; *729m; (G52); L57; NN474063; small, or pointed mountain*

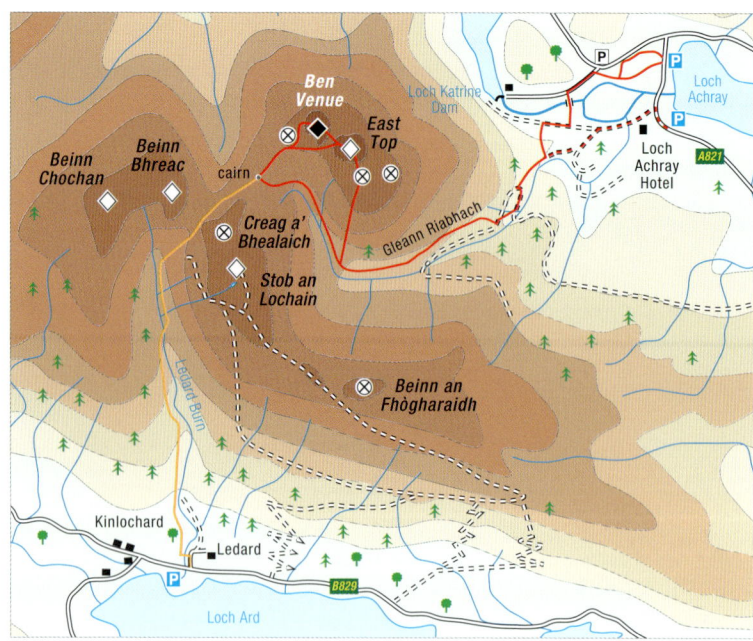

'High on the south, huge Benvenue
Down to the lake in masses threw
Crags, knolls, and mounds, confusedly hurled,
The fragments of an earlier world;'

Published in 1810, Walter Scott's epic poem, *Lady of the Lake*, heralds a change in the Lowland perception of the Highlands from an area of malevolence to be feared and avoided, to an area of romantic scenic beauty to be embraced and experienced.

Scott mentions a number of Trossachs mountains, but none as many times as Ben Venue. *Lady of the Lake* attracted the tourists and later the hillwalkers to Ben Venue, making it one of the country's best-loved small mountains, a position it retains to this day.

There are two principal approaches, from Loch Achray to the east or Ledard on Loch Ard to the south. Loch Achray lies at the heart of The Trossachs and has always been the most popular approach. However, much of the route is through forest which is being steadily felled with the path closures, tracks, and debris that entails. The approach from Ledard offers a more satisfying hillwalk, combining fine oak and birch woodland at the start with a traverse through dramatic mountain scenery to meet the Loch Achray route south-west of the summit.

The Loch Achray route can be started from three locations; the Ben Venue pay and display car park (NN506069), a pull-off at the start of the private road to Loch Katrine Dam (NN500068) and a layby on Loch Achray (NN506064). The path from the Ben Venue car park passes the parking on the Loch Katrine Dam road. The layby on Loch Achray allows a slightly shorter approach via the Loch Achray Hotel, about 200m to the north-west, and joins the Ben Venue car park route at NN494060.

From the Ben Venue car park, paths at the left and right corners form a loop, so follow either to where they join (the left is slightly shorter) then descend with views ahead to Ben Venue to meet the Loch Katrine Dam access road where there is parking for a few cars. Turn left and follow the road for about 560m, then take a path which goes off left to a footbridge over the Achray Water.

On the other side, ascend to a track and turn right, signposted Ben Venue. Follow the track for about 340m to a waymarked path on the left, with two large boulders at its base. A steep ascent through conifers is followed by a steep descent to a track; the route from Loch Achray Hotel.

The alternative approach via Loch Achray Hotel starts from the layby on Loch Achray. Walk north along the road then up the access road to the back of the hotel and a gated track signposted Ben Venue, which ascends into the forest above the Achray Water. Turn left at a track junction, signposted Ben Venue and continue to a second track junction. Veer right here, the mountain is straight ahead, to meet the car park route descending from the conifers on the right.

Both routes now continue as a prepared path leading to a forest

Ben Venue summit above Loch Katrine (Tom Prentice)

Ben Venue 113

Ben Venue and Loch Achray from the east (Tom Prentice)

track. Turn left and follow this for about 150m to a path on the right, marked by a cairn and beside a burn. Ascend this rough, mountain path through felling to reach a higher track, where a left then right turn regains the path. Further felled areas are passed on the ascent of Gleann Riabhach and the path can be waterlogged in places.

Exit the last of the forestry to the open hillside and cross a section of boardwalk. Continue north up the corrie on an obvious but rough and often boggy path, with views up towards the summit, the left-hand of Ben Venue's two highpoints. Ascend right of the Spùt Bàn waterfall and continue north-west for 600m to reach a col marked by a prominent cairn.

Ascend the eroded path to NN473063, where it traverses a small top above a col directly below the main peak. The path divides here, the right-hand branch dropping to the col, then traversing right below the main peak towards the lower East Top with its trig point. Follow the left-hand path to the far side of the col and ascend the rocky west ridge to the summit cairn on top of the rocky highpoint (**6.5km; 670m; 2h 35min**).

Continue south-east beside an old fenceline to meet the path left earlier, which leads to the East Top (727m). From there, descend south to a prominent knoll, then continue south-west down grassy slopes to regain the Gleann Riabhach path, which is followed back to the start (**12km; 730m; 4h**).

The southern route starts from a large pull-off (NN459023) on the B829 west of Aberfoyle, at the foot of the access road to Ledard Farm, on the shore of Loch Ard. Follow the access road, signed to Ben Venue, to a gate on the left and go through. Cross a bridge over the Ledard Burn and continue round Ledard waterfall to a path on its left side which ascends through oak woodland. Pass over a section of boardwalk and through a gate in a deer fence, protecting new broadleaf planting.

Higher in the woodland, the path divides at a marker post (NN459034). Turn sharp left uphill, the path soon levels out, and continue to open hillside. Higher up the path crosses the Ledard Burn at a rocky section where care is needed if the burn is in spate.

Go over a stile in the deer fence beyond and continue up the glen to the col between Creag a' Bhealaich and Beinn Bhreac. The Graham Tops of Beinn Bhreac (700m), Beinn Chochan (703m) and Stob an Lochain (684m) can be climbed from the col, although they add little aesthetically to the route and give rough going over wet and heathery terrain.

Cross the stile at the col and traverse north-east below Creag a' Bhealaich to the prominent cairn on the route from Gleann Riabhach described earlier. Ascend the eroded path to NN473063, where it traverses a small top above a col directly below the main peak. The path divides here, the right-hand branch dropping to the col, then traversing right below the main peak towards the lower East Top with its trig point. Follow the left-hand path to the far side of the col and ascend the rocky west ridge to the summit cairn on top of the rocky highpoint (**5km; 690m; 2h 15min**).

Continue to the East Top (727m), then descend on the main path back to the prominent cairn. From there, return to the start by the line of ascent (**10km; 720m; 3h 40min**).

Meall Mòr

Meall Mòr; 747m; (G16); L50, 56; NN383151; *big hill*

Located at the western end of the high ground separating Loch Katrine from Lochs Doine and Voil, Meall Mòr offers the hillwalker two routes with very different characters. Bikes can be used on both routes and will shorten the on foot return timings given by about 1h 30min.

Although the northern approach from Inverlochlarig allows Meall Mòr to be combined with the Graham Stob Breac, a more interesting and satisfying round can be had from Loch Katrine to the south. The only downsides are that new planting restricts access to the steep southern slopes and summer bracken can make for heavy going.

The route starts at Stronachlachar on Loch Katrine, gained by car from the B829 from Aberfoyle, or via the steamer Sir Walter Scott <www.lochkatrine.com> from Trossachs Pier to Stronachlachar (restricted winter service). The route can also be approached from the Trossachs Pier car park via a 16km bike ride along the private road on the north side of Loch Katrine, with a return via steamer if desired.

Meall Mòr above Loch Katrine and Glengyle house (Tom Prentice)

From the Stronachlachar car park and cafe, follow the road 5km to the track up Glen Gyle, about 300m north-west of The Dhu. The track leads below pylon wires to the Glengyle Water which is crossed on a sleeper bridge. Continue alongside a fence and after 200m cross a burn, turn right and follow it up the steep hillside to reach a fence. Cross this at a wooden section on the far right near the burn and continue to above a line of crags, where the angle eases.

Cross right over the burn and head north-east to the summit. This lies some distance back and is the right-hand of two similar knolls, east of a lochan and south of the fence posts (**8.5km; 630m; 3h**).

The view north to the Munro giants Beinn Chabhair, An Caisteal, Beinn a' Chroin, Cruach Ardrain, Stob Binnein and Ben More is spectacular.

The ridge is now followed south-east then north-east beside the fence posts and over the East Top and various knolls, to the much more attractive Graham Top of Stob an Duibhe overlooking the unnamed loch below Stob a' Choin. Descend south-east from here to the Bealach na Cloiche, followed by a steady ascent to An Garadh (**12km; 850m; 4h 10min**).

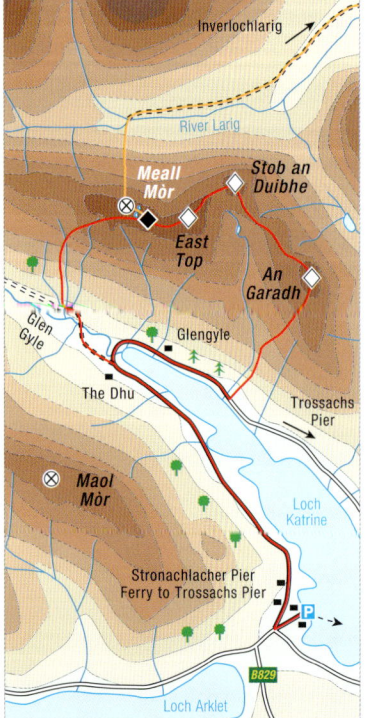

The summit of Meall Mòr and Ben Lomond (Tom Prentice)

Sgiath a' Chàise 115

Sgiath a' Chàise; 645m; (G180); L57; NN583169; wing-shaped hill of the cheese

Crowning the high ground dividing Strathyre and Glen Ample, Sgiath a' Chàise is a long grassy ridge surrounded by forestry and topped by a number of craggy summits. The smallest and most impressive of these is Creag a' Gheata, overlooking Loch Lubnaig and the A84.

The hill is easily climbed via the right of way from Loch Lubnaig to Loch Earn, which ascends the glen north of Ardchullarie More to the watershed, then descends Glen Ample to Edinample. It is a short though pleasant outing with fine views north to the Ben Lawers range and could be combined with an ascent of the fine Corbett Beinn Each on the east side of the glen.

Start at a layby on the north side of the A84 just west of Ardchullarie More, at the bend in Loch Lubnaig.

From the south end of the layby, take the path signposted to Loch Earn via Glen Ample, up the side of ▶

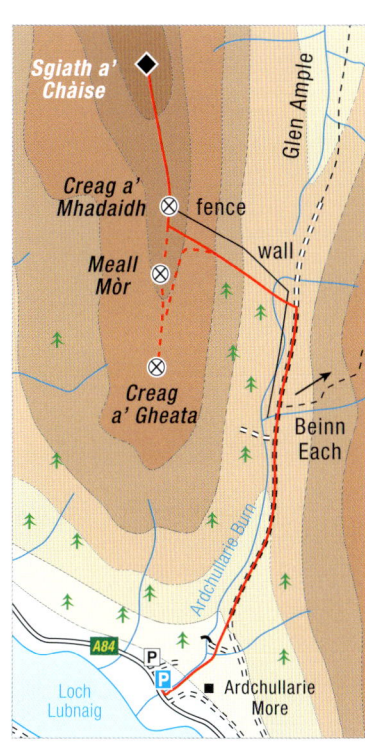

From there, descend south-south-west towards the burn in the corrie to reach the upper limit of a fence enclosing the lower part the hillside and a gate at NN399136. Go through and follow the fence and atv track to another gate, then straight down to a third gate to reach the road east of the white railing bridge over the burn. Turn right and follow the road past Glengyle back to Stronachlachar (**21km; 850m; 6h 30min**).

The northern ascent starts from the car park before Inverlochlarig (NN446185) and involves a 7.5km approach south-west beside the River Larig to where the track ends at NN384164 and the river forks. Cross the river, easy when the water is low, and make a steep ascent direct to the summit. The highest point is marked by a small cairn and is the furthest of two knolls, east of a small lochan and south of a line of fence posts (**9km; 620m; 3h**). Return the same way (**18km; 620m; 5h 15min**).

It is possible to continue east over Stob an Duibhe and the Corbett Stob a' Choin to Stob Breac (see p119). However, this will involve a lot of ascent and descent, and if a bike has been used for the approach, Stob Breac can more easily be climbed in a single day with Meall Mòr, by returning first to Inverlochlarig.

Sgiath a' Chàise, right, and Creag a' Mhadaidh above Glen Ample, from the flanks of Beinn Each (Tom Prentice)

Sgiath a' Chàise

The summit of Sgiath a' Chàise with Ben Lawers beyond (Tom Prentice)

Creag Mhòr; 658m; (G162); L57; NN510185; *big cliff*

Creag Mhòr lies at the north-eastern end of the high ground separating Lochs Doine and Voil from Loch Katrine, and is the lowest of the four Grahams in the area.

Its northern and eastern flanks are forested, complicating access from Balquhidder. However, the hill is easily ascended from Ballimore in Glen Buckie to the south and offers a delightful route over a knobbly, grassy ridge with fine views across the Braes of Balquhidder to the Graham The Stob and the Munro giants Ben More and Stob Binnein.

This ascent is short though, and while this presents an opportunity to bag another Graham in the vicinity on the same day, such as The Stob, the route over Creag Mhòr can also be extended to the nearby Corbett Beinn Stacach (previously known as Stob Fear-tomhais). This produces a fine round of the Fathan Glinne and is the route described here.

the Ardchullarie Burn, between it and the boundary fence around Ardchullarie More. At the top corner of the fence, cross a burn then continue up through the trees, crossing a hydro track, to emerge onto the main forestry track. Follow this to exit the forestry by a gate.

On the left, the craggy flanks of Creag a' Gheata give way to Meall Mòr and the pointed top of Creag a' Mhadaidh, with the grassy dome of Sgiath a' Chàise beyond.

Where the main track turns left, continue on the track through the glen. Shortly after fording a burn, Eas an Eoin, a signpost indicates the route to Beinn Each up the slope on the right; the inclusion of this adds 3.5km, 480m, 1h 50min to the route.

Continue for another 600m, almost to the watershed, to where a track goes off left towards the wall marking the lower boundary of the conifers.

Follow this track through a gap in the wall, swing left onto a grassy track and gain the hillside beyond. Climb the heathery hillside right of the trees to gain the crest just south of the pointed top of Creag a' Mhadaidh (557m). Now follow the broad grassy ridge across a shallow col cut by peat hags to gain an old fenceline which leads to the unmarked highpoint (**4km; 520m; 1h 45min**).

Another highpoint 750m to the north is 1m lower. Return by the route of ascent (**8km; 530m; 2h 45min**).

For anyone not in a hurry to descend, the route can be extended over Creag a' Mhadaidh and Meall Mòr to Creag a' Gheata for fine views south over Loch Lubnaig to Benvane and Ben Ledi. Unfortunately, there is no easy way through the forestry below, so a return must be made back past Meall Mòr; an added 2.5km, 100m, 50min to the route.

From Balquhidder, drive south up Glen Buckie to where the public road ends at a cattle grid and bridge over the river. Park on the left just before the access road to Ballimore farm.

Walk back along the road, turn left onto a track just before a bungalow and ascend to a gate in the high deer fence on the left. Up and right of this is another gate in a stock fence. Go through this gate and ascend diagonally up and right, heading for the corner of the conifer plantation, where a gap in the fence gives access to the open hillside.

Ascend the broad ridge with increasingly fine views to gain the hummocky summit ridge, marked by small, rocky escarpments of upturned mica-schist. The summit lies on one of these and is marked by a small cairn (**2.5km; 480m; 1h 20min**).

Immediately north-north-west across Loch Voil is The Stob, a hill whose summit is as hard to locate from a distance as it is close up! To the east, three lines of hills separate Glen Buckie, Strathyre and Glen Ample. The closest hill is knobbly

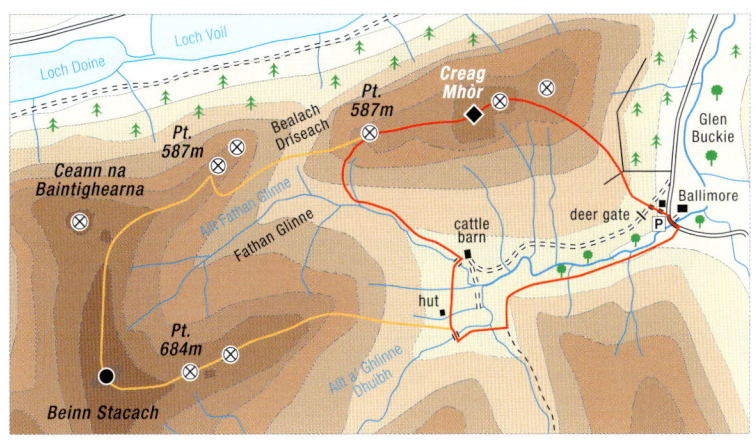

Beinn an t-Sìthein, a Sub 2000ft Marilyn. The middle hill is a long grassy ridge with forested lower regions, the Graham Sgiath a' Chàise, while the furthest line is formed by the impressive craggy buttresses of the Corbett Beinn Each and Munros, Stùc a' Chroin and Ben Vorlich.

Descend the ridge west, avoiding or taking in the last top to the south, towards the Bealach Driseach. From here it is possible to return to Ballimore by following animal paths south then south-east beside the Allt Fathan Glinne to a cattle barn. To do so, cross the bridge over the burn and traverse south towards a small hut with a corrugated iron roof, beyond which there is a footbridge over the Allt a' Ghlinne Dhuibh at NN508156. On the other side, follow the river east to a junction with the tributary joining from the south. Cross this and the fence beyond and ascend to a path; the right of way between Glen Buckie and Glen Finglas. Turn left and follow the boggy and occasionally ill-defined path north then east to the Ballimore road (**9.5km; 500m; 3h**).

If continuing to Beinn Stacach from the Bealach Driseach, continue south-west and climb grassy slopes on the south-west side of Pt.587m to gain a broad ridge. Climb this south-west alongside an old fence towards Ceann na Baintighearna. About 500m before its top, the fence swings south and broad slopes lead to the trig point on Beinn Stacach. A small pile of stones just to the east marks the highest point (**8km; 900m; 3h 20min**).

Descend south-east then east to gain the long north-east ridge and follow it over the distinctive pointed top of Pt.684m. Continue on the ridge until grassy slopes can be descended east to reach the footbridge over the Allt a' Ghlinne Dhuibh at NN508156, just south of the small hut with a corrugated iron roof. Cross the bridge to gain the right of way path and follow this back to Ballimore as described above (**15km; 950m; 5h**).

Creag Mhòr from Glen Buckie to the south (Tom Prentice)

The Stob

***The Stob**; 753m; (G9); L51; NN491231; the stub*

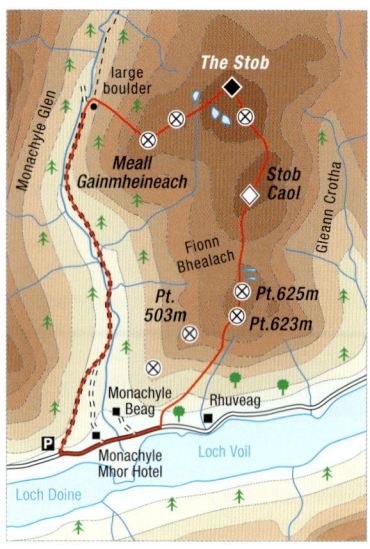

An illusive summit from all directions, near and far, The Stob marks the highest point on the ridge between the Monachyle Glen and Gleann Crotha above the Braes of Balquhidder.

Viewing the hill from a distance, the eye is drawn to the more prominent southern peak, the Graham Top of Stob Caol; 734m and a mere 19m lower. The actual summit lies further north, a rocky stub on a ridge of mica-schist. It rises only 20m above the surrounding moorland and is difficult to identify, making The Stob a navigational challenge in poor visibility. The summit area also carries the name Meall na Frean.

Park at the start of the track up Monachyle Glen, about 350m west of the turning to the Monachyle Mhor Hotel. Follow the track for 3.5km up the glen, first on the west side of the Monachyle Burn, then on the east, to where it ends at a footbridge over the burn (NN475230). Do not cross over but continue on the path on the east side of the burn, past a large boulder to a firebreak.

Follow the firebreak to where the trees end and continue steeply up the hillside, heading rightwards towards crags on the skyline to gain a deer fence. Follow this up and left to just left of the crags, where there are various gaps in the fence as it passes over a small rocky knoll at NN480227.

Continue ascending, either taking in the top of Meall Gainmheineach, or passing to its north then go over Pt.666m and on to Pt.687m beyond to gain the edge of the summit plateau. The summit lies some 750m to the north-east, marked by a cairn on a raised rocky ridge crossed by an old fence (**5.5km; 620m; 2h 25min**).

From the summit, go south over a small knoll, then leave the fence, descend to a col and ascend to the top of Stob Caol. Continue south across the Fionn Bhealach and over the slight rise of Pt.625m to Pt.623m overlooking Loch Voil. Leave the ridge at this point, descending south over open slopes (named Coire Bheathag on the OS 1:25k map) to reach a broad grassy gully with a burn.

Descend this, avoiding the bracken, to a fence enclosing the woodland below. Animal tracks lead west beside the fence to a wooden gate beside a wall at NN481199. Cross over, descend the left side of the wall to a gap, go through, and continue down to a ladder stile and the road. Follow the road right to the start (**10.5km; 730m; 4h**).

The broad summit of The Stob, centre left, with the more prominent top of Stob Caol just to its right (Tom Prentice)

Stob Breac

Stob Breac from the flanks of Stob Binnein (Tom Prentice)

Stob Breac; 688m; (G121); L57; NN447166; *speckled stub*

As the name states, Stob Breac is a bit of a stub, but it is a fine viewpoint and offers a number of routes.

All start from the car park before Inverlochlarig (NN446185). Exit right (south) from the car park onto an old tarmac road signposted Blaircreich Estate and keep left through a gate to cross a bridge over the Inverlochlarig Burn, then a bridge over the River Larig signposted to Blaircreich farm.

Go past a bungalow, then turn left at the next junction and through a gate in the deer fence, or over the stile, and zigzag up a grassy track to a junction. Firebreaks on both sides of the mountain offer ascent lines, but those on the west are steeper and harder to locate. A frontal ascent involves a deer fence and new planting and is not recommended.

Turn left (east) and traverse the hill to the first good firebreak on the east side (NN455174), which contains the Allt a' Choire Bhàin. Ascend beside this, the forest appears to close higher up but doesn't, to a narrow section requiring care beside a small waterfall, to exit the trees to open hillside. Continue beside the burn up the obvious rift, then ascend right (west) to the summit, marked by a cairn (**5km; 560m; 2h**). Return the same way (**10km; 560m; 3h 25min**).

A more interesting walk can be had by heading south along Stob Breac's elevated ridge. This leads over two distinctive tops and assorted knolls to An Stuchd (**7km; 650m; 2h 35min**), which has fine views south to Loch Katrine and the double-topped summit of the Graham Ben Venue.

A return is now possible down tracks on the west side of Stob Breac or over the Corbett Stob a' Choin. For the track route, descend south-west to a fence and follow it beside a burn to a firebreak in the trees. Where the burn joins the Allt Sgionie turn right and follow a path beside that burn to a track back to the outward route and the car park (**12.5km; 650m; 4h**).

For Stob a' Choin, continue beside the fence to a stile at NN442146, cross over and descend to the Allt Sgionie. From here, ascend north-west initially over grassy and hummocky ground, then more steeply to Pt.736m and a little further north to Pt.836m, marked by a small cairn atop a small crag. Continue north-west on the ridge over Meall Reamhar to reach the summit of Stob a' Choin (**11km; 1230m; 4h 35min**).

Carry on to the North Top and go down the north ridge for about 560m to near the 630m contour. From there, go east and north-east across the burn draining from the Bealach Coire an Laoigh to reach a footbridge over the River Larig at NN427175. Now follow a track to Inverlochlarig and the road (**15.5km; 1230m; 6h**).

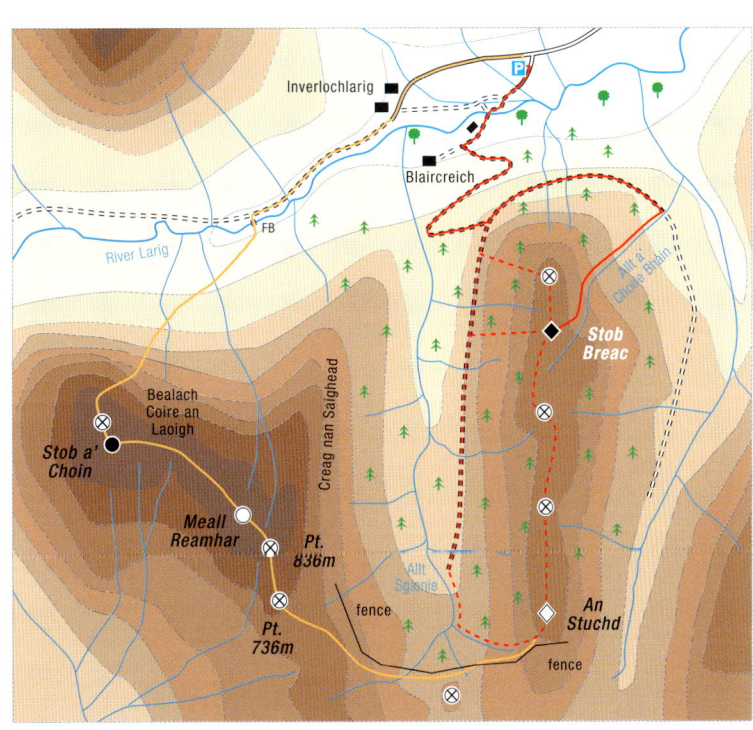

Creag na h-Eararuidh, left, and Beinn Dearg (Tom Prentice)

Creag na h-Eararuidh; *708m; (G86); L57; NN685189*

While the hills on the south side of Glen Artney lie in the Lowlands (see Uamh Bheag in Section 0c), two Grahams on the north side are in the Highlands; the Highland Boundary Fault running the length of the glen. These hills can be combined into a single round, but this involves climbing a deer fence, something which will not suit everyone. Thankfully Creag na h-Eararuidh and Mòr Bheinn also make enjoyable routes when climbed separately and are described in that way.

Beinn Dearg (707m) used to be the highest point, but surveys have confirmed that Creag na h-Eararuidh (formerly Stùc na Càbaig) is in fact 1m higher and now the Graham. The OS 1:25k map (but not the 1:50k map) has been updated to reflect this height change, but not the name. Both hills are climbed on a pleasant round of Coire a' Choire, starting from a car park (NN711161) below Glen Artney church.

Walk north-east back up the road to a track on the left and follow it down past Dalchruin to a bridge. Cross the Water of Ruchill, keeping right at the first junction, then left shortly after and pass through a gate to reach Dalclathick. Follow the now grassy track past ruins and a plantation on the left to a stile in a wall giving access to the open hillside. Continue ascending alongside a fence enclosing a broadleaf plantation on the south side of the Allt Coire Choire to reach a gate.

Ascend almost due west and climb the broad bulk of the Graham Top Sròn na Maoile (618m), initially rough then rocky. The worst of the peat hags are turned to the north to gain a gentler, broad ridge and the ill-defined summit. Descend to the start of a more prominent knobbly ridge and follow this onto Sròn nam Broighleag (679m) then across a col (Bealach na Moine) to Creag na h-Eararuidh (**6.5km; 630m; 2h 30min**).

Continue round the steep-sided corrie and ascend to Pt.680m, beyond which the ridge leads over assorted small tops to the Graham Top of Beinn Dearg, marked by a small cairn (**8km; 750m; 3h**).

To the east, the Graham Mòr Bheinn and the Graham Top Ben Halton (621m) face Beinn Dearg across the Allt Glas and can be included by descending the north-east ridge as described at the end. However, to return directly to the start, descend east then south,

Mòr Bheinn, left, and Ben Halton from Beinn Dearg (Rab Anderson)

Mòr Bheinn

keeping to the right-hand (due south) of the two ridges which fall from the summit, to gain the lower reaches of Coire Innein. Continue down to gain a vague atv track with the occasional sleeper bridge, aiming for the Àth na Mèine ford across the Allt Coire Choire at NN707175. This lies above a small but impressive jammed boulder forming a natural arch above a waterfall on the burn.

Cross over and follow the atv track to the corner of the fence enclosing the broadleaf plantation on the south side of the Allt Coire Choire and the gate crossed on the ascent. Retrace the ascent route by the fence to the stile in the wall and back to the start (**14km; 800m; 4h 30min**).

To include Mòr Bheinn, descend due north from the summit for about 300m to avoid the steep north-east face, then north-east to gain the north-east ridge. Weave down grass between the rocky knolls on the ridge until slopes lead eastwards to marshy ground and the deer fence in the glen. Cross this at about NN707204 and ascend beside the old fence enclosing the forestry to gain the col between Ben Halton and Mòr Bheinn. From here, animal tracks lead north up to the rocky summit of Mòr Bheinn with its trig point (**11km; 1080m; 4h 30min**). Return as described for Mòr Bheinn, opposite, taking in the Graham Top of Ben Halton (621m) if desired (**18km; 1230m; 6h 30min**).

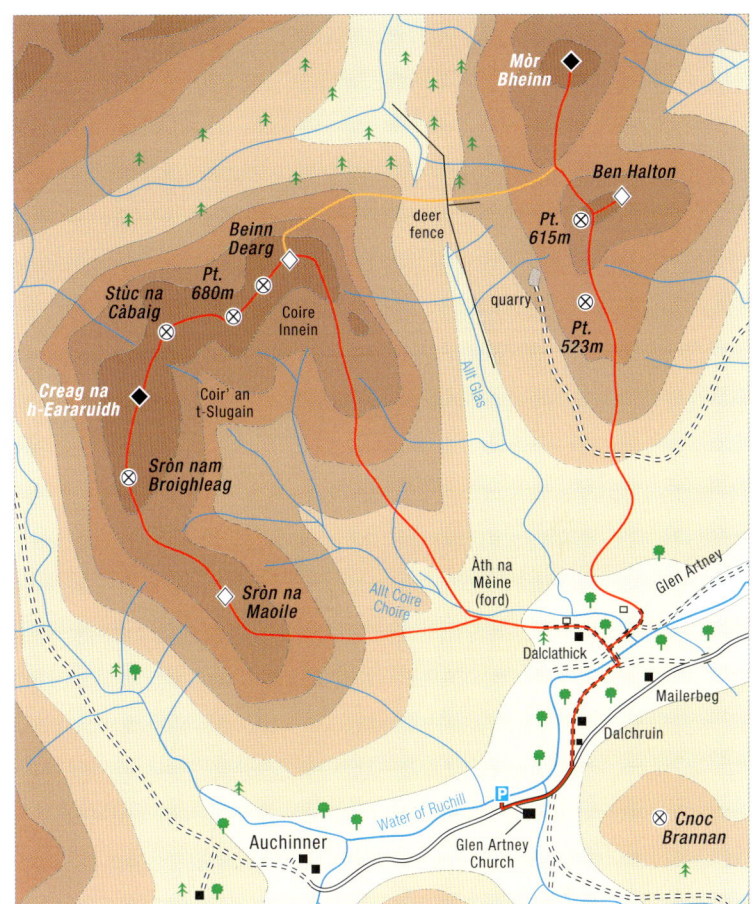

Mòr Bheinn; 640m; (G184); L51, 52, 57; NN716211; *big mountain*

Mòr Bheinn and its neighbour, the Graham Top of Ben Halton (621m), make a pleasant route by themselves, or they can be linked with Beinn Dearg opposite, providing you are prepared to scale the deer fence in the glen between them.

From the car park below Glen Artney church, walk north-east back up the road to a track on the left and follow it down past Dalchruin to a bridge. Cross over the Water of Ruchill and keep right at the junctions to cross a second smaller bridge.

About 60m past this bridge, turn left and ascend a grassy track to gain sheep pens, beyond which an atv track winds its way up through rough pasture to a wall. Go over this to a vehicle track and follow it left to a gate in the deer fence crossing it. Pass through, turn right and ascend the hillside on an atv track marked with wooden posts to a deer fence.

Cross the ladder stile and continue over boggy ground, keeping straight ahead where the atv veers right, and ascend the pathless heathery ridge to gain an elevated plateau of peat-encircled lochans and knolls, between Pt.615m and the Graham Top of Ben Halton (621m). Make a short detour north-east to the summit of Ben Halton before returning and descending north-west to the col below Mòr Bheinn, from where animal tracks lead up the south ridge to the rocky summit and trig point (**7km; 620m; 2h 35min**).

To the north-west, the Graham Creag Ruadh can be identified above St Fillans at the eastern end of Loch Earn, with the Graham Creag Each further to its west.

Return by the same route (**13.5km; 750m; 4h 25min**).

East across Glen Ogle to Meall Buidhe (Tom Prentice)

Meall Buidhe; 719m; (G66); L51; NN576275; yellow hill

Meall Buidhe, together with its adjacent neighbour, Beinn Leabhainn, provides a good short route with fine views. It makes an ideal ascent for a summer's evening, or a quick hit when passing up or down the A85.

Start from the car park at the picnic area on the east side of the road at the head of Glen Ogle (NN559285); the Làirig Cheile. For a number of months in the year there is a good mobile cafe here. Follow a track which heads east through a gate into a forestry plantation. After passing beneath an electricity pylon line, the track zigzags easily uphill through the forest out onto the open hillside, then climbs steadily around some crags to end at an incongruous communications aerial.

Leaving the aerial behind, the way ahead is south-east, aiming for a shallow col between Beinn Leabhainn and Meall Buidhe. The going is tougher, through heather and across boggy ground that is pathless save for the odd sheep track. Firmer ground is soon reached and this leads easily to the flat summit of Meall Buidhe (**3.5km; 430m; 1h 30min**).

There is a splendid view south down Glen Ogle over the head of Loch Earn to Ben Vorlich and Stùc a' Chroin. On her way to Lochearnhead in 1842, on one of her frequent visits to Scotland, Queen Victoria remarked in her diary of Glen Ogle's resemblance to the Khyber Pass!

Carrying on, descend north across a shallow col and climb to the top of the neighbouring and only slightly lower Beinn Leabhainn (709m), which is about 900m away. It is worth continuing north then south-west to take in the two northern highpoints. The view from here extends down the length of Loch Tay. Killin lies below, at the head of the loch, with Meall Tarmachan behind and the Ben Lawers group to the side. To the west along Glen Dochart lie Ben More and Stob Binnein.

The return is made by dropping steeply westwards through heather to regain the track, which is followed back (**7.5km; 500m; 2h 40min**).

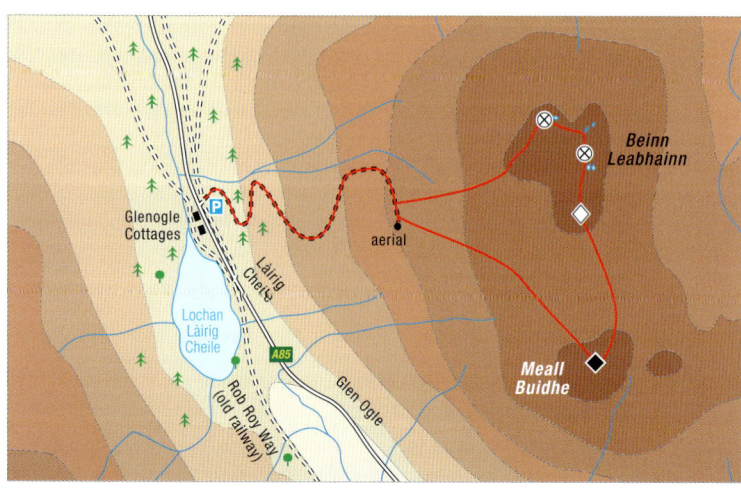

Creag Gharbh 123

Creag Gharbh; 637m; (G185); L51; NN632327; rough cliff

Located on the south side of Loch Tay, Creag Gharbh is a pleasant double-topped hill with a fine outlook across the loch to the Breadalbane Hills of the Meall Tarmachan and Ben Lawers groups. Start from Ardeonaig some 7 miles (11km) along the south Loch Tay road to the east of Killin. The Ardeonaig Hotel has a convenient car park and it should be possible to park here with permission.

At the post box opposite the hotel, walk uphill on the Braes of Ardeonaig road, following this past what was the Abernethy Trust Ardeonaig Outdoor Centre. This is the route of the Rob Roy Way long distance footpath. Beinn Ghlas and Ben Lawers dominate the view across the fields here. Shortly the road becomes a track and leads past a farm, then through gates onto more open hillside.

Cross a burn and, now on a path, head for a gate in a wall at the edge of a small plantation. Continue up the side of the burn in front of another small plantation, passing the ruins of old sheilings, and climb up onto a track traversing the hillside. This track runs alongside a pipeline carrying water to Loch Lednock Reservoir, which lies over the hills to

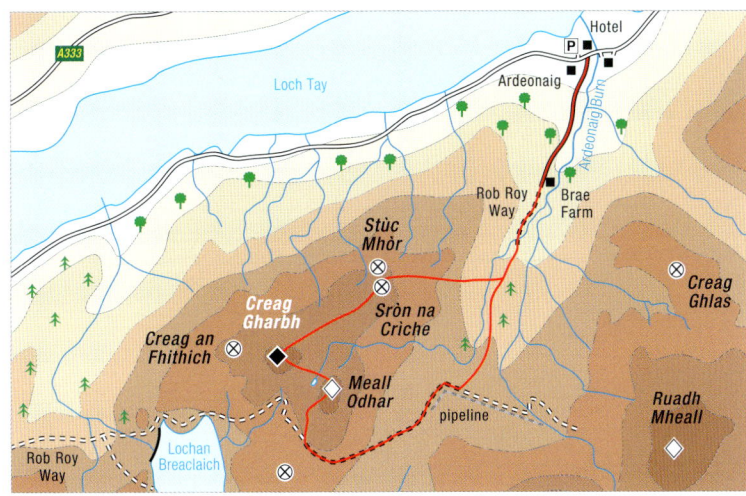

the south-east.

Walk south-westwards along the track, the pipeline soon disappears underground, then loop around the flanks of the hill and follow the track uphill to a communications aerial. Head across heathery ground and make the short ascent to the top of Meall Odhar (628m). The slightly higher summit of Creag Gharbh with its trig point lies on another knoll 900m to the north-west, reached across the somewhat boggy intervening ground (**7.5km; 570m; 2h 40min**). The view from here of the Ben Lawers and Tarmachan Hills is very fine indeed.

Descend the south-east shoulder back towards Ardeonaig, as far the knoll of Sròn na Crìche (562m) next to the knoll of Stùc Mhòr, then drop down east and follow first a fence then a wall back towards the small plantation passed on the ascent. A short distance before the gate, go through a gap in the wall and cut across to join the upward route, which leads back to the hotel car park (**13km; 590m; 4h**).

Creag Gharbh, far right, from Killin at the west end of Loch Tay (Tom Prentice)

Creag Each from the track in Glen Tarken (Rab Anderson)

Creag Each; 672m; (G142); L51; NN652263; horse cliff
Creag Ruadh; 712m; (G76); L51; NN674292; red cliff

Close to St Fillans on the sunny side of Loch Earn, these two hills are separated by the flat and boggy Glen Tarken but conveniently accessed by tracks. Start opposite the Loch Earn Sailing Club at Woodhouse, from one of two laybys on the A85, where a track (NN669247) leading up into Glen Tarken begins just west of a barn.

Follow the track which zigzags up through the trees past the old steadings of Wester Glentarken to swing round and ascend into the glen where Creag Each becomes visible on the left. Go through a gate in a wall by some sheep pens and after crossing the main burn (NN664261), which drains from beneath the top of the hill, leave the track just before it forks.

Climb the hillside to the right of the burn, aiming for an obvious cairn on the skyline to the east of the summit. The slopes to the left of the burn can

Clach Mhòr Na h-Airighe Lèithe, or the Glen Tarken Stone, with the summit of Creag Ruadh on the right (Rab Anderson)

also be climbed to gain the south shoulder of the hill. The top itself is defended by small crags, easily rounded (**3.5km; 580m; 1h 45min**).

To the north over the Graham of Creag Gharbh the Ben Lawers range dominates, while west beyond the Graham of Meall Buidhe lie Ben More and Stob Binnein. Ben Vorlich lies to the south over Loch Earn and to the east over Glen Tarken and Creag Ruadh is Ben Chonzie.

Descend by the north ridge, over heather and grass, passing some large boulders to reach a loop in the upper track, where it is joined by the lower track. This is just beyond an impressive huge boulder, Clach Mhòr Na h-Airigh Lèithe, or the Glen Tarken Stone; worth diverting to. From this descent, a gorge can be seen cutting into the hillside on the opposite side of the glen and the edge of this

Creag Ruadh from Creag Each (Ken Crocket)

provides the route up onto Creag Ruadh. The gorge is formed by the Allt Eas Domhain and has waterfalls. Although it is possible to cut directly across the glen to the gorge this is wet and boggy, so follow the track easily around the head of Glen Tarken to reach it.

Leave the track just to the east of the gorge and climb the hillside over grass and heather passing to the east of a small lochan; Loch Eas Domhain. The summit slopes are guarded by numerous outcrops and a delightful maze formed by them leads to the rocky top (**9km; 910m; 3h 30min**).

To the south-east over St Fillans and beyond the Graham Mòr Bheinn, the Ochils and the Lomond Hills complete the view.

To avoid a steep crag on the descent, initially go east to a col where easy grassy slopes lead down. Head for the outflow from Lochan na Creige Ruaidhe and pick up a faint path parallel to the burn, which leads down to the track in Glen Tarken again. Follow the track for 800m or so then take the right branch and descend to the floor of the glen and cross the Glentarken Burn via stepping stones. The track of the outward route is joined just above and this leads downhill back to the start (**15.5km; 930m; 5h 20min**).

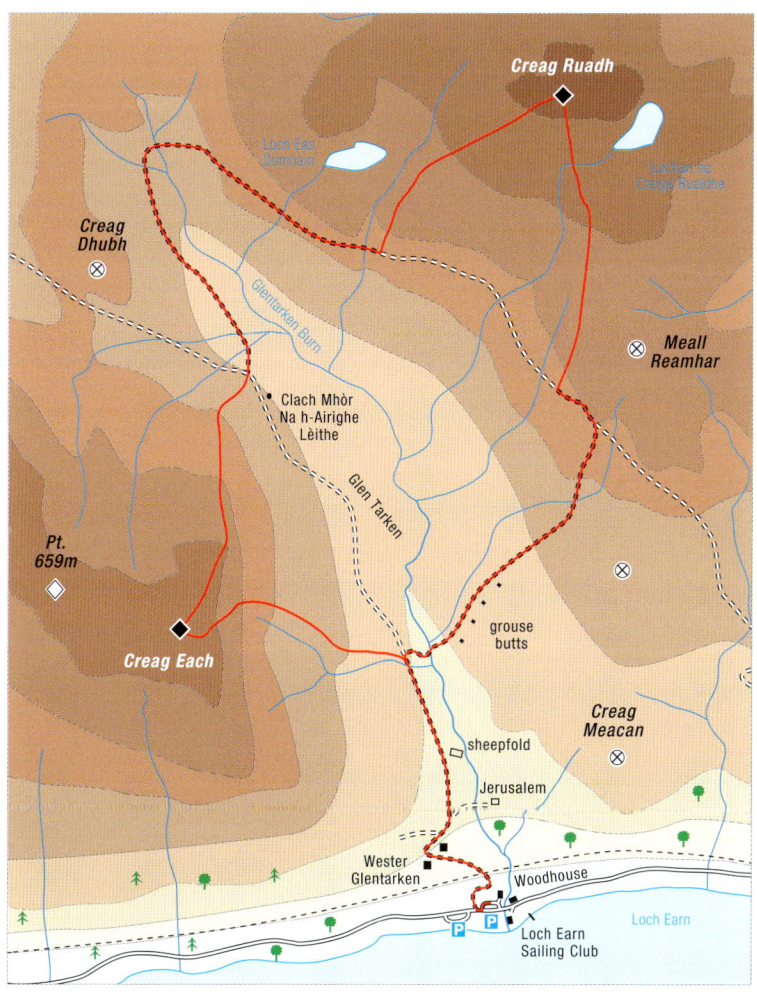

126 SHEE OF ARDTALNAIG Ciste Buidhe a' Claidheimh

> SHEE OF ARDTALNAIG; Pointed hill (above) Ardtalnaig
> **Ciste Buidhe a' Claidheimh**; 759m; (G4); L51, 52; NN729351; correctly Ciste Bhuidhe a' Chlaidheimh – the yellow chest of the sword, after the impressive rock-cleft north-east of the summit

Despite being flanked on both sides by higher and more extensive summits, this hill more than holds its own, thanks to its prominent profile when viewed from Loch Tay to the north and Glen Almond to the south-east.

Shee of Ardtalnaig relates directly to the whole hill and its profile, while the actual summit is named Ciste Buidhe a' Claidheimh. It offers an enjoyable short walk on its own, but it can also be linked with the two flanking Corbetts, most easily with Creagan na Beinne to the north.

Park at Milton of Ardtalnaig on the west side of the road just south of the bridge over the Ardtalnaig Burn (NN702392). Walk south up the hill, turn left just before the phone box and follow the road past the tennis courts (possible parking) and on for about 2km to Claggan farm.

Go rightwards through the farmyard to a track and cross a burn, beyond which the track divides. Take the right-hand track to a gate then leave the track and climb the frontal face to an atv track on the crest of the ridge. It is also possible to continue up the main track into Gleann a' Chloidh, from where it zigzags up to the ridge. Peat hags are a feature of this ridge and while they pose no problems in summer, the track does miss some of them and might offer pleasanter going if the weather is poor or conditions are very wet underfoot.

Follow the ridge through the hags, scattered with blocks of bleached mica-schist, silver sand and mountain hares. The worst of this ground is easily avoided by sticking to the east edge overlooking Gleann a' Chilleine. At the foot of the final steepening to the summit lies the impressive cleft of Bual a' Claidheimh, created by a rock slip. These features are common in mica-schist rock throughout the Southern Highlands, some of the most impressive being on the Corbett Ben Donich near Arrochar. A small pile of stones marks the summit (**5.5km; 630m; 2h 15min**).

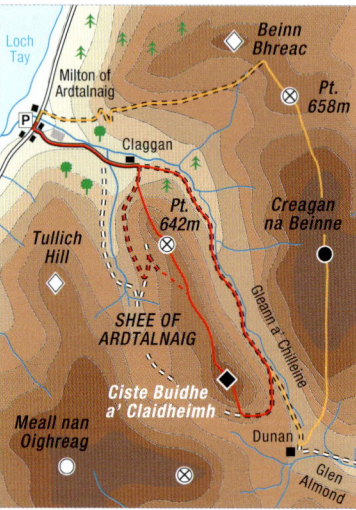

A descent can be made by the same route, or by a steep descent south to pick up a track which swings round into Gleann a' Chilleine, then leads north-west, back to Claggan and the start (**13.5km; 640m; 4h**).

Alternatively, the route can be extended over Creagan na Beinne (888m) by descending to the track in Gleann a' Chilleine and following it south to the moraine mounds by the cottage at Dunan. Gain the south ridge of Creagan na Beinne (named Dunan Hill) and follow it to the summit (**10km; 1100m; 4h 15min**).

Descend north beside the fenceline over boggy ground and pass over the hump of Pt.658, to a fence at the col below Beinn Bhreac (716m). A grassy track starts here and descends west into Corrie Cruinneachan to pasture and an exit onto the road at a gate with white gateposts, just north of the bridge over the Ardtalnaig Burn (**18km; 1140m; 6h 15min**).

Shee of Ardtalnaig across Gleann a' Chilleine with Creagan na Beinne, left (Tom Prentice)

Beinn na Gainimh   127

The rounded summit of Beinn na Gainimh and rocky Creag Grianain from the head of Coire Grianain (Tom Prentice)

Beinn na Gainimh; *730m; (G50); L52; NN837344; mountain of sand*

Beinn na Gainimh is the western most of four Grahams which occupy the high ground on either side of the road through the Sma' Glen and Glen Cochil, between Crieff and Aberfeldy, the line of one of General Wade's military roads.

Some 2.5 miles (4km) along the minor road that runs between Amulree and Kenmore on Loch Tay, there is verge parking next to the wall about 150m north-west of the entrance to Glenquaich Lodge. Walk down the road until opposite the entrance to Glenquaich Lodge, then take a track that leads around the side of Croftmill cottage and past the end of a plantation, out onto the hill. Continue up the glen for 800m and after passing through a gate in a wall, break off left away from the track. Cross the burn, gain the shoulder of Meall Mòr and climb steeply to the left of a small rock outcrop to gain easier ground leading to its 704m summit (**3km; 420m; 1h 25min**).

Now follow a somewhat unsightly electrified double fence, down and around the head of Coire Grianain, then ascend quite steeply to the summit of Creag Grianain (683m), an unusually shapely and rocky summit for these parts. Still following the fence, drop to a col, then ascend steeply up the side of the upper edge of a landslip and, where the ground flattens, cross through the fence. Although the current is not permanently on, it is possible to step through between the wires without touching them. The summit of Beinn na Gainimh is a large expanse of flat ground and a cairn in the middle appears to indicate the actual top (**5km; 620m; 2h 15min**).

Beinn Chonzie and Auchnafree Hill

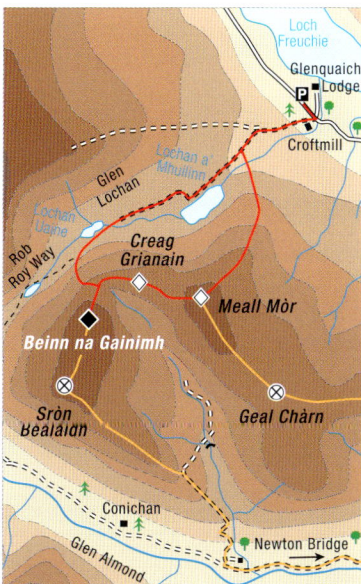

lie to the south-west on the other side of Glen Almond, whilst the three neighbouring Grahams, Meall Reamhar and Meall nan Caorach are to the east with Meal Dearg to the north-east across Loch Freuchie.

Return to the col, then make a zigzag descent to reach the floor of Glen Lochan, east of Lochan Uaine. At some point in the geological past there appears to have been a massive landslip here and the steep slope that falls away into Glen Lochan is riven with hollows and minor rock outcrops, requiring some care.

Cross the outflow from Lochan Uaine to gain the track (the route of the Rob Roy Way) and follow it past Lochan a' Mhuilinn back to the start (**9.5km; 620m; 3h 30min**).

Another route starts at the Newton Bridge car park in the Sma' Glen. Follow the track west along Glen Almond to NN852318, then ascend north-west on another track to gain the shoulder and climb this to Sròn Bealaidh and Beinn na Gainimh (**7.5km; 510m; 2h 30min**).

Traverse round over Creag Grianain to Meall Mòr then descend south-east over Geal Chàrn and Am Bodach to the trig point on Meall Reamhar (667m). A steep descent leads back to Newton Bridge (**15km; 860m; 5h**).

128 Meall nan Caorach, Meall Reamhar

Meall nan Caorach, left, and Meall Reamhar from Creag Liath (Rab Anderson)

Meall nan Caorach; 623m; (G199); L52; NN928338; sheep mountain
Meall Reamhar; 620m; (G204); L52; NN922332; fat, broad, mountain

Lying to the north-east of the Sma' Glen, this pair of Grahams sit on the line of the Highland Boundary Fault and are the highest points in the triangle of hills between Crieff, Dunkeld and Perth. They provide a quick and accessible circuit that begins less than 1km to the south of Amulree on the A822, where there is parking at NN903356 at the start of a track to the farmhouse at Girron.

Follow the track past the farmhouse to where it forks and continue on the grassy right-hand track for about 1.3km to the top of a short steep section above the Girron Burn where the track swings right. Leave the track here and climb the grassy slope to gain the Graham Top of Creag Chorm (611m) then continue south-east across a slight dip and turn south to gain the cairn and trig point on top of Meall nan Caorach (**4km; 370m; 1h 30min**).

Loch Freuchie in Glen Quaich is prominent to the north-west, with the Càrn Mairg group and Schiehallion beyond. A bit further right is the Graham Meall Dearg and to its right the distinctive pointed top of the Corbett Farragon Hill.

Follow the fence south-west and make a steep 160m drop to the col between the hills, cross the track then climb steeply up the other side to the cairn on top of Meall Reamhar where there is a fine view west to Glen Almond and the Graham Beinn na Gainimh (**5km; 525m; 2h 10min**).

Descend west beside the fence, being aware of some discarded fencing here and there, then gradually curve round west across heathery ground onto Càrn Liath (601m) and continue along the crest for about another 750m. One option is to drop off right here and descend north-east to cross the Girron Burn to regain the approach track at the foot of the short steep section, then follow it back (**9.5km; 565m; 3h 20min**).

The other option is to continue along the crest to a drystane dyke, which is followed for a short way to where it kinks left. Descend north from here to gain a grassy track which leads through a wall to a ford over the Girron Burn and the approach track near the start (**8.75km; 565km; 3h 10min**).

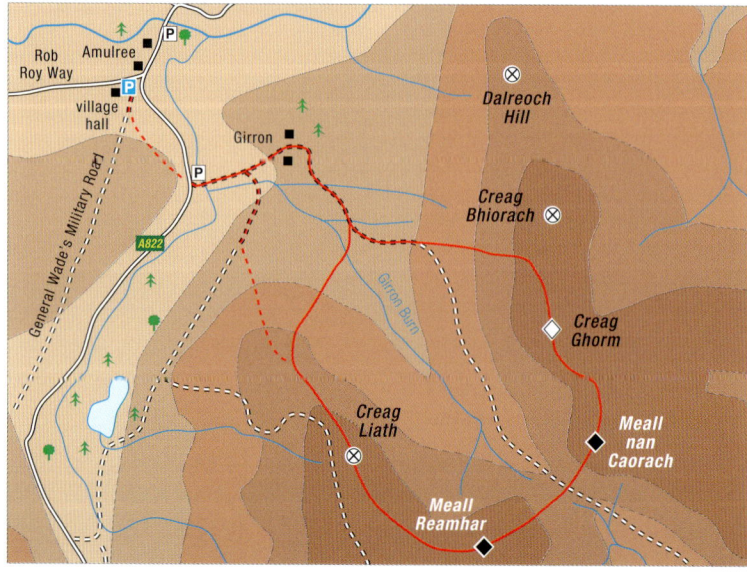

Meall Dearg

Meall Dearg; 690m; (G116); L52; NN886414; red hill

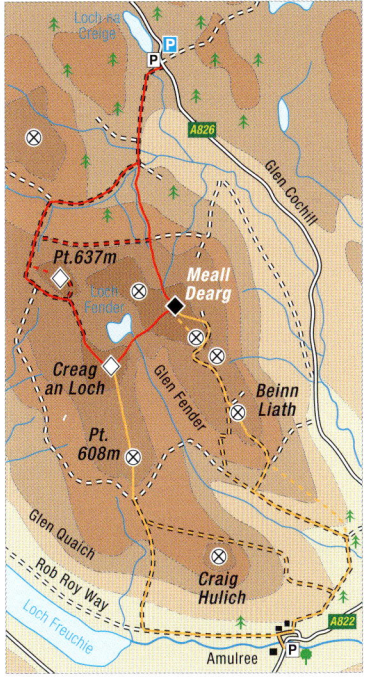

Meall Dearg is the highest of a number of small tops that make up the high ground between Glen Quaich and Glen Cochill to the south of Aberfeldy.

One route climbs it from a start at an elevation of 400m on the A826 to the south of Loch na Creige, where there is parking at the entrance to the Calliacher Wind Farm. The Griffin Forest car park is 100m to the north.

Go through a side gate and follow the main track through the forestry plantation, passing forks off to the right then the left, and swing westwards uphill to exit the forest by a gate. The wind turbines lie ahead with Loch Hoil in front and the peak of Schiehallion behind.

Take the track on the left and climb south, past a track off left along the top edge of the forest. The track passes just beneath the top of Pt.637m, an unnamed Graham Top, which can be included by a short diversion. At a junction go left, then swing right and follow the track to its end above Loch Fender nestling in the hollow between four hilltops. Creag an Loch (663m), another Graham Top, is easily gained after a short climb (**6.5km; 300m; 2h**).

Descend north-east to Loch Fender and cross the outflow then ascend to the trig point on Meall Dearg; a fine viewpoint (**7.5km; 410m; 2h 30min**).

Drop north-west towards the unnamed 640m central top and either climb this, or traverse its east side across a burn. Descend north beside another burn, crossing the track that traverses the hillside to reach the fence around the forest at a break. One option is to climb the fence and follow the right side of the break down and round to a side track to gain the main track, which leads back (**10.5km; 410m; 3h 30min**).

The other option is to go left along the track to regain the approach track and follow this back into the forest; an added 3km, 40min.

Another route starts from Amulree, from a layby opposite the former hotel. Cross the old bridge over the River Braan then go right along the road to follow a track northwards past the farm. Where the track bends left uphill, go through a gate and follow a grassy track down into Glen Fender.

Cross the bridge over the burn then continue uphill and cross a stile at NN908382 to gain the main track up the glen. Either go along this and take the first track up right, which is climbed to its end, to then gain the top of Beinn Liath (607m), or cut the corner and follow a series of sheep tracks to rejoin the track through a gap in a wall. Drop off Beinn Liath to gain another track and follow this towards Meall Dearg, then either climb to it over the knoll in front of it, or by going around the side of the knoll (**6.75km; 500m; 2h 20min**).

Drop to Loch Fender then climb Creag an Loch and descend south over Pt.608m to join a track. Descend past a track off left to reach a fork where either track can be followed. Left regains the approach, whilst right heads down by the Kinloch Burn to the track in Glen Quaich, which leads back (**15km; 640m; 4h 45min**).

Descending from Creag an Loch towards Loch Fender and Meall Dearg (Rab Anderson)

Beinn Suidhe from the Abhainn Shira Beinn nan Aighenan, Ben Starav and Glas Bheinn Mhòr beyond (Tom Prentice)

SECTIONS 2 & 3: Loch Tay to Loch Linnhe

SECTION 2 & 3

[1] *Meall a' Mhuic*	133
A' CHRUACH [2] *Stob na Cruaiche*	134
[3] *Beinn na Sròine*	136
[4] *Beinn Donachain*	137
[5] *Meall Tairbh*	138
[6] *Beinn Suidhe*	139
[7] *Meall Garbh*	140
[8] *Beinn nan Lus*	141
[9] *Màm Hael*, [10] *Beinn Mòlurgainn*, [11] *Beinn Mheadhonach*	142
[12] *Sgòrr a' Choise*, [13] *Meall Mòr*	144
[14] *Sgòrr na Cìche (Pap of Glencoe)*	146

Meall a' Mhuic 133

Meall a' Mhuic, viewed from the south over Glen Lyon (Rab Anderson)

Meall a' Mhuic; 745m; (G17); L42, 51; NN579508; *hill of the pig*

Meall a' Mhuic's location in Glen Lyon, one of the finest glens in the Southern Highlands, and the views it offers makes it a worthwhile short outing. It sits sandwiched between two Corbetts, Beinn Dearg to the east and Cam Chreag to the west and all three hills can be climbed together. For the round of all three hills, good tracks at the start and finish are helpful but steep featureless slopes between Meall a' Mhuic and Beinn Dearg are not, so although the link is there it is perhaps not the most pleasant. The westward link over Meall nam Maigheach to Cam Chreag is better. These extended outings are not described.

Start from the public car park on the Meggernie Estate at Innerwick (NN587475), behind which the summit of Meall a' Mhuic can be seen. Walk east along the road and cross the bridge over the burn then, just past the war memorial opposite the pretty white church, go left onto an estate track which heads north into the wooded glen between the hills. This is the Kirk Road, an old route used by people travelling from Loch Rannoch to the church in Glen Lyon.

After 500m, where the track rises away from the burn above a plantation, break off left to follow an old track beneath the plantation. This rejoins a branch of the track on the other side of the plantation where it descends to the junction of three burns. Take the track which crosses the right-hand burn by a bridge and ascend the hillside. It is a somewhat

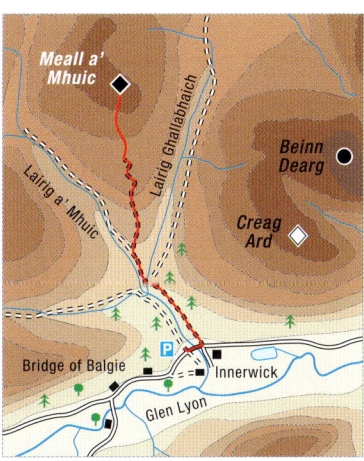

unsightly track but after 500m or so it is quit for an older grassy track which breaks off right; don't take the newer scar that traverses round the spur to the right, although from the start of this a section of old track runs parallel to the main track and can be followed to NN581488 where the old track swings uphill.

The old track leads pleasantly up the broad crest of the hill before petering out on easy-angled heathery terrain. This is crossed to reach the summit cairn where there are fine views north over afforested slopes to Loch Rannoch and the mountains beyond, as well as west to Glen Coe (**4km; 540m; 1h 45min**).

Although it is possible to vary the descent, unless one is planning to extend the outing to include one of the neighbouring hills, it is definitely better to return the same way. As well as avoiding the steep heathery slopes on either side, this has the advantage of allowing one to fully appreciate the splendid view south over Glen Lyon to the Ben Lawers massif and the hills to its west (**8km; 540m; 2h 45min**).

A' CHRUACH Stob na Cruaiche

> A' CHRUACH; the heap
> **Stob na Cruaiche;** 739m; (G33); L41; NN363571; stub of the heap

Stob na Cruaiche is the named summit of A' Chruach which sits on the edge of Rannoch Moor between Loch Laidon and Blackwater Reservoir. Due to the fact that it rises from the 300m contour, the hill presents a rather dull-looking squat ridgeline to those who pass on the road across Rannoch Moor. It is a reasonably high Graham though, however its principal feature is that being surrounded by mountains it is a fabulous viewpoint, which fully repays the effort involved in getting to it. The best route is the one that traverses much of the length of the hill from east to west, thereby making the most of the hill's situation and the views it affords.

Start from the car park at Rannoch Station (NN423578) at the end of a lengthy but scenic drive along Loch Rannoch, the only road in. Given there is a station here, it is an ascent that can be made by train, thereby saving time on the drive round. There is a tea room open from March until November, as well as a hotel.

Walk south past a cottage then take the track down to the railway, going through a gate and crossing this by a level crossing. The track leads north-west towards the forested

Stob na Cruaiche across Rannoch Moor to the south (Rab Anderson)

hillside across the head of Dubh Lochan at the end of Loch Laidon. To the north-east over the viaduct is Beinn Pharlagain, with the pointed top of Sgòr Gaibhre behind and the long ridge of Càrn Dearg to the left.

Go along the edge of the forest for 100m or so to a locked gate

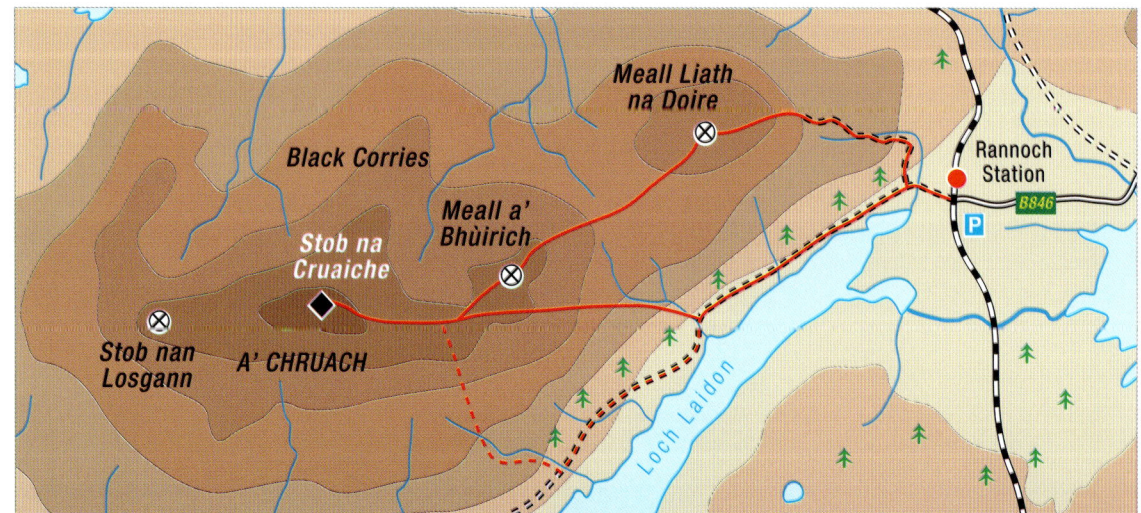

(NN418579) in the deer fence where another track heads off into the forest. To the left of the gate the barbed wire has been removed and access to the track is simplified. Follow the track uphill to emerge from the trees and continue up the hillside. At the highpoint (NN412585), where the main track goes down right, go to the end of the left-hand track then continue up the broad crest of the ridge following a vague atv track. Head towards an obvious boulder to gain the hill's 580m eastern top, Meall Liath na Doire. Schiehallion stands proud to the east, whilst Chno Dearg and Stob Coire Sgriodain are prominent to the north. The summit of Stob na Cruaiche is visible beyond another top, although it appears much further away than the map suggests. Drop down, dodging in and around peat hags, then climb to the subsidiary top of Meall a' Bhùirich (638m).

Descend a short way, again dodging in and out of small peat hags, then climb onto the shoulder of Stob na Cruaiche and pick up an atv track which leads to the summit trig point (**7.5km; 540m; 2h 35min**).

South across Rannoch Moor are the Bridge of Orchy Hills, then the Blackmount Hills and Meall a' Bhùirdh before the hills of Glen Coe. To the north-west across Blackwater reservoir are the Mamores then Ben Nevis and Aonach Beag, whilst closer to the north the vast bulk of one of the higher Corbetts, Leum Uilleim, blocks out much of the Grey Corries.

A return via the route of ascent (**15km; 640m; 4h 25min**) maintains the views, although an option is to descend the atv track back off the summit and out onto a little spur at NN377567, until the forest and Loch Laidon can be seen. Follow the atv track on a diagonal descent across the hill to enter the forest at NN391569 then cross the Allt a' Bhùirich and go down its north side to reach the forest track which leads back to Rannoch Station (**14km; 550m; 4h 5min**). A slightly longer route back by 1.5km, which gains the track quicker, descends south from the little spur to cross the burn draining the hillside to reach a gate in the deer fence at NN380556. An atv track then descends south-east onto the track leading into the forest.

A bike can be used on the track through the forest to the atv track at NN385555, and it is also possible to bike in from the Kingshouse Hotel past Black Corries Lodge.

Approaching the summit trig point of Stob na Cruaiche (Jim Teesdale)

Beinn na Sròine

Beinn na Sròine; 636m; (G188); L50; NN233289; mountain of the nose

Although surrounded by higher and grander mountains, the curve of Glen Lochy allows Beinn na Sròine to dominate much of the view when travelling west down the glen. The summit marks the highpoint of the western end of the long ridge separating Glen Lochy from Glen Orchy and is rather better defined than Beinn Udlaidh and Beinn Bhreac-liath, the two Corbetts at the eastern end.

With a starting altitude near the 200m contour, Beinn na Sròine is a direct and quick ascent from the A85, offering a pleasant diversion for anyone en route to or from other destinations, such as Oban and an Inner Hebridean ferry.

Start almost directly below the summit, at a small parking area on the A85 (NN246287), where a burn descends beside the conifer plantation flanking the eastern side of the hill. Care is needed when leaving the parking area at the end of the day as the traffic visibility westwards is poor.

Follow the burn to a fence, go through and gain the high ground left of the burn. Ascend steadily leftwards into the middle of the grassy face to

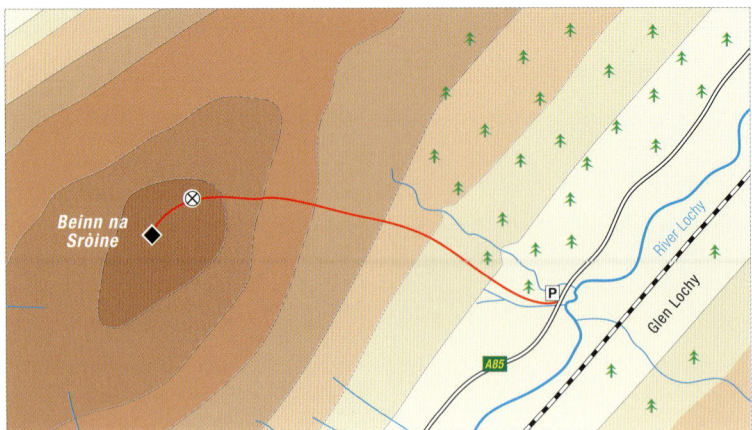

where the angle eases. The face is not as steep as it looks from below. Continue left below some small areas of scree to a final steepening leading to the eastern summit, marked by a rough cairn. A further 200m or so gains the cylindrical concrete trig point on the summit (**1.5km; 435m; 1h 5min**).

Across Glen Lochy, the pointed profile of Ben Lui fills the view, but there are also fine views west to Ben Cruachan and north to the peaks of Glen Etive and Glen Coe. A number of Grahams can also be identified including Beinn Bhalgairean and Meall nan Gabhar, south-west across Glen Lochy, and Beinn Donachain to the north-west across Glen Orchy.

Like the summit of nearby Beinn Udlaidh, the top of Beinn na Sròine is marred by concrete foundations and cable supports for an aerial, removed at some point in the past, but still marked on some OS maps. The best descent is via the line of ascent, which can be varied as desired (**3km; 435m; 1h 40min**).

Beinn na Sròine above the River Lochy (Tom Prentice)

Beinn Donachain 137

Beinn Donachain with Beinn Eunaich, right, from the east (Ken Crocket)

Beinn Donachain; 650m; (G174); L50; NN198316; bad or evil mountain

Rising above the northern end of Loch Awe, and sitting between the southern entrances to Glen Strae and Glen Orchy, Beinn Donachain is best climbed from the latter. Start from the Eas Urchaidh (Falls of Orchy) car park at NN243320 in the middle of Glen Orchy, reached by the single track road through the glen; either from the A82 at the north end near Bridge of Orchy, or from the A85 at the south end near Dalmally. The route to the Corbett, Beinn Mhic Mhonaidh, also starts here and follows the same initial approach.

An ascent via the suspension bridge over the River Orchy at Catnish is no longer possible since the bridge has been removed and the parking blocked-off.

Leave the Eas Urchaidh car park and cross the bridge over the River Orchy beside the falls. Follow the main track straight ahead for 500m then turn left up another track which runs above the Allt Broighleachan.

Continue ahead where the route to Beinn Mhic Mhonaidh crosses a bridge over the burn and go through a clearing to ascend into the Allt Broighleachan Caledonian Pinewood Reserve, passing through a gate.

Ford a burn, the Allt Coire Thoraidh, then climb steeply uphill to exit the reserve through another gate and follow the grassy track up the side of Coire Thoraidh. After crossing a small burn where the track levels off, turn right up a newer track and follow this steeply to its end at the upper limit of the trees where there is no fence.

Climb a grassy slope onto the rocky Cruach nan Nighean ridgeline, where Beinn Donachain's summit comes into view across Heart Loch, then head north-west along the ridge. Drop down and cut across the left (south) side of a small knoll (Pt.584m), then cross to the south of a smaller lochan, which is actually more heart-shaped than Heart Loch. Ascend to a deer fence and follow this to the right around the back of another knoll to where the fence can be climbed by an integral ladder.

Finally, climb steeply beside the remains of a fence then leave this where the angle starts to ease and go up right onto the summit. The obvious cairn sitting on the raised line of an old wall 170m or so to the south-west is apparently 1.6m lower (**7km; 630m; 2h 45min**).

To the south-west and west is the Ben Cruachan massif then Beinn Eunaich. To the right of these, beyond the impressive cleft of Coire Dubh on the other side of Glen Strae, is the Graham Meall Garbh, with Ben Starav, Beinn nan Aighenan, Glas Bheinn Mhòr and Stob Coire an Albannaich behind. Beinn Mhic Mhonaidh fills the view to the north, whilst to the north-east up Glen Orchy is the Graham Meall Tairbh and its neighbour Ben Inverveigh, with Beinn Dorain and Beinn an Dothaidh to the right again. Closer at hand, across Glen Orchy is Beinn Udlaidh, whilst to the south over the Graham Beinn na Sròine the great pyramidal summit of Ben Lui rises majestically above its neighbours.

Return the same way (**14km; 680m; 4h 30min**).

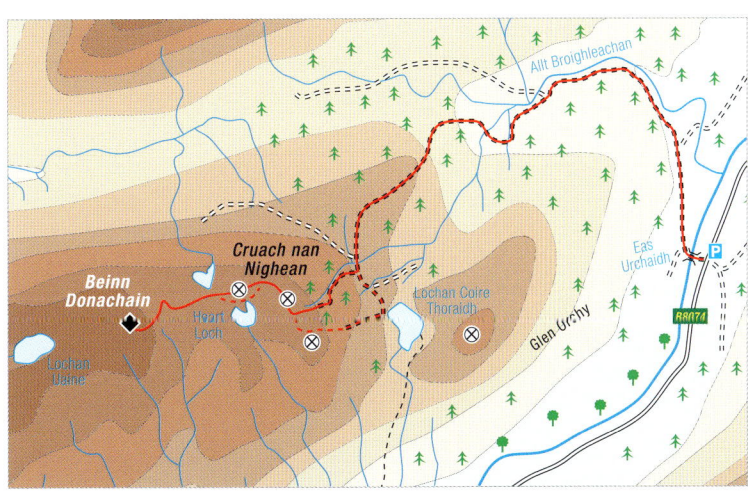

Meall Tairbh

Meall Tairbh and Lochan Coir' Orain from Ben Inverveigh, with Ben Cruachan in the distance (Tom Prentice)

Meall Tairbh; 665m; (G154); L50; NN250375; hill of the bull

Situated at the south-west end of Loch Tulla above the Inveroran Hotel, Meall Tairbh is usually combined with Ben Inverveigh, its lower but more shapely neighbour.

Park off the road where the West Highland Way (WHW) meets the road (NN275414) to the east of the Inveroran Hotel. Follow this route south-east onto the shoulder of Ben Inverveigh, as far as the highpoint at Màm Carraigh where the WHW descends to Glen Orchy. Break off southwards and follow a grassy track up the initial part of this long ridge onto Pt.546m where Meall Tairbh comes into view. Beyond another rise the rest of the ridge provides pleasant high-level grassy walking with scatterings of large flat rocks, leading past a tiny lochan and eventually on to the 639m summit of Ben Inverveigh (**4.5km; 470m; 1h 50min**).

There are fine views in all directions, including to the south, the unusual dyke which cuts across the north ridge of Beinn Udlaidh.

Ben Inverveigh only just falls short of Graham status, the drop to the col between it and Meall Tairbh being c144m. When descending south-west off Ben Inverveigh to gain this col it is best to keep to the ridge for as long as possible since the slopes on the west are heather-covered and awkward. The col is an amazing collection of glacial drumlins, including an unusual grass-covered pyramid. These are glacially-dumped hillocks, what geologists sometimes refer to as a 'basket-of-eggs topography'. The small Lochan Coir' Orain is easily lost to view in this jumble. Ahead, a brief but steep climb up heathery slopes leads onto the broad ridge, then the summit of Meall Tairbh (**7km; 640m; 2h 50min**).

The descent down the north ridge of Meall Tairbh is along a broad ridge, transected by numerous boggy hollows and burns. In compensation, the views ahead are excellent, with the Starav group, the Blackmount, and the upper parts of the Bridge of Orchy Hills. As the slope steepens the vegetation becomes lush and boggy. Towards the bottom break slightly right to avoid much boggier ground by aiming for the hotel, a forestry plantation and eventually the Allt Orain draining from the glen between the hills (**12km; 640m; 4h**).

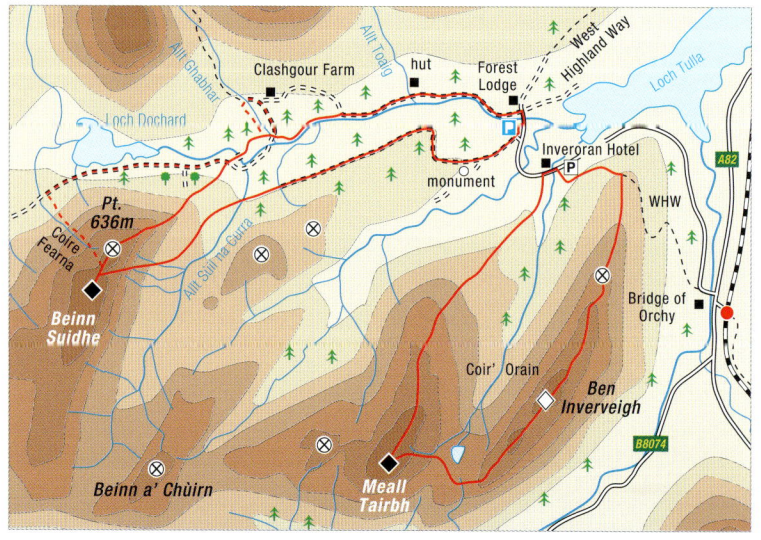

Beinn Suidhe

Beinn Suidhe; 676m; (G138); L50; NN211400; mountain of the seat or shelf

Starting from the Victoria Bridge car park at the west end of Loch Tulla (NN270419), Beinn Suidhe is best approached along the north bank of the Abhainn Shira. Take the path north onto the road leading over Victoria Bridge to Forest Lodge then follow the track west along the river, passing the tiny hut used by Glasgow University Mountaineering Club; once the local school! Beyond, the riverside path gives rutted, soft going with lovely views to the hill and leads eventually to the confluence of the Allt Ghabhar and the Abhainn Shira.

A bridge here has been washed away but the Allt Ghabhar is usually low enough to be forded. Cross the Allt Ghabhar then the stile in the deer fence enclosing the forestry, from where a path leads through a break in the trees to a bridge over the Abhainn Shira (NN232418).

If the Allt Ghabhar is high, head north to a small footbridge over the Allt Ghabhar (NN233426) to the west of Clashgour. On the other side, avoid the firebreak in the forestry which leads to a dangerously boggy area and follow the west bank back down to pick up the path leading to the bridge over the Abhainn Shira.

Beinn Suidhe rises steeply ahead and is climbed via the knoll of Tom Liath then the rocky rise beyond to reach a brief easing on the shoulder. The final steep slope is climbed by a zigzag line up grassy ramps on the north-east face, which avoids any difficulties and leads abruptly onto the north end of the main ridge.

Cross the northern top, Pt.636m, then drop slightly to a saddle and climb through rocky ground to gain the summit 800m further on (**7.5km; 510m; 2h 30min**)

It is an excellent viewpoint, not only for the surrounding Munros, but also for several neighbouring Grahams, including the remote Beinn nan Lus and Meall Garbh to the south-west, and the neighbouring Meall Tairbh to the south-east.

Return north to the saddle between the summit and the northern top then descend steeply eastwards through a gap in the rocky terrain to reach the moor below. From there, a contouring line leads through the shallow Beallach an Tailleir (NN227409).

Either return via the bridge over the Abhainn Shira and the approach route, or cross the Allt Sùil na Curra and go through a gate in the deer fence. A path then leads through a forestry break to reach a track.

This track leads back to the car park but there are a number of gates to be climbed. In the second forestry plantation, stay with the track where it doglegs up right, avoiding a tempting break on the left, and emerge from the forest with the Druimliart Memorial on the right. This is at the ruins of the house where the bard Duncan Ban MacIntyre was born in 1724; best known for his poem *In Praise of Ben Doran*, which there is a lovely view of from here. The track descends to the car park (**15km; 510m; 4h 20min**).

An alternative from the saddle between the summit and the northern top is to descend the uncomplicated slope north-west down Coire Fearna. This leads to the Glen Kinglass track which is followed back past idyllic Loch Dochard and the splendid amphitheatre this sits in; an extra 2km but worthwhile.

Beinn Suidhe from the north bank of the Abhainn Shira with Beinn nan Aighenan beyond (Tom Prentice)

Meall Garbh from the Làirig Dhoireann with Stob Coire an Albannaich in the distance (Ken Crocket)

Meall Garbh; 701m; (G101); L50; NN168367; rough mountain

Meall Garbh is a fine and remote hill between Glen Kinglass and Glen Strae. It could be approached via Loch Etive and Glen Kinglass as for Beinn nan Lus, which it sits opposite and can be combined with. However, the route described here is the shortest and the approach is made via Glen Strae.

Leave the B8077 at the apex of the loop road between the head of Loch Awe and Dalmally, taking the westmost of two tracks between bridges over the Eas Euanaich and the River Strae to park immediatley on the left at NN145295.

Walk up the track via its left branch for 2km, passing two marshy pond areas, to where the Allt Dhoireann flows under the road at a fine pool. Take the atv track up the west bank of the burn, through a gate and so onto the hill.

Glen Strae and Glen Kinglass are connected by the Làirig Dhoireann, which is followed by the initial section of the route. Continuing up the track, the cliffs of Beinn Eunaich gradually impose on the left, with the dark, forbidding cleft of the Black Shoot prominent. This was a favourite target of the Victorian mountaineers.

Either continue to follow the track, or make your own way over the drumlin-strewn and gully-incised slopes to reach the col (612m) where the Làirig Dhoireann crosses. The source of the burn is the small Lochan Dhoireann; several cairns and a perfectly positioned shelter mark the edge overlooking Coire Dhoireann to the north. Meall Garbh is now visible for the first time, peeking over the west shoulder of Meall Beithe.

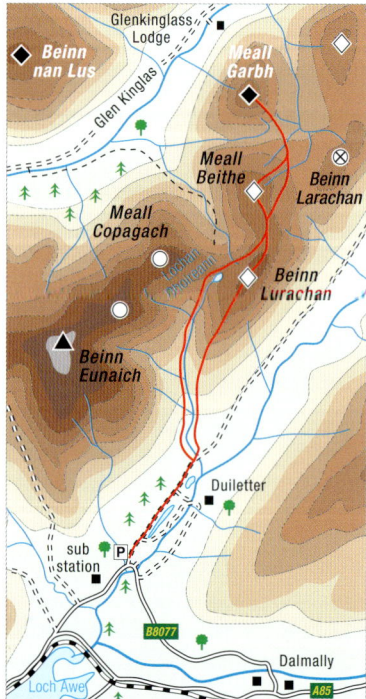

Make a slightly rising traverse to the north-east, across the side of Beinn Lurachan, to gain the col (626m) south of Meall Beithe, from where this 693m top is easily gained. Meall Garbh is now fully visible, as is its neighbour, Beinn nan Lus, on the other side of Glen Strae to the west.

Descend north-north-east to the col (444m) and make the steady 257m ascent of Meall Garbh. The summit is a delight of rocky outcrops and small lochans, with glacial erratic blocks of granite perched on metamorphics. The outlook in every direction is superb; (9km; 905m; 3h 45min).

Return to the col and cut across the eastern side of Meall Beithe to regain the col at 626m. Instead of retracing your steps, climb the ridge ahead onto Beinn Lurachan (719m), which narrows as it nears the top. Beinn Eunaich and its outliers look splendid from here, and there is a fine view over the Graham Beinn Donachain on the other side of Glen Strae to the Ben Lui group. The squat bulk of the Corbett Beinn Mhic Mhonaidh is also prominent, with the Bridge of Orchy hills beyond.

Descend the south-west ridge to the banks of the Allt Dhoireann then follow this past several enticing pools to regain the track and so back to the start (17.5km; 1215m; 6h 45min).

Beinn nan Lus 141

Beinn nan Lus; 709m; (G84); L50; NN130375; *mountain of the herbs*

This remote Graham lies on the north side of Glen Kinglass, the glen that runs eastwards from Loch Etive to provide a through route to Victoria Bridge and Loch Tulla. The hill is perhaps best accessed from near Taynuilt by biking in along the track on the east side of Loch Etive; a 42km round trip. The hill itself is relatively short and could be combined with Meall Garbh, the Graham facing it across Glen Kinglass. The track is a roller coaster with the odd rough section and some may find they have to push the bike up the steeper bits. However, the effort is eased by the stunning views of Loch Etive and the surrounding mountains.

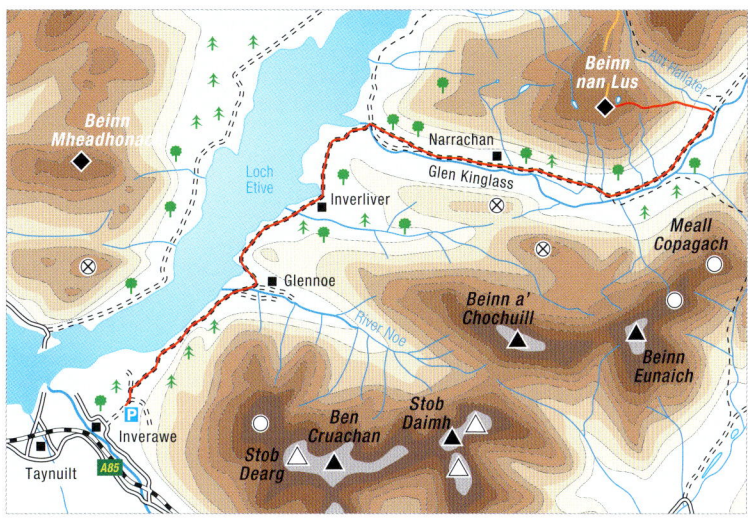

Leave the A84 to the east of Taynuilt and follow the minor road to Inverawe Country Park from Bridge of Awe for 2.25km. At a bend, turn up a track signed to a forestry car park 400m along the track at NN028319.

Follow the main track through the forest, past a track off right then one to the left, dropping down to cross the River Noe by a bridge. After an uphill section, the track leads downhill to a bridge over the River Liver then up and around Inverliver Bay before climbing over then down to a bridge over the River Kinglass. Turn right here and follow the track up Glen Kinglass. Pass Narrachan bothy and continue beneath the steep wooded southern slopes of Beinn nan Lus to where the Allt Hallater flows beneath a bridge into the River Kinglass from the north; bikes should be left here (**18.25km; 300m; 2h 45min by bike**), (**4h 30min** on foot). Times are now given on foot from and back to here.

Ascend the east shoulder of Beinn nan Lus, steep at first then easing, to pass a tiny lochan about 400m before the summit with its granite outcrops and boulders (**3km; 635m; 1h 45min**).

To the west over Loch Etive and Beinn Trilleachan are Beinn Sgulaird and Creach Bheinn, with the trio of Grahams, Màm Hael, Beinn Mòlurgainn and Beinn Mheadhonach to their south. North is Beinn Starav then Beinn nan Aighenan with Glas Bheinn Mhòr tucked behind it. East, on the other side of Glen Kinglass, domed Meall Garbh looks imposing, whilst Beinn Suidhe, another Graham, fills the upper part of the glen. Due south is pointed Beinn Eunaich with Beinn a' Chochuill then the splendid Cruachan range.

Descend as for the ascent route (**6km; 635m; 2h 45min**), then return along the track (**42.5km; 1220m; 8h with a bike**), (**11h 45min** on foot).

An ascent can be made from Glen Etive to the north, by way of Coileitir. This passes through the 766m col between Beinn Starav and Glas Bheinn Mhòr to gain the col with Beinn nan Aighenan. Drop to the Allt Hallater then go down beside this and cross it to gain the Bealach Cumhann. Finally, ascend across the slope to the summit (**11.25km; 1030m; 4h 30min**), (**22.5km; 1400m; 8h**).

Beinn nan Lus with Beinn Mheadhonach, left, from Meall Garbh (Ken Crocket)

142 Màm Hael, Beinn Mòlurgainn, Beinn Mheadhonach

Beinn Mòlurgainn from the ascent to Beinn Bhreac (Rab Anderson)

Màm Hael; 726m; (G56); L50; NN008408; 'màm' Gaelic breast. Also area between breasts, or cleavage. Name probably relates to pass, east of the peak. Hael problematic as no words begin H in Gaelic: the burn running north from the pass is Abhainn Teithil (pronounced approx tay-heel), but meaning obscure
Beinn Mòlurgainn; 690m; (G117); L50; NN019400; mountain of the bare hill of the long ridge
Beinn Mheadhonach; 715m; (G72); L50; NN019369; middle mountain

Sitting between Loch Creran and Loch Etive, these hills form the base of a chain of hills which gradually increases in height northwards to Bidean nam Bian above Glen Coe. This is one of a few walks where three Grahams can be conveniently linked into a suitable round, however the terrain is complex and good hill skills are required. The views are superb, especially to Ben Cruachan on the opposite side of Loch Etive.

Start in Gleann Salach at NM985367, on the B845 to Barcaldine, at the foot of Beinn Bhreac's long south ridge. This is almost at the top of the hill where there is a passing place on the west side of the road that can accommodate a car parked off the road; there is a better place on the east side of the road 50m downhill.

Just above the passing place, follow a track through a gate for a very short way then head up Beinn Bhreac's long and broad south ridge. Soon, this hill and the three Grahams come into view, as does Ben Cruachan revealing itself behind Beinn Mheadhonach. Cross a flat section halfway up then head up and right for a gate (NM994391) in a deer fence that cuts across the hillside. Continue up rockier ground to the large cairn on the 708m top of Beinn Bhreac (4km; 570m; 1h 50min).

Head north along the rugged summit with fine views to Mull, Ardgour and the Ballachulish hills then swing round and drop east to a col. Across Gleann Dubh to the north is the Eas Garbh chasm on the

Màm Hael from the ascent to Beinn Bhreac (Rab Anderson)

Corbett Creach Bheinn. Cross an old wall and climb to the top of Màm Hael past numerous tiny lochans. The hill is unnamed on OS maps and has been called Beinn Bhreac by some. However, the map clearly indicates this name refers to the hill to the south-west. It is more logical to use a different name from the map and Màm Hael just to the east has been chosen (**6km; 680m; 2h 30min**).

Descend east along a narrowing ridge and make a slight rise to a cairn before turning and dropping south to a col. An easy 150m ascent gains the right-hand of two knolls that is the summit of Beinn Mòlurgainn (**8km; 830m; 3h 10min**).

Drop steeply off this narrow hilltop and at the bottom cross a deer fence to reach the col. Tiresome mossy ground on the other side leads to the top of Meall Dearg; OS 1:25k and 1:50k maps show different knolls as being the 578m top.

Beinn Mheadhonach from the east (Rab Anderson)

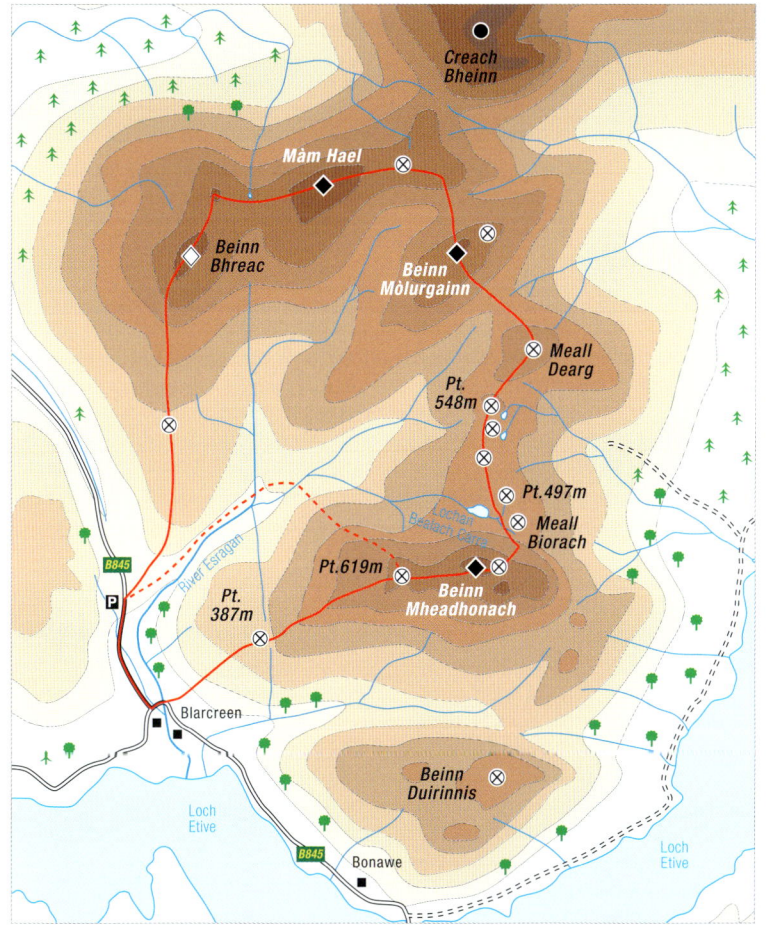

The onwards terrain is complex and best covered by pretty much staying on the high ground. Descend south-west then climb onto another knoll (548m) with a prominent boulder on its top; a small lochan lies below. Go down south and pass a smaller 528m knoll on its west side to ascend a third knoll (550m) at NN023380. Drop south-east off this knoll to a shallow col, aiming for the next in this chain of knolls (497m) but cut across beneath its top then descend to the Bealach Carra below Meall Biorach with Lochan Bealach Carra to the west.

Cross a fence, then from the high-point of the bealach climb the left-hand rocky skyline ridge, which is perhaps preferable to the slope on the right. A stiff climb gains the 710m east top of Beinn Mheadhonach, after which a rocky cleft is crossed to gain the main summit (**12km; 1270m; 4h 50min**).

Descend west across another similar but not so steep cleft and continue to Pt.619m. There is now a choice of descents. Either go down to the north-west and cross the river (possibly difficult in spate) to reach some old sheilings then follow a path that traverses the side of the slope above the River Esragan to get back to the start. Alternatively, descend the south-west ridge to a col, go through a gate in the fence and climb onto the final 387m top. Drop steeply down the other side and follow a burn to three fields below; there is a gate out of the middle field at NM990355. Follow the road north back to the start (**17km; 1430m; 6h 30min**).

Sgòrr a' Choise, Meall Mòr

Meall Mòr, from Sgòrr a' Choise, topped by the Aonach Eagach and Bidean nam Bian (Rab Anderson)

Sgòrr a' Choise; 663m; (G158); L41; NN084551; peak of the foot or leg (shape)
Meall Mòr; 676m; (G140); L41; NN106559; big hill

This is an excellent walk taking in a fine pair of Grahams with stunning views of Glen Coe and its surrounding peaks. Start from the car park at the Tourist Information office on the edge of Ballachulish (NN083585), just off the main A82.

Walk into the village, cross the road and go up Loanfern past the Co-op then the playing fields to cross the pedestrian bridge over the River Laroch. Turn left and go up a narrow road signposted as the Public Footpath to Glen Creran, passing the primary school. When the road ends, continue through gates into the open along firstly a track, then a footpath.

The day's first objective, the shapely peak of Sgòrr a' Choise, lies ahead and is gained by following the path beneath it into Gleann an Fhiodh with the Munro Top of Sgòrr Bhàn on the right. Cross a number of burns and continue almost to a large cairn at NN069548. Break off the main path which continues into Glen Duror and cross the River Laroch by stepping stones.

The map shows a path hereabouts, heading diagonally up the slope to the Màm Uchdaich, then over to Glen Creran. However, if it's there it's difficult to find and perhaps the simplest option is to make a direct assault up the steep, heathery slope to gain the long south-west ridge of Sgòrr a' Choise. Easy going then leads along this above the top edge of a forest, on a hill path following a line of old fence posts. Ahead, is the summit cone of Sgòrr a' Choise, flanked on the left by Sgòrr na Cìche (Pap of Glencoe) and on the right by Bidean nam Bian. A splendid narrowing rocky ridge leads to a delightful and airy summit with Meall Mòr ahead and the jagged ridge of the Aonach Eagach rising behind it (**6.5km; 660m; 2h 35min**).

Descend the steep south-east ridge, go through a walkers' gap in a deer fence at NN089548, then swing around over the top of Meall a' Bhuige and descend the grassy slope to gain the col at the foot of Meall Mòr. A long ascent ensues up the broad and grassy south ridge to gain the high ground where a traverse leads north-east to the summit cairn, perched above a low but impressively long crag (**9.5km; 1000m; 4h**).

Sgòrr na h-Ulaidh is prominent to the south and to the north the hooded bulk of Ben Nevis rises above the Mamores. It is worth walking down and out a bit for the wonderful view east along Glen Coe.

Sgòrr a' Choise, Meall Mòr 145

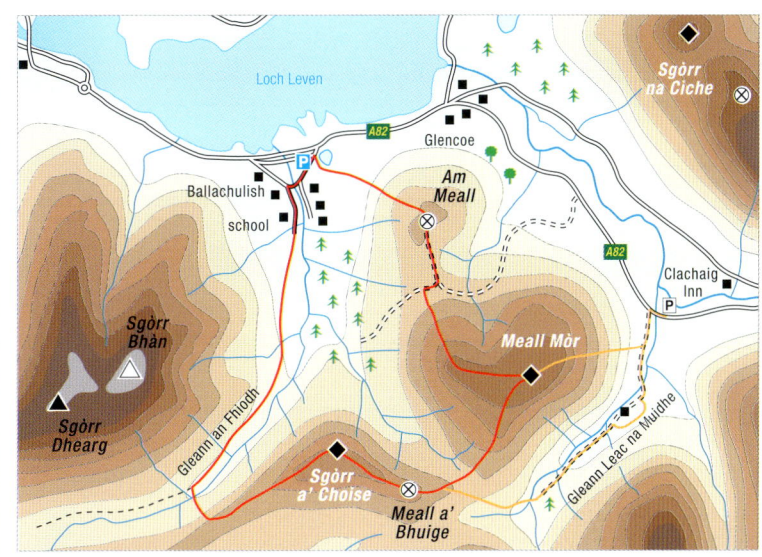

An alternative starts towards the west end of Glen Coe, from a parking area at NN120564 on the north side of the A82, at the apex of a bend.

Walk carefully west along this fast stretch of road (especially the vergeless bridge) then cross over and go along a track for 1km. Cross the bridge over the Allt na Muidhe, then in a further 100m, beyond the driveway to a house, skirt the cottages by a signposted path on the left to rejoin the track beyond.

Continue to where the track ends then in a further 100m, ford the Allt na Muidhe and strike west up the side of a tributary. Go over Meall a' Bhuige then through the gap in the deer fence and climb the steep southeast ridge to gain the top of Sgòrr a' Choise (**5.5km; 640m; 2h 20min**).

Retrace your steps to Meall a' Bhuige then drop to the col and climb Meall Mòr (**8.5km; 980m; 3h 45min**).

From the top, the quickest way back is to descend steeply east to the road with Glen Coe spread out at your feet (**10.5km; 980m; 4h 30min**).

However, it is perhaps less punishing, although longer, to return via the south ridge and the approach route through the glen.

Retrace your steps along the top, then swing around and descend the north-west ridge heading for the aerial on Am Meall to the north. There is a gate in the deer fence slightly to the left. Cross an area that has been clear felled to gain a forest track at the col then go right and break off on another track which leads uphill to the communications aerial on Am Meall. Cross the fence by a ladder stile and follow the fence downhill alongside the edge of the forestry plantation, crossing another stile. There are fine views back to Sgòrr a' Choise, while ahead lies the Ballachulish Bridge with the hills of Ardgour beyond. On the other side of Loch Leven is the long ridgeline of the Graham Tom Meadhoin.

Towards the bottom, pick up a path which swings west around the top of the old slate quarry through a gate, then down to the quarry entrance just out in front of the car park (**14km; 1070m; 5h 15min**).

Sgòrr a' Choise from the col with Meall Mòr (Rab Anderson)

146 Sgòrr na Cìche (Pap of Glencoe)

Sgòrr na Cìche from Am Meall (Rab Anderson)

Sgòrr na Cìche (Pap of Glencoe); 742m; (G27); L41; NN125594; peak of the breast

Despite its bigger neighbours, this distinctive little peak stands proud above Glencoe village. It is generally climbed by simply going up and down its south-west flank, however a better route is by the circuit described here, which ascends the west shoulder then descends by the south-west flank.

Park in the village and walk towards the Pap. Cross the Bridge of Coe and take the road off left to Glencoe Lochan. Where the road bends left after 100m, continue ahead on a footpath, through the trees to the right of the burn, then swing left across the burn to gain a forestry track. Go straight over, up some steps, and continue on the path to the left of the burn to reach another forestry track. Cross over this and follow the path through an old gate in a fence then up a clearing with a low overhead line. Ignore a route off right, which leads to the end of a track, and at the highpoint, about 50m past the second double pole on the overhead line, break off right to climb a narrow route through the trees. Exit the forestry by stepping over a fence to gain the open hillside then climb the shoulder above.

If this short cut is missed, continue downhill on the path to go through a gate then break off right and follow the forest edge uphill to meet the short cut at the fence. Higher up, traces of path begin as the summit dome is approached and the ground steepens and becomes rockier. The path leads through a rock band to gain the splendid summit with its stunning views (**3.5km; 730m; 2h**).

The surest descent is to head north-east towards Kinlochleven, on the path off the back, for 50m or so. The path drops down then swings round south beneath the craggy summit crown to cut diagonally down across the slope then descend more easily to the col at NN127591.

There are other ways but they involve a little scrambling and route-finding. It is a popular peak so take care not to dislodge any rocks and be wary of others who might. Sgòrr nam Fiannaidh, the Munro at the end of the Aonach Eagach, can be gained from here.

The peaty hillside below the col has been scarred by the passage of countless feet and, although a number of paths lead down, it is best to keep to the main path to contain any erosion. Ignore a path on the right before the col and descend the main path from the col to the left-hand burn; the Allt a' Mhuilinn. Another direct path down the side of the burn should also be ignored in preference for the main path. This swings away left downhill from the burn then cuts back right to zigzag down the side of its gully before crossing it.

Traverse the hillside on the path to cross a burn by a bridge and follow a track down to the road, which leads to the village (**7.5km; 730m; 3h 15min**).

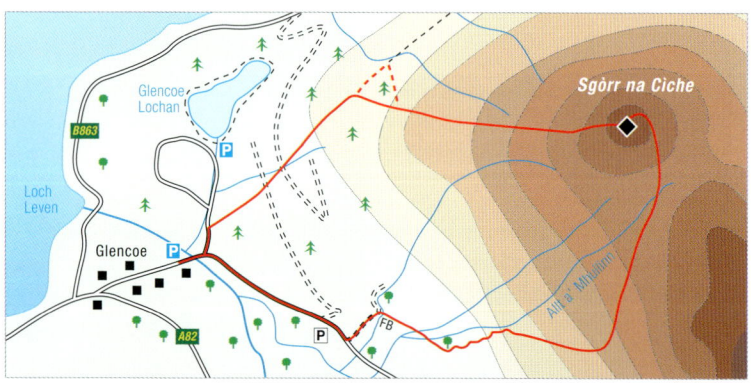

Sgòrr na Cìche from the west across Loch Leven with Garbh Bheinn, left, Sgòrr nam Fiannaidh, right (Jim Teesdale)

Sgòrr na Cìche from the south-west with Garbh Bheinn, right (Grahame Nicoll)

Binnein Shios with distant Creag Dhubh (Newtonmore) to its right then The Cairngorms (Rab Anderson)

SECTION 4
Loch Linnhe to Loch Ericht.

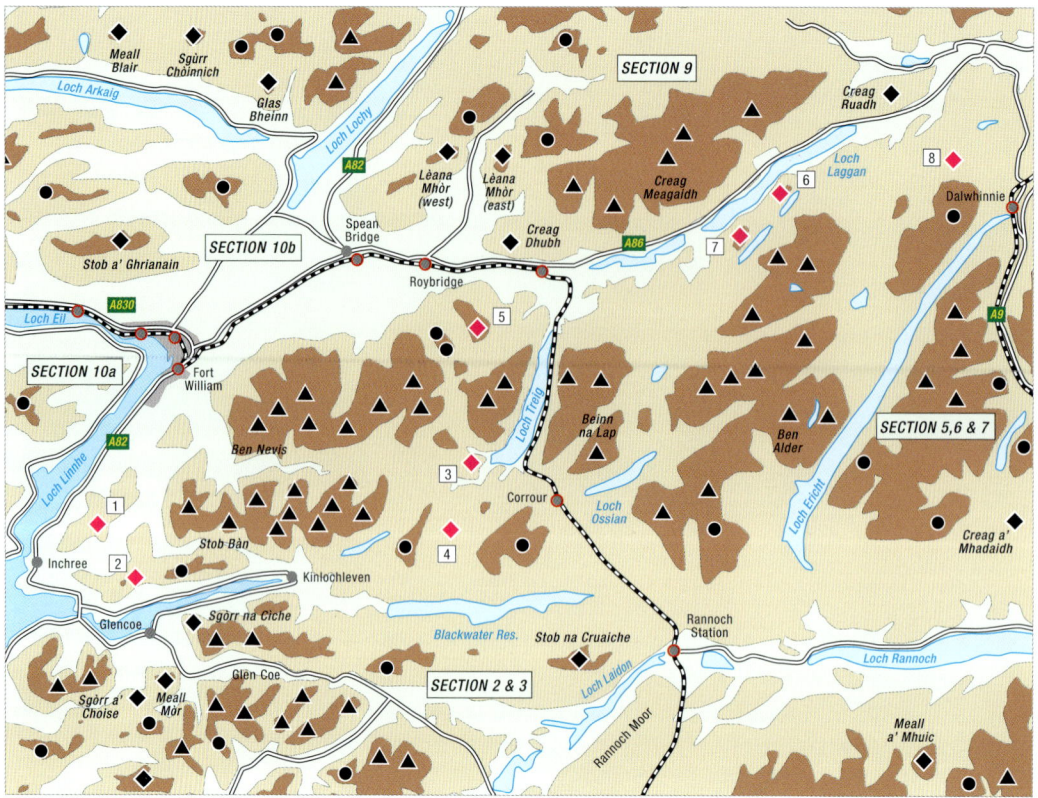

SECTION 4

[1] *Beinn na Gucaig*, [2] *Tom Meadhoin*	151
[3] *Creag Ghuanach*, [4] *Beinn na Cloiche*	152
[5] *Cnap Cruinn*	154
[6] *Binnein Shios*, [7] *Binnein Shuas*	155
[8] *Meall nan Eagan*	157

Beinn na Gucaig, Tom Meadhoin

Tom Meadhoin and Loch Leven from the flanks of Am Meall above Ballachulish to the south (Rab Anderson)

Beinn na Gucaig; 616m; (G211); L41; NN062653; *mountain of the little bell (probably bluebells)*
Tom Meadhoin; 621m; (G202); L41; NN087621; *middle knoll*

These two fairly low Grahams throw down long ridges to the south-west, either side of Gleann Righ, which reach the sea at Inchree and Onich on the point between Loch Leven and Loch Linnhe. These ridges enable a scenic but lengthy circuit to be made of both hills, although the drop and reascent in-between is not for the faint hearted! Start from the Glenrigh forestry car park at NN030634, accessed off the A82 via Inchree.

Exit the car park in the south-east corner to follow the 'Waterfalls' trail which climbs up the side of the splendid Abhainn Righ Falls to emerge onto a forest track. The south-west ridge begins here and atv tracks climb the hillside above onto this. However, it is perhaps better to walk along the track to the right for 400m, round the base of the ridge, following the An Drochaid circular trail and 50m before this turns off right to cross the river, break off left. Pass between two posts on an old track which soon disappears then continue up the edge of the forest behind a knoll onto the crest of the hill. The atv track is joined above, where the more defined ridge provides a splendid route to Pt.575m, the south-west top. Drop off the back and head slightly right to go through a gate in the deer fence then climb to the top of Beinn na Gucaig (**5.5km; 590m; 2h 10min**).

Descend south-east to the fence then swing gradually east beside this ▶

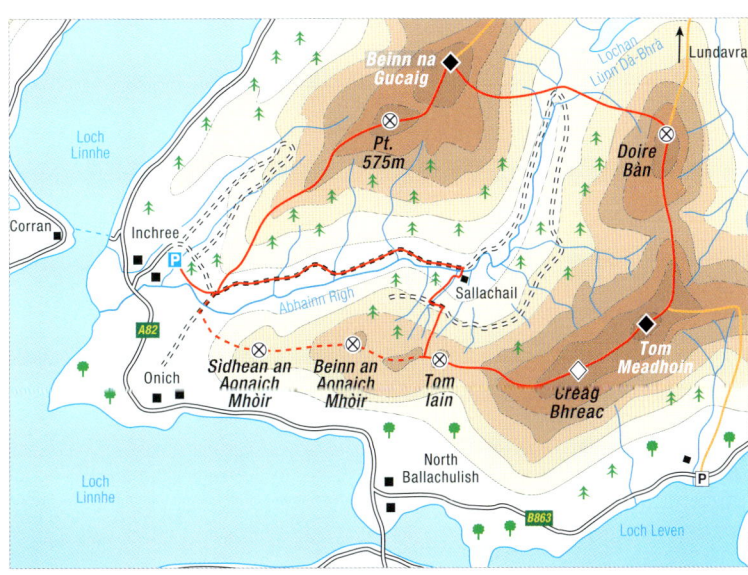

Creag Ghuanach, Beinn na Cloiche

and plunge down steeping slopes to gain the sanctuary of the floor of the glen; a 470m drop. Pause for breath then climb the other side to the left of the forest, directly to the top of Doire Bàn (566m); a sub 2000ft Marilyn. It is a 420m reascent followed by a 161m drop south to a col where a final weak-kneed ascent of 216m leads up the ridge to Tom Meadhoin (11.5km; 1230m; 4h 50min).

Continue westwards onto Creag Bhreac (615m) then descend the Leac Mhòr ridge to the top edge of the forestry and climb onto the knoll of Tom Iain (NN061617). It is possible to stay on the high ground and cross to the trig point on Beinn an Aonaich Mhòir then continue on to Sìdhean an Aonaich Mhòir (297m) before descending north-west to the bridge at NN035626 then back to the car park via the waterfalls (19km; 1440m; 6h 50min). However, the terrain is difficult at times and perhaps the better route is to cut north from midway between Tom Iain and Beinn an Aonaich Mhòir and cross the fence by a stile at NN059621. Descend to a forest track, follow it left over a burn, then descend beside the burn and the forest, crossing back over the burn at the bottom to the cottage at Sallachail. Cross the footbridge over the Abhainn Rìgh then follow the track through the glen and back down the side of the waterfalls (20.5km; 1330m; 7h 5min).

Tom Meadhoin is easily climbed (3.5km; 610m; 1h 50min) using the right of way that begins 100m to the west of a small parking area at NN097604 at the side of Loch Leven. This gains the col that links it to the Corbett Màm na Gualainn, which can also be included (6.5km; 940m; 3h 5min), (10km; 940m; 4h 15min).

Beinn na Gucaig can be climbed from Lundavra south of Fort William where there is good parking by the bridge at NN096665. Climb north-west up Sròn Garbh then south-west to Beinn na Gucaig (4km; 500m; 1h 45min). Tom Meadhoin can also be included (9.5km; 1050m; 4h), descending as above but avoiding the top of Doire Bàn, then taking this in on the return to descend its north ridge (14.5km; 1210m; 5h 30min).

Creag Ghuanach and Creaguaineach Lodge beside Loch Treig (Noel Williams)

Creag Ghuanach; 621m; (G201); L41; NN299690; *unsteady or nodding cliff*
Beinn na Cloiche; 646m; (G177); L41; NN284648; *mountain of the stone*

Approaches on foot to this pair of hills, which lie in remote country between Blackwater Reservoir and Loch Treig, are likely to involve a night in one of several bothies, perhaps Loch Chiarain bothy (NN289634) being the most convenient. However, they can be tackled in a single day by taking the train to Corrour, and it is this option that is described.

Catch an early train to Corrour, either from the north (Fort William & Tulloch) or the south (Glasgow & Crianlarich); check Scotrail. Watch for seasonal variations, restricted Sunday service and request stopping! Bikes can be taken. For the south-bound return there are two evening trains, and for the northbound return there is a mid-afternoon, then a late

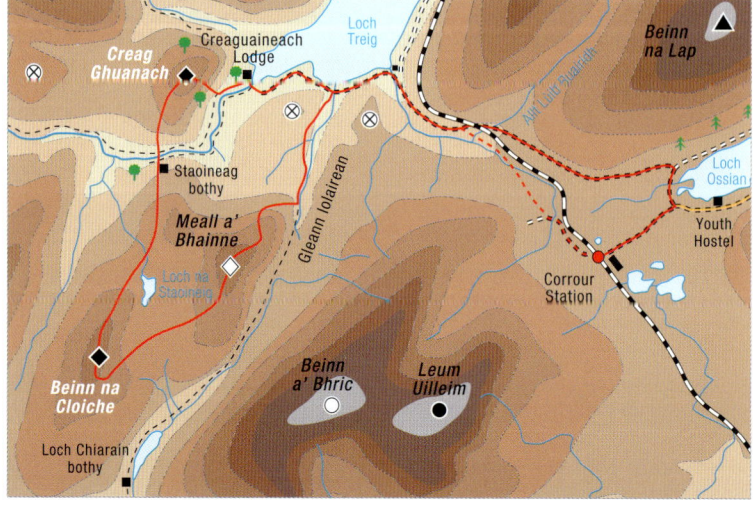

evening train. Plan well, take warm clothing for the wait and check the station house restaurant <www.corrour.co.uk>.

Leaving Corrour, a track then path on the west side of the railway can be followed, however the path can be boggy. A better option, which is double the length, follows a track towards Loch Ossian then turns left and left again towards Loch Treig. The track crosses a bridge over the Allt Lùib Ruairidh as it passes beneath the railway.

Follow the track quite steeply down towards Loch Treig then, just before a hydro building, turn left along another track which leads to a bridge over the Abhainn Iolairean. This is where the return route arrives down Gleann Iolairean. If bikes have been used they are best left here.

Continue on the rougher track across the head of the loch where there are fine views of Creag Ghuanach. The track ends at a bridge over the Abhainn Rath which leads to Creaguaineach Lodge.

The eastern end of Creag Ghuanach has some awkward craggy ground. So the best option is to cross the bridge, turn left and follow the path on the north bank of the Abhainn Rath upstream for about 600m to a prominent bend in the river. Turn right here and head for a grassy depression in the middle of the south-east face, which splits higher up into two narrow gullies. The aim is to eventually gain the right-hand fork. Ascend the hillside to a broad central area with much bracken in the summer. Traverse rightwards near a tree and eventually slant back leftwards to gain the right-hand grassy gully, which is then followed without difficulty. Weave a way up through minor crags to gain the crest of the hill. There are superb panoramic views from here, which include the Easains and Grey Corries to the north. Just to the west of a second small lochan, a tiny cairn on a rocky protuberance marks the summit (**10.5km; 410m; 3h 5min**).

Head easily down the south-west ridge from the summit and continue directly down the steeper hillside towards Staoineag bothy. There are stepping stones in the river immediately west of the bothy, however the crossing will normally entail getting wet feet. If a crossing cannot be made a lengthy detour will be required to recross the bridge at Creaguaineach Lodge.

From the bothy, ascend the hillside in a southerly direction initially passing some stone ruins. When the angle eases, slightly slant rightwards at first then contour along the hillside. Cross the burn from Loch na Staoineig then ascend the long but easy north-east ridge of Beinn na Cloiche. Head leftwards over a slight depression to reach the highest point which lies just east of a small lochan (**15km; 780m; 4h 55min**).

The views are not as spectacular as from Creag Ghuanach and it feels more desolate. Glas Bheinn lies to the west with Leum Uilleim to the east, both Corbetts, whilst Buchaille Etive Mòr is seen to the south-west across Blackwater Reservoir.

Go south past the summit for about 150m then descend the eastern face before heading north-eastwards to the broad bealach south of Loch na Staoineig. The natural continuation from here is to head for Meall a' Bhainne, a Graham Top failing by only a few metres of relative height to get separate Graham status. Ascend the south-western flank of the hill and continue up the broad plateau to the summit where there are fine views northwards to Loch Treig (**18km; 930m; 5h 55min**).

Descend the north-eastern ridge easily at first, but partway down it is best to slant leftwards to find the easiest way. Eventually gain a poor path in Gleann Iolairean and take this down to Loch Treig. Return along the track used in the approach for 7.5km, back to Corrour Station (**28.5km; 1110m; 8h 45min**).

A useful approach can be made by bike via the Road to the Isles track from 2km east of Kinloch Rannoch (NN446578). Bike the track north to the head of Loch Ossian then follow the above route to the bridge over the Abhainn Iolairean (**20.5km; 360m; 2h 30min** by bike). Continue on foot and return to the bridge (**13km; 890m; 5h** on foot). Bike to Corrour then the road (**54km; 1660m; 10h** with a bike).

Beinn na Cloiche from the traverse above Staoineag (Rab Anderson)

154 Cnap Cruinn

Cnap Cruinn; 742m; (G26); L41; NN302774; round knob

Broad and sprawling, Cnap Cruinn lies on the south side of Glen Spean, somewhat isolated from its neighbours. There are two approaches.

For the first, leave the A86 by a single track road leading to Fersit. Cross the railway then the River Spean and after 1.7km park with care where a forest track forks off to the right at Inverlair (NN339798); space is limited.

Ascend the track, initially in the open with good views back to the Graham Creag Dhubh on the north side of Glen Spean, then through the forest to where it runs beside the Allt Laire. At the point the track swings right, the east flank of Cnap Cruinn is visible straight ahead. Continue between plantations where the track coincides with the position of the former 'puggy line', the narrow gauge railway used in the construction of the tunnel for the Lochaber hydro-electric scheme. A mountain bike could be used on this 4km of track.

Leave the track soon after it exits the plantation and head over rough ground directly for the summit. Climb quite steeply to reach a sizeable cairn then continue southwards for a further 130m to the true summit, marked by a small cairn on a rocky rib (**6km; 540m; 2h 15min**).

There are fine views of Sgùrr Innse,

Cnap Cruinn from the Inverlair approach (George Archibald)

Cruach Innse and the Grey Corries to the south-west, as well as the Munros, Stob a' Choire Mheadhoin and Stob Coire Easain, to the south.

Rather than return the same way, descend north-west to a broad bealach where Buachaille Etive Mòr comes into view framed between Sgùrr Innse and Cruch Innse and continue over a minor top to reach Beinn Chlianaig (724m), a Graham Top, (**7.5km; 600m; 2h 40min**).

To the north past Creag Dhubh, the Parallel Roads indicating the water level marks of ancient glacial lakes can be seen in the lower reaches of Glen Roy, together with two Grahams, the Lèana Mhòrs, which sit opposite each other on either side of the glen.

Return to a dip below the summit, then slant leftwards (east) across a burn and descend the hillside beyond to cross the Allt Boidheach and make a beeline for the forest track used in the approach. Return by this to the start (**14km; 600m; 4h 25min**).

A good alternative starts at the Cille Choirill church car park (NN306812), as used for the ascent of Creag Dhubh on p195, and enables both hills to be climbed in the same day.

Walk down to the main road, go carefully straight over and cross the railway by a bridge, then swing right to gain the Monessie Gorge suspension footbridge at NN299811. Go through the farm at Monessie and climb the hillside onto the spur which leads to the lowest point between the tops then the summit (**5km; 610m; 2h 10min**).

Traverse over to Beinn Chlianaig then descend back to Monessie (**10.5km; 720m; 3h 40min**).

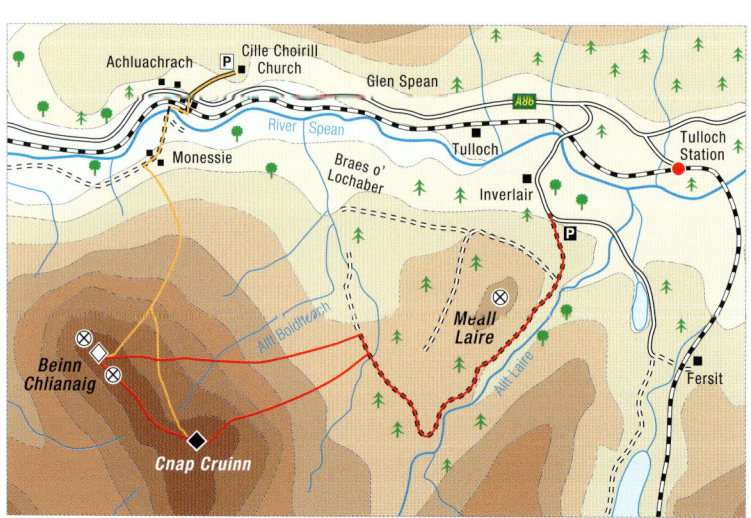

Binnein Shios, Binnein Shuas

Binnein Shios; 667m; (G149); L34, 42; NN492857; easterly pointed top
Binnein Shuas; 747m; (G15); L34, 42; NN463826; westerly pointed top

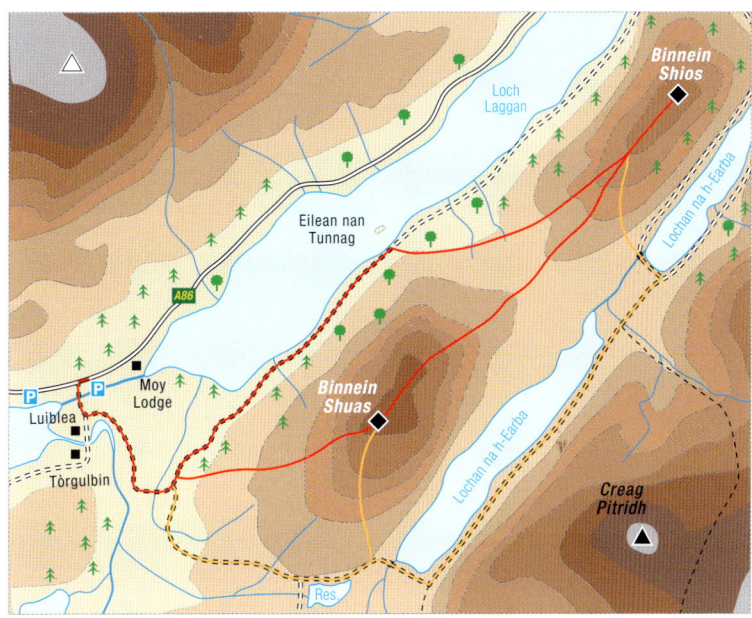

A very good outing can be made by combining these two fine hills on the south side of Loch Laggan, opposite Creag Meagaidh. Start between Loch Laggan and Laggan Dam Reservoir to the west, from a popular layby (NN433830) on the A86. This is on the east side of the concrete bridge over the River Spean. There is another layby 200m to the west.

Follow a track over the bridge and soon after take the left fork which leads to a high fence and gate. Continue on the east side of the Abhainn Ghuilbinn then climb more steeply eastwards to where the track divides after 1.9km. Take the left-hand track, which descends slightly and continue along the south side of Loch Laggan. There are fine exposures of pink and white pegmatite cutting the schist on the uphill side of the track. Follow the lochside for about 2km until just short of a tiny island in the loch called Eilean nan Tunnag.

Leave the track and head up eastwards through pleasant open woodland. Clamber through an old wire fence to gain the open hillside and head leftwards for the south-western end of Binnein Shios. Climb steadily up the grassy hillside for some distance and eventually rocky outcrops appear on the crest. From here there are good views southwards of the two long lochs which bear the same name, Lochan na h-Earba, and west across Loch Laggan to mighty Creag Meagaidh. ▶

Binnein Shios and Ardverikie House from across Loch Laggan (Grahame Nicoll)

Binnein Shios, Binnein Shuas

Binnein Shuas and Lochan na h-Earba from Binnein Shios (Noel Williams)

The angle eases and a long gentle climb eventually leads to the highest point which lies at the far end of the summit ridge (**9km; 450m; 2h 45min**).

Beyond, the northern slopes drop much more steeply to forestry and Ardverikie on Loch Laggan.

To reach Binnein Shuas, however, do an about turn and return south-west along the crest for about 1km and descend the end of the ridge slightly leftwards to reach the broad saddle between the two peaks.

The north-eastern end of Binnein Shuas is quite complex and has several steep crags, so it is important to try and identify the best way up this ground in advance. There is a broad gully well over to the left but the most direct way is to stay on the crest of the broad grassy ridge from the saddle and slant slightly right higher up. After this, follow a leftward slanting diagonal weakness up steep grassy ground with boulders and continue more easily in a broad runnel. The upper part of the mountain is somewhat confusing, especially in poor visibility. Slant slightly left to reach the upper tier and scramble up easy rocks to reach the highest point (**13.5km; 810m; 4h 30min**).

The views from the summit are very fine. Out of sight below is a rock face that is popular with rock climbers. Across the loch to the south-east is Creag Pitridh, with Geal Chàrn behind, whilst to the south is the great mass of Beinn a' Chlachair with its high central corrie. From the summit, go down the south-west ridge and follow the base of a long left-facing rock wall. Once past this, the track used in the approach can be seen. Descend the grassy hillside and head straight for the left end of a conifer plantation. The ground here is tussocky and somewhat boggy. The junction on the track is reached soon after. Return by the track to the start (**18km; 810m; 5h 45min**).

With the use of a mountain bike it is easy enough to climb these hills individually, biking to NN454809 to climb Binnein Shuas and return. Then biking to NN488842 and doing the same with Binnein Shios. This enables the lovely Lochan na h-Earba lochans to be explored and allows the cliffs of Binnein Shuas to be viewed, as well as avoiding the steep northern end of that hill.

Binnein Shuas, left, and Binnein Shios above Lochan na h-Earba (Jim Teesdale)

Meall nan Eagan   157

Meall nan Eagan through the Dirc Mhòr (Rab Anderson)

Meall nan Eagan; 658m; (G163); L42; NN596874; *mountain of the notches*

Meall nan Eagan is a small but fine peak to the north of The Fara whose top remains largely hidden from view, and although it can be glimpsed from various points on the road it is not easy to identify. The best approach follows the Allt an t-Sluic to the east of the hill.

Start from a parking area at the Crubenmore junction on the road north out of Dalwhinnie. This is at a bend just past the distillery, after the road crosses the railway. Walk up the road behind the distillery for 900m, passing a gated track into the forest, to reach a track towards the top of the brae signposted 'Old Drover's Route to Feagour'. Follow this to a track on the left which climbs onto the northern ridge of The Fara (a Corbett) and is the return route for walkers including that hill in the round.

Continue above the Allt an t-Sluic to the keeper's house, with its inevitable barking dogs. Go down left and where the track ends go uphill, as directed by a waymark, onto another track. This leads pleasantly through the glen, crossing the burn a couple of times; if the water is high, continue on the original side.

The track stops at a fenced plantation where the glen opens out and the hill is visible straight ahead. Ford the burn once more, then cross the flat floor of the glen and climb the heathery flank of the hill onto the east ridge. The ridge leads to a fine summit; steeply in places past rock outcrops and following a line of rusty fence posts (**5.5km; 310m; 1h 45min**).

Loch Caoldair with Creag Dubh beyond lie to the north-east, a view now spoiled by the Beauly to Denny pylon line that spans the glen. To the south the bulk of The Fara is close but cut off by two impressive rocky gashes slicing through the hillside. These are the Dirc Bheag and the Dirc Mhòr, particularly fine examples of glacial meltwater channels. The shortest route returns the same way (**11km; 310m; 3h 10min**).

However, a splendid extension explores the 'Dircs' and The Fara. Descend south-west to a col then traverse a deer track into the Dirc Bheag. Carefully go through the boulder-field to reach secluded Lochan Doire-uaine and beyond some crags climb steeply to the top of Creag nan Adhaircean. Traverse the rim of the Dirc Mhòr then cross the top of this and follow a line of fence posts to the 911m summit of The Fara (**11.5km; 810m; 3h 45min**). Descend the north-east ridge to gain a track and follow this to rejoin the approach route (**17.5km; 830m; 5h 15min**).

Meall nan Eagan can also be approached via Loch Caoldair to the north, although this is slightly longer and rougher going, as well as crossing beneath the pylon line. A track, then a path lead to the loch, thereafter deep heather, bog myrtle and deer fences have to be crossed to reach the hill's east ridge (**6.5km; 340m; 2h**), (**13km; 340m; 3h 40min**).

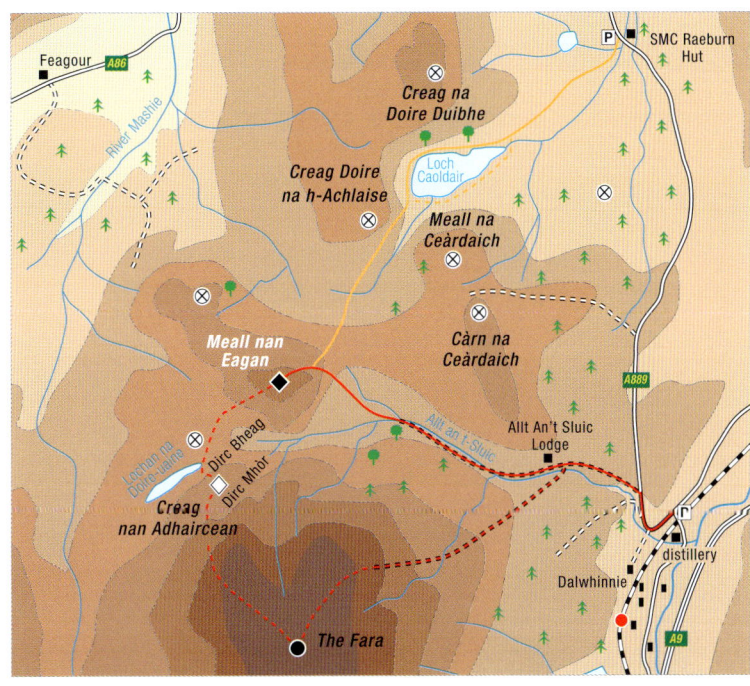

Hill of Wirren's expansive summit view Ben Avon, left, pointed Mount Keen and Mount Battock, right (Rab Anderson)

SECTION 5, 6 & 7
Loch Ericht to Glen Esk

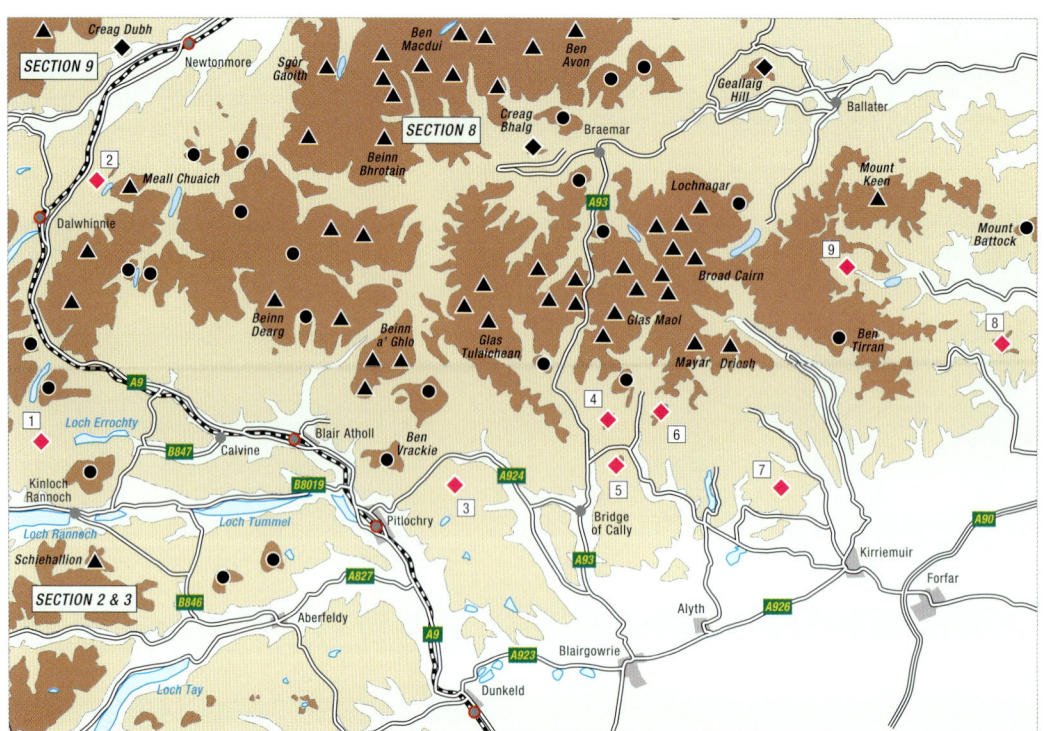

SECTION 5, 6 & 7

[1] *Creag a' Mhadaidh* — 161
[2] *Creag Ruadh* — 162
[3] *Blath Bhalg* — 163
[4] *Duchary Hill*, [5] *Mount Blair* — 164
[6] *Badandun Hill* — 166
[7] *Cat Law* — 167
[8] *Hill of Wirren* — 168
[9] *Hunt Hill* — 170

Creag a' Mhadaidh

The 'undistinguished' Creag a' Mhadaidh above Loch Errochty (Rab Anderson)

Creag a' Mhadaidh; 612m; (G215); L42; NN634650; cliff of the fox (dog)

Creag a' Mhadaidh lies in the remote and unfrequented ground between Drumochter and Rannoch. It is a rather undistinguished hill and the word 'creag' is misleading as the hill is no more than a highpoint in an area of rolling heathery moorland.

Approaches to the hill can be made from Dalnaspidal on the A9 to the north, from Loch Rannoch to the south, or via Loch Errochty to the east. The Loch Rannoch approach is the shorter and is the principal one described. Given that all of the approaches are on tracks then bikes could be used to shorten the timings.

A right of way begins 2.5km west of Kinloch Rannoch at Annat (signposted to Dalnaspidal). There is a small pull-off about 200m beyond this. Parking has become a problem on this road with many places blocked-off by boulders.

Walk up the track to Annat Farm and continue alongside an old stone wall until a sharp turn right leads into an old lane between high stone walls. There is a fine view of Schiehallion from here. A short while later the track turns left, still between walls, then emerges onto the open hillside. Before long the track forks and the ruins of Old Annat can be seen ahead. Either fork leads over the Annat Burn up to a forest. The track traverses below the forest before emerging onto a high open moor.

A little further on there is a junction with another track that comes up from Craiganour Lodge and Aulich. This is an alternative way up or down from this point. The track climbs gradually, passing a small dam where water is diverted to Loch Errochty, to gain the wide col between Gualann Sheileach and Creag a' Mhadaidh. Leave the track, cross the boggy col and ascend an easy heathery slope to the summit (9km; 400m; 2h 40min).

The cairn is substantial for such an unfrequented hill. The view of Schiehallion is now obscured by Càrn Fiaclach but the view east over Loch Errochty to Beinn a' Ghlo is splendid.

Although the Corbett Beinn Mholach lies to the west and the Corbett Beinn a' Chuallaich to the south-east, adding either into a walk with Creag a' Mhadaidh would make for a long day. Most walkers will be content to return by the approach route (18km; 400m; 4h 40min).

The ascent from Trinafour can be made via a pleasant circuit around Loch Errochty. There is limited parking at NN725649 at the start of the road to the Errochty Dam. Follow the road then track along the north side of Loch Errochty to its end then take the left-hand atv track. Ford the Allt Sleibh then pass below forestry and climb to the top (10.75km; 410m; 3h 5min).

Descend to a bridge at NN662642 then follow the track along the south side of the loch to reach the B847. Turn left and walk down the road to cross the bridge over the Errochty Water then turn left back to the start (22km; 500m; 6h).

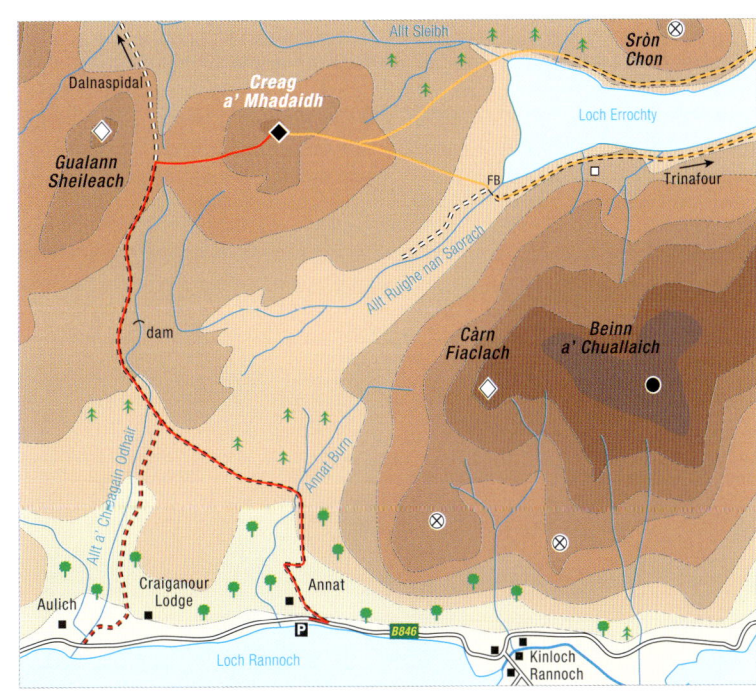

Creag Ruadh

Creag Ruadh, left, and Meall Chuaich from Glen Truim to the west (Rab Anderson)

Creag Ruadh; *658m; (G164); L42; NN685882; red cliff*

Creag Ruadh is an elongated hill overlooking the A9 between Dalwhinnie and Newtonmore. It appears as an insignificant heathery slope partially obscuring its grander neighbour, the Munro Meall Chuaich.

It is a hill that is probably best climbed on its own, albeit that the fit might consider adding it after an ascent of Meall Chuaich. However, for the Graham bagger it makes a convenient route to do on the way up or down the road, or in combination with one of the other single Grahams nearby. Although it could be climbed in less than an hour starting from Layby 96A, the closest point on the A9, the better route starts from Cuaich. This is the normal starting point for Meall Chuaich and makes use of the track leading to Loch Cuaich.

Park at Layby 94 on the east side of the A9, or in Layby 93 on the west side of the road, some 3km northeast of the Dalwhinnie turn-off and just south of the turning to Cuaich. Traffic moves fast here, so great care and attention are advised.

Almost opposite the entrance to Cuaich there is a gated track. Go through the gate and straight on to join the main track running alongside a concrete aqueduct. This was constructed in the 1950s and carries water from the Allt Cuaich and other nearby burns to Loch Ericht.

After about 20min the track crosses the aqueduct to reach Cuaich Power Station. Although the dam is easily crossed, a gate and two fences have to be negotiated. Perhaps better is to go through the gate to the side of the aqueduct crossing, to ford the usually small burn then go through the gate in the fence beyond to ascend the hillside past a line of shooting butts.

The going is rough but easier if you take advantage of the strips of muir burn. Before long the ground levels off and a sizable cairn and stone shelter are reached at the summit (**4km; 310m; 1h 25min**). The best views are to the north over Badenoch where Creag Dubh is prominent. Return the same way (**8km; 310m; 2h 20min**).

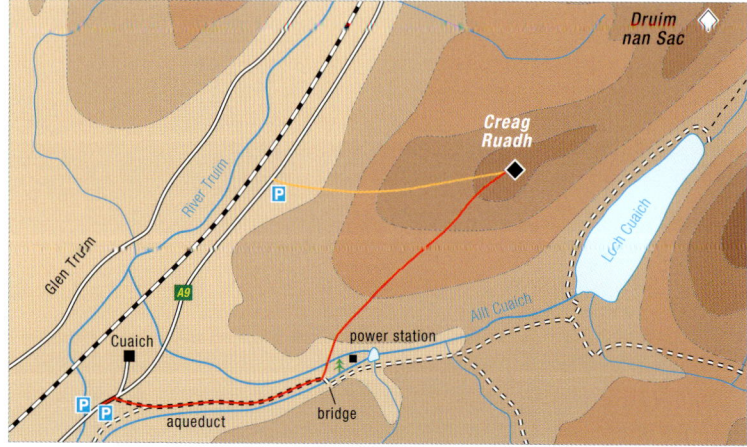

Blath Bhalg

Blath Bhalg; 641m; (G183); L43; NO019611; pleasant bulge

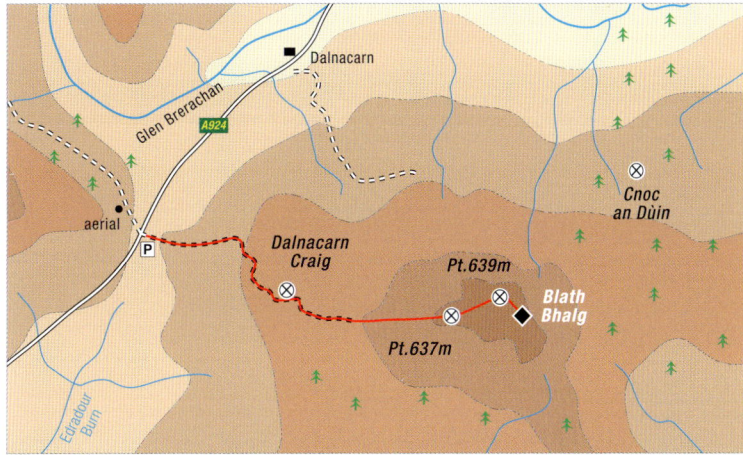

Pleasant bulge seems an appropriate description for this hill, which offers a pleasant excursion for a short day, or summers evening, or perhaps while travelling the A9.

The hill is readily accessed from the A924 north of Pitlochry via Moulin and Kinnaird. At the highest point of the road before it descends into Glen Brerachan, there is a parking area on the south-east side of the road at the start of a gated grassy track.

Follow the grassy track towards the north-to-south running ridgeline of Dalnacarn Craig. Some boggy areas at the start are easily avoided. The track leads up and rightwards to pass immediatley below the 526m high-point, which lies at the southern end of the ridgeline.

It is worth pausing here to take in the view. Ben Vrackie to the north-west does not present its best aspect, but behind and slightly further east the high peaks forming the long ridge of Beinn a' Ghlo are better appreciated.

The track continues rightwards across flatter heathery ground, gradually fading, to end in front of an old fence. Follow a rough path beside the fence up onto Point 637m, the first highpoint on the knobbly summit ridge. Drop steeply past a small rock outcrop then climb onto Point 639m and make a right-angled turn to the right past a boulder and follow the fence across a dip to the summit cairn (**3.75km; 315m; 1h 20min**).

The view is extensive for such a small hill. Beinn a' Ghlo remains prominent to the north and west, but the north-east is now dominated by the high hills of the West Mounth and Glas Maol above Glen Shee.

It is worth continuing for 150m to the end of the summit ridge. From the summit, it is perhaps tempting to descend north to a track leading to the A924 at Dalnacarn, but this would involve walking back up the road to the parking place and hardly seems worth the effort for such a small hill. Better to return by the outward route, enjoying the view ahead to Beinn a' Ghlo and Ben Vrackie, as well as west to Schiehallion and south over Loch Broom and Strath Tay (**7.5km; 365m; 2h 25min**).

The knobbly ridge leading to Pt.639m and the summit of Blath Bhalg (Rab Anderson)

Duchray Hill, Mount Blair

Duchray Hill from Mount Blair with the Corbett Monamenach beyond (Ken Crocket)

Duchray Hill; 702m; (G99); L43; NO161672; dark corrie, probably, from Gaelic 'dubh coire'. Also known as Mealna Letter, 'meall na leitir', hill of the broad slope

Mount Blair; 744m; (G19); L43; NO167629; hill-mass (above) the plain, from Gaelic 'monadh blair'

These two Grahams are easily combined into a pleasant circuit when ascended from the B951, which connects Glen Shee with Glen Isla, starting at a height of about 360m. Park off the road on the right opposite a strip of forestry, just beyond the highpoint of this road as it starts to descend to Glen Isla.

Walk downhill crossing over the Duchray Burn and about 50m beyond the entrance to the farm at Balloch go through a gate into the field on the left. Climb uphill to pass through a gate in a wall, then cross over a track and continue up onto the grassy ridge of Càrn an Fhidleir (518m). Continue north to ascend the south-east spur of Duchray Hill then swing left alongside a drystane dyke to gain the top,

Ancient and modern on the summit of Mount Blair (Rab Anderson)

Duchray Hill, Mount Blair 165

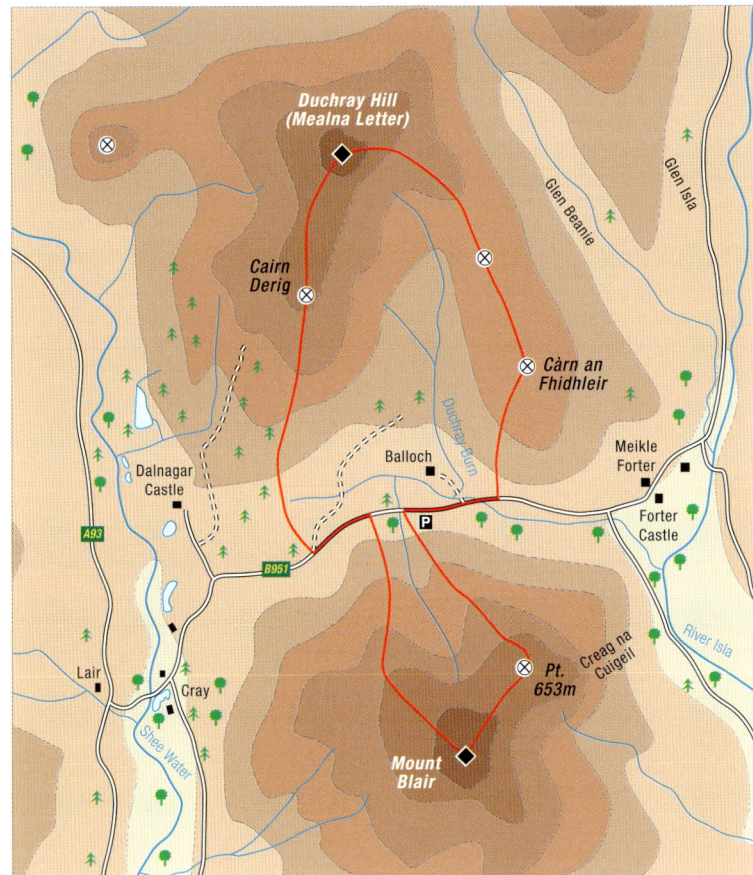

Forest prominent. Another Graham, Badandun Hill, can be seen across Glen Isla to the east.

Returning south, follow the drystane dyke downhill back to the B951, passing through a marshy section at the lowest point just before regaining the road, at the start of a track. Mount Blair is predominant, with its disfiguring communication tower an unwelcome if functional eyesore. Walk 200m east and start the ascent of Mount Blair at a gate, following a grassy track uphill to a second gate then the top (**9.5km; 780m; 3h 25min**).

There is a large prehistoric cairn, supplemented by the tower and a badly damaged circular viewpoint, which helpfully points to hills visible from here in good conditions. Mount Blair obviously has, despite its despoilments, a strong following in the neighbourhood, and it certainly stands out independently of any other hill.

Rather than return the same way, a better route heads north-east following a path to point 653m above Creag na Cuigeil. Descend from here via the north-west ridge passing through two gates at the bottom to regain the road next to the starting point. If it can be found, there is a rough atv track which eases the heathery descent (**12km; 790m; 4h 20min**).

which lies a few metres west of the dyke (**4km; 380m; 1h 35min**).

There are fine views to the north with the hills of the Caenlochan

Mount Blair from Duchray Hill (Rab Anderson)

Badandun Hill

> **Badandun Hill**; 740m; (G30); L44; NO207678; mapped as Baldendeen (1794). Probably Gaelic 'bad an dùn' or 'duine', tuft or spot, of the hill-fort, or of the man

This fine little hill lies tucked away from general view towards the head of lovely Glen Isla, opposite Duchray Hill. It can be accessed from the A93 through Glen Shee to the west by taking the B951 between Cray and Meikle Forter, then following the unclassified road up the glen almost to its end. The other option is to drive up the length of Glen Isla from the south via the B951.

Start just beyond the public telephone box at Delnamar, at the far side of a small forestry plantation where there is space to park around the entrance to the track to the Keeper's Cottage at Fergus.

Walk up this track and cross the River Isla to reach Fergus then take the uphill track through the trees onto the open hillside. Badandun Hill lies to the right but the track stays left, climbing up the Fergus Burn almost to the top of Craig Lair (711m).

The track to Badandun forks right just below the top of this hill, however it is worthwhile making the short detour onto its summit via the left-hand track then crossing through heather to the cairn on its top. The views north to the Glen Shee hills, Caenlochan Glen then the Munros of Mayar and Dreish are splendid.

Drop off the top of Craig Lair through some small rock outcrops to regain the track and follow this onto Badandun Hill. Where the main track starts to descend, take to a rough track which climbs the shoulder to the trig point on the summit; another excellent and panoramic viewpoint (**6km; 530m; 2h 15min**).

A direct descent to the track up the Fergus Burn shortens the walk. However, a better route descends south on a rough track which cuts through some peat hags then drops south-west towards Glen Isla before cutting across onto the track taken by the Cateran Way; a circular long distance footpath that starts in Blairgowrie, passing through Spittal of Glenshee, Forter, Kirkton of Glenisla and Alyth. Reach the road at Bridge of Forter then take the track which leads pleasantly along the east side of the River Isla back to Fergus (**14km; 590m; 4h 15min**).

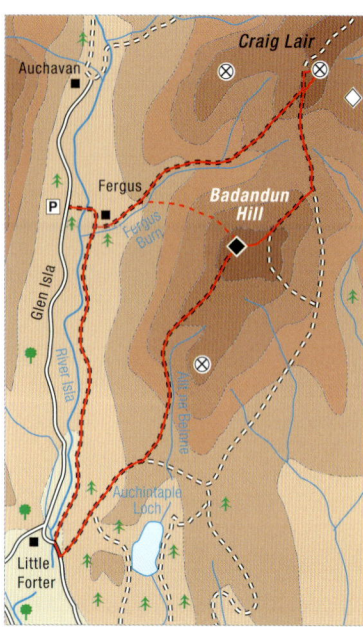

Badandun Hill across Glen Isla from Duchray Hill to the west (Ken Crocket)

Cat Law 167

Cat Law on the traverse from Long Goat (Rab Anderson)

Cat Law; 671m; (G144); L44, L53, L54; NO318610; probably (wild) cat hill. However, Gaelic 'cath', battle, is possible from long-held belief that in Roman times the battle of Mons Graupius was fought nearby

Rising to the north-west above Kirriemuir, Cat Law is a prominent sight at the entrance to the Angus Glens. It was previously best climbed from the north side together with Corwharn, as a round of Glen Uig. However, following the demotion of Corwharn as a Graham, Cat Law is now usually climbed on its own. This is best achieved from the south and east sides of the hill where parking is also easier, as well as perhaps being more readily accessible.

Cat Law and its environs are used for shooting, and the hill is criss-crossed by tracks for this purpose. Whilst these tracks make the approaches straightforward, there is a chance that during the shooting season one may have to alter ones plans for an approach via a particular part of the hill. For this reason three routes are described.

The best route is probably from the east, starting at NO357613 close to the highpoint of the road between Kirriemuir and Easter Lednathie; signed to Pearsie and Lednathie. There is a pull-off on the east side of the road just beyond the entrance to Muir Pearsie Lodge.

Walk north along the road for 650m then go through a red gate on the left and ascend a track up onto the crest of the hill to reach another red gate. Go through this and follow a path to, then alongside a fence, climbing onto the top of Long Goat (571m) where there is a boundary stone. Cat Law's domed summit can now be seen ahead some 2km away. ▶

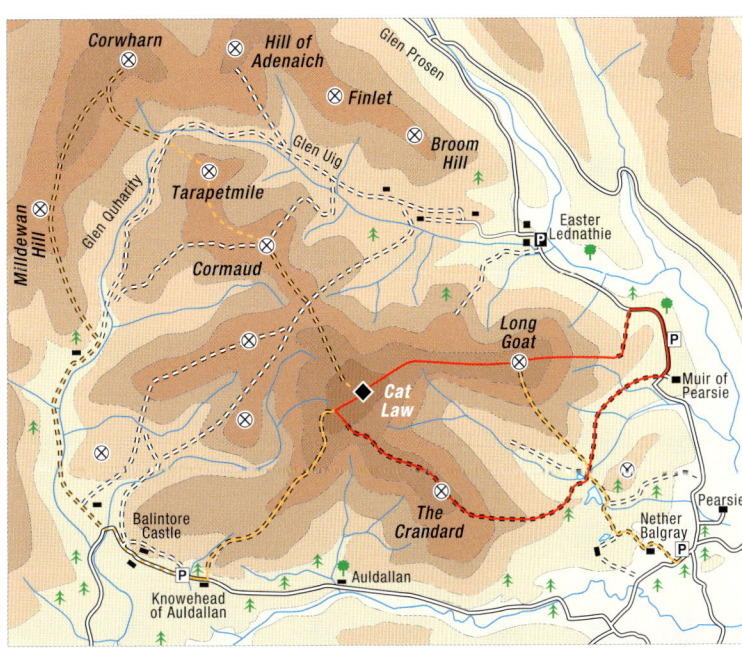

The ensuing traverse alongside the fence on an atv track then a rough path is scenic and provides especially fine views to the Glen Clova hills. On the final climb, a stone shelter on the other side of the fence is passed. At the top, cross a fence by a stile to gain the highpoint on the broad and flat summit. The slightly lower trig point is some 80m or so to the south (**5km; 450m; 1h 50min**).

A peat bank on one side of the trig provides shelter and on the other side, gained via a stile over the fence, are some wind-shelter cairns.

From the trig point side, descend south-west by the fence for about 400m and cross the fence by a stile at the corner to gain an atv track. Follow the track down to the south-east then up the slight rise onto The Crandard (560m).

Continue south-east downhill, quite steeply in places, then swing east and north-east, passing a track off right, to reach a small pond where a track breaks off uphill to Long Goat. Follow the main track across the base of the hill to gain the road opposite the entrance to Muir Pearsie Lodge, then turn left for 300m back to the start (**12km; 475m; 3h 30min**).

Another route leaves the Kirrimuir to Pearsie road, turning sharply left at a telephone box along a road signed to Kingoldrum. There is a pull-off on the right after 170m at NO360588.

Just beyond the pull-off, follow a track past Nether Balgray, then right and right again to reach a reservoir at Clash. Continue past this on another track then ascend a track steeply up onto Long Goat and traverse to Cat Law as for the previous route (**6km; 510m; 2h 10min**). Descend over The Crandard, then at the bottom, about 150m before a forestry plantation, go down a track on the right to cut the corner and rejoin the approach track south of the reservoir then return along this (**12km; 525m; 3h 40min**).

A popular ascent can be made from Burnside of Balintore where there is parking at NO295586 at the entrance gates to Balintore Castle, an impressive Scots Baronial style building currently being refurbished.

Walk east along the road for 200m to the farm then go through a gate and north up the field to pick up a track and follow this north-east to the summit of Cat Law (**4.25km; 400m; 1h 35min**). Most return the same way (**8.5km; 400m; 2h 35min**).

However, this route can be extended north-west then west on the track over Bodandere Hill. From Hill of Stanks, either continue westwards down the crest into Glen Quharity and return down this to the road then the start (**12km; 445m; 3h 30min**), or descend south to regain the road.

Another option is to continue north-west from Cat Law over Cormaud to Tarapetmile. Descend to the head of the glen then climb Corwharn via the track up Cairn Course. From there, follow a track southwards along the crest then down into Glen Quharity (**18.5km; 845m; 5h 45min**).

Hill of Wirren; 678m; (G133); L44; NO522739; *hill of springs from Gaelic 'fhuaran'. Mapped Worren (1755) and Warren Hill (1794)*

Prominently seen from the A90 between Dundee and Aberdeen, and lying some 10 miles (15km) north-west of Brechin, this broad sprawling hill throws out ridges, or 'shanks', in all directions. It sits on the Highland Line which possibly explains why there are no less than four aircraft wrecks on its slopes.

The ascent is best made from the south, from Bridgend to the west of Edzell. As well as offering a straight-forward route which follows a track to within a few hundred metres of the summit, this also enables it to be linked with the adjacent East Wirren for a pleasant circuit. Parking is possible out in front of Lethnot Primary School at Bridgend.

Zigzag up the track to the left of the school onto the brow of the ridge then go past the first house to where a track breaks off to the right and splits in two. This track, used for the return, can be taken via its left fork past a small man-made lochan then back onto the brow at another fork.

The Crandard, Cat Law and Long Goat from the south-east (Rab Anderson)

Hill of Wirren 169

Hill of Wirren, left, and East Wirren from the south (Grahame Nicoll)

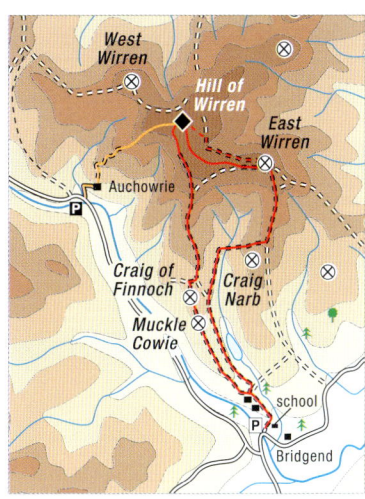

However, it is better and more scenic to continue past the second house then break off up a grassy track and through a gate. This leads up the crest over Muckle Cowie and through a gate to reach a track crossing the ridge at Craig of Finnoch. Follow this track right to another track then go left (or cut the corner) and continue up the ridge; the Shank of Ledmanie.

Not far below the plateau, and partway up a line of wood shooting butts, take the left fork. This traverses beneath the plateau, soon becoming rougher and fading, to reach a wooden gate. Go through the gate to reach the remains of an RAF Consolidated Liberator which crashed in October 1944; miraculously four of the eleven crew survived.

Continue in the same line by the fence to where it joins another fence then follow this up, passing through a metal gate, to reach the flat summit. The trig point lies on the other side of the fence, which can be stepped across (**6.5km; 560m; 2h 20min**).

The view of the rolling hills of The Mounth and the Grampians is fine, extending in an arc from Cat Law in the south-west to the Glen Clova hills, then Lochnagar, Beinn a' Bhuird, Ben Avon, Mount Keen, Mount Battock, then Clachnaben with its tor and out to the North Sea.

For the return, one option is to step over the fence then go back through the metal gate and follow that fence south-east then east through peat hags; not as bad as it looks. Beyond the hags, go right through a gate to gain a track on the right which leads to East Wirren and another trig point. The other option is to step back over the fence and head south-east for 400m to join a track which traverses below the peat hags to reach East Wirren (**8.5km; 580m; 2h 50min**).

On a clear day the view south to the Lowlands stretches beyond Fife's Lomond Hills to the Pentland Hills above Edinburgh. Much closer are the twin bumps of the Brown and the White Caterthun with their Iron Age forts and the Montrose Basin beyond.

To descend, follow the track south down the crest of the ridge then down the side of Torr na Menach. Just above the col with Craig Narb, turn right at a small hut onto another track and descend into the valley of the Burn of Drumcairn. Cross the burn and follow the track back to the start (**15km; 590m; 4h 20min**).

The summit can be gained in less than an hour from Glen Lethnot, by an up and back route via the access road to Auchowrie then the track up the hillside beyond this.

Hill of Wirren from the Muckle Cowie ridge (Rab Anderson)

Hunt Hill

![Craig Maskeldie, left, and Hunt Hill from Glen Lee (Rab Anderson)]

Craig Maskeldie, left, and Hunt Hill from Glen Lee (Rab Anderson)

Hunt Hill; 705m; (G91); L44; NO380805; hunt(ing) hill

Glen Esk runs north-westwards from Edzell and splits into Glen Mark and Glen Lee at Invermark. In turn, Glen Lee splits at the Waters of Lee and Unich. Hunt Hill stands prominently between these two Waters which drain the high plateau behind. The walk to and over Hunt Hill gives a very fine outing.

Start at the large car park at the end of the public road in Glen Esk; also the normal starting point for Mount Keen. Follow the road past the church and the track off right to Mount Keen and Ballater, taking the signposted route to Milton of Clova. Cross the bridge over the Water of Mark and pass a cottage, then Invermark Castle. This dates from around 1526 and was important in defending the vital pass between Glen Esk and Deeside. It's worth stopping to see if you can find the door! Continue along the track through birch woodland alongside the Water of Lee then pass out in front of Invermark Lodge and the old graveyard at Kirkton to reach the black waters of Loch Lee.

Further on, the dark crags of Craig Maskeldie dominate the glen and soon the steep face of Hunt Hill comes into view. Keep going on the main track to the end of the flat floor of the glen until it starts to rise and a footbridge can be seen; don't go to the rusty hut. Cross the bridge over the cascading Water of Lee to head towards the Falls of Unich and the

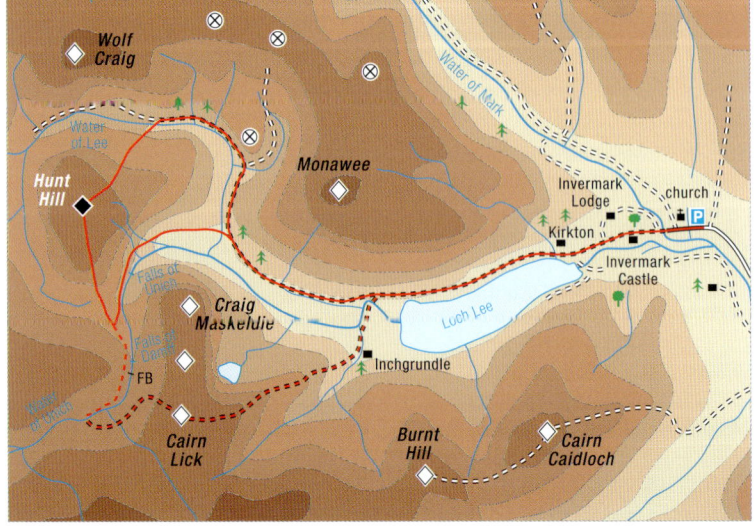

narrow glen beyond. The falls look diminutive from a distance but are more impressive close up and can have a large volume of water crashing over them.

The path now rises into the narrow rocky glen to provide a quite delightful route alongside the tumbling river. On emerging suddenly onto the plateau turn sharp right, or continue first a short distance to view the Falls of Damff, then traverse deep heather to a wide col. A steep pull now leads up to shorter-cropped heather and the summit. This is marked by a small quartz cairn (**9km; 460m; 2h 50min**).

The views are extensive over a vast area of barren high ground. Mount Keen is obvious to the north whilst Lochnagar is prominent to the west.

The best and quickest descent is to head north-east down gradually steepening slopes to the Water of Lee. This can be crossed by a rickety, steel girder bridge at NO388815, about 200m upstream of a forest, to gain the track on the other side. The lower part of the forest has been felled, exposing a tiny but well-frequented bothy. The track curves pleasantly downhill through the glen with the fine sight of Craig Maskeldie filling the view ahead. Join the upward route where it left the track earlier on the walk and follow this back (**18km; 460m; 5h**).

The Falls of Unich (Rab Anderson)

An alternative route, which is not that much longer than the route described here, is to ascend the track up the Shank of Inchgrundle from the head of Loch Lee onto Cairn Lick and hence to the Falls of Damff.

Hunt Hill from the top of the route through the Unich gorge with the top of Mount Keen far right (Grahame Nicoll)

Càrn a' Ghille Chearr across Glenlivet (Rab Anderson)

SECTION 8
Deeside to Speyside

Section 8 – Deeside to Speyside

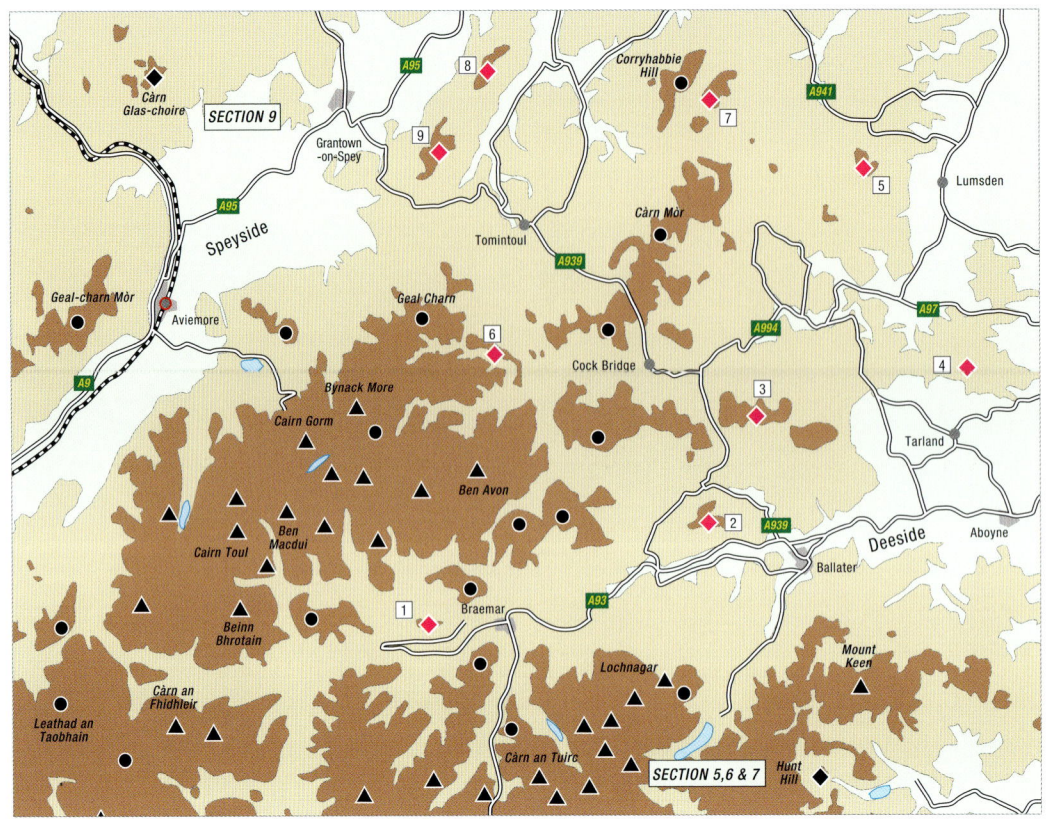

SECTION 8

[1] *Creag Bhalg*		175
[2] *Geallaig Hill*		176
[3] *Mona Gowan*		177
[4] *Pressendye*		178
[5] *The Buck*		179
[6] *Cnap Chaochan Aitinn*		181
[7] *Cook's Cairn*		182
HILLS OF CROMDALE [8] *Càrn a' Ghillie Chearr,*		
[9] *Creagan a' Chaise*		183

Creag Bhalg

Creag Bhalg across the River Dee from the Linn road (Fran Pothecary)

Creag Bhalg; 668m; (G147); L43; NO091912; bulge cliff

A modest hill situated on the edge of the Cairngorms extensive massif, Creag Bhalg presents two faces as you approach by road to the Linn of Dee from Braemar. The eastern face dropping to the Linn of Quoich is craggy and tree covered, while open heather and pine-clad southern and western slopes rise more gently above Mar Lodge and the valley of the upper Dee.

The main route starts from Linn of Dee, from a National Trust for Scotland pay and display car park with toilet facilities. A signed path out of the car park to the north leads to the track to Derry Lodge along the west side of the Lui Water. Alternatively, a short walk along the road to the east and across the bridge over the Lui Water then gives access to a pleasant stroll along the east bank of the river. This alternative route is a beautiful start to the walk and there is plenty of interest in the fast flowing lower reaches of the Lui where there is evidence of old dams and sluices.

Both routes meet at the bridge further up the Lui at NO003914 and take the track that leads back south-east toward Claybokie and Mar Lodge. About 500m from the bridge, branch off left on a track (shown as a footpath on the OS 1:50k map) which becomes increasingly overgrown as it rises through the open woodland of the Doire Bhraghad. The track is joined by another from the left and continues until it hits a deer fence with a stile at NO084908. A few metres short of the fence and stile, take an indistinct atv track which heads north past a lone dead pine onto the broad summit.

A low stone shelter affords a dramatic panorama of the heart of the southern Cairngorms, ranging from Cairn Toul and Ben Macdui, the remote corries of Sputan Dearg, Derry Cairngorm, the tors of Beinn Mheadhoin and over to the vast bulk of Beinn a' Bhuird and Ben Avon. Of the two cairns the rightmost is the true summit (**5km; 300m; 1h 40min**).

Continue east on a small path over the lower 657m top to where the ridge begins to narrow, and drop to the south-east. A fence blocks the route at the rightmost of two wooden masts (NO108908) and is crossed by a stile to follow a path with a wooden handrail south-west for 200m to the end of an old track. The track takes a delightful gently descending, sometimes undulating traverse, offering beautiful views over Mar Lodge and its grounds, and the Dee valley. Cross over two tracks, those branched off earlier on the walk, to emerge onto the road 500m to the west of Claybokie. A pleasant walk of just under 2km along the road leads back to the start (**11.5km; 320m; 3h 15min**).

An alternative route from Linn of Quoich gives the opportunity to take in the Clais Fhearnaig, a meltwater channel cut through between Glen Lui and Glen Quoich. The route leaves the parking area at the road end and heads up Glen Quoich on a track, branching west into the Clais Fhearnaig after 5km. From the Clais, the two north-western tops of Creag Bhalg can be gained, though 'tops' is maybe a slightly disingenuous description, situated as they are on a flat featureless expanse of moorland! From the main top (**9.5km; 340m; 2h 40min**), gain the east top and follow the south-east ridge back to the Linn of Quoich, with some quite steep ground through the trees (**12.5km; 360m; 3h 30min**).

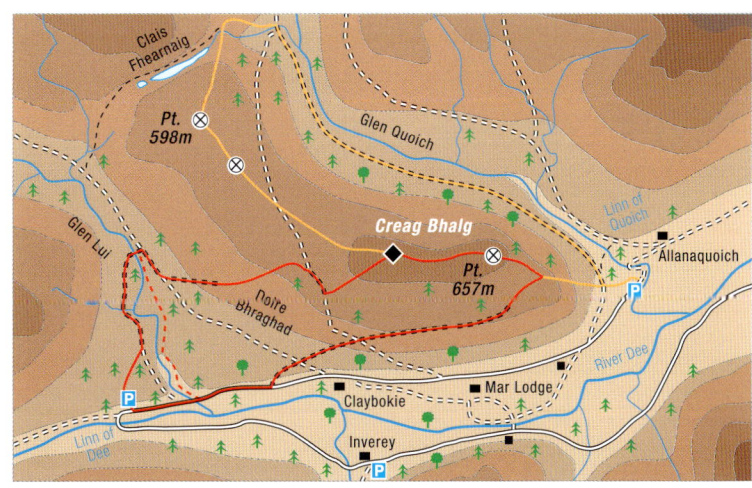

Geallaig Hill

Geallaig Hill from the B976 to the north-west (Rab Anderson)

Geallaig Hill; 743m; (G23); L37, 44; (NO297981); white one, probably from Gaelic 'geal', white. Mapped Mountains of Gallag (1725)

Commanding a fine position between the straths of the River Dee and the River Gairn, Geallaig Hill is a large and bulky Graham. With its open, featureless higher slopes, it appears to hold few secrets for the walker, but its lower slopes were once heavily farmed and supported a far greater population than today.

The obvious and quickest ascent up Geallaig Hill is from Glen Gairn, starting at a height of 360m from Braenaloin, a small farm on the B976. There is rough off-road parking opposite the farm at the base of a track. Simply follow this track all the way to the summit (**3km; 380m; 1h 20min**) and return the same way (**6km; 380m; 2h**).

A higher start, though taking a longer route, could be made from another track at 480m on the B976 to the south, and this could be combined into a circular route, albeit involving a section of road walking between the start and finish points.

However, if time and a second car, or driver, or strategically placed bike allow, the most interesting walk involves a traverse of the mountain from west to east, beginning at Crathie in Deeside and ending at the small farm on Gairnside. A large pay and display car park for the benefit of those visiting Balmoral Castle is sited on the A93 and makes as good a start point as any. Cross the main road and follow the small road up to Crathie Kirk. Just past the Kirk, take a left at the old quarry and head up onto the ridge of Creag a' Chlamhain. There is no path but the ridge guides you up through open birch and pine woodland, mossy boulders and steeper craggy ground.

The ridge opens out into heather

moorland and evidence of muirburn points to the importance of the area for grouse. On top of The Maim at 601m, the circular track of the northern route is picked up and is easily followed to the flat summit of Geallaig Hill, dominated by a trig point atop a large drystane circle (**5.5km; 470m; 2h**).

As with many of these intermediate hills, the view to the higher hills offers a different perspective on their traditional vistas. From Geallaig to the south over the Dee are the lower hills of Lochnagar, flanked by the Abergeldie triumvirate of Creag nam Bàn where 'French Katie' was burned for witchcraft; Creag Ghiubhais topped by twisted pines and the long light green spine of the Coyles of Muick. To the north-west the eye is drawn over the ruined farmhouses of upper Glen Gairn to the rolling featureless hills of the eastern Cairngorms and the complex bulk of Ben Avon itself.

Either return the same way (**11km; 480m; 3h 15min**) or descend to the road at Braenaloin (**8.5km; 470m; 2h 40min**). An alternative is to follow the ridge to the east over Creag na Creiche and Cairn Dearg, down to Bridge of Gairn or Torbeg.

Mona Gowan

Mona Gowan; 749m; (G13); L37; NJ335058; hill-mass (or moss) of the smith from Gaelic 'monadh' (or moine) 'gobhann'

Mona Gowan is one of the foothills of the Cairngorms and gives a high-level but easy and scenic walk. At the highest point of the A939 between the River Don and the River Gairn, a long layby at NJ303052 provides parking. From the centre of the layby, a well-defined but narrow path starts up stone steps and goes steeply to a cairn overlooking the road. Adders are common here and there is a warning sign about them on the road below, so the chances of a sighting are good. Although they generally slither away, they should not be approached too close.

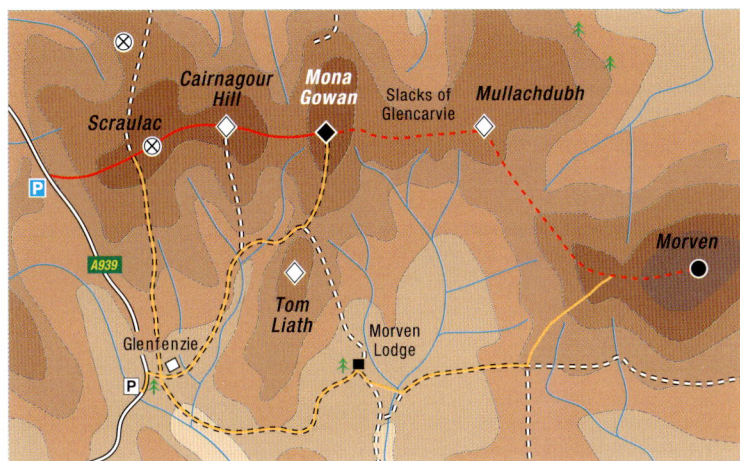

Walk easily across short heather and past ancient peat cuttings to a track which leads to Scraulac (741m). Cairnagour Hill (744m) lies in front of Mona Gowan and fills the view, though there are distant views of Ben Avon, Lochnagar and Mount Keen. Continue smoothly to Cairnagour Hill, then more roughly down and back up to the slightly higher Mona Gowan. A fence connects these hills; the path lies just out from it on the way down but close to it on the way up. The summit has a huge cairn, erected in 1887 for the Golden Jubilee of Queen Victoria (**3.5km; 300m; 1h 20min**).

For the return, a descent into Glen Fenzie is a possibility but the walk back over the tops, heading towards the high Cairngorms and the setting sun, is the better option and more direct (**7km; 400m; 2h 15min**).

Beyond Mona Gowan, the Corbett Morven beckons and the walk can be extended over the Slacks of Glencarvie and Mullachdubh to this (**9km; 660m; 3h 10min**).

Return the same way, cutting across the slopes of Mullachdubh (**18km; 1010m; 5h 50min**).

A good option for either hill, or both, is to start from the parking area further south on the A939 at NJ313027 and utilise the improved though unsightly tracks that run past the ruin at Glenfenzie. Either go direct to Mona Gowan, or take in Scraulac and Cairnagour Hill (**5.5km; 460m; 2h**).

From Mona Gowan, continue over Mullachdubh to Morven (**11km; 820m; 3h 50min**) and return via atv tracks then estate tracks past Morven Lodge (**19.5km; 920m; 6h**).

Mona Gowan and Morven from Cairnagour Hill to the west (Jim Teesdale)

178 Pressendye

Pressendye; 619m; (G205); L37; NJ490089; copse of the fire, probably, from Gaelic 'preas an daigh'

Pressendye lies at the east end of a long ridge forming the watershed between the rivers Don and Dee in the Cromar district, north of Dinnet and Aboyne. It is an extensive upland ridge with a great atmosphere and the view from the summit not only covers the lower hills towards Aberdeen, like Bennachie and Hill of Fare, but also the hills to the south, a line increasing in height from Kerloch to Clachnaben, Mount Battock, Mount Keen and finally Lochnagar.

There are many routes. Perhaps the best starts from a small car park at NJ485050 in Muirton Wood on the east side of the B9119 to Aberdeen, at the north-eastern edge of Tarland. The route, and its extension, is marked by blue waymark posts.

Cross the road and head towards Tarland, taking the first road on the right (north-west) to go past the MacRobert Trust's offices. The Trust has created a network of waymarked and signposted walks on its estate here. A mountain bike centre with trails is being built a short way along the B9119 from Tarland. The trails will extend to Pittenderich and Pressendye, crossing the paths.

About 300m beyond the MacRobert Trust's office, go through a gate on the right and follow a path up the middle of a magnificent 700m-long, narrow avenue of beech trees. Turn left at the top and continue alongside a line of beech trees forming the lower edge of the forestry on Doune Hill. On reaching the overhead power lines, drop down right onto a track and follow this as it curves back uphill to traverse across the side of the ridge. Leave this track and turn left up a grassy track onto the ridge where fine views open up to Mount Keen, Lochnagar and Morven.

Continue up the broad crest into the forestry to join a track and go left. In a further 300m make the short detour up right to gain the large cairn on top of Pittenderich (508m). Return to the track then after another 300m

Pressendye from Pittenderich (Rab Anderson)

go left then right and climb to the trig point and large cairn on top of Pressendye (**6.25km; 500m; 2h 10min**).

Return the same way (**11.75km; 510m; 3h 30min**).

A longer walk continues along the broad crest westwards beside the deer fence, passing through this at the first gate. If this is missed there is another gate further along and down. After crossing a dip, the track climbs onto Broom Hill. On the far side of this, where the track goes right, follow a path down left through a gate into the Davoch Plantation. At the bottom, go right through a gate, then 250m further on go through a gate to gain a track leading to the road at Easter Davoch. Follow the road for 3km back to Tarland where a left turn along School Road, then a left along Aberdeen road regains the start (**15.5km; 580m; 4h 25min**).

A good high-level walk approaches from the north. Park to the north-west at NJ424110 (spot height 333m) and follow an old drove road to Lazy Well. Go east along the open crest over Green Hill and Broom Hill to Pressendye (**8km; 400m; 2h 30min**).

Return towards Broom Hill but pass it to the north by a track and head down to a memorial above Mill of Culfork. Descend fields to the road and a 2.5km walk back along this to the start (**16km; 400m; 4h 20min**).

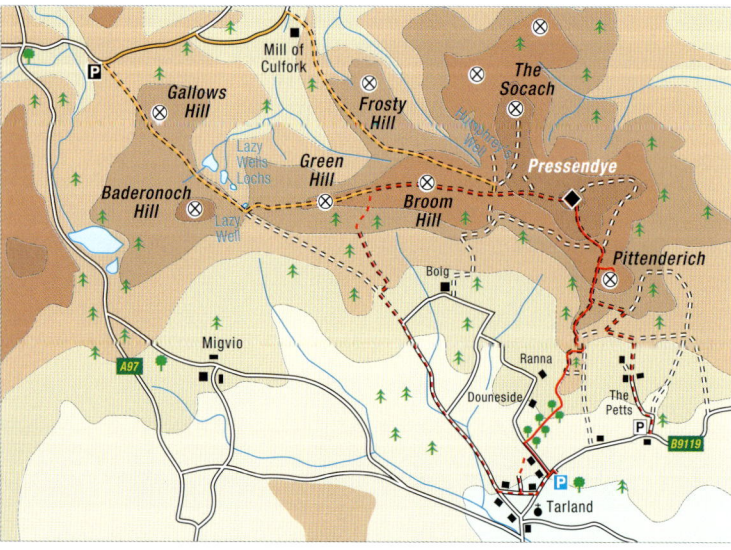

The Buck; 721m; (G62); L37; NJ412233; *from Gaelic 'boc', a male deer. Known locally as The Buck o' the Cabrach after the hamlet to the north-west*

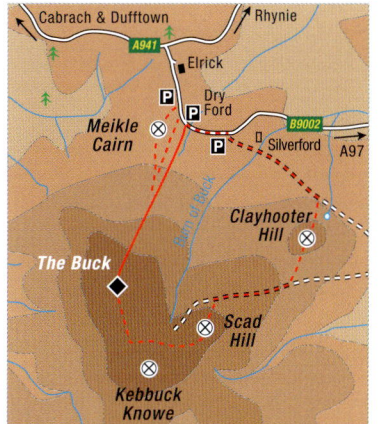

Set on the edge of the high moorland which leads north and east from the Cairngorms, The Buck offers fine views across the farmland of rural Aberdeenshire to the coast. It is a shapely hill which attracts attention from large distances around, even seen as a distant cone from the high Cairngorms, and its ascent provides a short but remarkably rough walk without the sizeable path one might expect of such a prominent and popular landmark.

Start at Dry Ford (NJ421251) at a height of 420m on the B9002, a minor branch off the A941 Rhynie to Dufftown road. There is limited parking on a bend with further parking to the north and east. This is just north of a boundary which consists of a decrepit fence leading to the top of the hill.

Step over the fence behind the parking and cross a grassy area. On reaching heather, there is a path on the left, some 10m from a burn. This follows the right edge of reeds in the bed of the burn to more heather. Head left on intermittent bits of path to the boundary fence and cross to its left side to reach Dry Know. Continue beside the fence on anything but dry ground until the path becomes more distinct once the going becomes steeper. The summit is a prominent little rocky tor atop which sits a trig point (**2km; 300m; 1h**).

An interesting but less direct start can be made by parking at NJ420254 and going over the rocky outcrops and juniper summit of Meikle Cairn. From here there is a good view of the route to the summit ▶

The Buck from the B9002 to the north-east (Andy Nisbet)

Cnap Chaochan Aitinn

Up the Burn of Buck over Silverford to The Buck (Rab Anderson)

> **Cnap Chaochan Aitinn;** *715m; (G71); L36; NJ145099; knob of the juniper stream*

The relative remoteness of this hill is offset by the ease of access to it, circumscribed as it is by vehicle hill tracks. In fact, the ascent of the hill could be taken in on a complete mountain bike circuit, with only a short walking section to the jumble of quartzite stones, a small wind turbine and telecommunications mast which grace the summit. An ascent by mountain bike would knock two to three hours off the time for the straightforward out and back route.

Whether an ascent is made on bike or by foot, the starting place is the car park at NJ165176 below Queen Victoria's viewpoint, about 1km to the south-west of Tomintoul. The private road to Inchrory and on through the Bealach Dearg to Deeside is rough and partially surfaced, perhaps as a deterrent to drivers hoping to drive into the heart of this area.

Glen Avon is a magical place by reason of the fact that it lies on the boundary between the granites of the Cairngorms and the softer calcareous rocks to the west, so the landscape is really quite different – almost reminiscent of the Yorkshire Dales with limestone grassland and grey shattered outcrops. It is worth keeping an eye out for the brown mosses and yellow saxifrages that characterise the stony wet flushes along the road.

The route takes the track on the east side of the River Avon. After going through the main gates onto the Inchrory estate at Birchfield, 3.5km from the start, cross the river by a hump-backed bridge then branch off uphill to the south-west.

Starting to climb, the track runs through grazing pastures beside a small tree-lined burn then passes the renovated cottage at Wester Gaulrig to run through birch trees.

Passing a track off right, then leaving the field system and the last of the trees behind, the track swings south to ford the Allt Bheithachan. Here, it makes a steady ascent up the hillside past the imperceptible top of

of The Buck, but then it is even rougher and wetter to reach the boundary fence.

There is a grand view from the summit over the colourful fields of Aberdeenshire. The higher hills of Ben Avon, Ben Macdui, Lochnagar and Mount Keen are clearly visible, but rather too distant to be spectacular. The three neighbouring Grahams can also be identified; Pressendye, Mona Gowan and Cook's Cairn with its wind turbines. To the south-west, open moorland with a mosaic of peat hags leads to Glen Buchat.

In the rocks beneath the trig point there is an incised motif of three intertwined fish, which is recorded as an ancient monument. Whilst thought not to be Pictish or Medieval, it is of unknown origin.

Returning the same way is quick and easy, but this may be too short and dull (**4km; 300m; 1h 30min**).

A nicer option is to head south along the boundary and a disused fence, with a small path leading almost to the col before Kebbuck Knowe. Where the path peters out, head east across a gentle soft slope which misses most of the peat hags to reach Scad Hill with its prehistoric-looking peat mounds. Some grouse butts are soon reached, then a track heading east which is followed a short way. Force yourself to leave the track and find better going than expected to reach Clayhooter Hill, which is what you'll get if you trip in the mud!

Continue on down, taking the more direct route across an atv track to reach another track (marked as a path on the OS 1:50k map) at the point it crosses a burn just west of a tiny lochan. Cutting the corner here is hard work. The track leads back to the road (**8km; 320m; 2h 20min**).

Approaching Cnap Chaochan Aitinn from above the Little Allt Bheithachan (Rab Anderson)

Cairn an' t-Sleibhe (589m) then turns south-east towards Geal Charn.

When the track forks above the Little Allt Bheithachan, take the right-fork to the south-west. This drops across the burn, above a hut on the left-hand branch, then climbs over the shoulder above the col between the summit and Càrn na Ruabraich to the west. Leave this track before it descends into Glen Loin in a series of steep and stony switchbacks and follow another to the south-east for 300m making a 50m ascent to gain the top of Cnap Chaochan Aitinn (**9.75km; 400m; 2h 50min** on foot), (about **1h 55min** by bike).

The best views are to the south across Big Garvoun to the northern corries of Ben Avon and Beinn a' Bhuird, as well as south-west across the Loch Avon basin to Ben Macdui and the main Cairngorm massif.

The simplest return is back the same way (**19.5km; 450m; 5h** on foot), (**3h** with a bike). However, for those who have biked this far it is worth making the exhilarating descent south into steep-sided Glen Loin and back down Glen Avon for a splendid circuit (**30km; 450m; 5h** with a bike).

A return can also be made via the tops of Càrn na Ruabraich and Càrn Ruabraich to provide a circular route on foot. If bikes are used, these should be left at the track on the right before the crossing of the Allt Bheithachan. From the summit, head north-west to the first top and descend northwards to climb to the second top above the Water of Ailnack. Unfortunately the convex slopes afford no views into this dramatic gorge. The somewhat heathery trudge is enlivened on the last section by a line of beautifully constructed and maintained Victorian grouse butts, lined with stone, disguised by heather and still draining freely (**21.5km; 580m; 6h** on foot).

Nearing the top with Ben Rinnes behind (Rab Anderson)

Cook's Cairn

The ruin at Suie with Cook's Cairn beyond (Jim Teesdale)

Cook's Cairn; 755m; (G8); L37; NJ302278; 1850s OS Name Book says Clinton's and Knox's Cairns, on the same hill, mark the spots where Lord Clinton, and Knox, future Lord Cavendish, 'shot their first deer'. Likely that Cook, an aristocratic friend, did likewise here. Roy mapped Corryhabbie Hill as Cook's Carn

Situated in the Ladder Hills, which lie north and east of the Lecht and the infamous Cockbridge to Tomintoul road, this is one of the more remote of the eastern Grahams. Despite a 10km approach, the going is fast on various tracks all the way to the top. Although there are a number of possible approaches, the easiest is perhaps from Glenlivet.

Glenlivet is the discreet end of the Cairngorms National Park, ideal for quiet walking away from the glamour and crowds of Aviemore. This area is more famous for distilleries than hills, with around 20 of them within 16km, considerably more than the number of Grahams. A mountain bike is helpful for this hill and although it saves about an hour on the day it is worth noting that the cycling is quite rough. However, cycling may be more entertaining than walking along tracks, particularly as the route is quite slippery when wet. Times given are on foot. Much of the ground on the approach forms part of The Crown Estate lands with walkers and bikers welcomed. For more information about low-level walks and mountain bike routes, see <www.glenlivetestate.co.uk>. There is an Information Centre at Tomintoul.

For the start of the walk to Cook's Cairn, turn off the B9008 just north of Tomnavoulin where there is a small sign for Tombae but no indication that this is also the direction for several of the Glenlivet walks. Drive to the end of the tarmac and the Allanreid car park (NJ237249).

The walk starts alongside the River Livet, on the continuation track sign-posted to Achdregnie and takes the old drove route to Cabrach known as The Steplar. Where the farm road track goes uphill, go down almost to a bridge over the river, but keep to the east side and follow the grassy river bank.

Although cyclists may worry about going off-road here, this is part of Glenlivet Estate's Cycle Trail 5. Walkers may also be surprised at the lack of path, but it is a right of way and marked as a path on the map; Walk 3 on the Estate's walking trail network. Go through a section of

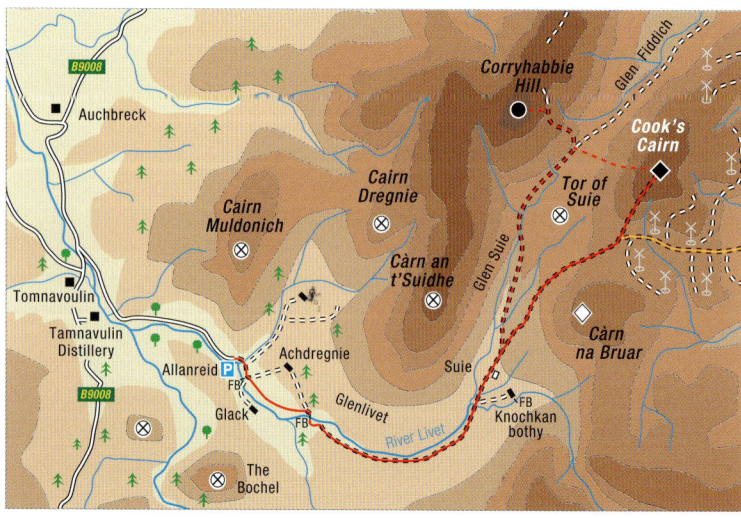

HILLS OF CROMDALE Càrn a' Ghille Chearr, Creagan a' Chaise

> **HILLS OF CROMDALE**
> **Càrn a' Ghille Chearr**; 710m; (G81); L36; NJ139298; hill of the unlucky (or awkward) boy
> **Creagan a' Chaise**; 722m; (G59); L36; NJ104241; little crag of the cheese

The Hills of Cromdale form a long ridge wedged between the River Spey and the River Avon before they join just to the north. The hills are quite prominent from a number of directions and their length makes them appear higher than they really are, especially when covered in snow. Since the summits of the two Grahams lie some 7km apart with a central col at 531m, they make one of the best high-level walks in the eastern highlands. However, be warned, for the traverse is no stroll, especially the soft going across the central col where only the hoofed, the winged and the hardy can cross with ease!

The hills can be climbed from either the east (Avon) or the west (Spey) side. Although there isn't much difference, the route from the east gives a slightly better circuit for climbing both Grahams on the same walk, as well as having better parking.

For the route from the east, start from the public car park at Ballcorach (NJ155265) next to the bridge over the River Avon. The route takes a track which is a signposted Right of Way over the hills to Cromdale. This leads north to the farmstead at Knock where another track is followed up the hillside crossing the Knock Burn a couple of times. When the track ends towards the top, a fading atv track then vague sheep-tracks lead to the ridgeline route.

The ground is heathery but managed for grouse, so there are usually large burnt areas for easier walking. Note how blaeberry and cowberry grow first ahead of the heather, hence the reason it's burnt. The rare orange-tailed bilberry bumblebee (Bombus Monticola) likes the sunny slopes and flowers in the morning, whilst cloudberry is much in evidence along the ridge.

Turn north and climb over Càrn Eachie via an atv track then a path to reach the flat summit of Càrn a' Ghille Chearr with its trig point (**6km; 490m; 2h 10min**).

▶

forest on a rough track then follow the base of fields to meet the farm track coming down from above. Follow the track to the river and cross via a footbridge, then continue along the south side of the river for 3km, sometimes rough, to reach a ford across the burn.

Although it is possible to bike on, the cautious will leave their bikes here. It may be possible to cross with dry feet. If not, there is a footbridge 300m upstream to the right. On the other side of the ford the track forks with the more obvious right branch going to Knochkan bothy. Take the fainter left branch up to Suie, now a grand old ruin. Walk past Suie, then an outhouse to reach another fork in the track. This is as far as most people will be able to bike.

Take the right fork and head up to the col between Càrn na Bruar and Cook's Cairn where the wind turbines of the Dorenell Wind Farm dominate the slopes of the Blackwater Forest to the east. Follow atv tracks uphill to the north-east to gain the summit of Cook's Cairn, which has a small but well-built cairn (**10km; 480m; 3h**).

The view west is dominated by the nearby Corbett, Corryhabbie Hill, with Ben Rinnes just poking out beside it. North are the rest of the 59 turbines of the Dorenell Wind Farm above Glen Fiddich. East is mostly moorland, but the nearby Graham The Buck is prominent. To the south-west are the Cairngorms, with Ben Avon the closest. Return by the same route (**20km; 480m; 5h 20min**).

The ambitious could descend west to a col then climb Corryhabbie Hill by an all too obvious snaking track which passes close to its summit (**13.5km; 760m; 4h 20min**) followed by a return via Suie (**25km; 760m; 7h**). For those on foot a return via Càrn an t-Suidhe, or the track down Cairn Dregnie is an option.

A shorter route comes in from Aldivalloch (NJ361264) to the east, via Dead Wife's Hillock and past the turbines (**7km; 540m; 2h 30min**); (**14km; 680m; 4h 20min**).

This is perhaps more convenient for those on that side of the hills since it could be combined with an ascent of The Buck which is nearby.

Càrn a' Ghille Chearr (Andy Nisbet)

HILLS OF CROMDALE Càrn a' Ghille Chearr, Creagan a' Chaise

Càrn a' Ghille Chearr, left, and Ben Rinnes, right, from the ascent to Creagan a' Chaise (Rab Anderson)

On the left there are views over the Paul's Hill Wind Farm to the Moray Firth with the hills of the North-west beyond. On the other hand, Ben Rinnes looks splendid with Corryhabbie Hill to its south. A cairn on a lower top just to the east is worth visiting for this view. The remains of a crashed wartime Armstrong Whitley lie just south of the summit.

Return south-west along the crest towards a distant looking Creagan a' Chaise with Ben Avon, Beinn a' Bhuird and the rest of the Cairngorms spread out ahead. The going is mostly easy except for the soft central col. Pass the end of a fence on the first top beyond the col to reach a large pointed cairn on the next. This is the Coronation Cairn, erected by the people of Cromdale on the site of the bonfire for King Edward VII's 1902 coronation. Continue on to Creagan a' Chaise with increasingly good views of the main Cairngorm massif. Unfortunately atv's have scarred this section. On the summit there is another trig point and a magnificently constructed cairncastle, which celebrates the 1887 Golden Jubilee of Queen Victoria (**13.5km; 720m; 4h 20min**).

There is a visitor book here which can be signed. To descend head towards Carlag, the north-east top, then drop down the east ridge to meet a track which reaches the road at Milton. A pleasant walk of 2.5km leads along the road back to the start (**20km; 720m; 6h**).

The approach from the west is likely to be via Cromdale itself. This was the original settlement in Strathspey, being at least a thousand years old and only bypassed when a new bridge was built across the Spey in 1754. Park at NJ102285 just west of Wester Rynabeallich (spelt Rynaballoch on the map).

Walk 150m south-west along the road to pick up a track, then head across rough ground to meet a new and prominent track snaking above. Ascend to its original top then take the line of the old and barely detectable path, east then south-east, to gain the crest of the ridge. Go to Càrn a' Ghille Chearr (**6km; 450m; 2h 5min**) then traverse the ridge to Creagan a' Chaise (**13.5km; 680m; 4h 10min**).

Return to the Coronation Cairn and descend a path down the spur to Clach nam Piobair (Piper's Stone) where a fatally wounded piper played for the Jacobites at the battle of Cromdale in 1690. The Jacobites were defeated, with 400 killed out of 800, and this battle marked the effective end of the Jacobite uprising. Continue down the track and if keen on Scotland's national flower, then cut across open ground to the start, otherwise follow the track to the road (**19km; 680m; 5h 40min**).

To climb the hills individually from the east, go up and down the ascent route for Càrn a Ghille Chearr and up and down the descent route for Creagan a' Chaise. To climb Creagan a' Chaise from the west, go to the top of the snaking track, then continue

HILLS OF CROMDALE Càrn a' Ghille Chearr, Creagan a' Chaise

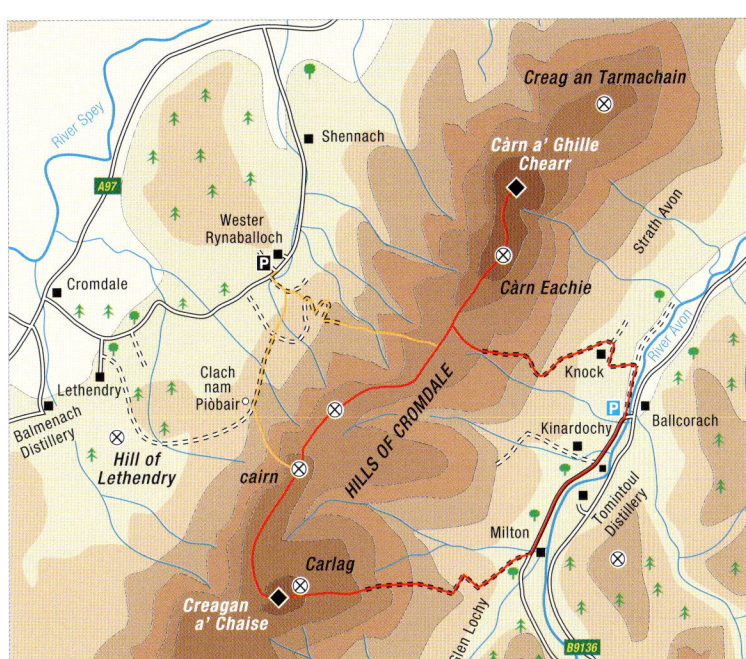

south up a rougher track and a line of grouse butts to gain the small top north of the Coronation Cairn; return via the Piper's Stone. To climb Càrn a' Ghille Chearr from the west, park at NJ111298, signposted to the Cromdale Hills, then go through a field to cross the Allt na Criche and follow its left side for about 1km before gaining the ridge of Càrn na h-Iolaire which leads to Càrn Eachie on the summit ridge.

Creagan a' Chaise (Andy Nisbet)

Cille Choirill and Creag Dhubh (Glen Spean) (Rab Anderson)

SECTION 9
Speyside to The Great Glen

Section 9 – Speyside to the Great Glen

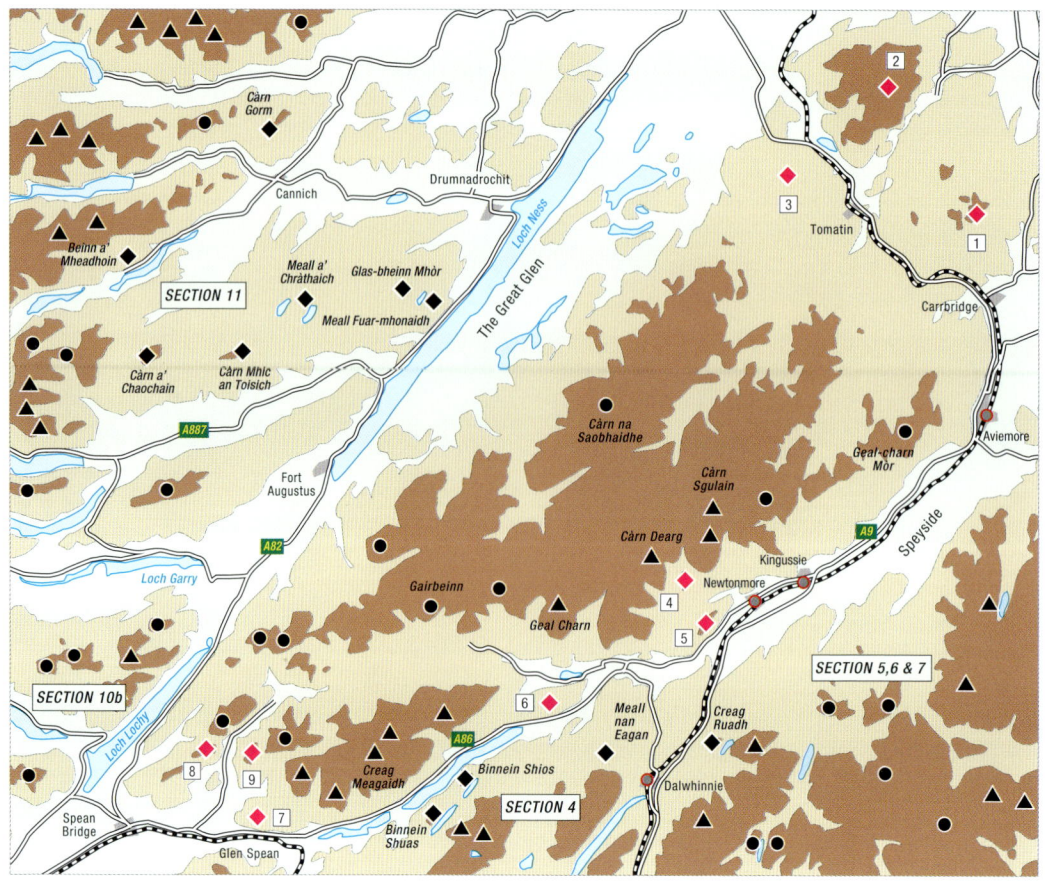

SECTION 9

[1] *Càrn Glas-choire*   189
[2] *Càrn nan Tri-tighearnan*   190
[3] *Càrn na h-Easgainn*   191
[4] *Creag Liath*   192
[5] *Creag Dhubh (Newtonmore)*   193
[6] *Creag Ruadh*   194
[7] *Creag Dhubh (Glen Spean)*   195
[8] *Lèana Mhòr (west)*   196
[9] *Lèana Mhòr (east)*   197

Càrn Glas-choire

Càrn Glas-choire from the south-east (Andy Nisbet)

Càrn Glas-choire; 659m; (G160); L35, 36; NH891291; *hill of the green corrie*

Càrn Glas-choire lies in the heart of the Dava Moor, an expanse of mostly heather moorland north-east of Slochd Summit on the A9, which is really an extension of the Monadh Liath. This is grouse country, with Cawdor Estate and this hill to the south-west and Lochindorb Estate to the north-east of the B9007, a minor but fast road which crosses the moor from near Carrbridge over towards Nairn and Forres.

The ascent of this hill is a great walk if east coast moorland interests you. The peak bagger may regard it as flat and featureless but this is a rarely visited hill, so the high moorland is largely unspoilt, the peat is untrampled and only animal prints are seen on the soft ground. Tracks go close to the summit and a bicycle can be used to make an easier outing; times given are for walking.

A track leaves the B9007 at NH929261, sign to Auchterteang and a Cawdor Estate sign which is a warning for the grouse season. There is possible parking 300m to the south where there is room at a track entrance into a forest on the east side of the road but forestry operations could affect this. There is also space for a few cars on the east side of the road at the end of the forestry plantation, 800m north of the walk start.

Follow the track beyond the keeper's house and kennels at Auchterteang, gently uphill staying with the main track as it contours round past a green hut, then take the uphill branch to a fork at NH906283 where bikes can be left. The left fork extends over the col to the east of the summit and enables a more direct approach but this would make a dull route and is better left for the return journey.

More interesting is to branch right and head uphill past Creag na h-Iolaire along a track which loops past a small hut to Càrn Mheadhoin and beyond, much further than marked on the map. Reach the boundary watershed and at the highpoint of the track, leave it to follow the boundary west. There are expansive views over the lower moors of Nairnshire with Lochindorb as the centrepiece. From here to the summit there is about 3km of high moorland to cross, with occasional peat hags.

Two steep little cnaps break up the flat moor and cloudberries grow on their slopes. Between them, stream channels up to 2m deep just reach down to a mixture of granite, schist and quartzite rocks in their bases and show the depth of the peat. There are also thick branches of bog wood, a surprising altitude for Scots pines of that size and the curved branches show how they must have battled against the wind. The number of hares here is notable.

This traverse along the watershed between the rivers Spey and the Findhorn gives great views, from the high Cairngorms to the Moray Firth coast and beyond to the Graham Morven in the far north. The summit has a trig point, the saviour of nervous navigators and there are some small walls offering marginal shelter in this exposed location (**8.5km; 400m; 2h 35min**).

To the east of the summit the left fork of the ascent track extends further than marked on the map, crossing a branch of the burn and continuing over the plateau. Descend east-north-east across the head of the burn to pick up the track and follow this to join the upward route which leads back (**15km; 400m; 4h**).

Over to the west there is extensive forest, but this is largely young forest managed for regeneration of native species. Protected by deer fencing and hare culling, it is amazing how quickly the pines have grown.

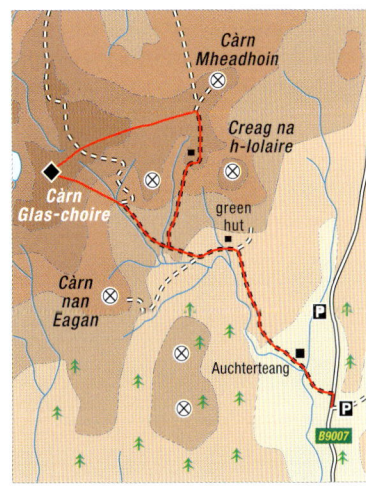

The southern flanks of Càrn nan Tri-tighearnan from above Daless on the approach (Andy Nisbet)

Càrn nan Tri-tighearnan; 615m; (G212); L27; NH823390; *hill of the three landowners*

This east coast moorland hill is remarkably flat and open, with distant views to match. Despite its lack of dramatic slopes it provides a good short outing, although the flat ground does give some soft going cut by peat hags.

Approach via the B9007 Carrbridge to Nairn and Forres road, turning off west to Dulsie where there is a fine bridge across a gorge on the River Findhorn and a viewpoint. On the north side of the bridge take a small road westwards along the north bank of the river. This tiny road almost makes a tunnel through beautiful birch woods with glimpses of the river in its clean-cut valley.

Beyond Drynachan Lodge, the road deteriorates and has a thick stripe of grass down the middle but is drivable with care to its end at a ford across the Allt Breac opposite Daless Farm where there is ample parking.

Cross the Allt Breac and take the track uphill behind Daless to a fine platform overlooking the River Findhorn. Continue past three rough tracks off right, which should be ignored since these lead to cages of partridges, then take the clear track off right at NH852384. This leads over the crest then drops down across the Allt Breac to join another track just above. Follow the track steeply uphill to its end just below the plateau then make a short climb to gain the flat ground and walk out to the trig point on top of Càrn an Uillt Bhric (599m) which lies over to the right. The view north across the Moray Firth to Morven and the other Grahams of the far north-east is fine, whilst to the south the nearest hill is another flat moorland Graham, Càrn Glas-choire, which is too low to block out the Cairngorm massif beyond.

An unusually flat plateau links this top with the main summit, although the going is not as bad as appearances suggest. The central section has many peat hags but as the ground is horizontal, they run in all directions so sometimes it is easy to climb into one and follow its stony base. Careful linking means the 1.5km crossing is not too tough and a second trig point is reached on the higher summit (**4.5km; 400m; 1h 45min**).

The view to the west has now opened and a myriad of distant hills can be argued over. Ben Wyvis, Sgùrr a' Mhuilinn and the Strathfarrar hills are there, but which is Mam Sodhail in Glen Affric, and are those the Glen Shiel hills, and is that really Ben Nevis in the distance?

A good return descends south-east on the other side of the Allt Breac, crossing a deep side branch, to reach a gentle ridge which leads to a series of grouse butts and finally a better track which soon joins the route of approach (**9km; 400m; 2h 45min**).

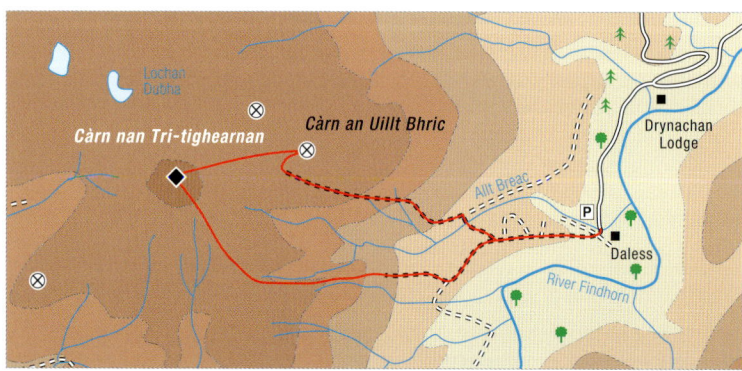

Càrn na h-Easgainn

Càrn na h-Easgainn; 618m; (G209); L27; NH744320; hill of the eel

Overlooking Strathdearn on the opposite side of the A9 from Càrn na Tri-tighearnan, Càrn na h-Easgainn is a useful hill with a track all the way to the summit. This means it can be quickly climbed when passing, or combined with one of the other nearby Grahams.

Turn south off the A9 at NH768340 onto a road signposted to Lynebeg. There is space to park by the first cattle grid and just along a track on the left. The road ends at a turning circle (no parking) by the houses and it may be possible to drive the track to just beyond Lynemore and park.

Follow the track to a junction 5m short of the trig point. The highest point is some 50m to the south-east (**3.75km; 310m; 1h 20min**).

There is a shooting bothy by the summit and the 40 wind turbines of the Farr Wind Farm lie on the south-west side. Despite these intrusions there are some fine views.

Return the same way (**7km; 310m; 2h 20min**).

A longer option, which is better for biking the hill, starts in Layby 162 (NH787321), on the west side of the A9. Follow a track under the railway then up beside the Allt a' Chùil to NH763311 where the right-hand track leads west then north-west to the summit (**5.75km; 350m; 1h.50min**).

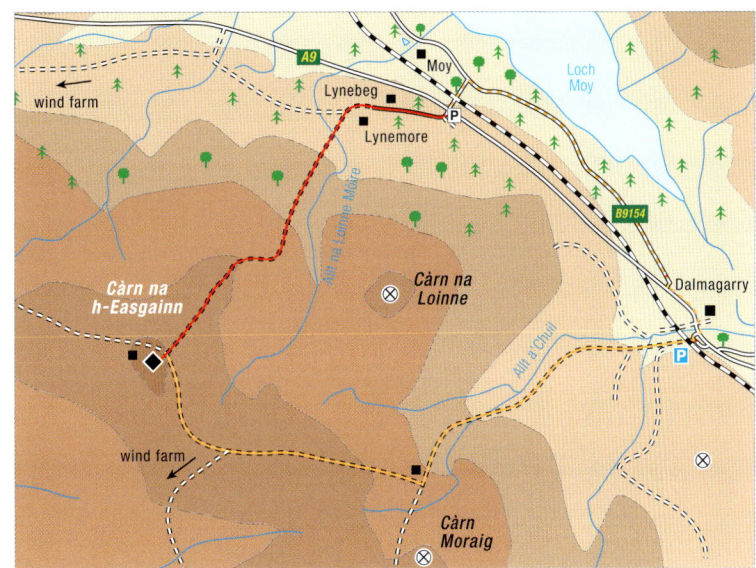

Return the same way (**11.5km; 360m; 3h 15min**).

A 12.75km bike circuit can be made by descending to Lynebeg and returning along Sustrans Cycle Route 7, which runs through Layby 162 via the B9154 parallel to the A9.

Càrn na h-Easgainn from the north-east across Strathdearn (Andy Nisbet)

Creag Liath

Creag Liath from just north of Glenballoch (Rab Anderson)

Creag Liath; 743m; (G25); L35; NH663007; grey cliff

Occupying a central position in the Monadh Liath mountains, Creag Liath is climbed by a short, looped walk. It can be combined with nearby Creag Dhubh, although this provides a nicer walk on its own from the south. It can also be included with Càrn Dearg and the other two Munros here, since the route to, or from Càrn Dearg passes through the c550m col to the north of Creag Liath.

In the centre of Newtonmore, turn northwards up Glen Road to reach Glen Banchor, which was heavily populated until the residents were cleared for sheep in the early 1800s. The landowner wasn't totally ruthless however for they were rehoused in newly built Newtonmore.

After 2km of grazed open ground, a parking area is reached just before the road drops to a gated bridge over the Allt a' Chaorainn, from where it becomes a track. Follow the track to a bridge leading to the ruinous buildings at Glenballoch. The quickest ascent would be to head for the top from here, but the terrain is generally rough and pleasanter in descent.

Turn right and follow a grassy then stony track up the glen beside the Allt Fionndrigh to where the track becomes an atv track. About 50m

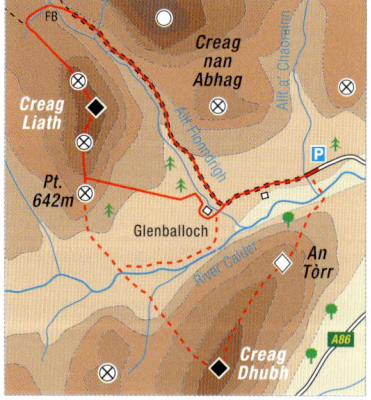

along this, at a small cairn, go left on a path leading down to a bridge at NH659019 (shown on the OS 1:25k, but not the 1:50k map).

On the other side, a path and atv track lead up a boggy gully to a col where the atv tracks turn right. Make a left turn here and gain the hill's northern ridge. Initially the ground is soft but soon a small path develops as the heather shortens on the crest of the ridge. The going becomes pleasantly easy and leads over a small top and final rise to the summit cairn (**6.5km; 450m; 2h 15min**).

The top is like an emperor's seat, facing an amphitheatre of Monadh Liath mountains to the north. To the east are the Glen Feshie Cairngorms and to the south-west, the upper reaches of the River Spey, while lying beyond are Ben Alder and Creag Meagaidh, better seen from the lower southerly top.

Turn south-west to gain the south summit (732m) and continue down the south ridge towards the prominent final top of Pt.642m. From the col before this, follow grass and heather slopes south-east, heading for the far corner of the plantation beside the Allt Fionndrigh. Follow the south side of the forest to the burn, from where an atv track leads to Glenballoch and the main track back to the start (**11km; 460m; 3h 25min**).

Inclusion of Creag Dhubh depends on the level of the River Calder, as there are no bridges, despite one being shown on the OS 1:50k map. From Pt.642m, continue down the south ridge to reach the river. This will need to be waded but it is generally shallow when water levels are low. A fairly direct line leads to the top of Creag Dhubh (**11km; 870m; 4h**).

The return leads down the north-east ridge, followed by a more crucial wade across the now wider river, although this is still easy when low (**14.5km; 880m; 5h**).

Creag Dhubh (Newtonmore)

Creag Dhubh; 756m; (G); L35; NN678972; black cliff

Attractive and unusually shapely for the area, Creag Dhubh overlooks upper Strathspey and offers a fine ridge walk to a popular summit.

Park at NN673958 on the A86 south-west of Newtonmore and opposite Lochain Uvie where there is room for about six cars. This is also the car park for Creag Dubh, the famous rock climbing cliff, which lies directly above.

Walk west along the road for 400m to a gate on the right, opposite and just before the gatehouse to Creagdhubh Lodge. Go through the gate and follow a grassy track into woodland for a short way to reach a gate in a fence. Leave the track and go through the gate then cross a burn and climb uphill beside this, through woodland beneath the left end of the line of cliffs. Emerge into the open then climb a steep grassy slope to swing round north-east above the cliffs on a rough path which becomes more distinct as height is gained.

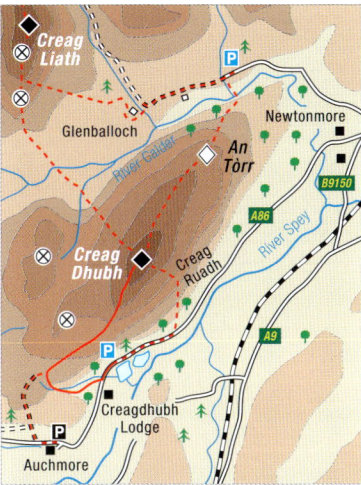

This point can be reached from Auchmore a little further west where a rough track starts at a gate (NN664947) 200m west of a small pull-off opposite the house.

Once on the main path, simply follow the fine crest. There is a small top first, then a drop to a stile, then up more steeply, almost scrambling. The crest narrows and there is another small top with gentle scrambling up to the summit of this miniature mountain. The east of the two cairns is probably the highest (3.5km; 520m; 1h 40min).

There are lovely views to the Cairngorms, especially Braeriach and the Glen Feshie hills, with Cairn Toul and Sgòr an Lochain Uaine just showing. The villages of Newtonmore and Kingussie show up well in the sun, as do the Monadh Liath and Creag Liath – see opposite for the combination of that hill with Creag Dhubh.

The best descent is to simply go back down the approach route (7km; 530m; 2h 40min).

A return can also be made straight down to Creag Ruadh, avoiding all the cliffs to reach the road 1.5km from the car. The further north-east you head along the summit ridge before descending, the longer you enjoy the view, but the longer the walk back.

Creag Dhubh across the River Spey from the south (Andy Nisbet)

Creag Ruadh

Creag Ruadh from the north-east across the Spey Dam Reservoir (Andy Nisbet)

Creag Ruadh; 622m; (G200); L35; NN558913; red cliff

Situated on the ridge between the A86 Newtonmore to Spean Bridge road and the upper River Spey above Laggan village, this hill offers inspirational summit views.

The best route is from the north. From Laggan village on the A86, take the Garva Bridge and Corrieyairack Pass road and park just before Sherrabeg where there is ample space on the grass at NN571930.

Walk towards Sherrabeg, cross the bridge over the burn in front of the cottage and go through a gate. Head up through sheep-cropped grass, with lots of bog asphodel and eyebright in summer, to a point which is shown on the map as a narrow gap between the two types of forest.

Go through a gate in a deer fence here then break out right onto a shallow ridge. Continue up this lovely ridge over various craggy bumps with hints of footpath to reach a cairn almost overlooking the high Loch na Lairige. Cross a deer fence on the left and follow old metal fence posts across nice short heather to the summit (**2.5km; 350m; 1h 20min**).

The finest view is that down Loch Laggan to the Grey Corries. Creag Meagaidh lies to the right and Binnein Shuas to the left with Ben Alder not far behind. To the north lie the Monadh Liath and east the Cairngorms. Return the same way (**5km; 350m; 2h**).

A fine circuit can be made by crossing south-east to Pt.560m, then heading north-east over the fence to the knoll of Pt.565m. From there, a waymarked path leads to a junction and interpretative board for the Dùn-da-lamh Pictish fort on the knoll to the north. A walk around this fort is recommended; return to the path junction. A direct route to the road can be contrived from here but this involves thrashing through forest, crossing a fence and descending steep, boggy ground.

Instead, leisurely descend the path south onto a forest track then turn north and follow this beneath the steep slopes below the fort. Turn left at the road and walk back to Sherrabeg (**10.5km; 560m; 3h 20min**).

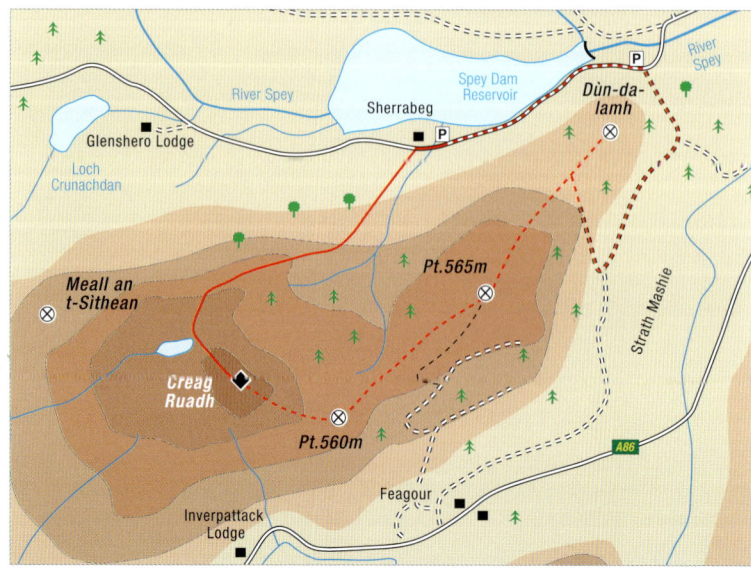

Creag Dhubh (Glen Spean)

Creag Dhubh; 658m; (G165); L34, 41; NN322824; black cliff

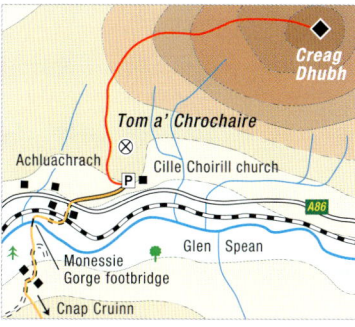

A somewhat rounded and rather dull looking hill, Creag Dhubh has an easy western flank which can be ascended quickly and without difficulty from Glen Spean. On the ascent it offers views of the two Glen Roy Grahams to the north, as well as Aonach Mòr and the Grey Corries to the south-east.

Another Graham, Cnap Cruinn (see p154), sits on the opposite side of Glen Spean and since one of the routes to this uses the same car park, it can be conveniently climbed as a second hill, accessed across the River Spean by the Monessie Gorge footbridge.

About 450m to the east of the Glenspean Lodge Hotel a narrow tarmac road rises to a car park at NN306812, just before a tiny church called Cille Choirill (Cairell's Church). If travelling from the east this turning comes up quickly after a bend, so care is needed here. The church was renovated in 1932 and is thought to have been built originally in the 15th century and named in honour of Saint Cairell, an Irish missionary who preached Christianity in the area around 600AD. There is a well-kept graveyard beside the church where many generations of Highlanders are buried. It has a commanding view eastwards up Glen Spean and is popular with tourists.

From the car park, head north-west away from the church and ascend a heathery slope, which has much tussock grass higher up. As the angle eases head northwards to the corner of a wire fence (NN304818), which corresponds with the level of a Parallel Road at 261m.

This feature can be traced for long distances around the hillsides on both sides of Glen Spean and marks the level of a huge body of water created some 12,000 years ago, when the western end of Glen Spean was blocked by glacial ice. The water escaped into the Spey Valley by spilling over a col through the Feagour channel, at the foot of the Graham Creag Ruadh (see opposite), about 4km to the east of Kinloch Laggan at the eastern end of Loch Laggan.

Step over the fence with care then head directly uphill on heathery ground and after a climb of 120m pick up a rough atv track. Turn right then follow this track steadily uphill and when it fades turn rightwards and ascend slightly steeper ground without difficulty. The summit area is slightly more interesting than expected and small outcrops of rock appear. The highest point is marked by a cairn 20m beyond the cylindrical trig pillar, where there are views east to the Creag Meagaidh range (**3km; 460m; 1h 25min**).

Return by the same route (6km; 460m; 2h 15min).

Creag Dhubh above Achluachrach, across Glen Spean from Monessie (Rab Anderson)

Lèana Mhòr (west)

Lèana Mhòr (west) from the north-east (Noel Williams)

Lèana Mhòr (west); 684m; (G124); L34, 41; NN284878; big meadow

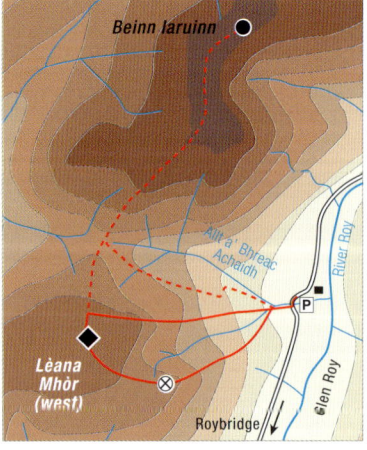

Glen Roy contains two Grahams named Lèana Mhòr which face each other on either side of the glen. This is the one on the west side of the glen and it gives an easier ascent than its partner. The outing can easily be extended to include the Corbett Beinn Iaruinn.

Leave the A86 in Roybridge and follow a single track road up Glen Roy to a viewpoint and interpretation board from where the Parallel Roads for which the glen is famous become apparent. These features represent different levels of ice-dammed lakes which were formed around 12,000 years ago when a glacier spread up into the mouth of the glen.

A further 3km up the glen, at a bend in the road, there is a bridge over the burn draining from the hill and the col to its north. There is good parking on the verge beyond the bridge. The route is well seen from here, taking the steep shoulder to the left of the narrow Coire an t-Seilich on the north-east face.

Walk over the bridge then climb the steep bank on the left to walk alongside a fence before heading up the hillside to climb the shoulder. Cross all three of the Parallel Roads which strike across the slope; there are good views of the matching Parallel Roads on the other side of the glen. Continue up the steeper ridge to a wide flattening then cross a slight dip and climb the slope above, curving gradually north to reach the broad summit. There is a small cairn on otherwise featureless ground (**2km; 500m; 1h 15min**).

The views across the Great Glen to the Meall na Teanga group and up Glen Roy are good, and the summit plateau of Lèana Mhòr east (see opposite) is conspicuous on the other side of the glen.

To descend, head north-east then go down a broad ridge on the other side of the corrie. Cross the burn where it joins the main burn draining from between the hills (**4km; 500m; 2h**).

To include Beinn Iaruinn, descend north to a col then climb the long but steady whaleback of a slope to a final short walk around the rim of a corrie to reach the 803m summit (**5km; 800m; 2h 30min**). The best descent, which also maintains the fine views, is to return to the col, then follow a deer track down and across Lèana Mhòr before dropping towards the start. Cross the burn coming from Lèana Mhòr where it joins the main burn draining from between the hills (**8.5km; 810m; 3h 30min**).

Lèana Mhòr (east)   197

Lèana Mhòr (east); 676m; (G139); L34, 41; NN317879; big meadow

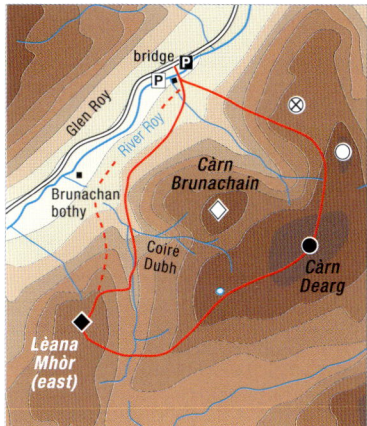

Approached from further up Glen Roy, this hill is harder to ascend than its namesake on the opposite side. It can only be reached conveniently by crossing the River Roy by a bridge a short distance before the end of the road up the glen. There is no longer a bridge across the river to Cranachan on the south side of the hill. In low water conditions it is possible to wade across to Brunachan Bothy on the north side of the hill.

As well as being more interesting, it is a natural combination to climb the hill as part of a round with Càrn Dearg, a Corbett to the north-east.

There is limited parking on the verge opposite a bridge and green shed at NN330909, about 500m before the end of the public road up Glen Roy; take care not to block access. In addition, there is good off-road parking 200m downstream, as well as 500m upstream where the public road ends.

Cross the bridge and head south a short distance, then cross the Allt na Reinich and continue up a broad ridge. The aim now is to slant rightwards up the hillside to the level of the third and highest of the Glen Roy Parallel Roads, which runs around the hillside at the 350m contour. The feature is not always obvious on the ground, but it should be possible to judge height from the equivalent Parallel Road on the opposite side of the glen. Contour in a south-westerly direction and gradually turn leftwards into the deep indent created by the Allt Brunachain.

If you find the correct level you should see a fork where the water from Coire Dubh joins the Allt Feith Bhrunachain. Cross this left-hand fork and ascend the ground between the two burns. Continue climbing southwards on the steep eastern bank of the Allt Feith Bhrunachain. After about 500m, cross the burn and head directly up the hillside, then climb a deer fence and continue up heathery ground to gain the crest of the north-north-east ridge.

An alternative, if coming up from Brunachan, or having traversed the lower 261m Parallel Road from the bridge then crossed the Allt Brunachain (if the burns are not running high) just below this, gains a gate in the deer fence at NN320894, then a rough atv track which climbs onto the crest of the ridge. The crest leads to what is an extensive plateau, where a small pile of stones marks the summit (**4km; 460m; 1h 35min**).

Head south-east off the summit then descend more steeply east to the floor of the glen. Cross a fence then a burn to ascend either side of a prominent straight gully and continue at a gentler angle. Pass to the right of a small lochan at Pt.745m and after 1km reach the pleasant 834m summit of Càrn Dearg where there are unusual views of the north side of Creag Meagaidh (**7.5km; 790m; 3h**).

Descend easily in a north-easterly direction to a saddle, then either gain the North Top, or avoid it by slanting down to another dip at about 645m. Trend leftwards, maintaining height for another 500m then descend the hillside on the north side of the Allt na Reinich directly to the bridge (**11km; 790m; 4h 5min**).

Lèana Mhòr (east), right, with Càrn Dearg behind (Rab Anderson)

Druim na Sgrìodain left
Sgùrr na h-Eanchainne right
and the Corran Ferry (Rab Anderson)

SECTION 10a
Loch Linnhe to Glenfinnan

Section 10a – Loch Linnhe to Glenfinnan

SECTION 10a

[1] Beinn Mheadhoin 201
[2] Beinn na Cille 202
[3] Druim na Sgrìodain 203
[4] Sgòrr Mhic Eacharna, [5] Beinn Bheag 204
[6] Sgùrr nan Cnamh 206
[7] Sgùrr a' Chaorainn 207
[8] Stob Mhic Bheathain 208
[9] Meall nan Damh, [10] Glas Bheinn 210
[11] Croit Bheinn, [12] Beinn Gàire 212

Beinn Mheadhoin

Beinn Mheadhoin viewed from the north across Coire Bàn (Noel Williams)

Beinn Mheadhoin; 739m; (G32); L49; NM799514; *middle mountain*

On the east side of Morvern, close to Loch Linnhe, there is a fine ring of hills facing the small community of Kingairloch, of which Beinn Mheadhoin is the highest.

From the Corran ferry, take the A861 towards Strontian and after 10km, just beyond Inversanda, turn south onto the B8043 for Kingairloch. Follow this single track road for almost 13km and take a left fork down to Kingairloch itself. Park by the shore just past the Boathouse Restaurant at the head of Loch a' Choire.

An ascent can be made most simply by the east-north-east ridge from the Old Mill in the floor of the glen via North Corry (**6km; 740m; 2h 35min**); (**12km; 740m; 4h 15min**).

However, the full circuit of the ring of hills makes a much finer expedition and this is the route described.

Walk along the road past the grounds of Kingairloch House then turn left and cross a bridge over the Abhainn na Coinnich, downstream of a power station. The first aim is to reach the eastern shoulder of Sgùrr Shalachain, called Sròn Seann. Ascend north-westwards on a forest

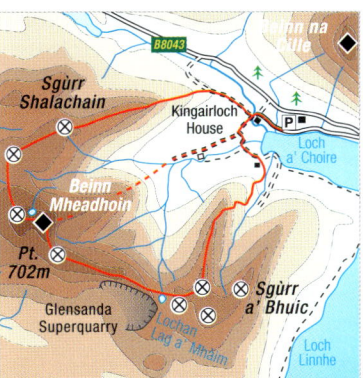

track. Ignore tracks off left and continue up the track until it starts to level off, then turn left and head up the open hillside. At a height of 200m start to follow the left flank of the shoulder and cross a burn before eventually regaining the crest. Steep grassy ground leads to the broad summit of Sgùrr Shalachain (538m), which has three tops of similar height (**3.5km; 540m; 1h 10min**).

Most of the hard work has now been done. Continue easily along the broad, undulating ridge for a further 1.5km to the flat top of Meall na Grèine (609m) from where there are fine views across Coire Bàn to Beinn Mheadhoin. Descend to lochan-peppered Bealach a' Choire Bhàin and climb more steeply to a subsidiary top 400m away from the summit. Descend to a broad dip with a shallow lochan and continue easily to the main summit (**7km; 830m; 3h**).

Although the quickest way back is to descend the east-north-east ridge, taking special care at a steep nose in the upper section (**13km; 830m; 4h 40min**), the better walk is to continue

To do so, head south around Coire nan Each, over Pt.702m then down the ridge, it is possible to get impressive views into the 1km-wide Glensanda Superquarry. From Lochan Lag a' Mhàim at the end of the ridge, skirt the next small top on the north side and descend northwards along the ridge of Meall an Doire Dhuibh.

Just in front of the last cairned knoll, pick up a stalkers' path on the left and follow this as it zigzags down rightwards to the west bank of the Allt na Carraige. From the buildings at South Corry, easiest is to follow a track across the Abhainn na Fearna to North Corry to join the approach route at the bridge over the Abhainn na Coinnich (**15km; 940m; 5h 25min**).

Beinn na Cille

Beinn na Cille; 652m; (G170); L49; NM854542; mountain of the church

This hill is situated just north of Loch a' Choire and overlooks the small community of Kingairloch. It forms the most southerly summit of a circle of hills, including two Corbetts, which surrounds Glen Galmadale to its east. Although it can be ascended most directly from the roadside by its south flank, a track up Coire Ghardail to the west gives slightly easier-angled access and allows a pleasant circuit to be made of that corrie. The route includes the Corbett Fuar Bheinn but is not as demanding as the full round of Glen Galmadale.

Parking along the B8043 above Kingairloch is limited. There is space for a car on the north side of the road immediately west of the bridge over the Abhainn Ghardail (NM829541). Otherwise, park with care in a passing place further to the west. The Coire Ghardail track leaves the north side of the road a few metres west of the bridge.

Climb steadily up the track into the corrie and follow it for just over 1km. Turn right at a junction and descend slightly to the Abhainn Ghardail where there is an intake for a small hydro scheme. Cross the burn and head directly up the hillside in an easterly

direction. It is hard-going on the lower slopes where there is much tussock grass but as the angle steepens the ground becomes easier. Higher up, where the angle starts to ease again, there is an outcrop of a distinctive, brown-coloured dyke. Once on the crest turn right to reach the summit of Beinn na Cille (**3.5km; 580m; 1h 45min**).

There are superb views east to the hills around Glen Galmadale and south-west to Beinn Mheadhoin, the neighbouring Graham. The whole island of Lismore is conspicuous further south in Loch Linnhe.

Although a quick return can be made the same way (**7km; 580m; 3h**), it makes for a more satisfying day to climb northwards across the Bealach Coire Mhic Gugain then up to the summit of Fuar Bheinn (**6km; 890m; 2h 50min**).

Descend the north western ridge to gain the Bealach a' Mhonmhuir then swing around the head of Coire Ghardail over Pt.626m and turn south onto the broad ridge of Glas Bheinn (**9km; 990m; 3h 45min**).

Drop south down the ridge then descend diagonally across the hillside to regain the track in the corrie floor (**12km; 990m; 4h 45min**).

Beinn na Cille can be climbed from the parking area at NM866531 at the entrance to Glen Galmadale. Head west along the road a short way then climb steeply between the forestry plantation and the burn (**2.5km; 650m; 1h 40min**). Returning the same way is quick (**5km; 650m; 2h 40min**), but continuing north over both Corbetts, then Maol Odhar and Meall nan Each for the Glen Galmadale horseshoe gives a classic but more arduous round (**16km; 1500m; 6h 30min**).

Beinn na Cille, right, with the Corbetts Fuar Bheinn, left, and Creach Bheinn, centre (Noel Williams)

Druim na Sgrìodain 203

Druim na Sgrìodain, centre left, and shapely Sgùrr na h-Eanchainne from the Corran road (Tom Prentice)

Druim na Sgrìodain; *734m; (G39); L40; NM978656; ridge of the scree*

Druim na Sgrìodain sits above the Corran Narrows on the west side of Loch Linnhe, towards which it presents a fine south-east facing corrie. As well as offering an excellent varied walk, the trip also involves a ferry crossing as a foot passenger, adding something a little unusual to the day.

Park beside the Corran ferry slipway and take the ferry over to Corran in Ardgour, which gives time to survey the objective; a round of Coire Dubh taking in two summits. Sgùrr na h-Eanchainne is the shapely peak on the right which dominates the view and tends to overshadow its marginally higher neighbour, Druim na Sgrìodain, which sits further back at the head of the corrie.

From the pier out in front of the Inn at Ardgour, walk north-west along the road for 2km, then go through a gate to Cille Mhaodain (the clan Maclean burial ground), beyond which another gate leads onto the open hillside. Steeply climb above the burial ground onto the rounded spur and continue over a knoll to a col. Swing round south and climb the ridge to the trig pillar and tremendous viewpoint on the summit of Sgùrr na h-Eanchainne (730m); (**5km; 730m; 2h 20min**).

Drop off the top and head west past tiny Lochan a' Choire Dhuibh, around the head of Coire Dubh, then make the short ascent to the summit of Druim na Sgrìodain, which sits atop a small knoll beside some tiny lochans (**7km; 830m; 3h**).

Descend the long curving ridge which drops southward, and follow it as it swings east to where steep slopes fall away to the forest below. Drop north into the corrie and cross the burn just before it cascades over the lip to form Tubhailt Mhic 'ic Eòghainn (Maclean's Towel), a lovely waterslide. Follow the path down the north side of the waterslide and at the bottom head for an aerial, beyond which a track leads down through the forest to Ardgour House.

Cross the bridge over the river, then take the track south-east through the woods to reach the minor road at Clovullin. A short section along the main road leads back to Corran and perhaps a brief refreshment while the ferry is waited on (**13km; 830m; 4h 40min**).

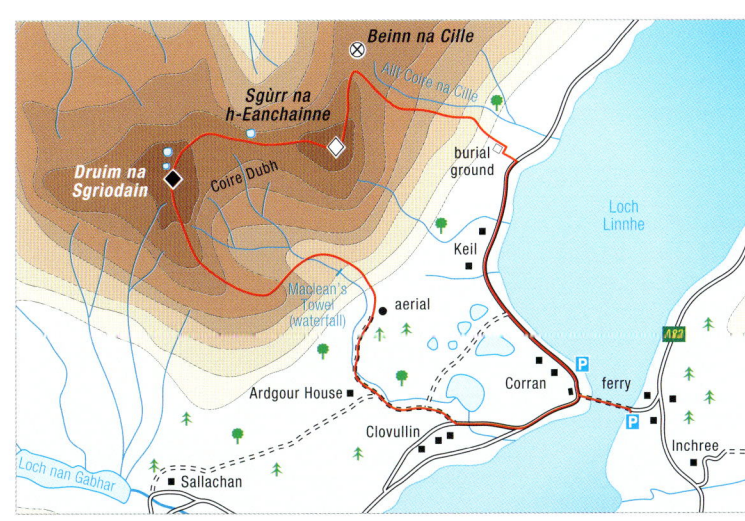

Sgòrr Mhic Eacharna, Beinn Bheag

Ascending the Druim an Iubhair towards Sgòrr Mhic Eacharna (Rab Anderson)

Sgòrr Mhic Eacharna; 650m; (G175); L40; NM928630; *MacEachern's peak*
Beinn Bheag; 736m; (G37); L40; NM914635; *little mountain*

Sgòrr Mhic Eacharna, Beinn Bheag and the Corbett Garbh Bheinn encircle Coire an Iubhair and offer a superb round through some of the rockiest and most dramatic mountain scenery in the area. Rough terrain with some steep descents and ascents requiring care and good navigation in poor visibility or wintery conditions, mean the route feels longer and more tiring than the time and distance might suggest. The round can also be extended to the north-west to include the Graham Sgùrr nan Cnamh (see the end of this description and p206).

Park off the A861 on a section of old road at the foot of Coire an Iubhair and follow the path up the corrie on the east side of the Abhainn Coire an Iubhair to join a track up the corrie. Cross straight over and ascend the hillside, passing west of Lochan Druim an Iubhair to gain Druim an Iubhair and follow this broad, rock-scattered ridge over assorted small knolls.

Increasingly rocky and steeper terrain leads towards the top of Sgòrr Mhic Eacharna to meet an old fenceline which is followed to the cairned summit (**4km; 640m; 2h**).

Garbh Bheinn dominates the view to the west, with the cone of the Corbett Sgùrr Dhomhnuill prominent to the north-west. To the south, beyond Mull, are Grahams Beinn Shiantaidh and Beinn a' Chaolais, two of the four Paps of Jura.

Descend west, nearer to the fenceline at the start then more to its south, to gain the Bealach nan Aingidh, with Beinn Bheag towering above. From here, a steep and surprisingly rocky ascent, initially close to the fenceline before it veers off west, leads to a small, craggy top followed by scree and boulders to the cairned summit (**6km; 910m; 3h**).

Beinn Bheag (Jim Teesdale)

Sgòrr Mhic Eacharna, Beinn Bheag

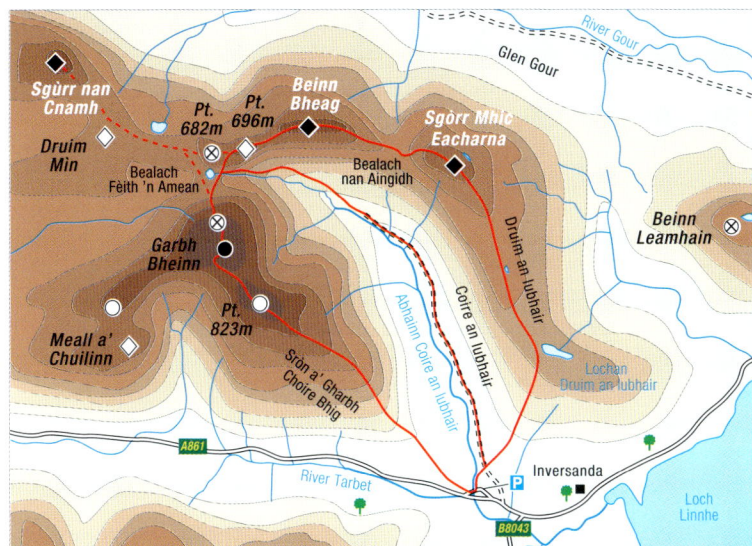

A fine elevated ridge now leads west then south-west over the craggy West Top (Pt.696m) to a grassy col before Pt.682m, overlooking Lochan Coire an Iubhair on the Bealach Fèith 'n Amean below. A possible extension continues west from here to pick up Sgùrr nan Cnamh; described at the end.

Continuing towards Garbh Bheinn, descend a steep grassy gully from the col to reach the eastern end of the lochan at the Bealach Fèith 'n Amean. A return can be made from here, east down Coire an Iubhair to pick up a rough path (12.5km; 950m; 4h 45min).

However, to complete the round, ascend above the lochan by taking a grassy zigzag line up the mixed slope between the large rounded buttress of the North Face cliffs on the left and a grassy gully on the right. Above, the rocky ridge of Sròn Lag nan Gamhna can be climbed direct by easy but fine scrambling to gain the top of Fiaclan Garbh-Bheinn; alternatively go right into the corrie, then up. Drop off the back and continue south up to the summit of Garbh Bheinn (9km; 1310m; 4h 30min).

From the summit, follow the path due west to clear the sheer South Face crags before descending south to the bealach. Continue on the ridge in a more easterly direction over Pt.823m then south-east down Sròn a' Gharbh Choire Bhig. The path fades in places and there are some short rocky sections, making the descent feel long and quite hard going (13.5km; 1380m; 6h 15min).

If continuing on to Sgùrr nan Cnamh from the ridge west of Beinn Bheag, climb over Pt.682m to drop steeply west off the back and cross the intervening col just south of Loch nan Dearcag. Gain a grassy traverse-line and follow this across the north-east side of Druim Mìn then cross gentle slabby ground and climb to Pt. 634m. Drop to a narrow col and climb steeply through a rocky band then on up to the summit of Sgùrr nan Cnamh. Return the same way and cut across to the Bealach Fèith 'n Amean; an additional 4.5km, 220m, 1h 45min on the day.

Garbh Bheinn, left, with Beinn Bheag, right, from Sgòrr Mhic Eacharna (Rab Anderson)

Sgùrr nan Cnamh

Sgùrr nan Cnamh; 701m; (G103); L40; NM886643; peak of the bones

Sgùrr nan Cnamh is a solitary hill rising from an extensive area of rough moorland south and east of the Strontian River. It is a north-westerly outlier of Garbh Bheinn, and lies to the south of the big ridges around Sgùrr Dhomhnuill, from which it is separated by deep glens.

Approach from the Loch Sunart side, from a car park at NM826633 inside the Ariundle Nature Reserve, 2.5km north-east of Strontian.

Follow a forest track gently uphill through beautiful pine and oak woods for 3km to a fork. Take the right branch and gradually descend north-east for 1km to the ruined croft at Ceann a' Chreagain.

Cross the potentially large Strontian River and follow the Allt a' Bhuic east, taking the left-hand tributary higher up. Clamber over rough, slabby ground to gain the subsidiary summit of Sgùrr a' Bhuic (461m). Undulating ground gives slow going for 1km before the final steady uphill climb to Sgùrr nan Cnamh's summit (**7.5km; 730m; 3h**).

Descend the same way (**15km; 750m; 5h**).

Sgùrr nan Cnamh can be combined with Sgùrr a' Chaorainn, in which case it is better to climb the latter hill first (see opposite for details of the link).

If connecting transport can be arranged, a better extended excursion is to continue east from Sgùrr nan Cnamh to traverse over the Grahams of Beinn Bheag and Sgòrr Mhic Eacharna, descending to the car park at the foot of Coire an Iubhair at NM928597. This makes a fine walk, passing the remote Loch nan Dearcag and scaling the grand prow of the west top of Beinn Bheag.

Sgùrr nan Cnamh can also be easily taken in after the Sgòrr Mhic Eacharna to Beinn Bheag traverse, returning to the col south of Loch nan Dearcag then the Bealach Fèith 'n Amean at the foot of Beinn Bheag. See p205 for details of that link.

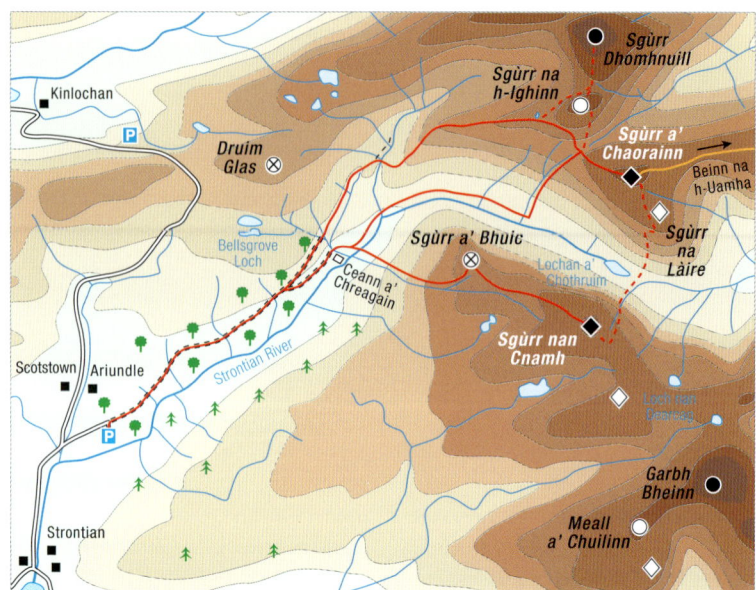

The craggy north-east face of Sgùrr nan Cnamh above Lochan a' Chothruim (Tom Prentice)

Sgùrr a' Chaorainn and Sgùrr Dhomhnuill from the south (Rab Anderson)

Sgùrr a' Chaorainn; 761m; (G2); L40; NM895662; peak of the rowan tree

Ardgour being an area of extremely rough terrain, it is no surprise that some of its Grahams give testing excursions; this is one of them. Sgùrr a' Chaorainn forms part of the high ridge on the north side of the Glen Gour to River Strontian divide, sitting between its Corbett neighbours, Beinn na h-Uamha, which is higher by just 1m, and Sgùrr Dhomhnuill, at 888m Ardgour's highest peak.

It can be climbed following an ascent of Beinn na h-Uamha, approached from Sallachan to the east. However, it is probably better approached from the west, starting from the car park at NM826633 inside the Ariundle Nature Reserve, 2.5km north-east of Strontian.

Follow a forest track through beautiful natural woodland for 3km to a fork. Take the left branch which leads in a further 1km to a bridge over a burn, the Allt Ruighe Spardain; it can be biked to here. On the other side, a path continues for 900m to the old Bellsgrove lead mines by the Allt Fèith Dhomhnuill.

Cross the burn at NM860663 and climb onto Druim Leac a' Sgiathain, the attractive long west ridge of Sgùrr na h-Ighinn. Follow this ridge to a height of around 600m, just east of a tiny lochan at NM879669.

Now traverse east below the steep south face of Sgùrr na h-Ighinn, passing below a band of crags. Once beyond the crags, drop south-east for 100m in height past a knoll to reach a col; the Bealach Màm a' Bhearna (493m). The ascent of Sgùrr a' Chaorainn's west ridge is straightforward, steep at first, then easing past a tiny lochan with a final blocky, almost gentle walk to the summit cairn (**8.75km; 870m; 3h 25min**).

To descend, return to the Bealach Màm a' Bhearna. If a bike has been left at the bridge, return past the mines. Otherwise drop steeply into Strontian Glen. Traces of a path can be picked up, which lead to the ruin at Ceann a' Chreagain where a track climbs gradually south-west for 1km to return to the fork on the track 3km from the start (**17km; 900m; 5h 40min**).

However, a good extension is to climb north from the Bealach Màm a' Bhearna onto Sgùrr na h-Ighinn (766m). From its summit, drop to the col (692m) with Sgùrr Dhomhnuill and climb the fine south ridge to the summit (**11.25km; 1360m; 5h 10min**).

To descend, return south to the col at 692m then traverse across the north side of Sgùrr na h-Ighinn, dropping down to rejoin the approach route at the tiny lochan. Retrace the route back down the Druim Leac a' Sgiathain and past the lead mines (**20km; 1370m; 7h 30min**).

Sgùrr a' Chaorainn can be linked with the neighbouring Graham, Sgùrr nan Cnamh, which lies 2km to the south. However, the hills are separated by a considerable 500m drop and the difficult link is only for the strong and the determined. It may also give some interesting moments!

To make this link, descend south to the col with Sgùrr na Làire (624m). This can either be included by a short 50m climb, or avoided by a descending traverse south-east beneath its crags, whilst staying above other crags below. After dropping about 100m, make a dogleg west then pick a way carefully down the steep and rocky hillside, especially if the slope is wet or frozen. Cross the top of the glen east of Lochan a' Chothruim to gain the craggy flanks of Sgùrr nan Cnamh.

On the ascent, initially follow the burn which emanates from the central corrie below the summit and then bear south-east up a gully to arrive at a small col just above a spur at NM893643. Above, some 250m of scruffy slab and vegetation lie in wait, requiring care. Higher up, the angle relents. Beyond a minor top there is a short but steep rocky climb to the summit (**12km; 1420m; 5h 35min**).

The way off Sgùrr nan Cnamh is down the north-west ridge to the col with Sgùrr a' Bhuic, then down by the burn to Ceann a' Chreagain. A reverse of the route for the ascent of Sgùrr nan Cnamh is described opposite (**19.5km; 1450m; 7h 35min**).

Easier than this link is the inclusion of Sgùrr nan Cnamh in the Sgòrr Mhic Eacharna to Beinn Bheag traverse (see p205), leaving Sgùrr a' Chaorainn to be climbed with one of its neighbouring Corbetts.

For the ascent from Sallachan via Glen Gour, ascend Beinn na h-Uamha (**8.5km; 770m; 3h 15min**). Traverse to Sgùrr a' Chaorainn (**11km; 975m; 4h 15min**) then descend into Glen Gour and return (**21km; 1000m; 6h 40min**).

Stob Mhic Bheathain

Stob Mhic Bheathain and Pt.706m, right, from the approach up Cona Glen (Noel Williams)

Stob Mhic Bheathain; 721m; (G63); L40; NM914713; MacBeth's peak

Situated on the south side of Cona Glen, in the northern part of Ardgour, there is a hidden range of hills which stretches almost from Loch Linnhe to Loch Shiel. Stob Mhic Bheathain lies on the western half of this range, more than 11km as the crow flies from the road at Inverscaddle Bay on Loch Linnhe.

Although it is little frequented, Cona Glen is one of the most delightful glens in the area. A rough vehicular track runs along the north side of the Cona River for most of its length. The only drawback in using this as an approach, is that there are no convenient bridges in the upper half of the glen, so any ascent from the north will entail fording the Cona River.

The quickest approach is by mountain bike on the initial 10.5km of track. This allows a rapid return down the glen at the end of the day and gives a saving of about 2h 30min on the Cona Glen approach and return.

However, if on foot, a more varied option is to approach by Cona Glen and return by Glen Scaddle, on the south side of the range. Both routes are described.

Park at NN022686, just off the A861 at Inverscaddle, at the start of a tarmac estate road. Follow the estate road through pleasant woodland past several buildings, turning left at a junction to continue on a rough track. After a few hundred metres the track re-enters natural

The summit from Pt.706m to the west (Noel Williams)

Stob Mhic Bheathain 209

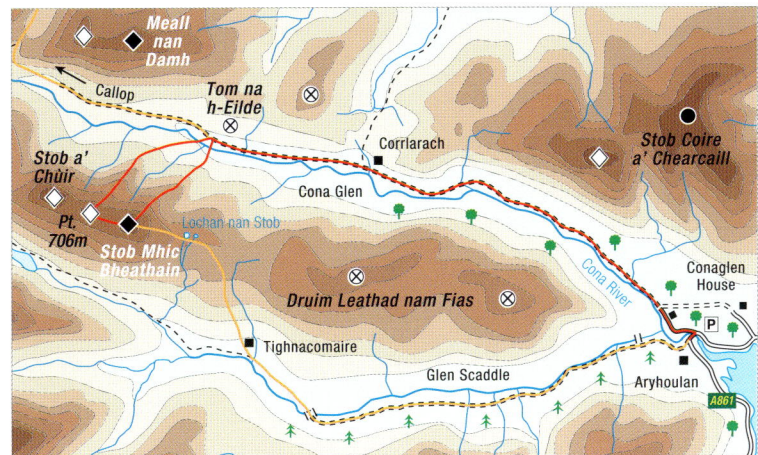

oak woodland and runs beside the Cona River. Continue past several more open areas with conspicuous lazy beds; a legacy of when the glen was extensively cultivated. Eventually, the track begins to undulate and there are distant views of Stob Mhic Bheathain in the upper glen. Shortly after, pass a locked bothy on the uphill side of the track called Corrlarach.

Just after some fine Scots pine trees, the track rises past Tom na h-Eilde (194m), an isolated hillock. There are some spectacular rapids in the Cona River nearby. When the track levels off, continue for a few hundred metres before looking for a suitable place to wade the river in the vicinity of NM930726.

The most straightforward option is to ascend the crest of Sròn a' Choire Lèith Mhòir, the ridge to the west of the summit. This runs up the west side of Coire Liath Mòr to gain Pt.706m. From there, continue east beside the remains of a wire fence over some fine rock slabs onto the summit (**14km; 760m; 4h 15min**).

There is a very slightly lower top 200m further east.

If the approach and return are being made via Cona Glen, it is best to make a clockwise circuit of Coire Liath Mòr. Wade the river opposite Tom na h-Eilde (where bikes are best left) just above the rapids and climb the rocky ridge directly to the summit. Descend via Sròn a' Choire Lèith Mhòir (**27km; 770m; 7h 30min** on foot), (**5h** with a bike).

For those continuing on foot via Glen Scaddle, head in an easterly direction, passing to the south of Lochan nan Stob. Go round the head of a gully at NM929708 then descend 350m to a building called Tighnacomaire. Follow an undulating track along Glen Scaddle for some 11km back to the start (**29km; 830m; 8h 20min**).

A high-level return along Druim Leathad nam Fias is also possible.

Stob Mhic Bheathain can also be approached via Callop to the north, from the car park at NM924792. A track goes as far as a dam at NM918770. This is used on the approach to the Grahams, Meall nan Damh and Glas Bheinn; see following route. A path continues through the hills to drop into the head of Cona Glen, from where the ascent is made (**10km; 910m; 3h 45min**), (**20km; 1000m; 6h 30min**).

Looking east along the rocky summit ridge towards Ben Nevis and The Mamores (Noel Williams)

Meall nan Damh, Glas Bheinn

Meall nan Damh from Sròn Meall nan Damh with Ben Nevis and The Mamores in the distance (Noel Williams)

Meall nan Damh; 723m; (G58); L40; NM919745; hill of the deer
Glas Bheinn; 636m; (G189); L40; NM938758 (NM939757); green mountain

These two Grahams lie above the west end of Loch Eil, west of Fort William, and are conveniently climbed together to give a fine round. They can be clearly seen from the roadside shortly after the A380 west passes under the railway some 2.5km to the east of Glenfinnan. At the apex of a wide bend, turn off south onto a track which leads over a bridge across the Callop River. Immediately on the right there is a car park at NM924792.

Head south on the track, which passes a small power station then Callop Cottage, and continue up the glen on a track constructed for the installation of a hydro-electric scheme. After 2km, note a track on the left which descends steeply to a bridge in the floor of the glen. This is used for the return route.

In another 300m or so, where the track loops round to end at a dam, take the signposted path through to Cona Glen. Follow the path as it loops away uphill then swings back across the foot of the spur leading to Meall na Cuartaige, coming closer to the burn below; now the Allt Fèith nan Còn. At a brief levelling, leave the path and go down to cross the burn above the upper limit of the bulk of the trees. The crossing is normally straightforward.

Now climb uphill to gain the broad and rocky crest of Sròn Meall nam Damh and go up this, zigzagging at times on the steeper sections. It is a splendid ridge with fine views west to the Corbetts on the opposite side of the glen and east across Coire Fada towards the main summit and its

Meall nan Damh summit with Ben Nevis beyond (Rab Anderson)

Glas Bheinn from Sròn Meall nan Damh with distant Stob a' Ghrianain left (Rab Anderson)

north ridge with Glas Bheinn beyond.

Eventually reach the western summit (722m), which is only one metre lower than the main summit. There are now views south across Cona Glen to the remote Graham Stob Mhic Bheathain and the prominent Corbett of Sgùrr Dhomhnuill. The highest point of Meall nan Damh lies some 900m further east and is reached by an easy ridge which drops only 40m at its lowest point (**6.5km; 770m; 2h 45min**).

There is no cairn on the summit itself. However, on slightly lower ground about 120m further along there is a prominent cairn with a large up-ended rock flake. Bidean nam Bian is prominent to the south-east whilst to the east there is an unusual view of Ben Nevis.

Descend the ridge more steeply eastwards. At a slight flattening, turn left and continue down, passing occasional lochans on increasingly rocky ground. Cross the lowest point on the ridge, Glas Bhealach, and ascend the broad south-west ridge of Glas Bheinn without difficulty to the summit plateau with its sprinkling of tiny lochans. A trig point sits on the first knoll and the Database of British and Irish Hills give a rock 3m south of this as the highest point. OS maps show a point on a knoll 80m further to the north-west as being 1m higher (**9.5km; 920m; 3h 45min**).

Since the west face of Glas Bheinn is fairly steep, the best descent option is to head north-west from the summit and to drop down for about 1km before turning more sharply westwards.

A bridge is obvious below, part of the hydro scheme, and the aim is to eventually reach this, or the head of the track which can be seen running north-west from it. To gain the track, either scale a fence and pick up a faint path heading north-west from one of the small dams on the Allt na Teanga Duibhe (NM925765), or take a longer route around the southern side of the fence and cross two burns before going through a gate and heading north.

Follow the track through a gate and continue through the forest. The track eventually becomes rather boggy and tree trunks have been laid across it. Exit the forest, go through another gate and descend to cross a bridge over the Allt na Cruaiche. Steeply ascend the other side to rejoin the track and return the 2km along this (**14.5km; 940m; 5h 20min**).

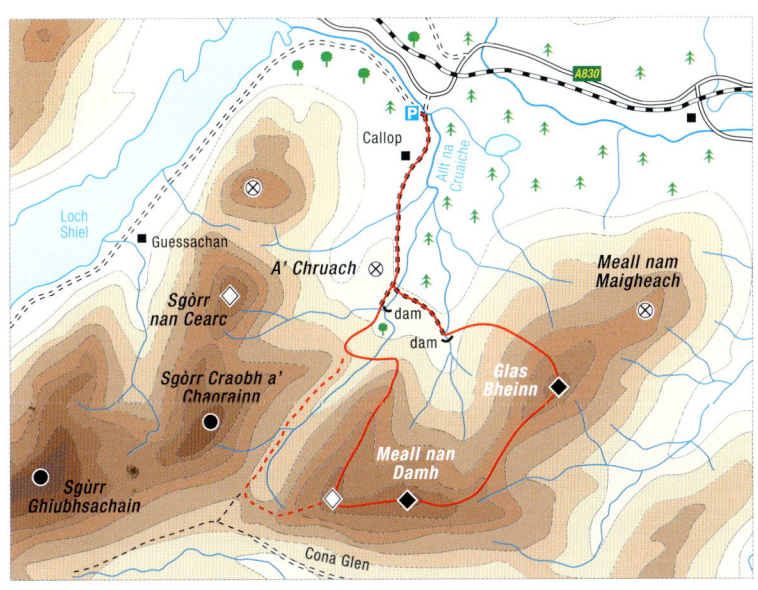

Croit Bheinn, Beinn Gàire

Croit Bheinn from the north-north-east (Jim Teesdale)

Croit Bheinn; 663m; (G157); L40; NM810773; hump mountain

Beinn Gàire; 666m; (G151); L40; NM781748; laughter or noise mountain (probably from burns)

Lying in a fairly remote part of Moidart, sandwiched between Loch Shiel on the east and Glen Moidart on the west, this pair of hills forms a broad mountain ridge. Consequently they are best climbed together.

From Lochailort on the Road to the Isles (A830), take the A861 south to Glenuig. Continue over the hill to Loch Moidart and after a further 4km, turn off at Ardmolich on a single track road up Glen Moidart. Cross the River Moidart at Brunery by a picturesque bridge and park at the end of the public road.

The road ahead leads to Glenmoidart House. Ignore this and go back along the road for 65m to take the track on the east side of the road, which crosses over a slight shoulder and passes Loch nan Lochan. After a further 1.2km, leave the track on the left and cross a footbridge over the River Moidart (NM754732). Head over rough ground in a north-westerly direction and join a track which leads up Glen Moidart.

Glen Moidart has an unfortunate claim to fame as one of the boggiest glens in Lochaber. In all but drought conditions the next 1km or so will be very wet underfoot, although eventually the going improves.

In the upper part of the glen there is plentiful evidence that numerous people once lived there. Ruined buildings and shielings can be seen at three separate locations; Inchrory, Assary and Ulgary. The remains of the latter settlement are somewhat hidden behind a rock-bar which guards a very flat stretch of glen floor. On the south-facing slopes above Ulgary there are numerous lazy beds. Families were cleared from Moidart in the middle of the 19th century and many emigrated to Australia.

The glen now changes character and the river runs through a narrow gorge. It is best to avoid the gorge and ascend the steep slope on the left (north) side of the river to a broad shoulder at about 220m. This is the Bealach na Lice and it is the key to reaching the upper glen. From there, descend very slightly at first, before gradually gaining height again to

Beinn Gàire across Loch nan Lochan in Glen Moidart (George Archibald)

contour along the hillside on the north side of the glen for some distance, staying well above the river. This upper section of glen is continuous with Glen Moidart but is given a separate name, Glen Gluitanen.

Continue contouring the hillside and eventually cross the burn in the floor of the glen in the vicinity of NM798770, at a height of about 250m. Gradually head away from this burn and climb more steeply eastwards to eventually reach the delightful little summit of Croit Bheinn (**10.5km; 660m; 3h 55min**).

The ground falls away steeply to the north and east where there are spectacular views across Glen Aladale, whilst to the west the whole Rois-bheinn to Druim Fiaclach ridge fills the skyline.

The next objective, Beinn Gàire, is of very similar height, but lies over 4km away. Descend in a south-westerly direction to the Bealach a' Choire Mhòir (c430m), then cross this rather complex col and go steeply up the other side to regain the crest of the ridge. Climb over a minor summit and descend to a slight dip, shortly after which the ridge broadens out considerably. At this point there are many outcrops of rock with very conspicuous dark crystals of hornblende.

Continue ascending to another higher top (Pt. 610m) and descend slightly to the shallow Bealach Gainmheach, with the summit still 1km away. Go round the north side of a lochan and continue ascending gently to yet another minor top then head south-west for 300m to reach the cairn on the summit of Beinn Gàire (**14.5km; 930m; 5h 25min**).

The summit plateau is quite extensive and peppered by several lochans. Though the views are not as dramatic as on Croit Bheinn, they are more wide-ranging. Beinn Resipol stands out to the south.

Head over to the westernmost top, which is 300m away, then descend in a west-south-westerly direction to the southern end of a wide saddle. Traverse across the slope on the right and descend the ridge of Sròn Dubh an Eilich, quite steeply, direct to Glenforslan in the floor of the glen. Pick up a rough track which leads back to the start (**20km; 950m; 7h 15min**).

Croit Bheinn from the north-eastern flanks of Beinn Gàire (Noel Williams)

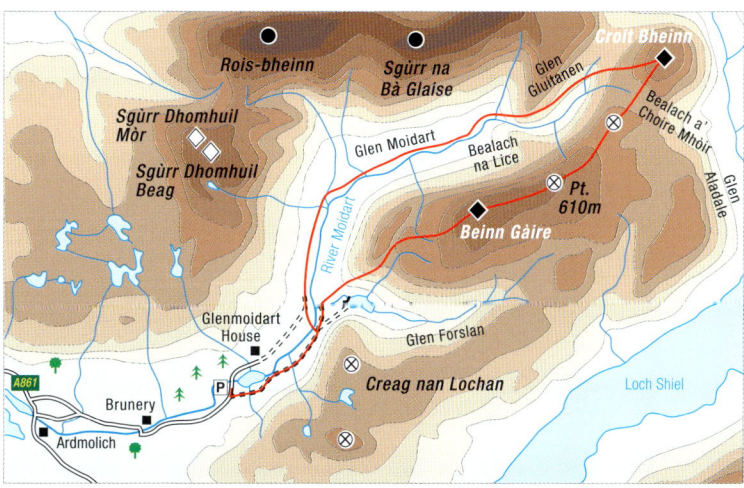

Sgùrr na Maothaich (Mèith Bheinn) and Loch Beoraid from near Prince Charlie's Cave on the approach. The Corbett Sgùrr an Utha and the Graham Glas-chàrn far right (Rab Anderson)

SECTION 10b
Glenfinnan to Glen Shiel

SECTION 10b

DRUIM FADA [1] **Stob a' Ghrianain**	217
[2] **Meall Onfhaidh**, [3] **Aodann Chlèireig**	218
[4] **Glas-chàrn**	220
MÈITH BHEINN [5] **Sgùrr na Maothaich**	221
[6] **Mullach Coire nan Geur-oirean**	222
[7] **Glas Bheinn**	223
[8] **Sgùrr Chòinnich**	224
[9] **Meall Blàir**	225
[10] **An Stac**	226
[11] **Slat Bheinn**, [12] **Meall nan Eun**	228
[13] **Beinn a' Chapuill**	230
[14] **Beinn Clachach**	231
[15] **Druim Fada**	233
[16] **Biod an Fhithich**	234

DRUIM FADA Stob a' Ghrianain

The summit of Stob a' Ghrianain from the west (Noel Williams)

DRUIM FADA; long ridge
Stob a' Ghrianain; 744m; (G18); L41; NN087824; peak of the sunny spot

North of Corpach and Loch Eil is the long and broad east-west ridge of Druim Fada, whose highest point is Stob a' Ghrianain. A traverse of this ridge makes a fine outing, although a shorter and very pleasant option is to make a circuit of Coire an Lightuinn at the eastern end of the ridge. The view across the Great Glen to Ben Nevis is superb. The best approach is by a signposted route to Stob a' Ghrianain through the forest from Glen Loy.

Turn off the B8004 between Corpach and Gairlochy into Glen Loy and follow the single-track road beside the River Loy. Look for the start of a forest track on the left, just before the road crosses to the north side of the river by a bridge. There is parking on the left at a gate into the forest.

Go through the gate and follow the track straight ahead; another track joins from the left after about 400m. Continue for 300m, where the track dips to cross a burn, and in a further 400m, where the main track curves to the right, take a less-used track off to the left. It is important then to find the start of a rough atv track which heads off on the right after less than 100m. This leads pleasantly through the forest with a dilapidated stone wall on the right-hand side. The track is boggy in places and climbs uphill to eventually emerge from the forest at a gate.

Walk on for about 200m and cross the burn in the floor of the glen by a hidden wooden bridge at NN112821. Climb straight up the hillside ahead by following a faint atv track up the line of a small burn to reach the ridge, which is then climbed. Higher up a couple of minor cols are crossed before the ground eventually begins to ease in angle.

Go along the top of Coire Odhar past the right-hand side of a lochan and make a slight detour to the right to visit a prominent cairn which overlooks Glen Loy. Turn left and head up to the tiny cairn which marks the highest point on the flat grassy summit (**5km; 680m; 2h 15min**).

Continue along the rim of Coire Dubh to a small pointed top on the other side of the ridge with fine views to the south. The slope beneath this is very steep, so to return go left and head east for 270m before descending the grassy hillside by the burn to where it drops into Coire an Lightuinn. Either descend more steeply into the corrie to follow the burn, or continue east along the ridge to Sròn Liath before descending north to the burn to rejoin the track used in the approach. Neither way is as easy as it looks (**11km; 700m; 3h 45min**).

From the summit, if time is not pressing, it is relatively simple and worthwhile to continue along the ridge, certainly to the far side of Coire Dubh for the view back, then westwards around Coire an Fhuidhir to the West Top (729m). The trig pillar at 716m lies some 700m beyond this (**9km; 770m; 3h 20min**). The Grahams, Aodann Chlèireig and Meall Onfhaidh sit on the other side of Gleann Sùileag to the west. Return along the ridge towards the summit then cut down the grassy hillside south-eastwards to join the descent described above (**17.5km; 800m; 5h 30min**).

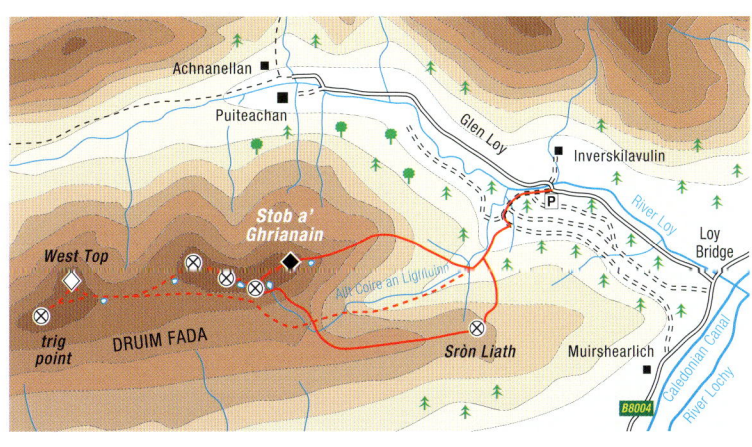

Meall Onfhaidh from Aodann Chlèireig (Noel Williams)

Meall Onfhaidh; 681m; (G127); L41; NN010840; *hill of the storm*
Aodann Chlèireig; 663m; (G156); L40; NM994825; *clergyman's face*

These two hills are accessed from Fassfern, a tiny settlement on a loop of the old road along the north side of Loch Eil. Turn off the A830 between Fort William and Mallaig at the signpost for Fassfern. After 800m, a car park is reached on the west side of the small bridge over the An t-Sùileag.

An anti-clockwise circuit of the two hills is described and those looking for a more demanding outing can easily include Meall a' Phubuill, the Corbett a little further to the north-east.

Cross the bridge over the An t-Sùileag and follow a track (signposted Public Footpath to Glen Loy) up the east side of Gleann Sùileag through lovely woodland. After 2km the track climbs rightwards away from the river then continues leftwards where another track joins, to eventually emerge from the main forestry plantation 3.5km from the start.

Continue on a rougher track through native woodland for just over 1km to cross a bridge over the An t-Sùileag and go through a gate; Glensulaig bothy is situated 350m further upstream. The track now climbs quite steeply up the other side of the glen to reach a bridge across the Allt Fionn Doire. Break off left here and head westwards up the hillside, initially on a rough atv track. The angle gradually increases until the broad south-east ridge is gained and leads more easily to the small cairn marking Meall Onfhaidh's summit (**8km; 670m; 2h 55min**).

A larger cairn some 90m to the south-west is apparently lower, though easily included. To the north, there are fine views of the neighbouring Munro, Gulvain.

From the bridge over the Allt Fionn Doire, Meall a' Phubuill can be climbed by its steep grassy southern slope. Meall Onfhaidh is then gained via the Fèith an Easain col (382m); an additional 1.5km, 390m, 1h 15min on the day. The descent of Meall a' Phubuill's south-west ridge is very steep and although some crags are easily avoided, it might be preferable to return by the ascent route to the bridge, certainly in winter.

To continue from Meall Onfhaidh, head westwards from the summit and descend the steep grassy hillside, gradually curving leftwards to reach the bealach (347m) below. Cross this and climb the broad northern shoulder of Aodann Chlèireig.

At a height of about 500m, a ramp slants rightwards below a small rocky escarpment on the north side of the summit and leads without any difficulty onto the western shoulder of the mountain. Turn left here and after about 200m reach the summit cairn which is situated on a rocky knoll (**11km; 990m; 4h 20min**).

Two slightly lower knolls are situated within 200m of the main summit and might cause confusion in poor visibility, especially when approaching from the south. There are splendid panoramic views.

To return, follow the remains of a

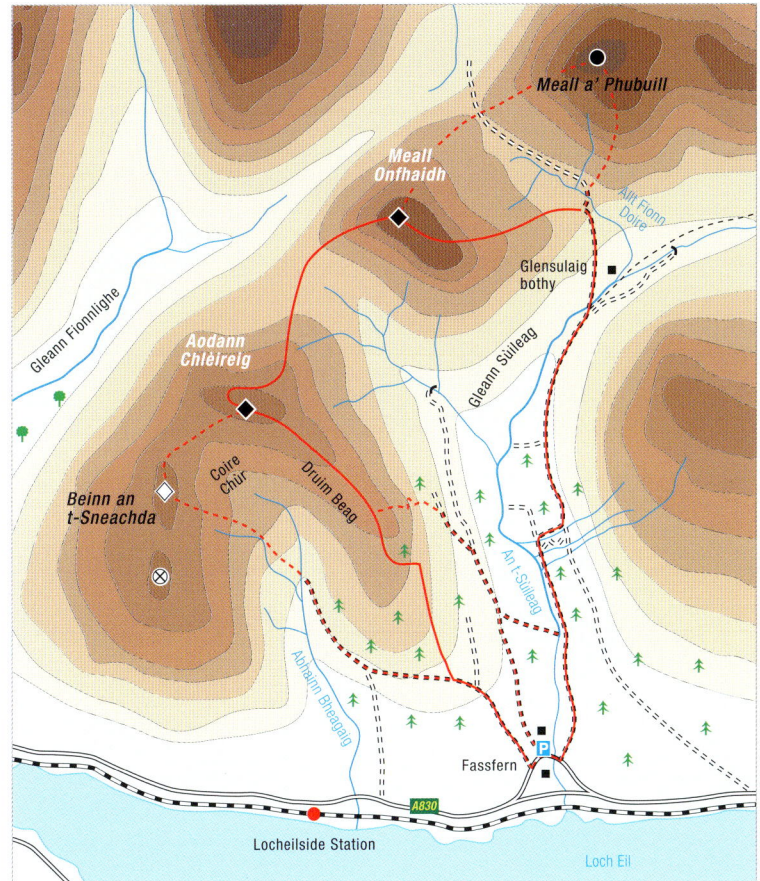

wire fence in a south-easterly direction until it veers off downhill and continue south-east down the broad ridge of Druim Beag. On the left side of the ridge, hidden from view, a gate in the fence around the forest at NN009811 offers a route onto the forest tracks which can be followed back. However, the felling of the trees here makes this not so attractive an option and it is probably better to stay on the ridge, crossing a stile over a deer fence to pick up a rough atv track. This leads downhill with fine views ahead to Ben Nevis, through breaks between younger trees onto a track. Turn left and continue downhill to be soon joined by another track from the left, then pass between two ponds where a short link path accesses the car park (**16.5km; 990m; 5h 50min**).

The Graham Top Beinn an t-Sneachda (625m) lies to the south of Aodann Chlèireig and can easily be included. From its summit, the descent is made via the track through the forest above the Abhainn Bheagaig, taking the left fork to Fassfern (**18km; 1040m; 6h 15min**).

Locheilside Station is close enough for these hills to be done by train from Fort William.

Approaching the ramp below the summit of Aodann Chlèireig (Noel Williams)

Glas-chàrn; 633m; (G191); L40; NM846837; grey-green hill

Situated a few kilometres west of Glenfinnan, Glas-chàrn is the highest point on a broad ridge of rugged country sandwiched between Loch Beoraid and Loch Eilt. Although its ascent gives a relatively short outing the upper ground is fairly complex and in poor visibility may require good navigational skills.

Park in a layby at NM873817 on the south side of the A830 just west of a bridge over the Allt Fèith a' Chatha. The route starts 200m to the east of the bridge at a gated forest track on the north side of the road. This is opposite a gated hydro track.

Squeeze round the gate and follow the track uphill through the forest for about 400m. Continue for a further 400m and, where the track swings rightwards, go straight on to cross the Allt an Utha by a footbridge.

Follow the vestiges of a boggy path in a north-westerly direction on the east side of the Allt Fèith a' Chatha for about 1.2km then leave the path and follow the burn in a more westerly direction. Cross a northern fork in the burn where there is a slabby rock pool. Stay on the north side of the main burn and shortly after this head directly up the hillside beyond. The ground is quite complex at times but a grid bearing of 282 degrees will lead directly to the summit, which is a fairly prominent rocky knoll with a tiny lochan just below it on its north-west side (**4km; 520m; 1h 50min**).

Another option is to continue to the col at NM865837 where an old fenceline can be followed across flat ground then up the side of the burn's right fork. The fence passes just beneath the top.

The deep glen to the north contains Loch Beoraid, which can be glimpsed by making a short descent northwards. There are good views north-west to the more remote neighbouring Graham, Meith Bheinn.

Instead of returning the same way, a pleasant circuit can be made by visiting Sgùrr a' Mhuidhe, a prominent hill to the south-east with outstanding views. Descend in a south-easterly direction and cross a broad section of plateau before dropping to a bealach at 454m. Continue over a broad rocky knoll to a slight dip with numerous small lochans then climb more steeply to the summit (**6km; 630m; 2h 35min**).

There are twin summits of similar height, with the more northerly one having a spot height of 562m. To descend, head quite steeply down the east-south-east ridge, which leads directly back to the start (**7.5km; 630m; 3h 15min**).

Including the Corbett Sgùrr an Utha, to the east, gives a longer and more substantial route, although this involves a significant 500m climb. Descend beside the fenceline to reach the col at NM865837 then break away from it and climb steeply up the hillside to the right of the main burn, past a huge boulder, keeping north of more complex ground.

Gain the col at the back of Sìthean Mòr, where the fenceline is rejoined, then climb the splendid rocky ridge to the summit of Sgùrr an Utha (**8km; 1020m; 3h 50min**). Traverse across to Fraoch-bheinn then descend south-west and cut across the side of Druim na Brein-choille to pick up the head of a track at NM881827 and follow this back (**13km; 1080m; 5h 30min**).

Below the rocky summit of Glas-chàrn (Noel Williams)

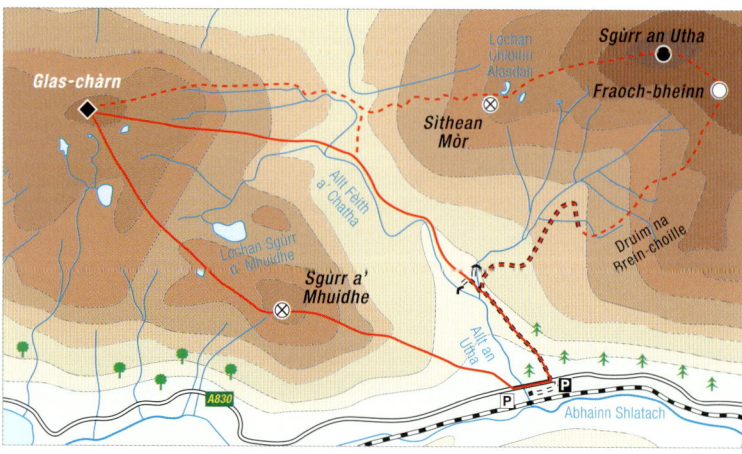

MÈITH BHIEINN *Sgùrr na Maothaich*

MÈITH BHEINN; fat, oily (as in boggy water) mountain
***Sgùrr na Maothaich**; 710m; (G82); L40; NM821872; peak of softness or moistness*

Set in fairly remote country between Loch Beoraid and Loch Morar, this great sprawling hill gives a splendid day out. It is best climbed by its south-west ridge, approached from Arieniskill on the A830 at the west end of Loch Eilt, although this does involve climbing to a height of 280m then dropping all the way down again.

Park in a layby at NM783831 on the south side of the road about 1.5km east of Lochailort. Walk east for 200m to the access to Craiglea B&B on the north side of the road then head off at a right angle to the road on a path which leads under the railway. Briefly follow the east bank of the Arienskill Burn then head eastwards behind some livestock pens and slant up the hillside following the west side of the Allt na Crìche. When the path splits, keep right and eventually cross to the east bank of the burn. Where the burn starts to turn westwards, head away from it and cross the remains of a fence. From here on the path now becomes difficult to follow.

Cross a boggy section at the watershed where there are distant views of Mèith Bheinn. Start to descend more steeply down the other side; care is required here due to hidden holes and fissures. One of Prince Charlie's Caves can be seen beneath a giant boulder on the right-hand side of the path. Continue down through open woodland then look carefully for a crossing place over the Allt a' Chuirn Mhòir. It is important to find the correct level to then follow a ledge system rightwards (east) on the steep northern bank until it is possible to turn left (north) away from this burn. Contour across the slope for about 200m then descend the hillside and cross a couple of footbridges by a hydroelectric scheme at the western end of Loch Beoraid.

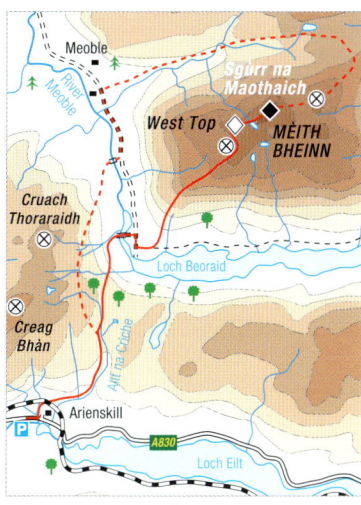

Follow a track to a junction and turn right, then a little way short of a boathouse, take a path on the left. After about 200m, leave the path and start to ascend the hillside in a slight depression then climb quite steeply up the long south-west ridge. From the broad West Top (660m), descend some 35m to pass a lochan by its western end. Climb north-east to another minor top and shortly afterwards gain the true summit, named Sgùrr na Maothaich, marked by a cairn and trig point (**7km; 950m; 3h 30min**).

Most return back down the south-west ridge (**14km; 1200m; 6h**).

An interesting return can be made by descending the north-east ridge until it flattens slightly at a height of 520m. Turn left off the ridge here and descend to a broad bealach before dropping into Slaite Coire. After 2.5km, pick up a path which leads to Meoble then follow a track south to cross the river by a bridge at NM799866. Ascend across the hillside on a faint path which soon becomes difficult to follow. The path rises to 310m before descending to join the path used on the approach (**17.5km; 1250m; 7h**).

Sgùrr na Maothaich and the surrounding summits of Mèith Bheinn above Loch Beoraid (Noel Williams)

Mullach Coire nan Geur-oirean

Section 10b – Glenfinnan to Glen Shiel

Mullach Coire nan Geur-oirean, right, across Loch Arkaig with the Corbett Meall a' Phubuill, left (Rab Anderson)

Mullach Coire nan Geur-oirean; *727m; (G55); L41; NN049892; summit of the corrie of the sharp edge or boundary*

Sandwiched between Loch Arkaig and Glen Mallie is a long and broad ridge, the highpoint of which is the remote summit of this hill. At its western end the ridge links with the Munro of Gulvain. The best approach is from the eastern end of Loch Arkaig. A mountain bike can be used on 8.5km of rough track. Times given are on foot and use of a bike should reduce the overall time by about 2h.

Start from the car park by the Eas Chia-aig waterfall at the western end of the Mìle Dorcha (Dark Mile), a deeply wooded and mossy glen. Head west along the road for 400m then turn off left and go round a locked gate to access a road that leads to Achnacarry. Cross a bridge over the River Arkaig where it flows out of Loch Arkaig then turn off right to follow a rough undulating track through the forest for 3km.

After exiting the forest, continue westwards on the main track which runs south of the bothy at Inver Mallie and cross the River Mallie by a bridge. Follow the track up Glen Mallie with its Caledonian pine trees for 4km to some isolated trees on the hillside. About 100m beyond these, at the highpoint of the track (NN098876), an atv track climbs the hillside and is the return route. Bikes are best left here.

Continue for another 1.5km to the end of the track by the ruin at Glenmallie then follow a rough track along the north bank of the River Mallie for a further 3km to the remains of a large shieling called Ruighe Mòr.

Now climb the steep and grassy hillside on the west side of the burns draining from Coire nam Fuaran, the shallow corrie directly below the summit. A steady plod eventually leads to the broad crest of the ridge where a right turn gains a small cairn which marks the highpoint on the flat summit (**15km; 730m; 4h 35min**).

A short diversion to the north gives the best view of the hills to the north of Loch Arkaig, including the Corbetts Sgùrr Mhurlagain and Fraoch Bheinn, with the distinctive chisel-like summit of the Munro of Sgurr Mor, behind. Then there are the three Grahams, Meall Blàir, directly opposite, with Sgùrr Chòinnich then Glas Bheinn to the east.

Descend eastwards along the broad ridge of Druim na Giùthsaich, with views of the Nevis range to the south-east, framed between Beinn Bhàn and the Graham Stob a' Ghrianain. Eventually leave the crest and descend more steeply in the same general direction to pick up the atv track which leads back to the track used in approach (**29km; 750m; 8h**).

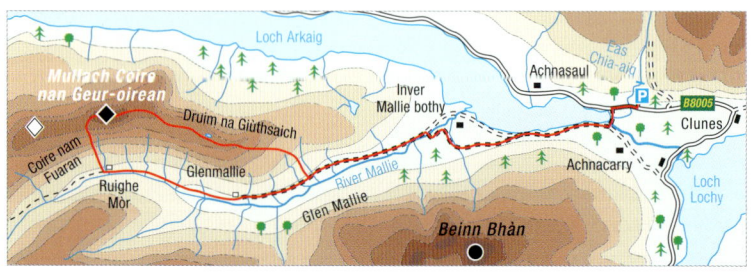

Glas Bheinn 223

Glas Bheinn; 732m; (G45); L34; NN171918; green mountain

Overlooking the eastern end of Loch Arkaig, Glas Bheinn is the most easterly of the three Grahams on the north side of the loch. It is a compact hill, set apart from its higher neighbours by deep glens on three sides. Although it can be approached from Gleann Cia-aig to the east, the preferred option is the unnamed glen of the Allt Dubh on its western side, since this gives the most open views and has the simplest return route. A north to south traverse gives the best outing.

Approach via the road through the Mìle Dorcha (Dark Mile) to reach the eastern end of Loch Arkaig then continue along the north side of the loch for just over 2km to Achnasaul. Parking is limited but perhaps best in a long grassy passing place at NN151893, just beyond Marine Harvest and a track to the loch.

Take the hydro track which heads north up the east side of the Allt Dubh. The track briefly follows the burn before swinging away from it to climb the hillside. There are some fine Scots pines below the track. After crossing several side burns the track

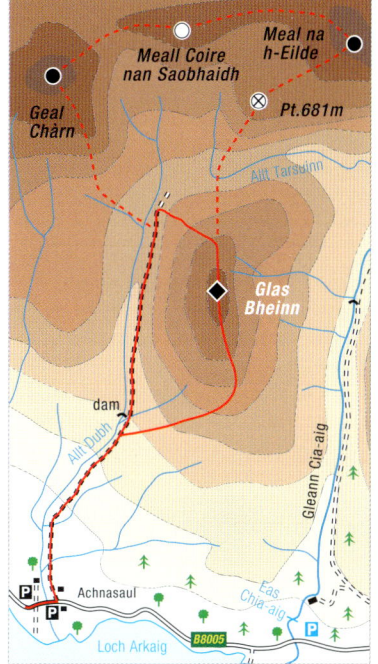

returns to the Allt Dubh where it ends at a dam.

Continue uphill above the burn on the original track and follow this almost to the head of the glen where it peters out then turn right and head up the heathery hillside for some distance. Eventually gain the crest of the hill at a slight flattening with fine views eastwards across Coire na Còsaig. Continue south up the crest to reach the cairn on the broad, flat summit (**5km; 680m; 2h 15min**). To the south there are distant views of Ben Nevis and the Grey Corries.

From the summit, head in a southerly direction at first before turning away to the right and descending much more steeply, directly down the south-western flank to regain the track used in the approach (**9km; 680m; 3h 25min**).

Glas Bheinn can be linked with the two Corbetts to the north for an excellent round. On Geal Chàrn, a grassy atv track runs up the burn from NN164927 which can be used in ascent, or descent, depending on whether Glas Bheinn is tackled first or last. The link with Meall na h-Eilde is made by the prominent steep spur of Pt.681m.

Either way, Glas Bheinn stands proud by a considerable 292m (**17km; 1360m; 6h 45min**).

Glas Bheinn from the approach above Achnasaul to the south (Rab Anderson)

Sgùrr Chòinnich

Sgùrr Chòinnich; 749m; (G12); L34; NN127949; peak of the moss

The middle and highest of the Grahams on the north side of Loch Arkaig, Sgùrr Chòinnich has a rather dull and sprawling south-western flank but more interesting northern and eastern sides. The best outing is to gain the north-east ridge via Coire Mhuic to the south.

Drive along the north side of Loch Arkaig for just over 6km to a car park at NN121912 on the north side of the road before the bridge over the Allt Mhuic. The start of the walk goes through Forestry Commission Scotland's Allt Mhuic Butterfly Reserve; one of the best places in Britain to see a rare chequered skipper.

Head directly uphill from the car park and follow a pleasant path through the reserve to a forest track. Cross over the track and continue up the pathless hillside to a wire fence. Clamber over the fence and ascend heathery ground for some distance. Continue by traversing the steep slope overlooking the Allt Mhuic. This is quite hard going initially but when the angle of the burn starts to ease-off slightly, drop down to reach its eastern bank and follow this a short distance, before crossing the burn. Continue up the corrie, gradually rising away from the bed of the burn, heading towards the watershed at Lochan an Fhithich between Sgùrr Chòinnich and Càrn Dubh.

Start to slant leftwards up the hillside towards the north-east ridge and follow the remains of an iron fence up onto the crest, then turn left to ascend this, still following occasional fence posts. At a short level section of ridge, cross over to the right and ascend some steeper ground which soon eases. The fence posts lead directly to the summit cairn (**5km; 700m; 2h 20min**).

There are views across Glen Garry to the north, east to the Corbett Geal Chàrn and Graham Glas Bheinn and west to Meall Blàir.

Continue along the summit ridge a short way, then turn leftwards and head due south. Descend the monotonous southern flank for almost 3km to a boundary fence and after a further 400m regain the forest track. Look for a gate on the south side of the track, which gives access to the return leg of the trail through the Butterfly Reserve. The road is reached a little to the west of the car park (**9.5km; 700m; 3h 40min**).

This hill can be linked with Meall Blàir to the west – see following page. From the summit, follow the fenceline

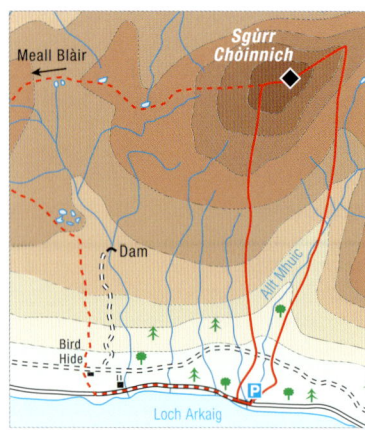

west to a lochan at NN110947, then north-west to another at NN105950 before heading across the watershed. Climb to the lochan-studded top of Meall Lochan nan Dubh Lochan, then past Lochan na Beinne Bàine to the top of Meall Blàir (**10.5km; 950m; 4h**).

Return downhill past Lochan na Beinne Bàine then continue south-east to pick up an atv track which leads to a cluster of lochans at NN093936. Carry on in the same direction on the atv, which drops south. Cross a forestry track at NN100917 where there is a bird hide, then gain the road below, 2km west of the start (**17.5km; 950m; 5h 50min**).

Sgùrr Chòinnich from the east with Spidean Mialach beyond (Noel Williams)

Meall Blàir and elevated Loch Blàir across Loch Arkaig from Mullach Coire nan Geur-oirean (Noel Williams)

Meall Blàir; 656m; (G168); L33; NN077950; hill of the plain

Meall Blàir is the most westerly of the three Grahams on the north side of Loch Arkaig and although it is generally climbed as a standalone hill it can be linked with Sgùrr Chòinnich; see previous page. It has a more complex summit area than the other two Grahams and scenic Loch Blàir lies to its west. The obvious approach is by its southern slope where a hydro track then an atv track can be followed for much of the way.

Follow the rollercoaster road along the north side of Loch Arkaig for about 13km and park in some natural woodland immediately beside the Allt Arcabhi (NN053923), about 1km beyond the house at Caonich. A hydro track leaves the road here on the east side of the Allt Arcabhi, next to a small hydro-electric substation.

Follow the hydro track uphill for about 1km, until just above a small waterfall at a height of 270m. The best option now is to probably leave the main track and follow an atv track up right without any difficulty until Loch Blàir eventually comes into view on the left. Continue more easily at first then ascend slightly steeper ground, with occasional marker posts, for some distance. Pass to the right of two minor tops to reach the cairn and trig point that mark the main summit (**4km; 600m; 1h 55min**).

The other option is to carry on up the main track to its end at a dam on the Allt Arcabhi. Loch Blàir now lies some 200m away, and the ascent to Meall Blàir can be made from there.

The summit area is peppered with tiny lochans and there are extensive views. Glen Kingie lies to the north with the Munro Gairich and a number of major hills at its western end. The Corbett Sgùrr Mhurlagain lies across Loch Blàir to the west, whilst to the east is Sgùrr Chòinnich with Glas Bheinn to its side, and to the south another Graham, Mullach Coire nan Geur-oirean, which sits straight across Loch Arkaig.

On the return, take in the various minor tops to the west of the summit and from the last of these (646m) take a direct line down the south-west flank. Rejoin the atv track and return down this then the hydro track, or all the way down the atv track, which may be easier (**8km; 630m; 3h**).

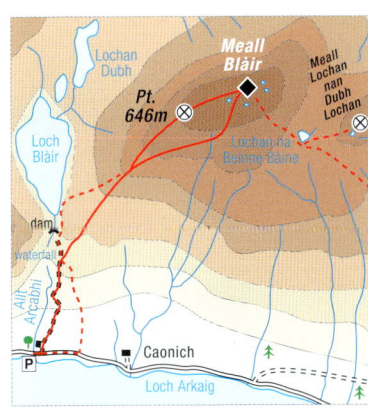

An Stac

Glenpean bothy and An Stac at the head of Glen Pean (Jim Teesdale)

An Stac; 718m; (G68); L40; NM866889; *the steep rocky hill*

This very remote hill overlooks the eastern end of Loch Morar. Any approach from the south would be long and entail a lot of ascent, descent and reascent. The described route along Glen Pean to the east of the hill, although long, is scenic and involves only a minor amount of height loss. A mountain bike can be used to advantage on the initial 5.25km of track through the forest for a saving of about 1h 30min on the final time given for the day.

An Stac can be approached most easily by boat along Loch Morar to Oban bothy (NM863901) at its foot, however, this is expensive (<*vivmorar@aol.com*>; 01687 462388).

For the Glen Pean approach, drive along the undulating single-track road on the north side of scenic Loch Arkaig to reach a good parking area where the tarmac ends.

Follow the continuation track and take the left-hand fork downhill past Strathan to cross the River Dessarry by a bridge. Shortly after this, enter a large forestry plantation, pass a track off right and head into Glen Pean. The track rises gently before descending through a felled area. When it ends, a rough track then a path lead to Glenpean bothy, which can be seen ahead.

Beyond the bothy, continue through the wonderful glen, following a fairly wet path and atv track for 2km on the north side of the River Pean to suddenly reach Lochan Leum an t-Sagairt. The route along the north

Looking down Glen Pean to An Stac (Noel Williams)

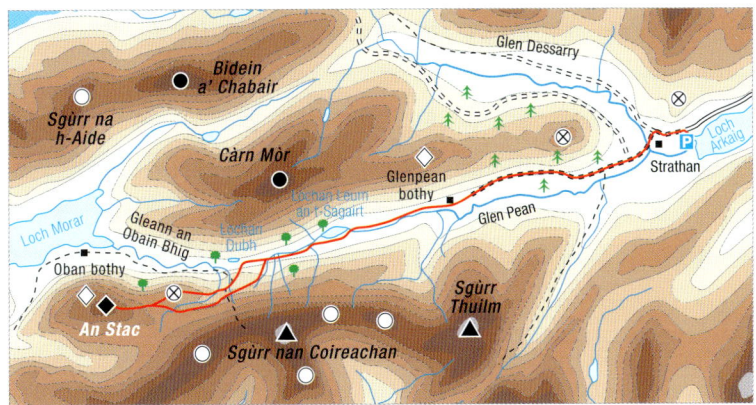

side is too difficult, so go downstream around a knoll and ford the river then ascend a path which traverses the steep hillside above the south side. Once beyond the lochan, descend to the floor of the glen again.

In a further 2km the glen narrows and has been filled by rockfall from a crag rising above it. Bypass this completely by a rough path crossing the steep slope on the left, or find a way through it and boulder-hop alongside the hidden reed-covered Lochan Dubh then clamber between some gigantic boulders. The floor of the glen has been filled by an enormous landslide originating from the impressive crag-strewn hillside of Meall nan Each to the north, and is similar in character to the famous Coire Gabhail landslide in Glen Coe.

Either way, climb the slope above the landslide-formed watershed on the south side of the glen to intersect a stalkers' path which comes up from Gleann an Obhain Bhig and Loch Morar to the west. This well-engineered but faint path climbs onto the Munro Sgùrr nan Coireachan and initially runs between the two burns that drain the hillside, then crosses the left-hand burn before crossing back over again higher up. Ascend the path to the 350m contour then leave it and cross the right-hand burn, the Allt an Toll Gainmhich, at the point it swings right into another valley. Climb up right onto a delightful slabby ridge, which leads to the minor summit of Cnoc Gorm (527m). At one point there are some impressive vertical clefts on the crest where the ground has started to slip away.

Descend slightly then climb the broad continuation ridge and weave a way up slightly steeper ground to arrive at the fine rocky summit of An Stac (**14km; 860m; 5h**).

There are superb views of Loch Morar with Rum behind. The neighbouring Graham of Mèith Bheinn lies some 5km to the south-west.

On the return it is perhaps better to follow the right bank of the Allt an Toll Gainmhich then, where this swings north, cross the next burn and the stalkers' path to continue heading east to a shallow bealach at NM892891. Descend diagonally across the hillside to the floor of Glen Pean then follow the approach route back (**27.5km; 1020m; 8h 50min**).

An Stac from the north-east ridge of Sgùrr na Maothaich, Mèith Bheinn, to the west (Noel Williams)

Slat Bheinn, Meall nan Eun

Slat Bheinn from the approach up Glen Barrisdale to the west (Noel Williams)

Slat Bheinn; 700m; (G105); L33; NG910027; *erect mountain*
Meall nan Eun; 667m; (G150); L33; NG903052; *hill of the birds*

Superbly situated in the north-eastern corner of the remote and rugged Knoydart peninsula, these two Grahams are best climbed together. Sitting opposite each other, either side of deep Glen Barrisdale, their ascent gives a demanding route. One option is to walk-in and spend the night at Barrisdale where there is a bothy, camping and self-catering accommodation.

The ascent of Slat Bheinn as described entails twice fording the River Barrisdale, which may well be a problem in spate conditions.

The best approach is from the road end at Kinloch Hourn, gained after a lengthy but scenic 22 mile (35km) drive along the single track road that branches off the A87 to the north of Invergarry. There are two car parks on the left side of the road. The closest one to the farm at Kinloch Hourn is for overnight visitors and has to be paid for in advance at the farmhouse. The day visitor car park is a little further on and has an honesty box. There is also a useful seasonal cafe at the farmhouse.

Follow the tarmac road for about 750m to where it ends at a turning area. A good, though in places rough, path now provides an undulating but scenic route alongside the fjord-like sea loch of Loch Hourn. The path initially stays beside the loch then heads inland to cross the Allt Coire Mhicrail by a footbridge. Pass above the building at Skiary, climbing to just over 100m before dropping back down to near sea-level. Head up and over a second shoulder at about 110m then descend to the shore again just after Runival.

After a further scenic section beside Loch Hourn, climb to a third and final highpoint of 90m before eventually descending to a track on the east side of beautiful Barrisdale Bay. Follow the track south for almost 2km, past Barrisdale Lodge, to the bothy at NG872042, just before a bridge over the River Barrisdale (**11km; 350m; 3h**).

Climbing Slat Bheinn first, continue on the east side of the River Barris-

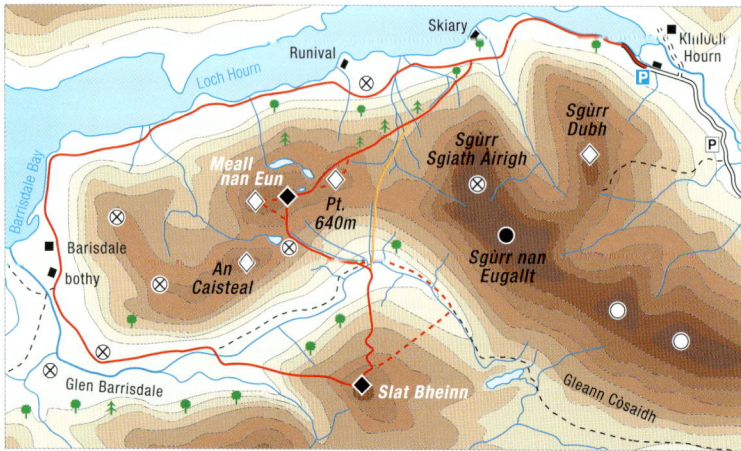

dale and follow a faint path southwards away from the bothy. This soon develops into a more prominent track and gradually rises to a shoulder before turning eastwards into Glen Barrisdale. Continue along the track for a further 1km with good views ahead to Slat Bheinn's western ridge. In normal conditions it is possible to cross the River Barrisdale with dry feet by hopping across rock outcrops in the riverbed at NG893032.

Skirt the steep buttress near the bottom of the west ridge on the left-hand side before climbing more steeply to gain a slight flattening on the crest of the ridge. Follow the ridge to another slight flattening with good views of the south flank of An Caisteal on the north side of Glen Barrisdale. The ridge now steepens significantly and at times it is necessary to zigzag to avoid rock buttresses, before the angle eventually eases. At this point there are good views of the second objective, Meall nan Eun, on the north side of Glen Barrisdale. Finally, turn rightwards and head south across a slight dip for about 100m to reach the summit itself (**16km; 1080m; 5h 20m**).

Sgurr a' Choire-bheithe and its Druim Chòsaidh ridge dominate the view to the south and Beinn Sgritheall stands out to the north-west.

The next objective is to descend to the floor of Glen Barrisdale to gain its most northerly point at NG913043 and then ascend the opposite flank in a north-westerly direction. Head north-north-east from the summit at first, then either turn right and descend the eastern ridge to gain the path in the floor of the glen, or take a more adventurous route northwards which, although shorter, involves some careful route-finding to avoid bands of steep rocky ground.

Ford the river and ascend diagonally leftwards beside a burn for some distance to gain the shoulder overlooking Lochan Coire Chaolais Bhig. Turn slightly right here and head up through very rocky ground to the central summit of Meall nan Eun (**19.5km; 1600m; 7h 20m**).

This is only 1m higher than the West Top, some 450m to the west, which can be included first if desired.

To descend, drop east to a small lochan in the dip then either climb onto the East Top, or skirt it to its north. Either way, head north to a minor rise (Pt.575m on the OS 1:25k map) then follow a grassy ridge north-east to just above the trees. Cross a burn then continue in the same line to gain a flattening at the 100m highpoint of the path west of Skiary. Follow the path back to Kinloch Hourn (**25.5km; 1650m; 9h**).

Another option for these hills is to reverse the route described above all the way to Slat Bheinn, then return up the slope and over the bealach between Meall nan Eun and Sgùrr Sgiath Àirigh. To do so, ascend Meall nan Eun via its East Top, climbing from the 100m highpoint of the Kinloch Hourn to Barrisdale path on the first of the rises after passing Skiary (**6km; 720m; 2h 30min**).

Head south from the summit for 300m or so, to the shoulder overlooking Lochan Coire Chaolais Bhig, then descend south-east to the floor of the glen. Cross the river and climb the north ridge of Slat Bheinn (**9.5km; 1280m; 4h 40min**).

Return down the north ridge and climb the slope above by the burn to gain the bealach with Sgùrr Sgiath Àirigh then descend to the approach route (**17.5km; 1650m; 7h 30min**).

On initial inspection this route would appear to involve more ascent than the other but interestingly, due to the undulations of the Barrisdale approach, it does not. This route also opens up the possibility of including the Corbett, Sgùrr nan Eugallt in the round.

Meall nan Eun from Slat Bheinn, with The Saddle and Sgùrr na Sgìne beyond (Noel Williams)

The eastern ridge of Beinn a' Chapuill (Noel Williams)

Beinn a' Chapuill; 759m; (G3); L33; NG835148; *mountain of the horse*

Three Grahams lie along the north side of Loch Hourn. They are approached by turning off the A87 at Shiel Bridge, at the end of the long north ridge of Biod an Fhitich, the final Graham in this Section. A single track road leads over Bealach Ratagain and makes the long descent to the village of Glenelg, which sits directly across the water from the three easternmost Grahams on Skye.

The road then continues southwards past the turning up Gleann Beag to Beinn a' Chapuill, and on round the coast for a further 9.5 miles (15.5km) to reach the Munro Beinn Sgritheall overlooking Loch Hourn, beyond which lies the tiny village of Arnisdale, from where the Grahams Beinn Clachach and Druim Fada can be approached.

Beinn a' Chapuill is first seen in the distance from the road over Bealach Ratagain en route to Glenelg. It can be combined with its higher neighbour Beinn Sgritheall but is described here on its own, as a traverse taking in its long and very fine eastern ridge.

The single-track road up Gleann Beag leads past the remains of two impressive brochs, Dùn Telve and Dùn Troddan. Parking is limited in the upper part of the glen but since the walk returns along the final bit of this road there are several places where it is possible to pull off onto the grass verge. The tarmac eventually ends at Balvraid Farm, where it would appear there is space for two or three cars.

Walk along a muddy track from the farm then continue up the glen on a better surface. Carry on for another 1km then pass under a pylon power line. After another 300m or so look carefully on the south side of the track for a small suspension bridge over the Abhain a' Ghlinne Bhig (NG866158). Go over the bridge and shortly after, cross a fence by a stile. Head south-west back under the pylon line and ascend to the crest of the eastern ridge.

Note: in 2022 the suspension bridge was signed as dangerous and not to cross. When the water is not high, a crossing can be made directly beneath the pylon line. This leads to a gate in the deer fence at NG8648 1577. An alternative would be to follow the tracks around the river

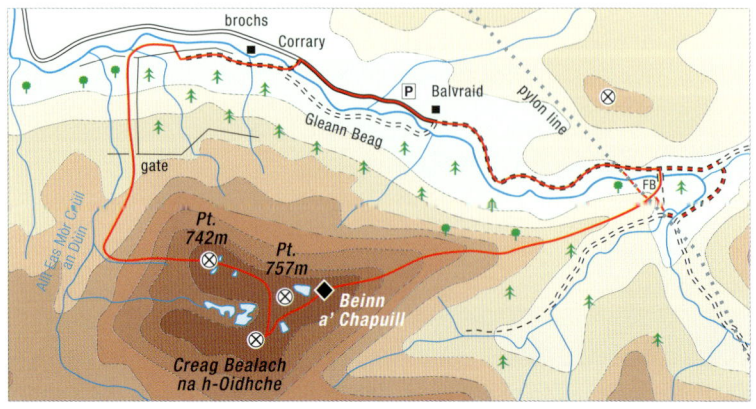

bend to a ford at NG86891547.

The pleasant and easy eastern ridge leads for just over 3km, all the way to the summit; marked as Pt.759 on the OS 1:25k map, but unmarked on the 1:50k map (**6km; 730m; 2h 35min**). There are fine views of Beinn Sgritheall directly to the south.

The undulating summit plateau is complex and extends westwards for another 1km. There is a lochan just west of the summit and others between the various small tops dotted about the plateau, all of which are lower than the summit. From the summit, go west-south-west to Creag Bealach na h-Oidhche (755m), then north skirting Pt.757m to its west, to reach the edge of the steep north face overlooking Gleann Beag.

Continue west-north-west round the corrie edge to Pt.742m, which sits above the western end of the north face. This is the top actually named Beinn a' Chapuill on OS maps, despite being one of the lowest points on the plateau. There are fine views westwards to Skye, with the Grahams Beinn na Caillich (Kylerhea) and Sgùrr na Còinnich clear across the water. Beyond these the rounded granite Grahams of Beinn na Caillich (Broadford) and both Beinn Dearg Mhòrs are prominent, backed by the jagged peaks of the Cuillin.

The north side of the hill is steep and although a way can be found down the northernmost buttress, it is not easy. The best option therefore, is to go west from Pt.742m and make a descent. Initially go down a depression with a small burn, zigzagging carefully down through rock outcrops, then towards the bottom start heading in a more northerly direction to gain the Allt Eas Mòr Chùl an Dùin.

Continue north above the burn and go through a gate at the left edge of the forest. Descend beside the forest to a gate and go through deciduous woodland to pasture beside the Abhainn a' Ghlinne Bhig below. Follow this rightwards until an opening in the forestry gives access to a forest track. After 1km, turn left where the track divides and cross the bridge over the river to reach the road in Gleann Beag, which leads back to the start (**12.5km; 760m; 4h 30min**).

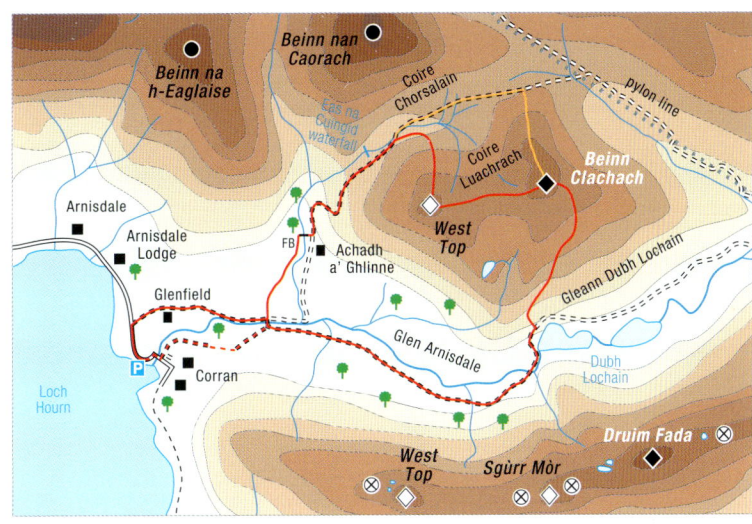

Beinn Clachach; 643m; (G181); L33; NG885109; *stony mountain*

Located on the north side of Glen Arnisdale, Beinn Clachach sits between the long ridgeline of Druim Fada, the neighbouring Graham on the south side of the glen, and two Corbetts to the north. Although it can be climbed with Druim Fada the drop between the pair is considerable, so it is generally climbed on its own. For those seeking an extended outing it is perhaps more conveniently climbed with the Corbett to the north, or even both. The approach to all of these hills starts to the south of Arnisdale, from a car park with toilets at the road end just before Corran.

Beinn Clachach is a double-topped hill whose actual summit is an unnamed top on the east side of Coire Luachrach, 1km east-north-east of the hilltop named Beinn Clachach on OS maps. The hill can be climbed by an up and back route utilising the track which rises into Coire Chorsalain to the north, but it is more interesting to make a traverse from the south. The initial part of the route is the same as for Druim Fada.

A track and path on the south side of the River Arnisdale can be boggy, so it is perhaps best to walk back along the road for 400m and turn right onto a track which leads eastwards past ▶

The West Top of Beinn Clachach from Corran (Noel Williams)

The summit of Beinn Clachach, right, from Druim Fada (Noel Williams)

Glenfield and up Glen Arnisdale.

In the distance a conspicuous dip called Bealach an Fheadain can be seen in profile on the south ridge of Beinn Clachach. After about 1.5km, cross a bridge over the river and continue for a further 2.5km, dropping north to cross the River Arnisdale by a bridge just before Dubh Lochain. Shortly before this the Druim Fada route heads up to the right.

The temptation is to immediately head up the south ridge of Beinn Clachach. However, the north side of Bealach an Fheadain is a tricky vegetated scramble, so the best option is to continue along the track for a further 400m to where it runs beside Dubh Lochain then head north-north-west up the hillside towards a broad heathery gully. Ascend the gully without difficulty to gain the grassy crest of the ridge at NG883098.

Continue up the broad ridge and soon get good views of a large lochan on the left. Eventually head north-east along an easier section of ridge to a minor top of just over 600m. Turn to the north-west here and soon after descend a grassy break rightwards to avoid a steep crag then cross a dip before climbing again towards the main summit. Go around a couple of lochans, the second is partly filled with reeds, to reach the cairn marking the highest point where there are fine views of the Corbett, Beinn nan Caorach to the north-west (**7km; 680m; 2h 40min**).

Leave the summit at first to the south-west then weave down to a broad bealach before following an easy ridge to the West Top (618m), to which the OS have assigned the hill name (**8km; 740m; 3h**).

The north-west flank of Beinn Clachach is rather steep, so descend initially in a north-north-east direction for about 300m before turning leftwards and dropping to the track in the floor of Coire Chorsalain. There are fine views of an impressive rock slope failure on the south-east flank of the Corbett Beinn Bhuidhe. The track drops past a waterfall before zigzagging down to Achadh a' Ghlinne to regain the track in Glen Arnisdale (**13km; 740m; 4h 30min**).

For the easier route via the Coire Chorsalain track, ascend the track to above the waterfall and climb the West Top first via its north ridge. Traverse to the summit then descend its north ridge to the track and follow it back (**12.5km; 710m; 4h 15min**).

Approaching the summit of Beinn Clachach (Noel Williams)

Druim Fada 233

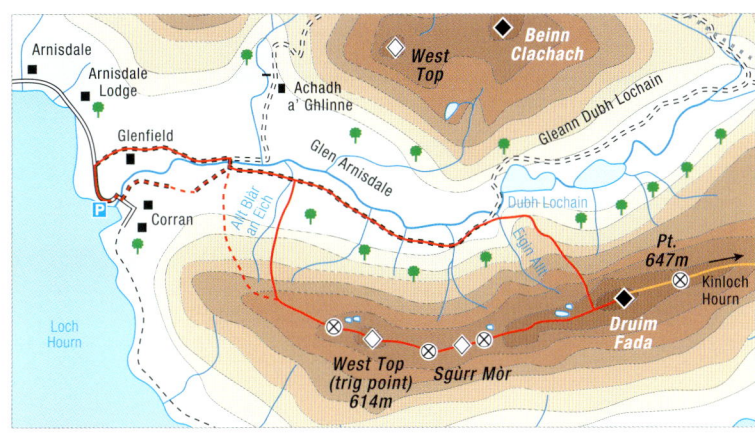

Druim Fada; 713m; (G75); L33; NG894083; long ridge

Druim Fada is the second of the Grahams approached from the car park at the road end just before Corran. It is the highpoint on a long undulating ridge running along the south side of Glen Arnsdale. The ridge forms the northern side of the Loch Hourn narrows, a familiar sight to those walking-in to Knoydart from Kinloch Hourn. It can be climbed with Beinn Clachach (see opposite) but the drop between them is significant and it is more pleasant to climb them separately. The initial part of the route is the same as Beinn Clachach.

The path on the south side of the River Arnisdale is poor so it is perhaps best to head back along the road for 400m and turn right onto a track heading east into Glen Arnisdale. Follow this for 1.5km to cross a bridge over the river. After a further 2km the track starts to climb more steeply and eventually there are good views of the small waterfall where the water drains from Dubh Lochain.

Leave the track on the right at NG884090, shortly before it starts to head northwards, and slant across a small burn, the Eigin Allt. Continue rising leftwards across the hillside by a grassy break through the crags and so gain the crest of the mountain's north-west ridge.

Follow this pleasant ridge with fine views to the north. At one point it is possible to scramble up some delightful easy slabs. Continue for some distance, eventually heading slightly leftwards to the first summit. The highest point is a knoll 130m further east (**6km; 710m; 2h 30min**).

The best option is to return along the fine undulating crest of Druim Fada over Sgùrr Mòr (627m). There is some interesting route-finding at times and on the penultimate top (614m) there is a fragmented trig pillar (**8.5km; 810m; 3h 15min**). Eventually start to head northwards and descend on the east side of the Allt Blàr an Eich before crossing it and descending to the track used on the approach (**13km; 840m; 4h 35min**).

Druim Fada can be climbed from Kinloch Hourn via the Cadha Mòr track and the stalkers' path up the east ridge to Lochan Chàrn nan Caorach. A bad step on the far side of Càrn nan Caorach is best avoided from about 50m above the lochan by traversing a deer track down and across a shelf below the crags on the south side. Continue over Pt.647m to the summit (**8km; 850m; 3h 15min**).

Return the same way (**16km; 970m; 5h 30min**).

East across Loch Hourn to Glen Arnisdale and Druim Fada (Noel Williams)

Biod an Fhithich

Biod an Fhithich; 646m; (G178); L33; NG950147; *point of the raven*

Although dwarfed by the impressive mountains that tower around it, Biod an Fhithich in Glen Shiel is a fine little hill which gives a lovely walk to a grand viewpoint. It has a distinctive pointed summit, well seen from the road as it descends through the glen past the old bridge and the 1719 battle site where government troops defeated a force of Jacobites and Spanish troops. The long north ridge and pointed summit are also clear in the background of the classic picture postcard view of Eilean Donan Castle looking up the glen.

This long, narrow ridge runs north from Shiel Bridge for 4.5km to the summit and although it provides the superior route, the peak is generally climbed from further up the glen where a convenient stalkers' path climbs Meallan Odhar to the Bealach na Craoibhe between it and Biod an Fhithich. This is the route to the Forcan Ridge and The Saddle, and Biod an Fhithich is often climbed as a quick addition from that route.

Lying a distance of only 600m to the side of the path to The Saddle, it

The long A' Mhuing ridge of Biod an Fhithich from Glen Shiel (Noel Williams)

Biod an Fhithich, centre left, and Eilean Donan Castle with the Corbett Sgùrr Mhic Bharraich above (Rab Anderson)

to the summit (**3km; 610m; 1h 40min**).

On the Glen Sheil side the slope plunges 600m to the road, giving a great sense of exposure. It is a fabulous summit and whilst there are no distant views, the view up and down Glen Shiel with the wall of mountains formed by the Five Sisters of Kintail across the glen, together with the Forcan Ridge and The Saddle opposite, is magnificent.

Return the same way (**6km; 610m; 2h 30min**).

A longer route, more befitting of this hill and its splendid surroundings, can be had by climbing the length of the long north ridge from Shiel Bridge. This narrow, knobbly ridge is called A' Mhuing, the English translation *mane of the horse* being particularly appropriate.

Start from the campsite car park (check with the petrol station first) and take the path alongside the Allt Undalain for 600m or so and before reaching the fence break off left up a spur onto the ridge. Although the ridge is narrow and the drop-offs on either side become increasingly bigger and steeper, the crest is grassy and leads without any difficulty over Pt.533m and the narrow gap beyond up to the exposed summit (**4.5km; 710m; 2h 10min**).

Drop north off the back to gain Bealach na Craoibhe and the stalkers' path coming up from Glen Shiel. The obvious onward extension is to continue up the Forcan Ridge onto The Saddle but the route described here simply descends west into Coire Caol to pick up a path that leads above the burn to Gob na Roinne where three burns meet. Cross over and follow the path on the other side along the foot of Sgùrr Mhic Bharraich back to the start (**10.5km; 710m; 3h 40min**).

can be a straightforward there and back diversion taking as little as 35min; an easy ascent for a Graham.

However, it is a fine hill in its own right and proves useful for when time is short, or when one is passing through Glen Shiel en route to or from another destination such as Skye.

A gate in the fence at NG968143 marks the start of a stalkers' path which climbs Meallan Odhar to the Bealach na Craoibhe. There is a large layby 150m or so to the north of this on the east side of the road. A path starts opposite the layby and follows the fence, thereby avoiding the walk along this fast stretch of road. It is a busy spot and there is further parking in a layby some 500m to the south of the start.

Follow the well-engineered path to the bealach then break off onto a small path, faint in places, which leads

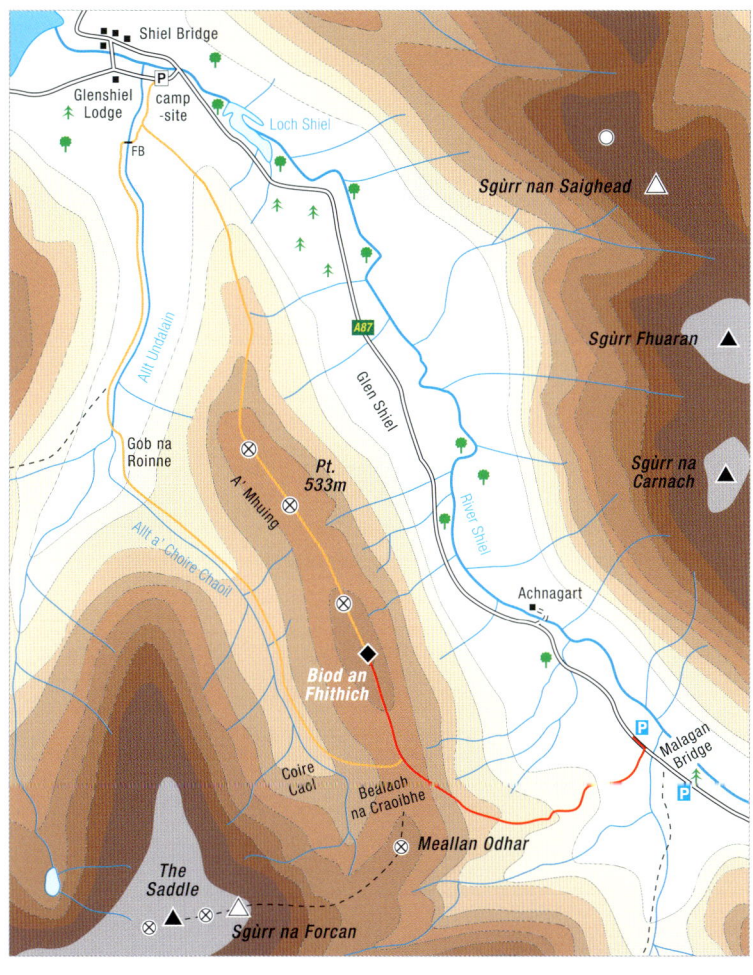

Meall Fuar-mhonaidh across Loch nam Breac Dearga from Glas-bheinn Mhòr (Rab Anderson)

SECTION 11
Glen Shiel to Loch Mullardoch

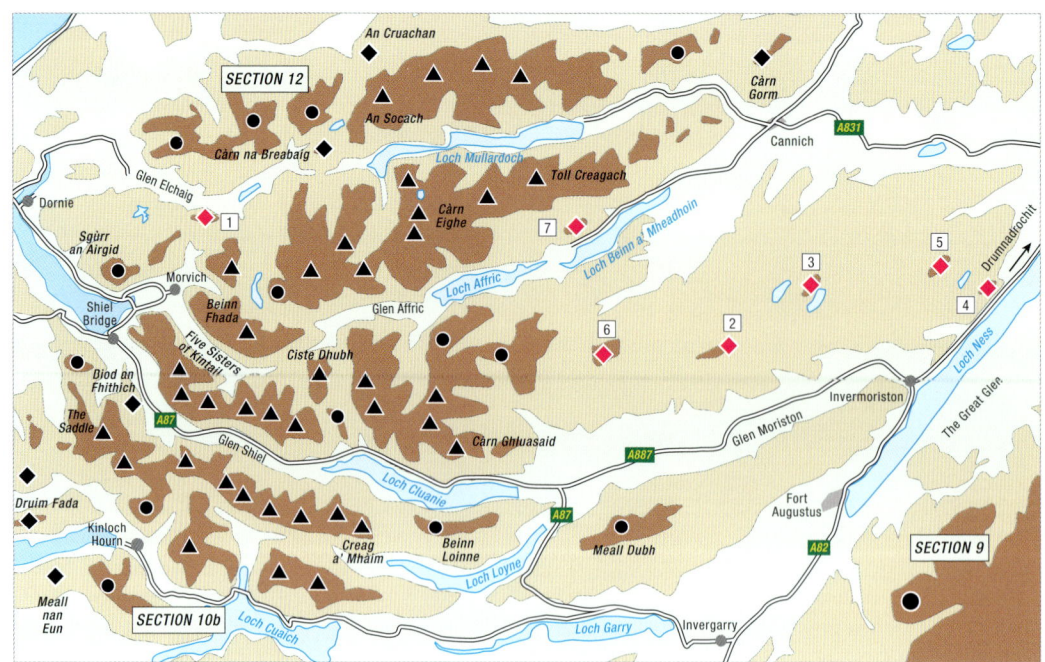

SECTION 11

[1] *Càrnan Cruithneachd* — 239
[2] *Càrn Mhic an Toisich,* [3] *Meall a' Chràthaich* — 241
[4] *Meall Fuar-mhonaidh,* [5] *Glas-bheinn Mhòr* — 243
[6] *Càrn a' Chaochain* — 245
[7] *Beinn a' Mheadhoin* — 247

Càrnan Cruithneachd 239

Section 11 – Glen Shiel to Loch Mullardoch

Càrnan Cruithneachd from Iron Lodge at the head of Glen Elchaig (Jim Teesdale)

Càrnan Cruithneachd; 729m; (G54); L25, 33; NG994258; hill of the Picts

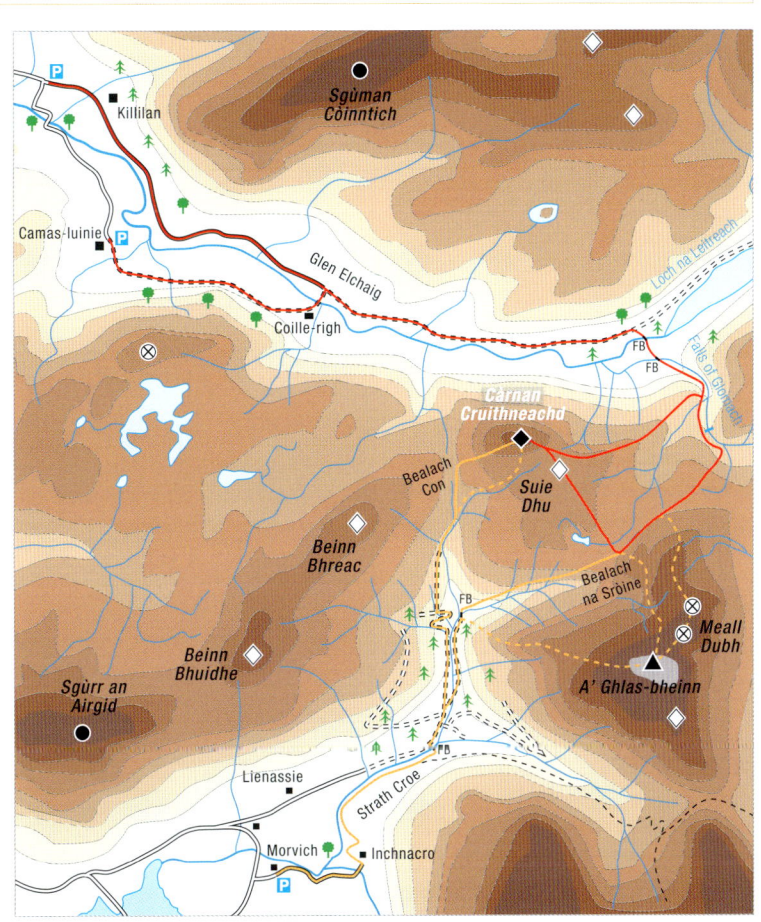

Càrnan Cruithneachd is a magnificent peak and a hill of extreme contrast. From the south its rolling moorland barely makes an impression, but to the north its slopes plunge dramatically into Glen Elchaig, a vertical drop of 650m in a distance of just 1km.

There are two main routes of ascent; one from Glen Elchaig to the north and the other from Strath Croe at the head of Loch Duich to the south. Both routes have their merits but the northern route approaches the hill via the splendid deep gorge of the Falls of Glomach and allows the majestic northern aspect of the hill to be fully appreciated.

The Glen Elchaig route has two start points depending on whether one approaches on foot, or by bike. The bike route along the north side of the glen starts from a car park at Killilan (NG940303) where a tarmac estate road leaves the public road at a right-angled turn at the head of Loch Long. The walking route starts at the end of the public road 2km further on, at a car park at Camus-luinie (NG948283) where a footpath on the south side of the glen leads to

▶

Càrnan Cruithneachd and the River Elchaig (Rab Anderson)

a bridge over the river to join the bike route on the north side. Both routes then lead through the glen beneath the steep slopes of Càrnan Cruithneachd to NH009271 where the Falls of Glomach path starts (**9km; 100m; 45min** by bike); (**7km; 100m; 1h 40min** on foot). Times and distances are now given from and back to here.

Follow the path across the bridge over the main river, then the bridge crossing the Allt a' Ghlomaich as it pours out of the mouth of the gorge ahead, and continue uphill into the gorge. After the first section is passed the gorge widens into a bowl; the return route descends into this. The upper fall lies above, and the path climbs a rib then traverses up and across to the top of the fall; with care a small path can be descended to view the fall.

Continue on the path to Morvich which turns to the south-west and climbs to the Bealach na Sròine. Leave the path and tramp north across bog and heather over the minor top of Suie Dhu (615m) towards Càrnan Cruithneachd. The final steep slope is climbed by a ramp which cuts up from right to left to gain the narrow pointed summit. It is a stunning viewpoint with the cairn perched in an exposed and lofty position (**6km; 690m; 2h 45min**).

To descend, return down the ramp then cut across to the north of Suie Dhu to gain the north-east ridge, which is followed to a slight rise at its end. Descend a steep but easy slope south-east into the bowl in the centre of the Glomach gorge. The path of the upwards route leads back to the track in Glen Elchaig (**10.5km; 700m; 4h**).

Return to Killilan (**28.5km; 830m; 5h 30min** with a bike), or Camus-luinie (**24.5km; 830m; 7h 20min** on foot).

The southern approach starts at the public car park at Morvich and follows the Falls of Glomach sign-posted route, first to the end of the road, then across the bridge past Inchnacro and alongside the river. Cross the bridge at NG982223 and go up the forest track on the Falls of Glomach route, but at NG983229 take the left fork. This leads to some zigzags, above which, turn right up an atv track to emerge from the forest.

Follow the track for 1km to a fork in the burn where the track crosses to the right. Either climb north towards the col by a path between the forks then pick a line up the rocky outcrops on the west ridge, which give good

Sgùrr nan Ceathreamhnan from Càrnan Cruithneachd (Rab Anderson)

but avoidable scrambling, or go up right by the burn then climb to the top (**7.5km; 720m; 2h 50min**).

Descend south-east from the summit, over the grassy minor top of Suie Dhu, then head southwards to gain the path through the Bealach na Sròine. This is followed to a bridge at NG985238 where a track leads back through the forest to the upwards route (**16km; 750m; 5h**).

A rewarding return from the Bealach na Sròine can be made over the Munro, A' Ghlas-bheinn (918m). Either ascend its north ridge by Meall Dubh and Creag na Saobhie, or climb steeply for about 120m from the path, then cut across in front of these tops by a traverse above a small waterfall. The climb to the summit of A' Ghlas-bheinn is steep but uneventful (**12km; 1200m; 4h 45min**). Return by the west ridge, which steepens just above the bridge and forest track at NG985238 (**19km; 1200m; 6h 45min**).

A return by the Bealach an Sgàirne to the south adds just over 1km.

Càrn Mhic an Toisich from Càrn na Caorach (Rab Anderson)

Càrn Mhic an Toisich; 678m; (G134); L34; NH310185; MacIntosh's hill
Meall a' Chràthaich; 679m; (G129); L26, 34; NH360220; hill of shaking

Standing just north of the Great Glen, on a clear day these two unassuming foothills of the Western Highlands give unparalleled mountain panoramas from their summits.

Start at the cluster of houses at Bhlàraidh in Glen Moriston, where a forestry and hydro track leaves the A887 immediately east of a bridge; verge parking either side of the road at the west end of a crash barrier over the bridge. Care is required as the traffic is very fast here. There are pros and cons to using a bike. The track has several steep sections, giving a hard climb but a fast descent. Times given are on foot.

Shortly after passing the houses, at the treeline, take the left fork which leads to the Bhlàraidh windfarm access track. Continue up this for 700m then fork left on a hydro track to pass Bhlàraidh Reservoir and continue almost to Loch Liath.

Climbing Càrn Mhic an Toisich first, leave the track at a fork (NH337194) just before the Liath dam and climb a slight ridge leading roughly west. A great wall of mountains starts to come into view, beginning with the Strathfarrar and Glen Affric hills.

Underfoot, the going is typical rough moorland, so there is little energy to be saved by avoiding the intermediate top of Càrn na Caorach, especially as the fine view continues to open out as height is gained. The summit cairn of Càrn Mhic an Toisich is capped with a luxuriant green cushion of vegetation, revealing a wonderful panorama extending from Ben Nevis and the Mamores in the south around to Ben Wyvis in the north. Be prepared to sit back and try to recognise many familiar hills, or simply be inspired. Unfortunately the line of pylons carrying the Beauly to Denny power line runs across the foreground, and to the north-east are the 30 turbines of the Bhlàraidh windfarm on Meall a' Chràthaich and its satellites, so the pleasure may not be perfect (**9km; 660m; 3h 10min**).

Return to the junction below the Liath dam and follow the right fork north below the turbines to the end of the track at the dam at the east end of Loch ma Stac. The climb north-east from here is rougher and more ▶

Meall a' Chràthaich and Loch Liath from Càrn na Caorach, before the wind turbines (Rab Anderson)

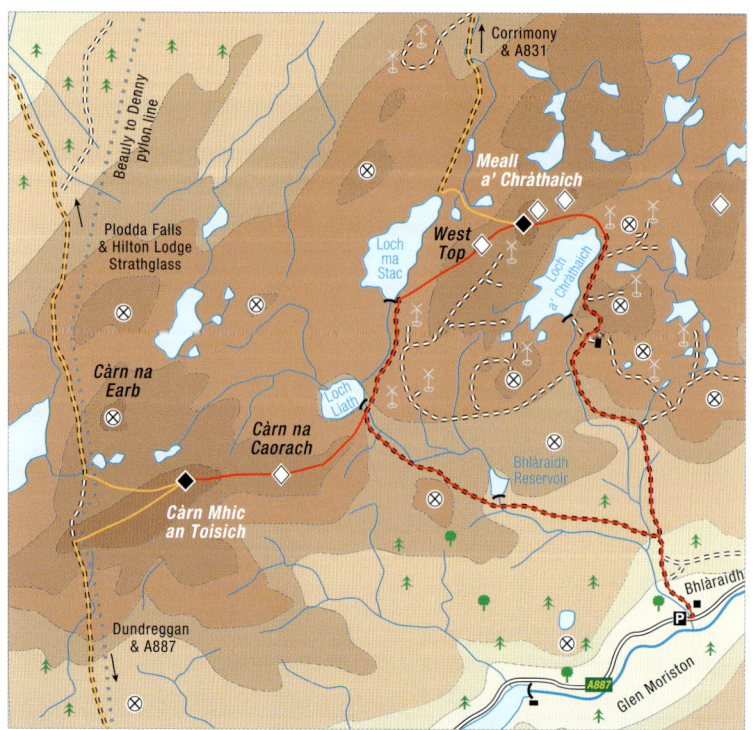

boggy, although the track up the crest past the turbines could be taken. The summit is hidden until the West Top (632m) is gained. From there, the line of a derelict and rusty wire fence leads up the final rise to the summit trig point on Meall a' Chràthaich. Although the wind turbines intrude on the view it is still fine. To the east overlooking a scattering of lochs there are glimpses of the more extensive waters of Loch Ness and the Moray Firth, whilst to the south-west is the bulk of Ben Nevis and the Aonachs (**16km; 1030m; 5h 20min**).

There are plans for some 17 turbines on the slopes to the west and north of Meall a' Chràthaich.

Without a bike to return to, a circuit can be made by descending north-east then east to go around the far side of Loch a' Chràthaich. This joins the windfarm access track and leads past the turbines to rejoin the route of ascent at the junction above Bhlàraidh (**24km; 1030m; 7h 15min**).

Meall Fuar-mhonaidh, Glas-bheinn Mhòr

> **Meall Fuar-mhonaidh**; 699m; (G106); L26, 34; NH457222; hill of the cold hill-mass
>
> **Glas-bheinn Mhòr**; 651m; (G173); L26; NH436231; big green hill

Càrn Mhic an Toisich can be climbed on its own from Glen Moriston to the south, or Strathglass to the north, utilising a track over the high ground in between; this is a right of way and the route used by Bonnie Prince Charlie in 1746.

Start at NH313138 in Glen Moriston where there is a pull-off opposite a signpost and gate. A path leads through woodland onto the track (known as Eve's Road), which starts 300m to the east at Dundreggan. Unfortunately the track follows the route of the Beauly to Denny pylon line. The track crosses the south-west shoulder of Càrn Mhic an Toisich at NH290177 at a height of 550m, and from there it is just over 2km to the summit (**7.5km; 560m; 2h 40min**), (15km; 560m; 4h 20min).

The track runs through to the Strathglass road at Hilton Lodge (NH285244) where it can be gained from, or by cutting though the woods from the Plodda Falls car park at NH280238 (**8km; 480m; 2h 35min**), (16km; 480m; 4h 25min).

Meall a' Chràthaich can be climbed on its own from the north via Corrimony where there is a chambered cairn signposted off the A831 through Glen Urquhart. Dating from the third millennium BC, the tomb is worth a visit. There is parking at NH384303 and a few spaces closer to where the track starts about 1km further on at a bridge (NH377302). Follow the track up the east side of the River Enrick for 250m, cross over then go left at a junction. Much of the approach route passes through an RSPB nature reserve.

The track leads to the Corrimony Windfarm. After 7km, and just before this, at NH355253 go left along a rough track by the burn. Bikes are not recommended beyond here, although future windfarm plans may create a new track. Continue to Loch ma Stac where there is an unusual semi-derelict three storey tower-like lodge perched on a tiny island just offshore, then climb to the summit (**11.5km; 550m; 3h 30min**), (20km; 570m; 6h 15min on foot). Including Càrn Mhic an Toisich would be an added 12km, 360m, 3h 30min. The use of a bike should save around 2h on the day.

Rising steeply half way along the west shore of Loch Ness, Meall Fuar-mhonaidh is one of the dominating features of the loch's landscape. Its lofty dome is an obvious sight from Inverness and it is a popular local walk. Due to the lush vegetation of its steep flanks, it is not normally climbed from the loch and the ascent is usually made by a well-worn path from the north-east. Combined with its modest western neighbour, Glas-bheinn Mhòr, it gives an enjoyable circuit.

Turn off the A82 Inverness to Fort William road at Borlum Bridge (NH513291) on the southern outskirts of Drumnadrochit and take the minor road to Bunloit for 6km, to a small car park at Grotaig.

Walk along the road for 100m then branch off on a signposted path which leads past fields then gains height through a birch forest. Emerge onto open moorland and continue up to a stile at NH477238. The well-used but rather soft path follows the ridge south-west, rising steadily, before rearing up steeply for the final climb onto the summit dome. The highpoint is at the furthest cairn (**4.5km; 510m; 1h 50min**).

The view up and down Loch Ness is superb and there is a tremendous panorama of the Affric, Cannich and Strathfarrar hills out west.

Most walkers return the same way. However, those after the second Graham now need to continue on pathless rough ground. Steep and craggy slopes lie west of Meall Fuar-mhonaidh, so it is best to descend to the south end of Loch nam Breac Dearga by dropping south-west for 1km to a grassy flattening at NH450215. Cut back north from here and descend steeply to gain the loch ▶

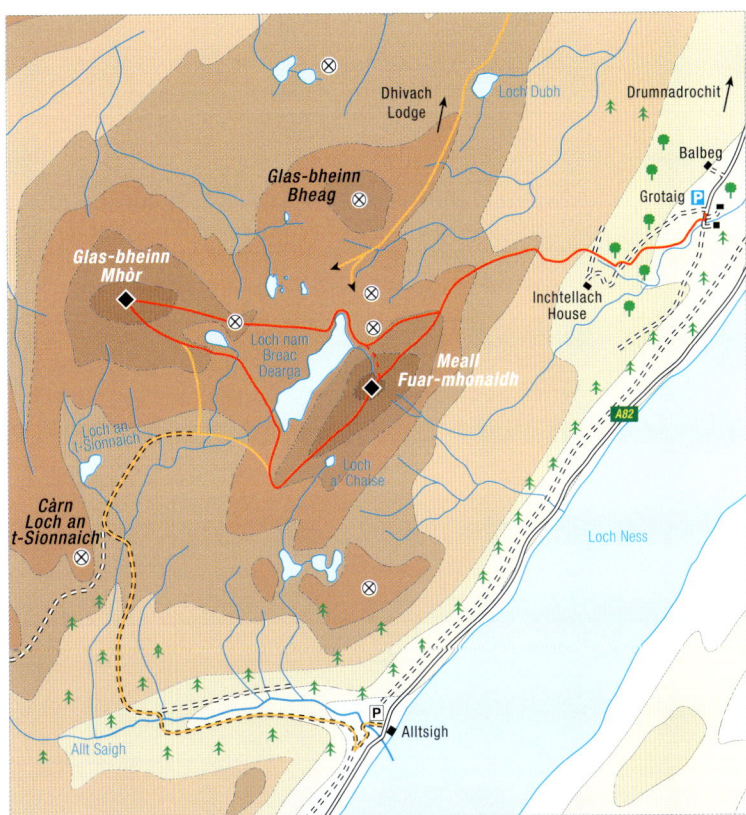

then cross its outflow. A steady ascent, passing west of the small Loch Ruighe an t-Seilich, gains the cairned highpoint just south of the trig point on Glas-bheinn Mhòr (**8km; 680m; 3h**).

The summit view, whilst fine, is less open than its neighbour's.

The best return descends around the east side of Loch Ruighe an t-Seilich, then crosses moorland to gain the north end of Loch nam Breac Dearga. Climb around the back (south) side of the knoll above then traverse east-north-east following animal tracks to regain the path of ascent 1km above the stile. Return by this to the start (**14km; 700m; 4h 30min**).

An alternative is the pleasant but lengthy Dhivach Lodge route, starting from the Divach Falls car park at NH494278, suitable for either or both hills. A track and a path lead to Loch Dubh to the north-east of Glas-bheinn Bheag. Continue towards Loch nam Breac Dearga then climb onto Glas-bheinn Mhòr (**9km; 500m; 2h 50min**). Reverse the previous route to Meall Fuar-mhonaidh via the south

Meall Fuar-mhonaidh from above the car park at Grotaig (Jim Teesdale)

Glas-bheinn Mhòr from Meall Fuar-mhonaidh with the Mullardoch hills left and Strathfarrar hills right (Rab Anderson)

Càrn a' Chaochain   245

Càrn a' Chaochain; 706m; (G87); L34; NH235177; *hill of the little streams*

Càrn a' Chaochain is the furthest west of the chain of five Grahams that occupy the tract of rolling hills which begins midway up Loch Ness and runs westwards between Glen Moriston and Glen Affric.

To its south-west the ground rises to Sgùrr nan Conbhairean and the other two Munros, one either side of it, which dominate the view with their wild east facing corries. Slightly closer to the west is the complex bulk of the Corbett, Aonach Shasuinn, whilst to the north and north-west lie the Munros of Glen Affric. To the south Ben Nevis rises above everything.

Therein lies the attraction of this hill, for although pretty nondescript in itself, it does provide a splendid vantage point from which to view the hills that surround it. The much smaller Graham, Beinn a' Mheadhoin (the last hill in this section), lies on the other side of Loch Beinn a' Mheadhoin in Glen Affric just to the north and since both hills are approached via Strathglass the pair could easily be climbed in a day, especially since the drive between them is not far. However, for those not in a hurry, both of these hills provide enjoyable if short outings on their own.

Càrn a' Chaochain is best approached from Cougie to its north since routes from the south are rather long and tedious. Cougie lies in the middle of nowhere some 16km south-west of Cannich in Strathglass. It is possible to drive to it along a forest track reached by forking left just beyond Tomich, and continuing to just beyond Balcladaich where the tarmac ends. Follow the forest track (signed to Plodda Falls and a sign for Pony Trekking) passing a pond and Hilton Lodge to reach the Plodda Falls car park then continue on the track signed to Pony Trekking Cougie.

On reaching Cougie (NH242211), pass a track off left at some sheds and loop round over the river to park as for the pony trekking centre.

Cougie is a pleasant spot situated in an area of woodland which is being targeted for natural regeneration of native species by the Forestry ▶

end of Loch nam Breac Dearga (**12.5km; 770m; 4h 10min**) then regain the approach route to the north of the loch (20km; 770m; 6h).

A quick mountain bike route to Glas-bheinn Mhòr can be made by a track along Glen Coiltie, to the north of Dhivach Lodge.

Another route starts next to Loch Ness Youth Hostel at Alltsigh (NH457190) where there is parking off the main road at the start of a forest track. The track leads left past a house then right up the south side of the Allt Saigh. Immediately north of a bridge at NH437192 a track goes west then north to join another track at NH434209. This terminates at a cut-off dam at NH438216 from where it is just over 2km to the top of Meall Fuar-mhonaidh (**8.5km; 680m; 3h**).

A link can be made with Glas-bhcinn Mhòr by descending north-east then steeply north and north-west by a burn to the north end of Loch nam Breac Dearga (**11.5km; 840m; 4h**). Descend south-east then south to the track (19km; 840m; 5h 50min).

West to the sprawling corries of Aonach Shasuinn (Meryl Marshall)

246 Càrn a' Chaochain

Looking north-east to the trig point, left, from near the summit of Càrn a' Chaochain (Meryl Marshall)

Commission. Already substantial stands of mixed Scots pine and birch are thriving.

Return over the river and take the track (NN241209) on its south side south-west for 375m or so. At a small cairn, follow a rough track which strikes uphill alongside the Allt na Fearna and continues through a gate onto the open moorland then onward to reach the Bealach Fèith na Gamhna at a height of 531m. Now climb steadily up the north-east spur of the hill, passing several small tops. The easiest ground is found in a direct line, firstly towards Loch Càrn a' Chaochain and then westwards to a trig point on the northern top (704m). The true top, which is 2m higher, lies some 400m to the south-south-west, with a short drop and reascent. There is a small cairn (**4.5km; 460m; 1h 45min**).

Rather than return the same way, an option which gives a circular route is to descend the north-west spur over rough terrain. Continue north towards the small rise of Meallan na Duibhre then the top edge of the cleared forestry plantation lower down.

Cross a deer fence and make for the furthest west branch of an unnamed burn, which offers a line of weakness leading to the forest track, south of the Allt Riabhach. Walk north-east along this for about 250m to a junction. Both tracks lead back to the start either side of the Allt Riabhach. However, much of the forest on the south side has been felled, so going left and crossing the river to take the track on the north side through pine woods is perhaps better (**9km; 460m; 2h 45min**).

Beinn a' Mheadhoin — 247

Beinn a' Mheadhoin; 613m; (G213); L25; NH218255; mountain at the middle

This small hill sits next to the loch named after it in beautiful Glen Affric and is somewhat overshadowed by the considerably bigger Munros to its north and west. It is sometimes climbed as an afterthought by those doing the shorter Toll Creagach and Tom a' Chòinnich Munro round but is generally either climbed on its own, or with one of the other nearby Grahams with a short drive in between.

Although a pleasant outing at any time of day, it makes a lovely evening walk and a fine place from which to appreciate Glen Affric, especially so in autumnal colours.

The walk starts from the Chisholme Bridge car park, located on the right about three quarters of the way along Loch Beinn a' Mheadhoin. From the back of the car park, follow a path westwards up through the trees to join the track up Gleann nam Fiadh, which is the approach to the Munros. In a further 240m, break off right just past the last trees to find a vague atv track and climb to the rocky summit of Beinn a' Mheadhoin. Whilst this may be a small hill, it is a grand summit with an even grander view (**2.5km; 380m; 1h 10min**).

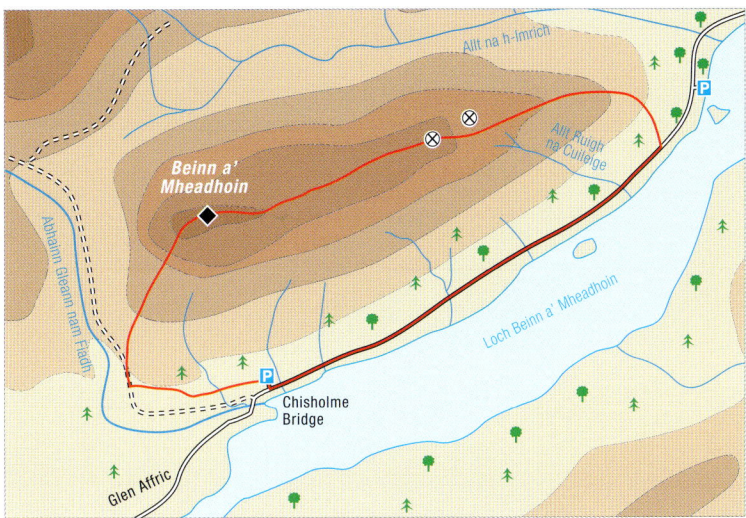

Quickest is to return the same way (**5km; 380m; 1h 45min**).

However, if not dashing off for another hill, a lovely walk can be had by descending east along the ridge onto a small knoll. Drop down in front of another knoll to the north-east and cross a deer fence by a stile at NH232259. Continue east close to the shoulder of the hill to enter woodland. Drop down south-east on a rough path to emerge onto the road at NH242258 by a large pine, about 500m south of the Loch Beinn a' Mheadhoin car park. A pleasant 3km stroll along the road leads back to the start (**8km; 400m; 3h 15min**).

Beinn a' Mheadhoin from Glen Affric (Rab Anderson)

Across Coire Odhar to Creag Dhubh Mhòr with Bidean a' Choire Sheasgaich and Lurg Mhòr beyond (Rab Anderson)

SECTION 12
Loch Mullardoch to Glen Carron

Section 12 – Loch Mullardoch to Glen Carron

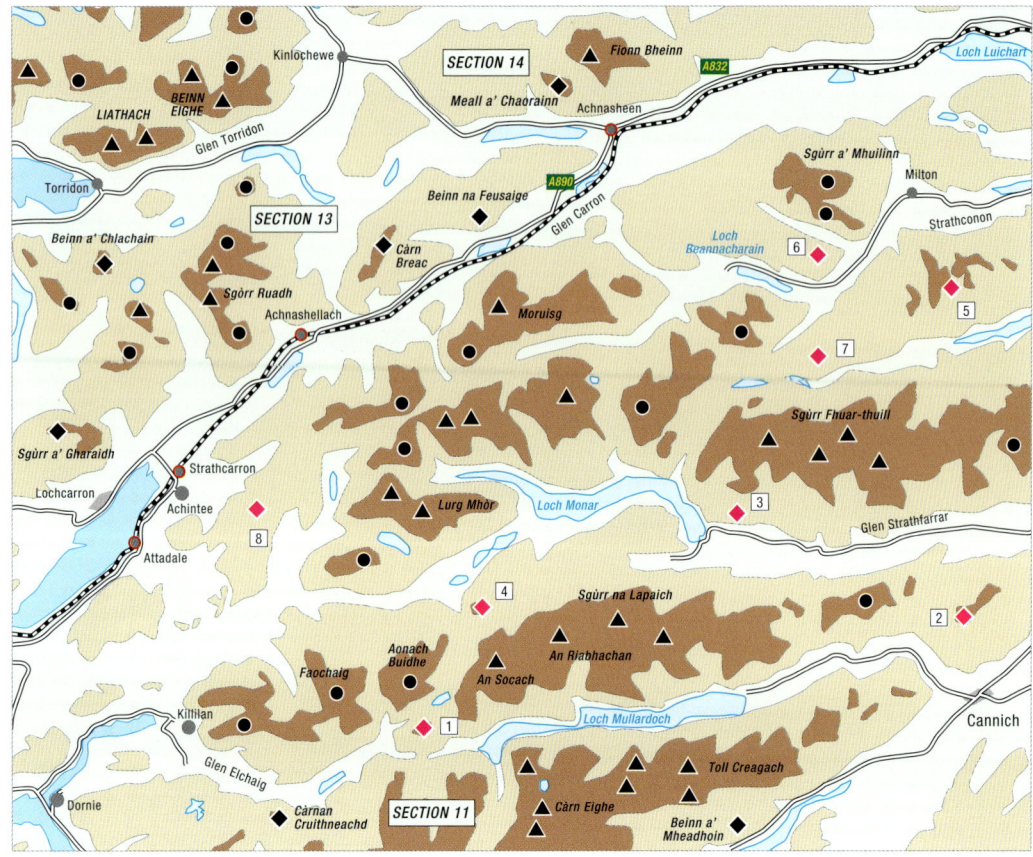

SECTION 12

[1] **Càrn na Breabaig** — 251
[2] **Càrn Gorm** — 252
[3] **Beinn na Muice** — 254
[4] **An Cruachan** — 255
[5] **Càrn na Còinnich** — 256
[6] **Meall na Faochaig** — 257
[7] **Beinn Mheadhoin** — 258
[8] **Creag Dhubh Mhòr** — 259

Càrn na Breabaig   251

Approaching Càrn na Breabaig, centre foreground, along Loch na Leitreach in Glen Elchaig (Rab Anderson)

Càrn na Breabaig; 679m; (G131); L25; NH066301; hill of the little brae, 'braigh beag', or hill of the little separate hill, 'breab beag'

Hidden away at the head of Glen Elchaig, this hill is overshadowed by its larger neighbours and as a result is not often climbed. It stands astride the main east-west watershed and has commanding views down Glen Elchaig and along lonely Loch Mullardoch. The best approach is to bike to the head of Glen Elchaig from where the peak is but a short ascent. It can be combined with an ascent of the Munro, An Socach, or the remote Graham, An Cruachan (see p255).

The bike route starts from a car park at Killilan (NG940303) where a surfaced estate road leaves the public road. The walking route starts at the end of the public road 2km further on, at a car park at Camus-luinie (NG948283) where a footpath leads to a bridge over the river to join the estate track on the other side.

Continue beneath the Graham of Càrnan Cruithneachd (p239), the Falls of Glomach and Loch na Leitreach and turn down to a rather neglected Iron Lodge (**13km; 130m; 1h 30min** by bike), (**11km; 2h 40min** on foot).Times are now given on foot from and back to here

Follow the zigzag track uphill to the south-east before breaking off up the south-west ridge of the mountain. The ascent is mainly grassy and passes a tiny lochan near the summit (**3.5km; 560m; 1h 45min**).

Descend to Iron Lodge the same way (**7km; 560m; 2h 45min**).

Return down Glen Elchaig to the start (**33km; 730m; 5h 15min** with a bike), or (**29km; 730m; 8h** on foot).

If continuing to An Cruachan there are two routes. One descends north-wards to the south-west end of Loch Mhoicean onto the track going north-east down the glen, before climbing to the bealach of Màm Ruisgte south of the summit; 7km, 360m, 2h 20min from Càrn na Breabaig. Return to Iron Lodge past Loch Mhoicean; an added 12.5km, 440m, 3h 45min.

Alternatively, climb Meall Shuas to the east then contour north across An Socach (initially steep) to Màm Ruisgte; more pleasant if the weather is good. Return past Loch Mhoicean; an added 13km, 600m, 4h 5min.

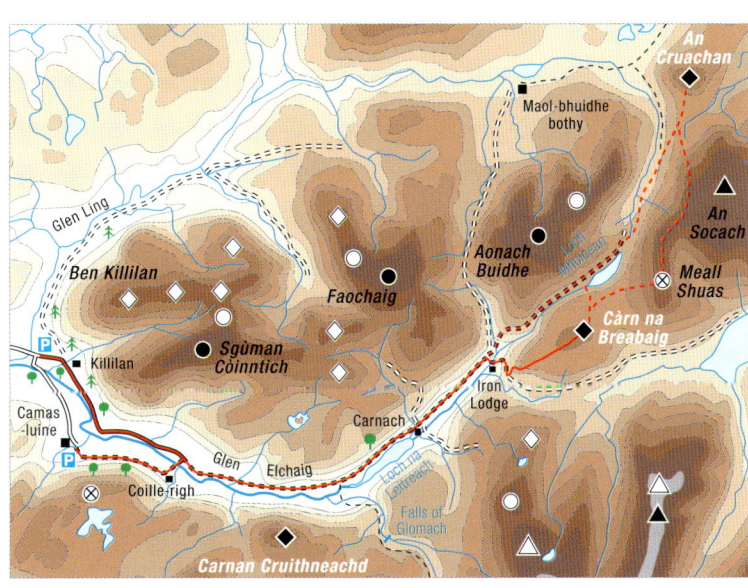

Càrn Gorm

Càrn Gorm; 677m; (G137); L26; NH328355; blue hill

Càrn Gorm is rather overlooked by most hillwalkers on their way to the bigger peaks to the west. It is ideal for a short day and can also be combined with Beinn na Muice, the other Strathfarrar Graham.

Although the shortest approach to the summit is from Glen Cannich to the south, the preferred route is from Glen Strathfarrar to the north. This is longer but more aesthetic, climbing through attractive Scots pine woodland and offering the potential for a good circuit of the whole massif, from Sgòrr na Ruadhraich in the west round to Càrn a' Mhuilt in the north.

Drive up Glen Strathfarrar to park in a lay-by on the left at NH329396, about 7.7km from the gate. For access information to the glen see opposite. It is possible to park in the car park at Inchmore and use a bike, thereby not being reliant on the gate times.

Walk back east along the road for about 100m to a small path leading off right down to a footbridge across the River Farrar at NH330397; the Pollcherian Bridge. Follow a path (indistinct in places) through the pine forest to the right of the Allt Coire nam Bràthan. At NH326384 there is a clearing with a deer fence and stile. Do not cross the stile but rather follow the fence to the left (south-west) parallel to the burn, emerging from the trees onto flatter, boggy ground. After another 1.5km or so, cross the burn and climb to the top of Sgòrr na Ruadhraich. Continue eastwards over heather and grass to a well-made cairn at the summit of Càrn Gorm (**6.5km; 690m; 2h 40min**).

Although a direct descent can be made to the north to pick up a path and rejoin the approach route, a more pleasant return continues along the ridge north-eastwards. This leads over the east top to Càrn a' Mhuilt then to the path at NH342374 in front of Càrn nam Barran. This is followed west then north-west beside the burn back to the trees where the approach route is joined after fording the Allt Coire nam Bràthan (**13.5km; 770m; 4h 20min**).

This route could be linked to the Corbett of Sgòrr na Dìollaid; 5km, 430m, 1h 50min from Càrn Gorm,

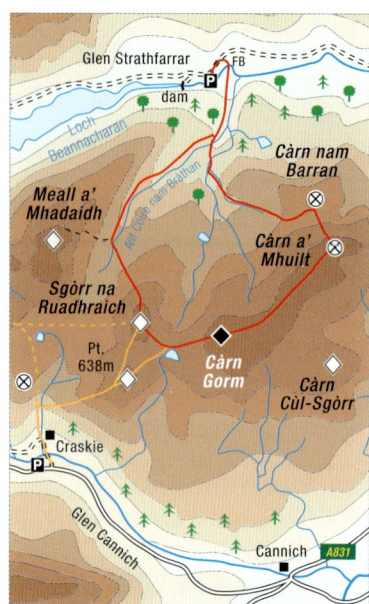

Càrn Gorm from the flanks of Sgòrr na Ruadhraich (Rab Anderson)

Vehicular access to the road up Glen Strathfarrar is restricted all year round (Noel Williams)

although this circuit is perhaps better done from Glen Cannich.

The ascent from Glen Cannich is made from Craskie, 4.5km from Cannich. It is a shorter approach and more easily combined with Sgòrr na Dìollaid. Parking is limited and perhaps best at a small pull-off about 100m west of the track to Craskie. Cross the causeway and follow the track to Craskie house, skirting round the west side of the garden to the bridge crossing the burn. Aim directly uphill on the west side of the wooded ravine onto the open hill, passing a tall cairn on the way to reach Pt.638m; rough going in places. Descend to the lochan and so to the summit (**4km; 620m; 2h**).

Return via Sgòrr na Ruadhraich (**8.5km; 720m; 3h 20min**).

To climb Sgòrr na Dìollaid, head west, over or round Sgòrr na Ruadhraich, then pass to the north of the small Loch Càrn na Toiteill and climb to the rocky summit (**9km; 1050m; 3h 50min**).

Return towards the small lochan then go over or round Càrn na Toiteill and descend back to Craskie (**13km; 1070m; 5h**).

Càrn Gorm can also be climbed direct from Cannich; useful for those without transport. Start up the edge of the forestry 500m north-east of the village on the A831 to Beauly.

Strathfarrar Access

The road up Glen Strathfarrar is private. There is a locked gate at its start (NH394406), at Inchmore near Struy Bridge. Vehicular access is restricted, but access on foot and by bike is unaffected. There is a car park on the left at Inchmore. For current access information check the Mountaineering Scotland website: www.mountaineering.scot/access/special-arrangements/strathfarrar.

Summer Access: This is controlled by a gatekeeper. Access is available from 1 April to 31 October from 9am until dusk (April 6pm; May 7pm; June 8pm; July 8pm; August 8pm; September 7pm; October 6pm). The glen is closed to vehicles all day Tuesday and until 1.30pm on Wednesday.

Winter Access: The gate is locked and there is no gatekeeper. Access is only available by telephone arrangement with Mountaineering Scotland (01738 493942). At the time of writing this is 1 November to 31 March. The following information is required; date of visit, car registration; occupant's names and a telephone contact number. A combination number for a lock on the gate will be issued. This number is changed regularly, so call Mountaineering Scotland every time a visit is planned. Each trip under the winter arrangements has to be notified to Mountaineering Scotland – there is no need to notify Mountaineering Scotland of summer access. Do not leave calls until the morning of the visit. The best times to call are between 10.30am and 3pm.

Access Rights: These apply to the glen using non-motorised vehicles at all times of day or night and include wild camping (away from road and buildings). These rights apply to responsible behaviour under the Scottish Outdoor Access Code. These rights do not extend to vehicles and overnight parking is not permitted in the glen. Anyone wishing to stay overnight should walk in, bike in or arrange to be dropped off and the vehicle driven out of the glen.

Notes: A maximum of 25 vehicles are permitted in the glen on a given day. Last vehicle access is one hour before closing time. Vehicles can be taken to the Loch Monar Dam, across it and 3km further to the Uisge Misgeach power station at NH183381.

The road through the glen runs for 15.5 miles (25km) and is single track with passing places and some potholes. It can take about 40min to drive its length. Plan this into your walk itinerary!

Beinn na Muice

Beinn na Muice from the Loch Monar Dam (Meryl Marshall)

Beinn na Muice; 695m; (G111); L25; NH 218402; *mountain of the pig*

This splendid little rocky peak is situated above the Monar Dam at the head of Glen Strathfarrar. It lies at the centre of a large tract of country which holds some of Scotland's remotest Munros. Beinn na Muice is in fact an extension of the Strathfarrar Munros and can easily be included with the westernmost of these, or indeed at the end of the full traverse of four Munros and two Munro Tops where the southward running ridge leads to it from Sgùrr na Fearstaig to provide a fitting finale; 4km, 290m, 1h 30min from Sgùrr na Fearstaig.

It can also be usefully combined with Càrn Gorm, the other short Strathfarrar Graham. However, it does offer a good short day in its own right.

Drive up Glen Strathfarrar (see p253 Strathfarrar Access) and 2.5km east of the Monar Dam, park at NH224392 at the foot of the track which follows the west bank of the Allt Toll a' Mhuic. Climb the track and after 1.3km, at the Eas na Muice waterfall, leave it and ascend the steep east spur of Beinn na Muice. A grassy gully provides easier going, and although it has a couple of short, steep sections these can easily be bypassed on the south side. The final 500m of ascent is along a pleasant gently rising ridge with several rocky knolls. The summit itself has a small cairn (**2.5km; 540m; 1h 30min**).

There are outstanding views of Maoile Lunndaidh and its neighbours to the west, the Mullardoch hills to the south-west and the Strathfarrar hills to the north-east.

Complete the traverse by going westwards along the broad rocky ridge for a further 500m. The views across Loch Monar are impressive.

The quickest descent is via the south-west spur to the 330m bealach with Meall an Tairbh (which can be ascended) then go south-east down a small glen to the road which is followed back (**6.5km; 540m; 2h 35min**).

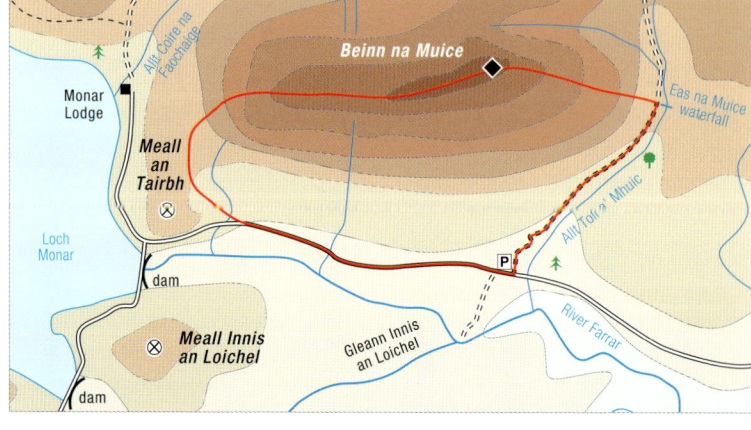

An Cruachan

An Cruachan; 705m; (G89); L25; NH093358; *the little heap*

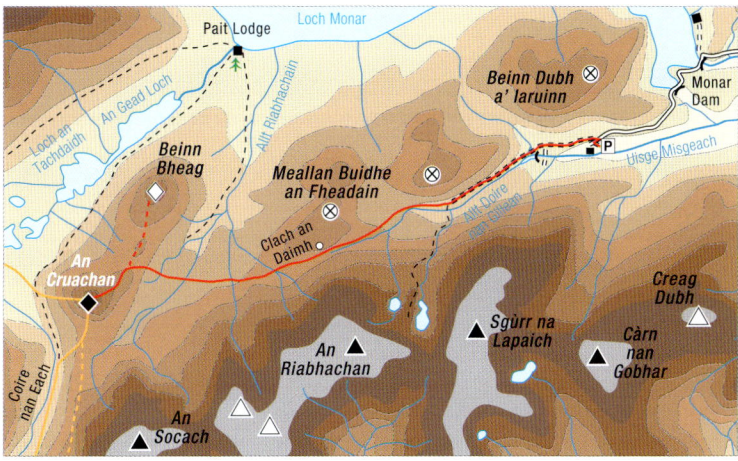

Rarely climbed An Cruachan is one of the most remote Grahams. It has a lonely feel with superb views. Given its central location there is a choice of possible routes. The fastest approach is probably from Glen Strathfarrar in the east; see p253 for Strathfarrar Access information.

Start from the end of the road at the parking area at the Uisge Misgeach power station (NH183381).

Walk west along a track then take the good path which continues south-west, uphill by the cascading burn, to peter out at NH137365 just short of the Clach an Daimh bealach. From there it is 4.5km to the summit of An Cruachan, westwards over the col and across an open expanse of rough country – not for the faint-hearted! There are occasional peat hags, some with remnant stumps of ancient trees. Whilst a little off route, a small bridge across the Allt Riabhachain at NH117371 could be useful if the burns are in spate, although there are no bridges across the other burns.

Ascend the grassy east slopes of the hill to the col below the summit cone then turn south-west up the ridge which is pleasant underfoot. The summit has a conical cairn, surprisingly well built for such a remote spot (**10km; 630m; 3h 30min**).

Return the same way (**20km; 740m; 5h 50min**).

Some who have come this far might wish to continue to the outlying top of Beinn Bheag to the north-east; an added 2.5km, 110m, 45min, bearing in mind the gate closing time.

Another route is from Glen Elchaig to the south-west, starting at Killilan at the head of Loch Long. Although longer than the eastern approach, it is an easy bike ride to the track junction above Iron Lodge (**13km; 130m; 1h 30min** by bike), (**11km; 2h 40min** on foot from Camus-luinie). Times are now given on foot from and back to here. The Graham Càrn na Breabaig can be included in this route.

From Iron Lodge, a rough track follows the Allt na Doire Ghairbhe and continues past Loch Mhoicean. About 500m beyond the loch, and just past a cairn, follow an atv track across the burn and along Coire nan Each. Once beyond a rocky rib, ascend the slope to the Màm Ruisgte bealach, south of An Cruachan. A short, steep pull leads to the summit (**9km; 670m; 3h 10min**). Return to Iron Lodge (**18km; 750m; 5h 35min**).

Return to Killilan (**44km; 920m; 8h 5min** with a bike), or Camus-luinie (**48km; 920m; 10h 50min** on foot).

Including Càrn na Breabaig only adds 1.5km, 270m, 55min; see p251. Easiest is to return to the south end of Loch Mhoicean then climb to the summit. Descend the south-west ridge to gain a track above its zigzags and drop down these to Iron Lodge.

Another approach is from Attadale on Loch Carron to the west, via tracks past Bendronaig Lodge and bothy. Bikes can be used to NH018391 (**12.5km; 365m; 1h 50min**) and perhaps further to Loch Calavie between Beinn Dronaig and Lurg Mhòr. There is a potentially tricky river crossing just past Loch Calavie (**9km; 600m; 3h** from the bike); (**18km; 720m; 5h 30min** back to the bike).

Return to Attadale (**25.5km; 1300m; 8h 45min** with a bike).

An Cruachan from An Riabhachan (Rab Anderson)

Càrn na Còinnich

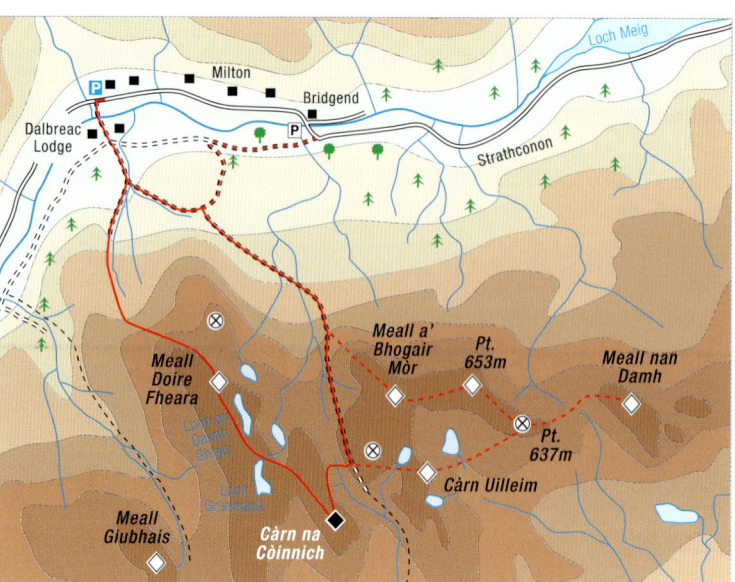

Càrn na Còinnich; 673m; (G141); L26; NH324510; hill of the moss

Càrn na Còinnich is an unusual Graham in being the highest point of a rolling plateau of peaks, three others of which are within 2-3m of the height of the main summit.

Confusingly, Meall nan Damh is given 671m on the OS 1:50k map, but on the 1:25k map it is given 673m. However, the Database of British and Irish Hills give Meall nan Damh 670.3m and confirm Càrn na Còinnich as being the highest point at 673.4m.

Start from a small car park at Milton Mill (NH304552) on the north side of the Strathconon road, 500m past the school in the village of Milton.

Walk west for 100m, cross the bridge over the River Meig and go through the Dalbreac Lodge estate buildings. Swing left then after 100m take the track leading uphill to a fork at a burn. The left fork is the return route, which can be used as an easier but less interesting line of ascent.

Instead, go right and follow the track until it enters forestry at NH302539. Strike south up heathery slopes to the right of the burn, cross a flat area, then either pass to the left of Creag a' Choire Riabhaich to gain the ridge, or climb steeply onto the ridge to its right. The ridge gives a pleasant and scenic route to the top of Meall Doire Fheara (671m); a good viewpoint from which to survey the Corbetts of Meallan nan Uan and Sgùrr a' Mhuilinn across the trench of Strathconon.

Continue south on easy terrain, crossing through the gap between Loch an Daimh Ghlais and Loch Gruamach, then follow a mossy ridge to the stark summit trig point of Càrn na Còinnich (**6km; 630m; 2h 30min**).

The view is extensive but less interesting than that from Meall Doire Fheara. To return, descend the mossy shoulder gently northwards for 500m to avoid some crags, then drop east and climb to a track. This is followed steeply down into Strathconon, going left at the fork (**12km; 630m; 4h**).

For the enhanced outing, gain the track then cross over and traverse round the south side of a knoll past a sometimes lily-bedecked lochan to climb Càrn Uilleim (651m). Drop north-east, passing the outflow of Loch na Caillich, and then make a rising traverse to reach point 637m. Descend to a col and climb by an old fenceline to the summit of Meall nan Damh (**10km; 900m; 3h 50min**).

To return, follow the fenceline back onto point 637m, then onto point 653m and Meall a' Bhogair Mòr (672m). Descend west for 500m onto the track, which leads back via the left fork (**17.5km; 1000h; 5h 50min**).

An alternative starting point is from a gated track entrance at Bridgend at NH323549. From there, the track is followed west for just over 1km to a track which connects to the one used in the descent route described above.

Càrn na Còinnich from Meall Doire Fheara (Rab Anderson)

Meall na Faochaig 257

Meall na Faochaig; 681m; (G128); L25; NH257525; hill of the shell, or spiral

Meall na Faochaig from above Inverchoran (Rab Anderson)

rocky crags of Creag Ghlas. On a clear day the outline of the hills of Torridon and the Fannaichs form a tremendous panoramic backdrop to the vast spaces of moorland lying to the north-west.

Most descend by the same route, especially if also climbing Beinn Mheadhoin (**7km; 560m; 2h 35min**).

Alternatively, extend the route by following Meall na Faochaig's north-west ridge past scenic Lochan na Croraig and over some peat hags to the top of Cnap na Feola (579m). From there, slant down to the east end of Loch Beannacharain via the shoulder of Meall Dubh and the Allt a' Chàrnaich (**16km; 650m; 5h**).

The steep south-east ridge of the hill provides a shorter circuit, down the side of Creag na Sàile to reach the road 400m from the start.

M eall na Faochaig is situated on the north side of the River Meig where it bends north-east after exiting Loch Beannacharain at the far end of Strathconon. It is an accessible and relatively undemanding hill, which has been helpfully equipped with a stalkers' path to make the ascent even easier. Beinn Mheadhoin, the third of the Strathconon Grahams, sits on the opposite side of the glen above Inverchoran; see p258.

Parking is common to both hills, at the start of the track to Inverchoran (NH261508). Both Grahams can be climbed in the day from here.

Walk west along the road for 300m and use the stalkers' path to gain height by a big dogleg up the hillside to where it terminates at a col. It is worth making a detour to visit Creag Iucharaidh (388m) for the striking views down and across the glen.

Return to the end of the path then climb the shallow south spur of Meall na Faochaig. This leads to the main ridge and a fenceline, which is followed eastwards for 500m or so towards the summit cairn (**3.5km; 560m; 1h 40min**).

There is a very fine view across the deep forested trench of Gleann Mèinich to Meallan nan Uan and the

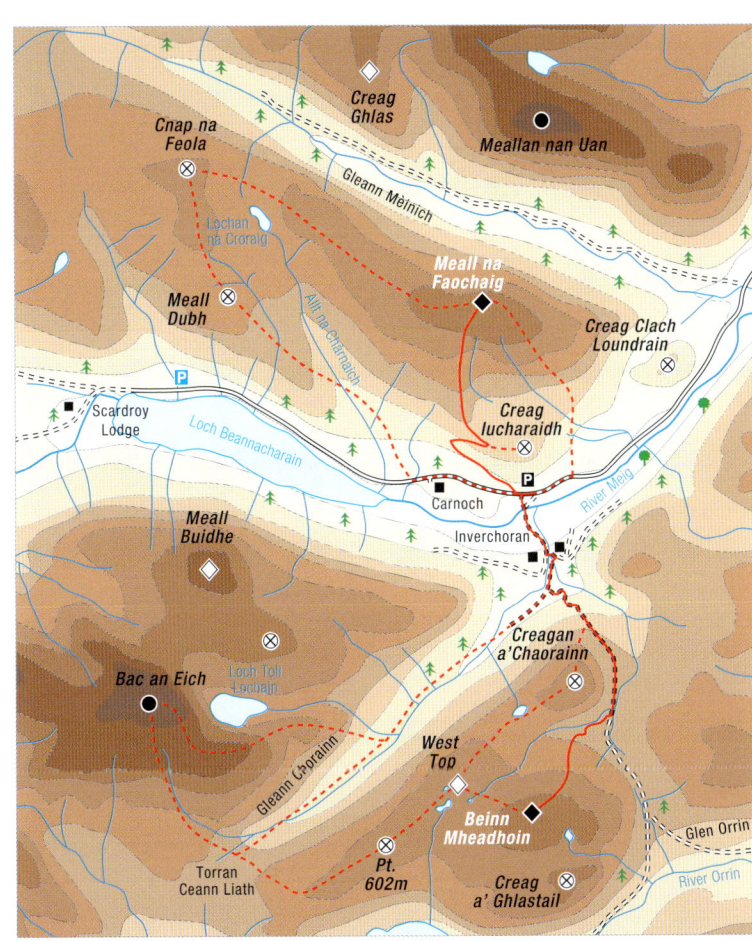

Beinn Mheadhoin

Beinn Mheadhoin from the east with Glen Orrin, left, and Bac an Eich, right (Jim Teesdale)

Beinn Mheadhoin; 665m; (G153); L25; NH258477; middle mountain

Lying on the south side of upper Strathconon above Inverchoran farm, Beinn Mheadhoin appears as a rolling area of hillside with no obvious summit to draw the eye. This is deceptive, although the hill's finest characteristics are reserved to the few who cross over into remote Glen Orrin to enjoy its southern features, which include the craggy flanks of Creag a' Ghlastail.

Park as for Meall na Faochaig (see p257), at the start of the track to Inverchoran (NH261508). Both Grahams can be climbed in the day from here.

Follow the track over the bridge and circumnavigate Inverchoran farm by a track on the left across a bridge then ford the burn to gain the track on the other side. Continue south on the track up Gleann Chorainn for 400m, then take the left fork, which leads steeply up and round to the east of Creagan a' Chaorainn.

There are good views north looking back over Strathconon to Meall na Faochaig and Meallan nan Uan.

About 100m after fording a burn, a stalkers' path leaves the track at NH267487 (not shown on the OS 1:50k map). Follow this path west-south-west onto a spur until it peters out at around NH263484 then continue up the spur and heathery slopes to the top. The upper part of the hill has a number of undulations and false tops, which may confuse the unwary in poor visibility. The summit cairn is on an outcrop and gives fine views west to Bac an Eich and south across Glen Orrin to the North Glen Strathfarrar ridge (**4km; 520m; 1h 45min**).

Most walkers return the same way (**8km; 520m; 2h 45min**).

However, a pleasant extension takes in the West Top (627m) whose summit sits amongst a number of craggy knolls. From there, descend north-east past the end of a tiny lochan then climb onto the triple-topped summit of Creagan a' Chaorainn (552m). Either descend steeply east back onto the track used on the ascent, or descend north towards Inverchoran a short way before heading right to pick up the track (**9km; 640m; 3h 15min**).

A longer option goes down the knolly south-west ridge via the West Top to reach the col at Torran Ceann Liath from where the Corbett of Bac an Eich (849m) can be climbed by its southern slopes (**9.5km; 990m; 3h 50min**).

Either return to the col and go down the path through Gleann Chorainn or descend the ridge south-east then east to join this path further on (**15km; 990m; 5h 15min**).

Rather than climb Bac an Eich, an easier option from the col at Torran Ceann Liath is to return down Gleann Chorainn to Inverchoran, or drop south to Loch na Caoidhe and walk east along the Glen Orrin path to reach the end of the track used in the ascent.

See preceeding page for map

Creag Dhubh Mhòr 259

Creag Dhubh Mhòr; 612m; (G219); L25; NG982404; big black cliff

Creag Dhubh Mhòr marks the high-point of a large tract of relatively unfrequented hill country between Strathcarron and the glen to the east which contains the bothies at Bendronaig and Bearnais. The hills are generally heathery and grassy but Creag Dhubh Mhòr is the culmination of a complex area of craggy knolls and lochans, bounded on its north-west side by a steep face. Traversing it provides an interesting and challenging exercise in route-finding, particularly in poor visibility. On a clear day the views to the north and west are particularly rewarding.

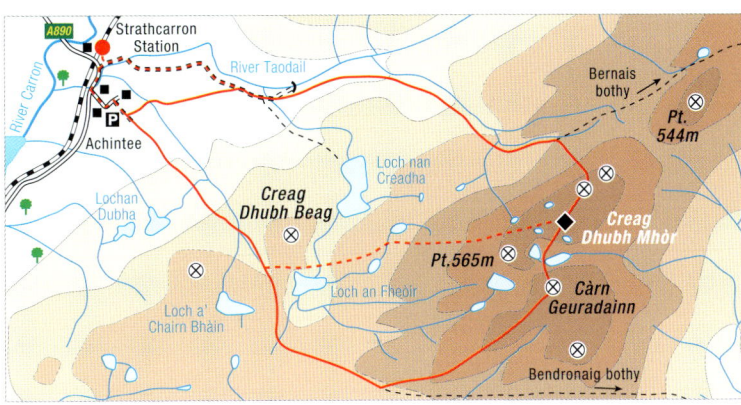

Several excellent hill paths serve the area, and a clockwise traverse of the hill makes good use of these. Start at Achintee (NG942417) where there is limited parking (beside the substation is a possibility). Achintee is 400m to the south of Strathcarron station and the timing of the trains is convenient if travelling from the east.

Follow the signposts through Achintee and go up a track past the electricity sub-station to a gate. About 60m beyond this, take the path on the left signed to Bearnais bothy. Cross a stile then a small burn and join a path coming up the north side of this burn. Climb uphill to the east for 500m to join a hydro track. This track can be followed from its start opposite the station, up and across the River Taodail.

Continue up the track to cross a bridge over a burn then break off right 120m further on at a cairn and follow a path up on the right. Leave this path after about 2.75km at NG982412 and head for a broad grassy gully in the crags on the right. This provides relatively easy going to a col about 550m to the north-east of the summit. A further 100m of ascent, initially steep and then over the false north-east top, gains the summit (**5.5km; 600m; 2h 10min**).

The shortest and the safest descent if the visibility is poor is west-south-west passing two small lochans and then westward to Loch an Fheòir to join the path from Bendronaig to Achintee (**10.5km; 600m; 3h 30min**).

However, continuing over Càrn Geuradainn (594m), 800m to the south-south-west of Creag Dhubh Mhòr, gives a more complete day. From the summit, take a line south-west, aiming between two lochans for a col, then make the short ascent to the trig point on Càrn Geuradainn. The south-west ridge gives an easy and interesting descent; avoid the steeper lower section by heading westward to gain the Bendronaig path (**12km; 670m; 4h**).

Looking north from Càrn Geuradainn across Coire Odhar to the summit of Creag Dhubh Mhòr (Meryl Marshall)

The view into Coire Mhic Fhearchair from Beinn a' Chearcaill's remarkable summit, with Ruadh-stac Mòr left and Sàil Mhòr right (Rab Anderson)

SECTION 1
Glen Carron to Loch Maree

SECTION 13

[1] *Càrn Breac*, [2] *Beinn na Feusaige*   263
[3] *Sgùrr a' Gharaidh*   265
[4] *Beinn a' Chlachain*   266
[5] *Beinn na h-Eaglaise*   267
[6] *An Ruadh-Mheallan*   268
[7] *Beinn a' Chearcaill*   269

Càrn Breac, Beinn na Feusaige

Beinn na Feusaige from Coille Bhreac (Rab Anderson)

Càrn Breac; 678m; (G135); L25; NH045530; speckled hill
Beinn na Feusaige; 627m; (G196); L25; NH090542; mountain of the beard

Càrn Breac and Beinn na Feusaige form a substantial and heathery retaining wall along the north side of the upper reaches of Glen Carron. The starting point for the ascent of both hills is to the south-west of Achnasheen, on the A890 to Lochcarron, where a loop of the old road leaves the main road at NH091530 at the west end of Loch Sgamhain. There is limited parking to the side of a locked gate here, as well as to the side of the access road to Loan on the opposite side of the road.

The most worthwhile route makes a clockwise circuit of the hills around the Allt Coire Crubaidh.

Cross the gate and walk along the old road, then go over the bridge and immediately go through a gate in the deer fence into an area of regenerating woodland. Climb rough ground through this and exit the enclosure by the gate at NH080528, which can be seen from the start, just south of the corner of the older plantation. Ascend tussocky slopes onto Coille Bhreac. The terrain becomes easier as height is gained and fine views of Moruisg and Sgùrr nan Ceannaichean open up to the south.

Continue along the top of Coille Bhàn then swing round past the head of the narrow Coire Dubh-riabhach to gain the upper slopes of Càrn Breac ▶

Trig point and shelter on the summit of Càrn Breac (Rab Anderson)

264 Càrn Breac, Beinn na Feusaige

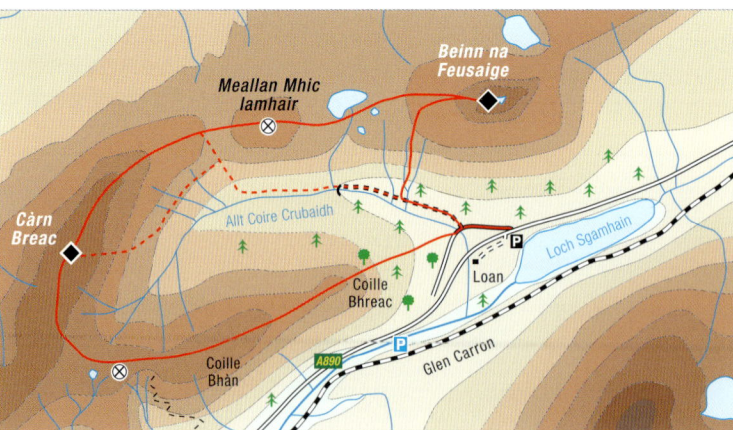

where a rising traverse leads northwards to the summit (**6km; 530m; 2h 15min**).

This final section crosses featureless slopes, where navigation could be challenging in poor visibility.

Càrn Breac's stone trig point and surrounding shelter provide an excellent grandstand from which to appreciate the superb panorama. To the west is the triple-peaked Beinn Liath Mhòr, with Sgòrr Ruadh rising behind and Fuar Tholl to the side, then the Torridon hills, Beinn Eighe and Liathach, which are seen across Loch Coulin. North is the Graham Beinn a' Mhùinidh with Slioch behind, then the Letterewe and Fisherfield hills with the Grahams, Beinn Bheag and Groban easily picked out. Not so readily identifiable are the Grahams Meall a' Chaorainn and Beinn nan Ramh lying in front of the Fannaichs and to the side of Fionn Bheinn. To the east are the Strathconan peaks then south, Moruisg, Sgùrr nan Ceannaichean and yet more hills.

Head north-east, gradually descending the long crest, then swing east and climb easily over Meallan Mhic Iamhair (499m) to reach the outflow of Lochan Meallan Mhic Iamhair. Beinn na Feusaige rises above and is gained by a steady 230m climb beside an old fence. Just below the summit area are the remains of a Martin B-26 Marauder which crashed in June 1943.

The top is located at the west end of the flat summit area, to the south-west of a small lochan (**11.5km; 830m; 4h**).

The OS 1:25k and 1:50k maps show a lower 625m height some 300m further east. The view is less fine than that from Càrn Breac.

To return, descend west for almost 1km, then veer south-west and drop steeply down a narrow, heathery buttress between two burns, to the west of a plantation, to gain a hydro track which is followed back to the road (**14.5km; 830m; 5h**).

Càrn Breac can be approached by the hydro track and path on the north bank of the Allt Coire Crubaidh. The path forks at the midway point at NH063538 by some old shielings and the right fork climbs steeply to run out on the north-east slopes, leaving easy walking to the summit. The rest of the route is as previously described. There is little difference in distance and time between the routes.

Càrn Breac from Meallan Mhic Iamhair (Rab Anderson)

The summit of Sgùrr a' Gharaidh from the east (Jim Teesdale)

Sgùrr a' Gharaidh; *732m; (G44); L24, 25; NG884443; peak of the cave or den*

With its outlying subsidiaries, Sgùrr a' Gharaidh is an extensive hill which couples a fine location with some rugged and exciting scenery. The hill's fine northern features are not obvious until after the A896 leaves Kishorn and heads towards Shieldaig.

The best starting point is from Loch an Lòin; parking at a passing place at NG852447, or 20m down the track to the loch. Walk along the track past the keeper's cottage and turn right after 1km to enter an enclosed section of regenerating birch woodland. The track deteriorates to a rough atv track which traverses through the Coille Dhubh woodland and leads to a small bridge over the Allt a' Ghiuthais at NG881455.

This point can also be reached by the Bealach a' Ghlas-chnoic path, which gives good views to the hill. However, whilst the path is good initially, it does fade.

Cross the burn and follow an atv track on the line of the path under the rocky flanks of Sgùrr a' Gharaidh. After 1km, recross the burn at NG893450 and follow a tributary south-south-east to a grassy flattening just west of a lochan at NG896447. Climb a scree shoot directly above to reach the upper slopes at NG896443. Locating this scree shoot requires precise navigation in mist, or in descent, and also suitable equipment in winter.

Having reached the upper slopes, made up of a confusing area of knolls, lochans, burns and gentle moorland, it is worth taking in Glas Bheinn. To do so, head south-south-east past a lochan to reach the trig point (711m), which gives a fine view down to Loch Carron, then return north to the actual top of Glas Bheinn (729m). Continue north-west past another lochan onto the top of Creag na h-Iolaire, then descend south-west.

Now follow the ridge west for 1km, past a series of lochans and steeply climb Sgùrr a' Gharaidh's summit cone, passing another lochan (**9km; 860m; 3h 30min**).

There are three descent options, which can also be used as quick there and back ascent routes. From the summit, all head westwards down the rough and rocky ridge to reach the north end of Lochan Meall na Caillich then continue west for 200m.
(i) Descend north-west beside an old boundary fence and wall to gain the west end of the Coille Dhubh track and drop to the lochside track south of Glasnock (**13.5km; 860m; 4h 50min**).
(ii) Continue west by the burn to the knoll of Cnoc nam Broc (NG862438) then descend easy slopes north-west to reach the south end of Loch an Lòin (**13km; 860m; 4h 45min**).
(iii) Descend westwards on a rough track which swings around the north side of Cnoc nam Broc to reach the road at Couldoran and follow this back (**14.75km; 890m; 5h 10min**).

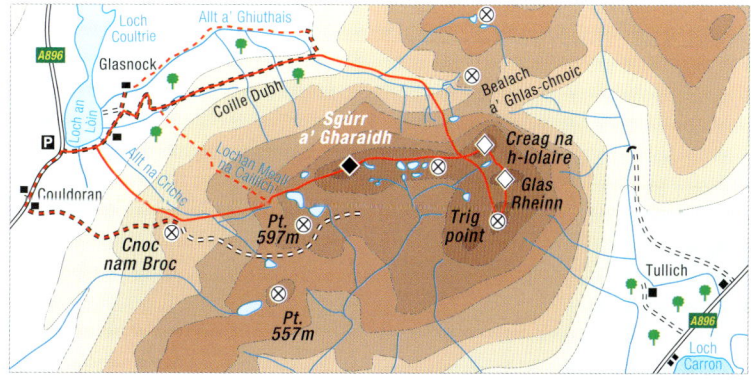

Beinn a' Chlachain

Beinn a' Chlachain; 626m; (G197); L24; NG724490; mountain of the clachan (church hamlet)

Like the nearby village of Applecross, from which it is separated by Applecross Bay, Beinn a' Chlachain is a secluded secret, only discovered by those prepared to pass the more obvious delights of Beinn Bhàn and Sgùrr a' Chaorachain. It is also a journey to get there starting from sea level at Loch Kishorn, crossing over the Bealach na Bà pass, at 620m the highest in Britain, then dropping back down to the sea again at Applecross.

Since the hill itself provides a relatively short outing it is worth taking the day to explore the Applecross Peninsula and savour the scenery. Applecross itself has a fascinating history and much can be learned about this at the Applecross Heritage Centre at Clachan.

Most of Beinn a' Chlachain is tussocky and undulating with long slopes, sprinkled with lochans, that run north-west down to the sea. However, on its south-east side the slopes drop steeply by terraced sandstone tiers into Srath Maolchaluim and this is the where the hill is best approached from.

Start at the north end of Apple-

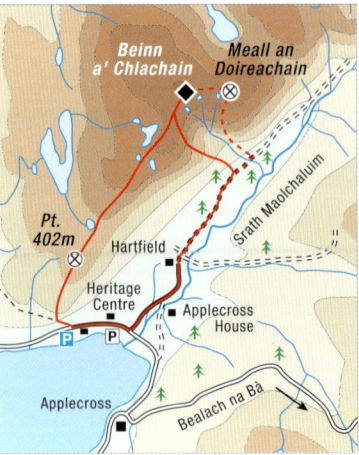

cross Bay, from the beach parking area opposite the Heritage Centre car park. Walk east along the road for 300m then take the road and track up cultivated Srath Maolchaluim for 3km. This runs alongside the River Applecross and passes Hartfield House hostel and bunkhouse. Leave the track at the east corner of a forestry plantation (NG731477) and head uphill to gain the western edge of Coire Glas, a fine recess that bites deep into the side of the mountain.

The angle, though steep, is never excessive and relents at around 530m. Easy walking then leads past a scenic small lochan to the summit trig point and its stone enclosure (**5km; 630m; 2h 10min**).

An alternative is to go up the right side of Coire Glas to climb Meall an Doireachain, then traverse to the top.

There are fantastic views across the Inner Sound to Rona and Raasay then across the Sound of Rassay to Skye. There are glimpses through to Torridon as well. The descent can be by the same route, particularly if the approach has been made by bike, (**10km; 630m; 3h 30min**).

However, it is better to make the most of the hill by walking down its long south-west ridge towards Applecross Bay, reaching Pt.402m after about 2.5km. Continue down the ridge past a large cairn then make a short and steep descent onto the coast path to Sand which leads to a parking area and alternative start point on the road just beyond Cruarg. A brief walk leads back along the road to the start (**10km; 650m; 3h 30min**).

Beinn a' Chlachain from the Bealach na Bà road (Tom Prentice)

Beinn na h-Eaglaise

Liathach from the summit of Beinn na h-Eaglaise (Rab Anderson)

Beinn na h-Eaglaise; 736m; (G36); L24, 25; NG908523; mountain of the church

What it lacks in height, Beinn na h-Eaglaise more than makes up for with the superb views it provides of its better known neighbours from its central Torridonian position.

Start from the large car park at The Torridon Inn (NG889541), signposted 'Beinn Damh Hill Track' from the A896 Torridon to Shieldaig road. The initial part of this route is the same as that for Beinn Damh, a Corbett.

Walk west along the road through the rear courtyard to a bridge over the Allt Coire Roill. Cross over then turn left onto a signposted path leading through woodland to reach the main road.

On the other side, go up a stalkers' path through the trees. The path climbs uphill above a gorge with waterfalls, through beautiful natural pine forest to emerge onto the more open, Caledonian pine and boulder-strewn hillside. Take the left fork at NG884533 and when this reaches the river, head upstream a little to make the crossing. To regain the path on the far side, go downstream for 50m.

Follow the path for another 600m onto the flanks of Beinn na h-Eaglaise then leave it and gain the ridge above. This becomes better defined as height is gained, although it is rough and offers short sections of easy scrambling on sandstone. The views to Beinn Damh and behind over Upper Loch Torridon to Beinn Alligin are excellent. The angle eases off towards the top. It is a superb viewpoint from which to appreciate the grandeur of the surrounding Torridonian scenery (**4km; 710m; 2h 5min**).

Descend rough, stony ground south-west to pass between a chain of lochans and climb onto the South Top (676m). Continue down, crossing a fine sandstone table, to reach the path by a small lochan at the Drochaid Coire Roill bealach. The quickest return is down the Coire Roill path (**10.5km; 750m; 3h 40min**).

An alternative from the summit is to descend the south-south-east ridge to Loch an Eoin to pick up the Glen Carron to Torridon path. This leads to the road at Annat, passing below Beinn na h-Eaglaise's craggy eastern flanks (**11.5km; 710m; 3h 50min**).

From the Drochaid Coire Roill, an excellent hill extension climbs to the summit of Beinn Damh (903m) via its east ridge (**7.5km; 1230m; 4h**) and traverses the length of that peak northwards before returning to the path then to the car park (**16.5km; 1500m; 7h**).

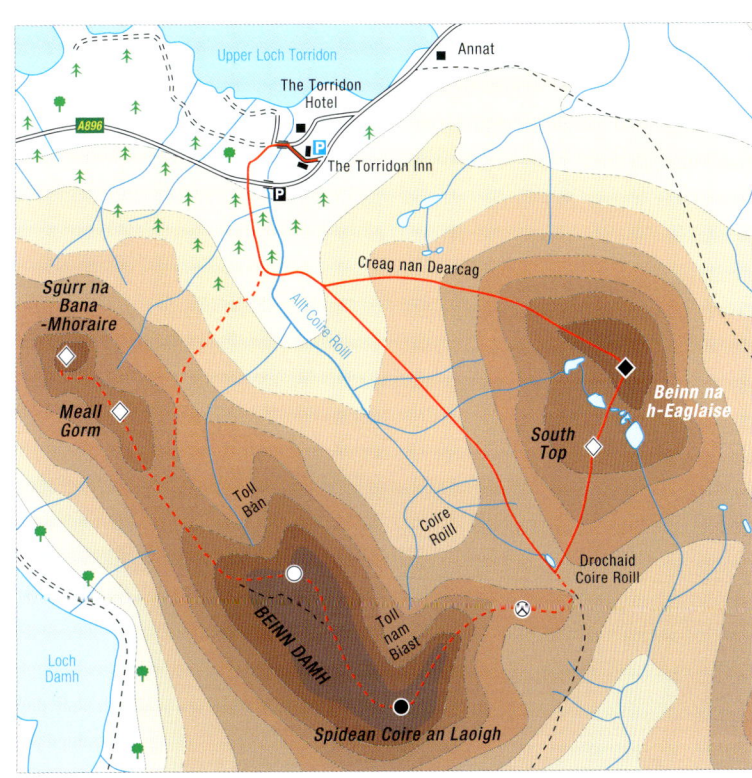

An Ruadh-Mheallan

An Ruadh-Mheallan from the parking to the south on the Diabaig road (Jim Teesdale)

An Ruadh-Mheallan; 671m; (G143); L19, 24; NG836614; *the little red hill*

Located on the doorstep of one of the country's grandest mountain arenas and usually overlooked, An Ruadh-Mheallan is a subtle hill worthy of exploration. A generally grassy peak with a steep sandstone summit cone, it rises north of the Diabaig road west of Beinn Alligin.

The approach starts from the aptly named Bealach na Gaoithe (pass of the wind) at the highpoint of the twisty single track road between Torridon and Diabaig. There is a layby on the west side at NG824593 (2-3 cars) with a bench overlooking Loch Diabaigas Àirde, just before the road starts the descent to Diabaig. There is also parking at the viewpoint 500m downhill to the south.

Head north, then cross a mixed landscape of heather, knolls and lochans to pass west of Loch nan Tri-eileanan. Continue north-east on gently rising rough ground, then climb more steeply north through slabby rocks to a small lochan at NG834611. The final climb up the summit cone is steeper still, with some avoidable scrambling, leading to large sandstone platforms (**3km; 430m; 1h 20min**).

The view is tremendous, stretching across the Minch and the Sound of Raasay to Skye with the Western Isles beyond. There is a good perspective of the Coulin hills and Beinn Damh. Beinn Alligin blocks the view east, from this side a grassy monolith, with the Graham Beinn a' Chearcaill visible beyond it.

To descend, continue by the east shoulder for 500m, and on gaining a flattish spur, turn south-east and drop into An Rèidh-choire. Descend its north-west side to a burn junction and shieling at NG838602. Climb briefly south-west to pass south of Loch nan Tri-eileanan and then continue south-west to regain the road (**7km; 470m; 2h 30min**).

Approaching the summit with Beinn Alligin behind (Rab Anderson)

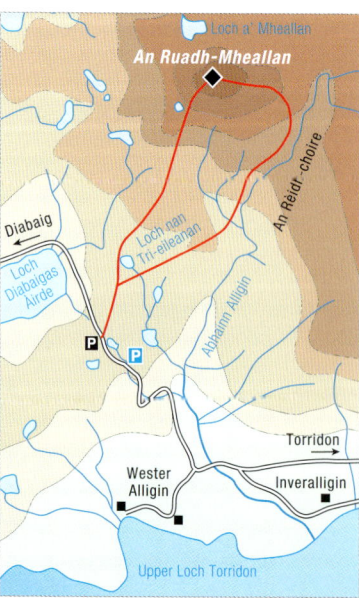

Beinn a' Chearcaill

Beinn a' Chearcaill; 725m; (G57); L19; NG930637; mountain of the circle

Beinn a' Chearcaill will often be observed from the main Torridon summits as a low, well-defended peak with an intriguingly flat summit. The usual approach is from the A832 Kinlochewe to Gairloch road by Loch Maree, from which side the hill is overshadowed by Beinn Eighe. The northern slopes are gentle and featureless, so the walk is best saved for a good day, which also allows the quality of the views and the unusual summit to be fully appreciated.

Start from a pull-off on the old road at NG962680. This is 500m west of Bridge of Grudie, the bridge over the river at the mouth of Glen Grudie.

Walk south-east along the road to the white cottage. Go up the left side of the lawn to pick up then follow a good stalkers' path up Glen Grudie for about 2km. Shortly before the path dips into Coire Briste, a less distinct path branches off right at NG953661 (cairn). Follow this path as it makes a gradual rising traverse up the back of the corrie to disappear near the outflow of a teardrop-shaped lochan at NG936653.

The top of the hill lies 1.8km to the south, with one short steeper section, and is reached up rough heathery slopes liberally covered in large blocks (**6.5km; 700m; 2h 35min**).

A detour east on the final ascent includes the outlying top of Creag na Feòl (641m) as a slightly longer but varied route; an added 15min.

The striking summit area is composed of a vast sandstone platform, reminiscent of a small airstrip, dotted with boulders.

Jagged Torridonian peaks rise on all southern aspects. There is a fantastic view straight into the jaws of Coire Mhic Fhearchair on Beinn Eighe, whilst Beinn an Eòin rises like a prow to the west.

Simplest is to return the same way (**13km; 710m; 4h 25min**).

Another option from the teardrop-shaped lochan is to rise slightly to A' Chòineach Beag (558m) for the great view of Loch Maree and Slioch. From there, head east-north-east for 1km to a spur, then trend north-east and drop gradually back to the Glen Grudie path (**13km; 770m; 4h 35min**).

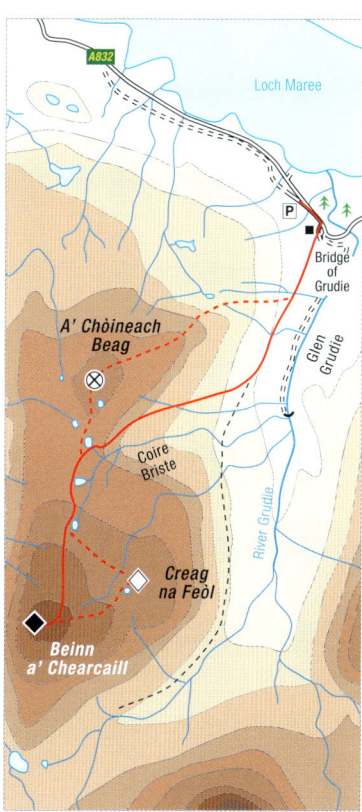

Beinn a' Chearcaill from the approach with Ruadh-stac Mòr, left, and Sàil Mhòr beyond (Tom Prentice)

Meall Mheinnidh's stunning summit view. Beinn a' Chlaideimh, Ruadh Stac Mòr, A' Mhaighdean, Mullach Coire Mhic Fhearchair, Beinn Tarsuinn and Beinn Làir (Rab Anderson)

SECTION 14
Loch Maree to Loch Broom

SECTION 14

[1] *Meall a' Chaorainn* — 273
[2] *Deinn nan Ramh* — 274
[3] *Beinn Bheag*, [4] *Groban* — 275
[5] *Beinn a' Mhùinidh* — 277
[6] *Meall Mhèinnidh* — 278
[7] *Beinn a' Chàisgein Beag* — 279
[8] *Beinn Ghobhlach* — 280

Meall a' Chaorainn

Meall a' Chaorainn from the approach across the peat hags (Rab Anderson)

Meall a' Chaorainn; 705m; (G92); L19, 20, 25; NH136604; hill of the rowan tree

Meall a' Chaorainn is an outlier of the Munro Fionn Bheinn, to which it is connected by a high col. It is a remarkably inconspicuous hill from below but offers a good and easily accessed viewpoint. Start from the railway station parking area just off the A832 in Achnasheen.

Walk back to the main road and cross over to go up the road to the left of a telephone box. Cross the bridge over the burn and take the first track right, through a gate, following signs to the hill. The track runs past a hydro building, opposite which is a gate that appears to be generally locked. This accesses a track that zigzags up the hillside to a dam. Whilst the track can be followed, the more pleasant route, albeit it can be boggy, is via the path up the east side of the burn, the Allt Achadh na Sìne.

This is reached by crossing a bridge over the burn to the Achnasheen Water Treatment Works where the path by the burn leads to a gate then continues up its side. Note a bridge on the left which can be used to avoid the gate if the return is made down the track.

Where the angle starts to ease, and the route to Fionn Bheinn swings away, cross the burn to gain the hydro dam. Now find a way through a level but contorted area of peat hags in a westerly direction for about 1km; easier on the descent when a slightly raised line can be seen. On gaining the drier slope beyond, make the climb to the flat summit, marked by a small cairn (**4km; 560m; 1h 50min**).

There is an extensive view towards Torridon, Slioch and the Fisherfield hills. It is an excellent balcony from which to try to name the many peaks spread out to the south.

Either return the same way, or via the track down the west side of the burn, crossing the bridge at the bottom if it has been noted that the gate is locked (**8km; 560m; 3h**).

To extend the route to include Fionn Bheinn, head north-north-east from Meall a' Chaorainn's summit for 200m to avoid its steeper eastern slope. Descend into the head of the unappealingly named Coire Bog then climb northwards to the summit (**7km; 980m; 3h 20min**).

Descend towards Creagan nan Laogh then regain the Allt Achadh na Sìne and return to Achnasheen (**11.5km; 980m; 4h 40min**).

Another approach can be made from verge parking about halfway along Loch a' Chroisg (NH125587) where a gated forest track leads into a plantation by the Allt Duchairidh.

Negotiate the gate and follow the track for 1.2km to emerge into patchier forestry. Just after a burn crossing, a possible short cut makes a rough way northwards up the steep hillside just north of a fence to gain the north-west ridge. However, the gentler approach, for those whose knees are no longer under manufacturer's warranty, follows the track to its end where a stalkers' path climbs up the Feadan Duchairidh, then trends north-east. Leave the path at its highpoint and follow the easy north-west ridge to the summit (**6.25km; 550m; 2h 15min**). Return the same way (**12.5km; 550m; 3h 45min**).

Map on following page

Beinn nan Ramh seen from the east across Loch Fannich (Jim Teesdale)

Beinn nan Ramh; 711m; (G77); L19, 20; NH139661; *mountain of the oars (or trees)*

A fine and remote hill at the west end of Loch Fannich, Beinn nan Ramh takes the form of a lengthy east to west whaleback ridge and fully repays the effort involved in getting to it.

The best approach uses a track which starts at NH199599, between forestry plantations about 4km east of Achnasheen. The nearest suitable parking is a layby about 1km east of here at Dosmuckeran; although it is possible to squeeze off-road closer to the track. There is a high metal gate at the start of the track, although the fence to its side is lower and a bike can be lifted over. The use of a bike should save about 2h 30min on the day for the on foot times given.

The track leads northwards over a low pass with views to the Fannaichs then drops to Loch Fannich before turning west to meet a hydro pipeline. At NH175649, turn right onto a track which is followed for 800m to where the steep lower part of the east ridge of Beinn nan Ramh is climbed (**9km; 210m; 2h 20min**).

The ridge eases and great views start to open. The final 3km to the summit gives easy walking with one short narrow section. A small cairn marks the top (**13km; 650m; 4h**).

There is a superb and open panoramic view of the Fannaichs, the Fisherfield hills, Beinn Eighe and south across Srath Chrombuill to Fionn Bheinn.

Beinn nan Ramh does not combine with other hills this way, so return the same way (**26km; 750m; 7h 15min**).

Beinn nan Ramh can also be climbed by its south-west flanks, although this lacks the grandeur of the Loch Fannich approach.

One route starts from Loch a' Chroisg, west of Achnasheen. Leave the road at NH125587 and follow a track through forestry up the Feadan Duchairidh. This turns into a stalkers' path which crosses the shoulder of Meall a' Chaorainn (see previous page) and drops to the hydro track in Srath Chrombuill. Leave the track, cross the river and grind up broad slopes to the top (**9km; 840m; 3h 25min**), (**18km; 1130m; 6h 15min**).

Meall a' Chaorainn can be taken in on the return, adding 1h to the trip.

Another option starts from the Incheril car park at Kinlochewe (NH037624). Walk or bike up the improved track past the Heights of Kinlochewe to Leckie (**7km; 110m; 1h 45min**).

A stalkers' path continues north-east for 2km to end near a burn. The summit lies a further 3km east across featureless moorland (**12km; 700m; 3h 50min**), (**24km; 730m; 6h 30min**). The use of a bike should save about 2h 15min on the day.

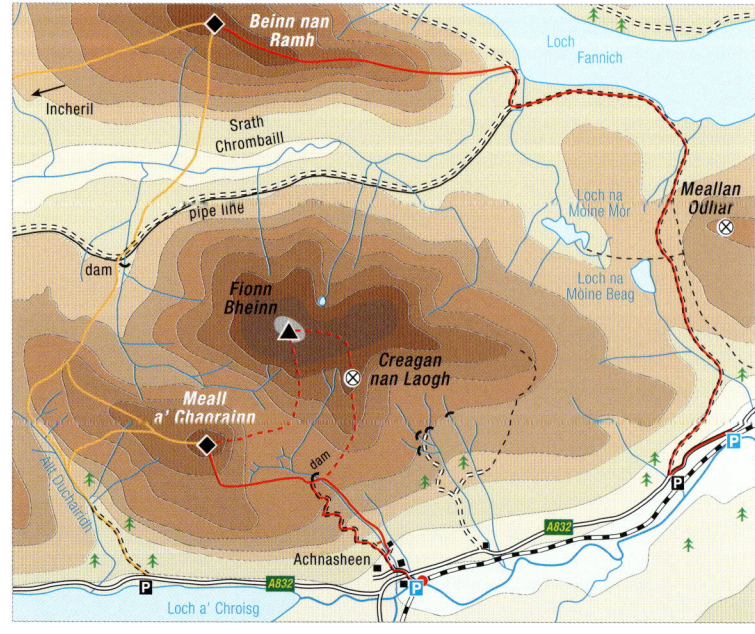

Beinn Bheag; 668m; (G146); L19, 20; NH085713; *little mountain*
Groban; 749m; (G11); L19, 20; NH099708; *little hill, swelling (it may refer to the large boulder at the summit)*

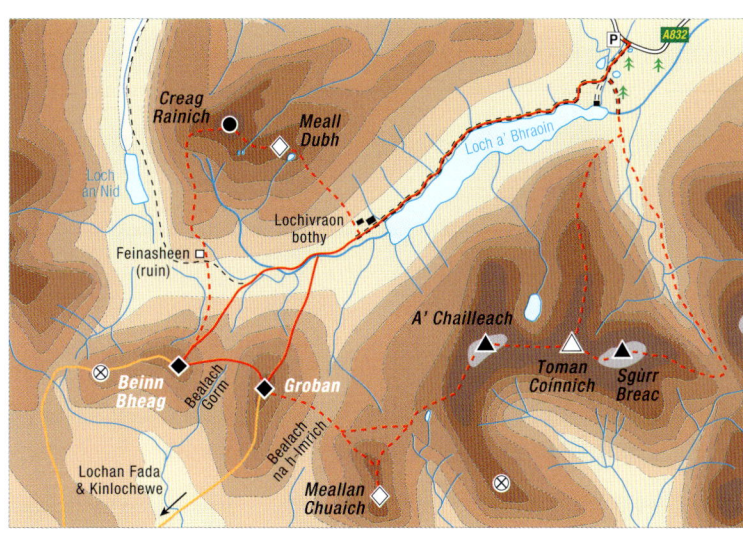

Beinn Bheag and Groban are a rounded and remote pair of peaks located in the rolling area of lower hills between the Fannaichs and the Fisherfield hills, and boast views to match their surroundings.

The best approach starts 6km beyond Braemore Junction on the A832 to Dundonnell, from parking in a layby at NH161761, just north of the start of a track to Loch a' Bhraoin. This is the same start point for the western Fannaich Munros and the eastern Fisherfield Munros.

Follow the track down towards the loch to a three-way junction and go right on an improved track. This leads along the north shore of Loch a' Bhraoin to the cottage and splendid bothy (one that boasts a flushing toilet!) at Lochivraon at the west end of the loch (**6km; 20m; 1h 20min** on foot), (**40min** by bike).

Times given are on foot and the use of a bike should save around 1h 20min on the day.

The domes of Groban and Beinn Bheag rise to the south-west of here and the farther of the two, Beinn Bheag, is best climbed first. Follow the rough track then footpath west for a further 1.7km then at a path junction, cross the burn at NH101728, as for the route to the Fisherfield hills. Leave the path here and follow the west bank of the burn towards the Bealach Gorm between the hills.

After some boggy ground, leave the burn and climb more steeply southwest. The angle relents and Beinn Bheag's summit is soon reached. There is more than one possible highpoint; OS 1:25k and 1:50k maps show different points 200m apart, but it may also lie somewhere in-between (**10km; 430m; 2h 55min**).

The western cairn makes the finer viewpoint. Particularly special are the views north to the turrets of An Teallach, the nearer slabby quartzite flanks of Sgùrr Bàn and Mullach Coire Mhic Fhearchair, whilst to the west there is a glimpse of Lochan-Fada with pointed Slioch beyond. ▶

South-west down Loch a' Bhraoin to Groban, left, and Beinn Bheag (Jim Teesdale)

Groban, left, and Beinn Bheag from the north-west (Rab Anderson)

Leave Beinn Bheag's summit and head east down steep grassy slopes to the Bealach Gorm (472m), then ascend the north-west shoulder of Groban to reach its summit (**11.5km; 710m; 3h 50min**).

A little removed from the most spectacular hills, Groban's view is not as good as Beinn Bheag's, despite its extra height.

The descent line, between north and north-east, depends on the level of the Abhainn Loch a' Bhraoin, which is forded to regain the approach path. Potentially high, the crossing is best made about 1.5km west of Lochivraon, upstream of some meandering loops, to regain the bothy (**15km; 710m; 5h**).

Return along the loch (**21km; 740m; 6h 20min** on foot, (**5h** with a bike).

Those for whom the two Grahams have made a good *hors d'oeuvre*, can make a great return over the western Fannaichs. From the summit of Groban, drop south-east to the Bealach na h-Imrich and either include the interesting Meallan Chuaich (690m) by its sinuous north ridge, or skirt it and head directly towards A' Chailleach. The ascent begins easily but the upper slopes rear up steeply to Ceann Garbh a' Chaillich (908m) where the ridge then leads to A' Chailleach (997m). Continue to Sgùrr Breac (999m) then descend to the east end of Loch a' Bhraoin, either by backtracking to Toman Còinnich and down the Druim Rèidh, or by continuing east to the col with Sgùrr nan Clach Geala and down the stalkers' path.

Another useful extension links Creag Rainich, a Corbett, into a round with the two Grahams, starting with Groban. On the descent northwards from Beinn Bheag, aim for the ruin of Feinasheen (NH092730) then climb to the summit of Creag Rainich (807m). Head south-east to Meall Dubh and either drop to the bothy if a bike has been used, or descend diagonally to Loch a' Bhraoin, or continue along the ridge before descending.

A longer but perhaps even better day can be enjoyed from Kinlochewe to the south, on a route where a mountain bike is recommended, saving about 2h on the overall time.

Start from the Incheril car park at NH037624 and head east up the glen by the Abhainn Bruachaig track. Fork left at the Heights of Kinlochewe, up the Gleann na Muice track (a high gate may need a bike lift) to its end at NH070666 (**7km; 240m; 2h** on foot), bikes are left here (**1h** by bike).

The Meallan Odhar stalkers' path starts here, but rather than approach the hills directly by this, it is better to continue up the Gleann na Muice path, which has been upgraded for its initial 1.6km, to a gate at NH063681. Continue on the path towards Lochan Fada then 1km beyond the gate, strike north over the rough heathery ground of Sìthean Bìorach.

There is a sense of being amongst great and wild mountains; Slioch and A' Mhaighdean sit either side of Lochan Fada, whilst the south-west corries of Beinn Tarsuinn and Mullach Coire Mhic Fhearchair lie ahead.

A line of small cairns marks a sketchy stalkers' path, which continues below and east of Loch Meallan an Fhùdair. Drop diagonally to the burn leading to the Bealach na Croise where another vague path is picked up on its east side. Gain the bealach (424m), or strike uphill earlier, and climb steeply to Beinn Bheag's west top (615m). There is then an easy stroll along the ridge by an old fenceline to the main summit (**14.25km; 720m; 4h 25min**).

Continue to Groban as previoulsy described (**15.75km; 1000m; 5h 20min**).

Descend via the long south-west slope, following the side of a prominent washed-out gully lower down, to gain the upper flats of Gleann Tanagaidh. Cross the river and locate the end of the stalkers' path at NH081683. If the river is high, use the unmarked bridge at NH082679. This upgraded path climbs over Meallan Odhar then drops to rejoin the track end in Gleann na Muice (**21.5km; 1150m; 7h 10min**).

Return to Incheril as for the approach (**28.5km; 1150m; 8h 45min**), (**6h 45min** with a bike).

Beinn a' Mhùinidh

Beinn a' Mhùinidh; 692m; (G113); L19; NH032660; mountain of pissing. (The huge waterfall dropping to Loch Maree is Allt na Still, burn of spouting)

Sitting at the south-east end of Loch Maree, Beinn a' Mhùinidh has been subjected to massive geological forces. It leans to the east displaying steep crags north-west towards Slioch (the Bonaid Dhonn) and south-west over Loch Maree, the latter containing the impressive Allt na Still waterfall. By contrast, the eastern aspects slope away into rolling moorland and small lochans.

Start from the Incheril car park at NH037624, gained by an access road across the river 500m to the east of Kinlochewe.

Follow the Loch Maree (and Slioch) footpath north-west for 3km to the burn which descends from the waterfall. Now climb a faint path up through steep heather and bracken on the right (south) side of the burn.

Bypass the band of crags to the right of the fall by a heathery gully on the right, up which gain a further 100m of height. The angle suddenly eases above the waterfall, on a shelf known as Coire Each.

Step over the burn feeding the fall and make a rising northwards traverse up the shelf to scramble through the upper quartzite tier at NH024657. A gentle ridge then leads north-east to the summit (**5.5km; 680m; 2h 30min**).

Throughout the ascent there are great views of Slioch and Beinn Eighe, as well as down the length of Loch Maree. The summit adds the Fisherfield and the Fannaichs to the panorama, and all four Grahams covered earlier in this section.

Descend southwards for just over 2km, between some lochans and passing Meallan Ghobhar on its east – as the name suggests, feral goats may well be seen hereabouts.

Cross the Allt Chnàimhean at around NH038638 above a waterfall at the entrance to a surprisingly deep and steep-sided gorge. Traverse deer tracks above the south side of the burn until clear of the gorge then drop steeply down a spur to its side to regain the Loch Maree path and

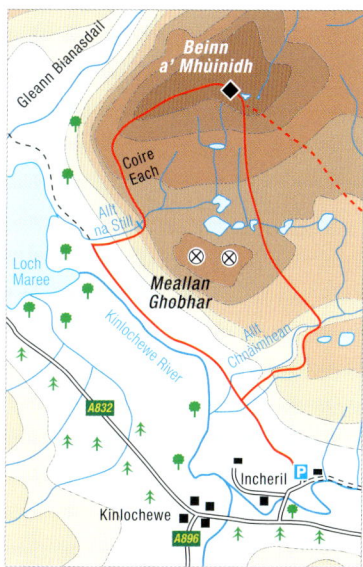

follow this back to the Incheril car park (**10km; 690m; 3h 50min**).

A more gradual descent can be made to the Heights of Kinlochewe track about 1.5km east of the car park (**11.5km; 690m; 4h 10min**).

The summit of Beinn a' Mhùinidh, centre, and the Allt na Still waterfall (Tom Prentice)

Beinn Làir, centre, with Meall Mhèinnidh, right, across Loch an Doire Crionaich from the approach (Rab Anderson)

Meall Mhèinnidh; 722m; (G60); L19; NG954748; hill of mining (bog iron was smelted beside Loch Maree)

To the north of Loch Maree lies a wild and empty area which stretches for more than 20km, and flanks the loch with steep slopes rising to a line of stunning mountains, of which Meall Mhèinnidh is the lowest. From the south side of Loch Maree, the hill appears as a gentle cone, sandwiched between its better-known Corbett neighbours Beinn Làir and Beinn Àirigh Charr; one or other of which it is often combined with.

Start in Poolewe, leaving the A832 on the east side of the River Ewe bridge, down the riverside road to a car park on the left (NG858808). A bike is recommended and can save about 1h 45min on the day.

Follow the road up the east bank of the river for 2km then a track, forking left to the keeper's cottage at Kernsary. In a further 500m, take a right fork to enter the forest, where the track deteriorates (**6km; 80m; 1h 25min**). Times are on foot. If a bike is used it is best left here (35min).

Continue on the track for 1.5km, then follow a path to exit the forest at NG910789. Not all maps show this path, which in a further 3km runs past Loch an Doire Crionaich. The scenery is fabulous, particularly the craggy north face of Beinn Àirigh Charr above. Continue to Srathan Buidhe and take the path that cuts across the burn; there is a bridge 500m upstream if the water is high.

Leave the path to gain Meall Mhèinnidh's prominent north-west ridge and climb this to the top over rough ground, which can give some scrambling on its occasional outcrops (**14.5km; 780m; 4h 30min**).

There is a superb view across the Fionn Loch to Ruadh Stac Mòr and A' Mhaighdean, and south across Loch Maree to Torridon. Return the same way (**29km; 760m; 8h** on foot), (**6h 15min** with a bike).

However, an excellent alternative is to drop roughly and directly into Srathan Buidhe to climb Beinn Àirigh Charr (791m) by its south-east corrie (**17.5km; 1380m; 6h 20min**).

Descend west then south-west to bypass Spidean nan Clach on its south side and pick up a stalkers' path at NG923761, which extends further than the map shows. Join a traverse path at NG911771 and follow this east to cut the corner and regain the approach route, which is followed back to Kernsary and Poolewe (**31km; 1430m; 9h 40min** on foot), (**7h 55min** with a bike).

On foot, it is some 2km shorter to go west down the path to the Ardlair track at NG893768 then cut the loop in the track by a path at NG891776.

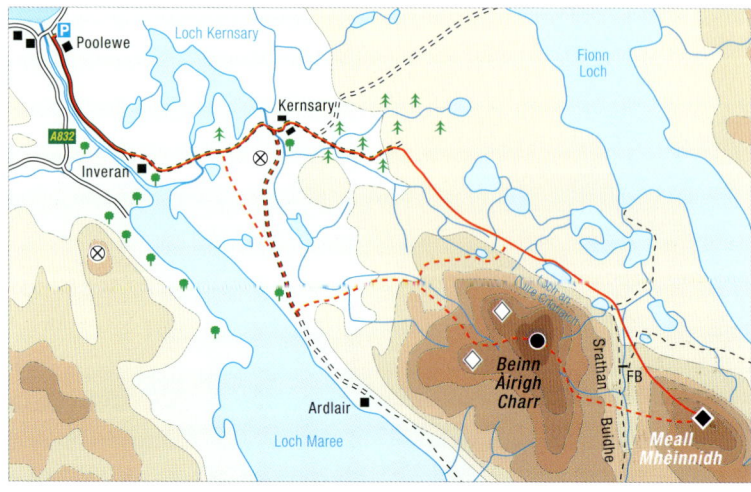

Beinn a' Chàisgein Beag; 682m; (G126); L19; NG966821; possibly big mountain of the tufts from Gaelic 'ceasg', plural 'ceasgan'

A satellite cone of remote Beinn a' Chàisgein Mòr, any ascent of Beinn a' Chàisgein Beag will be earned the hard way. All one day approaches are long and combinations with its neighbours longer still.

Start from the verge of the A832 at NG961911, and follow a track along the west bank of the Gruinard River. A mountain bike is recommended, saving about 1h 45min on the day, although the track is rough. Leave the track at NG993855, at a bridge over the Allt Loch Ghiubhsachain (**7.5km; 90m; 1h** by bike), (**1h 50min** on foot).

Times are now given on foot from and back to this point.

Follow the east bank of the burn and cross it after 1.5km at NG998840. Ascend the steep hillside and traverse southwards to gain a stalkers' path that starts at the foot of an outcrop at NG994833.

Follow this path round to where Beinn a' Chàisgein Beag at last comes into view, and drop down to cross the Uisge Toll a' Mhadaidh. Continue uphill for 1km, past an unlikely chalet off to the left, to reach the col (c505m) below the final slope.

Leave the path and climb northwest over grass and heather to Beinn

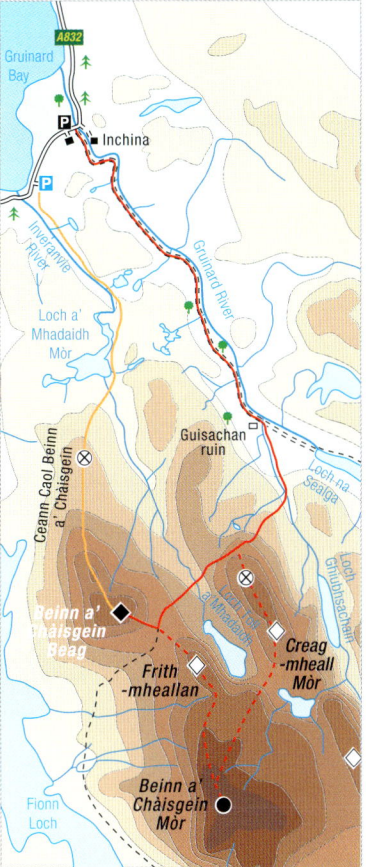

a' Chàisgein Beag's stone trig point; the highest point is some 50m southeast (**6.25km; 650m; 2h 30min**).

The view is superb, particularly out to sea and across the Fionn Loch to Beinn Àirigh Charr and Beinn Làir with Meall Mhèinnidh in-between.

Return to the track the same way (**12.5km; 700m; 4h 10min**).

Return to the start (**27.5km; 850m; 6h** with a bike), (**7h 45min** on foot).

However, it is worth continuing south from the col over easy slopes to Beinn a' Chàisgein Mòr (856m), a Corbett. The easiest return is the same way, but a good return can be made via Creag-mheall Mòr (628m) and the rough ridge enclosing Loch Toll a' Mhadaidh. Descend a grassy depression off the north end of this ridge to gain the eastern end of the stalkers' path used on the ascent; an added 10km, 540m, 3h 30min.

Another approach, on foot, starts from the Gruinard beach car park at NG952899. Take the path on the east side of the Inverianvie River to Loch a' Mhadaidh Mòr. Cross the Uisge Toll a' Mhadaidh to gain Ceann Caol Beinn a' Chàisgein and climb south up the final slopes (**9.5km; 700m; 3h 20min**), (**19km; 720m; 5h 30min**).

Beinn a' Chàisgein Beag from the stalkers' path to the north-east (Rab Anderson)

Beinn Ghobhlach from the north-east, across Loch Kanaird and Ardmair (Rab Anderson)

Beinn Ghobhlach; 635m; (G190); L19; NH055943; *forked mountain*

Beinn Ghobhlach is a distinctive twin-topped hill which sits across the water from Ullapool on a peninsula sandwiched between Loch Broom and Little Loch Broom. Its ascent gives a rewarding and scenic outing. Take the unclassified single track road which branches off to the north of the Corrie Hallie car park before Dundonnell. This crosses the river and leads past Dundonnell House through Strath Beag, climbing to 240m before dropping back down again, to end on the north side of Little Loch Broom at Badrallach. There is parking at the road end about 1km beyond the camp site and bothy; keep the turning circle free. A track continues from here to the remote community of Scoraig.

Follow the Scoraig Path for about 1km, to the end of the fence on the left, then leave it and climb directly up the steep south-facing hillside without any real feature to aim for; stiff but mercifully short, although height and views are gained quickly. Emerge onto a ridge just east of point 338m with the fine sight of Beinn Ghobhlach ahead, rising above two lovely lochans. Drop down and cross the isthmus between Loch na Coireag and Loch na h-Uidhe then climb the increasingly rocky sandstone slope beyond onto the summit shoulder where a final steep section gains the top (**3.5km; 660m; 2h**).

There are fine panoramic views, especially to Ben More Coigach to the north, Ben Dearg and the Inverlael Hills to the south-east, then Sàil Mhòr and An Teallach to the south.

Rather than return the same way (**7km; 730m; 3h 15min**), swing around the head of the west facing Coire Dearg and walk out to the north-west top above an impressive drop north down Coire nan Cnaimhean to Annat Bay. There is a distinct island feel out here and the view now extends over the end of the peninsula to a sea studded with islands. These are the lovely Summer Isles, through which the Ullapool to Stornoway ferry can often be seen threading a route on its way to the Isle of Lewis, visible to the west together with the hills of Harris.

Continue west a short way to the end of the ridge. The initial descent from here must be made in a slight south-easterly direction, heading towards the inner coire of Coire Dearg and the summit of Beinn Ghobhlach. Attempting to head west, or north-west, or north will end up in dangerous ground. Drop steeply down for about 100m or so then swing round and descend south-west, with

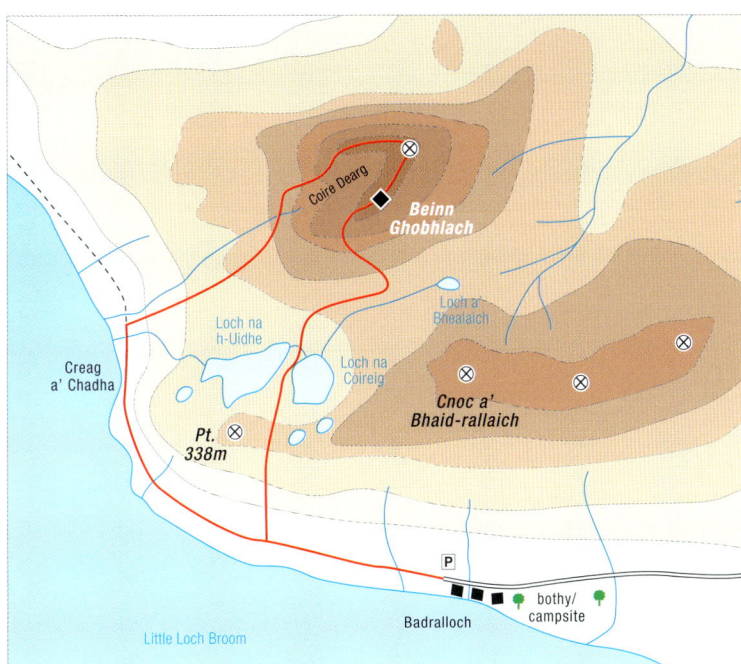

the angle gradually easing, to pick up the burn draining from the corrie. This is the Allt an Uisge Mhaith and is descended all the way to the Scoraig Path 30m above the sea. Follow this fine path which rises above Creag a' Chahda and leads around the point back to the start (**9.5km; 730m; 3h 45min**).

Another alternative is to take in Cnoc a' Bhaid-rallaich, the Sub 2000ft Marilyn to the south-east.

Loch na Coireag and Loch na h-Uidhe below the summit of Beinn Ghobhlach (Jim Teesdale)

*Càrn a' Choin Deirg from the South Top
Suilven and Canisp left
Conival and Ben More Assynt right
(Rab Anderson)*

SECTION 15
Loch Broom to the Cromarty Firth

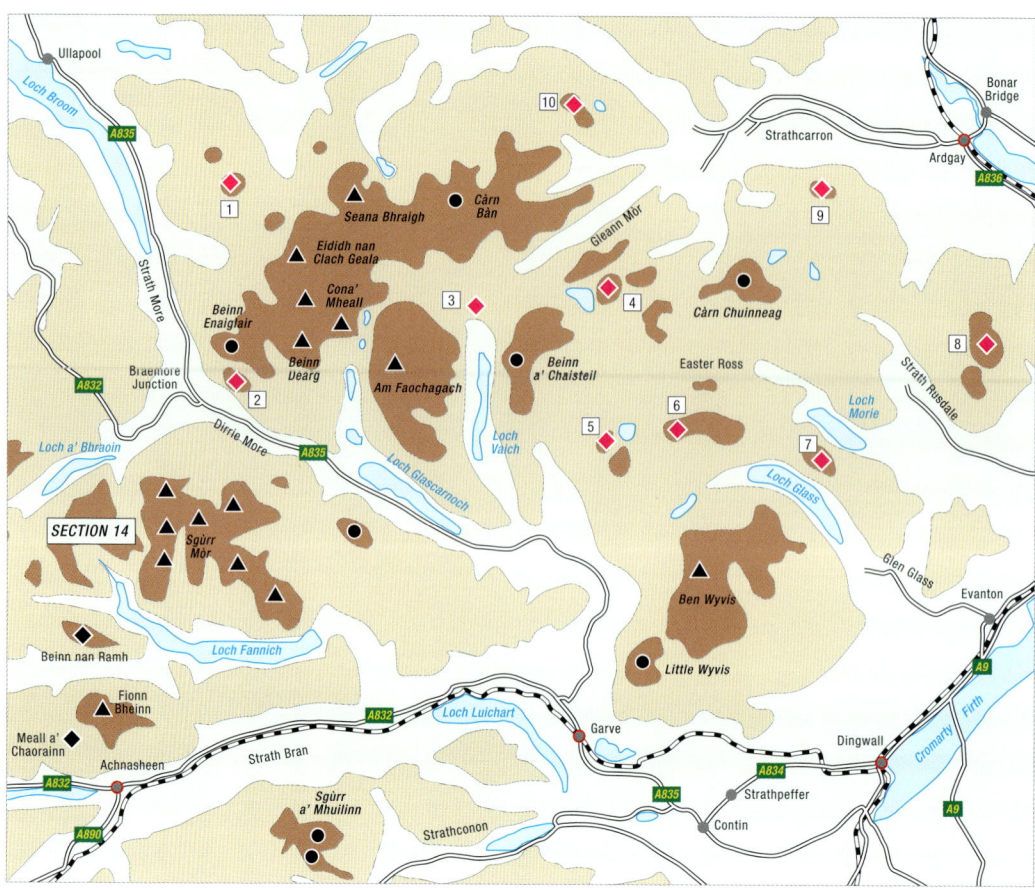

SECTION 15

[1] *Beinn Bhreac* — 285
[2] *Meall Doire Fàid* — 286
[3] *Meall a' Chaorainn*, [4] *Beinn Tharsuinn (Strath Vaich)* — 287
[5] *Càrn Loch nan Amhaichean*, [6] *Beinn nan Eun* — 288
[7] *Meall Mòr* — 290
[8] *Beinn Tharsuinn (Strath Rory)* — 291
[9] *Càrn Salachaidh* — 292
[10] *Càrn a' Choin Deirg* — 293

Beinn Bhreac 285

Beinn Bhreac; 667m; (G148); L20; NH225886; *speckled mountain*

Together with its tops, Meall Dubh to the north-west and Càrn Mòr to the south-east, Beinn Bhreac occupies a tract of high ground above Inverlael, between the Beinn Dearg hills and Ullapool. It is a retiring and difficult to discern summit, a great rounded featureless lump, which until recently was not named on any maps.

However, from its summit there is a quite magnificent panorama of some of the finest hills in Scotland. Clockwise from Ben More Assynt to the north, this encompasses, Ben Loyal, Ben Hope, Seana Bhraigh, the Beinn Dearg group, The Fannaichs, the Fisherfield mountains, An Teallach, Beinn Ghoblach, Ben More Coigach, Stac Pollaidh, Cùl Beag, Cùl Mòr, Suilven, and Canisp. So, despite it's dull-looking features, it is a hill certainly worth saving for a good day.

There are two approaches, both from the shores of Loch Broom. The principal route starts from the walkers' car park at Inverlael (NH182853) and follows the track east into Inverlael Forest. Shortly after going through a gate into the forest, break off left and take a track over a bridge, crossing the twin ravines of the River Lael, then go

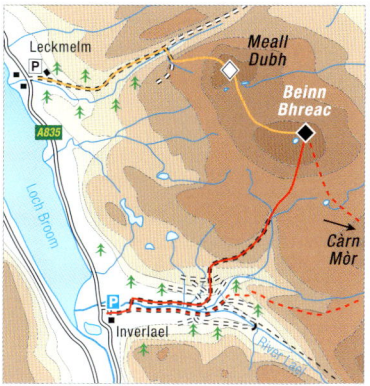

right on the main track running up the glen beside the river. After about 1km, pass a path off right to a bridge over the river and a track off left, staying with the main track as it swings round uphill above the ruins of Glensquaib.

Just above a cleared area, go left onto an overgrown track where a hidden track is revealed ahead. This hidden track zigzags steeply up through younger trees to emerge on the upper forest track. Climb the steep track opposite and leave the forest by a walkers' gate to the side of the vehicle gate.

Follow the track up and right across the hillside to where it eases above a steep drop into the Allt Badan Seasgach and the rounded summit of Beinn Bhreac comes into view. Where the track ends in boggy flat ground, cross a burn then continue on an atv track for 200m or so and break off left on an indistinct path, which soon fades. Climb the hillside onto the flat summit area, occupied by a small lochan. The top is on a small rise just to the north-east (**7km; 660m; 2h 40min**).

Return the same way (**14km; 660m; 4h 20min**).

Alternatively, drop off south-east to cross the Allt na Lairige, following an atv track across grassier ground, and climb to Càrn Mòr (649m). Descend south-west to join the Seana Bhraigh path and follow this pleasantly back with the fine sight of An Teallach ahead (**18km; 830m; 5h 30min**).

Another route starts from Leckmelm at NH171901, gained by turning north off the A835 at the sign for Leckmelm and parking just beyond some cottages. Ascend a track (shown as a path on some maps) steeply uphill through the forest above the Allt Raon a' Chroisg, swinging up left to emerge from the forest through a gate.

Continue past a shed then through some forestry into Srath Nimhe. At NH193903, break off right across the burn and follow a track up the other side to a bend in front of a small gully come waterslide. Ascend the slope up the left side of this and continue up the hillside to go through a decrepit deer fence. Meall Dubh, the north-west top, is gained via an obvious weakness on its north side; the 646m highpoint is 500m away at NH214900.

Beinn Bhreac itself lies some 2km to the south-east and is gained by initially heading south between two small lochans. The intervening ground is perhaps easier crossed slightly to the left, away from some fence posts, where traces of an atv track lead towards the summit (**7km; 670m; 2h 40min**). Return almost the same way (**13.5km; 670m; 4h 20min**).

Beinn Bhreac, with the snowy Beinn Dearg hills behind (Rab Anderson)

Meall Doire Fàid

Meall Doire Fàid and An Teallach (Meryl Marshall)

Meall Doire Fàid; 729m; (G51); L20; NH220792; hill of the prophet's grove

Lying above Braemore Junction at the head of Loch Broom, Meall Doire Fàid is a satellite of the Corbett Beinn Enaiglair, which can easily be included by extending either of the two suggested routes.

Both hills offer fine views to the south and to the west, where An Teallach looks magnificent and on a good day the Outer Hebrides can be seen.

The circuit of Coire Leacachain, to the east of the hill, offers a good high-level walk, maintaining a height of 600m for at least 7km and utilising stalkers' paths for half of that. Park in a layby 2km east of Braemore Junction, at NH229765. Cross the road and ascend the broad south-east ridge ahead, passing over Meall nan Doireachan (713m) to reach Meall Doire Fàid (**3.5km; 620m; 1h 50min**).

The north side drops steeply from the summit cairn and care is needed, particularly in poor visibility, when the onward descent is made to the Bealach nam Bùthan. To make this descent, go east for 200m and find easier ground, then turn west and bypass the steep craggy terrain immediately above the bealach on its west side.

From the bealach, a good stalkers' path is followed eastward for 1.5km to a junction of paths at NH238796 and then south-east for a further 2km along a broad ridge to Meallan Mhurchaidh (625m).

Beinn Enaiglair's summit lies directly above the Bealach nam Bùthan and can be quickly climbed from there, descending the south-east ridge to the junction of paths. An added 1.25km, 280m, 50min.

From Meallan Mhurchaidh, the most direct route to the starting point heads south-west down the Allt Leacachain, although the circuit continues onto Meall Leacachain (621m) then descends to the road at the start (**11km; 820m; 4h 10min**).

A longer and more pleasant route descends the stalkers' path south-east to Loch Droma, after which the line of the old road which runs parallel and to the north of the A835 can be followed back to the starting point (**13.5km; 710m; 4h 20min**).

Meall Doire Fàid can also be climbed from Braemore Junction where a path, marked by posts, climbs the hillside to the east of the forest plantation. The path passes to the east of Home Loch before joining a stalkers' path up the Allt a' Chumhainn. Leave this path at the 500m contour and go south-east to ascend the broad gully below the craggy north face of Meall Doire Fàid. This face does not ease off until east of the summit, from where it is an easy climb westwards (**4.5km; 540m; 1h 55min**).

Returning the same way is perhaps preferable to the direct thrash down the south-west slope (**9km; 540m; 3h**).

Again, Beinn Enaiglair can be included, although from its summit it is better to descend the north-west ridge to a stalkers' path then traverse round the hill to join the upward route at NH208797. An added 4km, 340m, 1h 25min. There are some newer tracks on this side of the hill.

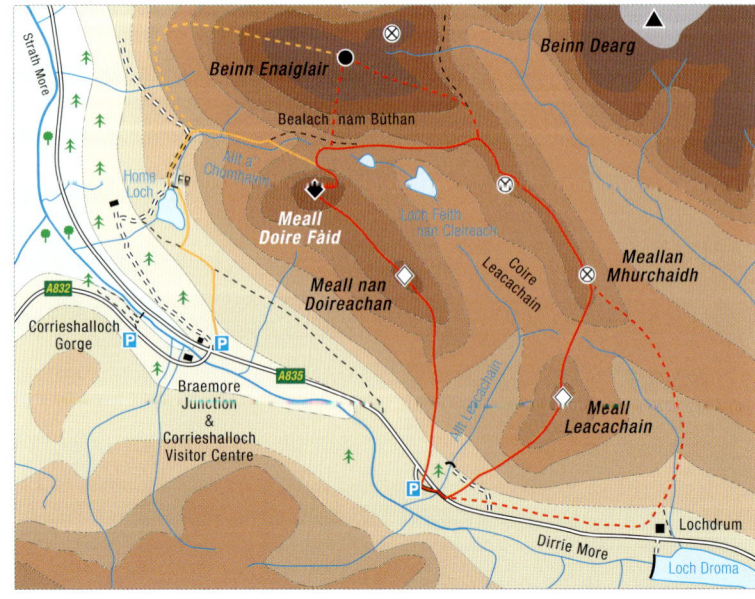

Meall a' Chaorainn, Beinn Tharsuinn (Strath Vaich)

Meall a' Chaorainn from the track to Loch Vaich (Rab Anderson)

Meall a' Chaorainn; 632m; (G193); L20; NH360827; hill of the rowan tree
Beinn Tharsuinn; 710m; (G80); L20; NH412829; transverse hill

Meall a' Chaorainn is a small hill, the northernmost summit of the crescent-shaped range of great rounded hills curving around Loch Vaich, with the Munro, Am Faochagach forming the highest peak. Beinn Tharsuinn sits tucked away on the opposite side of Strath Vaich, some 5km to the east of Meall a' Chaorainn and is the higher of the pair.

These are remote hills. Fortunately a private road then track cross 28km through the wilds from Black Bridge on the A835 Garve to Ullapool road, to the public road in Strathcarron, inland from Ardgay. This gives access to the hills from west or east and since it passes between them, it means they can conveniently be climbed as a pair, especially with the help of a mountain bike. Both ways in are almost equidistant, although it is the Black Bridge approach that is favoured. Any approach on foot is likely to entail an overnight stay.

There is ample parking at Black Bridge at the start of the road up Strath Vaich. After 3.5km, take the rougher track up the glen where the tarred road crosses the river towards Strathvaich Lodge and the hydro dam. After crossing a bridge over a burn the track passes a track off right then swings left and climbs to a highpoint where Meall a' Chaorainn comes into view. The track then drops down to pass through some gated fenced areas along the western shore of Loch Vaich. A long and gradual climb leads to the south-east shoulder of Meall a' Chaorainn. The highpoint of the track is at the watershed at 369m, where a track branches off right to the burn draining from Crom Loch beneath Beinn Tharsuinn. Bikes are left here (**13.75km; 220m; 1h 40min** by bike), (**3h 20min** on foot).

▶

Beinn Tharsuinn above Crom Loch (Rab Anderson)

Meall a' Chaorainn, Beinn Tharsuinn (Strath Vaich)

Times are now given on foot from and back to this point, although after descending from Meall a' Chaorainn, a track can be biked for another 1km towards Beinn Tharsuinn.

A short and ferociously steep climb north-west through heather gains the summit of Meall a' Chaorainn (**0.6km; 265m; 35min**).

The hill's size and location mean the views are somewhat truncated; Beinn Tharsuinn is a better viewpoint.

Return to the foot of the slope then climb Beinn Tharsuinn by following the track which goes east then north, traversing the hillside to a small hydro dam at NH373831; the end of the road for wheels. Follow the north side of the burn, upstream to Crom Loch, skirting the loch to the north by rough going to gain easy slopes leading to the top (**6.5km; 620m; 2h 40min**).

Return the same way to the track junction (**11.75km; 630m; 4h**).

With a bike nearby the Corbett Beinn a' Chaisteil might tempt some; an added 4.75km, 270m, 1h 40min.

Make the long return down Strath Vaich (**39.25km; 910m; 7h** with a bike), (**10h 30min** on foot).

The same point between these hills can be gained from Ardgay to the east, by following the road signposted to Croick, then turning left to pass Amat Lodge to reach the road end at Glencalvie Lodge; there is parking at the junction.

Follow the estate track west along the river towards Alladale Lodge. After 2.5km, just before the lodge, take the track on the left across the bridge over the river and continue up Gleann Mòr to join the Strath Vaich track just beyond Deanich Lodge, at the junction with Gleann Beag. The same approach and ascent times apply.

Càrn Loch nan Amhaichean; 697m; (G109); L20; NH411757; hill of the loch of the necks (isthmuses)

Beinn nan Eun; 743m; (G24); L20; NH448759; mountain of the birds

These hills share a remote location with fine views and can be climbed together, especially with the help of a bike. The best approach is from the A835 Garve to Ullapool road where a track leaves the road about 100m to the west of the Inchbae Lodge Hotel. There is parking 100m further west, just over the bridge, and it appears acceptable to drive up the track for 200m and park by a log stack.

Follow the river north up Strath Rannoch through forestry plantations then open moorland. Just beyond Strathrannoch Farm, leave the track at a sharp bend (NH387746) at the corner of a small plantation (**6km; 130m; 45min by bike**), (**1h 30min on foot**). Times are now given on foot from and back to this point.

A short section of track then a faint path lead up the north-west side of the Allt a' Choire-rainich, through an attractive rocky defile. Upstream of

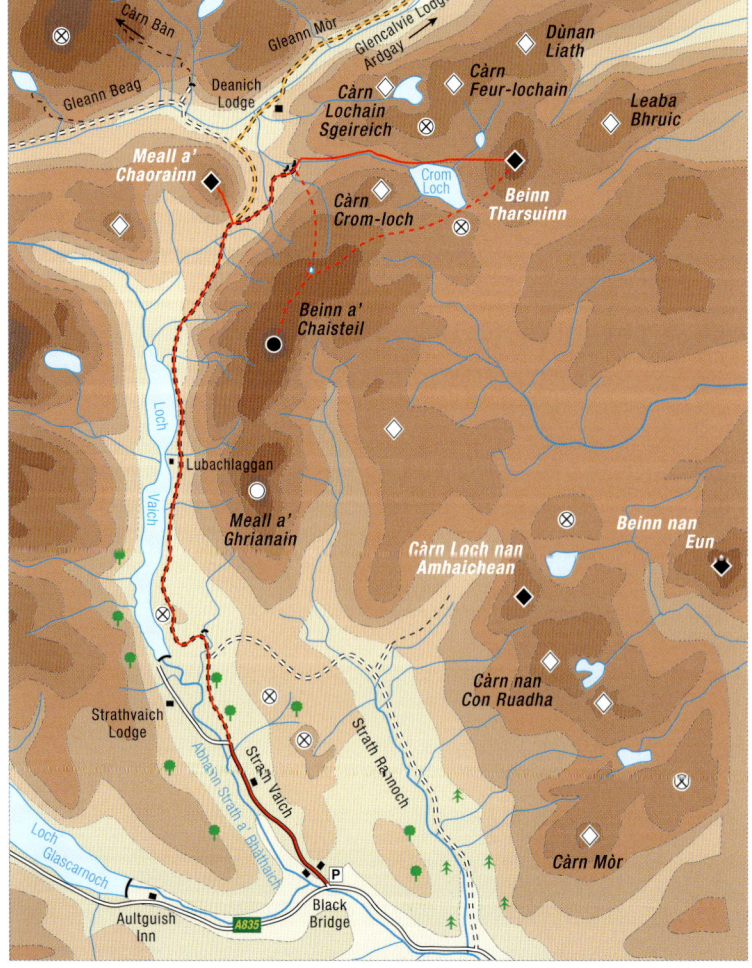

Càrn Loch nan Amhaichean, Beinn nan Eun

Beinn nan Eun across Loch nan Amhaichean (Rab Anderson)

upstream on a track along the south-west shore of Loch Glass to Wyvis Lodge where a hydro track continues 4km up the glen to an attractive waterfall (**12.5km; 150m; 1h 20min** by bike), (**3h** on foot). Times are now given on foot from and back to here.

Depending on the state of the Abhainn Beinn nan Eun, either cross early and climb the south-east slopes to the summit of Beinn nan Eun (**2km; 420m; 1h 10min**), or follow the stalkers' path upstream to join the previous route up the western spur.

From the summit, head west round the north side of the loch to climb Càrn Loch nan Amhaichean by its north ridge (**6.5km; 650m; 2h 40min**).

Either return past the loch to gain the upper Abhainn Beinn nan Eun and then the path, or descend the south ridge then cut across east and descend a burn to the path leading back to the waterfall (**11.5km; 650m; 3h 50min**).

Return along Loch Glass (36.5km; 820m; 6h 30min with a bike), (9h 35min on foot).

this, cross the burn by boulder hopping then climb the heathery hillside in a north-easterly direction, heading for a distinctive huge boulder on the skyline. The summit of Càrn Loch nan Amhaichean lies just beyond, with fine views of the neighbouring Easter Ross summits (**3km; 410m; 1h 20min**).

To continue to Beinn nan Eun, descend the north ridge, almost to a tiny lochan, then drop to the north shore of Loch nan Amhaichean and follow its eastern outflow for 1km until it joins the Abhainn Beinn nan Eun. On the other side, the easy western spur leads to the summit (**7.5km; 680m; 3h**).

The view is more extensive; from Morven and the Caithness hills some 76km to the north-east, around to Strath Spey's Ben Rinnes 90km to the south-east.

Return west and climb towards the tiny lochan at the foot of the north ridge of Càrn Loch nan Amhaichean. From there, drop into Coire Rhainich and descend the path beside the Allt a' Choire-rainich back to Strathrannoch (**14.5km; 750m; 4h 45min**).

Return along Strath Rannoch (26.5km; 880m; 5h 55min with a bike), (7h 35min on foot).

These hills can also be approached from the east by bike. The public road from Evanton climbs up Glen Glass as far as the bridge at Eileanach Lodge where there is parking. Continue

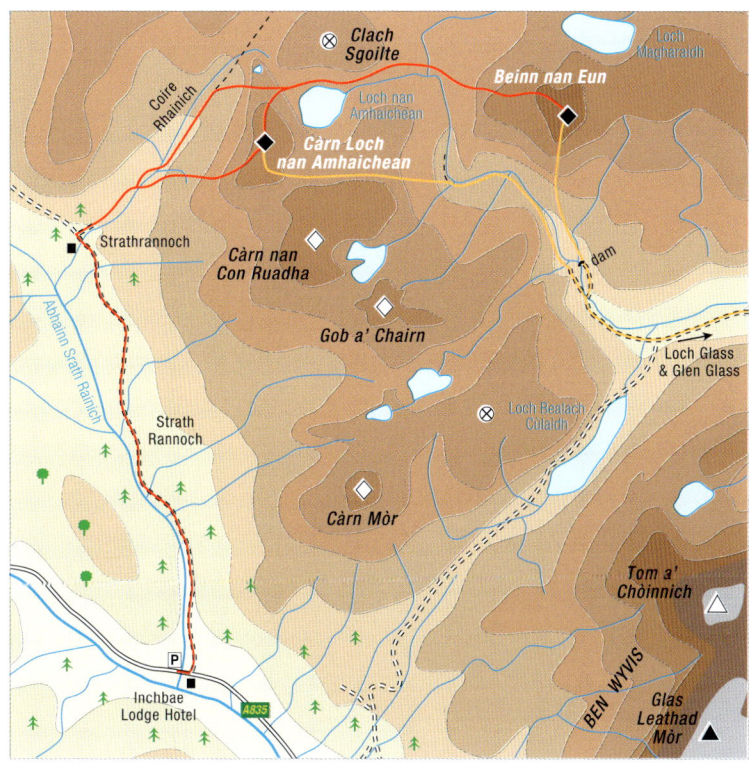

Meall Mòr

Meall Mòr; 738m; (G34); L20; NH515745; big hill

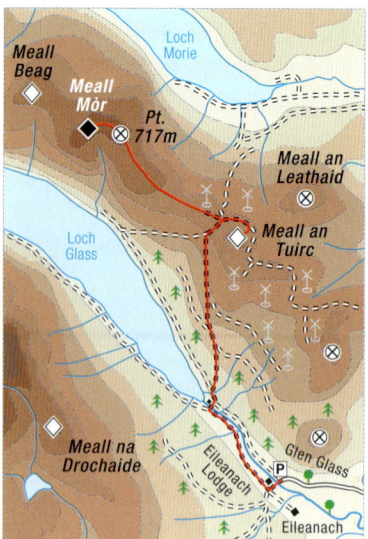

Meall Mòr's steep southern flanks present an impressive profile above the northern shore of Loch Glass. By way of contrast its summit ridge is open, grassy and rounded, making it prime wind turbine country. Not surprisingly perhaps, the lower top of Meall an Tuirc is populated by an extensive turbine development; the Novar Wind Farm.

Leave the B817 just north of Evanton and follow the minor road up Glen Glass to park short of the white iron gates and bridge over the River Glass, leading to Eileanach. Go over the bridge, past Eileanach Lodge and turn right onto a track leading north-west through forestry alongside the River Glass. At NH536701, turn right onto a short section of track leading to a deer fence and rickety stile and a concrete bridge over the River Glass.

Meall Mòr is now clearly visible to the north-west. Cross the bridge and continue past a white building to a track junction. Turn left here and carry on to another track junction, where a grassy track on the right is ascended through conifers. Keep left at the next junction, then right at the next, beyond which the upper level of the forestry has been felled, revealing the wind turbines on the flanks of Meall an Tuirc above.

Exit the forest and descend slightly to join another track coming up from Loch Glass and follow that up right to a four-way junction on the western side of Meall an Tuirc, above the col with Meall Mòr. Turn right and ascend the turbine access track then a short section of hillside to the rounded top of Meall an Tuirc (**6km; 420m; 2h**).

Return to the four-way junction and continue down past the turbines to the col. Pick your way through the peat hags to gain the broad south-east ridge of Meall Mòr and go over rounded Pt.717m to meet a ramshackle fence which is followed north-west then south-south west to the trig point on the summit (**9.5km; 600m; 3h 5min**).

The whale-backed mass of the Graham Beinn Tharsuinn can be seen across Loch Morie to the north-east and the rocky top of Càrn Salachaidh due north, beyond and right of the distinctive twin tops of the Corbett Càrn Chuinneag. However, all rather pale beside the massive presence of Ben Wyvis's Glas Leathad Beag, Tom a' Chòinnich and Glas Leathad Mòr to the south across Loch Glass.

Return by the same route (**18km; 650m; 5h 15min**).

The track on the west side of the loch provides an alternate route to Beinn nan Eun and Càrn Loch nan Amhaichean (see p289).

Meall Mòr from the southern end of Loch Glass (Tom Prentice)

Beinn Tharsuinn (Strath Rory)

Tòrr Leathann, left, and Beinn Tharsuinn from the approach up Strath Rory (Rab Anderson)

Beinn Tharsuinn; 692m; (G112); L21; NH606792; *transverse hill*

Beinn Tharsuinn is the culmination of a mass of rounded, largely grassy hills lying between the Dornoch and Cromarty Firths. It affords a fine bird's-eye view of the two firths and their associated features. The top is a broad plateau of undulating terrain where the only other breaks in this otherwise featureless countryside are the high windfarms that occupy the slopes either side of Sìthean a' Choin Bhàin to the north.

The most pleasant ascent starts at a bridge (NH660777) over the Strathrory River on the B9176, the old A9 Struie Hill road, where there is a large car park. Head north-west on a good track which ends at a quarry after 4km. Climb the broad north-east ridge leading to the Graham Top of Tòrr Leathann (637m); initially following a line of old turf shooting butts. It is reasonably easy going but marshy and tussocky in places.

Beinn Tharsuinn lies 1km to the north-west and is gained after a short descent to a col then a reascent over peat hags to reach the trig point (**7km; 570m; 2h 30min**).

Four of the other Grahams in this section are identifiable, from Càrn Salachaidh to the north-west, with the distinctive double-breasted Corbett Càrn Chuinneag between it and the other Beinn Tharsuinn, then Beinn nan Eun and closer to the south-east Meall Mòr with Ben Wyvis behind it.

Descend the eastern slopes to cross the burn coming down from the col and regain the approach track just below the quarry then follow this back (**13.75km; 570m; 4h 5min**).

Sìthean a' Choin Bhàin (689m), the Graham Top to the north-west, can be included across featureless haggy ground. From there, descend south-east by the burn; an added 2km, 30m, 30min.

An alternative starting point is Baldoon on the south-east side of the hill where a peat road can be followed for 2.5km to the foot of the hill. The slopes on this side give heavy going with tussocky grass and heather, so it is probably better to follow an old stalkers' path. This contours the base of the hill to the quarry where the previous route is joined.

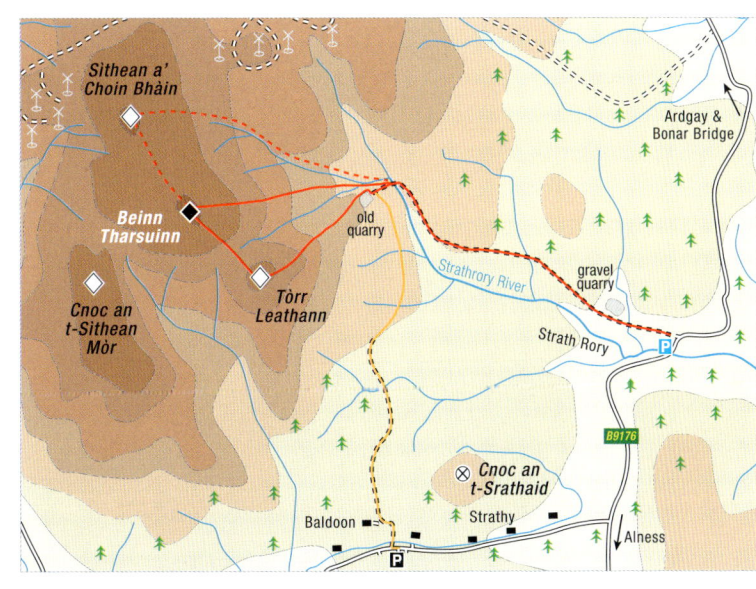

Càrn Salachaidh

The rocky summit of Càrn Salachaidh, centre, viewed from Croick (Rab Anderson)

Càrn Salachaidh; 647m; (G176); L20; NH518874; filth mountain

Viewed from Ardgay and Lower Gledfield on the northern approach up Strathcarron, Càrn Salachaidh's pointed double summit presents a distinctive profile. A similar profile can be seen from Croick to the north-west, but from most easily accessed locations, Càrn Salachaidh is obscured by the extensive high moorland which surrounds it.

One approach is on foot from Strathcarron in the north, via 6.5km of track and moorland. Park at NH524921 about 100m west of the entrance to Gruinards Estate, in a passing place on the south side of the road where a track starts. This is opposite a post box and metal pedestrian gate leading to Gruinards Lodge. There is room for passing and about two parked cars. Do not restrict access to the track. Passing places offer the only viable parking for some distance along this road.

From the passing place, follow the track south through woodland to a deer gate giving access to the open hillside. Càrn Salachaidh is now obvious straight ahead. Follow the track round Càrn Mòr to gain the deeply-cut river bed of the Allt a' Ghlinne. Cross over and follow assorted animal paths up the hillside, initially to the right of the Allt Coire Sheilich draining from Càrn a' Bhealaich, then to its left.

Gain the top of Càrn a' Bhealaich (508m) and follow the high ground to reach the broad north ridge of Càrn Salachaidh. Ascend this over granite slabs and boulders aiming south for Pt.633m, the rocky west peak, topped with an impressively perched granite slab and a small cairn.

From here, follow the summit ridge east to the trig point (646m) on Càrn Salachaidh. The 647m highpoint, as shown by the OS 1:25k map, is a large boulder about 50m to the north-east (**6.5km; 620m; 2h 30min**).

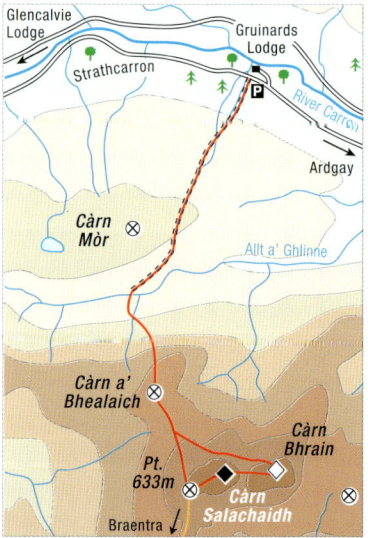

Descend south-east between small granite outcrops to a col and ascend to the east top of Càrn Bhrain (635m). Rather than return over the top of Càrn Salachaidh, it is easy to descend west into the shallow corrie and traverse below the main peak at about the 580m contour to gain the north ridge. From there, Càrn a' Bhealaich and the outward route lead back (**14km; 680m; 4h 30min**).

Another approach can be made up Glen Calvie from Glencalvie Lodge at the west end of Strathcarron; made easier by the use of a bike on the initial 5km of track. This also allows Càrn Chuinneag to be climbed with the link made via Loch Chuinneag.

A useful ascent can also be made from the south, from Braentra at the end of the road up Strath Rusdale at NH567780. A shorter drive from the south. Bike the track north-west to NH506854 beyond Lochan a' Chairn (**10.5km; 220m; 1h 30min** by bike).

A 1km section of track leads north onto Càrn Salachaidh; a return walk of (**5.5km; 240m; 1h 45min**).

The Corbett Càrn Chuinneag to the south-west is easily included; accessed via a stile, bridge, atv track and path, with the link via Loch Chuinneag. An added return walk of (**9km; 500m; 3h**). Return to Braentra (**35.5km; 960m; 7h 10min** with a bike).

Càrn a' Choin Deirg

Càrn a' Choin Deirg; 701m; (G102); L20; NH397923; hill of the red dogs

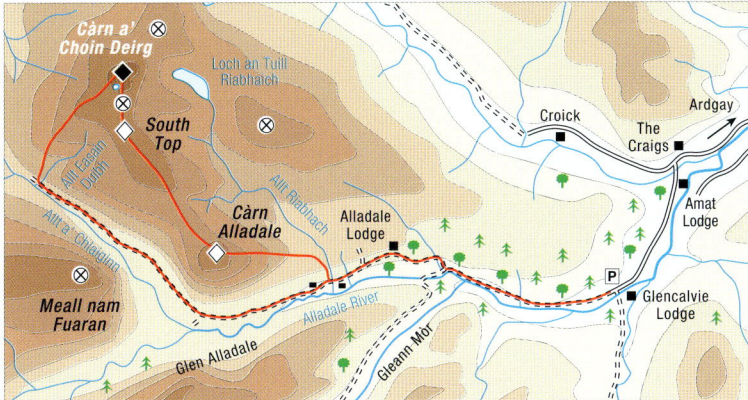

Càrn a' Choin Deirg is the most easterly summit of the range of hills known as the Freevater Forest and is situated inland to the west of Ardgay at the head of the Dornoch Firth. The summit sits at the north end of a curving undulating ridge some 3km in length and gives good views of the Sutherland hills to the north and Seana Bhraigh to the west.

The best approach is past Alladale Lodge to the south-east. This route affords some dramatic scenery with fine stands of Scots pine trees and good examples of U-shaped valleys.

The Alladale Estate is creating a wilderness reserve with plans to introduce European elk, wolves, lynx and bears, initially in a 500 acre enclosure situated on the spur of wooded hillside south of the described route.

From Ardgay, take the turn signed to Croick, along the north side of the River Carron. Turn left at the telephone box before Croick and pass Amat Lodge to reach the road end at the Glencalvie Lodge junction (NH464892) where there is parking.

Glen Calvie was subjected to an infamous clearance of its people in 1844 and an account in The Times brought this to the nation's attention and caused a considerable stir.

From the junction, go west on the estate road into Glen Alladale for 4km, passing the track off left to Gleann Mòr then on the right Alladale Lodge. Just past the first of the holiday lodges, cross the Allt Riabhach at NH426895 (a bike can be useful for this section) then strike up the hill on a rough atv track. This passes through natural planting then easy grass and heather to gain the summit of Càrn Alladale (635m).

Descend north-west and cross a fence (gate to the right) then traverse the broad ridge of Càrn a' Choin Deirg for 3km over several intervening tops. In the dip before the final rise to the trig point there is a small lochan (**9km; 720m; 3h 10min**).

The return to Glen Alladale can be made by the Allt a' Chlaiginn to the south-west. Descend to the small lochan then contour onto the spur of Leathad nan Con Dearga and drop down easy slopes on the west side of the Allt Easain Duibh with its waterfall. Gain an estate track and return to Glen Alladale around the base of Càrn Alladale (**20km; 720m; 5h 50min**).

Càrn a' Choin Deirg from the ascent to Càrn Alladale (Rab Anderson)

Sgùrr an Fhidhleir and Beinn an Eòin (Jamie Hageman)

SECTION 16
Loch Broom to the Pentland Firth

Section 16 – Loch Broom to the Pentland Firth

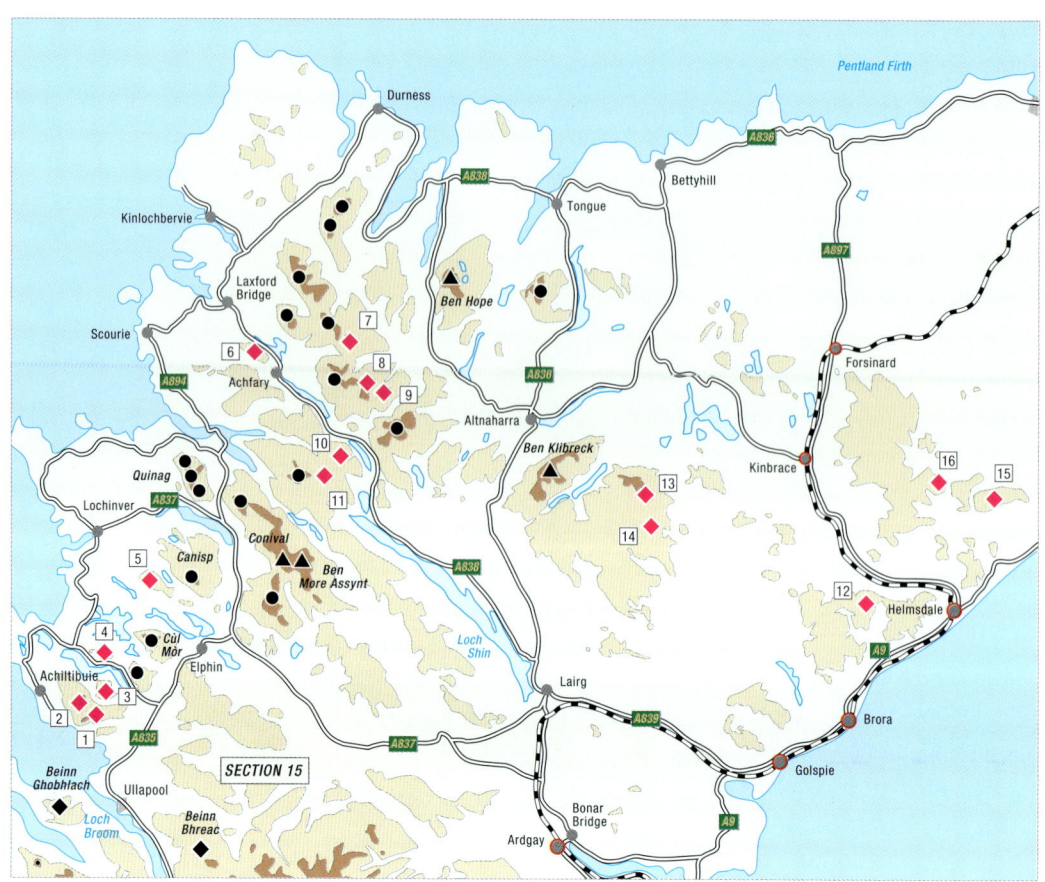

SECTION 16

[1] *Ben More Coigach*, [2] *Sgùrr an Fhìdhleir*	297
[3] *Beinn an Eòin*	300
[4] *Stac Pollaidh*	301
SUILVEN [5] *Caisteal Liath*	303
[6] *Ben Stack*	305
[7] *Sàbhal Beag*	306
[8] *Càrn an Tionail*, [9] *Beinn Direach*	307
[10] *Meall an Fheur Loch*, [11] *Meallan a' Chuail*	309
[12] *Beinn Dhorain*	311
BEN ARMINE [13] *Creag a' Choire Ghlais*, [14] *Creag Mhòr*	312
[15] *Scaraben*	314
[16] *Morven*	315

Ben More Coigach, Sgùrr an Fhìdhleir

Ben More Coigach and Sgùrr an Fhìdhleir, far left, from Speicein nan Garbh-choireachan (Noel Williams)

Ben More Coigach; *743m; (G22); L15; NC093042; big mountain of the Coigach district*
Sgùrr an Fhìdhleir; *705m; (G93); L15; NC094054; peak of the fiddler*

Ben More Coigach's unmistakable profile dominates the landscape on the road north from Ullapool. Looking like the vast hull of an upturned boat, it presents a long, forbidding buttressed wall beneath a high-level ridge. However, this conceals the fact that there are two Grahams here, which are part of a complex massif of seven separate summits, all over 500m in height. The views to mountain and sea, and the terrain, at times like a lunar landscape, are quite magnificent.

There are two principal approaches for climbing both Grahams, each with its own merits. A series of wild north-east facing corries containing the impressive rock prow of Sgùrr an Fhìdhleir makes an approach from that direction an attractive option.

However, it is perhaps better to drive the extra distance around the massif to the road end near Culnacraig where the full length of Ben More Coigach's ridge can be combined into a fabulous round of all seven summits. There is a parking area at NC062041, at the highpoint of the road before it turns the corner to run downhill to the road end; there is verge parking here also.

Walk towards the road end and on the other side of the bridge follow a path straight up the steep hillside. Where the angle eases at NC071042, break off the main path, which continues up the centre of the spur towards Sgùrr an Fhìdhleir, and traverse rightwards on a vague path above the steeper slopes, heading towards the end of the ridge ahead.

Drop down and cross the upper part of the Allt nan Coisiche ravine then continue to the foot of Garbh Choireachan. Although somewhat intimidating, with care, the ridge provides a relatively straightforward route. Once up, the path leads along a superb knife-edged ridge over Speicein nan Garbh-choireachan (738m) to reach the summit of Ben More Coigach, which is set back from the edge of the steep southern slopes on a promontory (**4.5km; 690m; 2h 10min**).

Regain the edge to complete the traverse, then detour south-east and drop down to ascend the fine conical peak of Speicein Còinnich (717m), which marks the end of the ridge. Return north-west and descend to the foot of Sgùrr an Fhìdhleir. Climb the slope and walk out to the summit of the Fhìdhleir, which is in an exposed position, perched on the point with dizzy drops on two sides (**8.5km; 930m; 3h 15min**).

Descend to the col to the north-west by heading south-west for 500m or so before swinging round north. The flat top of Pt.648m is easily gained and offers more fine views. Now head south-west to take in Beinn nan Caorach (649m) before descending west-north-west to climb Cairn Conmheall (541m), the final summit (**12.5km; 1170m; 4h 40min**).

There is steep rock at the western termination, so return towards the col then descend steeply to the side of ▶

Ben More Coigach, left, and Speicein nan Garbh-choireachan (Rab Anderson)

the Allt Tarsuinn to reach the road (**14.5km; 1170m; 5h 20min**).

The easiest and quickest way of climbing both Grahams is to start as for the above route but stay on the initial path which climbs to Sgùrr an Fhìdhleir. Drop off this and climb Ben More Coigach then return to the approach path to descend. This is quick and easy, but an inferior route.

The other favoured route starts as for Beinn an Eòin, (see p300 for details of parking and the initial approach). The path up the left side of the Allt Claonaidh leads through a gate in a deer fence to reach lovely Lochan Tuath where the mighty prow of Sgùrr an Fhìdhleir rears up ahead. Go round the south side of the lochan and continue up into the corrie to climb up the side of the burn beneath the peak. Towards the top, pass a stone gateway to emerge onto the shoulder and climb to the top of the Fhìdhleir (**5.5km; 650m; 2h 20min**).

It is possible to take in some of the peaks to the north and west, but this involves some back tracking. Otherwise, return to the head of the corrie then continue over onto Ben More Coigach (**8.5km; 840m; 3h 20min**).

The ridge is easily traversed, but again involves back tracking.

On the return, the fine conical peak of Speicein Còinnich is worth climbing, with a descent made back to the col at its base. From there, rather than return via the approach route down the corrie by the Fhìdhleir, descend a steep grassy slope north-east to go through a deer fence and climb onto Beinn Tarsuinn. Drop off this avoiding any craggy sections (the eastern termination is rockier than the map suggests) to rejoin the path alongside the Allt Claonaidh and follow this back (**14.5km; 970m; 5h**).

Although Beinn an Eòin gives a nice round on its own (see p300), it can be included with this round from Loch Lurgainn. If climbed on the way in, then it is best to return south-east from the summit for some way before descending to regain the path at the eastern end of Lochan Tuath. The steep ground directly above the loch is awkward to descend. If it is climbed on the way back then a number of ascent lines are possible, but will always be easier further east.

Speicein nan Garbh-choireachan left and Ben More Coigach right across Loch Kanaird from Ardmair (Rab Anderson)

Ben More Coigach, Sgùrr an Fhìdhleir 299

The impressive rock prow of Sgùrr an Fhìdhleir above Lochan Tuath (Jim Teesdale)

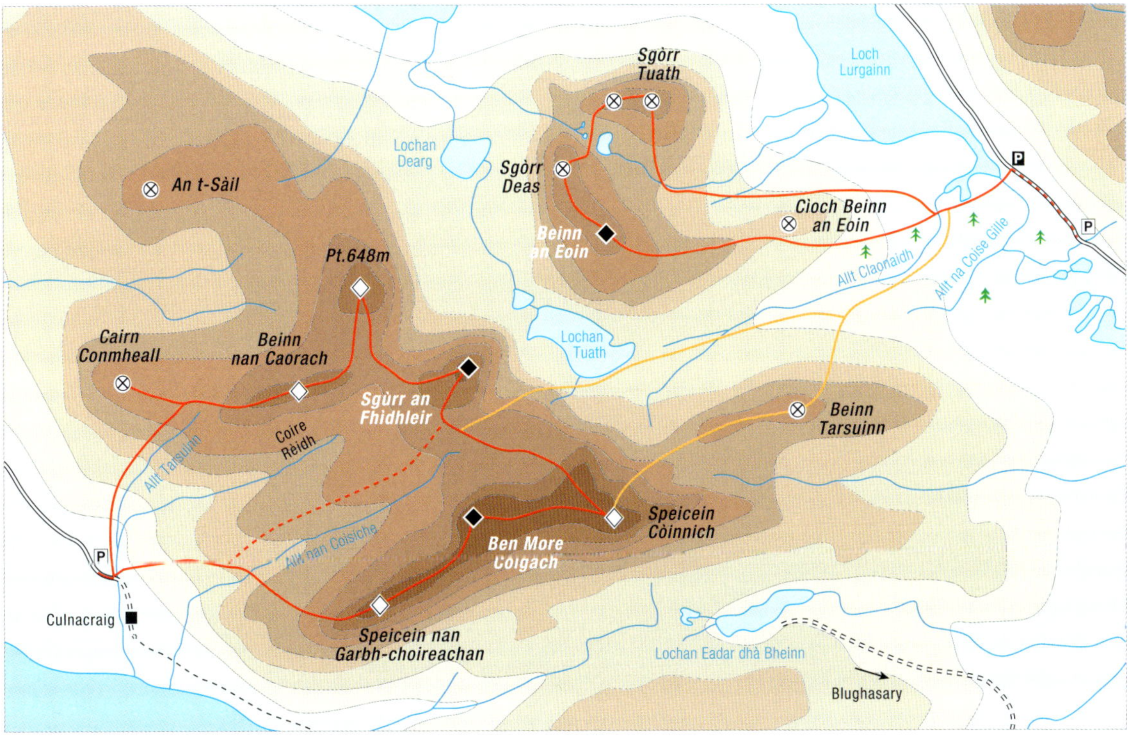

Beinn an Eòin

Beinn an Eòin; *619m; (G206); L15; NC104064; mountain of the bird*

This small but distinctive twin-peaked hill sits opposite Cùl Beag and Stac Pollaidh overlooking Loch Lurgainn. It is cradled by bigger Ben More Coigach and Sgùrr an Fhìdhleir behind, and a link with these is possible for a three Graham tick (see p298). However, this would miss out on what is a great little horseshoe walk taking in the northern top of Sgòr Tuath. It would also miss out on the best round of Ben More Coigach and Sgùrr an Fhìdhleir.

Start from a passing place at the head of Loch Lurgainn (NC139067); it is possible to squeeze a car in off the road here and in nearby passing places. Otherwise, the nearest suitable parking is 1km back up the road, either side of the burn at NC145062.

A path leads to a gate in a deer fence, then stepping stones across the Allt na Coise Gille flowing into Loch Lurgainn. If the river is high there is a bridge on the other side of the deer fence for access to a boat house, but this means that the deer fence then has to be climbed. The path leads to the Allt Claonaidh and an atv track which fords the burn at this point (NC133064). If a crossing is not made here (take footwear and a towel), and the path is followed up into the corrie, then the next easy crossing may not be until further upstream where the burn forks. It is also possible to cross the burn to the north, where the deer fence crosses.

After crossing via the atv track, head uphill to the left of the steep nose of Cìoch Beinn an Eòin to gain the ridge. Due to forestry planting somewhat tedious ground has to be crossed to reach the steeper slopes. The view is dominated by the immense rock prow of Sgùrr an Fhìdhleir. Follow the rounded ridge to the top (**4km; 560m; 1h 50min**).

Drop down northwards between bluffs of eroded sandstone and head out onto a little top. Descend off the southern peak, Sgòrr Deas, towards a lovely lochan nestling in the col, taking care not to stray too far north since there are cliffs at the end of the ridge. Cross over to the west of the lochan then climb steeply onto the northern peak, Sgòrr Tuath, dodging in and around little rock steps and boulders. A lower top is crossed, which has a curious deep fissure splitting it; take care under cover of snow! The slope to the north falls steeply to Loch Lurgainn and the view to Stac Pollaidh, Suilven, Cùl Mòr and Cùl Beag is magnificent. Traverse east past the head of an open gully with some fine pinnacles and climb to the summit (**6km; 720m; 2h 35min**).

The best descent is to head straight down south, towards the lip of the corrie. Stay fairly high to cross the burn then follow its right side aiming for some obvious boulders beneath Cìoch Beinn an Eòin where a shelf traverses around the hillside. Again, planting has made the terrain awkward here. Recross the Allt Claonaidh and return to the road (**10km; 730m; 3h 45min**).

Map on previous page

Beinn an Eòin, Sgòrr Deas and Sgòrr Tuath with Sgùrr an Fhìdhleir, back left, from below Cùl Beag (Rab Anderson)

Stac Pollaidh from the south (Rab Anderson)

Stac Pollaidh; 612m; (G215); L15; NC107106; *steep mountain at the pool*

Stac Pollaidh stands proud, a mountain in miniature, thrusting its weathered and battered Torridonian sandstone rock-ramparts skywards, in defiance to the elements that have worn it down over the millennia. There is a lot of rock on the summit ridge, much of which can be bypassed. However, attaining the summit itself involves some unavoidable exposed scrambling, probably making it the most technically difficult summit on the mainland. Many don't quite make the top, although getting close is good enough and certainly not without its excitement.

Start partway down Loch Lurgainn, from a sizeable car park at the foot of the hill; NC107095. Cross the road and go through a gate in the deer fence and follow a well-engineered footpath up through the trees. When the path splits, take the right branch and go through a gate onto the open hillside to continue up and across the south-eastern shoulder to the back of the hill. The views on this section are dominated by Cùl Beag and beyond this over the head of the loch to Seana Bhraigh and Beinn Dearg. Around the shoulder, Cùl Mòr appears, followed by Canisp and Suilven.

Take the left fork in the path, which slants steeply up towards a fenced enclosure with the odd zigzag to reach the narrow crest of the ridge at the central saddle (**1.5km; 460m; 1h 10min**). The Grahams on the south side now come into view across the loch; Beinn an Eòin, Sgùrr an Fhìdhleir and Ben More Coigach.

The East Top is only a short distance away and from it there is a fine perspective of the tower and pinnacle-bristling ridge ahead.

There is a Far East Top, but the scramble from the East Top down into the notch is quite difficult, especially if wet. A narrow traverse path on the north side leads to this top from the central saddle, avoiding all difficulty and the need for any scrambling. It is much the safer way if one wishes to include the Far East Top.

However, for the scrambler there are two options for the down climb (Grade 3), neither recommended for the inexperienced. From a boulder on the north-east corner, go right and down fairly smooth slabs. Better is to go left behind the boulder and using holds climb down, then step left across to the bottom of the other route to reach the base of the notch. The scramble up the other side and back down is easy.

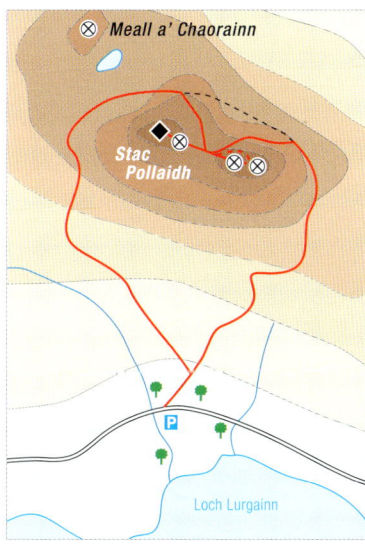

▶

Stac Pollaidh from the flanks of Cul Mòr to the north-east (Tom Prentice)

To continue from the central saddle, walk across to a flat area in front of the first tower, which bars progress along the ridge. The easiest scrambling options on the south side are described, although much can be bypassed on the north side by various traverse lines. Pass the tower on the left side (south) and continue past the first steep gully, then two more open ones.

At the third open gully, which is at the far side of a major gully coming up from below, there are two options. One is to traverse a path left around the edge past some boulders into a wide, loose gully and climb this easily to the crest. The other is to go up the gully to just beneath a steepening with a small jammed boulder and traverse out left on a path, then around the edge past some boulders into the wide loose gully and climb its right side over an easy step to gain the crest.

Either way, the right side of the ridge leads easily upwards past a cairned top to a tower. Here an awkward sidle has to be made across a short rounded slab above a gully – there is a good handhold for this short move. This allows a second cairned top to be reached. This short bit can be avoided by dropping down a gully on the left (south) and then ascending the gully on the other side until a traverse path leads up left onto the crest in front of the second cairned top. Ahead is a large and fine rock wall, above which is the highest point.

To reach the summit, drop to an airy col in front of a tower barring further access. Many get no further than this point; the knowledgeable use of a short rope here could be beneficial. This is perhaps the Grahams' version of the Inaccessible Pinnacle!

The tower can be climbed directly by a few moves graded Difficult. An easier option is to go down left (south) a short way to gain slabby rock and the base of a slanting, flared chimney-groove. An awkward move (squirm) gains a good hold, which enables one to pull up and pass through an easier narrowing to gain the crest behind the tower; take care on the final move back down this way. Remember the moves well for they have to be reversed!

It is a spectacular little summit with big drops all around and spacious views to land and sea.

Return the same way to the central saddle (**2.5km; 560m; 2h 10min**), avoiding the temptation to descend north earlier since this will add to the hill's erosion problem. Drop back down the main path then go left and follow the traverse path across the north side. The path swings around beneath the splendid western bastion, before dropping south back to the start (**4.5km; 560m; 3h 20min**).

Stac Pollaidh from Badnagyle to the west (Tom Prentice)

SUILVEN Caisteal Liath

SUILVEN; pillar mountain, from Old Norse 'sulr', pillar and Gaelic 'beinn', lenited as 'bheinn'
Caisteal Liath; 731m; (G48); L15; NC153183; grey castle

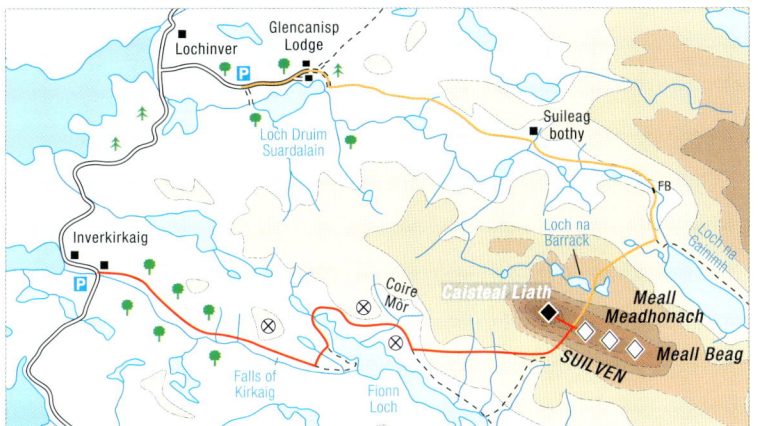

Not only is Suilven one of the finest Grahams, but it ranks as one of the best of all Scottish mountains. It is a mountain of superlatives and a much prized ascent. There are two principal approaches, both from the west near Lochinver. These are long but they allow time to enjoy the hill and the passage through a wonderful landscape.

The Inverkirkaig approach starts from a good car park (NC085193) beside the River Kirkaig to the southeast of Inverkirkaig. There is a café and bookshop up the hill above the car park.

Cross the road and follow a signposted path to the Falls of Kirkaig through lovely wooded terrain to reach the point where a path descends to the falls at NC111180 (55min). It is worth visiting the fall, but the hill is a long way off and it's better to save this for the return.

Continue for a further 800m, keeping an eye out for a cairn and a path up the banking on the left at NC118177, opposite a rapid on the river. Take this path, which cuts over the peninsula to cross the head of Fionn Loch. On the other side, the path loops round and after 1km crosses a flat area; Coire Mòr.

At the back of a knoll, Creag a' Choire Mhòir, at NC132179, take a cairned rough path which breaks off left and climb steeply through a craggy area. A vague path leads gradually up and across the slope with the majestic sight of sphinx-like Suilven ahead. This joins a path coming up from further along the lochside path (longer and perhaps less scenic) at a burn beneath the Bealach Mòr; the saddle in the middle of Suilven, and ▶

The impressive cliffs of Caisteal Liath, Suilven, from the Inverkirkaig approach (Noel Williams)

304 SUILVEN Caisteal Liath

Meall Meadonach from the ascent to Caisteal Liath (Rab Anderson)

the only chink in the hills defences.

A steep and eroded path leads to the saddle, which sits on a knife-edged crest where the route from Lochinver arrives from the north side. Head north-west through a wall that has been built here and climb to the fabulous summit of Caisteal Liath. There are a few easy rock steps to negotiate and some exposed sections which require care, especially in winter (**10.5km; 800m; 3h 45min**).

There is a definite sense of achievement in attaining this spot, so linger awhile then return the same way (**21km; 860m; 6h 30min**).

The other approach starts from the end of the public road, which leaves Lochinver on the north side of the Culag River, where there is a walkers car park at NC107220.

Walk along the road (not the track) to Glencanisp Lodge and pass behind this. Continue south-east on the main track, ignoring a path off left (the River Inver Loop), with the prow-like bastion of Caisteal Liath looking some distance away. After 4.5km (1h), pass a path off left to Suileag bothy and continue for 2km to reach a bridge across the river. Carry on for another 700m, uphill around the corner then down to a burn. Break off right here (NC168197) on a good path that climbs towards the Bealach Mòr. The path passes a small lochan then threads the gap between Loch a' Choire Dhubh and Loch na Barrack to reach the foot of the slope. A steep ascent leads up a shallow gully (Coire Dubh) to join the Inverkirkaig route at the Bealch Mòr. Turn right and continue to the top (**10km; 730m; 3h 25min**). Return the same way (**20km; 790m; 6h**).

Some may wish to prolong the experience and take in the two central Graham Tops, however the second of these involves some scrambling. A path leads easily up onto and along the splendid crest of Meall Meadonach West then down to a col. A steeper section follows with scrambling, where care should be taken in finding the easiest route and remembering the way back. The flat summit table is one of Suilven's most prominent features when viewed from the surrounding hills.

Anyone wishing to take in Meall Beag, the final Graham Top, might balk at the exposed descent down a noticeably less travelled route to the next col, and at the equally exposed tricky scramble to gain the sanctuary of the top of Suilven's tail fin. The descent off the back is easy, but a gully cleft that cuts into the top has to be watched out for.

Caisteal Liath, with its transverse wall (Rab Anderson)

Ben Stack from the A894 near Laxford Bridge (Rab Anderson)

Ben Stack; 720m; (G65); L9; NC269422; steep mountain

Rising from the rugged Sutherland landscape, this majestic little mountain presents a distinctive conical profile, particularly when seen from the north-west. From this direction Ben Stack bears an uncanny resemblance to the mountain in the Paramount Pictures logo.

There are two principal ascent routes, taking either the north-west or the south-east ridges. However, these are just up and down the same way routes, which do little justice to such a fine mountain. A better circuit, which combines these ridges, starts from Achfary to the south-east where there is parking in front of the estate office. The approach is made through Strath Stack.

Walk south past the school and turn right up a gravel track beside the public telephone box. Pass between the houses and the garages then go through a gate into the forest. The Allt Achadh Fairidh tumbles through the floor of the glen below and soon the track emerges into the open and continues alongside the top edge of the forestry plantation. About 500m past the last of the trees, opposite a cascade on the other side of the glen, break off right (NC263412) and follow the right bank of a burn up onto flatter ground.

Continue north out in front of the steeper slopes and ascend beside another burn, passing a distinctive large boulder with a small boulder perched on its top, to reach the north-west shoulder of the hill. The rough ascent path which comes up from Loch na Seilge is joined here and leads steeply up the splendid rocky ridge. At first sight this can look intimidating but it's straightforward with fine situations and superb views across to Foinaven and Arkle. Traverse the airy but easy knife-edged crest past the summit cairn then an incongruous solar-powered police aerial to reach the slightly lower trig point 100m or so to the south-east. The crest is split by a curious landslip fissure (**6km; 680m; 2h 30min**).

Descend the south-east ridge steeply to a small knoll, beneath which the slope fans out. Continue in the same line, down the prominent rock dyke of the Leathad na Stioma, to reach boggy ground, then a section of track and the road leading back to the start (**10km; 690m; 3h 30min**).

The above descent can be used to climb the hill since it provides the least intimidating route, although boggy ground is crossed at the start (**4km; 680m; 2h**); (**8km; 690m; 3h**).

The northern route starts at a small building beside the road where there is space for a few cars (NC266437). Ascend the track up the hillside to the west and leave this at NC258432 after crossing the burn that runs into Loch na Seilge. Follow the path and ascend the north-west ridge as for the previous route (**3km; 680m; 1h 50min**); (**6km; 680m; 2h 45min**).

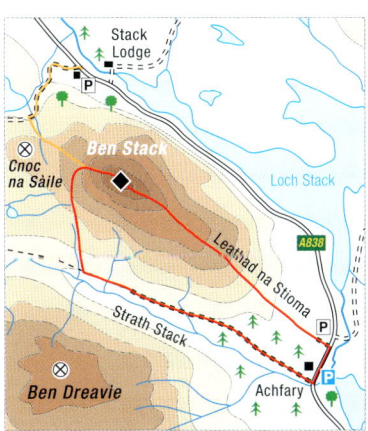

Sàbhal Beag

Sàbhal Beag; 732m; (G47); L9; NC373429; *little barn*

Sàbhal Beag is the northernmost Graham, a lonely lump of a hill to the south-east of its much finer neighbours, Foinaven and Arkle. In itself it does not have much to offer apart from good views of the neighbouring hills. However, when combined with Sàbhal Mòr, which in spite of its name is lower than Sàbhal Beag, and the Corbett, Meall Horn, it provides a very satisfying day.

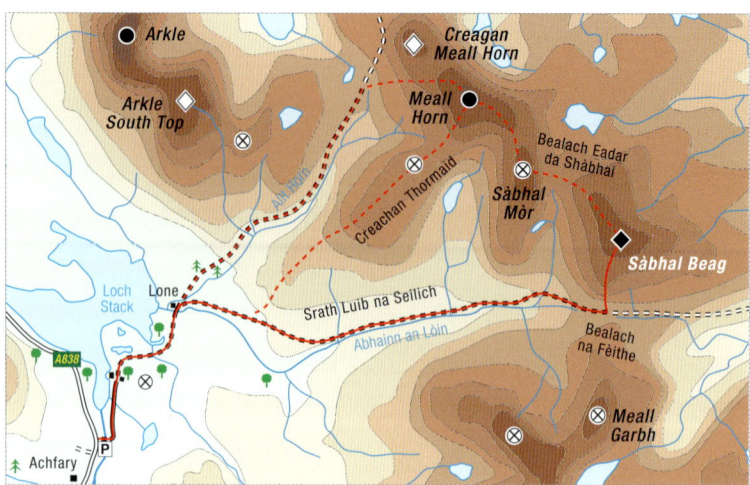

Begin at the south end of Loch Stack, 1km north of Achfary, where there is parking at the start of an estate road which crosses the river. A bike is useful for the first part of the route to Lone. Go along the estate road and track for 3km to Lone and thereafter on a good track that heads east up Srath Luib na Seilich. After an initial steep section, the glen flattens out and the track is followed for 6km to the Bealach na Fèithe. A mountain bike could be used on much of this track but it is rutted and steep in places. Timings given are on foot.

From the bealach, climb north up steep grassy slopes which ease higher; a small cairn tops the broad flat summit (**11km; 710m; 3h 40min**).

To the north-east, the views of Ben Hope and Ben Loyal are outstanding and almost the whole of the north-west corner of Scotland is spread out before you. The neighbouring Grahams of Ben Stack and Càrn an Tionail can be identified to the west and south-east. Descend the same way (**22km; 730m; 6h 20min**).

A more complete circuit takes in Sàbhal Mòr (703m) and the Corbett, Meall Horn (777m). From the summit of Sàbhal Beag go northwards over stony ground and descend to the boilerplate slabs of the Bealach Eadar da Shàbhal. Easily climb Sàbhal Mòr and follow the broad south-east ridge onto Meall Horn (**14km; 950m; 4h 50min**).

Descend the south-west slopes and the ridge of Creachan Thormaid back to Lone then the starting point (**23.5km; 1010m; 7h 15min**).

A return can also be made by cutting across westwards to the track at the bealach with Arkle then following this back to Lone.

Sàbhal Mòr and Sàbhal Beag, right, from Srath Luib na Seilich (Meryl Marshall)

Càrn an Tionail, Beinn Direach

Beinn Direach, left, and Meall a' Chlèirich from the track above West Merkland (Rab Anderson)

Càrn an Tionail; 759m; (G5); L16; NC392390; hill of the gathering (of deer, etc)

Beinn Direach; 688m; (G119); L16; NC406380; steep or perpendicular mountain

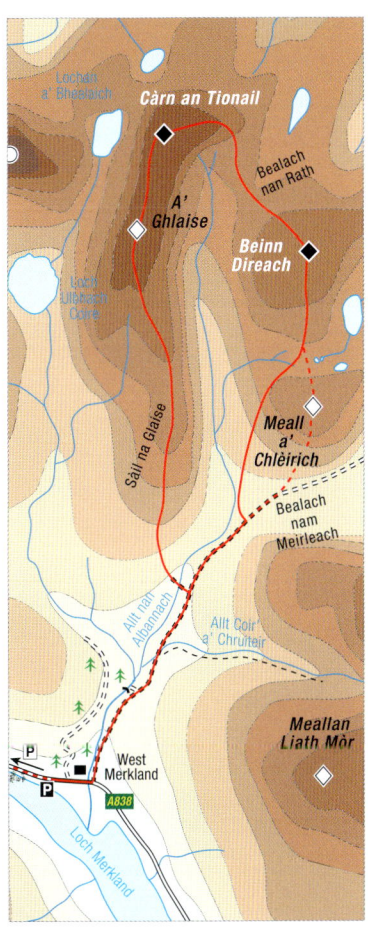

These two hills lie north of Loch Merkland on the A838 between Lairg and Laxford Bridge, at the southern end of the range of hills that include Foinaven, Arkle and several other Corbetts, as well as the Graham Sàbhal Beag. Càrn an Tionail is the higher of the pair with a fine and airy south ridge some 3km in length, whilst Beinn Direach is smaller and more rounded.

Both hills give relatively easy going with grassy slopes and stony upper reaches. A circuit combining the two provides a very pleasant horseshoe with good panoramic views of the surrounding hills.

Approach from West Merkland, towards the northern end of Loch Merkland where there is a cottage and a bridge over the Allt nan Albannach. Parking is difficult close to the start and it may be necessary to go 1km further along the road to the west, to the end of Loch Merkland.

Walk to the bridge and follow a good track up the east side of the Allt nan Albannach for 2km. This track continues over the Beallach nam Meirleach, the Robbers Pass, to the road which runs beneath Ben Hope in Strath More and was originally an old droving route.

A few hundred metres after crossing the Allt Coir' a' Chruiteir, which is the route of the path to the summit of the Corbett Ben Hee, break off left on a track which descends to a metal bridge over the Allt nan Albannach. Cross over, then head north up the grassy slopes of Sàil na Glaise, the long ridge leading to A' Ghlaise, the southern top of Càrn an Tionail. It is quite a steep initial ascent, although an atv track may be picked up from time to time, which helps the climb.

Once on the ridge the going is easier and a splendid walk along the edge of a steep drop-off into the corrie to the east leads to the top of A' Ghlaise (750m). Càrn an Tionail lies just over 1km away to the north and is easily

▶

Looking west to Meallan Liath Coire Mhic Dhughaill (Rab Anderson)

reached after a short descent and reascent (**8km; 700m; 3h**).

Large numbers of deer gather to graze on the steep slopes beneath the ridge and in the corrie, hence the name of the hill. The stony ground on the upper slopes gives a good habitat to several flocks of ptarmigan; also of note are a couple of small stone shelters just under the summit.

The view is grand, particularly north to Ben Hope and Ben Loyal, then west to the complex system of tops, ridges and corries that make up the Corbett Meallan Liath Coire Mhic Dhughaill. It is worth walking downhill a little to the west for the fine view over Lochan a' Bhealaich into the lovely corrie containing Coire Loch. To the north-west over the rounded and less defined neighbouring Graham of Sàbhal Beag lies the Corbett Meall Horn with Arkle and Foinaven beyond.

Descend the broad north-east ridge for 400m and then curve round to the south making for the slabby rocks at the remarkably rugged and scoured Bealach nan Rath, avoiding a line of crags on its north side. Beinn Direach rises ahead and the angle of the slope, together with the minimum reascent, means it is a quick and easy climb to the broad and flat summit (**10km; 850m; 3h 50min**).

The descent is made by going south down the short spur of Ceann Garbh na Beinne Dìrich towards the massive bulk of Ben Hee to reach a broad bealach. From here, the Graham Top Meall a' Chlèirich (631m) can be climbed although the descent south to the track below is quite steep. A descending traverse around the west side of Meall a' Chlèirich enables an atv track to be joined, which leads to the Allt na Glaise draining the corrie, then to the main track just west of the Bealach nam Meirleach.

The fact that it is a 600m ascent from here to the summit of Ben Hee is likely to put most off any thought of attempting to include this in the round. A pleasant 3km walk leads back down the track to West Merkland (**16km; 850m; 5h 30min**).

Càrn an Tionail from A' Ghlaise, Cranstackie and Beinn Spionnaidh left (Rab Anderson)

Meallan a' Chuail from the stalkers' path to the north (Grahame Nicoll)

Meall an Fheur Loch; 613m; (G214); L16; NC361310; hill of the grassy (reedy) loch
Meallan a' Chuail; 750m; (G10); L15; NC344292; little hill of coal (peat supplies?)

The ascent of this pair of Grahams gives a very good and scenic outing with the possibility of including the Corbett, Beinn Leòid. Start from the single track A838 between Loch Merkland and Loch More, just west of the highpoint where there is a small parking area at a passing place (NC358333) on the south side.

Walk west along the road for 100m to where a wooden bridge gives access to a stalkers' path which zigzags uphill between a break in the forestry. Height is gained quickly and the angle eases right off. At a flattish section, where there is a small, normally dried-up lochan, head up the slope on the left. At this point there is a boulder on the left and the stalkers' path veers away from the hillside, crossing some stepping stones.

Ascend the slope past two tiny lochans to climb easily up the rounded ridge with views across to the two neighbouring Grahams, Càrn an Tionail and Beinn Direach, as well as back to Ben Stack and Arkle. The summit of Meall an Fheur Loch is flat, and the cairn, which lies over to the left, could be difficult to find in mist (3km; 490m; 1h 30min). Ahead, Meallan a' Chuail's fine east face rises above the two lochans in its corrie; Ben More Assynt lies beyond.

▶

Meall an Fheur Loch above Loch a' Ghriama from the A838 (Jim Teesdale)

Meall an Fheur Loch, Meallan a' Chuail

Meall an Fheur Loch from the north ridge of Meallan a' Chuail (Rab Anderson)

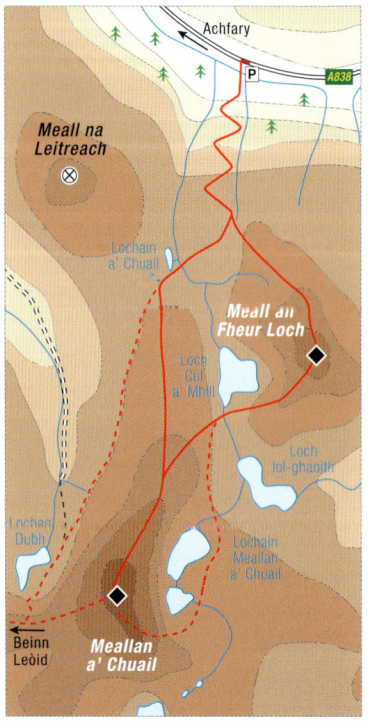

Head south-west off the top, down the curving ridge to a flatter section and a point where there is a view out over steeper slopes dropping to Loch Iol-ghaoith below. On the other side, a waterfall tumbles down the hillside from the lochan nestling in the corrie beneath the summit of Meallan a' Chuail. Swing round and descend westwards to the southern tip of Loch Cùl a' Mhill. Take care not to stray south here in poor visibility.

Cross the outflow at the end of the lochan and climb steeply to gain the narrow northern ridge of Meallan a' Chuail. Follow the ridge to the summit which is perched on the edge above a steep drop overlooking the lochans to the east (**6km; 790m; 2h 40min**).

A better alternative is to ascend the slope a short way from Loch Cùl a' Mhill, then cut south across the steep slope via a deer track to ascend past some boulders to reach idyllic Lochan Meallan a' Chuail. Go around the east side of this lochan and the unnamed lochan to its south then ascend the steep south-east ridge to the summit; about 1km and 15min longer.

Descend the long north ridge and continue north off the end above Loch Cùl a' Mhill on the higher ground, thereby avoiding most of the boggy terrain. The stalkers' path is reached a few hundred metres before a small lochan. Follow the path to the dried-up lochan then downhill to the start (**11km; 800m; 4h**).

Beinn Leòid can be included across the col at 546m to the west (Drochaid Beinn Leòid) then returning to it. One option is to climb back over Meallan a' Chuail and descend its north ridge; an added 5.5km, 450m, 2h 20min. Another option is to drop north into the corrie (Pollagan Dubha) on a stalkers' path, then about 160m beyond the end of Lochan Dubh, make a traverse across rough ground to reach the end of the stalkers' path used in the approach; an added 5.5km, 280m, 2h.

Beinn Dhorain

Beinn Dhorain; 628m; (G195); L17; NC925156; mountain of the wet place

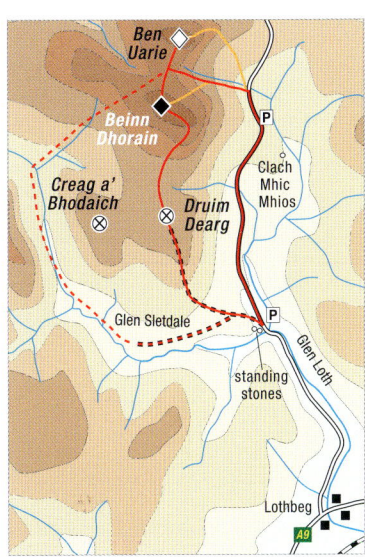

This summit forms the highest point of a large tract of hill country south of the Strath of Kildonan. It gives distant views of the Moray coast and most of the hills in the north-east part of Scotland, including the Cairngorms. The hills in this area are generally rounded and heathery but an exception to this is the steep east face of Beinn Dhorain.

The ascent is made from Glen Loth where a narrow road climbs to a height of 340m, cutting the corner between the A9 and the Strath of Kildonan. Glen Loth is uninhabited, but once held a considerable population, cleared to make way for sheep by the notorious Patrick Sellar, factor of the Duke of Sutherland. The remains of their settlements and other archaeological features, which indicate that the glen was settled in prehistoric times, can be seen. A visit to puzzle over the impressive Clach Mhic Mhios standing stone at NC941151 is worthwhile; park as for the short route to the top.

A pleasant route starts further down Glen Loth, some 200m north of a bridge over the Sletdale Burn, where a grassy track climbs the southern slopes of Druim Dearg. Park on the grass opposite the gate at the start of the track (NC936129). Follow the track into a planted area by a gate then by its less distinct right fork to exit the planted area by another gate. Continue over Druim Dearg to gain the saddle to the south of Beinn Dhorain then climb to the top, veering right for the view down into Glen Loth then gaining the summit to the north-west (**4km; 530m; 1h 45min**).

Continue across to Ben Uarie (623m) with its trig point, less than 1km to the north, where there are rewarding views into the Strath of Kildonan and to the splendid conical peak of Morven. The descent can be made from the col between the hills by the burn down the steep east facing corrie. Although this involves a 3km walk back down the road it can be combined with a visit to the Clach Mhic Mhios standing stone (**10km; 530m; 3h 15min**).

An alternative is to head south-west across easy featureless ground into Glen Sletdale and follow the burn, picking up a track for the last 2km (**12km; 530m; 3h 45min**).

For those wishing to gain the summit quickly, the shallow east facing corrie between Beinn Dhorain and Ben Uarie provides a steep and heathery ascent. There is a small parking area at NC937154. Walk up the road for 450m and cross a stile into a planted area. Follow the burn to exit the planted area by a stile then climb up and left to the summit (**1.75km; 360m; 1h**).

Cross the col to Ben Uarie then, either return to the col and descend by the burn, or descend steeply east to the side of a rocky band entering the planted area by a gate, or descending to the road by the fence (**4.5km; 360m; 1h 45min**).

Beinn Dhorain from Glen Loth (Rab Anderson)

312 BEN ARMINE *Creag a' Choire Ghlais, Creag Mhòr*

Section 16 – Loch Broom to the Pentland Firth

Creag Mhòr, centre, and Creag a' Choire Ghlais, right, from the south-east across Strath Brora (Rab Anderson)

BEN ARMINE; mountain of the hero, chieftain, steward
Creag a' Choire Ghlais; *705m; (G90); L16; NC694273; cliff of the grey-green corrie*
Creag Mhòr; *713m; (G74); L16; NC698240; big cliff*

These retiring and somewhat dull-looking hills are amongst the most remote Grahams. However, they are easily approached by mountain bike and the resultant walk over their summits ends up providing an excellent day out in the rugged far north.

The start point for the hills is normally reached by a lovely drive up the A897 beside the River Helmsdale through the Strath of Kildonan, then via the B871 up Strath Beg. To the south of Badanloch Lodge an estate track begins at NC801330, at the entrance to which there is good parking. The track runs west past Loch Badanloch, Loch an Alltan Fheàrna then on to Loch Choire Lodge at the head of Loch Choire beneath Ben Klibreck.

Follow this track to NC687310 where a good stalkers' path heads south-south-east to run beneath the steep east-facing slopes of both hills (**13.5km; 70m; 1h 30min** by bike), (**3h** on foot). The best route is probably to climb across the hills and to return by this path. Times given are now on foot, from and back to here.

Strike off up the hillside to gain a slight spur descending from Meall nan Aighean. Swing right before the summit of this Graham Top to reach a col then make the short ascent west onto Creag na h-Iolaire, another Graham Top (**3km; 500m; 1h 30min**).

A lovely cover of moss carpets the ground, a feature of the hilltops on this round. The view across the top of Scotland is expansive; Ben Klibreck is close and large, Ben Hope, Ben Loyal, the island of Hoy then Ben Griam Mòr and Ben Griam Beag rising out of the flatland. Creag Mhòr looks a long way from here but the intervening terrain is generally good for walking and can

The summit of Creag Mhòr, Morven in the distance (Rab Anderson)

BEN ARMINE Creag a' Choire Ghlais, Creag Mhòr

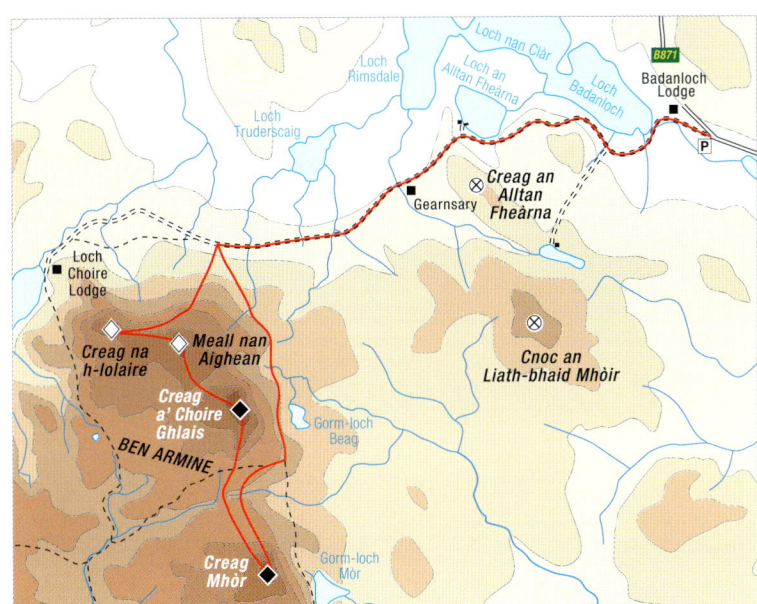

be crossed with ease. There are some peat hags but these are easily crossed, or avoided.

Return to the col and climb east onto Meall nan Aighean (695m), then drop south-east to a col where hag-riven ground looks like it will be a problem. However, the hags are small and a line through them is easily found to gain the mossy dome of Ben Armine and the summit, named Creag a' Choire Ghlais on OS maps (**5.5km; 650m; 2h 30min**).

Descend south-south-west across a stalkers' path passing between the hills, then head south across the col. Avoid the hags on the right, or left, and make a long but steady climb to the trig point on the summit of Creag Mhòr (**9km; 800m; 3h 40min**).

Over to the east is the final pocket of mainland Grahams; Beinn Dhorain, Scarben and majestic Morven.

On the descent the natural drift is to initially head down the north-east shoulder past a large cairn to a point where the map suggests a steep drop north-east to the stalkers' path below.

However, it is perhaps better to avoid the reascent that this entails and to continue north-north-west down the slight spur, not far from the line of ascent. Swing round across Coir' an Eas and make a descending traverse to join the stalkers' path that crosses between the hills, then descend a short way to the junction with the northbound stalkers' path at NC703261.

This excellent path leads above Gorm-loch Beag, through a dip in front of Coire na Saidhe Duibhe, back to the track. It is a long, but pleasant walk of 5.5km back to the bike (**17.5km; 850m; 5h 50min**), aided by the knowledge of what turns out to be a swift and enjoyable bike ride back (**44.5km; 940m; 8h 50min** with bike), (**11h 50min** on foot).

Looking towards Creag a' Choire Ghlais, Ben Armine from Creag Mhòr (Rab Anderson)

Scaraben

East Scaraben, Scarben and West Scaraben from Smean to the north-west (Jim Teesdale)

Scaraben; 626m; (G198); L17; ND066268; incised mountain, from old Norse 'skora' and Gaelic 'bheinn'

In complete contrast to the neighbouring peak of Morven, Scaraben takes the form of a linear quartzite ridge with three distinct rounded tops. The summit sits in the middle and the traverse of all three tops gives a pleasant walk.

Start from Braemore where there is a small parking area at the end of the minor road which leaves the A9 on the edge of Dunbeath. The Morven approach starts here too.

Cross the bridge then turn off left along another track and continue all the way along it as it becomes grassier. Once beyond the buildings and fields, climb south on a gradually steepening slope, crossing quartz scree to gain the top of East Scaraben (590m).

Not far below the top at ND083276 is the 1941 wreckage of a crashed Coastal Command Armstrong Whitley, with an impact crater probably caused by an exploded depth charge.

Head westwards across the dip to the main central summit and trig point (**5km; 560m; 2h**) then drop down and climb onto West Scaraben (609m).

Descend by the north spur, avoiding a steeper section lower down on the east. Cross the Allt Aoil and head for the left side of a strip of forestry to avoid the fields at Braeval to the west. On reaching the Morven track, turn right back to the start (**11.5km; 650m; 3h 50min**).

Including Smean and Maiden Pap in this route is straightforward (**14.5km; 1030m; 5h 15min**).

Including Morven via Smean is longer (**20km; 1310m; 6h 30min**) and including the Maiden Pap is awkward (probably best back over Càrn Mòr), adding 1km, 300m, 50min.

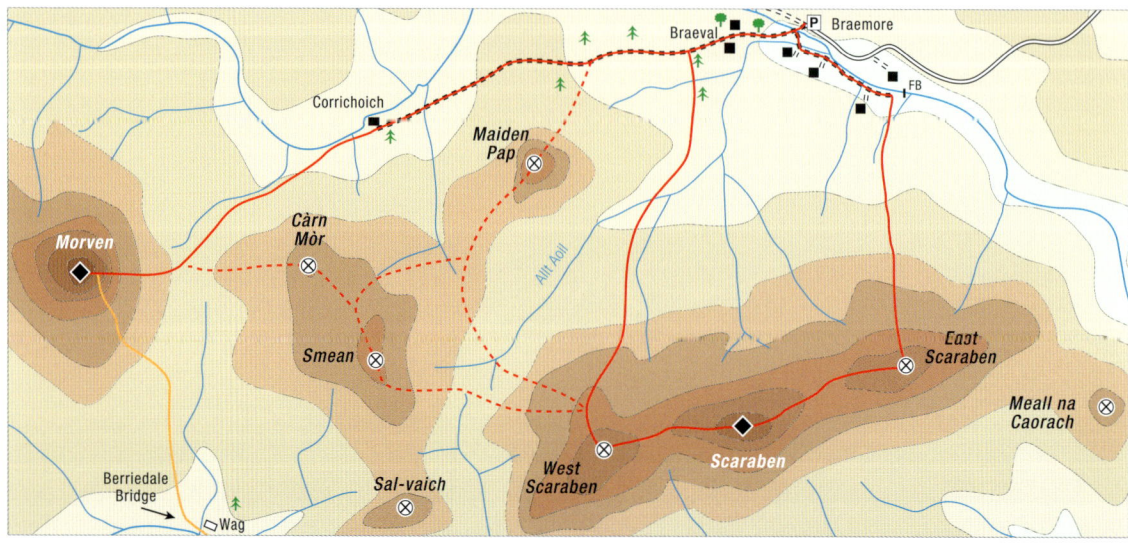

Morven; 706m; (G88); L17; ND004285; big mountain

Morven is the highest point of Caithness and one of Scotland's most prominent mountains; a great conical mass rising out of the water-logged flatness of the Caithness Flow Country, the largest expanse of blanket bog in Europe. Its distinctive shape can be seen from as far away as the Moray coast and the Cairngorms beyond. There is a sense of space here and the expansive view extends from the Sutherland hills in the west, along the Caithness coast in the north to the islands of Orkney and Hoy, with its sea-stack the Old Man of Hoy, then east to the rigs of the Beatrice oilfield.

Start from Braemore at the road end as for Scaraben. Follow the track over the bridge then west through Braeval to pass beneath the fine mini-peak of Maiden Pap to reach the end of the track at Corrichoich.

Head south-west over moorland following a rough atv track, then a vague path, to gain the broad col below Morven's eastern slope. A steep ascent over heather and scree, where a rough path might be found to ease some of the way, gains the shoulder. Pass south of a rock tor then climb easy slopes to the final rise and a fabulous summit (**7.75km; 590m; 2h 45min**).

Return the same way (**15.5km; 620m; 4h 45min**).

Alternatively, for a three Marilyn day, climb east onto the rocky top of Càrn Mòr then traverse across onto the fine tor-topped summit of Smean (509m) (**11.25km; 850m; 4h 10min**).

Descend steeply to the north-east then cross the intervening flat ground to reach the Maiden Pap. Climb this via the obvious line of weakness on its south side to gain a narrow col from where a final short climb gains an impressive little summit (484m) (**13.75km; 1020m; 5h 10min**).

To descend, return to the col then drop steeply north on a path to regain the track of the outward route beside a forestry plantation and return to Braemore (**16.75km; 1020m; 6h**).

From Smean it is possible to ascend Scaraben but this makes for quite a long day and Maiden Pap is awkward to include, being off the natural round. See Scaraben opposite for the link timings from there.

An interesting and unusual route to Morven is from the south via the track along the Langwell Water; a bike is useful. Park at the Berriedale bridge and take the estate road (ND118226) for Langwell House. A locked gate at the edge of the wood necessitates a high bike lift; thereafter take the middle of three tracks. Leave bikes at Wag (**13km; 180m; 1h 30min** by bike), (**3h 10min** on foot).

Times are now given on foot from and back to here. Head north over rough moorland to homesteads marked on the map then go north-west up an obvious shallow gully to the summit; a steep and sustained 450m climb (**3km; 520m; 1h 30min**).

Return the same way (**6km; 520m; 2h 30min**) and then return to the start (**32km; 180m; 5h 15min** with a bike), (**8h 50min** on foot). This can be extended east to take in Smean, or west then south to include Creag Scalabsdale.

Morven from the approach track to Corrichoich (Jim Teesdale)

*Trollabhal from Ainshval
The Skye Cuillin and Blabheinn beyond
with Marsco in-between (Rab Anderson)*

SECTION 17 The Islands

SECTION 17

ARRAN
[1] **Mullach Buidhe**   322

JURA
[2] **Beinn Shiantaidh**, [3] **Beinn a' Chaolais**   324

MULL

[4] *Creach Beinn*, [5] *Ben Buie*	326
[6] *Beinn Talaidh*, [7] *Sgùrr Dearg*	328
[8] *Corra-bheinn*, [9] *Cruach Choireadail*	330
[10] *Beinn Fhada*	332

Section 17 – The Islands

RUM	
[11] *Trollabhal*	334
SKYE	
[12] *Beinn na Caillich (Kylerhea)*, [13] *Sgùrr na Còinnich*	336
[14] *Beinn na Caillich*, [15] *Beinn Dearg Mhòr (Broadford)*	338
[16] *Belig*	340
[17] *Beinn Dearg Mhòr (Sligachan)*	342
[18] *Marsco*	344
[19] *The Storr*, [20] *Hartaval*	346

SOUTH UIST	
[21] *Beinn Mhòr*	348
HARRIS	
[22] *Uisgneabhal Mòr*	350
[23] *Oireabhal*, [24] *Tiorga Mòr*	351

Mullach Buidhe, centre, from Casteal na h-Iolaire (Tom Prentice)

ARRAN
Mullach Buidhe; 721m; (G64); L62, 69; NR901427; *yellow mountain*

Arran's western hills lack the jagged peaks and alpine ambiance of the main range, being rather more rounded in appearance. Nevertheless, they harbour some rocky ridges and corries which would not be out of place in the Cairngorms.

The village of Pirnmill on the west coast offers the most direct access to Mullach Buidhe. Park at the southern end of the village in a roadside layby just north of Pirnmill Village Store and Post Office and the bridge over the Allt Gobhlach. The footpath is signposted from here.

Ascend the access road directly opposite the parking area, first diagonally left then more directly. Where it starts to curve left, look out for a footpath sign on the right on the edge of woodland. The path leads through scrubby birch, muddy in places, to gain the Allt Gobhlach. Ascend over various stiles and alongside a deer fence to leave the trees and get the first view of the hills. Continue past a waterfall on the right then alongside the burn, now flowing through a narrow wooded gorge, to a point directly below the nose of Coire Roinn's right-hand ridge, which descends from the Graham Top of Beinn Bharrain (717m). The left-hand ridge offers an alternative scrambling ascent (see next page).

At the head of a track by a small dam, cross the burn and the moorland to gain the ridge. A path appears as the ridge becomes better defined and leads round the top of Coire Roinn to the cairn on the summit of Beinn Bharrain. Continue east then north-east over the prominent granite tor of Casteal na h-Iolaire, then

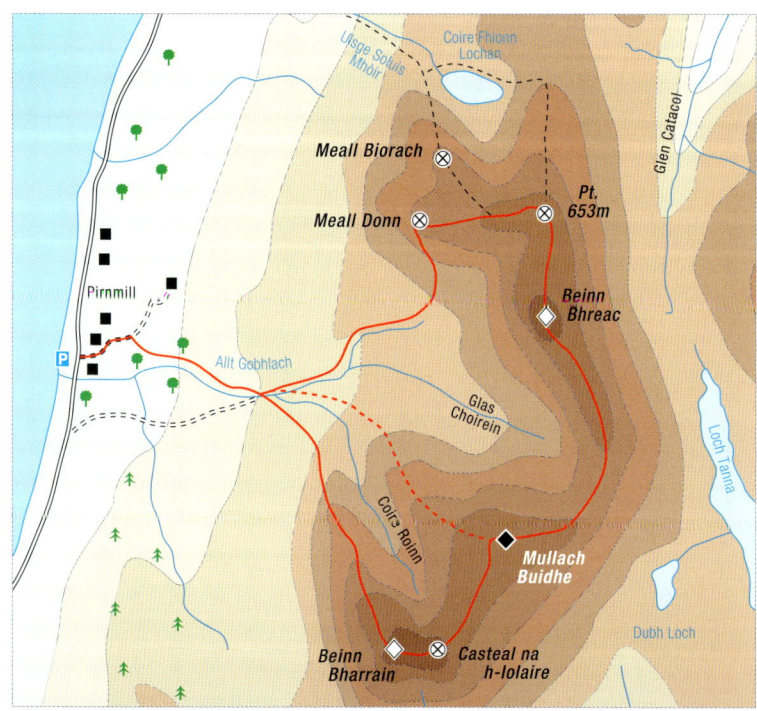

The Islands

Caledonian MacBrayne is the major operator of ferries to the islands calmac.co.uk. Highland Council operates a few small crossings and there are some private companies operating crossings. Online searches for ferry crossings to the island name should reveal the relevant information. The Caledonian MacBrayne website timetable contains a section 'Useful Ferry Timetables (Non Calmac)' which is certainly useful. In addition to the standard crossings, Caledonian MacBrayne offer a Hopscotch Ticket which covers various ferry crossings to from and between the islands, valid for a limited period.

Arran & The Inner Hebrides

The Isle of Arran, and the group of islands known as the Inner Hebrides contain a total of 11 Grahams on four islands. Arran has one Graham whilst Jura has two, Mull has seven and Rum has one.

Arran is reached by Caledonian MacBrayne ferry from Ardrossan to Brodick. Another ferry crosses from Claonaig on the Kintyre Peninsula to Lochranza calmac.co.uk.

Jura is reached by Caledonian MacBrayne ferry from Kennacraig at the northern end of the Kintyre Peninsula, either to Port Ellen or Port Askaig on Islay calmac.co.uk. Another ferry crossing is required from Port Askaig to Feolin on Jura; (ASP Ship Management Ltd) details on isleofjura.scot, through the Argyll & Bute Council website and in the Caledonian MacBrayne timetable. A passenger-only ferry crosses directly to Craighouse on **Jura** from Tayvallich (NR742782) on Knapdale, details on jurapassengerferry.com and on calmac.co.uk.

Mull can be reached by ferry from Oban to Craignure, although the more convenient and less expensive crossing from Lochaline on Morvern (probably gained via the Corran ferry crossing operated by Highland Council) to Fishnish makes day trips possible. There is a spring, summer and autumn only crossing to Tobermory from Kilchoan on Ardnamurchan. The Mull crossings are operated by Caledonian MacBrayne calmac.co.uk where details of the Corran ferry can also be found.

Rum contains one solitary Graham and the island can be reached by ferry crossing from Mallaig via the Caledonian MacBrayne Small Isles service calmac.co.uk.

Isle of Skye

The Isle of Skye contains 9 Grahams and most walkers will choose to arrive on the island via the Skye Bridge from Kyle of Lochalsh. However, the Kylerhea ferry crossing from near Glenelg is an alternative. This ferry is seasonal and it takes vehicles, but it is also possible to cross as a foot passenger and climb the two easternmost Grahams on Skye; Beinn na Caillich and Sgùrr na Còinnich. The ferry is operated by the Isle of Skye Ferry Community Interest Company skyeferry.co.uk. Details are on the Caledonian MacBrayne website calmac.co.uk who also operate a ferry crossing from Mallaig to Armadale.

The Outer Hebrides

Despite their size and their hilly nature, in contrast to the islands of the Inner Hebrides, the islands of the Outer Hebrides only contain four Grahams: Beinn Mhòr on South Uist then Uisgneabhal Mòr, Òireabhal and Tiorga Mòr on Harris. Caledonian MacBrayne calmac.co.uk is the sole ferry operator.

South Uist can be reached from Oban on the mainland by ferry to Lochboisdale on South Uist, a service which alternates with Castlebay on Barra. A ferry also crosses between Barra and Eriskay, connected by causeway to South Uist. Another ferry crosses from Uig on Skye to Lochmaddy on North Uist, connected by road with South Uist. A ferry also provides a link between The Uists and Harris, see below.

Isle of Harris can be reached from Uig on Skye by ferry to Tarbert. A ferry crosses from Ullapool on the mainland to Stornoway on the Isle of Lewis, which is joined to the Isle of Harris. The final link is a ferry between Leverburgh on Harris and the island of Berneray, connected to The Uists by causeway.

---

descend slabby ground to the corrie edge and follow it to the cairn and trig point on Mullach Buidhe, overlooking Glas Choirein (**5km; 780m; 2h 25min**).

An alternative approach can be made up the north ridge (the left-hand of the two ridges enclosing Coire Roinn), which is easily gained from the Allt Gobhlach and offers an excellent Grade I/II scramble on rough granite. The main difficulties are near the top and would be awkward to avoid, however the exposure is moderate and the scrambling is not sustained. Descending by this route is not recommended.

A return can be made back over Beinn Bharrain, but it is more enjoyable to continue north round Glas Choirein to Beinn Bhreac, at 711m a Graham Top, then on to the smaller summit of Pt.653m. From there, traverse west round the corrie overlooking picturesque Coire Fhionn Lochan to spot height 586m, where the path makes a distinct turn to the north-west and contours round the corrie towards Meall Biorach. Do not follow this route, but leave the path at NR901542 and descend in a south-westerly direction towards Meall Donn, from where heather and grass lead down to a path on the north bank of the Allt Gobhlach, which leads back to the main path to Pirnmill (**13km; 960m; 4h 45min**).

It is also possible to descend north to Coire Fhionn Lochan from Pt.653m and Meall Biorach and follow a well-travelled path beside the Uisge Soluis Mhòir to Mid Thundergay on the coast road, 2.5km north of Pirnmill. This traverse is popular with walkers using the coastal bus service for transport, rather than private car.

324 JURA Beinn Shiantaidh, Beinn a' Chaolais

JURA
Beinn Shiantaidh; 757m; (G6); L61; NR513747; *probably holy mountain; locally 'a' bheinn sheunta'*
Beinn a' Chaolais; 733m; (G40); L60, 61; NR488734; *mountain above the narrows*

Jura's mountains have a reputation for uncompromising toughness requiring similar stamina and mountain skills to another great island round in this guide; the Cuillin of Rum. Known by all as the Paps of Jura, there are actually three main mountains and a lesser outlier, rather than the two that might be expected from the 'breasts' of the Gaelic title.

The two Grahams and Beinn an Oir, the Corbett in-between, form the north and west sides of Gleann an t-Sìob', making a round of all three the logical expedition for most hillwalkers. Just 52m separates the highest and lowest of the three and the amount of ascent from the cols in between ranges from 330m–350m.

Effort is fairly evenly distributed through the day, but when combined with the rugged and boggy approach and descent, ankle-twisting scree, some ill-defined paths and mountain route-finding, it is easy to see where Jura's reputation comes from.

The popular ascent begins from a car park on the north side of the Corran River (NR544720) at the start of the minor road to Knockrome. From here, there are two options.

The main route crosses back over the bridge and follows the signposted path and subsequent atv track on the

Beinn Shiantaidh from the head of Gleann an t-Sìob' (Tom Prentice)

west side of the Corran River, first north then west towards Loch an t-Sìob'. The route is very marshy in places, but leads directly to stepping stones at the eastern end of Loch an t-Sìob'. Cross then leave the lochside path and ascend Beinn Shiantaidh directly north-west on ill-defined paths through heather and scree tongues. On reaching the west side of the south-east ridge the scree starts in earnest. Although a path becomes more obvious there are two options. After a left traverse one heads up the left side of the ridge to the summit, the other gains the ridge and follows it to a levelling which leads south-west over grass and scree mounds to the cairn (**4.75km; 740m; 2h 25min**).

The alternative is via the signposted 'Evans's Walk', which starts opposite a car park at NR550731, and is reached by walking north up the road. This route is less marshy, the best approach if including Corra Bheinn in the round, and also misses out the lower flanks of Beinn Shiantaidh. However, it is slightly longer and requires a little more route-finding. Follow the left-hand path when the route divides near the start and leave it at a small cairn

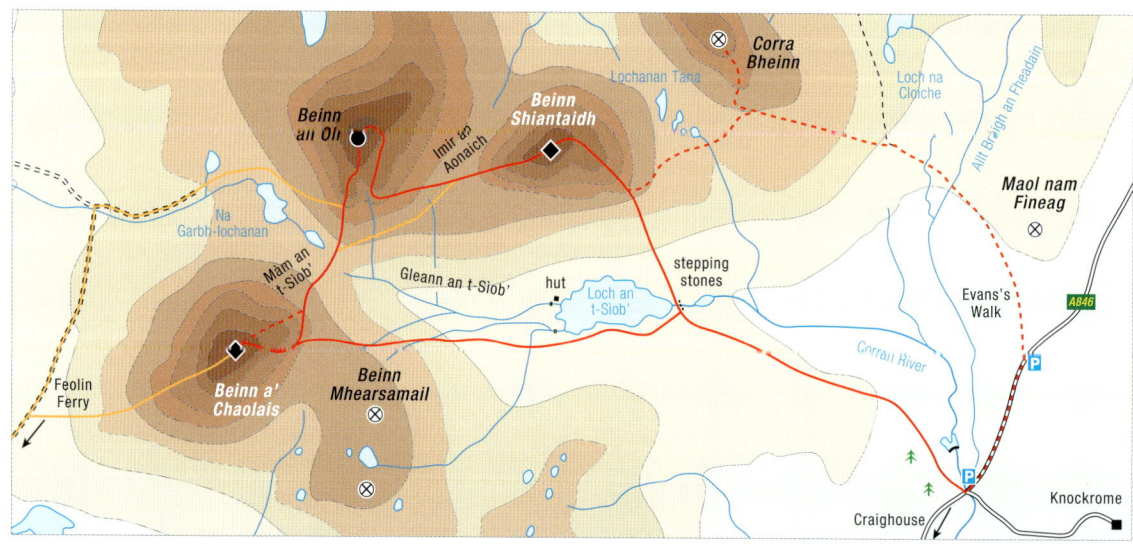

(NR539747), just before it bends sharp right and ascends north towards Loch na Cloiche. Traverse north-west on animal tracks to the base of Corra Bheinn, which can be climbed up and down via the same route in 50min from here; 1.5km. From the Lochanan Tana lochans, a distinct path follows the screeline south-west below Beinn Shiantaidh's south-east ridge to the join the previously described ascent route. Excluding Corra Bheinn, this route is 1.5km longer than via the River Corran but with the same height gain and takes an extra 20min.

From the summit of Beinn Shiantaidh, descend the ridge west, which broadens into a mixture of grass and scree. About halfway down, where the ridge steepens, break through a band of rock by a gullyline a little to the right, then continue down to the Imir an Aonaich col.

Beyond the col, follow a path westwards across the flanks of Beinn an Oir to a burn draining the shallow corrie formed by the obvious rake that slants rightwards across the mountain. Turn north up the right side of the burn and follow the path up the rake into the upper corrie to a stone shelter where the scree starts. There are now two options.

(i) Ascend grass between the scree slopes above, and directly below an obvious tor formed by an igneous sill, to reach another two stone shelters. These are thought to be the remains of a 'Colby Camp' occupied by the Ordnance Survey during the first Triangulation of Great Britain in the first half of the 19th century.

(ii) Continue up the rake on a rough path into a depression then onto the north-east ridge and turn south-west past a cairn to reach the Colby Camp.

A stone pathway leads to the trig point (**7km; 1080m; 4h**).

Descend south on a superb ridge of blocky quartzite with fine views west to the Sound of Islay and south-west to Beinn a' Chaolais, then veer south-west onto a subsidiary ridge and weave down through scree and crags to skirt the lochans of Na Garbh-lochanan to the south.

Either climb directly up the left side of the east face of Beinn a' Chaolais by a line left of the scree to gain the east ridge, or traverse round the base of the ridge, then ascend gentler-angled scree, heather and rock to its crest. Follow the ridge to the summit (**9.5km; 1445m; 5h 40min**).

Go back down the east ridge and take the easier right-hand line to reach the bottom then drop into Gleann an t-Sìob'. Pick up a wet and muddy path along the southern edge of Loch an t-Sìob' to reach the east end then follow the main path back to the start (16.25km; 1445m; 7h 30min).

These mountains can also be approached from the Feolin Ferry. Follow the bikeable track north above the shore through woodland to a crossroads. Take the track that leads east, uphill to the Lochan Gleann Astaile dam then follow the track on the other side a short way, leaving bikes after 7.25km, 170m. Now climb to the summit of Beinn a' Chaolais via its south-west ridge (**8km; 730m; 3h 25min**). Times are given on foot.

Descend the north-east ridge then scree to the col then drop down a bit and cut across the front of Beinn an Oir to climb Beinn Shiantaidh (**11km; 1140m; 4h 30min**). Return to below Beinn an Oir and ascend it as previously described (**13.5km; 1470m; 5h 45min**), then descend the south ridge to regain the Beinn a' Chaolais col. Skirt the Na Garbh-lochanan lochans to their west and descend by the burn to reach a track. Continue down to NR479744 then cross the burn and take the track south to rejoin the approach route and return (26.75km; 1500m; 10h 10min); the use of a bike should save about 2h on the day.

Beinn a' Chaolais with Islay beyond, from the south ridge of Beinn an Oir (Tom Prentice)

Creach Beinn from Loch Buie (Tom Prentice)

> **MULL**
> **Creach Beinn**; 698m; (G107); L49; NM642276; craggy mountain
> **Ben Buie**; 717m; (G69); L49; NM604270; yellow mountain

Creach Beinn and Ben Buie are the biggest hills in the south of Mull. They have a lot of steep, exposed gabbro giving them the appearance of rugged little mountains, in contrast to the rounded, grassy hills just to the north. Creach Beinn lies above the sheltered, wooded freshwater loch, Loch Uisg, whilst Ben Buie overlooks the marine loch, Loch Buie, which is surrounded by yellow gorse blooms. Loch Spelve, Loch Uisg and Loch Buie are part of the Great Glen Fault which cuts through to Inverness.

Start on the east side of a small bridge in Gleann a' Chaiginn Mhòir, about 1km from the road end at Loch Buie; there is a small parking area at NM615256, used by people visiting the Lochbuie Stone Circle.

The glen runs northwards between the two hills and is more interesting than many on Mull, containing several small crags of glacier-smoothed gabbro with a few hardy holly trees clinging to them. Fallow deer have been introduced here whilst those at Gruline near Salen have been established for longer. Mull is well known nowadays for white-tailed eagles but these hills are the territory of golden eagles, with both hills having highpoints named Creag na h-Iolaire (Eagle's Cliff) on their northern flanks.

Climbing Creach Beinn to the east first, go through a gate on the opposite side of the road and follow a stalkers' path that runs gently up to the east of the burn leading through

The Loch Uisg flanks of Creach Beinn (Tom Prentice)

MULL Creach Beinn, Ben Buie

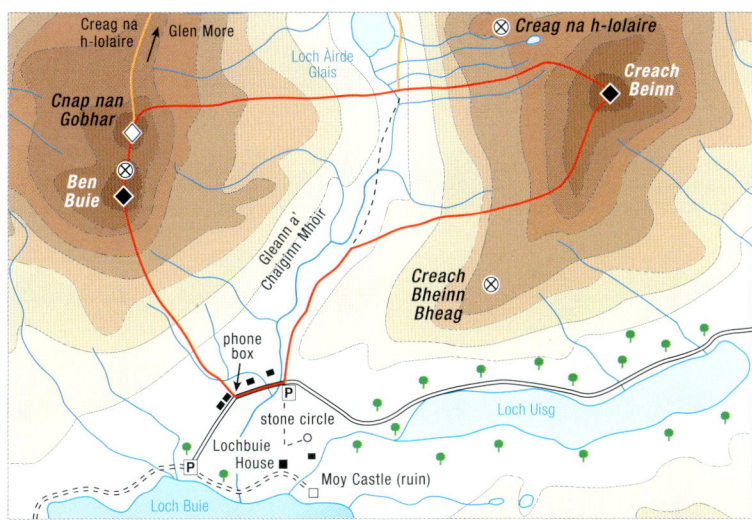

the glen towards Loch Àirde Glais, the first of 'the three lochs'. After less than 2km of gentle walking, above a step in the floor of the glen, break off right and climb steeply to reach the easy broad ridge, which is followed north-east to the summit of Creach Beinn (**4km; 690m; 2h**).

There is a cylindrical trig pillar then a small ring cairn just to the east, which offers a little shelter. This is a good viewpoint for the mainland hills such as Ben Nevis, Beinn Sgulaird, Ben Cruachan and also Rum to the north and Jura to the south.

To descend it is best to first walk north-west from the summit then drop west back down to the glen. Descending to the west from the summit leads to a scree covered slab, and whilst this can be descended with care, it is unpleasant. Continue down to the glen past various crags to join the vague path just south of Loch Àirde Glais; a substantial 550m drop.

On the other side, climb the broad ridge ahead which leads up to the north of Ben Buie; some of the ridge is on perfect gabbro slabs. From the top of the ridge, a short walk leads south to Cnap nan Gobhar (714m), the north top of Ben Buie. There are three tops of similar height. Continue south for 500m over the central top (700m) to reach the large cairn on the main summit overlooking Loch Buie (**9km; 1310m; 4h 30min**).

There are cliffs below the summit, to the south and east, so care is needed to descend. A path just south of the summit runs down to the right (west) under the cliffs. Alternatively, walk down to the west to avoid the cliffs then walk back east. Descend the rounded ridge with scree soon giving way to vegetation. Continue down overlooking the burn of the Allt a' Ghoirtein Aird then avoid the houses just before reaching the road on the bend by the telephone box. A short walk along the road leads back to the car park (**12km; 1310m; 5h 30min**).

These hills can also be ascended from the top of Glen More on the A849 to the north using public transport. Start from the highpoint at NM617303; there is also a layby for parking at NM622394. The top of Ben Buie is easily reached via Creag na h-Iolaire. Return over Cnap nan Gobhar before dropping east to reverse the previously described ascent route to climb Creach Beinn. It is perhaps best to descend this via the line of ascent then traverse along either side of Loch Àirde Glais.

Ben Buie from the Loch Buie seashore (Tom Prentice)

Beinn Talaidh from Glen More (Colin Moody)

MULL

Beinn Talaidh; 762m; (G1); L49; NM625347; possibly mountain of the view, from Gaelic 'beinn an t-seallaidh'
Sgùrr Dearg; 741m; (G29); L49; NM665339; red mountain

Together with its neighbour Sgùrr Dearg, these two hills dominate the head of Glen Forsa and provide a short but energetic outing from Glen More. The lowest point for the crossing between the two hills is only 80m above sea level, which is lower than the starting point of the walk!

Start in Glen More, at the junction of a forestry track and the A849 at NM642328 where there is space for several cars. Less than 100m up the forestry track, at a slight bend, a vague atv track/path runs off to the left. Follow this to quit the forestry at a stile where the steep, grassy hillside leads to the shoulder of Maol nam Fiadh and the start of the curving south ridge of Beinn Talaidh. This gives a gradual ascent above Coire Ghaibhre to the broad summit dome (**3km; 650m; 1h 45m**).

A cylindrical trig pillar sits on the top, from where there are stunning views in all directions.

For those wishing to ascend the outlier Beinn Bheag (537m) a steep, straight descent over scree gives access to the linking col, from where Beinn Bheag is a short ascent.

Immediately north of the col, at the very head of Gleann Lèan, lie the remains of a Dakota aircraft which crashed at the col in 1945, en route from Iceland to Prestwick.

From the summit, descend the steep south ridge, then skirt the foot of Beinn Bheag northwards to a wide break in the forestry in the glen. The same point can be reached

The curving upper ridge of Beinn Talaidh (Rab Anderson)

with more ease from the trig pillar on Beinn Talaidh, by initially heading south-east then swinging east to descend grassy terrain between the two main burns in Coire Ghaibhre.

The right side of the forest break is less boggy, but crossing the burn here after heavy rain would be problematic since there is no footbridge. In these circumstances it might be better to head back to the car then climb Sgùrr Dearg from the road; see the alternative description which follows.

Continuing though, head up the hillside to follow a slight burn (not shown on OS maps) and thence onto the craggy nose of Beinn Bheàrnach. A wide, gently rising ridge of about 1km, leads to the summit cairn of Sgùrr Dearg which lies close to the edge of its precipitous north face (**8.5km; 1360m; 4h 30min**).

Descend the south ridge towards the other Beinn Bheàrnach until a strange tumbled down wall is encountered. Follow the wall into Coire nan Each and then descend the north bank of the Allt Caisreagach passing some attractive cascades, to reach the A849 at the roadside ruins of Torness. A short walk along the road leads back to the starting point (**11km; 1360m; 5h 35m**).

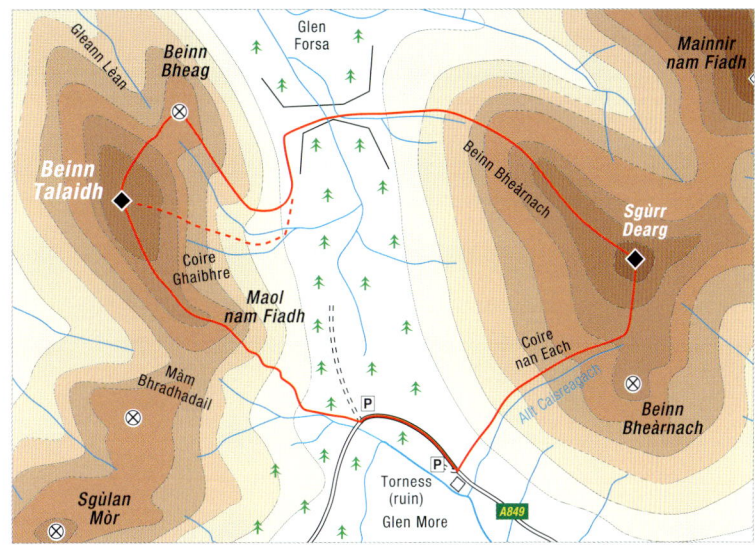

A useful option is to ascend Beinn Talaidh then return the same way (**6km; 650m; 2h 45min**). Drive east for 750m to park on the south side of the road at the ruin at Torness, or walk. From there, simply reverse the principal descent route by ascending the slope up and right to the main burn, the Allt Caisreagach. Follow this up Coire an Each to pick up the old wall, then veer left at the top to gain the summit of Sgùrr Dearg and return the same way (**5km; 630m; 2h 30min**).

A significantly longer ascent of these hills can be made from the north via Tomslèibhe bothy, accessed by mountain bike along the track from the main road at NM595427 by the Glen Forsa Hotel. The classic north ridge of Beinn Talaidh is climbed and Glen Forsa crossed via the previously mentioned forestry break. The return from Sgùrr Dearg gives rough walking above the forestry on the east side of Glen Forsa by the old settlement of Rhoail.

Sgùrr Dearg and Beinn Bheàrnach from Beinn Talaidh (Rab Anderson)

Cruachan Dearg, Corra-bheinn, Beinn a' Mheadhain and Cruach Choireadail from Glen More (Colin Moody)

MULL

Corra-bheinn; 705m; (G94); L48; NM573321; steep mountain

Cruach Choireadail; 618m; (G210); L48; NM594304; heap above An Coireadail (perhaps 'coire na dail', corrie of the meadow)

These fine hills, whose rocky southern flanks give depth and atmosphere to the northern side of Glen More, are infrequently ascended and consequently have no established ridge paths. Although somewhat dominated by Ben More to the west, they give splendid walking with ever-changing views. The so-called twin peaks of Cruachan Dearg and Corra-bheinn, with summits over 1km apart, do have similarities of form although the former is undoubtedly the most striking and elegant.

Start at the western end of Glen More, at a prominent holly tree and stone bridge carrying the old road over the Allt Teanga Brìdeig burn, at the ruins of Teanga Brìdeig (NM563306). There are several parking spaces on the old road, just west of the stone bridge. Take the track over the bridge to the ruins and follow a wet path leading up the east side of the glen to the col of Càrn Cùl Righ Albainn (330m). Head eastwards, contouring around rocky knolls, then climb the steep west flank to the summit of Cruachan Dearg (4.5km; 670m; 2h 10min).

An OS ratified survey measured Cruachan Dearg at 704m and confirmed Corra-bheinn as the higher of these former twins at 705m.

Descend steeply south and cross

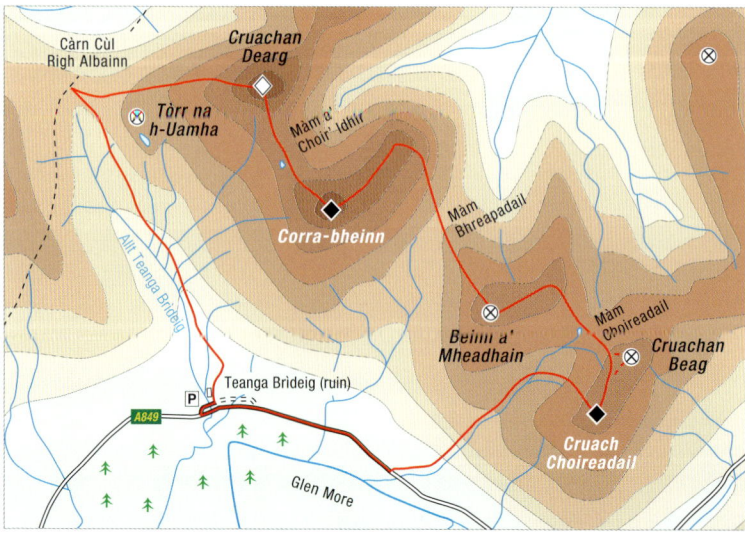

the Màm a' Choir' Idhir col (c575m) to climb past a tiny lochan onto the dark summit of Corra-bheinn (**5.75km; 800m; 2h 45min**).

Traverse along the wide north-east ridge for about 500m to just before it is truncated by the rugged little Coire na Lice Duibhe. Descend southwards across the surprisingly steep slope over scree, linking grass patches, to the pass of Màm Bhreapadail (c385m), where an ancient path links Glen More and Glen Cannel.

The bonus hill of Beinn a' Mheadhain (602m) lies straight ahead, with its distinctive north-west spur giving a 210m ascent directly to the top. A straightforward descent east then south-east leads to the col of Màm Choireadail (464m).

Either climb south-east onto Cruachan Beag (596m) then south-west, or climb southwards past it, to the summit of Cruach Choireadail (**9.75km; 1200m; 4h 35min**).

Descend north-west to the near level floor of An Coireadail (a hanging valley) and then head down the glen, crossing the burn just before it plunges ove the edge. Just beyond the lip, a fine little waterfall drops over an overhanging barrier into a

Cruach Choireadail from the south-east (Grahame Nicoll)

deep pool – the perfect place to cool off on a hot summer's day!

A short distance below, the Uisgeacha Geala cascades over gabbro walls and slabs. These can be avoided by descending on the north side of the burn, passing a prominent perched block lower down and thence to the road. Teanga Brìdeig is a 20min walk along the road (**13.5km; 1200m; 5h 40min**).

An even more challenging circuit of these hills can be made from the north by starting at the ruin of Gortenbuie at the head of Glen Cannel; a 7.5km mountain bike ride from Knock along the south side of Loch Bà. The circuit, probably best done by starting with Cruach Choireadail, gives a splendid wilderness experience (**12km; 1230m; 5h 20min** from Gortenbuie).

Corra-bheinn's summit with Ben More and A' Cìoch, left, and Beinn Fhada, right (Rab Anderson)

Approaching the stepped nose, with the summit tower of Beinn Fhada beyond (Andrew Fraser)

> **MULL**
> **Beinn Fhada**; 702m; (G97); L47, 48; NM540349; long mountain

While many hillwalkers will link Beinn Fhada with the nearby Munro of Ben More, it is also easily combined with its two northerly lower neighbours to make an excellent round in its own right.

It is an impressive and surprisingly rocky peak, every bit as good as its more illustrious neighbour and, as with all Grahams, the lower altitude means it is often clear when Ben More is cloud-bound.

Park at NM516374 on the north side of the B8035 in the vicinity of a Mile Post, some 200m south of the bridge over the Scarisdale River. There is ample parking on the grassy coastal pasture. Cross the heather moorland, wet initially, in a south-easterly direction to gain Beinn Fhada's prominent north ridge and make the steep ascent to the summit of Pt.563m, admiring the fine sea views north-west across Loch na Keal to the islands of Eorsa and Ulva.

Climb the ridge left of a lochan to a stepped nose leading to a broader ridge and follow that over grass and rock towards the summit cone. After the larger of two lochans, a short section of scrambling gains the final

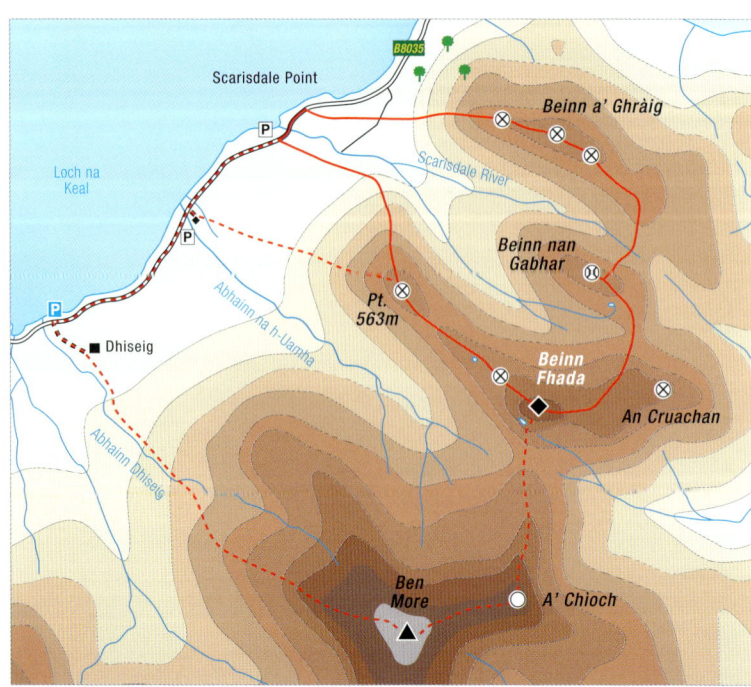

ridge leading to the summit cairn (**4km; 740m; 2h 5min**).

Continue eastwards from the summit, then north-east past the col below An Cruachan, to grassy slopes leading north to the col below Beinn nan Gabhar. From here, ascend north then north-west to the cairn marking the highest point on the broad, rocky ridge of Beinn nan Gabhar (572m). Return south-east for about 250m, then east down scree and cross the infant Scarisdale River at the head of the corrie.

A line of small cliffs form a distinctive feature slicing straight up the southern side of Beinn a' Ghràig. Ascend left of these to quickly gain the long ridge and follow it over rocky tops and the 591m summit (a Sub 2000ft Marilyn) to the final lower cairned top, which is separated from the main ridge by a col. Descend west from the cairn, weaving through areas of steep ground divided by slabby rock steps. In poor visibility or wet weather, care is needed here in order to find the easiest route to the grassy runnels and scree at their base.

Continue descending west towards the coast to pass through a boundary wall, beyond which the driest line is taken across rough sheep pasture to reach the road then back to the start (**11km; 950m; 4h 15min**).

The distinctive summit tower of Beinn Fhada from the west (Colin Moody)

Ben More can be included by descending south-west from the summit of Beinn Fhada to a col, reached by walkers making a circuit of Ben More from the road. Climb the fine north ridge of A' Chìoch (867m) to its top, then descend west to the base of Ben More's steep east ridge and climb this to the summit (**7km; 1280m; 3h 45min**).

The standard ascent route up Ben More is now followed north-west then west down to the Abhainn Dhiseig. Cross over and continue to reach the track to Dhiseig then the road, which is followed back along the coast to the start (**14.5km; 1280m; 5h 45min**).

The far west top of Beinn a' Ghràig and Loch na Keal from the flanks of Beinn Fhada (Tom Prentice)

RUM
Trollabhal; 702m; (G100); L39; NM377952; troll fell

Trollabhal is the only Graham on Rum and one of the six principal hills forming the Rum Cuillin ridge. Askival and Ainshval are Corbetts, while Hallival and Sgùrr nan Gillean, the first and last of the round of six when starting from Kinloch, are fine summits in their own right. The latter is a Corbett Top, whilst Hallival and Pt.759m between Ainshval and Sgùrr nan Gillean are Graham Tops.

Getting to Rum requires effort and planning, and most hillwalkers will want to make the most of their visit, especially if it coincides with good weather. A full round of the Rum Cuillin ridge is usually the objective, or at the very least, an ascent of Trollabhal and the two Corbetts. Accordingly, a full round is described here, along with a variety of alternative return routes and descents which can be utilised to climb Trollabhal, with or without Askival and Ainshval, should time and weather be against you.

Check the Calmac website for current ferry times. The rescheduling of the timetable in 2022 has meant that a day trip to climb any of these hills is not possible. Western Isles Cruises in Mallaig do charters which may be suitable for larger groups.

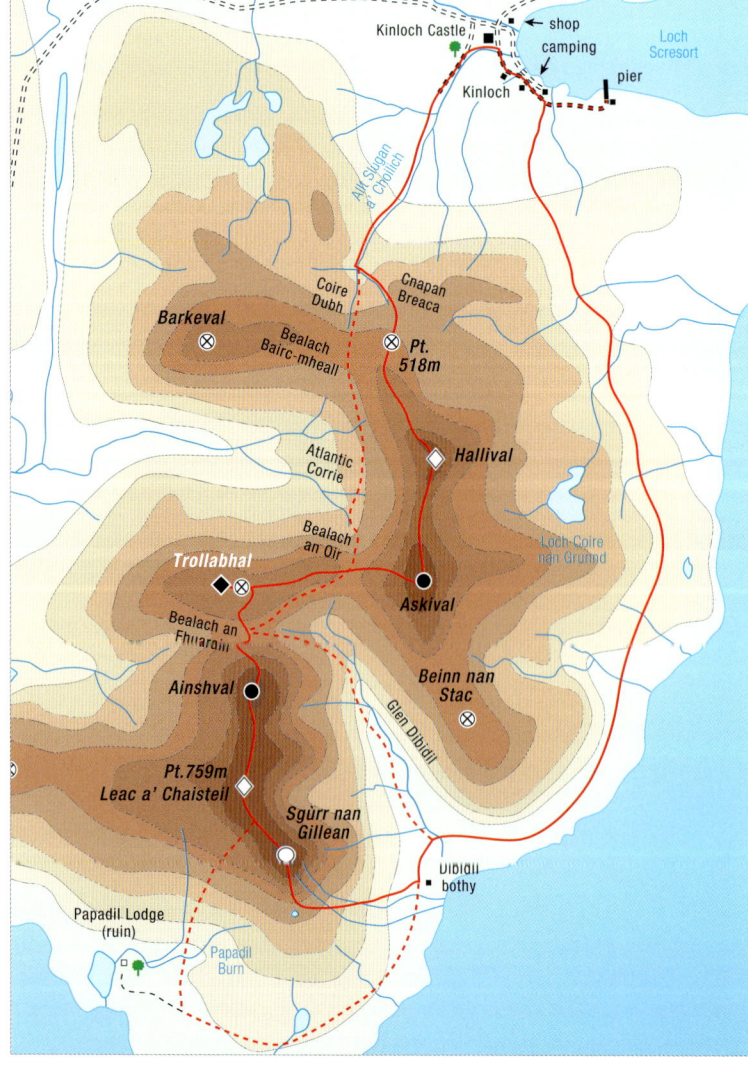

The route is described starting from the south side of Kinloch Castle, which is reached from the main track across the bridge over the Allt Slugan. This is a 10-15min walk from the pier past the toilets, pods, campsite and bunkhouse. Go left alongside the castle then left through a gate and head into woodland passing an old bridge over the river. Pass to the left of a powerhouse building onto the end of a track then ascend the prepared path beyond to its end at a hydro dam.

Continue by a rougher path and climb into Coire Dubh to a causeway breached by the burn then cross. This is the old dam that once supplied Kinloch Castle with water for electricity; the first Scottish castle to be lit this way.

The path now forks and is less distinct; the right branch continues up the corrie to Bealach Bairc-mheall, the other branch veers left (southeast). Follow the left-hand path up beside a small burn to a col named Cnapan Breaca then ascend the rocky hillside to gain the lower northwest ridge of Hallival, just above the Bealach Bairc-mheall. Ascend the ridge, at first grassy then steeper and rocky, to reach Hallival's summit (**4.5km; 730m; 2h 15min**).

There are fine views south to Askival and the hills of Mull beyond. The island of Eigg sits 'afloat' in the sea below and the mainland hills stand out to the east. The ground is covered in Manx Shearwater burrows; a large portion of the world's population breed here on Rum.

Descend the crest south from Hallival, negotiating a steeper section via a series of rocky steps (be wary of dampness early in the day), then drop through boulders to gain the col.

Continue up and along an amazing narrow grassy ridge to the first rocks of Askival's rocky crest and the Askival Pinnacle (more of a slab than a pinnacle). Follow the path left here and make a rising zigzag ascent up the easier ground to the left of the crest. At the top, a trickier move gains easy ground then Askival's summit (**5.75km; 945m; 3h 30min**).

A surprisingly long and tiring descent of the steep and mostly grav-

Approaching the spectacular summit of Trollabhal (Noel Williams)

elly west ridge leads to the Bealach an Oir; be wary of being sucked too far down left at the top.

The east ridge of Trollabhal lies ahead, its broad and grassy lower section leading easily to the narrow upper section which, despite its rocky profile, is straightforward. The easiest line is just right of the crest and leads to the south-eastern and slightly lower summit. The main summit lies some 50m further on to the north-west across a gap. A short descent then an exposed scramble up rock and grass gains the top of one of the most impressive summits among the Grahams (**7.5km; 1200m; 4h 45min**).

Return to the lower summit and descend the south ridge, first south-east then weaving south-west and south between small rock steps to reach the Bealach an Fhuarain.

Avoid the steep lower buttress of Ainshval's north ridge by traversing right (west) for a short way then zigzag up the left side of the screes to gain a grassy col on the ridge.

Although the ridge ahead can be scrambled up (tricky when wet) it is generally bypassed to the left (east) via a small path up the corrie; Grey Corrie. A couple of minor slabby rock steps and some loose ground leads to the grassy top close to the large cairn that marks the summit of Ainshval (**8.5km; 1470m; 5h 45min**).

With the main summits climbed, a return can be made from here. However, unless pressed for time, it is better to complete the traverse. To do so, descend the grassy ridge south to a col then follow a pleasantly airy ridge up and over the broad Pt.759m (Leac a' Chaisteil) and on to Sgùrr nan Gillean (**10km; 1590m; 6h 20min**).

There are three principal ways back to Kinloch from Sgùrr nan Gillean.

(i) Probably the most popular is via Dibidil bothy and the path above the eastern coast. Descend the south ridge for about 600m to where the ground flattens at a tiny lochan at NM381925. The last 100m can involve scrambling down short rocky gullies and requires care. Head east from the flatter ground to pick up the burn draining the east face and follow it eastwards to gain the path above Dibidil bothy. Follow this around the coast, rough and boggy in places, to Kinloch (**20.5km; 1780m; 9h 20min**).

Sgùrr nan Gillean's east ridge looks tempting as a direct descent, but it leads to steep and rocky ground and is not recommended. Other than (i) or (ii), the only safe route into Glen Dibidil is from Bealach an Fhuarain.

(ii) Easier but longer to the bothy is to return to the col between Sgùrr nan Gillean and Pt.759m, then descend south-west and south to cross the Papadil Burn and gain the coastal path to Dibidil and Kinloch (**23.5km; 1810m; 10h 10min**).

(iii) Return over Ainshval to Bealach an Fhuarain then traverse north-east below the rocks at the base of Trollabhal to Bealach an Oir. Drop north into Atlantic Corrie and make a long traverse north across it beneath Askival and Hallival. There is a rough path in places and it is important to drop far enough down to only make a short crossing over the boulders at the foot of the large boulder field and recent rockfall. Beyond this, make a rising ascent on rough paths to the Bealach Bairc-mheall. Descend into Coire Dubh and follow the path back to Kinloch (**18.25km; 1900m; 9h**).

Anyone wishing to climb Trollabhal in isolation from the rest of the ridge should ascend to the Bealach Bairc-mheall between Barkeval and Hallival and then traverse across Atlantic Corrie (reversing the route described in (iii) above) for the approach and return route (**6.25km; 840m; 3h**), (**12.5km; 990m; 5h**).

A shop to the north of the castle offers refreshments; ice cream, soft drinks and a well-earned beer!

Beinn na Caillich from Sgùrr na Còinnich (Noel Williams)

> **SKYE**
>
> **Beinn na Caillich**; 732m; (G42); L33; NG770229; *peak of the old woman*; said to be named after the Norse princess who barred the Kyleakin narrows with a chain to collect taxes
>
> **Sgùrr na Còinnich**; 739m; (G31); L33; NG762222; *peak of the moss*

Situated in a fairly quiet and less frequented part of Skye, these two hills are prominent in the view west from Glenelg on the mainland side of Kyle Rhea. They also feature in the view across Loch Alsh from the road to Kyle of Lochalsh and the route onto the island via the Skye Bridge, which passes to the north.

A turntable vehicle ferry crossing to Skye still operates from April to October at the ancient Glenelg to Kylerhea crossing point. It is also possible to cross from the mainland as a foot passenger to climb these hills. The road from Kylerhea climbs to a highpoint at Bealach Udal before dropping through Glen Arroch to join the A87 north coast road between the Skye Bridge and Broadford.

The hills are climbed from Kylerhea where there is a car park 300m up a side road that runs north from the road above Kylerhea and is directly above the ferry slipway. The road is signposted 'Kylerhea Otter Haven'.

Climb directly up the heathery hillside on a slope with occasional rock outcrops. These hills are actually built of Torridonian sandstone, a rock more usually associated with the hills on the mainland further north.

Eventually the slope eases off onto the broad stony flattening of Beinn Bhuidhe (488m). Sgùrr na Còinnich and Beinn na Caillich now lie ahead.

Cross a shallow neck, then head slightly rightwards towards the dip between the peaks; Bealach nam Mulachag. Once on this broad col, turn right to ascend Beinn na Caillich. The initial ascent is steep and is tackled up a short section of scree, then by weaving a way through the dipping rock strata. Continue more easily on grassier ground to the cairn

Sgùrr na Còinnich from Beinn na Caillich (Rab Anderson)

SKYE Beinn na Caillich (Kylerhea), Sgùrr na Còinnich

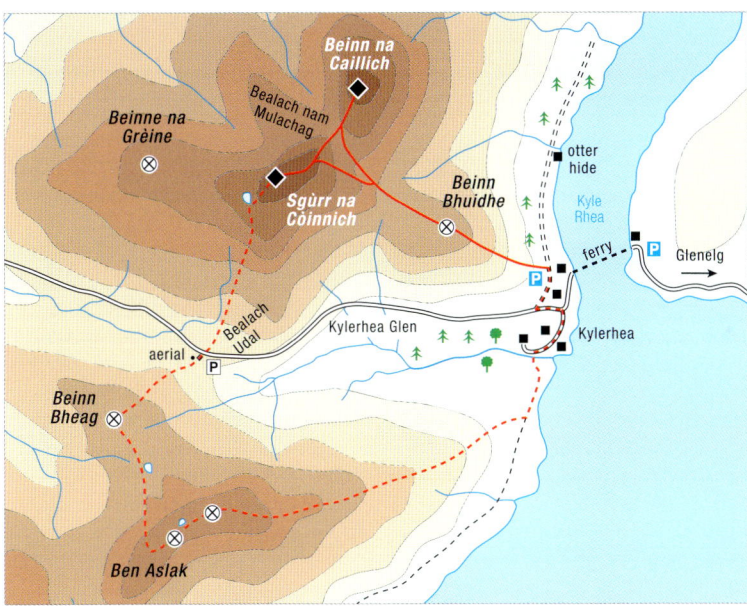

on the summit (**3km; 690m; 1h 50min**).

There are superb views in all directions. North over Kyle Akin, the Skye Bridge and Kyle of Lochalsh to Applecross with the Graham Beinn a' Chlachain visible. To the south-east above Glenelg is the Graham Beinn a' Chapuill with Beinn Sgritheall beyond, whilst to the west behind the other Beinn na Caillich are the jagged peaks of Blabheinn and The Cuillin. South is Ben Aslak.

Return to Bealach nam Mulachag and climb a grassy slope trending rightwards with the slanting rock strata to reach the cylindrical trig pillar on the summit of Sgùrr na Còinnich (**4.25km; 850m; 2h 30min**).

If only doing the two Grahams, descend the south-east ridge to regain Beinn Bhuidhe and drop to the car park (**7km; 870m; 3h 35min**).

However, to make more of a day of it, a good extension is to cross south to Ben Aslak (609m), once a Graham but now 1m short on stature.

Leave Sgùrr na Còinnich's summit and head south-west to a small lochan. Descend southwards, as directly as possible to Bealach Udal and the highpoint on the road up the Kylerhea Glen; a rough 460m drop.

On the opposite side of the road follow a short section of track to a mast. Beyond this, continue up a broad slope in a south-westerly direction to the minor Beinn Bheag (468m). Turn to the left here, then after 100m, descend more steeply to a dip. Continue heading in a south-easterly direction and go past a sizeable hidden lochan. On the final section, either make for a prominent grassy runnel and at the top turn right to reach the summit, or slant rightwards towards more rocky ground and find some pleasant scrambling which leads back left to the summit (**8.25km; 1230m; 4h 15min**).

Descend north-east to a dip and go past the right-hand edge of a lochan then continue easily onto the eastern top of the hill. The view to Sgùrr na Còinnich on the other side of the glen is good, whilst on the mainland Beinn a' Chapuill is better seen, with the Munro Beinn Sgritheall to its side.

Now make a long descent of the east ridge, which is at a pleasant angle for most of the way. On the lower section, go past a minor top on its northern flank and continue for another 500m. The bottom part of the ridge is rather steeper and the vegetated slope gives hard going. Fight across the lower ground and head in the direction of a rusty metal shed.

Pick up a faint path along the coast and follow this inland to a hidden bridge across the Kylerhea River at NG784204. Emerge between the houses and turn right along a track which leads back to the road from the ferry. Turn left then right back to the start (**13.75km; 1300m; 6h**).

Sgùrr na Còinnich's south-east ridge from the approach to the Bealach nam Mulachag (Rab Anderson)

SKYE Beinn na Caillich, Beinn Dearg Mhòr (Broadford)

SKYE
Beinn na Caillich; *732m; (G41); L32; NG601233; peak of the old woman: a gigantic Fingalian woman (and a pot of gold) is said to be buried under the huge summit cairn*
Beinn Dearg Mhòr; *709m; (G83); L32; NG587228; big red mountain*

These hills of the Red Cuillin form a distinctive backdrop to the west of Broadford, especially the conical Beinn na Caillich, which is prominent when seen from the Skye Bridge crossing. The circuit of the two Grahams, together with the lesser Beinn Dearg Bheag, provides a splendid and scenic outing. It is a popular walk and there is a rough path in places, though not for all of the circuit.

It is possible to start the circuit by parking at NG620230, close to the end of the cul-de-sac road to Old Corry, gained off the A87 to the west of Broadford. The parking is to the side of the bridge over the Allt a' Choire, however, space can be difficult to find at times and the end of the road is a turning circle. Another option starts from the B8083 to Torrin at NG627220 where there is good parking on the grass opposite a chambered cairn. A prepared path joins a track which leads to a footbridge over the Broadford River and the road end at Old Corry (about 15min). There is a good view of all three hills on the circuit from this approach.

From the road end at Old Corry, where the distance and times are given from, head north-west directly towards the summit of Beinn na Caillich, following a faint path then crossing a burn to continue up its south side. The going steepens and the path disappears as the upper cone-shaped slope of scree and boulders is gained. Height is attained quickly to reach the trig point and large cairn which sit on the summit (**2km; 710m; 1h 45min**).

Descend westwards out along the broad ridge to gain the lowest point between the hills then continue up the elegant ridge which curves round to the top of Beinn Dearg Mhòr (**3.5km; 860m; 2h 25min**).

This sits at the head of the corrie and as well as offering fine views down this to the east, there is a tremendous view to the west over the head of Loch Slapin to Blàbheinn, Sgùrr nan Each, Garbh-bheinn then the Graham Belig which sits at the end of the ridge connecting this group. Poking up behind these peaks is the Cuillin.

Descend steeply down scree to the south-east to gain the Bealach Sgreamhach then climb the ridge onto 582m-high Beinn Dearg Bheag (**4.5km; 970m; 3h**).

Descend the long north-east ridge, cross the burn that issues from the corrie, Allt Beinn Deirge, then continue across the slope to the road at Old Corry (**8km; 970m; 3h 50min**).

Beinn na Caillich above Loch Cill Chriosd (Rab Anderson)

SKYE Beinn na Caillich, Beinn Dearg Mhòr (Broadford)

Beinn Dearg Mhòr from Beinn na Caillich with Blàbheinn, Garbh-bheinn and the Cuillin beyond (Rab Anderson)

A pleasant circuit of Beinn Dearg Mhòr and Beinn na Caillich can also be made from the north, around Coire Rèidh. The ascent begins from a section of the old road at Strollamus, parking at NG603267, just after a left-hand bend on the main road between Broadford and Portree.

Walk west along a track for almost 1km to cross the Allt Strollamus then take to a path which runs up the side of the burn. Follow this for 800m or so, to where it forks, then go up beside the left fork, the Allt na Teangaidh. Gain Pt.535m above the prominent dark crag ahead, Creagan Dubh, by a grassy runnel on the left of the north-east ridge; there are some alternative scrambling options. Continue across a change in rock type and climb to the top of Beinn Dearg Mhòr (**5km; 720m; 2h 20min**).

Descend north-east, then east to cross the head of Coire Rèidh, then climb to the top of Beinn na Caillich (**6.5km; 900m; 3h**).

The descent is via the north-west ridge between Coire Rèidh and Coire Seamraig; the going is a little easier closer to the right-hand edge. A descent of slabby rocks regains the Allt na Teangaidh which is followed back to the start as for the approach (**11.5km; 900m; 4h 40min**).

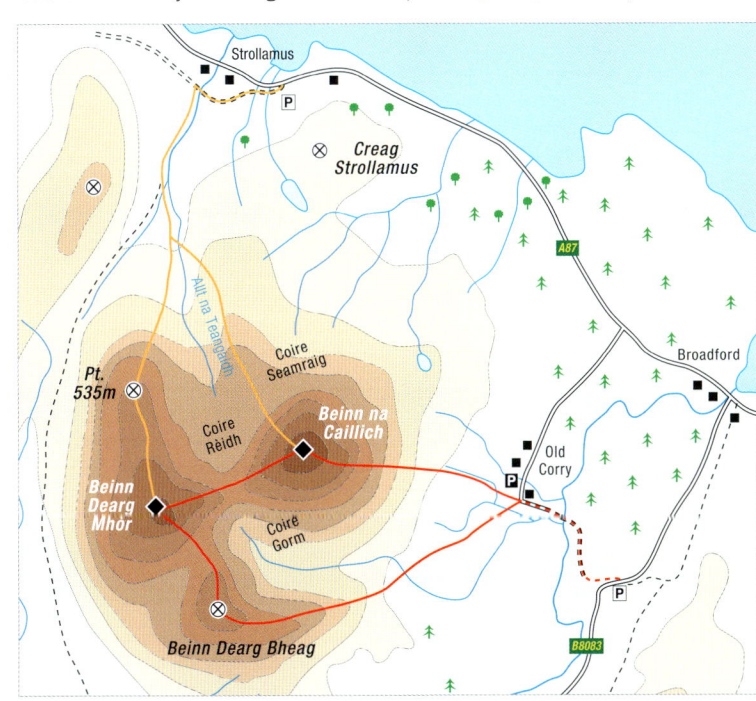

Belig, left, and Garbh-bheinn from the north (Rab Anderson)

> **SKYE**
>
> **Belig**; 702m; (G98); L32; NG544240; fore tooth, perhaps, from Gaelic 'beulag'; or a corruption of Gaelic 'bealach', pass, from Bealach na Beiste high on its west flank

Belig and its bigger neighbour, the Corbett Garbh-bheinn, occupy a prominent position overlooking the A87 where it loops around the head of Loch Ainort. The hills are linked by a fine ridge and although Belig gives a pleasant short outing on its own, it is normal to climb both hills together.

The best starting point for this traverse is the long layby (NG534267) in front of the Eas a' Bhradain waterfall, just around the bend where the A87 straightens for the uphill climb. Starting here also enables Marsco to be included if desired.

Walk down the road and cross the bridge over the Abhainn Ceann Loch Ainort; there is a small parking area on the west side of the bridge here. Leave the road and follow the left bank until a suitable place to cross the tributary which joins it can be found. This gains the slope at the foot of Belig's north ridge. It is possible to cut across to the ridge directly but the main burn, though not deep, might have to be waded. Climb the slope, which gradually steepens and narrows to a rocky section. This is bypassed via the scree slope to its right, although if taken more directly it gives a Grade 2 scramble; see the SMC guidebook *Skye Scrambles*.

Above this, the narrow, grassier crest is gained and leads to a fine summit (**3.5km; 690m; 2h**).

This point can also be reached by following the left-hand burn towards the col between Belig and Glas Bheinn Mhòr before climbing onto the shoulder at the top of the south-east ridge; also a possible descent should one wish.

Continuing with the round, descend towards Garbh-bheinn beside an old wall that runs down the rocky south-west ridge to gain the Bealach na Bèiste. Any steeper ground is easily bypassed. It is possible to drop north into the corrie to return from here but this misses the splendid north-east ridge of Garbh-bheinn, which gives a stiff but interesting 350m climb that passes remarkably quickly. The broad ridge starts easily, steepening to scree then narrowing to rockier ground with an easy but airy ridge to finish. Any difficulties are avoidable but if taken directly give a Grade 1/2 scramble (**5km; 1040m; 3h 15min**).

The views are stunning, especially south to the rocky Sgùrr nan Each, Clach Glas, Blàbheinn traverse and west to the main Cuillin ridge.

The descent curves around the corrie then drops down the long north ridge. Again, any difficulties can be avoided but if taken directly they give Grade 1/2 scrambling. The ridge kinks to the north-west for a 60m climb over Pt.489m then continues as the Druim Eadar Dà Choire, which leads to the waterfall above the road at the start (**9km; 1100m; 4h 35min**).

To include Marsco, from the col beneath Pt.489m, traverse west beneath scree to gain the col (323m) at the head of Coire nam Bruadaran. Follow a line of old fence posts up the fine and rocky south-east ridge of Marsco to reach its south summit (643m). Continue along the crest across a dip then up and along the splendid narrow arete to the summit (**8.5km; 1470m; 4h 45min**).

Return to the dip then descend a path north-east following the fence posts down the side of Coire nan Laogh. Cross the burn to gain the south side of Màm a' Phobuill then

SKYE **Belig** 341

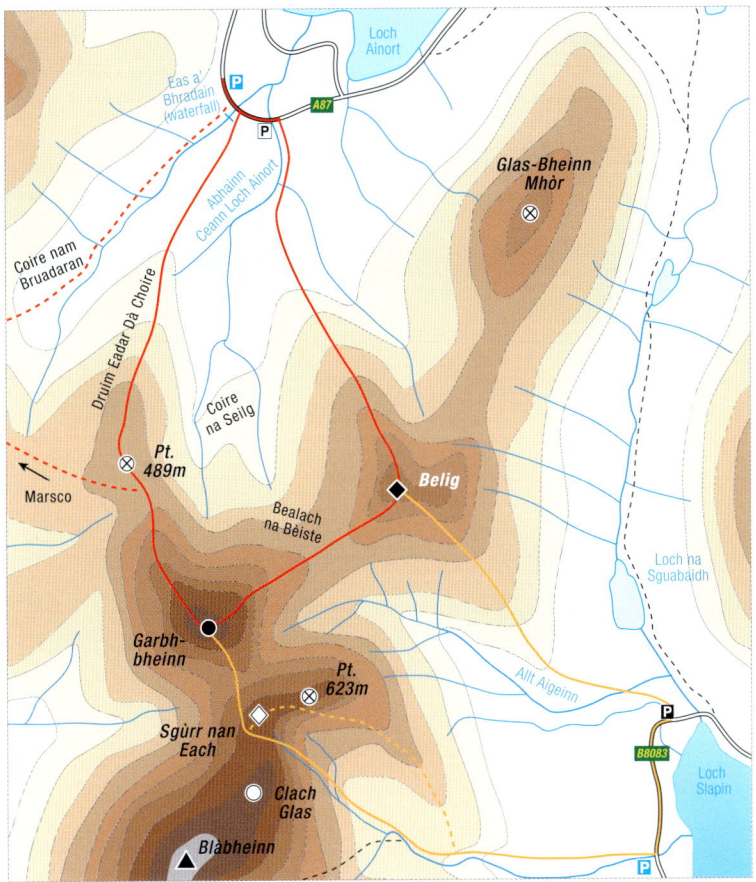

beyond Torrin. This is perhaps best done in an anti-clockwise direction starting with Belig, which also allows for variations or extensions at the end of the day. Either park at NG561224 on a loop of old road where a rough path heads across to the south-east ridge of Belig, or in the main car park for Blàbheinn then walk north along the road to this point. Once across the Allt Aigeinn the ridge quickly steepens and provides a stiff but fine route to first the east shoulder, then the summit (**2.5km; 700m; 1h 45min**).

Descend the south-west ridge to Bealach na Bèiste then ascend the north-east ridge of Garbh-bheinn to reach its summit, as for the previous route (**4km; 1050m; 3h**).

Descend the rocky south-east ridge which has some Grade 1 scrambling to reach the col with Sgùrr nan Each (636m). This peak can be skirted by a traverse south to reach the col with Clach Glas where a descent east down steep scree leads into Choire a' Càise to gain the Blàbheinn path where it runs down the burn back to the road (**8.5km; 1060m; 4h 20min**).

If Sgùrr nan Each is included, the ridge leading to the summit beyond its western top (Pt.623m) gives some Grade 1/2 scrambling. From a dip in front of the eastern top, descend the south-east ridge to join the Blàbheinn path (**9km; 1160m; 4h 40min**).

cross another burn and make a descending traverse to follow the Allt Coire nam Bruadaran back to the road (**12.5km; 1470m; 6h**).

A circuit of Belig and Garbh-bheinn can also be made from the south-east, from the B8083 where it loops around the head of Loch Slapin just

Belig from the flanks of Garbh-bheinn (Noel Williams)

342 SKYE Beinn Dearg Mhòr (Sligachan)

Beinn Dearg Mhòr's prominent profile from Marsco, with Glamaig, The Storr and Hartaval beyond (Noel Williams)

> **SKYE**
> **Beinn Dearg Mhòr;** *731m; (G49); L32; NG520285; big red mountain*

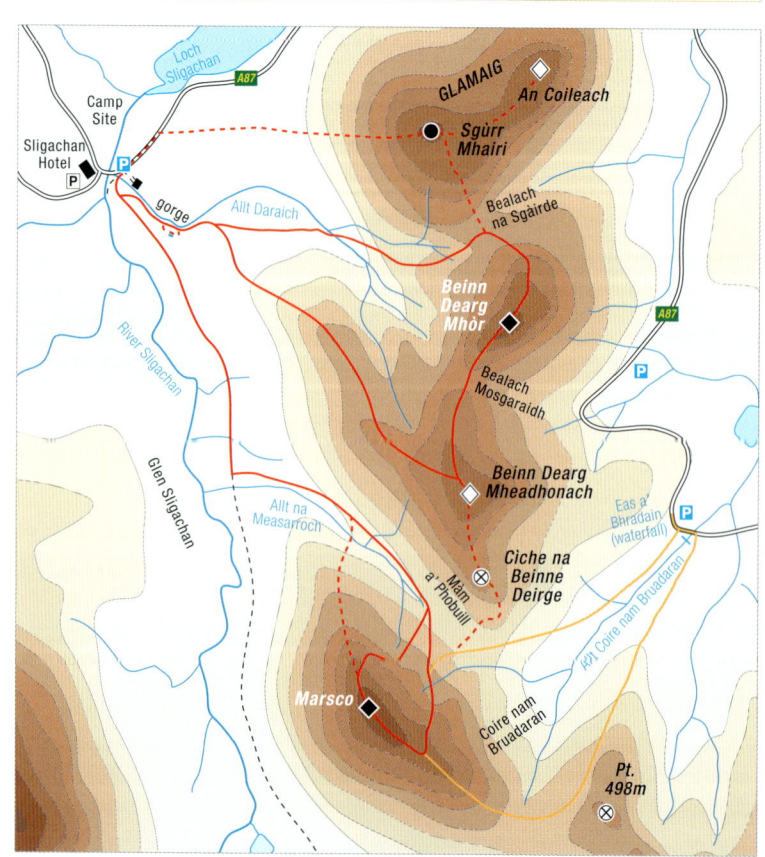

The hills of the Red Cuillin prominently form the east side of Glen Sligachan opposite the northern termination of the Cuillin Ridge. Sitting at the entrance to the glen is the great pyramidal cone of the Corbett Glamaig, then the two Grahams, Beinn Dearg Mhòr, which has a subsidiary top in Beinn Dearg Mheadhonach, and Marsco. This whole group can be climbed in one fine outing, but Beinn Dearg Mhòr and Marsco are described here as separate, more manageable walks.

Start the approach to Beinn Dearg Mhor from the car park on the east side of the bridge in front of the Sligachan Hotel, beside the entrance of the road to Sligachan self-catering bunkhouse and cottages.

Walk along the old road towards the picturesque old bridge and take the Loch Coruisk footpath past the statue of Mackenzie and Collie, keeping to the left-hand path. In a further 200m, when the path forks, go left through a gate and follow the path up the side of the Allt Daraich gorge. Pass a hummock to its left then go through a gate on the left and follow the path as it crosses boggy ground and curves round to the base of the ridge.

After the initial steepening, the ridge provides a fine highway leading to the final slopes of red-coloured scree, up which the path zigzags onto Beinn Dearg Mheadhonach (651m). The top lies a short distance to the south-east and is worth walking out to for the view (**4.5km; 660m; 2h 5min**).

Now head northwards around the edge of the eastern corrie, whose slopes plummet steeply to the road below, then descend to the Bealach Mosgaraidh. The steep pyramidal cone is climbed surprisingly quickly by a path which zigzags up through scree and juniper to reach the top of Beinn Dearg Mhòr (**6.25km; 880; 3h**).

Descend north and continue easily along the shoulder overlooking Coire nan Laogh, towards a small cairn at the end. Turn left towards Sligachan and drop down to pick up paths which descend steeply through scree to the Bealach na Sgàirde (415m).

Glamaig's long and very steep southern shoulder rises dauntingly upwards from here. For the fit this gives a steep, stony ascent to the western summit of Sgùrr Mhairi. The east top of An Coileach can be taken in if desired. A punishing descent can be made directly towards Sligachan, although it is perhaps easier to return to the Bealach na Sgàirde; an added 2km, 360m, 1h 20min to the day for Sgùrr Mhairi, or 4km, 520m, 2h 5min for An Coileach and Sgùrr Mhairi.

However, most will be content to leave Glamaig for another day and simply drop west off the Bealach na Sgàirde to Sligachan. A path leads across to the spur between the burns and is descended to their junction at NG505292. Either cross over to briefly follow the left bank, then cut across to the upward route, or cross to the right-hand burn and follow its right bank then cut the corner to regain the car park (**11km; 880m; 4h 30min**).

Steep scree runnels on the west face of Beinn Dearg Mhòr (Jim Teesdale)

Glamaig, left, Beinn Dearg Mhòr and Beinn Dearg Mheadhonach from Sgùrr nan Gillean (Rab Anderson)

Marsco from Glen Sligachan, flanked by Garbh-bheinn and Blàbheinn (Rab Anderson)

SKYE
Marsco; 736m; (G35); L32; NG507251; meaning obscure

One of the finest Grahams, this shapely hill is a distinctive member of the Western Red Hills group. Its eastern flank is seen clearly from the A87 coast road where it runs alongside Loch Ainort. A more familiar view is the impressive profile seen from the Sligachan Hotel when looking south along Glen Sligachan. An obvious crag stands out on its western flank, the Fiaclan Dearg.

The shortest approach is from the north-east but the route in Coire nam Bruadaran is rather boggy. A much better path runs along Glen Sligachan and this approach is preferred. Start from the same car park as for Beinn Dearg Mhòr, on the south side of the road a short distance to the east of the bridge over the River Sligachan.

Walk along the old road towards the old bridge and take the Loch Coruisk footpath past the statue of Mackenzie and Collie, keeping to the left-hand path. When the Beinn Dearg Mhòr path breaks off left through a gate after 200m, continue ahead. It is further than it looks and it takes an hour to reach the foot of the mountain. After 3km it is important to take the left fork in the path and stay on the north bank of the Allt na Measarroch, climbing steadily in a south-easterly direction to a broad bealach called Màm a' Phobuill.

Before the bealach is reached, a route can be taken up the steep northern end of the mountain. However, it is perhaps slightly more interesting to continue to the bealach for a route. From there, rather than go up and down the same way by the path beside the fenceposts, a circuit can be made by ascending the faint north-eastern spur to the right of the central corrie; Coire nan Laogh.

Slant off to the right just before the highpoint of the bealach and head towards a rather indistinct, broad, rocky spur which separates this corrie from another shallow corrie to the right. The way to tackle this spur is by a faint grassy ramp which slants gently upwards from left to right. To do this, when the slope steepens, ascend a grassy patch to the left of a

Marsco's summit ridge with Sgùrr nan Gillean beyond (Noel Williams)

train of boulders then clamber over boulders to reach the start of the ramp and follow this rightwards without undue difficulty. Eventually emerge in the upper part of the corrie where a distinctive reptilian-like rock can be seen in profile on the skyline. Continue up the slope above to gain the crest of the north ridge at the southern end of a horizontal section.

Turn left and ascend a pleasant stretch of ridge directly to the narrow summit, marked by a small and precariously perched cairn (**6.5km; 730m; 2h 40min**).

The views are breathtaking. The whole Cuillin range lies across Glen Sligachan to the west, Blàbheinn, Garbh-bheinn and Belig are close by to the south and the rest of the Western Red Hills lie to the north.

Descend the delightful south ridge with superb views straight ahead of Blàbheinn and its neighbours. At a dip (NG511249) before the small south-east top, turn left and descend northwards by a line of old fence posts. Towards the bottom, cross a burn to regain the Màm a' Phobuill col and return by the approach route (**13.5km; 730m; 4h 30min**).

From the bealach Màm a' Phobuill, Marsco can be linked with Beinn Dearg Mhòr, via the small but finely proportioned summit of Cìche na Beinn Deirge (509m) to the south-east of Beinn Dearg Mheadhonach.

Marsco from the Allt Coire nam Bruadaran to the north-east (Tom Prentice)

This is done by ascending north-east from the bealach to a path running east below the extensive screes on the south side of Cìche na Beinn Deirge. Follow this path, a little faint in places, round to the south-east face with views north-east to Loch Ainort, to gain heathery and rocky sections in the scree which can be ascended north with more ease to gain the cairned summit.

From here, follow the broad ridge to a col, then ascend straight up Beinn Dearg Mheadhonach's south ridge to the summit. Continue to Beinn Dearg Mhòr (**11.5km; 1350m; 5h 5min**), then return as described on p343 (**15.25km; 1350m; 6h 35min**). Including Glamaig as described on p343 is an additional 2km, 360m, 1h 20min.

The ascent of Marsco from the north-east starts from the car park at the bend in the road by the Eas a' Bhradain waterfall. Ascend the Druim Eadar Dà Choire ridge which extends from Garbh-bheinn. Cut off right before Pt.489m to gain the bealach, then climb the south-east ridge to the summit (**4.5km; 735m; 2h 15min**).

Descend as for the main route then return alongside the boggy Allt Coire nam Bruadaran (**8.5km; 735m; 3h 30min**).

Marsco can also be included in an extended round with Belig and Garbh-bheinn from this starting point (see p340).

See previous pages for map

Marsco, left, Beinn Dearg Mheadhonach in shade, Beinn Dearg Mhòr and Glamaig from Garbh-bheinn (Tom Prentice)

The Storr and the Old Man of Storr from across Loch Leathan (Rab Anderson)

> **SKYE**
>
> **The Storr**; 719m; (G67); L23; NG495540; the steep high cliff, from Gaelic 'stòr'. Possibly a Gaelicisation of original old Norse 'stor', large
>
> **Hartaval**; 669m; (G145); L23; NG480551; hill of the stag. Old Norse 'fjall', mountain, has been Gaelicised to '-bhal', and Anglicised to '-val'

The two Grahams of The Storr and its more retiring partner, Hartaval, form the highest points on the fabulous Trotternish Ridge which snakes its way up the length of the Trotternish Peninsula in northern Skye.

The ascent to the summit of The Storr passes one of the island's most iconic landmarks, the leaning rock pinnacle of the Old Man of Storr. The scenery and the rock architecture of the landslip area around the Old Man are spectacular and it is one of the 'must see' places in Scotland. As a result the main car park is busy. However, there is a choice of parking depending on the route chosen.

There are effectively two routes, which start about 900m apart, some 6 miles (10km) to the north of Portree, at the end of the Storr lochs; Loch Fada and Loch Leathan. There is an area of felled forest here which has somewhat affected the aesthetics of the surroundings, at least until new growth occurs.

Perhaps the more popular route starts from the large but busy pay and display tourist car park located at NG510531, directly below the Old Man and the felled forestry. From there, a good path leads steeply through the felled area, then on up boulder-strewn slopes to pass to the right of the Old Man who leans skywards from his precarious perch on a mound, amidst a mass of attendant pinnacles and twisted rock formations in Coire Faoin. Swing right on a path that runs north between Needle Rock and the impressive cliffs

Needle Rock, left, and The Old Man of Storr (Iain Thow)

to make a rising traverse below the cliffs, which gradually diminish in height. Cross a fence, then a small rock band marking the end of the cliffs and emerge on the east shoulder of the hill.

There are two options from here.

(i) The easiest route, suited to those of a more nervous disposition, follows a fairly level path that makes a wide arc across Coire Scamadal to reach the north ridge on the corrie's far side. This ridge then leads pleasantly south up to the trig point on the amazingly flat and grassy summit of The Storr, which sits on the very edge of the precipice high above Coire Faoin and the rock formations of The Sanctuary (**4.25km; 560m; 1h 55min**).

(ii) A steeper and more direct line from the east shoulder follows the left-hand edge above the cliffs, which although shorter is perhaps more time consuming. Traces of path lead up a barren slope of scree and through small rock bands where there is much looseness. However, it is a spectacular way to the top and passes the head of a number of impressive gullies that split the massive cliffs and offer glimpses of the Old Man far below. Towards the top it is possible to climb onto the pinnacle which is The Storr East Top (c710m). However, this sits above big drops and although relatively easy, great care should be taken. Beneath this top, traverse right and either go up a small rock bluff, or traverse

Hartaval, centre, and The Storr, left, from the north (Tom Prentice)

beneath it then ascend to regain the path and a ladder of steps up a steep grassy slope in a shallow gully that forms an obvious break in the upper rocks. Emerge onto the flat grassy slopes leading to the summit.

Leave the summit of The Storr northwards and descend a short way along the rim of the corrie before dropping more steeply west off the back to reach the Bealach a' Chuirn below Hartaval. Continue up the shoulder and follow a line of old fence posts, crossing the head of a fine corrie, to reach Hartaval's summit (**6.25km; 740m; 2h 45min**).

Return to the Bealach a' Chuirn then gain the northern shoulder of The Storr by climbing diagonally left up the slope above a rock outcrop, aiming for a small rock bluff. Traverse across Coire Scamadal and return by the route of ascent past the Old Man (**11.25km; 840m; 4h 15min**).

The other route starts to the south at NG502524, where there is a gated parking area, or verge parking, and is the least used by tourists. It is also the better route for a circuit, returning via the Bealach Beag. Climb northwards to gain then follow the wall and fence up the side of the felled area. Swing round through a gap into Coire Faoin to reach an area known as The Sanctuary. Massive impregnable cliffs, riven with dark gullies tower above here and form an impressive backdrop to the chaotic landscape. Various paths allow the many nooks and crannies to be investigated.

The previous route is joined on the north side of the Old Man and followed onto the east shoulder then via option (i) or (ii) to the summit of The Storr (**4.5km; 580m; 2h**) and on to Hartaval (**6.5km; 760m; 2h 50min**).

Return to the Bealach a' Chuirn then contour south around the west flank of The Storr, initially following the fence posts, then a line below them to reach the Bealach Beag. Aim for the lowest point then pick up the burn and follow this steeply down a break in the cliffs with little rock steps. Care is required here, although there is nothing of any difficulty. Beneath this, grassy slopes lead back to the start (**10.5km; 760m; 4h**).

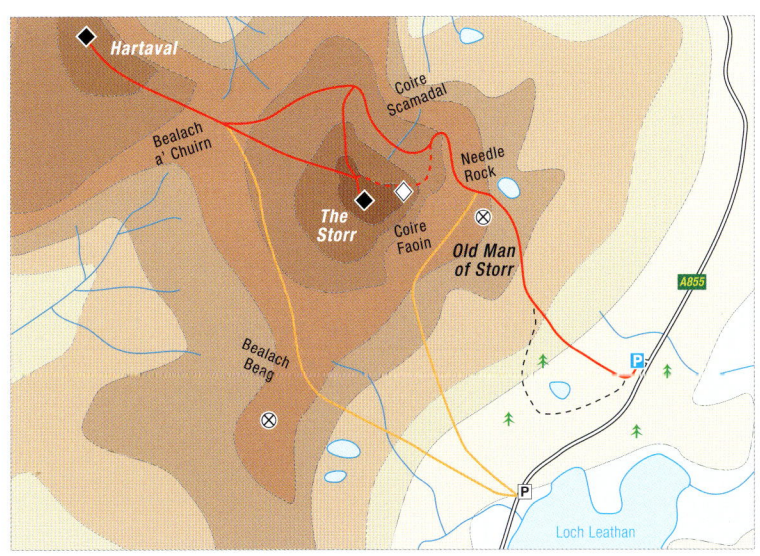

SOUTH UIST
Beinn Mhòr; 620m; (G203); L22; NF808310; big mountain

A rugged chain of hills runs down the eastern side of The Uists, and their highpoint on South Uist, Beinn Mhòr, is a fine hill with a splendid lofty ridge. On one side this looks out over a sprinkling of lochans and long sandy beaches into the Atlantic Ocean with St Kilda visible to the north-west, whilst on the other it gives views over The Minch to Skye with the mainland beyond. The ascent of Beinn Mhòr provides a memorable day out.

Start at Àirigh nam Bàn at the road end along the north side of Loch Aineort, taking care not to block the turning circle (NF787282).

Walk east through the trees and fuchsias on a well-constructed footpath just above the sea, passing a ruin and crossing a bridge over the head of a small inlet. A little further on, at another ruined building there is a deeper inlet and the path, now less distinct, runs up the west side of this. Pass around the head of the inlet and cross the two burns that drain into it, then climb a stile over a low fence

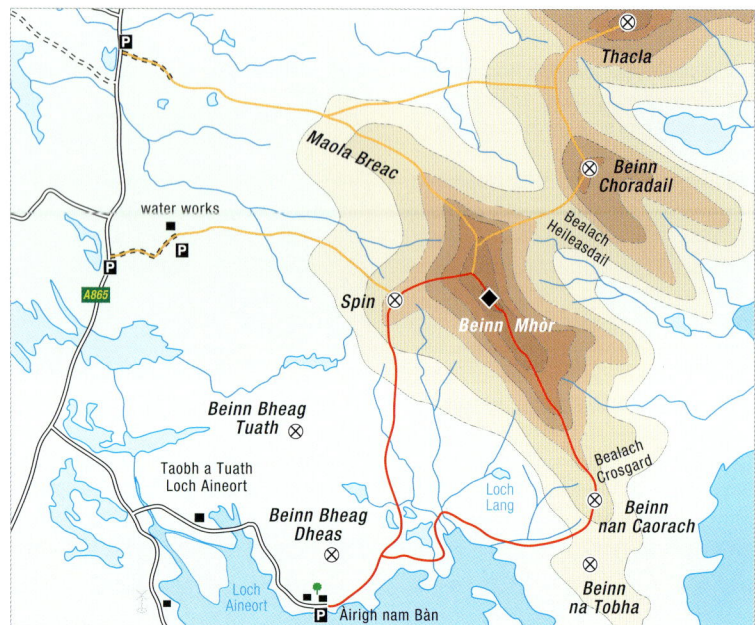

and continue up and around the other side to pick up a path. This traverses the slope away from the obvious notch of the Bealach Crosgard, which is the direction you feel you should be going in. However, the direct approach to the bealach gives steeper and tougher going.

Cross a small bridge over the burn draining from Beinn nan Caorach and

The south ridge of Beinn Mhòr above Bealach Crosgard (Rab Anderson)

Looking south to Beinn Mhòr's summit and the Heileasdale Buttresses with Skye in the distance (Noel Williams)

Beinn na Tobha, then start to climb upwards beside the right-hand burn and curve up onto Beinn nan Caorach (347m), which is crossed to gain the Bealach Crosgard. Now with fine views opening up all around, climb grassy slopes onto the whaleback ridge which provides a pleasant climb past a false top to the summit trig point, perched on the edge of some cliffs (**6km; 700m; 2h 40min**).

After a short descent, continue to the slight rise that is the northern top, along a splendid narrow ridge with steep slopes plummeting dramatically into Gleann Heileasdail to the east. Drop down steeply due west using the grassy slopes between the boulders to reach a small lochan then the top of the spur of Spin (356m). Descend,the broad rocky ridge south towards Loch Aineort. Cross the flats below and head between two small lochans to pass the western end of Loch nam Faoileann to reach the path at the first small inlet, which leads back to the start (**11.5km; 710m; 4h 15min**).

A quicker route, though not as good, starts from the road to the water works that goes through an unlocked gate to the side of the A865 past the standing stone at NF770322. This gains a helpful 50m of height. Go round the north side of the knoll of Beinn a' Charra then cross the burn and climb Spin via its north-west shoulder. Thereafter climb steeply to the north top of Beinn Mhòr and traverse the ridge to gain the summit (**4.5km; 590m; 2h**). Return the same way (**9km; 610m; 3h 20min**).

Another route uses the peat track which starts at NF768346 on the A865 at the north end of Loch Dòbhrain; verge parking. This is the better start point for the fine round which takes in Beinn Corradail and Thacla. Follow the peat track to its end then pass a group of three small lochans to climb onto Maola Breac, the north-west ridge of Beinn Mhòr, and continue up the narrow upper section to gain the north top. Thereafter the splendid level crest leads to the summit (**6km; 620m; 2h 25min**).

Return to the north top then descend the north-east ridge to the Bealach Heileasdail. From there, gain the south-east ridge of Beinn Choradail by a slanting climb due east up its steep but easy south-west flank, crossing a small subsidiary grassy top to gain the Fèith-Bhealach then the 527m summit of Beinn Choradail (**9km; 870m; 3h 45min**).

To reach Thacla from here, it is important to avoid the steep buttresses that flank the north side of Beinn Choradail. Do this by first heading north-north-east for 50m or so along the short summit ridge from the summit cairn to find a small scree gully. Descend this to a sloping grassy traverse which leads down north-west to the broad bealach between the hills, at the head of Gleanns Uisinis and Dorchaidh. The summit of Thacla (606m) is then easily reached by a steep, grassy and stony ascent of its south-west flank (**11.5km; 1170m; 5h**).

The best descent is to return to the bealach then descend the north-west spur of Beinn Choradail, Maoladh Creag nam Fitheach, and traverse west across the foot of the north-west ridge of Beinn Mhòr to the head of the peat track and follow this back to the road (**18km; 1170m; 6h 50min**).

The linear traverse of Beinn Mhòr, Beinn Choradail and Thacla, starting from Àirigh nam Bàn and finishing at Loch Sgioport, is a splendid outing but with the obvious problem that the finish is some way from the start.

Uisgneabhal Mòr and Tèileasbhal from Aird Asaig to the south (Rab Anderson)

> ### HARRIS
>
> **Uisgneabhal Mòr**; 729m; (G53); L13, 14; NB120085; *Old Norse 'fjall', mountain, has been Gaelicised to '-bhal'. The first element is probably old Norse but Gaelicised to 'uisge' water*

Uisgneabhal Mòr and its smaller neighbour Tèileasbhal form the central part of the beautiful and rugged North Harris Hills. Lying to the west of the higher An Cliseam group of hills and to the east of the other two Harris Grahams, Oireabhal and Tiorga Mòr, they are a shapely pair of peaks that catch the eye when travelling north on the road from Tarbert.

Park either side of the bridge over the river at the sea inlet of Loch Mhiabhaig, at the start of the track up Gleann Mhiabhaig. This track is the return route past the mighty rock prow of Sròn Scourst, seen in profile ahead.

Walk beside a fence on the east side of the river for 300m and, where this veers off right, strike up the hillside. There is no path and initially the going is quite tough, but once the knoll of Creag na Speireig is reached it becomes easier and the elegant south ridge of Uisgneabhal Mòr leads upwards with ever expanding views.

Broad at first, the ridge gradually narrows down and traces of a path are picked up, which lead along the top of some cliffs to the east to a large cairn perched right on the edge (**4km; 730m; 2h 10min**).

There are fine views east across the narrow rift to Mulla bho Thuath and Mulla bho Deas in the An Cliseam group, as well as west to Oireabhal.

Descend north through a boulderfield, then down steep grassy slopes

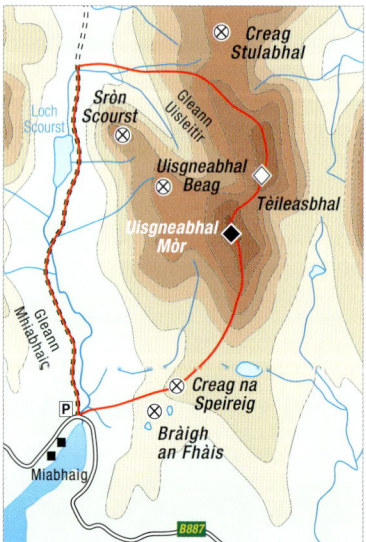

around the edge of the corrie and down through another boulder field to reach the col between the two peaks. The ascent to Tèileasbhal (697m) is steep but short-lived, and a small crag which bars the way up the crest is easily bypassed (**5km; 870m; 2h 45min**).

A shorter return is possible, but it is better to drop down and follow the summit spur north to its end before heading down the long north-west shoulder through boulders, aiming for two lochans that can be seen ahead at the end of the track in the main glen. The line of descent runs along the head of the hanging-valley of Gleann Uisleitir, on the other side of which the rocky profile of Sròn Scourst holds the view.

Eventually drop off this shoulder, just after a steepening, and descend to the burn, which leads to the track in Gleann Mhiabhaig. A fairly level 4.5km walk along this track leads back to the start, passing beneath Sròn Scourst, whose rocky slopes tower above the track and the lochan at its foot (**12.5km; 870m; 4h 45min**).

HARRIS

Oireabhal; 662m; (G159); L13, 14; NB083099; Old Norse 'fjall', mountain, has been Gaelicised to '-bhal'. The first element is possibly Old Norse 'orri', moorfowl, i.e. red grouse. There are also two peaks of this name on Harris and one on Rum

Tiorga Mòr; 679m; (G130); L13, 14; NB055115; Tiorga is obscure, 'mòr' is Gaelic for big

Together with their satellite tops, these two Grahams lie either side of Gleann Chliostair and are the highest points of the westernmost hills of North Harris. Oireabhal forms part of a 7km-long ridge that runs along the east side of the glen and terminates with the great rock promontory of Sròn Uladail. Tiorga Mòr lies on the other side of the glen and is the higher and more rugged of the pair. The traverse of the hills on the east side of the glen, followed by a visit to view the dramatic cliffs of Sròn Uladail then the ascent of Tiorga Mòr gives a superb outing.

The views from these hills are stunning and extend north beyond the Harris Hills to the Uig Hills on Lewis then north-west to the sand-fringed island of Scarp. To the south is the island of Taransay, the sands of Luskentyre and hills of South Harris. If you are lucky, out west will be the islands of St Kilda, sitting on the edge of the Continental Shelf.

The best starting point for the full circuit is at the northern end of Loch nan Caor where there is off-road parking at a bend on the B887 (NB065073), about 1km to the west of the highpoint of the road at Cliasmol. Alternatively, park further west, at the start of the access road to Loch Chliostair (see below) and walk the 1.5km east along the road at the start, rather than the end.

Climb east onto the south-west shoulder of Cleiseabhal (511m) and follow this to the trig point on the stony top (**2km; 460m; 1h 15min**).

Crags fall steeply to the north of the summit, and the route descends north-east onto the connecting ridge, which runs north above crags on the east side, to reach a well-defined bouldery bealach. From here, the ridge continues north over the small intermediate summit of Bìdigidh (500m) then on to the summit of Oireabhal (**4km; 740m; 2h 15min**).

Drop down the slope to the north-north-east to gain the bealach then climb the ridge onto the fine Ulabhal (659m). Descend northwards towards the lesser top of Muladal then swing westwards and descend close to the burn to reach the path running along the floor of the glen at the north end of Loch Aiseabhat. The simple option from here is to make the 340m climb straight up the other side onto the ▶

Tiorga Mòr from Oireabhal across Gleann Chliostair (Grahame Nicoll)

Oireabhal and Bìdigidh from near Amhuinnsuidhe (Rab Anderson)

unnamed rounded grassy top at NB061121, which is probably Tiorga Beag; the OS place this name further north where there is no summit. From here, a short drop south-west and a final 130m climb gain the trig point and cairn on Tiorga Mòr (**9.5km; 1210m; 4h 30min**).

However, a longer and better route descends the path north, out in front of the remarkable overhanging cliffs of Sròn Uladail, which sits sphinx-like at the head of the glen. Regarded as the most impressive crag in the British Isles, the Sròn is home to some of the hardest rock climbs in the country. Continue to Loch Uladail out in front of the nose itself, on the left of which is where pioneers in the late 1930s recorded the area's first climbs. Now, either retrace your steps to Loch Aiseabhat for the onward ascent, or climb west up the steep hillside to gain a shallow col south of Màs a' Chnoic Chuairtich then traverse south along the rocky ridge above the crags of Creagan Leathan. Ascend Tiorga Beag and continue to Tiorga Mòr. This detour adds another 4km, 180m, 1h 15min onto the final time given below.

Two options exist for the descent off Tiorga Mòr. The most obvious is to go down the fine south-east ridge to cross the dam at the south end of Loch Chliostair then follow the track back. However, although there are no real difficulties there is a lot of rough, rocky terrain. The other option is to head south down less complicated slopes, either directly to the track, or perhaps easier to the path through Gleann Leòsaid then the track.

Follow the track then access road to the B887 just to the east of the gates to Amhuinnsuidhe, where a 1.5km road walk leads back to the start (**16.5km; 1250m; 6h 40min**).

Oireabhal can be climbed on its own starting at (NB065073), as for the main traverse described above (**4km; 740m; 2h 15min**), then returning over Bìdigidh and descending south-west from the bealach south of this, first

Sròn Uladail with the summits of Ulabhal and Oireabhal beyond (Noel Williams)

steeply, then west more gently to the small Loch Collas Sgairbhe. From here, a descending traverse of the west flank of Cleiseabhal leads easily back to the start (8km; 780m; 3h 30min).

Another option is to park along the road signposted to Chliostair Power Station and Marine Harvest's Amhuinnsuidhe Hatchery. Do not park in the entrance since large vehicles require this for turning. There is limited space beside the gates to Amhuinnsuidhe and a short way up the track where the riverside verge is wide enough to accommodate a number of vehicles opposite a passing place. There is also limited parking at the locked gate 400m further on where the road forks right to the fish farm. Follow the track past Loch Leòsaid and the power station towards the dam, then head east to gain the south ridge of Oireabhal (5km; 650m; 2h 10min).

Tiorga Mòr from the south across Lochan Beag (Rab Anderson)

Either of these options can be extended north over Ulabhal, with a possible visit to view Sròn Uladail, then a return past Loch Aiseabhat and Loch Chliostair.

To climb Tiorga Mòr on its own, park along the start of the track to Loch Chliostair and follow it to the bridge across the burn flowing into Loch Leòsaid. Head north-west up Gleann Leòsaid, picking up a path after 500m or so and following it for another 500m before striking north up the steep but easy south flank of Tiorga Mòr to reach the summit (4km; 670m; 2h). Alternatively, carry on up Gleann Leòsaid to the bealach at NB040111 then head north, first to the attractive small Loch Bràigh Bheagarais, then to the bealach with Ceartabhal. Now head south to climb the north-east ridge to the top of Tiorga Mòr (7km; 670m; 2h 40min).

Another option is to continue past the power station, cross the dam and climb the south-east ridge, described in descent opposite. The ridge gives some easy, though avoidable, scrambling (5.5km; 670m; 2h 20min).

A return can be made by one of the other ascent options, or the outing can be extended down the north-east ridge to return past Loch Aiseabhat and Loch Chliostair.

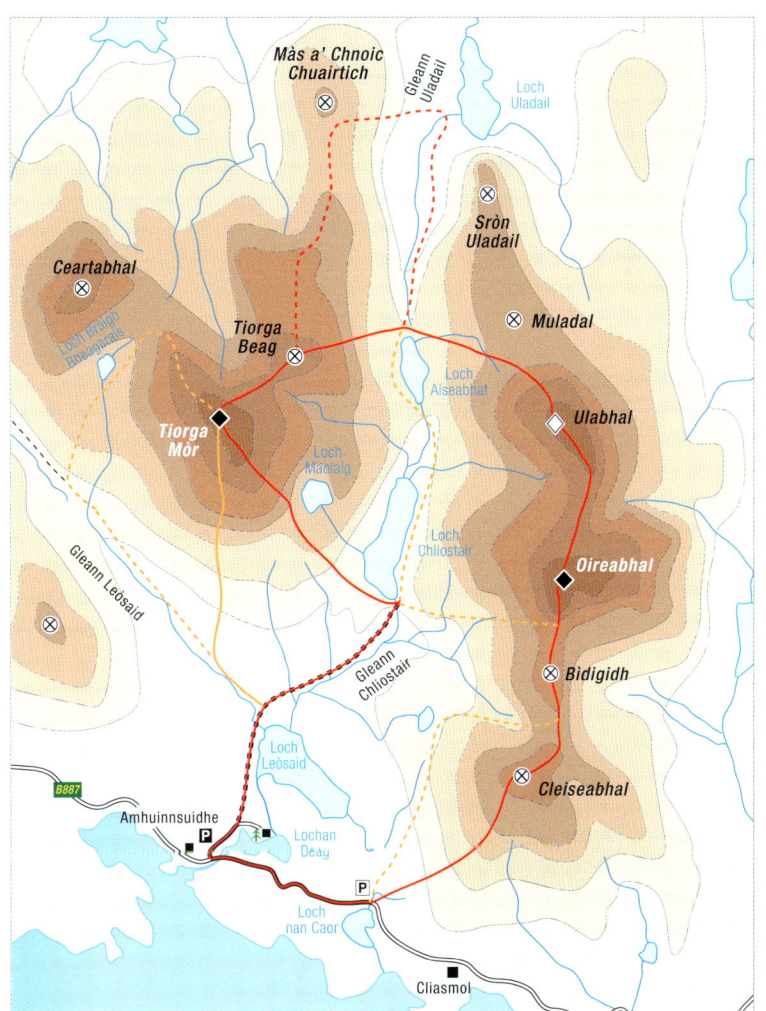

Scottish Hills over 2000ft (609.60m) and less than 2500ft (762m) in Height

The Table that follows lists 219 Scottish hills that are over 2000ft (609.60m) and less than 2500ft (762m) in height, which have an all round drop, or prominence, of 150m. Despite the metrication of UK mapping, the traditional method of grouping hills into their original imperial measurement height bands in feet has prevailed, in accordance with the height Tables for The Munros and The Corbetts, albeit that this creates odd metric equivalents for use with contemporary maps.

Hugh Munro's *Tables Giving All the Scottish Mountains Exceeding 3000ft in Height* was published in 1891 and John Rooke Corbett's *List of Scottish Mountains 2500ft and Under 3000ft in Height* was published in 1952. However, unlike Munro before him, Corbett set a separation criterion to illustrate how distinct each hill on his list was from those around it. This was based on a set number of map contour rings, subsequently interpreted to mean that hills on his list had to involve a reascent of 500ft (152.4m) on all sides, thereby illustrating their prominence, or what has become known as their drop.

A definitive list of the hills between 2000ft and 2500ft was finally agreed in 1992 between Alan Dawson and Fiona Torbet (neè Graham). They too continued the practice of grouping hills within a height band measured in feet, but a metric height separation criterion of 150m was applied, this being the closest round metric equivalent to 500ft. The hills were named The Grahams.

Alan Dawson maintains the official hill listing for The Grahams and that differs from the Table here because Dawson is actively resurveying hill heights, summit locations and cols to update the official list. Although the results of these surveys are noted in the Database of British and Irish Hills (DoBIH), at the time of writing not all are sent to the Ordnance Survey, with only significant data being passed to them for possible inclusion on their mapping. The Table here also differs from the official list in that it has been presented to run in the same order as the text and lists hills geographically rather than by height.

The Ordnance Survey is the national mapping authority responsible for the maintenance of the definitive record of Britain's geographic features. The OS produces the most widely-used maps for hillwalkers, and in order that this guidebook aligns with these maps, OS hill heights are used in the Table and throughout walk descriptions. The SMC recognises the ongoing survey work by Alan Dawson, and others, so has included the height information held in the DoBIH where it is different or more accurate than that on OS maps. See note at the end of Table on the DoBIH. The SMC hopes that the results of all independent surveys can be incorporated into the OS database for potential inclusion in future mapping.

Table/Column Explanations

Section Number & Name: For the purpose of this guidebook, the layout of this Table of Grahams differs from the official list maintained by Alan Dawson. For ease of use, the Grahams have been grouped into geographical Sections which correspond to the established Sections numbered 1-17 used by the SMC for *The Munros*, with the addition of a Section 0 to include the Lowland Hills for *The Corbetts*.

Where necessary, due to the size of a particular geographical Section and the resultant number of hills it contains, that Section has been subdivided by the use of an alphabetic letter. Section 0 has been divided into 0a, 0b and 0c, Section 1 into 1a and 1b and Section 10 into 10a and 10b. Due to the lack of Grahams in an area, some Sections have been combined for this book, namely Sections 2 & 3, and Sections 5, 6 & 7.

As with previous SMC Tables, these Sections are generally ordered in a logical snake-like progression through Scotland from the south-west to the north-east, finishing with The Islands. The official List of Grahams lists hills in each Section in descending order of height. However, again for ease of use in connection with this book, the Table here lists hills in a geographic order, which also has the advantage of having hills that are generally linked and climbed together appearing together in the Table.

Name: The name is generally that according to the OS. When there are two hills with the same name, standard brackets give a relevant location. When there is an overall name for a hill massif, or a second, or an alternative name for a hill, this is shown in square brackets.

Height: This is in metres and taken from OS maps. The next column lists the heights from the DoBIH that differ from and are more accurate than the OS heights.

G No: Grahams in order of height, (G1) being the highest, which is Beinn Talaidh (761m) and G219 being the lowest, which is Creag Dhubh Mhòr (611m).

OS Map & Grid Ref: The first two digits refer to the relevant OS 1:50k Landranger series map which covers the hill. An eight figure OS grid reference, prefixed by two grid letters, is given in the following Table, which provides the location of a summit to within 10m, and a six figure grid reference has been given in the text, which provides the location of a summit to within 100m.

Munro's Tables and Donald's Tables both included Tops. As a result Munro's Tables lists 508 summits, of which 282 are classed as separate mountains, or Munros, and 226 are subsidiary Munro Tops. Donald did the same, but fortunately Corbett did not do this and neither did Torbet and Dawson at the time, so Graham Tops are not listed here. For the uninitiated, Graham Tops do not just occur on Grahams, as indeed Munro Tops only occur on Munros, they occur on Grahams, Corbetts and Munros, and they number around 1000. Being higher, Corbett Tops occur on Corbetts and Munros and number around 700. Complete lists of Grahams, Graham Tops and Corbett Tops were published by TACit Press. At the time of writing, Pedantic Press are to publish a book on the official Grahams listing; check the Pedantic Press website.

Name	Height	(DoBIH)	G No	OS Map	Grid Ref	Page	Date climbed
SECTION 0a – Galloway & The Lowthers							
Cairnsmore of Fleet	711		G78	83	NX 5016 6707	16	
Lamachan Hill	717		G70	77	NX 4352 7690	18	
Millfore	657		G167	77	NX 4779 7545	18	
Mullwharchar	692		G115	77	NX 4542 8664	21	
Craignaw	645		G179	77	NX 4592 8333	21	
Windy Standard	698		G108	77	NS 6201 0146	32	
Blackcraig Hill	700	(700.9)	G104	71,77	NS 6476 0640	32	
Queensberry	697		G110	78	NX 9890 9975	34	
Ballencleuch Law	689		G118	78	NS 9356 0497	36	
Green Lowther	732		G43	71,78	NS 9003 1203	38	
SECTION 0b – The Borders							
Tinto	711		G79	72	NS 9532 3437	44	
Culter Fell	748	(748.3)	G14	72	NT 0528 2908	46	
Gathersnow Hill	688		G120	72	NT 0587 2570	48	
Andrewhinney Hill	677	(677.3)	G136	79	NT 1975 1387	50	
Croft Head	637		G186	79	NT 1530 0565	52	
Capel Fell	678		G132	79	NT 1639 0690	52	
Ettrick Pen	692	(691.8)	G114	79	NT 1999 0765	52	
Dun Rig	744		G21	73	NT 2534 3155	68	
Blackhope Scar	651		G172	73	NT 3152 4833	70	
Windlestraw Law	659	(659.2)	G161	73	NT 3712 4309	72	
Cauldcleuch Head	619	(618.6)	G207	79	NT 4565 0068	74	
SECTION 0c – The Midland Valley							
Ben Cleuch	721		G61	58	NN 9027 0063	79	
Uamh Bheag	666	(665.8)	G152	57	NN 6911 1185	83	
SECTION 1a – Loch Fyne to Loch Lomond							
Cruach nan Capull	612		G216	63	NS 0957 7954	87	
Beinn Ruadh	664		G155	56	NS 1557 8837	88	
Beinn Mhòr	741	(741.5)	G28	56	NS 1078 9081	89	
Beinn Bheag	618		G208	56	NS 1259 9320	89	
Creag Tharsuinn	643		G18	56	NS 0882 9136	91	
Beinn Lochain	703	(702.9)	G96	56	NN 1602 0062	92	
Cruach nam Mult	611	(611.2)	G218	56	NN 1682 0563	94	
Stob an Eas	732		G46	56	NN 1853 0738	95	
Beinn Chaorach	713		G73	56	NS 2875 9236	96	
Beinn a' Mhanaich	709		G85	56	NS 2691 9460	96	
Beinn Eich	703		G95	56	NS 3021 9467	98	
Cruach an t-Sìthein	684		G122	56	NS 2752 9651	98	
Doune Hill (a)	734		G38	56	NS 2905 9708	98	
Mid Hill	657		G166	56	NS 3214 9626	98	
Tullich Hill	632		G194	56	NN 2935 0064	101	
Beinn Bhreac	681	(680.8)	G126	56	NN 3213 0005	101	
Beinn Damhain	684		G123	50,56	NN 2820 1730	103	
Fiarach	652	(652.2)	G171	50	NN 3448 2615	104	
Meall Odhar	656		G169	50	NN 2980 2984	105	
Beinn Bhalgairean	636	(636.8)	G187	50	NN 2026 2410	106	
Meall nan Gabhar (b)	744		G20	50	NN 2357 2402	106	
SECTION 1b – Loch Lomond to Loch Tay							
Cruinn a' Bheinn	632		G192	56	NN 3654 0514	111	
Ben Venue	729		G52	57	NN 4746 0633	112	
Meall Mòr	747		G16	50,56	NN 3837 1515	114	
Sgiath a' Chaise	645	(644.2)	G180	57	NN 5836 1694	115	
Creag Mhòr	658		G162	57	NN 5103 1851	116	
The Stob	753	(753.6)	G9	51	NN 4913 2318	118	

Grahams

Name	Height (DoBIH)	G No	OS Map	Grid Ref	Page	Date climbed
Stob Breac	688	G121	57	NN 4473 1661	119	
Creag na h-Eararuidh (c)	708 (708.3)	G86	57	NN 6851 1899	120	
Mòr Bheinn	640 (640.3)	G184	51,57	NN 7162 2117	121	
Meall Buidhe	719	G66	51	NN 5768 2757	122	
Creag Gharbh	637 (637.4)	G185	51	NN 6323 3273	123	
Creag Each	672 (673.7)	G142	51	NN 6525 2637	124	
Creag Ruadh	712	G76	51	NN 6742 2925	124	
Ciste Buide a' Claidheimh [Shee of Ardtalnaig]	759	G4	51,52	NN 7295 3515	126	
Beinn na Gainimh	730 (729.3)	G50	52	NN 8372 3446	129	
Meall nan Caorach	623 (623.7)	G199	52	NN 9286 3389	128	
Meall Reamhar	620 (617.8)	G204	52	NN 9220 3326	128	
Meall Dearg	690 (690.3)	G116	52	NN 8865 4149	121	
SECTION 2 & 3 – Loch Tay to Loch Linnhe						
Meall a' Mhuic	745	G17	42,51	NN 5793 5080	133	
Beinn na Sròine	636	G188	50	NN 2339 2894	136	
Beinn Donachain	650 (651.4)	G174	50	NN 1988 3165	137	
Màm Hael	726	G56	50	NN 0085 4089	142	
Beinn Mòlurgainn	690 (688.3)	G117	50	NN 0195 4006	142	
Beinn Mheadhonach	715	G72	50	NN 0198 3689	142	
Beinn nan Lus	709	G84	50	NN 1307 3757	141	
Meall Garbh	701 (700.3)	G101	50	NN 1679 3672	140	
Beinn Suidhe	676	G138	50	NN 2117 4004	139	
Meall Tairbh	665 (664.4)	G154	50	NN 2509 3758	138	
Sgòrr a' Choise	663	G158	41	NN 0844 5515	144	
Meall Mòr	676	G140	41	NN 1061 5596	144	
Sgòrr na Cìche [Pap of Glencoe]	742 (742.4)	G27	41	NN 1252 5943	146	
Stob na Cruaiche [A' Chruach]	739	G33	41	NN 3636 5710	134	
SECTION 4 – Loch Linnhe to Loch Ericht						
Beinn na Gucaig	616	G211	41	NN 0629 6533	151	
Tom Meadhoin	621	G202	41	NN 0873 6210	151	
Creag Ghuanach	621	G201	41	NN 2999 6900	152	
Beinn na Cloiche	646 (645.1)	G177	41	NN 2847 6487	152	
Cnap Cruinn	742	G26	41	NN 3028 7748	154	
Binnein Shuas	747 (747.2)	G15	34,42	NN 4630 8268	155	
Binnein Shios	667 (667.1)	G149	34,42	NN 4924 8571	155	
Meall nan Eagan	658	G163	42	NN 5967 8747	157	
SECTION 5, 6 & 7 – Loch Ericht to Glen Esk						
Creag a' Mhadaidh	612 (611.4)	G217	42	NN 6346 6501	161	
Creag Ruadh	658	G164	42	NN 6852 8821	162	
Blath Bhalg	641 (640.4)	G183	43	NO 0194 6112	163	
Mount Blair	744	G19	43	NO 1674 6297	164	
Duchray Hill [Mealna Letter]	702	G99	43	NO 1615 6725	164	
Badandun Hill	740	G30	44	NO 2074 6788	166	
Cat Law	671	G144	44	NO 3188 6108	167	
Hill of Wirren	678	G133	44	NO 5228 7393	168	
Hunt Hill	705	G91	44	NO 3800 8053	170	
SECTION 8 – Deeside to Speyside						
Creag Bhalg	668	G147	43	NO 0917 9123	175	
Geallaig Hill	743	G23	37,44	NO 2979 9817	176	
Mona Gowan	749	G13	37	NJ 3359 0583	177	
Pressendye	619	G205	37	NJ 4903 0897	178	
The Buck	721	G62	37	NJ 4121 2339	179	

Name	Height	(DoBIH)	G No	OS Map	Grid Ref	Page	Date climbed
Cnap Chaochan Aitinn	715		G71	36	NJ 1458 0996	180	
Cook's Cairn	755		G8	37	NJ 3022 2783	182	
Creagan a' Chaise	722		G59	36	NJ 1042 2415	183	
Càrn a' Ghille Chearr	710		G81	36	NJ 1396 2985	183	

SECTION 9 – Speyside to the Great Glen

Name	Height	(DoBIH)	G No	OS Map	Grid Ref	Page	Date climbed
Càrn Glas-choire	659		G160	35,36	NH 8915 2916	189	
Càrn nan Tri-tighearnan	615		G212	27	NH 8231 3903	190	
Càrn na h-Easgainn	618	(617.0)	G209	27	NH 7440 3207	191	
Creag Liath	743		G25	35	NH 6637 0077	192	
Creag Dhubh (Newtonmore)	756		G7	35	NN 6780 9723	193	
Creag Ruadh	622		G200	35	NN 5580 9138	194	
Creag Dhubh (Glen Spean)	658		G165	34,41	NN 3226 8245	195	
Lèana Mhòr (west)	684		G124	34,41	NN 2847 8787	196	
Lèana Mhòr (east)	676		G139	34,41	NN 3171 8791	197	

SECTION 10a – Loch Linnhe to Glenfinnan

Name	Height	(DoBIH)	G No	OS Map	Grid Ref	Page	Date climbed
Beinn Mheadhoin	739		G32	49	NM 7991 5144	201	
Beinn na Cille	652		G170	49	NM 8543 5420	202	
Druim na Sgrìodain	734	(734.6)	G39	40	NM 9784 6561	203	
Sgòrr Mhic Eacharna	650	(650.5)	G175	40	NM 9284 6304	204	
Beinn Bheag	736	(737.4)	G37	40	NM 9145 6353	204	
Sgùrr nan Cnamh	701	(701.8)	G103	40	NM 8866 6432	206	
Sgùrr a' Chaorainn	761	(760.6)	G2	40	NM 8950 6620	207	
Stob Mhic Bheathain	721		G63	40	NM 9140 7139	208	
Meall nan Damh	723		G58	40	NM 9194 7450	210	
Glas Bheinn (d)	636		G189	40	NM 9388 7584	210	
Beinn Gàire	666	(666.1)	G151	40	NM 7811 7488	212	
Croit Bheinn	663	(664.5)	G157	40	NM 8108 7733	212	

SECTION 10b – Glenfinnan to Glen Shiel

Name	Height	(DoBIH)	G No	OS Map	Grid Ref	Page	Date climbed
Sgùrr na Maothaich [Mèith Bheinn]	710		G82	40	NM 8215 8725	221	
Stob a' Ghrianain [Druim Fada]	744		G18	41	NN 0870 8240	217	
Aodann Chlèireig	663		G156	40	NM 9946 8254	218	
Meall Onfhaidh	681		G127	41	NN 0104 8408	218	
Glas-chàrn	633	(633.3)	G191	40	NM 8464 8373	220	
Mullach Coire nan Geur-oirean	727		G55	41	NN 0490 8927	222	
Glas Bheinn	732		G45	34	NN 1715 9189	223	
Sgùrr Chòinnich	749		G12	34	NN 1277 9497	224	
An Stac	718	(717.8)	G68	40	NM 8667 8890	226	
Meall Blàir	656	(656.5)	G168	33	NN 0774 9503	225	
Slat Bheinn	700	700.6)	G105	33	NG 9100 0274	228	
Meall nan Eun	667		G150	33	NG 9035 0522	228	
Beinn a' Chapuill	759	(759.8)	G3	33	NG 8351 1485	230	
Beinn Clachach	643	(642.3)	G181	33	NG 8859 1091	231	
Druim Fada	713	(710.7)	G75	33	NG 8946 0833	233	
Biod an Fhithich	646	(645.9)	G178	33	NG 9508 1473	234	

SECTION 11 – Glen Shiel to Loch Mullardoch (or Glen Cannich)

Name	Height	(DoBIH)	G No	OS Map	Grid Ref	Page	Date climbed
Càrnan Cruithneachd	729	(727.8)	G54	25,33	NG 9944 2582	239	
Càrn Mhic an Toisich	678		G134	34	NH 3105 1858	241	
Meall a' Chràthaich	679	(678.9)	G120	26	NH 3007 2209	241	
Meall Fuar-mhonaidh	699		G106	26	NH 4570 2221	243	
Glas-bheinn Mhòr	651		G173	26	NH 4368 2316	243	
Càrn a' Chaochain	706	(706.6)	G87	34	NH 2351 1778	245	
Beinn a' Mheadhoin	613		G213	25	NH 2186 2555	247	

Name	Height (DoBIH)	G No	OS Map	Grid Ref	Page	Date climbed
SECTION 12 – Loch Mullardoch (or Glen Cannich) to Glen Carron						
Càrn na Breabaig	679	G131	25	NH 0667 3015	251	
Càrn Gorm	677 (677.3)	G137	26	NH 3286 3551	252	
Beinn na Muice	695	G111	25	NH 2188 4023	254	
An Cruachan	705	G89	25	NH 0937 3587	255	
Càrn na Còinnich	673 (673.4)	G141	26	NH 3245 5105	256	
Meall na Faochaig	681	G128	25	NH 2575 5251	257	
Beinn Mheadhoin	665 (664.3)	G153	25	NH 2588 4777	258	
Creag Dhubh Mhòr	611 (611.0)	G219	25	NG 9828 4047	259	
SECTION 13 – Glen Carron to Loch Maree						
Càrn Breac	678 (677.8)	G135	25	NH 0451 5300	263	
Beinn na Feusaige	627 (626.8)	G196	25	NH 0900 5423	263	
Sgùrr a' Gharaidh	732	G44	24	NG 8841 4436	265	
Beinn a' Chlachain	626	G197	24	NG 7242 4904	266	
Beinn na h-Eaglaise	736	G36	25	NG 9088 5235	267	
An Ruadh-Mheallan	671	G143	19,24	NG 8361 6148	268	
Beinn a' Chearcaill	725 (725.4)	G57	19	NG 9306 6378	269	
SECTION 14 - Loch Maree to Loch Broom						
Meall a' Chaorainn	705	G92	19	NH 1360 6041	273	
Beinn nan Ramh	711	G77	19	NH 1396 6615	274	
Beinn Bheag	668	G146	19	NH 0859 7138	275	
Groban	749	G11	19	NH 0997 7089	275	
Beinn a' Mhùinidh	692	G113	19	NH 0321 6604	277	
Meall Mhèinnidh	722	G60	19	NG 9549 7484	278	
Beinn a' Chàisgein Beag	682 (682.3)	G125	19	NG 9655 8214	279	
Beinn Ghobhlach	635	G190	19	NH 0557 9435	281	
SECTION 15 – Loch Broom to the Cromarty Firth						
Beinn Bhreac	667	G148	20	NH 2257 8865	285	
Meall Doire Fàid	729	G51	20	NH 2208 7920	286	
Meall a' Chaorainn	632	G193	20	NH 3600 8272	287	
Beinn Tharsuinn (Strath Vaich)	710	G80	20	NH 4125 8294	287	
Càrn Loch nan Amhaichean	697	G109	20	NH 4112 7576	288	
Beinn nan Eun	743	G24	20	NH 4482 7597	288	
Meall Mòr	738	G34	20	NH 5153 7455	290	
Beinn Tharsuinn (Strath Rory)	692	G112	21	NH 6063 7928	291	
Càrn Salachaidh	647	G176	20	NH 5188 8744	292	
Càrn a' Choin Deirg	701	G102	20	NH 3975 9234	293	
SECTION 16 – Loch Broom to The Pentland Firth						
Ben More Coigach	743	G22	15	NC 0939 0426	297	
Sgùrr an Fhidhleir	705	G93	15	NC 0944 0545	297	
Beinn an Eòin	619	G206	15	NC 1049 0643	300	
Stac Pollaidh	612 (612.4)	G215	15	NC 1071 1061	301	
Caisteal Liath [Suilven]	731 (731.4)	G48	15	NC 1532 1836	303	
Ben Stack	720	G66	9	NC 2693 4229	305	
Sabhal Beag	732	G47	9	NC 3732 4291	306	
Càrn an Tionail	759 (758.5)	G5	16	NC 3923 3903	307	
Beinn Direach	688 (688.9)	G119	16	NC 4061 3806	307	
Meallan a' Chuail	750	G10	15	NC 3446 2923	309	
Meall an Fheur Loch	613	G214	16	NC 3619 3107	309	
Beinn Dhorain	628 (628.3)	G195	17	NC 9253 1566	311	
Creag a' Choire Ghlais [Ben Armine]	705 (705.3)	G90	16	NC 6948 2732	312	
Creag Mhòr	713	G74	16	NC 6984 2401	312	
Scaraben	626	G198	17	ND 0661 2684	314	
Morven	706	G88	17	ND 0047 2854	315	

Name	Height (DoBIH)	G No	OS Map	Grid Ref	Page	Date climbed
SECTION 17 – The Islands: Arran, Jura, Mull, Rum, Skye, Uist & Harris						
Mullach Buidhe (Arran)	721 (721.4)	G64	62,69	NR 9018 4278	322	
Beinn a' Chaolais (Jura)	733 (735.2)	G40	60,61	NR 4888 7344	324	
Beinn Shiantaidh (Jura)	757	G6	61	NR 5134 7477	324	
Creach Beinn (Mull)	698 (698.7)	G107	49	NM 6427 2762	326	
Ben Buie (Mull)	717	G69	49	NM 6041 2701	326	
Beinn Talaidh (Mull)	762 (761.7)	G1	49	NM 6255 3470	328	
Sgùrr Dearg (Mull)	741	G29	49	NM 6654 3399	328	
Corra-bheinn (Mull)	705 (704.8)	G94	48	NM 5732 3218	330	
Cruach Choireadail (Mull)	618	G210	48	NM 5947 3048	330	
Beinn Fhada (Mull)	702	G97	47,48	NM 5400 3490	332	
Trollabhal (Rum)	702	G100	39	NM 3773 9520	334	
Sgùrr na Coinnich (Skye)	739	G31	33	NG 7624 2225	336	
Beinn na Caillich (Kylerhea-Skye)	732	G42	33	NG 7704 2297	336	
Beinn Dearg Mhòr (Broadford-Skye)	709	G83	32	NG 5877 2285	338	
Beinn na Caillich (Broadford-Skye)	732	G41	32	NG 6014 2330	338	
Belig (Skye)	702 (701.6)	G98	32	NG 5440 2405	340	
Beinn Dearg Mhòr (Sligachan-Skye)	731	G49	32	NG 5203 2849	342	
Marsco (Skye)	736	G35	32	NG 5075 2519	344	
Hartaval (Skye)	669	G145	23	NG 4800 5510	346	
The Storr (Skye)	719 (718.7)	G67	23	NG 4954 5404	346	
Beinn Mhòr (South Uist)	620 (620.4)	G203	22	NF 8085 3109	348	
Uisgneabhal Mòr (Harris)	729	G53	13,14	NB 1209 0858	350	
Oireabhal (Harris)	662	G159	13,14	NB 0839 0997	351	
Tiorga Mòr (Harris)	679	G130	13,14	NB 0555 1150	351	

(a) Highest point is a small cairn 45m SSW of the trig point.
(b) Summit height of 744m on the south-east top at NN23572402 (OS 1:10k) confirmed by survey. OS 1:25k & 1:50k show 743m highpoint at NN23452417 on the top 200m to the north-west.
(c) Replaces Beinn Dearg (708m) at NN685189 (now a Graham Top) as the highpoint and the Graham.
(d) DoBIH give a rock 3m south of the trig point at NM93957575 as being 1m higher than that shown on OS maps 80m further to the north-west.

The Database of British and Irish Hills (DoBIH) was founded by Graham Jackson and Chris Crocker in 2001 with the intention of providing a comprehensive, up-to-date resource for British hillwalkers. It has grown considerably in the intervening years and is currently maintained by a team of seven. The DoBIH is offered as a downloadable database on its website, and as an online database on the Hill Bagging webite. Both formats offer logging facilities and there is a facility for transferring personal ascent records from one to the other. The majority of bagging websites and apps take their data from the DoBIH, though not always from the latest release. The version used here is 17.4.

The DoBIH pioneered the use of differential GPS instruments and line surveying by automatic level and staff to obtain accurate measurements of height, drop and location. Amongst many surveys are the more well-known ones resulting in the subsequent reclassification by the SMC of Sgurr nan Ceannaichean and Beinn a' Chlaidheimh from Munro to Corbett status, Cnoc Coinnich from Graham to Corbett, the de-twinning of Sgurr a' Bhac Chaolais and Duidhe Dheinn to a single Corbett, the deletion of Knight's Peak from the list of Munro Tops and the addition of Mullach Coire nan Cisteachan as a Munro Top.

The SMC acknowledges the survey programme carried out by G & J Surveys, the results of which were passed to the OS and DoBIH. In support of the work of the DoBIH team and contributing surveyors, a donation has been made by the Scottish Mountaineerng Club to the Database of British and Irish Hills fund.

The Donalds

All Hills in the Scottish Lowlands, 2000ft (609.60m) in Height and Above

Percy Donald's *Tables Giving All Hills in the Scottish Lowlands 2000ft in Height and Above* was first published in the Scottish Mountaineering Club Journal in 1935. This list was subsequently published by the SMC in its book *Munro's Tables and Other Tables of Lower Hills* and has been maintained by them ever since.

Percy Donald visited every elevation over 2000ft in what he considered The Scottish Lowlands. He developed a complex formula to distinguish between those points which he classified as Hills and those which he considered to be Tops. The format of his list was similar to the earlier Munro's Tables where summits were classified as Hills and Tops, now simply known as Munros and Munro Tops. Likewise the summits on Donald's List once classified as Hills and Tops are now simply known as Donalds and Donald Tops.

It has been suggested that Donald's List should conform to a metric equivalent and that the definition should be more precise and relate to a specific measure of reascent from neighbouring summits. However, albeit antiquated, it is felt that Percy Donald left us a clear definition of his categorisation which has produced a list of historical interest that is still relevant to today's hillwalker. It would be an aberration for any of these historic hill listings to be forced down this route in order to conform to a more precise definition. So, like The Munros, the table that follows adheres to the traditional definitions. This is Donald's List and these are The Donalds. Those who compleat the list are known as Donaldists.

An interesting point about Donald's Tables is that they are seen as a complete entity. So, most of those collecting The Donalds elect to climb all 141 Hills and subsidiary Tops on Donalds list; the Donalds and Donald Tops. This is unlike the Munros where the majority complete only the 282 principal Hills, or the Munros as they are known, and a remarkably low percentage, perhaps less than 20%, complete the 226 subsidiary Munro Tops as well.

The exact geographic compass of Donald's Tables was never made clear but the inclusion of the Ochill Hills suggests that his definition of Lowland was a geological one; namely, all of the country south of the Highland Boundary Fault. If this definition is strictly applied, it is clear that Donald overlooked a small group of hills lying to the south of Glen Artney which rise above the 2000ft level. Although appearing to be part of the Highlands, this group of two Hills and two Tops lies south of the Highland Boundary fault and was subsequently added to the tables.

Hills and Tops were determined by Percy Donald in accordance with the following rules: *Tops are all elevations with a drop of 100ft (30.48m) on all sides and elevations of sufficient topographical merit with a drop of between 100ft and 50ft (15.24m) on all sides. Grouping of Tops into Hills, except where inapplicable on topographical grounds, is on the basis that Tops are no more than 17 units from the main top of the Hill to which they belong; where a unit is either one twelfth of a mile measured along the connecting ridge or one 50ft contour between the lower Top and its connecting col.*

While the rules as they stand lack mathematical precision, the actual result of their application is that, with but few exceptions, an 80ft (24.38m) drop determines a Top and the 17-unit rule a Hill.

Table/Column Explanations

Section Number & Name: Section 0 – The Lowlands has been split into three; 0a, 0b (effectively west and east of the M74 corridor) and 0c (north of the M8).

Name & Height: Ordnance Survey spellings and heights in metres have been used. Survey information that has not been ratified by the OS has been noted.

Hill No & Top No: Hill No refers to the actual Donalds (D1) to (D89) and Top No refers to a summit placing in the full list of Donalds and Donald Tops, 1-141.

OS Map & Grid Ref: The first two digits refer to the relevant OS 1:50k Landranger series map which covers the hill. An eight figure OS grid reference, prefixed by two grid letters, is given in the Table below, which provides the location of a summit to within 10m, and a six figure grid reference has been given in the text, which provides the location of a summit to within 100m.

Name	Height (DoBIH)	Hill No	Top No	OS Map	Grid Ref	Page	Date climbed
SECTION 0a – Galloway & The Lowthers							
Galloway Hills							
Cairnsmore of Fleet	711	D28	42	83	NX 5016 6707	16	
Knee of Cairnsmore	657		88	83	NX 5096 6563	16	
Meikle Mulltaggart	612		137	83	NX 5120 6781	16	
Larg Hill	676	D49	67	77	NX 4247 7574	18	
Lamachan Hill	717	D26	39	77	NX 4352 7690	18	
Curleywee	674	D51	71	77	NX 4546 7695	18	
Millfore	657	D62	86	77	NX 4779 7545	18	
The Merrick	843	D1	1	77	NX 4275 8554	21	

Name	Height (DoBIH)	Hill No	Top No	OS Map	Grid Ref	Page	Date climbed
Benyellary	719		37	77	NX 4148 8390	21	
Mullwharchar	692	D39	54	77	NX 4542 8664	21	
Dungeon Hill	620	D83	128	77	NX 4604 8507	21	
Craignaw	645	D68	94	77	NX 4592 8333	21	
Kirriereoch Hill	787 (786.8)	D11	13	77	NX 4209 8695	24	
Tarfessock	697 (696.4)	D35	50	77	NX 4090 8919	24	
Tarfessock South Top	620		129	77	NX 4136 8862	24	
Shalloch on Minnoch	775 (774.2)	D13	15	77	NX 4075 9056	24	
Caerloch Dubh	659 (659.5)		84	77	NX 4001 9202	24	
Carlin's Cairn	807	D8	9	77	NX 4969 8836	26	
Meaul	695	D37	52	77	NX 5005 9098	26	
Cairnsgarroch	659	D60	83	77	NX 5155 9135	26	
Corran of Portmark	623	D80	122	77	NX 5092 9367	26	
Bow	613		135	77	NX 5080 9282	26	
Meikle Millyea (a)	749 (748.6)	D14	20	77	NX 5161 8255	28	
Milldown	738	D18	24	77	NX 5112 8394	28	
Millfire	716		41	77	NX 5082 8479	28	
Corserine	814	D6	6	77	NX 4978 8706	28	
Carsphairn Hills							
Cairnsmore of Carsphairn	797	D10	12	77	NX 5946 9799	30	
Beninner	710		44	77	NX 6057 9716	30	
Moorbrock Hill	650 (651.4)	D65	91	77	NX 6206 9838	30	
Windy Standard	698	D33	48	77	NS 6201 0146	32	
Dugland (b)	612		138	77	NS 6026 0089	30	
Keoch Rig	611 (612.4)		140	77	NX 6170 9998	30	
Alhang	642	D71	100	77	NS 6422 0102	32	
Alwhat	628		114	77	NS 6466 0203	32	
Meikledodd Hill	643		98	77	NS 6609 0276	32	
Blacklorg Hill	681	D45	62	77	NS 6538 0423	32	
Blackcraig Hill	700 (700.9)	D30	45	71,77	NS 6476 0640	32	
Lowther Hills							
Queensberry	697	D34	49	78	NX 9890 9975	34	
Earncraig Hill	611	D88	139	78	NX 9732 0137	34	
Gana Hill	668	D54	76	78	NS 9543 0107	34	
Wedder Law	672	D52	72	78	NS 9387 0251	36	
Scaw'd Law (c)	663	D58	81	78	NS9226 0350	36	
Glenleith Fell	612		136	78	NS 9223 0238	36	
Ballencleuch Law	689	D42	57	78	NS 9356 0497	36	
Rodger Law	688		60	71,78	NS 9453 0580	36	
Comb Law	645	D67	93	71,78	NS 9438 0738	36	
East Mount Lowther	631	D76	112	71,78	NS 8785 1000	38	
Lowther Hill	725	D23	32	71,78	NS 8900 1075	38	
Cold Moss	628		115	71,78	NS 8989 0947	38	
Green Lowther	732	D21	30	71,78	NS 9003 1203	38	
Dun Law	677	D48	66	71,78	NS 9166 1364	38	
Lousie Wood Law	619	D84	132	71,78	NS 9319 1527	38	

SECTION 0b – The Borders

Tinto & Culter Hills

Name	Height (DoBIH)	Hill No	Top No	OS Map	Grid Ref	Page	Date climbed
Tinto	711	D29	43	58	NS 9532 3437	44	
Culter Fell	748 (748.3)	D15	19	72	NT 0528 2908	46	
Chapelgill Hill	696	D36	51	72	NT 0665 3037	46	
Cardon Hill	675		70	72	NT 0652 3148	46	
Hillshaw Head	652	D63	89	72	NT 0483 2460	48	
Coomb Dod	635		108	72	NT 0461 2383	48	

The Donalds

Name	Height	(DoBIH)	Hill No	Top No	OS Map	Grid Ref	Page	Date climbed
Gathersnow Hill	688		D43	58	72	NT 0587 2570	48	
Coomb Hill	640			102	72	NT 0695 2636	48	
Hudderstone	626		D78	119	72	NT 0221 2714	50	
Moffat Hills								
Swatte Fell (d)	728	(729.9)	D22	31	78	NT 1184 1138	54	
Nether Coomb Craig	724			34	78	NT 1293 1097	54	
Falcon Craig	724			33	78	NT 1223 1272	54	
Hart Fell	808		D7	8	78	NT 1136 1357	54,56	
Whitehope Heights	637		D73	106	78	NT 0956 1389	56	
Under Saddle Yoke	745		D16	21	78	NT 1424 1262	54	
Saddle Yoke	735	(735.5)		27	78	NT 1440 1239	54	
Lochcraig Head (e)	801	(800.8)	D9	11	79	NT 1670 1761	58	
Nickies Knowe	761			17	79	NT 1639 1915	58	
White Coomb	821		D4	4	79	NT 1632 1509	58,60	
Carrifan Gans	757			18	79	NT 1593 1388	58,60	
Firthhope Rig	800			10	79	NT 1535 1539	58,60	
Cape Law	722		D24	35	78	NT 1311 1508	60	
Din Law	667			77	78	NT 1242 1568	60	
Garelet Dod	698		D32	47	78	NT 1262 1726	60	
Erie Hill	690		D41	56	78	NT 1241 1873	60	
Laird's Cleuch Rig	684			61	78	NT 1250 1959	60	
Garelet Hill	681			63	72	NT 1240 2015	60	
Great Hill	774	(774.8)		16	78	NT 1459 1639	60	
Molls Cleuch Dod	785		D12	14	79	NT 1511 1794	60	
Carlavin Hill	736			26	78	NT 1420 1887	60	
Ettrick Hills								
Bodesbeck Law	665	(664.2)	D57	78	79	NT 1699 1040	50	
Mid Rig	616			133	79	NT 1802 1227	50	
Bell Craig	623		D79	121	79	NT 1864 1286	50	
Andrewhinney Hill	677	(677.3)	D47	65	79	NT 1975 1387	50	
Trowgrain Middle (f)	628			116	79	NT 2068 1504	50	
Herman Law	614	(614.4)	D87	134	79	NT 2135 1570	50	
Croft Head	637		D72	105	79	NT 1530 0565	52	
Loch Fell	688		D44	59	79	NT 1701 0472	52	
West Knowe	672			73	79	NT 1630 0524	52	
Capel Fell	678		D46	64	79	NT 1639 0690	52	
Smidhope Hill	644			96	79	NT 1681 0767	52	
White Shank	622			126	79	NT 1690 0830	52	
Wind Fell	665	(665.2)	D56	79	79	NT 1789 0613	52	
Hopetoun Craig	632	(633.1)		109	79	NT 1876 0679	52	
Ettrick Pen	692	(691.8)	D38	53	79	NT 1999 0765	52	
Manor Hills								
Talla Cleuch Head	691		D40	55	72	NT 1334 2183	62	
Broad Law	840	(840.1)	D2	2	72	NT 1464 2353	62	
Cramalt Craig	831	(830.2)	D3	3	72	NT 1684 2473	62	
Hunt Law	639			103	72	NT 1500 2646	62	
Clockmore	641			101	72	NT 1831 2287	62	
The Scrape	719			38	72	NT 1760 3241	64	
Pykestone Hill	737		D19	25	72	NT 1730 3125	64	
Middle Hill	716	(717.2)	D27	40	72	NT 1594 2946	64	
Taberon Law	636	(636.7)		107	72	NT 1464 2888	64	
Drumelzier Law	668		D53	75	72	NT 1494 3121	64	
Black Cleuch Hill	675			69	73	NT 2222 2900	66	
Black Law	698		D31	46	73	NT 2226 2793	66	

The Donalds

Name	Height (DoBIH)	Hill No	Top No	OS Map	Grid Ref	Page	Date climbed
Conscleuch Head	624		120	73	NT 2203 2627	66	
Deer Law	629		113	73	NT 2229 2555	66	
Greenside Law	643	D70	97	72	NT 1979 2562	66	
Notman Law	734		28	72	NT 1850 2602	66	
Fifescar Knowe	811		7	72	NT 1751 2708	66	
Dollar Law	817	D5	5	72	NT 1780 2783	66	
Dun Rig	744	D17	22	73	NT 2534 3155	68	
Glenrath Heights	732	D20	29	73	NT 2416 3226	68	
Stob Law	676	D50	68	73	NT 2301 3327	68	
Birkscairn Hill	661	D59	82	73	NT 2747 3317	68	

Moorfoot Hills

Name	Height (DoBIH)	Hill No	Top No	OS Map	Grid Ref	Page	Date climbed
Blackhope Scar	651	D64	90	73	NT 3152 4833	70	
Bowbeat Hill	626	D77	118	73	NT 2920 4690	70	
Dundreich	623	D81	123	73	NT 2746 4908	70	
Windlestraw Law	659 (659.2)	D61	85	73	NT 3712 4309	68	
Bareback Knowe	657 (656.0)		87	73	NT 3622 4206	68	
Whitehope Law	623	D82	124	73	NT 3303 4456	68	

Roxburgh & Cheviot Hills

Name	Height (DoBIH)	Hill No	Top No	OS Map	Grid Ref	Page	Date climbed
Cauldcleuch Head	619 (618.6)	D86	130	79	NT 4565 0068	74	
Windy Gyle	619	D85	131	80	NT 8553 1521	74	
Cairn Hill West Top (g)	743		23	80	NT 8957 1930	74	

SECTION 0c – The Midland Valley

Ochil Hills

Name	Height (DoBIH)	Hill No	Top No	OS Map	Grid Ref	Page	Date climbed
King's Seat Hill	648	D66	92	58	NN 9337 9998	79	
Andrew Gannel Hill	670		74	58	NN 9185 0060	79	
The Law	638		104	58	NS 9102 9965	79	
Ben Cleuch	721	D25	36	58	NN 9027 0063	79	
Ben Ever	622		125	58	NN 8933 0010	79	
Blairdenon Hill	631 (631.9)	D75	111	58	NN 8657 0185	81	
Innerdownie	610	D89	141	58	NN 9666 0315	82	
Whitewisp Hill	643		99	58	NN 9551 0136	82	
Tarmangie Hill	645	D69	95	58	NN 9421 0140	82	

Glen Artney Hills

Name	Height (DoBIH)	Hill No	Top No	OS Map	Grid Ref	Page	Date climbed
Meall Clachach	621 (618.9)		127	57	NN 6883 1258	83	
Uamh Bheag	666 (665.8)	D55	80	57	NN 6911 1185	83	
Beinn Odhar (h)	626		117	57	NN 7144 1277	83	
Beinn nan Eun	631	D75	110	57	NN 7236 1312	83	

(a) Survey confirms summit is SW top 748.6m (749m), NE top (trig) is 746.7 (747m).
(b) OS 1:25k & 1:50k give 612m (DoBIH 611.5m), which is over 2000ft and a new addition to Donalds Tables.
(c) DoBIH suggest that a point 300m to the north at NS9221 0378 may be higher.
(d) OS 1:50k marks summit here with a height of 728m. DoBIH confirm this as summit with a height of 729.9m (730m). OS 1:25k shows a point 300m north east at NT12031154 as 729m, but DoBIH confirm cairn here is lower.
(e) DoBIH give highpoint 130m further north at NT16661774.
(f) Summit lies 150m north-west of cairn and fence.
(g) The highest point on the border between Scotland and England. It is not an actual summit and cannot therefore be classified as a separate 'hill'.
(h) West top confirmed as summit at 665.8m (666m), east top is 663.4m (663m) and trig point between the two is lower again.

Grahams by Height

G No	Name	Height	Page
G1	Beinn Talaidh	762m	328
G2	Sgùrr a' Chaorainn	761m	207
G3	Beinn a' Chapuill	759m *	230
G4	Ciste Buide a' Claidheimh [Shee of Ardtalnaig]	759m	126
G5	Càrn an Tionail	759m	307
G6	Beinn Shiantaidh	757m	324
G7	Creag Dhubh (Newtonmore)	756m	193
G8	Cook's Cairn	755m	182
G9	The Stob	753m *	118
G10	Meallan a' Chuail	750m	309
G11	Groban	749m	275
G12	Sgùrr Chòinnich	749m	224
G13	Mona Gowan	749m	177
G14	Culter Fell	748m	46
G15	Binnein Shuas	747m	155
G16	Meall Mòr (Loch Katrine)	747m	114
G17	Meall a' Mhuic	745m	133
G18	Stob a' Ghrianain [Druim Fada]	744m	217
G19	Mount Blair	744m	164
G20	Meall nan Gabhar	744m	106
G21	Dun Rig	744m	68
G22	Ben More Coigach	743m	297
G23	Geallaig Hill	743m	176
G24	Beinn nan Eun	743m	288
G25	Creag Liath	743m	192
G26	Cnap Cruinn	742m	154
G27	Sgòrr na Cìche [Pap of Glencoe]	742m	146
G28	Beinn Mhòr (Cowal)	741m *	89
G29	Sgùrr Dearg	741m	328
G30	Badandun Hill	740m	166
G31	Sgùrr na Còinnich	739m	336
G32	Beinn Mheadhoin (Kingairloch)	739m	201
G33	Stob na Cruaiche [A' Chruach]	739m	134
G34	Meall Mòr (Loch Glass)	738m	299
G35	Marsco	736m	344
G36	Beinn na-h Eaglaise	736m	267
G37	Beinn Bheag (Ardgour)	736m *	204
G38	Doune Hill	734m	98
G39	Druim na Sgrìodain	734m *	203
G40	Beinn a' Chaolais	733m *	324
G41	Beinn na Caillich (Broadford)	732m	338
G42	Beinn na Caillich (Kylerhea)	732m	336
G43	Green Lowther	732m	38
G44	Sgùrr a' Chaoraidh	732m	265
G45	Glas Bheinn (Loch Arkaig)	732m	223
G46	Stob an Eas	732m	95
G47	Sàbhal Beag	732m	306
G48	Caisteal Liath [Suilven]	731m	303
G59	Beinn Dheary Mhòr (Sligachan)	731m	342
G50	Beinn na Gainimh	730m *	127
G51	Meall Doire Fàid	729m	286
G52	Ben Venue	729m	112
G53	Uisgneabhal Mòr	729m	350
G54	Càrnan Cruithneachd	729m *	239
G55	Mullach Coire nan Geur-oirean	727m	222
G56	Màm Hael	726m	142
G57	Beinn a' Chearcaill	725m	269
G58	Meall nan Damh (Loch Eil)	723m	210
G59	Creagan a' Chaise	722m	183
G60	Meall Mhèinnidh	722m	278
G61	Ben Cleuch	721m	79
G62	The Buck	721m	179
G63	Stob Mhic Bheathain	721m	208
G64	Mullach Buidhe	721m	322
G65	Ben Stack	720m	305
G66	Meall Buidhe	719m	122
G67	The Storr	719m	346
G68	An Stac	718m	226
G69	Ben Buie	717m	326
G70	Lamachan Hill	717m	18
G71	Cnap Chaochain Aitinn	715m	180
G72	Beinn Mheadhonach	715m	142
G73	Beinn Chaorach	713m	96
G74	Creag Mhòr (Sutherland)	713m	312
G75	Druim Fada (Kinlochhourn)	713m *	233
G76	Creag Ruadh (Loch Earn)	712m	124
G77	Beinn nan Ramh	711m	274
G78	Cairnsmore of Fleet	711m	16
G79	Tinto	711m	44
G80	Beinn Tharsuinn (Strath Vaich)	710m	287
G81	Càrn a' Ghille Chearr	710m	183
G82	Sgùrr na Maothaich [Mèith Bheinn]	710m	221
G83	Beinn Dhearg Mhòr (Broadford)	709m	338
G84	Beinn nan Lus	709m	141
G85	Beinn a' Mhanaich	709m	96
G86	Creag na h-Eararuidh	708m	120
G87	Càrn a' Chaochain	706m *	245
G88	Morven	706m	315
G89	An Cruachan	705m	255
G90	Creag a' Choire Ghlais [Ben Armine]	705m	312
G91	Hunt Hill	705m	170
G92	Meall a' Chaorainn (Achnasheen)	705m	273
G93	Sgùrr an Fhidhleir	705m	297
G94	Corra-bheinn	705m	330
G95	Beinn Eich	703m	98
G96	Beinn Lochain	703m	92
G97	Beinn Fhada	702m	332
G98	Belig	702m	340
G99	Duchray Hill [Mealna Letter]	702m	164
G100	Trollabhal	702m	334
G101	Meall Garbh	701m	140
G102	Càrn a' Choin Deirg	701m	293
G103	Sgùrr nan Cnamh	701m *	206
G104	Blackcraig Hill	700m *	32
G105	Slat Bheinn	700m *	228
G106	Meall Fuar-mhonaidh	699m	243
G107	Creach Beinn	698m *	326
G108	Windy Standard	698m	32
G109	Càrn Loch nan Amhaichean	697m	288
G110	Queensberry	697m	34
G111	Beinn na Muice	695m	254
G112	Beinn Tharsuinn (Strath Rory)	692m	291
G113	Beinn a' Mhùinidh	692m	277
G114	Ettrick Pen	692m	52
G115	Mullwharchar	692m	21
G116	Meall Dearg	690m	129
G117	Beinn Mòlurgainn	690m *	142
G118	Ballencleuch Law	689m	36
G119	Beinn Direach	688m *	307

Grahams by Height

G No	Name	Height	Page
G120	Gathersnow Hill	688m	48
G121	Stob Breac	688m	119
G122	Cruach an t-Sìthein	684m	98
G123	Beinn Damhain	684m	103
G124	Lèana Mhòr (west)	684m	196
G125	Beinn a' Chaisgein Beag	682m	279
G126	Beinn Bhreac (Loch Lomond)	681m	101
G127	Meall Onfhaidh	681m	218
G128	Meall na Faochaig	681m	257
G129	Meall a' Chrathaich	679m	241
G130	Tiorga Mòr	679m	351
G131	Càrn na Breabaig	679m	251
G132	Capel Fell	678m	52
G133	Hill of Wirren	678m	168
G134	Càrn Mhic an Toisich	678m	241
G135	Càrn Breac	678m	263
G136	Andrewhinney Hill	677m	50
G137	Càrn Gorm	677m	252
G138	Beinn Suidhe	676m	139
G139	Lèana Mhòr (east)	676m	197
G140	Meall Mòr (Glen Coe)	676m	144
G141	Càrn na Còinnich	673m	256
G142	Creag Each	672m *	124
G143	An Ruadh-Mheallan	671m	268
G144	Cat Law	671m	167
G145	Hartaval	669m	346
G146	Beinn Bheag (Letterewe)	668m	275
G147	Creag Bhalg	668m	175
G148	Beinn Bhreac (Loch Broom)	667m	285
G149	Binnein Shios	667m	155
G150	Meall nan Eun	667m	228
G151	Beinn Gàire	666m	212
G152	Uamh Bheag	666m	83
G153	Beinn Mheadhoin (Strathconon)	665m *	258
G154	Meall Tairbh	665m *	138
G155	Beinn Ruadh	664m	88
G156	Aodann Chleireig	663m	218
G157	Croit Bheinn	663m *	212
G158	Sgòrr a' Choise	663m	144
G159	Oireabhal	662m	351
G160	Càrn Glas-choire	659m	189
G161	Windlestraw Law	659m	72
G162	Creag Mhòr (Balquhidder)	658m	116
G163	Meall nan Eagan	658m	157
G164	Creag Ruadh (Dalwhinnie)	658m	162
G165	Creag Dhubh (Glen Spean)	658m	195
G166	Mid Hill	657m	98
G167	Millfore	657m	18
G178	Meall Blàir	656m *	225
G169	Meall Odhar	656m	105
G170	Beinn na Cille	652m	202
G171	Fiarach	652m	104
G172	Blackhope Scar	651m	70
G173	Glas-bheinn Mhòr	651m	243
G174	Beinn Donachain	650m *	137
G175	Sgòrr Mhic Eacharna	650m *	204
G176	Càrn Salachaidh	647m	292
G177	Beinn na Cloiche	646m *	152
G178	Biod an Fhithich	646m	234
G179	Craignaw	645m	21
G180	Sgiath a' Chàise	645m *	115
G181	Beinn Clachach	643m *	231
G182	Creag Tharsuinn	643m	91
G183	Blath Bhalg	641m *	163
G184	Mòr Bheinn	640m	121
G185	Creag Gharbh	637m	123
G186	Croft Head	637m	52
G187	Beinn Bhalgairean	636m *	106
G188	Beinn na Sròine	636m	136
G189	Glas Bheinn (Loch Eil)	636m	210
G190	Beinn Ghobhlach	635m	280
G191	Glas-chàrn	633m	220
G192	Cruinn a' Bheinn	632m	111
G193	Meall a' Chaorainn (Strath Vaich)	632m	287
G194	Tullich Hill	632m	101
G195	Beinn Dhorain	628m	311
G196	Beinn na Feusaige	627m	263
G197	Beinn a' Chlachain	626m	266
G198	Scaraben	626m	314
G199	Meall nan Caorach	623m *	128
G200	Creag Ruadh (Loch Laggan)	622m	194
G201	Creag Ghuanach	621m	152
G202	Tom Meadhoin	621m	151
G203	Beinn Mhòr (South Uist)	620m	348
G204	Meall Reamhar	620m *	128
G205	Pressendye	619m	178
G206	Beinn an Eoin	619m	300
G207	Cauldcleuch Head	619m	74
G208	Beinn Bheag (Cowal)	618m	89
G209	Càrn na h-Easgainn	618m *	191
G210	Cruach Choireadail	618m	330
G211	Beinn na Gucaig	616m	151
G212	Càrn nan Tri-tighearnan	615m	190
G213	Beinn a' Mheadhoin	613m	247
G214	Meall an Fheur Loch	613m	309
G215	Stac Pollaidh	612m	301
G216	Cruach nan Capull	612m	87
G217	Creag a' Mhadaidh	612m *	151
G218	Cruach nam Mult	611m	94
G219	Creag Dhubh Mhòr	611m	259

* Denotes a summit where the Database of British and Irish Hills has a different height - see tables.

Donalds by Height

Cairnsgarroch, right, and distant Cairnsmore of Carsphairn (Tom Prentice)

Hill No	Name	Height	Page
D1	The Merrick	843m	21
D2	Broad Law	840m	62
D3	Cramalt Craig	831m *	62
D4	White Coomb	821m	58,60
D5	Dollar Law	817m	66
D6	Corserine	814m	28
	Fifescar Knowe	811m	66
D7	Hart Fell	808m	54,56
D8	Carlin's Cairn	807m	26
D9	Lochcraig Head	801m	58
	Firthhope Rig	800m	58,50
D10	Cairnsmore of Carsphairn	797m	30
D11	Kirriereoch Hill	787m *	24
D12	Molls Cleuch Dod	785m	60
D13	Shalloch on Minnoch	775m *	24
	Great Hill	774m *	60
	Nickies Knowe	761m	58
	Carrifran Gans	757m	58,60
D14	Meikle Millyea	749m	28
D15	Culter Fell	748m	46
D16	Under Saddle Yoke	745m	54
D17	Dun Rig	744m	68
	Cairn Hill West Top	743m	74
D18	Milldown	738m	28
D19	Pykestone Hill	737m	64
	Carlavin Hill	736m	60
	Saddle Yoke	735m *	54
	Notman Law	734m	66
D20	Glenrath Heights	732m	68
D21	Green Lowther	732m	38
D22	Swatte Fell	728m *	54
D23	Lowther Hill	725m	38
	Nether Coomb Craig	724m	54
	Falcon Craig	724m	54
D24	Cape Law	722m	60
D25	Ben Cleuch	721m	79
	Benyellary	719m	21
	The Scrape	719m	64
D26	Lamachan Hill	717m	18
D27	Middle Hill	716m *	64
	Millfire	716m	28
D28	Cairnsmore of Fleet	711m	16
D29	Tinto	711m	44
	Beninner	710m	30
D30	Blackcraig Hill	700m *	32
D31	Black Law	698m	66
D32	Garelet Dod	698m	60
D33	Windy Standard	698m	32
D34	Queensberry	697m	34
D35	Tarfessock	697m *	24
D36	Chapelgill Hill	696m	46
D37	Meaul	695m	26
D38	Ettrick Pen	692m	52
D39	Mullwharchar	692m	21
D40	Talla Cleuch Head	691m	62
D41	Erie Hill	690m	60
D42	Ballencleuch Law	689m	36
D43	Gathersnow Hill	688m	48
D44	Loch Fell	688m	52
	Rodger Law	688m	36

Hill No	Name	Height	Page
	Lairds Cleuch Rig	684m	60
D45	Blacklorg Hill	681m	32
	Garelet Hill	681m	60
D46	Capel Fell	678m	52
D47	Andrewhinney Hill	677m	50
D48	Dun Law	677m	38
D49	Larg Hill	676m	18
D50	Stob Law	676m	68
	Black Cleuch Hill	675m	66
	Cardon Hill	675m	46
D51	Curleywee	674m	18
D52	Wedder Law	672m	36
	West Knowe	672m	52
	Andrew Gannel Hill	670m	79
D53	Drumelzier Law	668m	64
D54	Gana Hill	668m	34
	Din Law	667m	60
D55	Uamh Bheag	666m	83
D56	Wind Fell	665m	52
D57	Bodesbeck Law	665m *	50
D58	Scaw'd Law	663m	36
D59	Birkscairn Hill	661m	68
	Caerloch Dubh	659m *	24
D60	Cairnsgarroch	659m	26
D61	Windlestraw Law	659m	72
D62	Millfore	657m	18
	Knee of Cairnsmore	657m	16
	Bareback Knowe	657m *	72
D63	Hillshaw Head	652m	48
D64	Blackhope Scar	651m	70
D65	Moorbrock Hill	650m *	30
D66	King's Seat Hill	648m	79
D67	Comb Law	645m	36
D68	Craignaw	645m	21
D69	Tarmangie Hill	645m	82
	Smidhope Hill	644m	52
D70	Greenside Law	643m	66
	Meikledodd Hill	643m	32
	Whitewisp Hill	643m	82
D71	Alhang	642m	32
	Clockmore	641m	62
	Coomb Hill	640m	48
	Hunt Law	639m	62
	The Law	638m	79
D72	Croft Head	637m	52
D73	Whitehope Heights	637m	56
	Taberon Law	636m *	64
	Coomb Dod	635m	48
	Hopetoun Craig	632m *	52
D74	Blairdenon Hill	631m *	81
D75	Beinn nan Eun	631m	83
D76	East Mount Lowther	631m	38
	Deer Law	629m	66
	Alwhat	628m	32
	Cold Moss	628m	38
	Trowgrain Middle	628m	50
	Beinn Odhar	626m	83
D77	Bowbeat Hill	626m	70
D78	Hudderstone	626m	50
	Conscleuch Head	624m	66
D79	Bell Craig	623m	50
D80	Corran of Portmark	623m	26
D81	Dundreich	623m	70
D82	Whitehope Law	623m	72
	Ben Ever	622m	79
	White Shank	622m	52
	Meall Clachach	621m *	83
D83	Dungeon Hill	620m	21
	Tarfessock South Top	620m	24
D84	Lousie Wood Law	619m	38
D85	Windy Gyle	619m	74
D86	Cauldcleuch Head	619m	74
	Mid Rig	616m	50
D87	Herman Law	614m	50
	Bow	613m	26
	Glenleith Fell	612m	36
	Meikle Mulltaggart	612m	16
	Dugland	612m	30
D88	Earncraig Hill	611m	34
	Keoch Rig	611m *	30
D89	Innerdownie	610m	82

* Denotes a summit where the Database of British and Irish Hills has a different height - see tables.

Index of Grahams

Name	Page
A' Chruach	134
An Cruachan	255
An Ruadh-Mheallan	268
An Stac	226
Andrewhinney Hill	50
Aodann Chleireig	218
Badandun Hill	166
Ballencleuch Law	36
Beinn a' Chaisgein Beag	279
Beinn a' Chaolais	324
Beinn a' Chapuill	230
Beinn a' Chearcaill	269
Beinn a' Chlachain	266
Beinn a' Mhanaich	96
Beinn a' Mheadhoin	247
Beinn a' Mhùinidh	277
Beinn an Eòin	300
Beinn Bhalgairean	106
Beinn Bheag (Ardgour)	204
Beinn Bheag (Cowal)	89
Beinn Bheag (Letterewe)	275
Beinn Bhreac (Loch Lomond)	101
Beinn Bhreac (Loch Broom)	285
Beinn Chaorach	96
Beinn Clachach	231
Beinn Damhain	103
Beinn Dhearg Mhòr (Broadford)	338
Beinn Dhearg Mhòr (Sligachan)	342
Beinn Dhorain	311
Beinn Direach	307
Beinn Donachain	137
Beinn Eich	98
Beinn Fhada	332
Beinn Gàire	212
Beinn Ghobhlach	280
Beinn Lochain	92
Beinn Mheadhoin (Kingairloch)	201
Beinn Mheadhoin (Strathconon)	258
Beinn Mheadhonach	142
Beinn Mhòr (Cowal)	89
Beinn Mhòr (South Uist)	348
Beinn Mòlurgainn	142
Beinn na Caillich (Broadford)	338
Beinn na Caillich (Kylerhea)	336
Beinn na Cille	202
Beinn na Cloiche	152
Beinn na Feusaige	263
Beinn na Gainimh	127
Beinn na Gucaig	151
Beinn na Muice	254
Beinn na Sròine	136
Beinn na-h Eaglaise	267
Beinn nan Eun	288
Beinn nan Lus	141
Beinn nan Ramh	274
Beinn Ruadh	88
Beinn Shiantaidh	324
Beinn Suidhe	139
Beinn Talaidh	328
Beinn Tharsuinn (Strath Vaich)	287
Beinn Tharsuinn (Strath Rory)	291
Belig	340
Ben Armine	312
Ben Buie	326
Ben Cleuch	79
Ben More Coigach	297
Ben Stack	305
Ben Venue	112
Binnein Shios	155
Binnein Shuas	155
Biod an Fhithich	234
Blackcraig Hill	32
Blackhope Scar	70
Blath Bhalg	163
Buck, The	179
Cairnsmore of Fleet	16
Caisteal Liath	303
Capel Fell	52
Càrn a' Chaochain	245
Càrn a' Choin Deirg	293
Càrn a' Ghille Chearr	183
Càrn an Tionail	307
Càrn Breac	263
Càrn Glas-choire	189
Càrn Gorm	252
Càrn Loch nan Amhaichean	288
Càrn Mhic an Toisich	241
Càrn na Breabaig	251
Càrn na Còinnich	256
Càrn na h-Easgainn	191
Càrn nan Tri-tighearnan	190
Càrn Salachaidh	292
Càrnan Cruithneachd	239
Cat Law	167
Cauldcleuch Head	74
Ciste Buide a' Claidheimh	126
Cnap Chaochain Aitinn	180
Cnap Cruinn	154
Cook's Cairn	182
Corra-bheinn	330
Craignaw	21
Creach Beinn	326
Creag a' Choire Ghlais	312
Creag a' Mhadaidh	151
Creag Bhalg	175
Creag Dhubh (Glen Spean)	195
Creag Dhubh Mhòr	259
Creag Dhubh (Newtonmore)	193
Creag Each	124
Creag Gharbh	123
Creag Ghuanach	152
Creag Liath	192
Creag Mhòr (Balquhidder)	116
Creag Mhòr (Sutherland)	312
Creag na h-Eararuidh	120
Creag Ruadh (Dalwhinnie)	162
Creag Ruadh (Loch Earn)	124
Creag Ruadh (Loch Laggan)	194
Creag Tharsuinn	91
Creagan a' Chaise	183
Croft Head	52
Croit Bheinn	212
Cruach an t-Sìthein	98
Cruach Choireadail	330

Index of Grahams

Cruach nam Mult	94
Cruach nan Capull	87
Cruinn a' Bheinn	111
Culter Fell	46
Doune Hill	98
Druim Fada (Kinlochhourn)	233
Druim Fada (Stob a' Ghrianain)	217
Druim na Sgrìodain	203
Duchray Hill	164
Dun Rig	68
Ettrick Pen	52
Fiarach	104
Gathersnow Hill	48
Geallaig Hill	176
Glas Bheinn (Loch Eil)	210
Glas Bheinn (Loch Arkaig)	223
Glas-bheinn Mhòr	243
Glas-chàrn	220
Green Lowther	38
Groban	275
Hartaval	346
Hill of Wirren	168
Hills of Cromdale	167
Hunt Hill	170
Lamachan Hill	18
Lèana Mhòr (east)	197
Lèana Mhòr (west)	196
Màm Hael	142
Marsco	344
Meall a' Chaorainn (Achnasheen)	273
Meall a' Chaorainn (Strath Vaich)	287
Meall a' Chrathaich	241
Meall a' Mhuic	133
Meall an Fheur Loch	309
Meall Blàir	225
Meall Buidhe	122
Meall Dearg	129
Meall Doire Fàid	286
Meall Fuar-mhonaidh	243
Meall Garbh	140
Meall Mhèinnidh	278
Meall Mòr (Loch Glass)	299
Meall Mòr (Loch Katrine)	114
Meall Mòr (Glen Coe)	144
Meall na Faochaig	257
Meall nan Caorach	128
Meall nan Damh (Loch Eil)	210
Meall nan Eagan	157
Meall nan Eun	228
Meall nan Gabhar	106
Meall Odhar	105
Meall Onfhaidh	218
Meall Reamhar	128
Meall Tairbh	138
Meallan a' Chuail	309
Mealna Letter	164
Mèith Bheinn	221
Mid Hill	98
Millfore	18
Mona Gowan	177
Mòr Bheinn	121
Morven	315
Mount Blair	164
Mullach Buidhe	322
Mullach Coire nan Geur-oirean	222
Mullwhachar	21
Oireabhal	351
Pap of Glencoe	146
Pressendye	178
Queensberry	34
Sàbhal Beag	306
Scaraben	314
Sgiath a' Chaise	115
Sgòrr a' Choise	144
Sgòrr Mhic Eacharna	204
Sgòrr na Cìche	146
Sgùrr a' Chaorainn	207
Sgùrr a' Gharaidh	265
Sgùrr an Fhìdhleir	297
Sgùrr Chòinnich	224
Sgùrr Dearg	328
Sgùrr na Còinnich	336
Sgùrr na Maothaich	221
Sgùrr nan Cnamh	206
Shee of Ardtalnaig	126
Slat Bheinn	228
Stac Pollaidh	301
Stob, The	118
Stob a' Ghrianain	217
Stob an Eas	95
Stob Breac	119
Stob Mhic Bheathain	208
Stob na Boine Druim-fhinn	84
Stob na Cruaiche	134
Storr, The	346
Suilven	303
Tinto	44
Tiorga Mòr	351
Tom Meadhoin	151
Trollabhal	334
Tullich Hill	101
Uamh Bheag	83
Uamh Bheag East Top	77
Uisgneabhal Mòr	350
Windlestraw Law	72
Windy Standard	32

Index of Donalds

Ben Ever, left, The Law and Andrew Gannel Hill from above Mill Glen (Tom Prentice)

Alhang	32
Alwhat	32
Andrew Gannel Hill	79
Andrewhinney Hill	50
Ballencleuch Law	36
Bareback Knowe	72
Beinn nan Eun	83
Beinn Odhar	83
Bell Craig	50
Ben Cleuch	79
Ben Ever	79
Beninner	30
Benyellary	21
Birkscairn Hill	68
Black Cleuch Hill	66
Black Law	66
Blackcraig Hill	32
Blackhope Scar	70
Blacklorg Hill	32
Blairdenon Hill	81
Bodesbeck Law	50
Bow	26
Bowbeat Hill	70
Broad Law	62
Caerloch Dubh	24
Cairn Hill West Top	74
Cairnsgarroch	26
Cairnsmore of Carsphairn	30
Cairnsmore of Fleet	16

Cape Law	60
Capel Fell	52
Cardon Hill	46
Carlavin Hill	60
Carlin's Cairn	26
Carrifran Gans	58,60
Cauldcleuch Head	74
Chapelgill Hill	46
Clockmore	62
Cold Moss	38
Comb Law	36
Conscleuch Head	66
Coomb Dod	48
Coomb Hill	48
Corran of Portmark	26
Corcorine	28
Craignaw	21
Cramalt Craig	62
Croft Head	52
Culter Fell	46
Curleywee	18
Deer Law	66
Din Law	60
Dollar Law	66
Drumelzier Law	64
Dugland	30
Dun Law	38
Dun Rig	68
Dundreich	70
Dungeon Hill	21

Earncraig Hill	34
East Mount Lowther	38
Erie Hill	60
Ettrick Pen	52
Falcon Craig	54
Fifescar Knowe	66
Firthhope Rig	58,60
Gana Hill	34
Garelet Dod	60
Garelet Hill	60
Gathersnow Hill	48
Glenleith Fell	36
Glenrath Heights	68
Great Hill	60
Green Lowther	38
Greenside Law	66
Hart Fell	54,56
Herman Law	50
Hillshaw Head	48
Hopetoun Craig	52
Hudderstone	50
Hunt Law	62
Innerdownie	82
Keoch Rig	30
King's Seat Hill	79
Kirriereoch Hill	24
Knee of Cairnsmore	16
Lairds Cleuch Rig	60
Lamachan Hill	18
Larg Hill	18
Law, The	79
Loch Fell	52
Lochcraig Head	58
Lousie Wood Law	38
Lowther Hill	38
Meall Clachach	83
Meaul	26
Meikle Millyea	28
Meikle Mulltaggart	16
Meikledodd Hill	32
Merrick, The	21
Mid Rig	50
Middle Hill	64
Milldown	28
Millfire	28
Millfore	18
Molls Cleuch Dod	60
Moorbrock Hill	30
Mullwharchar	21
Nether Coomb Craig	54
Nickies Knowe	58
Notman Law	66

Pykestone Hill	64
Queensberry	34
Rodger Law	36
Saddle Yoke	54
Scaw'd Law	36
Scrape, The	64
Shalloch on Minnoch	24
Smidhope Hill	52
Stob Law	68
Swatte Fell	54
Taberon Law	64
Talla Cleuch Head	62
Tarfessock	24
Tarfessock South Top	24
Tarmangie Hill	82
Tinto	44
Trowgrain Middle	50
Uamh Bheag	83
Under Saddle Yoke	54
Wedder Law	36
West Knowe	52
White Coomb	58,60
White Shank	52
Whitehope Heights	56
Whitehope Law	72
Whitewisp Hill	82
Wind Fell	52
Windlestraw Law	72
Windy Gyle	74
Windy Standard	32

Scottish Mountaineering Club

Established in 1889, the Scottish Mountaineering Club is at the forefront of climbing and mountaineering in Scotland. We want our guidebooks, covering hillwalking, scrambling and climbing, to be the first book you reach for when you head for the cliffs, hills and outcrops of Scotland.

www.smc.org.uk/publications

Scottish Mountaineering Press

The Scottish Mountaineering Press exists to promote and share Scotland's natural wonders. We do this by embracing the creativity and art born out of an explorer spirit. Whether it's poetry, photography or prose, our publications capture the moments when nature stuns us into silence and stops us in our tracks.

www.scottishmountaineeringpress.com

Scottish Mountaineering Trust

All profits from Scottish Mountaineering Press books go to help fund the Scottish Mountaineering Trust, a charity that provides grants to projects and organisations that promote recreation, knowledge and safety in the mountains, especially the mountains of Scotland.

www.thesmt.org.uk